Eleventh Edition

Psychology for Living

ADJUSTMENT, GROWTH, AND BEHAVIOR TODAY

Steven J. Kirsh
State University of New York—Geneseo

Karen Grover Duffy
State University of New York—Geneseo

Eastwood Atwater

Boston   Columbus   Indianapolis   New York   San Francisco   Upper Saddle River
Amsterdam   Cape Town   Dubai   London   Madrid   Milan   Munich   Paris   Montreal   Toronto
Delhi   Mexico City   São Paulo   Sydney   Hong Kong   Seoul   Singapore   Taipei   Tokyo

Editorial Director: Craig Campanella
Editor in Chief: Jessica Mosher
Acquisition Editor: Amber Chow
Associate Editor: Diane Szulecki
Editorial Assistant: Alexis Rodriguez
Director of Marketing: Brandy Dawson
Senior Marketing Manager: Nicole Kunzmann
Production Editor: Meghan DeMaio
Creative Director: Jayne Conte
Cover Designer: Suzanne Duda
Cover Art: Kudryashka/Shutterstock
Media Director: Brian Hyland
Senior Digital Media Editor: Peter Sabatini
Media Project Manager: Tina Rudowski
Full-Service Project Management/Composition: Niraj Bhatt, Aptara®, Inc.
Printer/Binder: Edwards Brothers Malloy
Cover Printer: Lehigh-Phoenix Color
Text Font: TimesStd

Credits and acknowledgments borrowed from other sources and reproduced, with permission, in this textbook appear on appropriate page within text or on page 405.

Library of Congress Cataloging-in-Publication Data
Kirsh, Steven J.
  Psychology for living : adjustment, growth, and behavior today /
Steven J. Kirsh, Karen Grover Duffy, Eastwood Atwater.—11th ed. p. cm.
  Duffy's name appears first on the 7th-10th eds.
  ISBN-13: 978-0-205-90902-5
  ISBN-10: 0-205-90902-7
  1. Conduct of life—Textbooks. I. Duffy, Karen Grover. II. Atwater, Eastwood, III. Title.
  BF335.A88 2014
  158--dc23
2012037266
Student Version

10 9 8 7 6 5 4 3

PEARSON

ISBN-10: 0-205-90902-7
ISBN-13: 978-0-205-90902-5

For my father-in-law, Sri Ram Bakshi. Thanks for the love and support you've given me over the years ... not to mention the goat curry.

~SJK

To Hugh, Ted, Al, and all our other veterans, past, present, and future:

Welcome Home.

~KGD

BRIEF CONTENTS

CONTENTS

PART 4 Being Social

Chapter 8 Making and Keeping Friends   150

Chapter 9 Groups: Belonging, Following, and Leading   170

PREFACE

This book is intended for readers interested in applying psychological insights and principles to their own lives as a way of achieving a better understanding of themselves *and* of living more effectively. To this end, we have included material from the major perspectives of psychology, including the psychodynamic, cognitive, behavioral, and humanistic viewpoints. Since a well-rounded text cuts across several branches of psychology, we have included contributions from clinical, personality, social, and developmental psychology, as well as from the important fields of cognitive, biological, and health psychology. Our aim is to increase readers' understanding as well as their knowledge about personal adjustment, in order that they may continue learning on their own.

Major Features of this eleventh edition are explained in the following sections.

NEW TO THIS EDITION

We have made some changes to the content of the book to reflect changes in the field of psychology in addition to world events. First, there are nearly 320 new references as well as new glossary terms. Second, you will also find new or additional information on the following topics:

- Technology and how it is benefiting yet at the same time perplexing our lives.
- Applications from the field of positive psychology.
- The ecological perspective on human development.
- The impact of parental monitoring and different parenting styles on youth.
- The impact and proliferation of handheld devices such as PDAs and cell phones.
- The malleability versus fixedness of personality.
- The definition and application of defensive pessimism.
- Bullying and cyber-bullying.
- Children's understanding of death.
- Why we make up excuses for or misdeeds.
- Obesity, the obesity stigma, and body image.
- The insanity defense.
- Academic dishonesty.
- What to do when someone tells you they are suicidal.
- Panic disorder and dysthymia.
- The relationship between music and suicide.
- Infertility, infertility treatments, and adoption.
- Updated U.S. census figures (and world population growth) throughout the book.
- Recent research on body image and the influence of the media.
- New research on post-decision regret, including hindsight bias.
- Frenemies.
- What makes a face attractive?
- Women in management positions and their experience with the glass cliff.
- Updated research on the impact of electronic communication at work.
- The issues surrounding having a therapist of a similar or different race.
- The resurgence of interest in the trait approach to leadership.
- Inclusion of new information on posttraumatic stress syndrome.
- The prominence of resilience in everyday life and in coping with stressors.
- The influence of the media in promoting eating disorders.
- Data on the prevalence of personality disorders.
- The concept that well-being is different from the mere absence of disorder and stress.
- The movement away from theories of stages of bereavement and toward interest in growth theories of bereavement.

- The continuing threat of terrorism and how it has changed the way we live and cope.
- Expanded information on the concepts of individual and collective societies.
- Changes in the American family and how they affect individual members.
- The effects of the baby boomers on society as they enter late adulthood.
- Thoughtful analysis of the role ethnicity and race play in health care, psychotherapy, and other areas.
- More coverage on cultural effects of nonverbal communication.
- Additional information on child pornography and sexual assault.

ORGANIZATION

The chapters of this book stand alone; that is, you can read them out of order and still understand all of the material even though you have not read a preceding chapter. The introductory chapter on self-direction and social change remains at the beginning, of course. The second large unit is about development or the state of "becoming." The chapters on childhood and adulthood can be found here. The third large unit pertains to the individual in the present or in a state of "being." Here you will find the chapters on self-concept, health, personal control, and decision making, as well as on emotion and motivation.

The next large unit is about the social side of adjustment and growth. Here are located the chapters on friends, groups (leaders and followers), and work and leisure. This unit is followed by an apt unit about closer intimate relationships. This short unit contains two chapters, one each on sexuality and on committed or intimate relationships. Finally, any book about personal growth and adjustment would be incomplete without including material on the challenges each of us faces. The last unit contains chapters on stress, mental disorders, therapy, and death and dying. Please let us know how you feel about this organization, and remember that the chapters are self-contained so they can easily be read in any order you wish. We can be reached at kirsh@ geneseo.edu and duffy@geneseo.edu.

LEARNING AIDS

Several features have been included to assist the student in making the best use of this book:

- A How to Study section at the beginning of the book provides suggestions for studying and test taking.
- Chapter outlines at the beginning of each chapter give students an overview of what will be covered.
- Learning objectives identify what students are expected to attain in regard to knowledge, understanding, and application.
- Terms that may be new to students are boldfaced and are followed by an italicized definition that is repeated in the glossary.
- Special-interest boxes, figures, and tables contain interesting and important material supplemental to the text.
- A glossary at the end of the book defines key, boldfaced terms in the text.
- End-of-chapter summaries, arranged by learning objectives, help the reader to grasp the main points of the chapter.
- Self-tests, consisting of 10 multiple-choice questions, help students to assess their understanding of the material covered.

APPLICATIONS

- One or two self-scoring inventories in each chapter enable students to apply the concepts and principles covered in the text. These inventories are designed by us, so please note that

they have no scientifically derived validity or reliability. They are merely meant to be tools for self-exploration and self-understanding and should be interpreted as such.
- End-of-chapter exercises heighten the student's involvement in the material.
- Questions for self-reflection encourage students to relate the material in the text to themselves.

SUPPLEMENTS

Instructor's Manual (0-205-90947-7)

The instructor's manual is a wonderful tool for classroom preparation and management. Each chapter in the teaching aids section includes a chapter overview, lecture suggestions, discussion questions, class activities, and media resources.

Test Bank (0-205-90948-5)

A set of tests, containing representative multiple-choice, true-false, short-answer, and essay questions, each with a page reference, difficulty rating, and type designation, are available for each chapter. The tests are also available in the **MyTest (0-205-95088-4)** computerized version for ease in creating tests for the classroom.

PowerPoint Presentation (0-205-90906-X)

Completely revised, the PowerPoint presentation is an exciting interactive tool for use in the classroom. Each chapter pairs key concepts with images from the textbook to reinforce student learning.

MySearchLab with Pearson eText (0-205-90958-2)

For over 10 years, instructors and students have reported achieving better results and better grades when a **Pearson MyLab** has been integrated into the course. **MySearchLab** provides engaging experiences that personalize learning, and comes from a trusted partner with educational expertise and a deep commitment to helping students and instructors achieve their goals. Features of **MySearchLab** include:

eText
Just like the printed text, you can highlight and add notes to the eText online or download it to your iPad.

Writing & Research
Access to various academic journals, census data, Associated Press news feeds, and discipline-specific readings. Also, a wide range of composition and grammar tools aid students throughout the writing process, helping them to produce more effective papers.

ACKNOWLEDGMENTS

Many thanks to Dr. Eastwood Atwater for providing us with the opportunity to take over this well-established book. While he is no longer with us, we hope that he would approve of our continued efforts at producing the same high-quality book he wrote. Many thanks to the professors who adopted past editions and provided feedback to us. We really do appreciate your comments and take them to heart. Special thanks goes to Amber Chow and Diane Szulecki at Pearson Education for all of their patience and excellent guidance. To our friends and family, a big thank you for nudging us along when we got discouraged about getting this and other books completed, especially given the vicissitudes of daily life and the distracting tug at our heart strings of the sun, moon, stars, spouses, children, and many critters who needed petting.

Many thanks to the following reviewers for their insightful comments and helpful suggestions:

Norma Caltagirone
Hillsborough Community College

Christopher Dyszelski
Madison Area Technical College

Rebecca Francis
West Virginia State University

Paul Herrle
The College of Southern Nevada

Rod Hoevet
Maryville University

Gloria Howell
Blue Ridge Community College

Andrew Ornberg
Central Oregon Community College

Courtney Ryan
Ball State University

Victoria Schultz
Wharton County Junior College

HOW TO STUDY

Students give many excuses about why they haven't done well on a test. Occasionally, they will admit outright, "I just didn't study." But more often they will say, "I really studied for that test. I can't understand why I did so poorly." A common problem is waiting until the last minute to study. But in many instances, students just don't know how to study. Regardless of whether you fall into this category, chances are you could improve your studying habits by applying one of the following time-honored methods of studying.

THE PQ4R METHOD

The PQ4R method gets its name from the six overlapping stages for studying material such as textbook chapters—preview, question, read, reflect, recite, and review.* Extensive experience has shown that this method can improve your understanding and memory, and thus your test performance.

Preview

It's a good idea to look over the chapter as a whole before you begin it. When you read a novel, you usually start at the beginning and read straight through so as not to spoil the surprise ending. But with concepts and factual material, it's just the opposite. Here, it's important to get an idea of the material as a whole so you can put the details in context as you read.

- First, look over the table of contents.
- Next, skim through the chapter, looking at the headings and subheadings.
- Then, read the chapter summary.
- Finally, decide how much you want to read at a sitting.

Question

Once you've looked over the chapter, you may be curious about the material. A helpful technique is to ask yourself questions about the material. Then read the chapter with the aim of finding the answers to your questions. One way to do this is to turn each boldfaced heading and subheading into a question. For example, the first major heading and subheadings in Chapter 1 on self-direction are

- Social Change
- Living in a Technological World
- Living with Other Social Changes
- How Certain Is Our Future?

Now use these headings and subheadings to think up some questions. Here are some examples: What is social change? I know I live in a technological world, but how does that relate to social change and self-direction? What are some of the other social changes that I have witnessed? With terror alerts and other dramatic changes, just how certain is my future? Your use of such questions may prove even more effective if you jot them down, and then, as you read, write down your answers.

Read

Make it a point to understand what you're reading, digesting the material in one section before proceeding to the next. Skimming through material without comprehending it leads to superficial

*E. L. Thomas and H. A. Robinson, *Improving memory in every class: A sourcebook for teachers* (Boston: Allyn & Bacon, 1972).

understanding at best, but more often, to downright confusion. In contrast, when you take the time to understand what you read, you'll also retain it better. If you're not clear about the meaning of a word, check the glossary of terms at the end of the book. If you can't find the word in the glossary, look it up in one of the better dictionaries such as *Webster's New World Dictionary*. Also, feel free to make explanatory notes to yourself in the margins of the pages of your textbook.

Reflect

A good way to improve your understanding of something is to pause periodically and reflect on it. Ask yourself: Do I really understand this material? Could I explain it to someone else? If the answer is "no," then you'll need to reread the material. It's also helpful to mark or underline key passages in the chapter. This makes you an active participant in reading and provides you with key passages to review for tests. Some students prefer to mark or underline as they read. Others prefer to read through the material and then go back and highlight the most important points. Experts prefer the latter approach, because we usually have a better idea of the key passages after we've read through the material. Here are some suggestions for marking or underlining:

- Read through each section before marking or underlining.
- Mark only key passages or ideas.
- Use a marker or pen. Pencil often smears.

Recite

Perhaps you've had this experience: You look up someone's telephone number, but no sooner have you closed the phone book than you've forgotten the number. You reopen the book and find the number again. But this time as you close the book, you repeat the number to yourself, either silently or audibly. You're improving your memory through recitation—the act of repeating or speaking aloud. Recitation improves your memory in several ways. First, by focusing your attention on the page a bit longer, you can encode the material better, thereby ensuring accurate storage of the material. Repeated practice may also help you to retrieve the material when you need it.

There are several ways to use recitation. First, the act of reflection, or asking questions about the material, mentioned earlier, is itself a form of recitation. Second, you may also recite by closing the book and mentally recalling what you've just read. A third way is to recite aloud, either by discussing the material with a classmate or by sharing your reactions or asking questions about it in class. A fourth way is to make a written outline of what you've read. We highly recommend this method because it forces you to select the main ideas in the material. Occasionally, students attempt to escape the thinking process by simply copying down the headings and subheadings, including little else. Others include too much detail, which becomes distracting. Instead, be selective. You should be able to outline an entire chapter of this book in just several written pages, depending, of course, on how large you write. The entire process of selecting the major ideas and writing them down is an excellent form of recitation. It also provides you with a handy guide to review for the test.

The amount of time spent on recitation depends on the material covered. When you're trying to remember isolated bits of information, like names or numbers, up to 80 percent of your time should be spent in recitation. But when you're learning ideas or concepts that are highly meaningful and well organized, perhaps you would spend only 20 percent of your time in recitation. Personal experience will help you to determine which method of recitation works best for you.

Review

When you're ready to review, reread the summary at the end of the chapter to give yourself a sense of the material as a whole. Then look back over the material in the chapter, paying special attention to the key ideas you've marked or underlined under each heading and subheading. If you've made a written outline of the chapter, review this, too. Ideally, you should review the material periodically, to offset the rapid decline in retention once you've learned something. It's recommended that you review the material within 24 hours of the initial reading, and then again 72 hours later. After this, it's a good idea to review the material about once a week until you're tested on it.

When you're ready, do the self-test at the end of each chapter. Then check your responses against the list of correct answers provided in the back of this book. When you miss a question, it's important to go back and look up the correct answer. Otherwise, you may make the same mistake again. You may observe that the order of test items parallels the sequence of material in the chapter, thus facilitating your use of the self-test for study purposes.

WHERE AND WHEN TO STUDY

Once the semester is under way, you're ready to plan your study schedule. Consider your class schedule, the workload in each course, and other commitments, such as a part-time job or family responsibilities. Be realistic. Don't try to study too much material at one time.

First, it's important to find a place to study that is free from distractions. Then use this place only for studying. In this way, you'll develop a set of associations that will strengthen your study habits. One of the worst places to study is on your bed. The bed is associated with fatigue; thus, you may find yourself falling asleep rather than studying. When you find yourself daydreaming or worrying about something else, take a short break and return when you're ready to study. When you finish studying, leave this place. By consistently doing so, you'll associate this place with studying and feel more like studying only there.

It's also important to set aside particular times for study. You may wish to study for a given block of time and quit at the end of this period regardless of how much you've read. Or you may want to study until you've covered a certain amount of material. Either way, it's best to study in reasonable blocks of time, about one to three hours. After a long stretch, you may have difficulty concentrating on the material at hand. That's why it's a good idea to take a short break at least once an hour, or even on the half-hour when you're covering very difficult material. Also, you might select other things you enjoy doing and make them contingent on completing your study goal for a given time slot. For instance, if you'd like to call a friend or watch television, do your studying first. Then make your call or watch TV as a reward to yourself.

Above all, don't procrastinate. Distribute your study times realistically so you don't try to absorb too much material at a time. For instance, if you must cover four chapters in this book for a test, plan to read no more than one chapter in a given time slot. Spacing out your study time cuts down on boredom and fatigue and also allows your memory time to consolidate the material. Your mind may continue absorbing the material in the intervals between study periods. This is especially important to keep in mind when you're learning complex or difficult material.

TAKING TESTS

When taking a test, stay calm and reasonably relaxed. By keeping your anxiety at a mild to moderate level, you minimize its interference with your thinking process. If you encounter a question that makes you especially anxious, note this on the question sheet or test itself. Then proceed to do the remaining questions before returning to tackle the difficult question(s). Realizing that you've completed most of the test helps you to concentrate on the more difficult items.

Regardless of the type of test, take time to read the questions carefully. Make certain you understand what the instructor is asking. Don't read things into a question, making it more complicated than it is. If the item looks particularly confusing, raise your hand and ask the instructor to rephrase the item. Be sure also to read every single choice for multiple-choice questions before selecting the correct one.

Before answering an essay question, take a few moments to jot down a brief outline on the back of a page. This helps to keep your thoughts on the subject while you write. If your test includes both multiple-choice and essay questions, first outline the essay question. Then complete the multiple-choice questions before writing out the essay answer.

After you've read a multiple-choice question and selected an answer, it's best to reread the question to make certain your answer matches the question. This helps to avoid simple "forgetting" mistakes, because material stays in our short-term memory for only about 30 seconds. By the time you've decided on the correct answer, chances are you've forgotten the exact wording of the question. Consequently, it's helpful to reread the question before marking your answer. This time, read the answer choices in reverse order.

Learn to eliminate incorrect answers before settling on the correct one. For instance, if there are four possible answers, eliminate the two that are the least plausible. With only two remaining answers to choose from, you have a 50–50 chance of selecting the correct one. Answers containing words like *always, never, only, must,* and *totally* often imply sweeping assertions and can usually be eliminated early on.

Should you ever change your answer? It all depends. If you have studied reasonably well and feel good about your answer, stick with it. If you have strong doubts about an answer, however, especially if you're not well informed on the subject, it might pay to reconsider. At the same time, a lot depends on the individual. In going over tests with students, we've found that anxious, impulsive students may initially choose an incorrect answer and would benefit from taking another look at their answer. On the other hand, students who lack self-confidence will often change a correct answer to an incorrect one because they distrust their own abilities. As a result, we suggest keeping track of the answers you change. Then go over each test, recording the number of answers you changed from wrong to right, and vice versa. Take this information into consideration throughout future test taking.

Finally, there are other ways you can learn from your test results. If your instructor goes over the test in class, make it a point to attend that day. Find out what you missed and, equally important, why. Were the questions different from what you expected, requiring, say, the understanding of concepts rather than factual information? If you didn't do well on an essay test, ask your instructor how you can do better next time. Try not to waste time making excuses or blaming your instructor or yourself. Find out what you need to do in order to improve your test performance next time. Then modify your study habits and test taking accordingly. Good luck!

ABOUT THE AUTHORS

Steven J. Kirsh is a Professor of Psychology at The State University of New York at Geneseo. He received his Ph.D. in developmental psychology from Pennsylvania State University. Dr. Kirsh's primary areas of research focus on the influence of violent media on emotion recognition and social information processing. He has published *Children, Adolescents, and Media Violence: A Critical Look at the Research, 2nd Ed.* (2012) and *Media and Youth: A Developmental Perspective* (2010) as well as numerous scientific articles and book chapters.

Karen Duffy is a Distinguished Service Professor–Emerita, at the State University of New York at Geneseo. She received her Ph.D. in social and personality psychology from Michigan State University. Dr. Duffy served as a family mediator for the New York Unified Court System. She has also served on the executive committee and as the chief instructor for the training institute for the New York State Employee Assistance Program (EAP), as well as on the board of directors for a shelter for domestic violence and on an educational committee for a family planning agency. She has consulted to a variety of work settings on stress management, EAPs, and other work issues. She is a member of the American Psychological Society. Dr. Duffy has written several other books, including *Community Mediation: A Handbook for Practitioners and Researchers and Community Psychology.* She has also edited several hard-copy and web-based annual editions for another publisher, on topics including psychology of personality, social psychology, introductory psychology, and adjustment. She has held two Fulbright Fellowships to St. Petersburg State University, St. Petersburg, Russia. While in Russia, she worked with AIDS International, several children's shelters, and other community agencies. More recently, she completed two humanitarian aid trips to Mongolia.

Chapter One

Self-Direction in a Changing World

*Z*achary is a freshman in college in the late 1800s. He is among the privileged few to attend an institute of higher learning, mostly because his family is sufficiently well off to send him to school. Zachary travels to college by train, passing through miles of farmland and forests along the way. He keeps in touch with his family by letters. Zachary hopes to be a physician, an occupation pretty much closed to women in the 1800s. Zachary lives at a boardinghouse for male college students. He takes his meals there but studies at the library, where he reads by gaslight. He writes papers by hand. No one, absolutely no one, is using a mobile phone in Zachary's library.

Karen, Zachary's great-granddaughter, is a first-year college student of the twenty-first century. She is able to attend college because of financial aid from private lenders and the government. Karen travels back and forth to college by plane several times a year. To keep in touch with her family, she has only to pick up her walkie-talkie enabled phone, send a text message, or post a status update on Facebook or Twitter. Electricity lights up the room in which Karen reads and powers the computer she uses for term papers and correspondence. Karen, who lives in a coed dormitory, is accustomed to mingling with students from different ethnic and racial groups on campus, and about half of them are women.

Karen hopes to be a physician, as did Zachary, who planned to be a general practitioner. Zachary knew some patients could not give him money, so he would take produce, wool, or other products in payment. Karen, on the other hand, wants a posh office, working hours from 9 a.m. to 5 p.m., and an answering service so she can enjoy her private life. She knows she will set up her financial accounting system to accept credit cards, not eggs and bacon.

SOCIAL CHANGE

LEARNING OBJECTIVES

1.1 Explain how technology is changing the way we communicate and live.
1.2 Discuss other recent social changes unrelated to technology.

Living in a Technological World

Both Zachary and Karen lived in eras of rapid **social change**, defined as *changes in social patterns and institutions in society*. Social change can occur in any time period and be planned in advance

BOX 1–1	Did you know that . . .

- You would have to sit motionless for 8 hours in order to have the first camera invented take your picture.
- A child playing with a Game Boy (in 2000) had more available computing power than NASA did when it first sent men to the moon.
- There are more than 17 billion devices connected to the Internet.
- The first Apple II hard drive could only hold 5 megabytes worth of data.
- It took only 4 years for there to be 50 million users on the World Wide Web. By contrast, it took TV 13 years and radio 38 years to accomplish the same feat.

Source: Based on "Technology Facts," from FunFactz.com, 2012.

or totally unplanned. Planned changes are those created and engineered by humans, for example, building a new housing development wired for the most current technology. Unplanned changes are created by nature or by social accident, such as tsunamis and hurricanes or unexpected shifts in the population of a country due to disease or famine (Moritsugu, Wong, & Duffy, 2010).

In Zachary's lifetime, America slowly transformed from an agrarian society to an urban one, and numerous inventions of the industrial revolution made transportation, farming, and manufacturing better and easier. Shortly thereafter, America was transformed from a frontier society to an industrial giant. Karen, in turn, takes technological change for granted. She believes that medical advances will soon have a cure for many life-threatening illnesses, including AIDS and cancer. She worries that the shortages of fossil fuels in addition to increased greenhouse gases are changing the world she knows. Meanwhile, she has learned that spiraling social change is normal and inevitable, although she occasionally wonders what lies ahead. Karen knows that social change is not always planned or positive.

All of us now realize that the galloping rate of technological, scientific, and social change occurs worldwide and has far-reaching (global) consequences. For your consideration, many of the demonstrations and acts of civil disobedience that ultimately led to the over overthrow of Egyptian President Hosni Mubarak's regime were organized through Facebook, with 20-year-old Khaled Kamel's page, "We are all Khaled Saeed," leading the path to revolution (Hauslohner, 2011). Social change seems to be a pervasive condition of our time, and technology has expanded interconnectedness of peoples and increased awareness of a common, global humanity (St. Clair, 2011).

Across the globe, Internet use has spiked in the past decade. Since 2000, the number of Internet users has increased by 2527 percent in Africa, 1987 percent in the Middle East, 1037 percent in Latin America/Caribbean, 709 percent in Asia, and 150 percent in North America. Moreover, 44 percent of the world's Internet users are located in Asia; only 13 percent are found in North America (InternetWorldStatistics.com, 2012). Table 1–1 reveals current home media and Internet use in the United States and comparable countries.

Table 1–1	Media in the Home: A Comparison of Three Countries

Medium	United States	New Zealand	United Kingdom
TV	>99	>99	>99
Video game console	87	66	66
Internet access	84	72	79
iPod or MP3 player	76	56	69

Source: Broadcasting Standards Authority (2008), and Childwise (2010). "Generation M2: Media in the Lives of 8- to 18-Year-Olds" by Victoria J Rideout, et al. Henry J. Kaiser Family Foundation, 2010.

Technology makes relationships among people more fluid, flexible, and portable and has freed us from the constraints of being in only one place. Technology connects us to more people more of the time; it also equips us to work both at home and at our job sites, blurring the boundaries between them (Amichai-Hamburger, 2009). Technology, in fact, may be the most powerful engine of change in today's world (Sood & Tellis, 2005). People in almost every country are growing up in a world of greater interdependence because of technology. The revolution in communication, in particular, is re-creating the world in the image of a "global village," in which every aspect of life—every thought, act, and institution—is being reconsidered in light of what is happening to people in other parts of the world (Shah, 2007).

Exploration 1.1: Technology

www.cpsr.org   A site supported by computer professionals concerned about the responsible use of technology in society. Their motto is "Technology is driving the future; it is up to us to do the steering."

Although people recognize the fact of change, they often disagree on the direction in which we're headed (Kohut & Wike, 2008). Is it changing for better or worse? Some assume that the world as we know it will last indefinitely and that all the changes around us will not shake the familiar social, economic, and political structures that hold our society together (Moen & Roehling, 2005). A larger proportion of people, however, fed by a steady diet of bad news about crime, economic problems, world crises, the threats of terrorism, natural disasters, and possible nuclear destruction, have adopted a bleaker view (Huddy, Khatib, & Capelos, 2002). And yet others worry that digitalization and technology will damage or threaten local cultures and economies (Shah, 2007). However, worries about the negative effects that new technologies have on society are nothing new, as they have been around for hundreds of years. In the late 1800s, scholars believed that reading novels lead to bloated imaginations, over-exited nervous systems, and distorted views of reality. Newspapers were thought to cause unnatural, rapid shifts in attention, which ultimately undermined the mental health of the reader. During the early 1900s, movies were thought to teach depravity and immorality, and the cinema was marked as a training ground for criminals. Moreover, the comic books of the 1940s–1950s were believed to glorify violence, stimulate unhealthy ideas about sex, laud delinquency, and teach lawlessness. Simply put, throughout history, new technological advances, especially those related to media, have been vilified as "evil influences" on society (Starker, 1989).

From this generation forward, many forms of employment are and will be affected by automation and computerized systems. The increasing need for technical solutions places a premium on intellectual and technical knowledge. In turn, educated, middle-class workers will make up a larger proportion of the workforce in comparison to blue-collar workers, at least in the United States. One major problem related to increasing people's knowledge and use of technology, however, is that *some people fear technology, a phenomenon referred to as* **technophobia** (Wagner, Hassanein, & Head, 2010). For example, some people are apprehensive about using computers because they worry they will break the computers, make costly errors, or look stupid. This has created a seeming digital divide. Those individuals who are already less powerful use technology least; they are perhaps the very individuals who could benefit from knowledge about technology in order to improve their jobs, social standing, and economic conditions (Mehra, Merkel, & Bishop, 2004).

Interestingly, the overall technology picture is changing, as "on the go" technology (cell phones and other wireless handhelds) is reducing this digital divide (Horrigan, 2008).

Table 1–2	The Social/Cultural Dimension of the Information Revolution: How the World Has Changed

- More information flowing with less obstruction
- Information flowing independent of distance
- Increasing opportunities for economic cooperation across borders
- Greater opportunities to profit globally
- The erosion of censorship
- People being inundated with vast quantities of information
- The democratization of information
- A growing gap between rich and poor
- Empowerment individuals vis-à-vis their governments
- Gradual adaptation to a surplus of information

Source: Alterman (1999).

These technological changes, along with other scientific discoveries, are moving Americans, Canadians, Koreans, Swedes, and other technologically advanced societies away from manufacturing and industry to service-oriented and technological employment, just as the Industrial Revolution moved Zachary's generation from agricultural to manufacturing jobs. For an interesting summary of other ways in which technology has changed our world, see Table 1–2.

Living with Other Social Changes

What other changes can we expect in today's global village? One additional change will be continued population expansion and attendant worries about the health of our environment, including sufficient water and arable land, increased pollution, poverty, unemployment, and a plethora of related problems (Worldwatch.org, 2012). The world population stands at around 7 billion, with almost 150 new people born every minute. Furthermore, pollution as well as exhaustion of natural resources are problems for all countries and are contributed to by our increasing population. As mentioned above, another dramatic change will be the increase in the diversity of the population in the United States. Table 1–3 documents some of these

Table 1–3	Changes in Our Population

As you can see from this table, the percentage of the population made up by minorities as identified by the U.S. Census Bureau is increasing.

Population	1990—% of total	2010—% of total
White	75.6	72.4
Black or African-American	11.7	12.6
Hispanic*	9.0	16.3
Asian	2.8	4.8
American Indian or Alaska Native	0.7	0.9
Race other than above	0.1	6.4
Two or more races	Not available	2.9

*Hispanics are the fastest growing segment of our population.
Source: U.S. Census Bureau, Census (2012). http://www.census.gov/.

historic changes. Beyond the data in the table, the U.S. Census Bureau projects that by 2042 minorities will no longer be "minorities" and that by 2050 they collectively will represent 54 percent of the population (U.S. Census Bureau, Census, 2012). An increasing number of immigrants from various regions of the world are entering this country too, bringing with them a wealth of cultural ideas, languages, and customs. Accommodating these individuals, and the **cultural diversity** that they bring, will not always be easy, for some people are closed-minded, and rather ignorant of, insensitive to, or bigoted about cultures different from their own (Lamb, 2009).

Exploration 1.2: Cultural Diversity

www.edchange.org/multicultural/   Find songs, quotations, speeches, documents, and research related to multicultural issues.

How Certain Is Our Future?

How each of us understands the changes and trends in today's world is somewhat like the proverbial question of whether we perceive a partly filled glass as half empty or half full. Pessimists tend to see the glass as half empty; optimists see it as half full. Social forecasters, who speculate on our long-term future, admit that we live in uncertain times—both good and bad (Kohut & Wike, 2008). They nevertheless project a fairly optimistic future. Although they do not necessarily agree on what the future holds for us, they typically see it as promising. Do you?

Social forecasters view many of the problems of our time as the growing pains of success rather than the harbingers of doom. While the problems of overcrowding, unemployment, environmental pollution, social inequality, and poverty cannot be dismissed, such issues perhaps should be seen as temporary phenomena with which society must deal rather than the inevitable foreshadowing of the end of civilization. Societies can and do rebound from problems that at the time appear to be insurmountable (Moritsugu et al., 2010).

THE CHALLENGE OF SELF-DIRECTION

LEARNING OBJECTIVES

1.3 Explain the concept of self-direction.
1.4 Compare individualistic and collectivist societies.
1.5 Define positive psychology.
1.6 Summarize the humanistic perspective.
1.7 Discuss what it means to take charge of your life.

Self-Direction and Society

Rapid social changes and the growing importance of information and access to technology heighten the challenge of **self-direction**, which is *the need to learn more about ourselves and our world as a means of directing our lives more effectively*. Self-direction helps us respond to many life events as either a threat or a challenge. For example, some individuals find on-line dating to be both exciting and stimulating; they relish the opportunity to quickly meet so many new, and different, types of people. Others view on-line dating as overwhelming and are fearful about making their personal lives available for inspection to so many people with just the click of a mouse.

Another issue is that the world is seemingly changing and shrinking, in large part due to the technological changes discussed earlier. Given this, there are bound to be cultural clashes, disputes, and sometimes out-and-out warfare. On a daily basis, people from one society are bound to conflict with or misunderstand others from a different society (Moritsugu et al., 2010). Here's a specific cultural example related to technology. A study of electronic advertising (i.e., SPAM) found that whereas Korean SPAM includes an apology for the unsolicited nature in which the product information was sent, SPAM in the United States does not. Not surprisingly, Koreans are more likely than Americans to think it is rude to complain about receiving unsolicited electronic advertisements (Park, Lee, & Song, 2005).

We are increasingly exposed to other cultures due to the diversity of the U.S. population, ever-changing technology, and easier modes of travel.

The study of culture, then, is extremely important to our understanding of one another. **Culture** is broadly defined as *the ideas, customs, arts, and skills that characterize a group of people during a given period of history*. To that end, one commonly used system for classifying cultures is via the orientation taken toward the individual in that culture. **Individualistic societies** are *societies in which individual gain is appreciated more than general societal gain*. Individualistic societies are sometimes referred to as *independent or autonomous* cultures, where the sense of self is developed based on privately held attitudes, preferences, and judgments. Another term for individualistic culture is *individual-level* culture. Individualistic societies can be contrasted to **collectivist societies**, *in which collective or societal gain is cherished over individual advancement*. Collectivist societies are also known as *interdependent* societies, where the sense of self is based on attitudes, preferences, and judgments held by others. Another way to refer to collectivistic cultures is as *consensual-level* (or *group-level*) or *embedded* cultures (Kitayama & Uchida, 2005; Matsumoto, 2007). Thus, the pressure to conform to group or cultural pressures in collectivist societies is far greater than in individualistic societies.

If you have only lived in the Western world you may be familiar with individualistic societies but unfamiliar with collectivist ones. Describing his childhood in a collectivist society, Joseph

Lemasolai Lekuton, born Maasai in Kenya, said about his childhood in this nomadic society, "In my tribe, the village is you, and you are the village. . . . Everyone older than you will tell you what to do. And you never defy their orders" (Court, 2003, p. 5). In contrast, people from Western cultures enjoy personal freedom, independence from others, and take greater pride in personal achievements than do people in collectivist cultures. By the same token, people from individualistic societies may be more vulnerable to insecurity, confusion, and loneliness. Rest assured that there are other dimensions along which societies and cultures vary (Cohen, 2009), many of which will be pointed out in subsequent chapters.

In contrast to North American and European societies, many Eastern and Asian cultures remain collectivist in nature. Some contemporary scientists argue, however, that the contrasts are not as sharp between individualistic and collectivistic societies as once thought (Oishi et al., 2005). Ask yourself whether this could be because of the technological revolution we are experiencing today. In the same vein, it is important to remember that any label applied to a culture *cannot and does not* capture the individual variations that exist within that culture (Matsumoto, 2007). For example, although there is culture-level consensus in many Western societies about the value of equality, prejudicial viewpoints, such as ageism, racism, sexism, and homophobia, are still prevalent.

Positive Psychology and the Humanistic Perspective

Positive psychology is *an umbrella term for the study of positive emotions, positive character traits, and positive actions that allow individuals and institutions to thrive* (Seligman, 2011). Those in the field of positive psychology investigate diverse areas, such as teaching techniques that help students flourish, managerial strategies that maximize the productivity of workers, and the virtues that people possess, like the capacity for courage, love, and compassion. Thus, a major goal of positive psychology is to explore the best of human behavior, rather than the worst, which has been the traditional focus of much of psychological research (Baumgardner & Crothers, 2009).

Similarly, psychologists in the humanistic perspective focus on what makes human existence distinctive, such as the meaning and richness of subjective interpretations, the holistic characteristics of experience, and our capacity to willfully choose and determine behaviors and thoughts for ourselves (Fischer, 2003; Lenderking, 2005). The **humanistic perspective** consists of *a group of related theories and therapies that emphasize the values of human freedom and the uniqueness of the individual*. Thus, both positive psychology and the humanistic perspective have called our attention to the constructive side of psychology. Individuals are now being viewed in the light of their potential for health and fulfillment as well as in terms of their vulnerabilities and maladjustments. Two of the main ideas in the humanistic perspective are the phenomenal self and self-actualization. Let's take a look at each.

Exploration 1.3: Positive Psychology

http://www.ppc.sas.upenn.edu/ Learn more about the field of positive psychology by reading articles or becoming a participant in online experiments. This site is sponsored by the leading researcher in the field of positive psychology, Martin Seligman.

THE PHENOMENAL SELF   The **phenomenal self** is *the individual's overall self-concept available to awareness.* Here, the term *phenomenal* refers to that which is apparent to or perceived by the senses—in short, reality as experienced by the individual. Carl Rogers (1980), a leading humanistic psychologist, emphasized that it is this "perceived reality," rather than absolute reality, that is the basis of behavior. Essentially, human behavior is the goal-directed attempt by individuals to satisfy needs as they experience or perceive them. In other words, how a person sees and interprets events in the environment determines how the person reacts to them.

Rogers assumed the existence of an actualizing tendency at the biological level—a human's tendency to develop and fulfill the self. As individuals become aware of themselves, they automatically develop a need for **positive regard** or *acceptance by others*. In the course of actualizing, the individual engages in a valuing (evaluation) process. Experiences that are perceived as enhancing are valued positively and sought after; those that are perceived as blocking fulfillment are valued negatively and avoided. The degree to which individuals trust this valuing process depends in a large measure on their self-concept, especially the **self-image** derived from one's experience with significant others (such as parents) during the formative years of childhood.

SELF-ACTUALIZATION   Self-actualization is *the process of fulfilling our inborn potential*. The term *self-actualization* is usually associated with Abraham Maslow, who gave it its fullest explanation (Hanley & Abell, 2002). Maslow, like Rogers, assumed the existence of an inborn actualizing tendency in the individual. Each child and adult has an inherent need to actualize his or her potentialities. However, in Maslow's conceptualization, the core of growth operates in relation to a hierarchy of needs. Only as the individual's most basic needs are met do the higher growth needs become a potent force in motivation. As long as the individual's needs of hunger, safety, and human companionship remain *un*satisfied, the person is motivated to fulfill them. Once these needs are relatively satisfied, the individual becomes more aware of growth motivation, such as the desire to fulfill needs related to self-esteem, achievement, and personal development (Reiss & Havercamp, 2005). Maslow's concepts will be discussed in greater detail in the chapter entitled Managing Motives and Emotions.

Maslow (1971) held that certain people have reached a healthier, more optimal level of functioning than the average person. He called them *self-actualizing* people and held that studying them may teach us much about our potential for growth. Such people are relatively free from major psychological problems and have made the best possible use of their talents and strengths. Compared to the average person, self-actualizing people have certain characteristics in common, such as a continued freshness of appreciation of everyday realities; greater acceptance of themselves and others; high creativity; and high resistance to conformity (Delle, Massimini, & Bassi, 2011). **Self-actualized** individuals *accept responsibility for their lives and carefully scrutinize the alternatives available to them. They also keep their eyes open and have the courage to admit when they are wrong and need to change.* If self-actualization is indeed a positive process, we should seek out means by which to become more actualized. Activity 1–1 contains a questionnaire designed to assess how much you are moving toward your self-actualization.

ACTIVITY 1–1

ARE YOU BECOMING MORE SELF-ACTUALIZED?

The following survey can help you determine how far you have progressed on the road to self-actualization. Each statement is followed by a scale of 1 (disagree) to 7 (agree). Please mark the extent of your agreement by circling the appropriate number.

1. I experience life fully in the present moment rather than dwelling on the past or worrying about the future.

   Disagree   1   2   3   4   5   6   7   Agree

2. I make choices that will enhance my growth by taking reasonable risks that will develop my potential rather than keep me safe and secure.

   Disagree   1   2   3   4   5   6   7   Agree

3. I listen to my own needs and reactions rather than let others influence me.

Disagree   1   2   3   4   5   6   7   Agree

4. I am honest with myself and with other people.

Disagree   1   2   3   4   5   6   7   Agree

5. I strive to do my best in accomplishing tangible goals in everyday life.

Disagree   1   2   3   4   5   6   7   Agree

6. I am assertive in expressing my needs, ideas, and values.

Disagree   1   2   3   4   5   6   7   Agree

7. I recognize and live by the inspiration of special moments or peak experiences in which I feel especially close to fulfilling my potential.

Disagree   1   2   3   4   5   6   7   Agree

8. I relish new experiences and new knowledge.

Disagree   1   2   3   4   5   6   7   Agree

9. I can identify my defenses and am willing to put them aside in order to revise my expectations, ideas, and values.

Disagree   1   2   3   4   5   6   7   Agree

10. I commit to concerns and causes outside of myself because I recognize that self-actualization comes as a by-product of unique experiences.

Disagree   1   2   3   4   5   6   7   Agree

11. I remember that self-actualization is a lifelong process; it is never fully achieved.

Disagree   1   2   3   4   5   6   7   Agree

12. I trust my own experiences to be my guides in life.

Disagree   1   2   3   4   5   6   7   Agree

Now add up your scores. The higher the score, the more you may have progressed toward optimal being or self-actualization. Find topics (questionnaire items with low scores) that might need more work. Also, keep in mind that few people are truly self-actualized. Actualization is a process, not a final end state. Remember, this questionnaire was specifically devised for this book and thus should be interpreted with caution.

Source: Based on *The Farther Reaches of Human Nature* by Abraham H. Maslow. Viking, 1971.

Our inner core of growth needs may be relatively weak and undeveloped, making it easily stifled by discouraging circumstances. Many people fail to actualize themselves because of the lack of supportive circumstances. However, countless people have been significantly creative despite deprived circumstances, and Maslow acknowledged that it is something of a mystery why wealth and prosperity releases some people for growth while stunting others. As a result, Maslow suggested that a favorable environment is not enough to ensure growth. Individuals must also have an intense desire to grow to offset the fear and resistance to growth.

All things considered, Maslow envisioned personal development as a struggle between growth-fostering forces and growth-discouraging forces, such as fear of the unfamiliar. He felt that society discourages growth by overvaluing safety and physical comfort, as, for example, overly protective parents do. Instead, he suggested that we should minimize the attractions of security and maximize its hazards, such as boredom and stagnation. At the same time, he felt we should emphasize the attractiveness of growth while minimizing its dangers. Maslow (1968) repeatedly emphasized that "growth is, in itself, a rewarding and exciting process, thereby overcoming much of our resistance to self-actualization" (p. 30).

APPLYING IT TO YOURSELF Positive psychology and the humanistic perspectives encourage us to see ourselves in terms of our positive potential, or what we can become. As such, they are more concerned with our **personal growth** than with sheer survival. Problems and conflicts are neither necessary nor inevitable. When these occur, it's likely to be the result of our restrictive self-images, faulty choices, or an unsupportive environment. We may improve ourselves by changing the way we see ourselves and achieving more of the potential control we have over our lives. Such changes occur more readily in an environment conducive to growth, whether a challenging job or a happy marriage, not simply in psychotherapy.

The Ambiguity of Personal Freedom

The above discussion brings us to another issue related to self-direction—freedom. Nobody has written more eloquently about the ambiguity of human freedom than Erich Fromm (1963), the distinguished psychoanalyst. His experience of growing up in Germany during the Nazi regime and his subsequent move to the United States gave him tremendous insight into the problems of totalitarianism and human freedom. According to Fromm, those in individualistic societies have freedom to direct their lives—from the details of their daily existence to more crucial choices, such as what career to pursue. On the other hand, the challenge of freedom can make them feel more anxious, insecure, and isolated. Fromm contends that such isolation may be so unbearable that many people are inclined to escape from the burden of freedom into new dependencies. Examples of such dependencies included looking to experts and the government for assistance, or in our modern society, becoming reliant on the Internet for help in all walks of life, from researching health-related information, to finding new romantic partners, to shopping for clothes, books, and food; and all without leaving the comfort and safety of our homes.

The ambiguity of human freedom is especially evident when making important life choices, for example, *who* we want to be and *how* we want to live our lives. We may find ourselves coping by becoming anxious and "freezing up" in the face of important decisions. Another common strategy is *drifting*. Instead of choosing how to live, people simply drift along, either by living according to the status quo or by dropping out, becoming people whose lives are guided by no ties, codes, traditions, or major purposes.

Another strategy is based on *shared decision making*, as in committee work, marriage, and family life, and assumed agreements among friends. Instead of really making a decision, people just talk until something happens. They presume a consensus, often never questioning it, but if things turn out badly, no one feels responsible: Each merely goes along. Another frequently used strategy for making choices is based on an *appeal to some type of authority*—an expert, a movement, a religion, the government, or some institution. Truly autonomous people rely on none of these strategies. Case in point, many Russian writers working under communist rule in Soviet times, such as Alexander Solzhenitsyn, made one decisive choice after another in order to maintain their personal integrity. They often made these decisions in the face of overwhelming criticism and the threat of severe punishment from their oppressive governments.

Taking Charge of Our Lives

Today, many people the world over are pursuing an odyssey of freedom. Much of the dissatisfaction that occurs in other countries reflects people's desire for the greater liberty and economic opportunity they see in the more economically advanced societies. Case in point, many of the people who immigrate to the United States seek freedom of speech, freedom of religion, and freedom of movement. Moreover, the majority of Americans today feel they have more freedom and control over their lives than their parents did, who were hemmed in by all kinds of social, educational, and economic constraints. For example, most of today's middle-aged Americans did not face the Great Depression or World War II, which delimited their parents' options. They believe they have more opportunities in the important areas of education, work, sex, marriage, religion, family, friends, travel, possessions, where to live, and how to live.

Before you proceed further, make an honest assessment of whether you are actively taking charge of your life by completing the survey in Activity 1–2.

ACTIVITY 1–2

Do You Take Charge of Your Life?

INSTRUCTIONS: *For each statement below, circle T if the statement is generally true of you; circle F if the statement generally is not true of you.*

1. I enjoy being interconnected to others—both friends and family members.　　T　F

2. Sometimes I have difficulty making the choices that make the most sense for my life.　　T　F

3. I have many options from which to select in terms of my education, career, social circle, etc.　　T　F

4. My friends are better than I am at making efficient and sound decisions.　　T　F

5. I get a great deal of satisfaction out of helping others less fortunate than I.　　T　F

6. If I have a choice, I much prefer to do the safe rather than the risky thing.　　T　F

7. I strongly feel that a promise is a promise and should not be broken.　　T　F

8. Difficult decisions daunt me because I have little confidence in my decisional abilities.　　T　F

9. No matter where I am (e.g., at work or at college), I accept my responsibilities.　　T　F

10. Sometimes I call in sick when I am healthy because I do not want to work or study.　　T　F

11. I'd invest my money in a risky but challenging venture.　　T　F

12. During times of stress, I feel as if my life is out of control.　　T　F

13. I am fully aware of who, where, and what I am as well as my personal goals.　　T　F

14. I am disturbed that some charities call me for donations and invade my privacy.　　T　F

15. When and if I ever borrow money, I make sure that I pay it back.　　T　F

16. I do not like it when others expect me to be the one to choose our leisure activity.　　T　F

SCORING: *Even-numbered items* are phrased in a negative direction, so if you answered "F" (false), you may have a "take-charge" attitude or exercise self-direction. The *odd-numbered items* are phrased such that a "T" (true) indicates agreement with an item demonstrating that you probably have self-direction.

Score 1: Total number of "Fs" for even-numbered items _____
Score 2: Total number of "Ts" for odd-numbered items _____
Total for self-direction = Score 1 + Score 2 _____

The higher your grand total, the more self-direction you may have. Now return to the regular reading with your score in mind. Pay attention to how and in what areas of self-direction you can improve.

Freedom, however, has its challenges. Exercising our positive freedom means facing up to the necessity of decision making in our lives, especially the life choices that shape our destinies. At the same time, the fear of making the wrong decision in front of others is so great that many youths speak of "keeping my options open," living in an "extended holding pattern," and being "leery of commitment." Much of this reaction is understandable in light of the uncertainties of our times. However, individuals extrinsically motivated by financial success, an appealing appearance, or social recognition have lower vitality and lower self-actualizing potential and report more health problems than individuals who are more intrinsically or internally inspired. Intrinsically motivated, autonomous, self-actualized individuals appear to be healthier, more self-accepting, and more community-minded as well as better adjusted and less distressed (Baker, 2004; Kasser & Ryan, 1996).

Taking charge of our lives means that we *can and must choose for ourselves*, that is, we must be self-directed. A lack of decisiveness, by default, becomes its own decision. Also, we must make choices in a timely fashion so that our choices do not make us miss opportunities that lead to personal growth. On the other hand, it is fortunate that not all decisions are cast in stone. We can and often do change many decisions as we grow and mature, such as switching college majors or starting a new career. Meanwhile, the realization that our decisions are only as good as the information they are based on reminds us again of the value of continuous learning and critical thinking.

Acting on our *positive* freedom also means *assuming responsibility for our choices*, without blaming others or fate for what happens to us. In fact, those who are self-actualized or internally directed experience less interpersonal distress and more interpersonal closeness, perhaps because they are less likely to blame others (Baker, 2004; Sheffield, Carey, Patenaude, & Lambert, 1995). Interestingly, self-actualized individuals are also more likely to demonstrate **altruism**, or *the desire to help others at cost to the helper* (Koltko-Rivera, 2006).

Admittedly, we had no choice about being thrust into the world, but we have a great deal of choice in the manner in which we live. However, we often hear people say things such as "I can't help it because that's the way I am" or "Naturally I'm this way because of the way I grew up." These people fail to realize that free choice and responsibility go hand in hand. As a constant reminder of this fact, Viktor Frankl (1978) suggested that the Statue of Liberty on the East Coast be supplemented by the Statue of Responsibility on the West Coast.

Self-realization also involves taking calculated risks and making commitments in spite of uncertainty. Where would the world be without the risks taken by, for example, Thomas Edison, Mikhail Gorbachev, the Dalai Lama, and Steve Jobs? Personal growth involves stepping into unfamiliar and potentially risky situations, thereby leaving us more vulnerable to hurt and disappointment. Perfectionists are especially prone *not* to take risks and to be satisfied with low levels of actualization. Self-actualizers are more tolerant of failure (Flett, Hewitt, Blankstein, & Mosher, 1991). With regard to these issues, it is important to ask yourself the following questions: How self-directed are you? How does perfectionism interfere with your taking risks? How actualized are you?

The decision to grow or actualize our potential often has to be made in spite of risks and therefore requires courage. This is the "courage to be," that is, the courage to affirm ourselves and our possibilities in spite of the perils that lie ahead. On the other hand, we run a risk whenever we avoid growing. Each time we pass up an opportunity to develop a new skill or when we value security over challenge, we run the risk of becoming stagnant or succumbing to boredom. When we habitually suppress or deny the inherent growth tendency of humans, we risk becoming maladaptive, sometimes in obvious ways, sometimes in subtle ways, sometimes immediately, or sometimes later in life. Fortunately, mechanisms for growth, such as higher education and continual learning, help individuals self-actualize (Barnes & Srinivas, 1993; MacKay & Kuh, 1994). Abraham Maslow (1968) once observed that many of the characteristic disorders of our time such as the "stunted person," the "amoral person," or the "apathetic person" result from the fundamental failure to grow.

Living in Today's Individualistic Society

Interestingly, the times in which we live afford us a more supportive environment because of the technological advances that bring friends and family on the other side of the continent "closer" to us. In fact, we can contact whole group of supportive people at once by merely pressing a few buttons on our handheld devices. Just as important, though, is the increased number of hazards in our social and physical environments: We meet more people, some of whom are highly critical of us and judgmental; we become bewildered by the increasing number of available consumer choices; and we worry about the proliferation of hazards in our environment, from threats of child victimization on the Internet to pandemics such as H1N1 (Swine) flu and AIDS. These, in turn, heighten the challenge of self-direction.

The cumulative impact of these social changes has given rise to newer social values and newer rules by which people live in comparison to older generations. Generally, these changes mean greater interest in shaping the environment to meet *our* needs (i.e., increased personal control) rather than society's needs and goals. Ask yourself this: In today's society, to what extent are people preoccupied with themselves?

THEMES OF PERSONAL GROWTH

LEARNING OBJECTIVES

1.8 Describe some of the problems of using self-help books.
1.9 List some characteristics that change over time and list some that remain the same.
1.10 Describe the three-phase cycle by which we experience personal growth.
1.11 Explain why it is important to move beyond individualism.

Living with Contradictions and Uncertainty

All of us face the challenge of reconciling old rules with new rules and old values with new values. Many of us feel we must honor the old values of hard work, frugality, and moderation to complete an education and secure our careers and, thus, the means to enjoy the new values associated with personal pleasure and freedom (Moen & Roehling, 2005). In many ways these two sets of values contradict each other, making it difficult to reconcile them. For example, we know we must work to support our families, but at the same time we may also want to drive an expensive convertible and experience the thrill of the wind blowing through our hair—a symbol of independence and freedom.

Those of us who seek guidance about personal growth from popular self-help books, television shows that entertain more than they educate, and movements that blend pop psychology with quasi-religious thought do not always fare well. Many of these sources oversimplify the process of personal and social change, generating grossly unrealistic and disappointing results, while at the same time garnering the purveyors of such drivel millions upon millions of dollars (Salerno, 2005). In contrast, psychological research (such as that found in this book) can provide sound principles of personal development and growth as well as guidance related to self-direction and social responsibility. Throughout this book we attempt to show how the principles and findings of contemporary psychology can help us better understand ourselves and others and, thus, to cope more effectively with our environment and fulfill more of our potential.

This statement does not mean that personal growth can be achieved by simply reading a book on the subject. Neither does mere exposure to scientific knowledge or interesting examples guarantee that you will use the information. Now, let's look further at some other issues related to seeking self-direction.

Continuity and Change

A key issue for psychologists and the public alike is the extent to which people change over a lifetime. Do our personalities really change, or do they remain stable? Do we change in fits and starts or gradually? What makes us change—many small experiences or cataclysmic events? As it turns out, many positive aspects of our personalities, such as levels of warmth, assertiveness, and sociability, tend to remain stable throughout the life span; however, so to do many negative traits, such as depression, anxiety, hostility, and impulsiveness. Thus, individuals who were expressive and outgoing in their teens are apt to remain that way in adulthood. In contrast, those who were inhibited and shy in their teens tend to remain inhibited and shy.

Psychologists supporting the stability thesis state that even when individuals do change because of personal maturation or life experiences, the unique differences among people remain. This means that a rather impulsive 20-year-old like Karen may be a bit less impulsive by the time she is 55, but she is still likely to be more impulsive than her age-mates at any given time. In addition, as people grow older, the stability of their personalities becomes more evident. Thus, there is more stability of personality from ages 30 to 40 than there is from 20 to 30 (Pfaffenberger, 2005). Part of the reason for increased stability with age is that we tend to select and stay in environments and marry people that help sustain our traits (Caspi & Herbener, 1990).

Nevertheless, our lives are also filled with change, especially in the areas of self-esteem, sense of personal mastery or control over their environment, and values. Additionally, personal beliefs (e.g., about the malleability of personality) can play a significant role in altering personality across the life span (Dweck, 2008). Individuals who *believe* that they can change are more open to learning, more willing to confront challenges, and are better able to bounce back from failures. Those who *believe* that their traits are fixed have a more difficult time facing challenges, such as stressful business tasks or conflict-laden relationships. The emphasis on the potential for change has been embraced by those who want to foster change, from weight watchers to social watchers, all of whom stress openness to change throughout the course of adulthood.

The tension between continuity and change is found not only in academic debates but also in each of us. How much personal growth or change in a desirable direction we want depends greatly on the different priorities we assign to stability or change, that is, *how much we want to change* and *how differently we want to live our lives*. Thus, people with traditional values tend to exhibit a high degree of stability in their lives unless something happens to make them change. For them, the events most likely to cause change are usually quite dramatic, such as an unwanted divorce, the death of a child, failure in one's career, or witnessing a traumatic event. In contrast, those who put value on personal growth will experience positive change throughout their lives, and without the need for a dramatic or traumatic event to propel them forward.

The Experience of Personal Growth

To believe we can change is one thing. To *pursue and actively achieve personal change* is something else. Think about all the times you have vowed to exercise but didn't or swore to quit smoking cigarettes and failed. These are but small instances of attempts to change. Like all patterns of development, our inner experience of growth tends to be uneven, with spurts and plateaus. We may be willing to try out something new one minute and retreat to the familiar the next. Because we experience our inner world more as a continuous flow of ideas, feelings, and meanings, we are more apt to realize that we've grown in *retrospect* than while we're in the midst of personal growth.

Exploration 1.4: Personal Growth

www.best-personal-growth-resources.com   A site dedicated to personal growth, with lots of free resources, including information on growth-promoting activities.

In fact, the experience of personal growth tends to follow *a three-phase cycle*:

1. *Acknowledging change.* Growth usually begins with the acknowledgment of change. Actually, changes occur all the time, but we're not always aware of them. A constant awareness of change would be too disrupting to our daily lives. Instead, we strive to construct an image of ourselves and our world that pictures reality as under our control and more stable than it really is. As a result, we become more acutely aware of changes at some moments than at others. Sometimes, we become aware of change rather suddenly, for example, by receiving an unexpected compliment or criticism. Taking on new responsibilities, such as a marriage, parenthood, or promotion at work, forces us to acknowledge change, too. The common denominator in all these experiences is *the realization that things are different from what they were*—or what we believed or expected they would be.

2. *A sense of dissonance or dissatisfaction.* Whether the awareness of change leads to growth depends on how we react. Sometimes we may respond to change defensively, with little awareness of our real feelings—positive or negative. In contrast, when someone feels disappointment, he or she actually may be aroused or motivated to seek further change or confront the challenge of disappointment. Thus, the growth cycle can often be triggered by disappointment and failure as well as by success. This phase of growth (dissonance) is inevitably accompanied by a certain degree of anxiety and discomfort. When our motive for growth proceeds out of a sense of challenge or mastery, we may be more stimulated and less apprehensive about the outcome. But when our motive springs from profound dissatisfaction with ourselves, our feelings tend to be more agonizing.

3. *Reorganizing our experience.* In conventional psychological terms, *reorganizing* is often defined as acquiring new ideas and then altering our attitudes, behaviors, and values in response. As an example, we may adopt a new attitude toward another person, becoming more willing to listen to someone's criticism because we know that the person wants to help rather than hurt us. Growth may also take the form of new self-perceptions, for example, increased self-acceptance and confidence from an achievement, such as earning a college degree. The main point is that each inner adjustment or change we make affects the whole of our experience, so that growth consists of the continuous reorganization of that experience.

Beyond Individualism

At times, the language of individualism has the potential to limit the way people think. For example, we have long celebrated "independence" on July 4, but we are only now slowly recognizing our "interdependence" on others via *Make a Difference Day*. Being responsible to the self alone limits the influence of both culture and society, rendering people less committed to the common purposes of humanity. This is in sharp contrast to collectivist societies in which self-orientation is held in check by strong ties to family and community. That is not to say, however, that those from individualistic society think solely about themselves. For instance, each year millions of Americans volunteer their time and money to help those in need. And witness how the whole nation pulled together following the terrorist attacks of September 11, 2001.

Exploration 1.5: Interdependence

www.change.org   A site dedicated to those interested in creating social change.

A major reassessment of the search for self-fulfillment may be giving rise to a more realistic view of life and personal fulfillment. Millions of people are discovering, often through

Terrorist acts and disasters sometimes stimulate collectivism in Americans who are otherwise fairly individualistic.

such painful experiences, such as watching their adult children or parents become unemployed, that preoccupation with their own personal needs is not a direct path to fulfillment. The heart of this new outlook is the realization that *personal fulfillment can be achieved only in relation to others*—through a web of shared meanings that transcend the isolated individual. Personal fulfillment in the deeper sense requires commitments that endure over long periods of time and perhaps require self-sacrifice. The term *commitment* shifts the focus away from unduly individualistic notions of the self, either self-denial or self-fulfillment, toward the more inclusive "self connected to others." This is a positive change, because almost all of our activity occurs in relationships, groups, and community, structured by institutions and interpreted by cultural meaning. As we've seen, human fulfillment is more complex than popularly thought and requires a better balance between the interests of self and of society.

Activity 1–3 is designed to help you discover the extent of your own individualism in our interdependent world. When you have finished the activity, ask yourself if you need to be more interconnected with your family, friends, and community.

ACTIVITY 1–3

How Individualistic Are You?

Go back to your e-mail account, your diary, letters you have written to your friends and family, or some other written document developed by you. Count how many times pronouns related to yourself such as I, my, me, mine, etc., occur and how many time pronouns such as you or we or they (or pronouns indicating that you were taking into account another's feelings, needs, or desires) occur.

PRONOUNS RELATED TO SELF _____

PRONOUNS RELATED TO OTHERS _____

Which type of pronouns prevailed? Are pronouns indicating the importance of others more predominant or are pronouns related to you more predominant? In terms of individualism and social connectedness, what do your results suggest about you?

Chapter Summary

SOCIAL CHANGE

1.1 Explain how technology is changing the way we communicate and live.

Technological changes have given rise to a global outlook in which people are influenced by what they see happening in other countries. Technology has made relationships more fluid, flexible, and portable, but it has also blurred the boundaries between work and home.

1.2 Discuss other recent social changes unrelated to technology.

In the United States, there is an increasingly diverse population. Across the globe, the population expansion has resulted in concerns about poverty, unemployment, and the health of our environment.

THE CHALLENGE OF SELF-DIRECTION

1.3 Explain the concept of self-direction.

Self-direction refers to the need to learn more about ourselves and our world as a means of directing our lives more effectively.

1.4 Compare individualistic and collectivist societies.

In an individualistic society, individual gain is appreciated more than general societal gain. In contrast, in a collectivist society societal gain is cherished over individual advancement.

1.5 Define positive psychology.

Positive psychology is an umbrella term for the study of positive emotions, positive character traits, and positive actions that allow individuals and institutions to thrive.

1.6 Summarize the humanistic perspective.

The humanistic perspective focuses on what makes human existence distinctive, such as the meaning and richness of subjective interpretations, the holistic characteristics of experience, and our capacity to willfully choose and determine behaviors and thoughts for ourselves.

1.7 Discuss what it means to take charge of your life.

Taking charge of your life means that you face up to the importance of decision making, taking calculated risks for the sake of growth, and assuming full responsibility for your lives.

THEMES OF PERSONAL GROWTH

1.8 Describe some of the problems of using self-help books.

People looking to self-help books for advice tend to find an oversimplified idea of self-fulfillment, leading to unrealistic expectations that end in disappointment. In contrast, the field of psychology offers sound principles and tested knowledge that may help to achieve realistic self-direction and growth.

1.9 List some characteristics that change over time and list some that remain the same.

Many positive aspects of our personalities, such as levels of warmth, assertiveness, and sociability, tend to remain stable throughout the life span; however, so to do many negative traits, such as depression, anxiety, hostility, and impulsiveness. Characteristics that can change include self-esteem, sense of personal mastery or control over their environment, and values.

1.10 Describe the three-phase cycle by which we experience personal growth.

The subjective experience of growth involves a three-phase cycle: (1) the acknowledgment of change within ourselves or our environment, (2) a sense of dissonance or dissatisfaction within, which in turn leads to (3) reorganizing our experience in some way, such as adopting a new attitude toward ourselves or others.

1.11 Explain why it is important to move beyond individualism.

Today, a major reassessment of the self-fulfillment movement is under way, giving rise to a more realistic view of life and personal fulfillment. The core of this new approach is the call for a realignment of the interests of self and society so that personal fulfillment can be realized in relation to others—through a web of shared meanings that transcend the isolated individual.

Self-Test

1. Facebook has transformed the way that people network for jobs, interact with others, and stay in touch with family and friends. In other words, Facebook helped establish _____ throughout the world.

   a. mesosystems
   b. social change
   c. collective modifications
   d. universal reforms

2. Eddard is very old fashioned. He likes to read books printed on paper, watch re-runs of *Gunsmoke* on a black and white TV, and listen to music on vinyl records. For over 40 years, he successfully avoided using all of those new electronic gizmos and gadgets that kept popping up. Based on this profile, Eddard may be classified as having _____.
   a. electrophobia
   b. mediaphilia
   c. digital fright
   d. technophobia

3. Which of the following activities is least likely to promote self-direction?
   a. learning how to use Photoshop
   b. attending a workshop on cultural diversity
   c. playing with your dog in the park
   d. seeing a counselor to deal with emotional issues resulting from a divorce

4. Cultures in which individual gain is appreciated more than general societal gain are referred to as _____societies.
   a. individualistic
   b. collectivist
   c. interdependent
   d. consensual level

5. The statement "It takes a village to raise a child" would most likely be used to guide behavior in a _____ society.
   a. collectivist
   b. intradependent
   c. individualistic
   d. autonomous

6. Which group is increasing fastest in the United States?
   a. Hispanics   b. Asians
   c. African-Americans   d. Whites

7. What is the correct ordering for the three-phases associated with the experience of growth
   a. a sense of dissonance, reorganizing our experience, acknowledging change
   b. acknowledging change, a sense of dissonance, reorganizing our experience
   c. reorganizing our experience, acknowledging change, a sense of dissonance
   d. a sense of dissonance, acknowledging change, reorganizing our experience

8. After suffering a career-ending injury to her knee, Whitney realized that her life would never be the same. Which phase in the experience of growth does this example illustrate?
   a. acknowledging change
   b. a sense of dissonance
   c. reorganizing our experience
   d. none of the above

9. People need to realize that _____ are a necessary component of self-fulfillment.
   a. relationships with others
   b. egocentrism
   c. self-denial
   d. isolation

10. The individual's overall self-concept available to awareness is called the _____.
   a. actualized self
   b. archival self
   c. phenomenal self
   d. developmental self

Exercises

1. *Social change.* What two or three societal changes are having the greatest impact on your life (e.g., changes in technology, the economy)? Write a page or so about how your life is affected by these changes. For example, think about how a computer has altered your academic, business, and personal life. Are most of the societal changes having a negative or positive impact on your life? Are you coping with the changes appropriately? Are the changes helping you grow?

2. *Change as a challenge or threat.* Select some change that has occurred in your environment recently, such as a new professor, a marital engagement, or layoffs at work. Then write a page or so describing how you feel about this change, especially whether you see it as a challenge or a threat and why.

3. *Identify your level of interdependence.* Identify at least one important aspect of your life, such as a job, a friendship, or marriage. Then describe in a few paragraphs how much you're prepared to give to this relationship and how much you expect in return. Are your expectations fair? If the give and take is unbalanced, how do you think your expectations will affect your relationships?

4. *How important is self-fulfillment to you?* Think about what you do that is fulfilling. What are your life goals? Are they generally other-centered or self-centered, and is this adaptive and growth-oriented? What do you do to actively meet these goals?

5. *Self-fulfillment and personal and social involvement.* Select some area of your life that has been very gratifying to you (an accomplishment, relationship, etc.) and describe the extent to which your sense of fulfillment depended on involvement with others.

Questions for Self-Reflection

1. Are you more optimistic about your own personal future than that of our society or the world?
2. Are you so concerned about keeping your options open that you may suffer from the inability to make decisions? Are you too perfectionistic?
3. How much control do you feel you have over your life? How much control do you think you need? Are you a self-directed person?
4. Would you agree that many of the ground rules in our society have changed from one century to the next? How so?
5. Have you met people who act as if there are no rules—that anything goes? What are such people like?
6. How important are self-fulfillment values to you?
7. Do you expect more out of life than your parents did?
8. Can you remember a difficult time in your life and, in retrospect, realize it was a time of growth?
9. Would you agree that personal fulfillment is achieved mostly in and through our relationships with others?
10. What keeps you from self-actualizing?

Chapter Two

The Puzzle of Childhood

*T*hree-year-old Sara was having the time of her life. This was her first trip to the zoo and she was excited to be near the animals that she had only previously seen on TV. Sara was especially fond of the black bears because they looked just like Teddy, the stuffed animal she was carrying under her arm. But then her parents told her it was time to go. Sara, having been in this situation before, knew just exactly what to do . . . she became enraged, refusing to get back into the stroller. She yelled and screamed, and even tossed her beloved Teddy to the ground. Exasperated, her parents gave up trying to get Sara into the stroller, and let her walk around the zoo until she was tired. At preschool the next day, Sara told her friends what a great time she had at the zoo. Her friends then talked about their favorite animals; even the teacher joined in on the fun. When she was 14, Sara found herself smiling as she remembered this event, as well as the many other times she had gotten her way by having a huge hissy-fit in public. She had plenty of time to think about these sorts of things, as she was grounded in her room for doing something her parents did not like, even though she wasn't quite sure what it was.

PERSPECTIVES ON CHILD DEVELOPMENT

LEARNING OBJECTIVES

2.1 Explain why a perspective approach of development is important.

2.2 Explain Bronfenbrenner's theory of ecological development and the four contexts of the environment that comprise it.

2.3 Describe Erikson's theory of psychosocial development.

2.4 Explain Bandura's concept of modeling and social learning.

From infancy through adolescence, the ways in which youth think, feel, and interact with others is dramatically transformed. For example, whereas infants cry when left alone, adolescents desire solitude; while 4-year-olds think that monsters live under beds, teenagers believe no such thing, rather, they are afraid of their parents embarrassing them in front of their peers; and for young children "friends" are people you play with, in contrast, for older youth friendship requires trust, intimacy, and being "friended" on Facebook. Each of these examples illustrates the concept of **development—**defined as *the relatively enduring changes in people's capacities and behavior as they grow older because of biological growth processes and people's interaction with their*

BOX 2–1   Did you know that . . .

- Babies have more brain cells (close to 200 billion) than adults.
- Around 18 months of age, toddlers start learning close to 50 words per day.
- In today's society, girls get their periods nearly 2 years earlier (around age 12) than girls of previous decades.
- Children are unable to recall memories of events that occurred before age three.
- Most children start telling lies between 3 and 4 years of age.

Source: Based on *Child Development: Its Nature and Course* by Ganie DeHart, L. Alan Sroufe and Robert G, Cooper. The McGraw-Hill Companies, 2004.

environment. Remember, when studying children, generalizing the findings from adults to adolescents or from older children to younger children can lead to incorrect and misleading conclusions. Developmental status matters!

On the Importance of Childhood

Historically, children were once thought to be miniature versions of adults. That is, children had the *same* thoughts, feelings, and capabilities as adults do, only they were a lot smaller (Stearns, 2006). When children and adults are alike in every meaningful way, childhood becomes unimportant. Today, not only are children and adults viewed as having different physical and psychological characteristics, but childhood is looked upon as one of the most important contributors to a healthy adulthood. For instance, the quality of the relationships between infants and their mothers has been shown to influence friendships during elementary school, self-esteem during adolescence, and interactions with spouses and children decades later (Cassidy & Shaver, 2008). Likewise, the choices parents make about raising their children (such as whether to spank, show affection, etc.) is heavily influenced by the type of parenting they received growing up (Kovan, Chung, & Sroufe, 2009).

Psychologists liken child development to the building of a house. Childhood is the foundation upon which the remainder of development rests, just as the house's foundation is the support for the rest of the home—the floors, walls, roof, and so forth. If the foundation is weak, the future of the house is in jeopardy as problems such as cracks in the walls or sticky windows develop when the foundation sags. If the foundation of the house is sound, however, the house may well withstand duress such as floods and high winds. If not, it can certainly be easily rebuilt. Many perspectives on development take this same tack—that a healthy childhood can create resiliency that helps the person overcome problems later in life.

Psychologists approach development from different viewpoints or perspectives. Although there are dozens of different theories of development, most of them generally can be grouped into four basic types: biological, ecological, psychodynamic, and social learning. Each perspective emphasizes certain aspects of development, while minimizing, if not overlooking, others. What *each* view offers us, then, is a limited understanding of how children grow, think, feel, and interact with others over time. When looked at as a whole, however, a more complete picture of childhood emerges. So, rather than attempting to prove which view of development is more correct, it is more helpful to learn the best that each perspective has to offer (Johnson, Slater, & Hocking, 2011). Think of each perspective as a piece in the puzzle that is child development.

Before proceeding further, look at Box 2–2, which presents some interesting and often startling statistics about childhood in America.

The Biological Perspective on Child Development

Today, the rapid increase in knowledge about brain functioning and genes provides scientific evidence for a biological basis for some aspects of development. Although the exact proportions

BOX 2–2   Focus on Family: America's Children: Will They Make It?

Here are some revealing statistics—both positive and negative—about America's children. Decide for yourself whether you think today's children have a good start on a happy and productive life:

- The number of children in the United States is projected to increase to 88 million by 2030.
- In 2010, 66 percent of children lived with two parents.
- About 21 percent of children under the age of 17 live in poverty.
- Nearly 41 percent of U.S. children are born out of wedlock.
- Each year, close to 3 percent of children join their families through adoption.
- Close to 20 percent of children are taken care of by their fathers while their mothers work.
- Around 10 out of every 1000 children experiences some form of maltreatment.
- Nearly 60 percent of children are covered by private health insurance; another 37 percent are covered by public policies.
- The percentage of children under the age of 18 who are clinically obese is 19.
- Almost 5 percent of children and adolescents are reported by parents as having serious behavioral or emotional problems.
- About 21 percent of school-aged children speak a language other than English at home.
- After graduation, close to 70 percent of teens immediately enroll in a 2-year or 4-year college.
- Around 46 percent of high school students report having sexual intercourse.
- Close to 24 percent of 12th-grade students report recently using illicit drugs. About 23 percent also report recent alcohol use.

Source: Childstats.gov.

remain unknown, genetic influences account for between 25 percent and 75 percent of the differences in characteristics among the general population (Plomin, DeFries, McClearn, & McGuffin, 2008). For instance, genetic factors have been cited for a wide range of psychological outcomes in adulthood, including alcoholism, depression, and phobias. During childhood, the evidence seems strongest for such characteristics as intelligence, sociability, emotionality, and activity level (Bazzett, 2008).

Exploration 2.1: Child Well-Being

www.hfrp.org   Provides information that promotes well-being for children and their families.

Some psychologists argue that biology influences almost all of our personal qualities and development (Bouchard, 2004). Biological aspects of development include **heredity** (*the transmission of traits from parents to offspring*), aspects of the nervous system related to behavior, and the influence of hormones. For instance, preschool children's preference for arousing or sedentary activities is affected by the amount of the hormone testosterone that they are exposed to during prenatal development (Cohen-Bendahan, van de Beek, & Berenbaum, 2005). In most arguments about development, heredity comes to the forefront as the most important biological determinant of who we are and how we develop.

APPLYING IT TO YOURSELF   According to the **biological perspective**, *many of our personal attributes and much of our personal development may be attributable to genetic and other biological influences.* Have you ever considered the dominant traits in your family tree? At the next family gathering, observe your relatives for a while. You might notice that a favorite uncle or aunt exhibits the same warmth and sociability that you do. How is it possible that you are more similar to this more distant relative than to your siblings on this trait? The

BOX 2–3	Focus on Family: Do Birth Order Effects Really Exist?

Are only children really pampered, spoiled, self-centered, and uncooperative? Do first-born children strive to please others and have the highest IQs? Are they controlling of others but conforming to parental desires? Do second-born children always rebel and feel as if they are in a constant race to catch up to their older sibling? Surely middle children always view life as unfair, feel unloved, and are destined to be viewed by their families as having problems. In thinking of your own family, or those of your friends, supporting cases easily come to mind. Whether the portrayal involves Jan and Peter from *The Brady Bunch* or Malcolm from *Malcolm in the Middle,* television and movies often depict siblings along the lines of the birth order stereotypes mentioned above. Nevertheless, psychologists have had great difficulty finding consistent support for the idea that personality, social relationships, and intelligence systematically vary by the order of one's birth (Dunkel, Harbke, & Papini, 2009). At this point, birth order effects appear to be more myth than reality!

answer may be heredity; you may simply share more genes with this person than with your brothers and sisters.

As we've seen, characteristics like intelligence and sociability may have a marked genetic influence. Nevertheless, even these characteristics are determined not so much by a single gene as by a complex combination of genes that gives rise to a range of potential responses. How much or how little of our potential we develop, however, depends largely on our interaction with the environment. For instance, a first-born girl might earn high grades and go on to become a physician. Her younger sister, who is equally smart but impatient about waiting to start her career, may choose an occupation as an emergency medical technician. The schooling required is less demanding and time-consuming, and therefore may appeal to her hasty tendencies. While both sisters may get similar scores on an intelligence test, they have different perceptions about their futures and interests. Do such sibling differences occur in reality? Absolutely, but are such differences characteristic related to birth order, such as being a first- or second-born child? Take a look at Box 2–3 for a discussion of the interesting topic.

The Ecological Perspective on Child Development

Although biology is an important influence on development, so too are the environments in which development takes places. For instance, Sara's parents took her to the zoo because they felt that she would benefit from real-life encounters with interesting animals. Each year, youth come across hundreds, if not thousands, of different environments, such as school, houses of worship, and parks. Although the settings for each of these environments differ, they all have one thing in common: The child experiences the environment first hand. However, children can also be influenced by environments they did not actually experience. For your consideration, the *No Child Left Behind Act* of 2001 required that children in grades 3 through 8 take standardized tests every year. Although children were not involved in the legislation of this act, they are still influenced by it every time they take a mandated test!

Urie Bronfenbrenner's (1993) **ecological perspective** emphasizes the role of such environmental *contexts* on children's development. Bronfenbrenner organized the environments that influence youth into four interrelated contexts (or systems) of development: microsystem, mesosystem, exosystem, and macrosystem. Let's take a look at each.

MICROSYSTEM   A **microsystem** *refers to the setting that the child is currently in, such as the home or daycare center.* Typically, the first microsystem that youth encounter is the hospital in which they are born. Within each microsystem, youth engage in activities (e.g., playing, eating) and interact with others (e.g., talking, fighting). Some of these activities/interactions are initiated by the child and some are started by other individuals, such as parents and siblings. As such, microsystems are dynamic contexts of interaction. Over time, children are influenced by the different microsystems that they encounter and the varying experiences they had within. For instance, in the United States, Japan, and Israel, children and adolescents with TVs in their bedroom watch more TV, get less sleep, and report feeling more tired than youth without TVs in their bedroom (Kirsh, 2010; Oka, Suzuki, & Inoue, 2008; Shochat, Flint-Bretler, & Tzischinsky, 2010).

MESOSYSTEM   As mentioned above, while at preschool Sara told her classmates about the great time she had at the zoo and they responded positively. Thus, what happened to Sara in one microsystem (the zoo) influenced her, a short time later, in a *different* microsystem (preschool). *In the ecological environment, the linking of microsystems* is referred to as a **mesosystem.** It is important to remember that mesosystem influences take place over time, as the child is directly involved in each microsystem. The concept of the mesosystem is extremely central to the understanding of child development, for it states that not only are the experiences within each microsystem important to the child in that particular setting, but potentially in other settings as well. For instance, children experiencing sensitive, responsive care at home are better liked by their peers at school (Dwyer et al., 2010); and for adolescents, watching multiple hours of music videos per week at home increases the odds of drinking alcohol when going out by 239 percent (Van den Bulck, Beullens, & Mulder, 2006).

EXOSYSTEM   In the third context of development, the **exosystem,** *children and adolescents are influenced by social settings that they do not take part in.* How is it possible that children can be affected by a context that is unknown to them? The answer is simple: Someone the child knows was in that setting and what happened to *him or her* causes a change in how he or she acts toward the child in a *different* setting. For example, when single mothers are stressed due to work-related conditions, the home environment of their preschool children suffers (e.g., the parent is less sensitive and more hostile) (Lleras, 2008). In this case, a context unfamiliar to the child (mom's workplace) influenced the child's life.

MACROSYSTEM   The last of Bronfenbrenner's systems, the **macrosystem,** refers to the larger sociocultural context in which development takes place, including cultural (e.g., American, Japanese), sub-cultural (e.g., gender, race, religion), and social-class (e.g., wealthy or poor) distinctions. Essentially, the macrosystem refers to *the set of shared values, goals, practices, and attitudes that characterizes a group of people.* In turn, these values, goals, etc., influence all other systems within the ecological environment, which correspondingly affect the child's development. Here are some examples: Youth brought up in cultures that are more accepting of real-life violence tend to be more violent themselves (Tolan, Gorman-Smith, & Henry, 2003). And adolescents raised to believe that religion is important are less likely than other youth to drink alcohol and engage in binge drinking (Dunn, 2005).

APPLYING IT TO YOURSELF   Because of macro- and exosystem influences, each of us plays a role in the development of all children, even those we do not know. By reinforcing cultural ideology, attitudes, and values (macrosystem influences) and by our interactions with coworkers, siblings, and strangers (as part of an exosystem), we indirectly influence the children around us. Of course, whenever we encounter children directly, we have entered into a microsystem, and therefore become a direct influence in their lives. And the lessons learned in these microsystems can be taken by children to other environments, affecting a whole new group of children (via the mesosystem). Thus, the welfare of children is influenced by environments both big and small. Not only can improvements in society, such as gender and racial equality, positively affect children for generations to come, but so too can our own *personal* growth and development be beneficial to those around us. Through the ecological environment, personal growth becomes a gift that keeps on giving.

Exploration 2.2: Understanding Children

kidshealth.org   A website providing helpful information on a variety of developmental topics to parents, children, teenagers, and educators.

The Psychodynamic Perspective on Child Development

The **psychodynamic perspective** *views personality and behavior as resulting from unconscious forces (such as desires, anxieties, and conflicts), especially those originating in childhood.* According to this viewpoint, individuals are inevitably caught in the clash between conflicting dynamics of life, such as those between impulses and inhibitions. For the child, the conflict occurs between the child's own desires and the demands of placed on him or her by parents and society (Doerr, 2007). Although Sigmund Freud's theory introduced the psychodynamic perspective to the world, and subsequently revolutionized the field of psychology, it does not encompass a *realistic* view of child development. As such, we'll focus on Erik Erikson's psychosocial perspective, which details *key* issues that people face during specific periods of development. (See Box 2–4 for Freud's stages of psychosexual development.)

ERIKSON'S STAGES OF PSYCHOSOCIAL DEVELOPMEN   Erik Erikson (1964) widened the potential application of psychodynamic theory by transforming Freud's psychosexual theory of development into a more inclusive view of personality development. Whereas Freud focused on the child's psychosexual development with the family, Erikson takes into account the individual's psychosocial relationships within the larger society. And whereas Freud's stages covered only the years between birth and puberty, Erikson's stages extend throughout adulthood into old age. Each of the eight psychosocial stages is presented as a polarity (or crisis), with a positive ability to be achieved along with a related threat or vulnerability. At every stage of development, key social agents help the individual resolve the current crisis, with the resolution (be it successful or unsuccessful) influencing the outcome of the next crisis encountered. Thus, human development is thought to be both sequential *and* cumulative, with one's overall personality composed of the strengths and weaknesses acquired during each psychosocial stage. In the current chapter, the first five stages related to child and adolescent development are presented. The remaining three stages will be discussed in the following chapter, which focuses on adulthood.

STAGE 1: TRUST VS. MISTRUST   The first year of life corresponds to the first psychosocial stage, *Trust versus Mistrust.* Being completely helpless, infants must rely on others to meet (1) their physical needs for food, clothing, diaper changes, bodily comfort, etc.; and (2) their psychological desires for affection, emotional sensitivity, and timely responsiveness to their signals for care. When infants' physical and emotional needs are *consistently* met, the world seems like a safe place and, correspondingly, they learn to trust the people around them. If, however, their needs are not met, infants become anxious and mistrustful, for the world has proven to be unresponsive to their needs and therefore dangerous to be in. During this stage, the key social agent (whose *behavior* creates in the infant a sense of trust or mistrust) is the primary caretaker, typically the mother.

BOX 2–4	Focus on Psychology: Freud's Psychosexual Stages of Development

Since Freud regarded **libido**, or *psychic energy related to sexuality*, as fundamental, he interpreted development in terms of a series of **psychosexual stages**. In each stage, *the child seeks to gratify the drive for pleasure in the various body zones: the mouth, the anus, and the genitals. The manner in which children handle the conflict between their impulses and environmental restrictions is decisive for development.* Too little or too much gratification at a certain stage may result in **fixation**, *by which the person becomes emotionally fixed at a particular anxiety-ridden stage and continues to act out symbolically the wishes that were overly inhibited or indulged.*

Stage	Approximate Age	Major Characteristics
Oral	Birth–1 year	The mouth is the primary means of gratification. Fixation may result in either a passive personality associated with addictive eating, smoking, or drinking or in sarcasm in a person who is always criticizing everyone else's ideas without offering any of his or her own.
Anal	1–3 years	The major source of physical pleasure becomes the releasing or retaining of feces. Fixation in the early phase of this stage may result in adult tendencies toward disorderly, messy behavior. By contrast, fixation in the later phase of this stage would give rise to the stubborn, compulsively orderly personality in adulthood.
Phallic	3–5 years	The child experiences sensual pleasure through handling of his or her genitals. Too little or too much gratification sets the stage for later difficulties, such as the individual who feels guilty about his or her sexuality or engages in sex to reduce anxiety. Children develop an *Oedipus* (boys) or *Electra* (girls) *complex*, in which they are sexually attracted to the opposite-sex parent and envy the same-sex parent. Resolution of these complexes results in children identifying with the same-sex parent, thus incorporating their parent's sexual orientation, mannerisms, and values.
Latency	5–12 years	Early sexual feelings are forgotten and sexual urges lie relatively dormant. Children focus on sports, schoolwork, and same-sex friendships.
Genital	12 years onward	Sexual interests are reawakened and focus on gratification through genital or sexual activity. The well-adjusted adult experiences genital strivings so that he or she is capable of genuine love and adult sexual satisfaction. Most adult problems with sex derive from fixations at the earlier oral, anal, or phallic stages.

STAGE 2: AUTONOMY VS. SHAME AND DOUBT Erikson's second psychosocial stage, *Autonomy versus Shame and Doubt,* which occurs between 1 and 3 years of age, focuses on the toddler's increasing desire to be independent and self-reliant. As parents (the key social agents of this stage) encourage children to walk, talk, and do things for themselves, children will develop age-appropriate autonomy. However, as Sara's behavior at the zoo illustrated, autonomy can quickly turn into defiance, and if parents are coercive or overprotective, children will experience self-doubt and feel ashamed of themselves.

STAGE 3: INITIATIVE VS. GUILT From 3 to 6 years of age, children are faced with the crisis of *Initiative versus Guilt.* During this third psychosocial stage, preschoolers readily roam about and attempt to plan new activities, make new friends, and develop a sense of judgment (e.g.,

Erik Erikson's theory asserts that children in grade school pass through a crisis of industry versus inferiority.

knowing when it is appropriate to cross a road). Rather than simply imitating the actions of others, which is commonplace during the toddler period, youth are now initiating them. If such efforts are supported by family members, children will enjoy exploring their environment and trying new things, and consequently develop a sense of initiative. However, if such actions conflict with the goals of parents and siblings, and are thus unduly restricted or punished, children may become passive and guilt-ridden about taking the initiative. As this description illustrates, *all* family members are now key social agents. As such, frequent conflicts with siblings and **sibling rivalry**—*jealousy and resentment between siblings*—are threats to the successful development of initiative.

STAGE 4: INDUSTRY VS. INFERIORITY   *Industry versus Inferiority* is the fourth crisis that children face. Taking place from about 6 to 11 years of age, children are tasked with mastering both academic and social skills. Aiding children during this crisis are newly developed cognitive abilities that allow youth to not only compare themselves with their peers, but also consider how their peers view them! The resolution of this crisis is aided by teachers and peers, the key social agents of this stage. Industrious, self-assured youth succeed at developing various abilities at home, school, and play. The more competent youth become in dealing with their environment, the better they feel about themselves as persons. Undue frustration and failure evoke the sense of inferiority or worthlessness.

STAGE 5: IDENTITY VS. ROLE CONFUSION   Throughout adolescence, roughly 12 to 18 years of age, individuals are busily redefining their identities in ways that incorporate the various changes occurring in their bodies, minds, and sexual development. Thus, during the fifth psychosocial stage, known as *Identity versus Role Confusion*, adolescents strive to answer the question, "Who am I?" The more successful teens are in facing this identity crisis, the stronger their sense of personal identity becomes. The more difficulty experienced, however, the more confusion adolescents feel about who they are and about what lies in store for them in the future. During adolescence, identities are primarily explored through real-world interactions with others, thus, it is not surprising that peers are the key social agents of this stage.

For today's youth, the Internet also affords additional ways to explore one's identity (Subrahmanyam, Smahel, & Greenfield, 2006). When online, adolescents can try out virtually any persona: smart or dumb, skinny or obese, young or old, rich or poor, nice or mean, etc. Outlets for identity exploration include social networking sites, Twitter, blogs, and online gaming. For instance, players in the popular Internet-based game *Second Life* can create any type of persona they would like, even if it is nothing like how they are in reality. One advantage of online identity exploration, over real-world ones, is that the relative anonymity of the Internet allows youth to try out identities with little concern about real-life negative social consequences. It is not surprising then, that more and more identity exploration is occurring online (Kirsh, 2010).

APPLYING IT TO YOURSELF   In the psychodynamic perspective, each of us is driven by motives, needs, and conflicts we're not fully aware of. Accordingly, at times we're beset by ambivalence and indecision, such as whether we really want to remain in a given relationship or job. However, much of the way we cope with life and relate to others depends on how we've grown up and, specifically, how we've resolved the various psychosocial crises that we have faced. Our adjustment to life, therefore, has evolved through a developmental process in which later experiences are influenced by earlier ones.

When thinking about your own resolution to Erikson's psychosocial stages, it is important to keep in mind that each stage brings with it new opportunities for success, not just failure. Even if one has had an unsuccessful resolution during the previous stage, the possibility of a positive outcome during the next stage is still there. Optimal adjustment, therefore, comes from figuring out what must be done to meet the challenges ahead. Essentially, this

When parents model patriotism, social learning theory suggests that their children will be patriotic, too.

consists of increasing our self-understanding and self-mastery so that we can make meaningful accommodations between our deepest needs and desires, on the one hand, and the conflicting social demands made of us, on the other. Our goal, therefore, should be to maximize the satisfaction of our needs while minimizing guilt, self-defeating tendencies, and harm to others and society. As Freud observed, and as Erikson's stages reveal, if we are able "to love and to work"—to establish satisfying relationships and find meaningful work—we are indeed fortunate.

Social Learning Theory and Child Development

Much of what we know and learn, especially as children, is acquired in a social context—hence the term **social learning**. As such, central to social learning theory is the concept of **observational learning**—*the process in which we learn by observing other people, or "models."* Here's an example: After watching an episode of *The Power Rangers* (an action-adventure television show filled with martial arts violence), elementary school-aged children imitate many of the flying kicks, punches, and blocks that they had just seen (Boyatzis, Matillo, & Nesbitt, 1995). Observational learning depends on four components: attention, retention, reproduction, and motivation (Bandura, 1986). In other words, we must *pay attention* to what is going on around us, *retain* what we have learned, *be motivated* to perform the observed behaviors, and, finally, *reproduce* those behaviors at some point in the future.

According to social learning theory, observational learning is often combined with direct reinforcement (or "reward") to enhance learning. **Reinforcement** is *the addition of something that increases the likelihood of a behavior occurring again*. As a concrete example of this, let us again re-examine Sara's behavior at the zoo. Prior to her bad conduct in front of the animals, Sara had a history of whining and fussing in order to get her way. In effect, each time her parents gave in to her tantrums (either out of exhaustion or fear of embarrassment), they were actually reinforcing her bad behavior—that is, increasing the likelihood of her tantruming in the future! Rather than experiencing reinforcement directly, during observational learning the observer sees whether or not the model's behavior was reinforced and adjusts their own behavior accordingly. For instance, after watching her cousin Lisa successfully tantrum at home to get more dessert, Sara replicated Lisa's yelling and arm flailing in order to get a candy bar while waiting in the checkout line at the store. Sara's reproduction of the Lisa's tantrum is an example of observational learning; receiving a candy bar at the store for her bad behavior exemplifies reinforcement.

Moreover, observational learning is thought to have its greatest influence when there is an agreement between our own views and the messages observed in the environment. As an example, adolescents desiring to become some of the toughest kids on the block should learn more and be affected to a larger extent by witnessed acts of aggression than their more passive peers. Nevertheless, once a given characteristic or behavior has been learned, it is not necessarily expressed uniformly in all situations. A lot depends on the extent to which the behavior is valued or rewarded in a setting. For instance, whereas pushing and shoving is deemed acceptable when children are playing in a rough-and-tumble manner during recess, the same behavior is clearly unacceptable when standing in the lunch line at the cafeteria. Current behavior is therefore best understood in terms of the interaction between a child's past learning and the demands of the present circumstances.

SOCIAL LEARNING THEORY IN ACTION   Even young children can become aggressive through observational learning. For your consideration: After watching a short movie of an adult hitting, kicking, and yelling at an inflatable "Bobo" doll, preschoolers imitated these behaviors the most when the adults were reinforced for their aggressive actions. In other words, these children learned to be aggressive by watching others act aggressively (Bandura, 1965). On a related note, children are more apt to imitate their parents' aggressive behavior than their verbal warnings to

Table 2–1	Media Consumption of American Youth

1. Each day, 56 percent of infants and 81 percent of toddlers watch TV. By age 3, children consume TV for at about 2 hours on the average day.
2. The daily exposure of media for youth between 8 and 18 years of age is about 7 hours and 30 minutes.
3. Adolescents listen to music for about 3 hours each day.
4. Televisions, VCR/DVD players, radios, and CD players are found in 99 percent of homes in the United States.
5. The averages number of TVs per household is 4.
6. Computers are found in 93 percent of homes, with 84 percent having Internet access.
7. In their bedrooms, nearly 71 percent of elementary school-aged children have TVs; 50 percent have video game consoles; and 33 percent have access to the Internet.
8. Around 30 percent of media-related activities occur at the same time (i.e., media multitasking), such as watching TV while using a computer.

the contrary (Bandura, 1973). Thus, the old adage said by many parents, "Do as I say and not as I do" does not appear to work!

Children and adolescents have voracious media appetites (see Table 2–1). And video games, television, comic books, the Internet, etc., all provide youth with ample opportunities for observational learning. As an example, let us look at the potential effects of media violence consumption on youth. Regardless of the type of media consumed, children and adolescents are constantly witnessing media-based characters being reinforced for their violent actions. The results of numerous studies clearly show that violence in films, television, video games, and other media not only desensitize us to violence (that is, make it less bothersome) but also induce aggressive thoughts, feelings, and behavior in children and adults (Kirsh, 2012). Unfortunately, because the level of televised and other forms of media aggression in our society remains very high (Rideout, Foehr, & Roberts, 2010), so too does the opportunity for the observational learning of aggression.

Exploration 2.3: Media and Children

www.commonsensemedia.org   A great resource for information on the effects of media on youth. This site also contains reviews of movies, games, and apps so parents can make informed decisions.

APPLYING IT TO YOURSELF   According to the social learning perspective, much of a child's personality and behavior patterns have been acquired through interaction with the environment, especially the significant people in their lives and the messages they encounter in the media (Kirsh, 2010). Although past experience may affect present functioning, it need not determine the whole of life. That is, through the learning process, many of the same mechanisms that are involved in childhood can be also used to improve adult adjustment. For instance, a teen who acquired a habit of cursing when excited may give up this habit as an adult when sufficiently motivated and encouraged by positive role models.

Similarly, children often act the way they do because of specific influences in their immediate environments, whether at school or at home. As such, maladaptive behavior is often more attributable to inadequate circumstances and faulty learning than deficiencies in a child's psychological makeup. Conversely, the possibility of positive change involves providing youth with new, more positive models from which they can learn! Consider the following study as an example of this. In an attempt to reduce racial stereotyping in third-grade children, youth were shown a series of videos entitled, *Different and the Same: A Prejudice Reduction Video Series*. In this series, racially diverse puppets modeled racially unbiased behaviors (e.g., resisting peer pressure, problem solving), thought processes (e.g., challenging stereotypes), and attitudes. As a result of viewing these videos, children showed marked reductions in their racial stereotyped attitudes and beliefs. Additionally, these youth were more likely to make cross-race friendships, offer help to a child of a different race, and report knowing how to effectively handle inter-racial conflict (Graves, 1999).

Piecing the Puzzle Together

Each of the four perspectives mentioned above places a piece in the puzzle that is childhood. Erikson's stages of psychosocial development illuminate some of the key issues that children face as they grow. The theory highlights the fact that individuals face different challenges across the lifespan and that previous life experiences influence future growth and adaptation. At each stage of development, influential elements in the environment are identified. Similarly, Bronfenbrenner's ecological perspective explains the numerous ways that the environment can influence youth, ranging from interpersonal interactions to societal values. The biological perspective highlights the role that genes, hormones, etc., play in facing the challenges of development. Finally, the social learning theory suggest through direct experience with others and by watching those around them, children learn how to interact with the world.

In summary, child development is a product of both inherited or biological factors *and* environment or learning. Just how much or how little of our genetic potential we realize depends greatly on our interaction with the environment, especially our selection and reaction to particular environments. However, such determinations are difficult to make, for biology and environment interact to influence youth in what could be described as a dance of intertwined partners. While each partner is responsible for the elements of the performance to varying degrees, together they produce something beautiful that when looking at each partner alone, may not necessarily be apparent.

KEY FOUNDATIONAL ELEMENTS OF CHILDHOOD

LEARNING OBJECTIVES

   2.5 Identify four key foundational elements of childhood.
   2.6 Distinguish between the three main types of temperament.
   2.7 Discuss the importance of attachment to children.
   2.8 Explain the connection between self-recognition and self-concept.
   2.9 Compare Baumrind's four parenting styles.
   2.10 Describe the outcomes associated with physical punishment and poor parental monitoring.

In addition to the various perspectives mentioned above, psychologists have documented important *foundational* elements of development. That is to say, each is present during infancy or early childhood and each has the potential to influence youth decades later. Included in this list are temperament, attachment, and self-concept. Beyond these child-centered characteristics, one cannot deny the importance of parents to a child's well-being. As such, some central aspects of parenting are also presented below.

Temperament

Temperament is defined as *an individual's characteristic pattern of emotional response and behavioral reactivity to situations and stressors*. When we describe an individual as "easy-going," "laid-back," or "intense," we are basically describing that individual's temperament. Sara's negative reaction after being told that it was time to leave the zoo, in part, resulted from her more intense temperamental style. Three basic styles of infant temperament have been identified: "easy," "difficult," and "slow-to-warm." Infants classified as "easy" are happy and cheerful for the most part, have very regular biological rhythms, and adapt to new situations well. "Difficult" infants are irritable in their responses, unpredictable with regard to their eating and sleep habits, and intense in terms of their emotional expression. And babies with a "slow-to-warm" temperament are cautious and restrained in new situations, but as they "warm up" they become more open and playful in their responses.

Today, the consensus among researchers is that temperament is inborn, strongly based on our biology and surprisingly consistent over time—even through adulthood (Thomas & Chess, 1984). For example, children's temperament at age 3 is not only highly predictive of their personality in adolescence and young adulthood, but also of how successful (or unsuccessful) they are in relationships with family, friends, coworkers, and romantic partners (Caspi & Silva, 1995). Think of Sara, who frequently got into trouble as a preschooler and was still getting into trouble for her high level of reactivity as a teenager. However, temperament is not necessarily the defining feature of who you are and how you adjust—most certainly the experiences that we have and the interactions we have with others throughout our lifetimes affect our personality in a number of ways. But based on the fact that temperamental patterns can be observed in infants, we can say that temperament serves as one of the building blocks for our social and emotional functioning (Rothbart, 2011).

Attachment

Attachment is often defined as *a close, emotional tie with another person.* Throughout our lives we develop attachments to various individuals, including parents, grandparents, siblings, and spouses (Dykas & Cassidy, 2011). Across child development, attachment is characterized by the tendency to seek out caregivers for comfort and support in times of stress. Of note, such supportive individuals are referred to as "attachment figures." During infancy, children typically require physical contact to derive a sense of comfort from attachment figures. However, with increasing age children can feel comforted by sight of their caregivers or the sound of their voices. Even pictures of caregivers can make children feel safe and secure. *Feeling comforted by an attachment figure without actual contact* has been termed by attachment researchers as **felt security** (Greenberg, Cicchetti, & Cummings, 1990). In Box 2–5, the concept of felt

---

BOX 2–5	Focus on Psychology: Explaining the Power of the Teddy Bear

The concept of felt security can also be used to explain a very commonplace behavior of childhood: namely, the carrying around of blankets, stuffed animals, and other special objects by young children. As you recall, Sara went everywhere with her stuffed animal, Teddy. As another example, think of the cartoon character Linus, from *Peanuts,* who not only has his blanket with him at all times, but also cuddles and squeezes it whenever he is feeling insecure. Over 60 percent of U.S. children derive comfort and felt security from such objects (Hobara, 2003).

Teddy bears, blankets, pacifiers and the like are referred to as **transitional objects** because they *help the child transition from dependence on a caregiver for comfort and support to more independent forms of coping.* Even thumb sucking fits into this category. Do transitional objects give youth a sense of felt security? Yes, they do: Transitional objects allow children to feel secure and self-sooth during times when the caregiver is not available to meet their needs (Green, Groves, & Tegano, 2004). Does the use of transitional objects mean that children cannot derive comfort from their mothers and other attachment figures? Absolutely not! In fact, it has been argued that children cannot develop emotional connections with *objects* unless they've developed an even stronger relationship with their mothers first (Winnicott, 1953).

security is used to explain why so many very young children carry teddy bears, blankets, etc., around with them.

TYPES OF ATTACHMENT   For human infants, who cannot care for themselves and who are particularly vulnerable to the dangers in their surroundings, attachment has survival value (Bowlby, 1977). Thus, the *ability* to form attachments is rooted in biology and hardwired into our genes. All the same, the *quality* of attachment is very much determined by environmental experiences, and in particular, early interactions with the caregiver (Ainsworth, Blehar, Waters, & Wall, 1978).

So, just how is the quality of attachment measured? Back in the 1970s, Mary Ainsworth and her colleagues developed the "Strange Situation," a procedure which involves observing the interactions between a mother, child, and a stranger in a playroom filled with toys. Over the course of about 21 minutes, the infant meets a new person and experiences the mother leaving and returning to the room, not once, but twice. Near the end of the procedure, infants are even left by themselves in the playroom for upwards of 3 minutes! Although a variety of actions and interactions are measured, the quality of the attachment is primarily determined by how the infant reacts when the mother leaves the room, and, more importantly, how the infant responds upon her return.

Based on the history of sensitive and response caregiving (or lack thereof), two main types of attachment can develop: *secure* and *insecure*. Infants with a secure attachment wholeheartedly believe that their emotional needs will be met by their caregivers. As such, following a brief separation from their mothers during the Strange Situation, secure infants greet her upon return, get comforted if upset, and then quickly return to exploration and play in their new environment. Simply stated, secure infants use their mothers as a secure base for exploring their physical and social worlds and a haven of safety if they should be frightened, hurt, or otherwise in need of support. In contrast, children with insecure attachments believe that their emotional needs will not be met by their caregivers; instead, their emotional needs will be ignored, rejected, or some combination of the two.

Three subtypes of insecure attachments have been identified: *insecure–avoidant, insecure–ambivalent,* and *insecure–disorganized.* Based on a history of having their emotional needs rejected, insecure–avoidant children minimize their emotional expressions (e.g., suppress the expression of anger) and minimize the use of their caregivers for comfort and support. Thus, during the reunion episodes of the Strange Situation, insecure–avoidant infants ignore and avoid their mothers. By comparison, after having their emotional needs responded to inconsistently, insecure–ambivalent children maximize their emotional expressions and maximize the use of their mothers for comfort and support. These infants are extremely upset during the reunion episodes of the Strange Situation: They cry a lot, have difficulty soothing, act angry toward their mothers, and tantrum. Finally, because they have been abused as infants and toddlers, insecure–disorganized children fail to develop a clear strategy for interacting with their mothers during the Strange Situation. Upon the return of the mother to the room, such infants demonstrate bizarre actions (such as spinning in circles or remaining immobile), display a fearful expression, or show a mixture of avoidant and ambivalent behaviors (Ainsworth et al., 1978; Main & Solomon, 1990).

DOES ATTACHMENT MATTER?   Just how important is the quality of attachment to the well-being of youth? Quite a bit, actually, as a variety of positive cognitive, emotional, and social characteristics develop as a result of having a secure attachment. Here's a sampling: Securely attached toddlers generally display positive emotions (like joy) the most, whereas insecurely attached toddlers often show more negative emotions (such as anger, fear, and distress). Insecurely attached youth are also more likely to be aggressive, antisocial, and bullies. Children with secure attachments have larger vocabularies, are more sociable, and are better problem solvers than same-aged peers with insecure attachments. And securely

BOX 2–6	Focus on Family: Recognizing the Importance of Fathers

Here are some facts about the importance of fathers to their children.

- When fathers are involved in their children's schooling, the children complete more years of school and have higher wages as adults than children whose fathers were uninvolved.
- When both the mother and the father are present in the family, the children have fewer behavioral problems and earn better math and reading scores in school.
- When no father is present in a son's life, the son is more likely to become a father as a teenager and to live apart from his children.
- When fathers are present and have warm relationships with their daughters, the daughters are less likely to engage in early sexual activities.
- The more sons and daughters report feeling supported by their fathers, the more likely they are to show initiative in engaging in prosocial activities outside the home.

Fathers indeed make a difference. Remember, all parents—whether fathers or mothers—need to do the best parenting job they can in order to raise well-adjusted, healthy children.

attached children tend to have closer, more stable friendships during childhood and early adolescence. This finding occurs, in part, because secure children have better social skills than insecure children. Patterns of attachment first apparent during infancy remain fairly stable across childhood and adolescence. It is not surprising then, that early interactions with our caregivers help set the stage for our interactions with others later in life. In fact, security of attachment in childhood predicts security in adult relationships (Cassidy & Shaver, 2008; Zayas, Mischel, Shoda, & Aber, 2011).

In previous decades, the primary caregiver of children was the mother. Not surprisingly, most research examined the mother–child relationship, at the exclusion of fathers (Stolz, Barber, & Olsen, 2005). Nevertheless, fathers are also important attachment figures, a finding echoed by current research (Veríssimo et al., 2011). See Box 2–6 for an understanding of the role that fathers play in the lives of their children.

Self-Concept

Self-concept *refers to the set of abilities, characteristics, and values that an individual believes defines who he or she is.* However, the development of a sense of self is contingent upon a *child's ability to differentiate him- or herself from others in the social environment,* or what is termed **self-recognition**. Of course, this differentiation is made possible by the natural progression of neurological and cognitive development. But when does an infant develop the ability to recognize him- or herself?

In an ingenious study, researchers asked mothers to gently and inconspicuously smudge a dab of rouge on their infants' noses and place their babies in front of a mirror. The researchers observed that infants between the ages of 18 and 24 months reliably touched their noses in a seeming attempt to rub off the strange marks (Lewis & Brooks-Gunn, 1979). Infants younger than 18 months, although capable of touching their noses, rarely did so. Other researchers placed stickers on toddlers' legs in a variation on the "rouge test" and discovered that even when sitting in a high chair with a tray obstructing their view, children between 18 and 24 months reliably attempt to remove the sticker from their legs when they see themselves in a mirror, indicating that self-recognition at this age extends beyond the face (Nielsen, Suddendorf, & Slaughter, 2006). Another indication of self-awareness is when children begin to use first-person pronouns like "I" and "me," a feat that occurs between 20 to 24 months (Lewis, 1997). Interestingly, children with mental retardation and other developmental disabilities also display evidence of self-recognition during the rouge test, but only when they achieve a *mental age* of 18 to 20 months, regardless of how old they really are (Hill & Tomlin, 1981).

Once a child can distinguish him- or herself from the others in the social environment, the stage is set for the development of self-concept. In answer to the question "Who are you?" most preschool-aged children define themselves by their physical characteristics ("I have brown hair") or by what they own ("I have a tricycle") (Keller, Ford, & Meacham, 1978). Self-concept during the preschool years is colored by the concrete, tangible characteristics that define a child's impressions of self. As a child progresses through the school years into adolescence, behavior-based characteristics and physical attributes are gradually replaced by more reflective, abstract, psychologically based qualities in self-descriptions (Damon & Hart, 1988). Examples of statements reflecting a more advanced sense of sense include "I am trustworthy," "I am a good friend," and "When I can, I help others out."

Sense of self is a very important aspect of personal and social functioning that will influence us as we navigate the social world throughout our lives. The types of environments we seek out, the decisions we make, and the values we hold are all influenced by how we view ourselves. For instance, many adolescents will value abilities that they are good at (e.g., skateboarding) and devalue those that they are not (e.g., academic achievement), even if the latter are highly valued by society (Harter, 2006). As this example illustrates, once youth can differentiate the self from others, they start comparing themselves to others. This social comparison process, which starts around the time children enter kindergarten (about age 5 or 6), is a key component in determining whether children, as well as adults, will feel good or bad about who they are (Dijkstra, Gibbons, & Buunk, 2010).

Parenting

Parents take care of their children's needs on a daily basis: they shuttle them to and from school, lessons, and activities; they clothe and feed them; they read to, play games with, and hang out with them; and they take care of them when they are sick. In addition to being influenced by these parental undertakings, the adjustment and personal growth of children is impacted by the following three factors: parenting style, use of physical punishment, and parental monitoring. Each is examined below.

PARENTING STYLES   Parenting can be described based along two major dimensions: *warmth/hostility* and *permissiveness/control*. The warmth/hostility dimension refers to the degree to which parents interact with their children in a warm or hostile manner. Parents high in warmth are typically caring, responsive, and affectionate toward their children. In contrast, hostile parents criticize, belittle, and act harshly toward their children while rarely displaying any warmth. The permissiveness/control dimension refers to the level of behavioral control exerted over their children. Parents high in permissiveness have few rules, and the rules they do have are inconsistently enforced. Furthermore, permissiveness is associated with limited supervision of children and the implicit transference of decision-making control to their children. Finally, parents high in control have lots of rules and enforce them consistently. Additionally, controlling parents supervise their children regularly and make most of the decisions for them.

By crossing the warmth/hostility dimension with the permissiveness/control dimension of parenting, four unique parenting styles are formed: *authoritative*, *authoritarian*, *permissive*, and *uninvolved* (Baumrind, 1991). Authoritative parenting is characterized by high levels of warmth and flexible control. These parents are responsive to their children's needs while at the same time are consistently enforcing rules and providing justification for those rules. Consider the following as an example of authoritative parenting: In the classic 1970s TV series *The Brady Bunch*, Greg, Peter, and Bobby refuse to share their newly built clubhouse with Marcia, Jan, and Cindy. In retaliation against being discriminated against, the girls destroy the boys' clubhouse. To resolve this conflict and prevent further escalation, the patriarch of the family, Mike Brady, warmly and moralistically talks to his three children and three stepchildren about the importance of sharing and respecting the rights of others.

Authoritarian parents tend to display little warmth, affection, and responsiveness. Also, these parents exert tremendous control over their children by rigidly enforcing strict obedience to parental commands. To authoritarian parents, rules are meant to be followed, not explained. In J. K. Rowling's popular Harry Potter series, Petunia and Vernon Dursley make use of an authoritarian parenting style when interacting with their nephew Harry Potter. As evidence, consider the following: The Dursleys show no positive effect toward Harry, they force him live in a tiny closet under the stairs, and they require that Harry receive permission to speak. Furthermore, when Harry is perceived to be disobedient, he is sent to his room without dinner.

Permissive parenting is typified by a great deal of warmth and affection along with an equally impressive lack of control over and supervision of their children. Consider once again the Dursleys, who when interacting with their son Dudley, utilize a permissive parenting style. For instance, after finding out that he has *only* received 36 birthday presents (two less than the previous year), Dudley begins to have a tantrum. In response to this display of negative emotionality, Petunia quickly tells Dudley that she will get him more gifts. Giving in to excessive demands from children, especially to stop or avoid tantrums, is characteristic of permissive parenting.

Finally, the absence of control, supervision, affection, and warmth along with the presence of hostility and insensitivity comprise the uninvolved parenting style. Typically, the children of uninvolved parents are merely provided with the bare essentials: food, warmth, clothing, and shelter. Beyond that, their parents have little to do with them. Uninvolved parents do not go to parent–teacher conferences, they do not arrange play dates for their progeny, and they do not sign their children up for extracurricular activities. Essentially, children are required to raise themselves.

Over the last 35 years, a great deal of research has investigated the impact of these four parenting styles on child and adolescent development. In general, authoritative parenting produces the best social, emotional, and cognitive outcomes for youth (Steinberg, Lambom, Darling, Mounts, & Dombusch, 1994). For instance, children of authoritative parents are more friendly, outgoing, emotionally expressive, and they display higher levels of self-esteem and academic achievement than children of authoritarian, permissive, or uninvolved parents. In addition, children experiencing permissive and uninvolved parenting show the greatest levels of aggressive behavior across development. However, acts of violence and delinquency are more likely to be committed by children raised by uninvolved parents than by children reared under any other parenting style (Maccoby & Martin, 1983).

PHYSICAL PUNISHMENT Spanking is a form of discipline in which an open hand is used to hit a child on the buttocks or extremities without leaving bruises (Kazdin & Benjet, 2003). Spanking tends to be fairly prevalent among in the United States, as 94 percent of parents spank their toddlers and preschoolers (Larzelere, 2008). A pertinent question therefore arises: Is spanking a good idea? In other words, does spanking eliminate or lessen undesirable behaviors in children, or does spanking actually make undesirable behaviors worse? Most experts on learning and behavior strongly suggest that spanking should not be used (Durrant, 2008), as it does not typically lessen the punished behavior. In fact, new studies find that spanking not only increases current undesirable outcomes (including aggression, depression, conduct problems, and delinquency), but years later, aggression toward significant others (Christie-Mizell, Pryor, & Grossman, 2008; Mulvaney & Mebert, 2007; Taylor, Manganello, Lee, & Rice, 2010).

Researchers have found that the primary *positive* outcome of spanking a child is rapid compliance with the parent's request to stop the undesired behavior (Owen, 2004). As much as spanking seems efficient, most psychologists far prefer that parents find some other means for managing the behaviors of their children, because the long-term consequences of spanking are simply too serious. Instead, parents should use other methods, such as time-outs, removal of privileges, rewarding or reinforcing the positive behaviors of a child (e.g., praising a child for working hard to get good grades at school). The take-home message from these studies is clear: For a better-behaved and less aggressive child, avoid spanking (Durrant & Smith, 2011).

Exploration 2.4: Positive Parenting

www.positiveparenting.com   A website that has the main goal of making parenting a positive experience, for example, other ways to discipline children besides spanking.

PARENTAL MONITORING   Parental monitoring refers to *the degree to which parents know about their children's whereabouts, day-to-day activities, and activity partners.* Research has consistently found that a lack of adequate parental monitoring is associated with higher levels of behavior problems, delinquency, and antisocial behaviors, including physical and sexual aggression (Miller, Gorman-Smith, Sullivan, Orpinas, & Simon, 2009). For your consideration, the parents of Eric Harris, one of the Columbine killers, failed to notice that their son had stored guns, ammunition, and bombs in his bedroom in preparation for his murderous rampage (Bartels, 2004). For the optimal development of children, when asked "Do you know where your kids are and what they are doing?" the answer should be "yes."

APPLYING IT TO YOURSELF   Are you an easy-going person or are you generally suspicious of others until you get to know them? When you look in the mirror, what do you see? If you were to describe yourself, what qualities would you identify as characteristic of you? Are you happy with the person you are, or do you have different ideas regarding who you want to be? Are you secure in your relationships with friends and lovers, or do you sometimes feel betrayed or suspicious of their actions or intentions? The answers to these questions all have their roots in some of the major concepts examined in early childhood by developmental psychologists. And as the previous review revealed, some of these influences are related to the characteristics of the child, while others are associated with the type of parenting received.

Chapter Summary

PERSPECTIVES ON CHILD DEVELOPMENT

2.1 Explain why a perspective approach of development is important.

Psychologists approach development, adjustment, and growth from differing perspectives, each of which offers an optimal range of explanations rather than a comprehensive truth. Thus, by examining the distinctive contributions of all four major perspectives, we may attain a more inclusive, balanced understanding of personality and behavior. The four major perspectives are biological, ecological, psychodynamic, and social-learning.

2.2 Explain Bronfenbrenner's theory of ecological development and the four contexts of the environment that comprise it.

The ecological perspective highlights the importance of four distinct, but interrelated settings on children's development: microsystem, mesosystem, exosystem, and macrosystem. Moreover, this perspective emphasizes the fact that what happens in one setting can influence youth in other settings, in both direct (microsystem, mesosystem) and indirect (exosystem, mesosystem) manner.

2.3 Describe Erikson's theory of psychosocial development.

According to Erikson's psychosocial theory, youth develop in a sequential process (via psychosocial stages) in which they are faced with a specific crisis to resolve at different points of development. From cradle to grave, the manner in which the individual handles these crises has a decisive influence on his or her current and future development. Key elements in the environment influence the outcome of each psychosocial stage.

2.4 Explain Bandura's concept of modeling and social learning.

Social learning is a process in which we learn by observing events and other people, or "models," without receiving any direct reward or reinforcement.

KEY FOUNDATIONAL ELEMENTS OF CHILDHOOD

2.5 Identify four key foundational elements of childhood.

The key foundational elements of childhood are temperament, attachments, self-concept, and parenting.

2.6 Distinguish between the three main types of temperament.

There are three main types of temperament: easy, difficult, and slow-to-warm. Easy children are happy and cheerful and adapt to new situations well. Difficult youth are irritable, have irregular eating and sleeping habits, and intense emotional reactions. A temperament of slow-to-warm is characterized by being cautious and restrained in new situations, followed by a period of warming up (e.g., becoming more open and playful).

2.7 Discuss the importance of attachment to children.

The quality of our early attachment to our caregiver (secure, insecure-avoidant, insecure-ambivalent, and insecure-disorganized) tends to influence childhood outcomes related to emotional, cognitive, and social functioning, as well as frame the ways we relate to significant others later in our lives.

2.8 Explain the connection between self-recognition and self-concept.

Self-recognition, critical to the development of self-concept, emerges at around 18 months. Self-concept in young children is based on their concrete personal characteristics, but as a child develops cognitively, psychological attributes tend to color self-characterization.

2.9 Compare Baumrind's four parenting styles.

Authoritative parents use rational discipline and warm and affectionate style of interaction. Authoritarian parents strictly enforce all rules (without explanation) and are hostile towards their children. Permissive parents are incredibly warm, but lack discipline (rules are not enforced). Uninvolved parents basically let children raise themselves; there is little discipline and lots of hostility.

2.10 Describe the outcomes associated with physical punishment and poor parental monitoring.

Parents do matter, and the style of parenting received, the presence or absence of physical punishment, and the monitoring of behavior all influence youth greatly. Both spanking and poor parental monitoring are associated with aggression, conduct problems, and delinquency.

Self-Test

1. Which of the following examples best illustrates the biological perspective?
   a. Nate's activity level increases after experiencing the hormonal changes of puberty
   b. Stuart's math scores improve after going to a tutor for four weeks
   c. Lilly's vocabulary expands after watching a Baby Einstein DVD
   d. Ariel can't remember how to play a song on the piano because she "forgot" to practice

2. Robert is having a hard time sleeping at night because he stays up late watching movies on his iTouch. As a result, Robert has a hard time focusing while at school and his grades have dropped. According to the ecological perspective, the above scenario illustrates the _____.
   a. microsystem
   b. mesosystem
   c. exosystem
   d. macrosystem

3. Which of the following is not one of Erikson's psychosocial stages?
   a. Belief vs. Hope
   b. Identity vs. Role Confusion
   c. Initiative vs. Guilt
   d. Industry vs. Inferiority

4. Isaac loves to go up and down the escalator stairs at the airport. His favorite part is jumping off the final step onto the floor. When Isaac's mom tries to prevent him from doing this activity or if she tries to hold his hand while he is doing it, Isaac has a big tantrum. According to Erikson, Isaac is dealing with the crisis of:
   a. Trust vs. Mistrust
   b. Autonomy vs. Shame and Doubt
   c. Intimacy vs. Isolation
   d. Generativity vs. Stagnation
5. Which of the following is an example of observational learning?
   a. becoming more angry when frustrated
   b. jumping off a tree stump and trying to fly after watching Superman on TV
   c. sharing toys to avoid having to go into "time out" for the second time that day
   d. receiving a sticker for "good listening" during snack time
6. Which of the following parenting styles involves providing the child with warmth and affection, while at the same time using rational discipline and making sure that rules are enforced?
   a. uninvolved
   b. permissive
   c. authoritative
   d. authoritarian
7. James recently found his "baby book" which described his infancy. He was surprised at how little had changed in 15 years. As a baby, James had difficulty sleeping, irregular eating habits, and tended to fiercely emotional. According to Thomas and Chess, James had (and still has) a _____ temperament.
   a. easy
   b. slow-to-warm up
   c. difficult
   d. insecure
8. Wherever toddler Michelle goes, so goes her stuffed bear, Brownie. When Michelle is scared, Brownie makes her feel safe. When Michelle is upset, hugging Brownie makes her feel better. For Michelle, Brownie functions as a _____.
   a. transitional object
   b. attachment figurine
   c. emotion avatar
   d. phenomenal self
9. Children that avoid their mothers during the reunion episodes of the strange situation are called:
   a. insecure-ambivalent
   b. secure
   c. insecure-avoidant
   d. insecure-disorganized
10. _____ refers to knowing where your children are and what they are doing.
    a. attachment
    b. parental monitoring
    c. temperament
    d. corporal punishment

Exercises

1. *Apply Erikson's stages to your childhood.* Write approximately a page explaining how well you mastered the appropriate developmental task for any of Erikson's stages while you were growing up. If possible, comment on how your past development affects your current state of well-being.
2. *Identifying ecological influences.* Think about the various ecological influences in your life. Identify two examples for each system in the ecological environment.
3. *Barriers to personal growth.* Each of the four major perspectives covered in this chapter offers a different view of the barriers to personal growth. The biological view reminds us of the importance of heredity to our temperament, the ecological perspective highlights the importance of the interrelated environments we face, the psychodynamic view stresses the cumulative effect of the crises we face across development, and the social learning view emphasizes faulty models, environments, and maladaptive behavior. Write a paragraph or so explaining how each of these views may help to account for the barriers to your own personal growth.
4. *What can you learn from watching violence on TV?* According to the social-learning theory, we learn by observing others. Watch a show containing real violence (such as that shown in the evening news), realistic violence (e.g., a dramatic series), and cartoon violence (makes sure it's a funny cartoon). What did you learn about violence when watching each of these shows? Write your experiences down so you can compare and contrast what you learned.
5. *Which major perspective most reflects your views?* Select one of the four major perspectives that is most compatible with your own thoughts on adjustment and development. Then write a page or so explaining why you prefer this viewpoint. To what extent are you receptive to viewpoints different from your own? Would you agree that no one perspective possesses the whole truth?

Questions for Self-Reflection

1. Why is it important to take a perspective approach to the study of development?
2. Given what you now know about development, do America's children stand a reasonably good chance of being happy and well adjusted?
3. Are there personal characteristics that seem to run in your family tree?
4. Do you agree with Erikson that across development we are faced with specific crises?
5. How do you feel about Freud's psychosexual stages of development? Are they realistic?
6. Why is attachment in infancy important to relationships later in life?
7. Have you experienced birth-order effects? What might account for differences between siblings, other than the order that they were born?
8. Do you think that if caregivers knew more about adjustment and child development, the world would be a different place? How so?
9. What is your self-concept like? Describe yourself and identify the different types of characteristics (e.g., appearance, race, intelligence, etc.) you believe capture who you are.
10. Thinking about your own childhood, what type of parenting style were you exposed to? Was it more than one type?

Chapter Three

Affirmative Aging—Adulthood

*Z*ena sat on the edge of her bed. She felt stiff this morning and didn't know why. She thought, "The funny thing about getting older is the way it sneaks up on you. One minute you're 30 or 40. Before you know it, you're 64." She continued her thoughts as she rubbed her sore, stiff hands. "I don't feel 64, but my birthdays betray me. So do my arthritic hands," she thought. Zena continued to think of herself as someone in her late 40s, though she was reminded otherwise each time she looked in the mirror. It usually came as a surprise when her body rebelled. She didn't feel older, except in those rash moments when she overexerted herself, such as walking too quickly up a steep hill, or when she awoke to morning hand stiffness. As had Zena at times in her life, virtually all of us have been hit with the admonishment "Act your age." As Zena sat on the edge of the bed, she wondered, "But what if your real age isn't the age you feel?"

ADULT DEVELOPMENT

LEARNING OBJECTIVES

3.1 Explain the difference between age-related and non-age-related development.

Fresh tasks, different challenges, and unforeseen sources of happiness and frustration mark each new period of our lives. Consequently, the process of personal growth continues as we age. Perhaps more than ever before, people are deliberately trying to change themselves, so that with age and experience they have greater coping skills and self-mastery; affirmative aging, if you will. On the other hand, people often like to feel settled and connected to the familiar. Older adults, for example, prefer to stay in their own homes rather than move to an assisted living facility or move in with their children (Administration on Aging, 2012). As Carl Rogers (1980), one of the pioneers in the field of personal growth, grew older, he became convinced that the phrase "older but still growing" is a more apt description of adult development than the conventional cliché "growing old." With age, we all develop our own individual identities to a greater extent, feel more confidence in ourselves, and can achieve greater personal control and mastery over our lives (Pfaffenberger, 2005). Of note,

BOX 3–1	Did you know that each of the following is a myth?

- It is normal for older people to be confused and disoriented.
- After age 65, a person is too old for sex.
- Most older people are in poor health.
- It is almost impossible for most older people to learn new things.
- Intelligence always decreases with age.

Source: Arcnec.org.

the segment of the population known as "old" has been growing dramatically in recent years due to healthier lifestyles and medical advances. Case in point, in 2000, there were 35 million Americans aged 65 and older. By 2010, that number had risen to 40.2 million. And by 2050, it is estimated that the number of elderly will more than double to over 88 million (Vincent & Velkoff, 2010).

From infancy through adolescence, much of our development is associated with **age-related changes**—*changes that occur at a given age*, such as learning to talk or walk. In contrast, adult development is increasingly influenced by **non-age-related changes**, or *events and influences that are unique to each of us and may occur at any age or not at all*, such as marriage or the decision to change careers. Nevertheless, because the physiological well-being, self-perceptions, emotional experiences, and social circumstances of adults vary with each additional decade of life, we'll examine adult adjustment and growth in terms of three broad stages across the lifespan: early, middle, and late adulthood. Keep in mind that the age boundaries between these stages are fuzzy and that people differ considerably in their own individual patterns of development. Before you read further, take the quiz in Activity 3–1 to examine how much knowledge you possess about the aging process.

ACTIVITY 3–1

HOW MUCH DO YOU KNOW ABOUT AGING?

Write either "true" or "false" by each of the following statements. Then check your responses with the answers at the end of this chapter.

_____ **1.** All five senses tend to decline in old age.

_____ **2.** People lose about one-third of their brain cells or neurons by late adulthood.

_____ **3.** Drivers over 65 years of age have fewer traffic accidents per person than those under 30.

_____ **4.** Most older people are pretty much alike.

_____ **5.** Older adults become less susceptible to short-term illnesses, such as the common cold.

_____ **6.** Recognition memory declines sharply with old age.

_____ **7.** Reaction time generally becomes slower with age.

_____ **8.** About one-fourth of those over 65 live in nursing homes.

_____ **9.** People become more fearful of death as they grow older.

_____ **10.** Widows outnumber widowers about three to one.

DECISIONS, DECISIONS, DECISIONS—EARLY ADULTHOOD

LEARNING OBJECTIVES

3.2 List the three main challenges of early adulthood.

3.3 Explain why after venturing out on their own early adults return home.

3.4 Discuss issues related to choosing a career and starting a family.

3.5 Explain the connection between infertility and adoption.

3.6 Describe how having children affects a marriage.

Early adulthood begins with an "early adult transition," *roughly from the late teens or early 20s and lasting well into a person's 30s.* At this time, young adults are faced with many new opportunities for growth, including leaving home, choosing and preparing for a career, establishing close relationships with others, and starting a family of one's own. In Erikson's (1964) theory of psychosocial development, this stage is called *Intimacy versus Isolation.* A successful resolution here will result in individuals forming satisfying, close relationships with peers of both sexes as well as an intimate relationship with another person. The inability to establish rewarding relationships with friends, including a lover or spouse, results in a painful sense of isolation or loneliness.

Because the decisions young people make will affect them for 50 years or more, these developmental tasks can be quite stressful. On the other hand, young adults' relationships with their parents become more positive and connected during early adulthood; after all, parents and adult children now share increasingly similar roles in life (e.g., spouse, employee, parent). Thus, young adults often rely on their parents, and other family members, to help them with the difficult decisions that lie ahead (Masche, 2008; Whitbourne, Whitbourne, & Whitbourne, 2011).

Leaving Home

Leaving home involves more than just packing your things, loading up the car, and changing residences; as the old saying goes "Home is where the heart is." Of course, one aspect of leaving home does include moving out of the house or apartment that you grew up in. But there are other changes as well, such as becoming less dependent financially on parents, entering new (and more adult-like) roles and responsibilities, and engaging in more autonomous decision making. It is these latter psychosocial transitions that are essential for entering adulthood. Some individuals may run away from an unhappy home at an early age but take a long time before growing up emotionally; others, may remain home well into their 30s (Strom & Strom, 2005). In both cases, it is the "symbolic" leaving from home that is so crucial to attaining emotional self-sufficiency.

At the same time, a curious thing has been happening in the last decade. Like birds flying back to the nest, more young adults are moving in with their parents after years of absence from home. For this so-called "boomerang-generation," around 56 percent of males and 48 percent of females between the ages of 18 and 24 still live at home. And immediately following college, nearly 85 percent of degree holders return home for a brief period of time. Between 25 and 34 years of age, close to 20 percent of young adults continue to live with their parents (Reuters, 2010; Roberts, 2010). After experiencing emotional, psychological, and behavioral independence from parents, why would adult children return home? In large part, the increase in these "boomerangers" is due to both personal and economic situations. It is often difficult for young people to maintain their own apartments or homes because housing prices generally continue to increase, and many young people are having a hard time finding a suitable job. In fact, the unemployment rate for 20- to 24-year olds is about twice that of adults 25 and over (U.S. Bureau of Labor Statistics, 2012).

As you might expect, there are pros and cons to a "nesting" arrangement. For instance, food bills increase and parents may ask about their child's whereabouts and activities, such as, "Where were you last night?" Parents in this situation are encouraged to foster the growth of their adult children by including them in the creation of a new household budget and the establishment of ground rules for living together, having them contribute to the household financially (e.g., pay for room and board), and requiring participation in the basic upkeep of the home. Moreover, parents are encouraged to teach financial stewardship to their adult children, so that when they are on their own for good they are better able to track their finances, budget their money, and save for the future (Reuters, 2010). Noteworthy is the fact that individuals and their parents often find that this is a satisfying time for sharing and strengthening their ties before a son or daughter leaves home again, usually for good (Strom & Strom, 2005).

Choosing a Career

In choosing a career, young adults must strike a balance between two somewhat contradictory tasks. One task is to explore the possibilities in the adult world, keeping their options open. The other task is to create a stable life structure with the aim of making something of themselves (Miller, 2010). Young adults often agonize over the important decisions they must make at this stage, whether they are making the right choice, and if not, how difficult it will be to change. If you experience some personal distress about career options as you progress through college, you are not alone!

Over the past several decades, earning potential has become an increasingly important issue when choosing an academic major and/or career, especially for men (Associated Press, 2011). Many students now plan to major in biology (for medical school), business, or economics, almost double the number several decades ago. Additionally, for the benefit of their careers, many young adults decide to delay (or forego altogether) starting a family. See chapter 10 for more detailed information on how to choose a career and land a good job.

Exploration 3.1: Researching Careers

www.employmentguide.com   A rich source of information on careers, internships, networking, resume development, and other useful information for job seekers.

Starting a Family

THE DECISION TO HAVE CHILDREN   Early adulthood is usually the time for starting a family. In today's world, however, starting a family occurs nearly as often for those who are married as for those who are not, as close to 41 percent of all childbirths in the United States occur out-of-wedlock (National Center for Health Statistics, 2011). Now, more than ever, adults are waiting longer to have children. For instance, in the 1970s the average age for a first-time mother was 21, today that number is 25. A finding that has been echoed across most European countries and Japan, where the average age for having a first child is between 28 and 29 (NationMaster.com, 2012). Moreover, in the last 40 years, the proportion of first births to women age 35 and over has increased nearly eight times (Jayson, 2009). Couples are giving more thought to whether they want children and if so, when to have them. One result is more voluntary childlessness. Nearly 10 percent of couples choose this option (Mueller & Yoder, 1997); however, few couples resolve this issue directly. Usually, couples decide to postpone having children until they eventually make the postponement permanent. For women who choose to work *and* start a family, discrimination may soon follow. The **motherhood penalty**, as it is called, refers to the fact that working mothers are viewed as less competent and less committed to work than non-mothers. As such, they are discriminated against when making hiring decision and determining salaries. In fact, working mothers are paid 5 percent less, *per child*, than non-mothers (Correll, Bernard, & Paik, 2007; Quast, 2011).

INFERTILITY   For the nearly 7.3 million women in the United States who are infertile or have impaired fecundity (i.e., extreme difficulty having a child), childlessness is not by choice. The reasons for infertility are many and varied, affecting both females (e.g., problems producing ova, ovarian cysts, tumors) and males (e.g., low sperm count, hormone deficiencies) alike (Healthline.com, 2012). Although the number of live births resulting from assisted reproductive technologies (e.g., in vitro fertilization, hormone treatments, surgery) has doubled over the past decade, millions of women remain infertile despite extensive, and expensive, treatments (SART.org, 2012).

For those who wish to have children, but cannot due to infertility, general health concerns, gender, etc., adoption becomes a viable alternative. **Adoption** refers to *the legal establishment of a new, permanent parent–child relationship.* Currently, around 2 million children live with their adoptive parents. Of these, 38 percent were adopted privately through lawyers and adoption agencies, 37 percent were adopted through the foster care system, and 25 percent were adopted internationally. Somewhere around 125,000 children are adopted each year. Interestingly, whereas most private and international adoptions involve infants and toddlers, the vast majority foster care children are over age of 2 when they are adopted. This difference may occur because the goal of foster care is to reunite the child with the birth family; adoption occurs only after all other options have been exhausted, a process that can take years to complete (Adoption.com, 2012; ChildStat.gov, 2012).

EFFECTS OF HAVING CHILDREN   Having children biologically, or through adoption, may affect a couple's marriage in several ways. On the positive side, many couples report that having children makes them feel more responsible and adult. They also report increased satisfaction in sharing affection and experiences with their children, which enhances their sense of purpose in life. On the minus side, taking care of small children is an added stress on the marriage, leaving less time for the parents to do things on their own. Even without children, there can be a great deal of marital stress as individuals question their marriages and their relationships to their partners (Doss, Rhoades, Stanley, & Markman, 2009). For working couples, the stress increases as the couple may wish to spend lots of quality time with their children but cannot. Studies show that today's parents have 22 fewer hours a week to spend with their children (Kornblush, 2003). Many people have children before they realize how children can alter parents' lifestyles, sleep habits, and other matters of daily life. At times, raising children can be overwhelming, leaving parents unable or unwilling to cope with the financial, psychological, and emotional challenges of rearing youth. When such difficulties arise, other family members, especially the grandparents, take over child-rearing responsibilities. Demographers estimate today that close to 3 million children are raised by their grandparents. A similar number of elderly have both their adult children and their grandchildren living with them (Livingston & Parker, 2010).

Exploration 3.2: Adoption

adopting.adoption.com   A comprehensive website for finding information on a variety of issues related to adoption.

SAME OLD, SAME OLD?—MIDDLE ADULTHOOD

LEARNING OBJECTIVES

3.7   **Describe the main challenges of middle adulthood.**

3.8   **Explain the mid-life transition.**

3.9 Summarize the physical changes of middle adulthood.

3.10 Discuss the effects of sexual changes on men and women.

Sometime between the late 30s and mid-40s people enter **middle adulthood,** defined as *that era between the late 30s and the 60s that is generally characterized by fulfillment of career and family goals.* According to Erikson (1964), individuals are now faced with a new crisis, *Generativity versus Stagnation.* Generativity refers to the ability to look beyond one's self, family, and job and to contribute to the welfare of others. The successful resolution of this stage results in an individual who is both happy and a productive member of society. However, for many individuals, especially those developing a sense of isolation during young adulthood, such societal responsibilities can be overwhelming. For those that fail to meet the challenges set forth for them by society, stagnation occurs, and the person becomes increasingly self-absorbed.

Midlife Transition or Midlife Crisis?

During this period of aging, people begin to think about what they would like to do with the rest of their lives. Such self-questioning may lead to changes in their careers, marriages, or personal relationships (Helson & Soto, 2005; Lindgren, 2002). It often leads individuals to take up new interests or become active in community or national affairs as a way of making their world a better place in which to live. Middle age, then, is a time for shifting gears and developing new interests and values; a transition, if you will.

Essentially, the **midlife transition** is *a period of personal evaluation that comes sometimes with the realization that one's life is about half over.* The individual gradually pays less attention to the "time since birth" and starts thinking more in terms of "time I have left." Some people at this age may hide some of the more obvious changes of age or compensate by trying harder to appear young. For example, Americans spend 10 billion dollars each year on cosmetic surgery in an attempt to obtain a more youthful or pleasing appearance (Cafferty, 2010). It is sometimes difficult for middle-aged individuals to ignore other fundamental changes. For one thing, their parents retire, become ill, and die during these years. And if the aging parent has significant health issues, their own health may also suffer (Di Mattei et al., 2008). More of their friends and acquaintances are also lost through death; with death from all causes rising sharply at this time of life. Their children grow up and leave home, and middle-aged parents feel more aware of the mistakes they have made raising their children. Nevertheless, close to 75 percent of adults make it through midlife without experiencing a crisis, of any sort (Wethington, 2000).

Box 3–2 examines well-being in adulthood with information that may surprise you, because it indicates middle-aged people and older adults are remarkably happy.

Physical Changes

The most obvious signs of middle age are physical changes in appearance, such as skin wrinkles, weight gain, and hair turning gray or receding (Ellis & Sinclair, 2008). These changes reflect a

---

BOX 3–2   Focus on Wellness: Well-being throughout Adulthood

Drawing from the tenets of positive psychology, aging research is increasingly focusing on successful aging. And as it turn out, life satisfaction tends to peak at about 65 years of age (Mroczek & Spiro, 2005). Compared to younger adults, individuals at these older ages experience more autonomy in their lives and also feel that they are an integral part of their communities. Additionally, older individuals are more likely than younger ones to experience personal growth as they successfully address some of life's challenges (Bauer, McAdams, & Sakaeda, 2005). Also, as people age, they find themselves experiencing negative emotions less often and positive emotions more often, resulting in a greater sense of well-being (Mather & Carstensen, 2005; Sheldon, Kasser, Houser-Marko, Jones, & Turban, 2005).

gradual slowing down in the overall physical system. People get tired more easily and take more time to bounce back from fatigue or illness; and there are decreases in strength, coordination, and reaction time. Presbyopia, also known as farsightedness (i.e., difficulty seeing things up close), and presbycusis (i.e., difficulty hearing high-pitched sounds) become commonplace. High school students have begun to take advantage of the latter by setting their cell phones to ring at a frequency too high for most middle-aged adults to hear. When used during class, these "mosquito" ringtones, as they are called, allow teens to know when a text has arrived, without alerting the teacher (Vitello, 2006). Additionally, during middle age, individuals become more susceptible to chronic and serious illnesses, such as diabetes, heart attacks, strokes, and cancer. As a result of these changes, there is increasing concern over one's health (Malmberg, Miilunpalo, Pasanen, Vuori, & Oja, 2005). But do not abandon all hope, for there are ways to compensate for many of these changes. Diet and exercise can lead to a more youthful body type and a reduction in health risks for stroke and heart disease; glasses allow for reading with ease; and becoming more cautious at the gym or when driving (where reaction time is an issue) can reduce the chance of both accidents and injury.

Sexual Changes

The most significant physical change in women is **menopause**, or *cessation of monthly menstrual cycles*, which signals the loss of childbearing capacity. Menopause tends to occur sometime between 45 and 55 years of age. Physical effects vary from a certain degree of atrophy in the uterus, vagina, and breasts to a variety of other changes such as hot flashes. Some women find menopause mostly a negative experience, with adverse effects on their appearance and their physical, emotional, and sexual lives. Other women feel little or none of these effects. Some positive changes also occur during this period, thus evening out the quality of life between pre- and postmenopausal women (özkan, Alatas, & Zencir, 2005). The lessened fear of pregnancy often leads to increased sexual responsiveness for many women. Other events of middle adulthood, such as changes in the marriage relationship, freedom from child-care responsibilities, and return to work outside the home, can be more important to women than the physical changes.

Middle-aged individuals who stay active or take up new hobbies remain happier and healthier.

BOX 3–3	Focus on Health care: That Little Blue Pill

Who would think a little blue pill would make such a big splash? Viagra (generically known as silde-nafil), the little blue pill described here, was introduced in 1998 as a treatment for **male impotence** or **erectile inhibition** —*the inability to experience an erection*. Around 52 percent of the men between the ages of 40 and 70 years old suffer from erectile dysfunction (Cappelleri, Bell, Althof, Siegel, & Stecher, 2006). However, men who have regular intercourse are less likely to experience impotence (Ma & Qin, 2009). Clearly, this is a case of "use it or lose it!" Within months of the introduction of Viagra, sales reached 4.5 million prescriptions a month, breaking the all-time record for all new drug sales. Since then, Viagra has been tried by more than 30 million men in 120 different countries (Hill & McKie, 2008). Given its success, Viagra was quickly followed in the intimacy products market by Cialis (generically named tadalafil) and Levitra (vardenafil).

These drugs do not work for every man and have some unwelcome physiological side effects, such as a flushed face and, worse, sudden blindness (Harder, 2005). That is one reason why a doctor's prescription is really important. There are many causes of sexual dysfunction, such as depression and side effects from some of the medications used to treat high blood pressure, diabetes, and prostate cancer. That is why a regular physician's checkup is also important.

Although medications for erectile dysfunction can have a positive effect on marriage by increasing sexual satisfaction and intimacy, such medications may lead to two additional side effects: adultery and sexually transmitted diseases (STDs). According to newspaper reports, Viagra-fueled adultery has led to an increase in older women seeking divorces from their sexually meandering husbands (Hill & McKie, 2008). With regard to STDs, although the greatest number are contracted during late adolescence and early adulthood (15 to 24 years of age), the incidence of HIV and AIDS is growing faster among individuals 50 and older compared to those under 40 (Levy, Ding, Lakra, Kosteas, & Niccolai, 2007). Nevertheless, the true psychological and societal value of such drugs may be that they bring sexual dysfunction out into the open and motivate more men to see physicians for physical exams.

Today, middle-aged women have the opportunity to address menopausal changes with hormone supplements, usually a combination of estrogen and progesterone. As a result of replacing these hormones, women experience a decline in post-menopausal symptoms, such as hot flashes, night sweats, dry skin, and mood swings. Additional benefits of hormone replacement therapy include a reduction in osteoporosis, colorectal cancer, migraine, urinary tract infections, and heart disease. However, this treatment is not without controversy because of such possible side effects as increased risk of certain cancers, as well as gallstones and asthma (Slowik, 2011).

Although men are not subject to menopause, they do go through a male **climacteric**, defined technically as *the loss of reproductive capacity*. In men, the climacteric is accompanied by a gradual reduction in fertile sperm, a diminution of testosterone, and reduced sexual vigor, sometimes with increasing impotence in men. However, men tend to reach their climacteric 5 to 10 years later than women reach menopause and do so in a much more gradual way, with fewer physiological consequences. The drug Viagra for men has added an interesting element to the aging male's sexuality, as revealed in Box 3–3.

Men and women who take these changes in stride often find their lives even more satisfying than before, including the sexual aspects of their lives. For one thing, the changes and anxieties of this period may make each individual more aware of the need for a spouse and the security of marriage. In fact, at middle age and older, men and women's friends and family are very important to their quality of life (Jaccoby, 1999). Perhaps nothing helps a person through this stage as much as an understanding and supportive partner (Spotts et al., 2005). Actually, there is a rise in marital happiness among many couples as they age, with individuals in their late 40s and 50s reporting levels of marital happiness surpassing couples in their 20s (Bookwala & Jacobs, 2004). As you can see, although sexual changes can create anxiety for both men and women, they also represent new opportunities for personal growth.

AGING GRACEFULLY—LATE ADULTHOOD

LEARNING OBJECTIVES

3.11 Explain ageism and its impact on the elderly.

3.12 Explain differences between the young elderly and the old elderly.

3.13 Describe the physical and cognitive changes accompanying late adulthood.

3.14 Describe the factors that lead to satisfaction during retirement.

3.15 Explain the different pathways to successful aging.

Late adulthood is *the final stage of adult development, from the mid-60s to death and is characterized by adjustment to changing health, income, and social roles*. Today, more than 40 million men and women are 65 years of age or older. By the year 2050, there will be nearly 89 million Americans 65 or older and 19 million 85 and older (U.S. Bureau of the Census, 2012). The "graying of America" will alter every aspect of society—business, education, government spending, housing, medical care, and leisure. The elderly often discover that old people don't fit well into our society. Bottle caps are too hard to get off, restaurants are too noisy, and doors are hard to open. Older adults frequently report problems using everyday items, and sometimes such problems can negatively impact the health of the individual (Fisk & Rogers, 2002). For instance, because of poor eyesight the elderly are at risk for misreading over-the-counter and prescription medications, resulting in adverse drug reactions (Pawaskar & Sansgiry, 2006).

Ageism

At the beginning of this chapter, you were asked to answer some questions on what it is like to be old. In comparing your answers to those in the back, how did you do? Younger adults tend to provide stereotypical answers to these types of questions, and these stereotypes tend to be quite negative (Pecchioni & Croghan, 2002). Significantly, age stereotypes sometimes translate

---

BOX 3–4   Focus on Wellness: Healthy Aging

Regardless of what part of the lifespan we are in, each of us can start practicing healthy techniques that can ensure a healthier life as we age. The sooner we start, the longer our life is likely to be and the better the quality of our health.

- Exercise, exercise, exercise. Study after study shows the benefits even for the very old. Exercise lowers the risk of heart attacks, results in fewer hip fractures, and promotes better mental health.
- Stop smoking. No matter how long you have smoked, when you stop your health improves. Avoid the use of drugs (other than medications), and if you drink alcohol, drink only in moderation.
- Eat well. Avoiding sugars and fats also improves overall health and helps ward off diabetes and arteriosclerosis.
- Avoid stress. This is easier said than done in today's modern world. If stress is overtaking your life, refer to the chapter on stress and stress management.
- Develop and maintain outside interests.
- See a physician regularly. Some of the infirmities of aging are silent, such as high blood pressure. Preventive checkups earlier in life can ensure healthier aging later in life.
- Find and maintain a social support system. Social support for the elderly increases their morale, buffers the effects of the loss of loved ones, and enhances their self-esteem.

into age discrimination, as evidenced by the number of age-bias suits that have surged in recent years (Baldas, 2007). Such discriminatory experiences have led gerontologists to coin the term **ageism**, which refers to *negative attitudes toward and treatment of the elderly*. Ageism can be seen in the readiness with which people attribute all sorts of negative qualities to the elderly, mostly because of their age. For example, many younger people assume that the typical older person is helpless and frail and resides in a nursing home, despite the fact that over 90 percent of older adults are not in need of custodial care. Another symptom of ageism is that the elderly are often **infantilized** or *treated like infants*, as, for example, when other adults speak to them in baby talk. Such instances of ageism generate false generalizations about the elderly, thereby restricting their opportunities, undermining their personal dignity, and alienating them from the larger society. We need to become more sensitive to ageism because as the largest cohort group, the baby boomers, moves through historic time, the elderly American population will continue to grow (Teichert, 2002).

Physical and Cognitive Changes

The literature on aging has identified two distinct groups of elderly: one group aged 65 to 74, known as *the young elderly*, and another group aged 75 and beyond, known as *the old elderly*. These two groups differ psychologically and physically. Many of the young elderly are free of infirmity, whereas those in the old elderly experience more disability.

PHYSICAL CHANGES   With increasing age, the physical changes that started during middle adulthood endure: the skin continues to wrinkle and thin, the hair keeps receding and becomes grayer, there is a further reduction in the sharpness of vision and hearing, and reflexes slow down even more (Wingfield, Tun, & McCoy, 2005). Some older people eat less because their sense of taste diminishes, they exercise less, and they have less physical energy for life. They also sleep less restfully, although they spend more time in bed compensating for this lack of sleep. The old elderly sometimes have more trouble maintaining their sense of balance. Deaths from falls occur twice as frequently as deaths from other accidents. Deaths from high blood pressure, cancer, and heart disease are also more common among the old elderly. These changes, however, do not necessarily have to result in disability, especially in the young elderly and those older elderly who continue to exercise and adopt healthy lifestyles (Fries, 2002; Kolata, 2002). Even mild involvement in less strenuous activities, such as reading, can result in feelings of well-being and reduced mortality (Menec, 2003). It is worth noting that many of the negative changes associated with aging are due to stress, disease, and lifestyle rather than to the aging process itself. Box 3–4 offers some tips to promote healthy aging.

BOX 3–5   **Did You Know That Each of the Following People Accomplished Greatness during Late Adulthood?**

- Sophocles wrote *Oedipus Rex* when he was 70 and *Electra* when he was 90.
- Michelangelo began work on St. Peter's Basilica at age 70.
- Laura Ingalls Wilder didn't publish her first book until age 65 and wrote children's stories during her 70s.
- Mother Teresa continued her missionary work around the clock, helping less fortunate people throughout the world, until her death at age 87.
- Mahatma Gandhi led India's opposition to British rule when he was 77.
- Frank Lloyd Wright completed New York's Guggenheim Museum at 89 and continued teaching until his death.

COGNITIVE CHANGES   Cognitive functions are also affected by the aging process, although rarely to the extent that justifies the stereotype of the absent-minded old person having a "senior moment" (Wingfield et al., 2005). In fact, cognitive decline in late life is *not* inevitable, as is often assumed (Wright, Kunz-Ebrecht, Iliffe, Foese, & Steptoe, 2005). For instance, the ability to use accumulated knowledge to make judgments and solve problems often remains the same, and in many instances can improve with age! Individuals can also maintain their creativity well into late adulthood, depending on their type of work. Artists hit their peak in their 40s; scientists maintain their creativity well into their 60s; and those in the humanities (e.g., historians and philosophers) may show a steady increase in creativity through their 70s. Box 3–5 showcases other individuals who seemed at their peak of achievement in their old age. It may be that any decreased creativity ordinarily seen among older people is due more to their restricted environments than to aging. Consider this, about 16 percent of America's elderly have mobility limitations (especially elderly women who are more prone to osteoarthritis than men) that curb the types of environments they can enter.

However, cognitive declines do occur in late adulthood. For instance, older adults tend to have more difficulty remembering information related to the timing of events, such as the order of their occurrence or how recently they happened (Hartman & Warren, 2005). Moreover, the ability to quickly process new information also declines in late adulthood (Phillips, 2005). This finding, along with slower reaction times, partially explains why the rate of car accidents for the elderly is second only to that for teenagers. Of note, because of their frailty, elderly drivers are also more likely to die in car accidents, relative to their younger counterparts (Skyving, Berg, & LaFlamme, 2009). Box 3–6 discusses the debilitating cognitive disorder that may, in fact, begin to develop in midlife but is more often associated with old age: **Alzheimer's disease**.

Exploration 3.3: Alzheimer's Disease

www.alzheimers.org   An excellent website for all sorts of information on Alzheimer's disease, including content for both patients and their families.

BOX 3–6   Focus on Health care: Alzheimer's Disease

Alzheimer's disease refers to the loss of memories and other intellectual abilities serious enough to interfere with daily life. Symptoms of Alzheimer's include:

- Difficulties in planning or solving problems
- Misplacing things
- Challenges in completing familiar tasks
- Increases in confusion and poor judgment
- Confusion with time or place
- Difficulty completing familiar tasks
- Poor judgment
- Changes in mood and personality

Alzheimer's, for which there is no prevention or cure, is the sixth leading cause of death in the United States. Between now and 2050, the number of people with Alzheimer's will increase from an estimated 5.4 million up to 14 million (Alzheimer's Association, 2012). But help is on the horizon. Scientists appear to be on the brink of discovering much-needed treatments and even a preventive vaccine for Alzheimer's disease. One promising treatment involves the use of an enzyme that would block brain cell degeneration caused by Alzheimer's. The vaccine, which thus far has been tested with some success in humans and monkeys, might eventually immunize people if serious side effects are not found (Alzheimer's Association, 2009).

Personal and Social Adjustment

During late adulthood, individuals experience a time of contemplation and reflection, or as Erikson (1964) calls it, *Integrity versus Despair*. Individuals that reflect upon a life fulfilled will feel happy with themselves during this final developmental stage. But for those that view their lives as disappointing, meaningless, and a failure, despair will follow. In actuality, most elderly ordinarily experience both integrity and despair, but the healthier the person, the more self-acceptance and personal satisfaction will prevail.

FEELING IN CONTROL   Elderly who concentrate on what they *can* do rather than on what they cannot do age more gracefully and experience less anxiety about aging. Thus, if the elderly are resilient and motivated rather than bitter and passive, aging is more successful. Those people with positive attitudes toward aging also live longer. According to positive psychology, one of the most important ingredients of successful aging is the ability to maintain an **internal locus of control** such that *an individual believes that something within him- or herself controls life events.* When the elderly feel that they have control over their fates, they tend to live longer, healthier lives (Gruenewald, Karlamangla, Greendale, Singer, & Seeman, 2009). Due to significant losses, such as the death of loved ones, the elderly sometimes perceive less control than younger adults. Older adults who cope with loss of control by maintaining or enhancing their competencies or by shifting the subjective importance of their personal goals adjust better to the aging process (Schulz & Heckhausen, 1996).

LIVING ARRANGEMENT   An important area of psychosocial change, and therefore feelings of control, involves living arrangements for the elderly. The young elderly, those individuals from 65 to 74 years of age, are more likely to live at home, be in better health, and be more financially comfortable than the old elderly. Nearly twice as many older women as men live alone. Conversely and logically, more than twice as many men as women live with their spouses. As mentioned earlier, many elderly prefer to stay in their own homes, but a small number of older people find they are unable to care for themselves. These individuals generally are the frail or old elderly. In fact, 97 percent of nursing home residents have at least one disability. Contrary to stereotypes, however, only a small portion of individuals 75 and older (7.5 percent) reside in nursing homes (Administration on Aging, 2012).

By the age of 85, only about one-half of all the old elderly live alone. Unfortunately, a significant proportion of the old are at or below the poverty level, making any living arrangement difficult. Poverty is a special problem for elderly women, especially elderly women of color (Administration on Aging, 2012). A much smaller proportion of old elderly lives with others, such as with a grown child, because of a desire for independence (i.e., autonomy or control) and privacy not found in facilities for the elderly. Other older people live near a grown child who visits frequently. In some instances, as mentioned earlier, elderly parents can assist their children with childcare, and the latter can help their parents with finances and emotional support in times of illness.

Exploration 3.4: Elder Care

www.aging-parents-and-elder-care.com   A helpful resource providing information on the care of elderly loved ones.

RELATIONSHIP CHANGES   Because most married women will outlive their husbands, there are more widows than widowers among the elderly. Half of the women in the United States are widowed by their early 60s, and 80 percent by their early 70s. Among those over 65, widows outnumber widowers three to one. Women tend to adjust to the loss of their spouse more

Cell phones and computers help maintain contact with friends and family. Widely embraced by teens and young adults, older adults are also adopting these technologies.

readily than men. Although, as mentioned earlier, older men are usually better off financially than older women, they tend to have more difficulty coping with routine household tasks, are lonelier, and are less happy than widows and older women. People who have remained single throughout their lives often feel more satisfied in late adulthood than do widows or widowers of the same age, possibly because they have chosen a single lifestyle and have become better adjusted to it.

Friendships play an important role in the lives of the elderly (Giles, Glonek, Luszcz, & Andrews, 2005). Interestingly, women often have an easier time making and keeping friends in their old age, partly because of the way they have been socialized and partly because of the disproportionate number of older women. Yet with the reduction of social contacts at this age, friends become even more significant to both sexes. People who continue to live in the same neighborhood as they get older, an increasingly frequent phenomenon, may keep in touch with their friends from the past. Other friends may be deceased, so the social networks of the old elderly are smaller, but they are just as close as those of younger people. Those who move elsewhere must make new friends. In both instances, friends play an influential role in preventing loneliness and disengagement from life (Thanakwang, 2009). This is perhaps why some people prefer to live in a retirement home or assisted living community, often in the Sunbelt of the South or Southwest. Today, elderly residents can also keep in contact with friends and family, no matter how distant, over the Internet. In fact, such communications have been shown to ward off loneliness in the elderly. However, when older adults attempt to find *new* friends via the Internet, feelings of loneliness continue (Sum, Mathews, Hughes, & Campbell, 2008).

Retirement

The retirement experience, which varies considerably from one person to another, usually depends on several factors. Generally, the more voluntary the decision to retire is, the better the adjustment to post-employment life. Second, whereas retiring with reasonably good health leads to feelings of satisfaction, retirements resulting from poor health reduce feelings of well-being. Third, an adequate income during retirement is also very important (Petkoska & Earl, 2009). Many seniors plan on living on Social Security, but the retirement age to receive this income is slowly rising. And Social Security alone is generally not sufficient for the retired to maintain a reasonable standard of living (Moreau, 2002). Those who have insufficient income after retirement are likely to continue to work, a phenomenon known as *bridge employment*. In fact, a "need for money" is the leading reason people continue to work after retirement from their primary jobs (Gobeski & Beehr, 2009). On note, the recent recession, which dramatically reduced the value of investment portfolios, has caused more and more elderly to raid their savings account, seek out bridge employment, or delay retirement altogether (Fleck, 2011). Not surprising, people from upper-level careers generally report a more favorable retirement experience, partly because they have ample income (Pinquart & Schindler, 2007).

Exploration 3.5: Retirement

www.aarp.org   The website for the largest advocacy group for the elderly, the American Association for Retired Persons. It contains general information on aging, as well as material on the association's advocacy programs and government lobbying.

Research on retirement demonstrates that retirees have the same levels of self-esteem as those who continue to work, and retirees are generally as well adjusted as non-retirees (Drentea, 2002); if anything, research demonstrates that retirement improves mental health (Mandal & Roe, 2008). Other factors that influence the decision to retire or continue to work include the need to be a caregiver, especially for women, and whether the spouse will also retire (Dentinger & Clarkberg, 2002; Pienta & Hayward, 2002). In retirement, volunteer work, such as becoming a teacher helper for elementary school children, is the "work" most favored by retirees especially those who have sufficient funds (Carey & Ward, 2000).

Successful Aging

Which person does a better job of growing old gracefully—the individual who continues to work actively as a lawyer and keeps up an active social life or the person who retires to a rocking chair on the porch? Gerontologists who favor the **activity theory of aging** suggest that the more active a person remains, the more satisfied and better adjusted that person is likely to be, regardless of age. Those who adhere to the **disengagement theory of aging** point out individuals tend to disengage from society with advancing age. As it turns out, there is no single way to age successfully, and different people adapt to old age in their own way. In fact, people tend to select a style of aging that best suits their personality, needs, and interests. Thus, an energetic, hardworking person will continue to tackle new projects, whereas a more contemplative person will probably do more reading (Neugarten, 1986).

Older people also obtain a sense of their lives as a whole by engaging in the **life review**, *a naturally occurring process of self-review prompted by the realization that life is approaching an end*. Although such a process can lead to wisdom and serenity, it may also evoke some negative feelings, such as regret, anger, guilt, depression, or obsessively thinking about negative events from their past (Kraaij, Pruymboom, & Garnefski, 2002). The process consists of **reminiscence**—*thinking about oneself and reconsideration of past events and their meanings*. Some older people prefer to reminisce in private, whereas others may enjoy doing it more publicly, such as by making a family tree or telling their children and grandchildren about the significant aspects of their lives and family history. Such reminiscing serves to give them a final perspective of their lives while leaving a record of the past to their family and friends.

Chapter Summary

ADULT DEVELOPMENT

3.1 Explain the difference between age-related and non-age-related development.
Age-related changes occur at a given point in development. Non-age-related changes can occur at any time during the lifespan or they might not occur at all.

DECISIONS, DECISIONS, DECISIONS—EARLY ADULTHOOD

3.2 List the three main challenges of early adulthood.
Early adults are tasked with leaving home, entering the workforce, and starting a family.

3.3 Explain why after venturing out on their own early adults return home.
A combination of an extremely high rate of unemployment, the expenses required to live on their own, and personal reasons explains why half of all early adults are boomeranging back home.

3.4 Discuss issues related to choosing a career and starting a family.
Both choosing a career and starting a family can cause early adults a great deal of anxiety. Whether for personal reasons, or for their careers, many decide to postpone having children, and as a result, the average age for starting a family has increased.

3.5 Explain the connection between infertility and adoption.
Millions of women experience infertility or impaired fecundity, which makes having a biological child impossible or extremely difficult. As a result, millions of women have decided to start their families through adoption.

3.6 Describe how having children affects a marriage.
Starting a family can have both positive and negative effects on a marriage. On the positive side, having children can provide couples with a clearer sense of purpose. The negative effects include an increase in stress resulting from child care, a reduction in quality time with your spouse, and difficulties trying to balance work and family life. As a result of these stressors, many couples rely other family members to take over child-rearing responsibilities.

SAME OLD, SAME OLD?—MIDDLE ADULTHOOD

3.7 Describe the main challenges of middle adulthood.
The main challenges of middle adulthood include looking beyond the self in order to contribute to the welfare of society, the evaluation of both career and family goals, and the development of new interests and values.

3.8 Explain the mid-life transition.
Sometime in between the late 30s and the mid-40s, people experience the midlife transition—a time of personal evaluation that comes with the realization that life is half over. This does not necessarily mean a midlife crisis. Midlife sometimes brings changes in careers for both sexes, with both women and men changing jobs or careers to fulfill their aspirations, and many traditional women taking a job outside the home or returning to school.

3.9 Summarize the physical changes of middle adulthood.
The most obvious signs of middle age are physical changes, such as skin wrinkles, weight gain, graying hair, and more difficulty seeing things up close and hearing high-pitched sounds. The physical system as a whole slows down and takes longer to repair. Billions of dollars are spent each year on cosmetic surgery to give middle adults a more youthful appearance.

3.10 Discuss the effects of sexual changes on men and women.
The biological and psychological changes that accompany the loss of reproductive abilities pose both new anxieties and new opportunities for both men and women. Menopause can cause a variety of uncomfortable physical, emotional, and psychological effects, though hormone replacement can ease them. Many women experience an increase in sexual responsiveness. Despite impotency or reduced sexual vigor, drugs such as Viagra allow men to continue having sex. Having a supportive partner makes the aforementioned changes easier to handle as well as producing a more satisfying sex life.

AGING GRACEFULLY—LATE ADULTHOOD

3.11 Explain ageism and its impact on the elderly.
Ageism, which refers to negative attitudes towards the elderly, stereotypes those in late adulthood as being infirmed and feeble minded. Ageism can undermine the personal dignity of the elderly, alienate them from society, and restrict opportunities for work.

3.12 Explain differences between the young elderly and the old elderly.

The young elderly are between the ages of 65 and 74; the old elderly are 75 years of age and older. The young elderly experience less disability (as well as other physical and cognitive declines) and are generally healthier than the old elderly.

3.13 Describe the physical and cognitive changes accompanying late adulthood.

During late adulthood, physical functions progressively slow down and energy levels drop. Balance suffers, reaction time decrease, and sensory abilities related to hearing, vision, and taste worsen. However, people's basic adaptive abilities tend to remain remarkably stable throughout adulthood. Adopting a healthy life style can help ward off many of the aforementioned declines.

3.14 Describe the factors that lead to satisfaction during retirement.

Satisfaction in retirement depends on a variety of factors, such as the reasons for retiring, one's attitude toward retirement, health, income, and involvement in meaningful activities such as volunteer work.

3.15 Explain the different pathways to successful aging.

There is no single best way to age successfully, however, and each individual adapts to old age in his or her own way. Aging is an individualized process. Successful aging depends on one's social network, maintaining a sense of control, and positive reminiscing.

Answers to Aging Quiz

1. *True.* Various aspects of hearing, vision, and touch decline in old age. In many cases, taste and smell also become less sensitive.
2. *False.* People lose very few of their neurons. The loss starts at about the age of 30 rather than in later adulthood.
3. *True.* Aged drivers have fewer accidents than those under 30 but more accidents than middle-aged people.
4. *False.* There are at least as many, if not more, differences among older individuals as among people at other age levels.
5. *True.* Because of the accumulation of antigens, older people suffer less from short-term ailments such as the common cold. However, the weakening of the immune system makes them more susceptible to life-threatening ailments, such as cancer and pneumonia.
6. *False.* Recognition memory shows little or no decline with age, in contrast to the marked decline in recall memory.
7. *True.* Slower reaction time is one of the best-documented facts about older people.
8. *False.* Less than 5 percent of the population over 65 lives in a nursing home during a given year.
9. *False.* Although older people become more aware of death, they tend to have less fear of it than other age groups.
10. *True.* There are more widows than widowers.

Self-Test

1. On her 40th birthday, Lisa attained one of her lifelong goals by receiving a master's degree in education. According to developmental psychologists, the above example illustrates a:
   a. transactional development
   b. cross-sectional change
   c. age-related change
   d. non-age-related change
2. The transition to early adulthood:
   a. can be quite stressful given the long-term consequences of decisions made during this stage
   b. has many challenges, including leaving home, preparing for a career, and starting a family
   c. often results in adult children becoming closer to their parents
   d. all of the above
3. Compared to couples in the past, married couples are
   a. starting their families later.
   b. having more children.
   c. more likely to include a working husband and a stay-at-home wife.
   d. more desirous of girl than boy babies.
4. On Stephen's 40th birthday he thought to himself, "I've got a stable job (that I hate), a 401K plan (with too little money in it), two kids in high school (who spend more time texting me than talking to me), and a 10-year old minivan (that plays cassette tapes). Is that all there is? Is this my life from now until I die?" Stephen is probably experiencing:
   a. feelings of well-being
   b. a midlife transition
   c. a sense of generativity
   d. a climacteric

5. The most obvious signs of middle age are
   a. more colds and allergies.
   b. fewer chronic illnesses.
   c. significant memory losses.
   d. changes in physical appearance.
6. The legal establishment of a new, permanent parent–child relationship is called:
   a. adoption
   b. foster care
   c. alternate care
   d. surrogate parenting
7. At the age of 50, Matt married Marcia, who was in her early thirties. After months of trying to have a baby without success, Matt went to a doctor who told him he had few fertile sperm and a general loss of reproductive capacity. Matt was probably experiencing:
   a. the climacteric.
   b. impotence.
   c. male menopause.
   d. sexual senility.
8. Because of the recent downturn in the economy, 60-year-old Jack saw his retirement saving quickly dwindle. As a result, Jack decided to go back to work in advertising. Much to his surprise, he had great difficulty finding a job. He wasn't sure why until he overheard one of his interviewers telling his potential boss that Jack was "an old man, who is probably out of touch with today's retail market." Jack's treatment was probably the result of:
   a. gender stereotyping
   b. infantilization
   c. ageism
   d. retail bias
9. What factors are most important in determining how people will adjust to retirement?
   a. health status.
   b. income status.
   c. whether retirement was voluntary.
   d. all of these are important.
10. After retirement Jose decided to volunteer at the local school helping children learn how to read. He also spent several days each week volunteering at the food kitchen. Jose's behavior supports the:
    a. disengagement theory of aging
    b. concept of bridge employment
    c. activity theory of aging
    d. process of life review

Exercises

1. *How have you grown as an adult?* Write a brief paragraph describing your personal development since adolescence. In what ways has your personality changed or remained the same? Comment on the factors that have contributed to your personal growth, such as success at school, disappointment in love, or new responsibilities at work.
2. *Leaving home.* Describe your experience with leaving home. If you're already living on your own, how peaceful or stormy was your departure? If you're still living at home or are away at college part of the year, how well are you coming to terms with this developmental task? How helpful are your parents in this matter?
3. *The midlife transition.* If you're going through the midlife transition or have completed this stage, write a page or so describing your experience. If you are not middle-aged, write about what you think the experience will be like. To what extent has this been, or do you think this will be, a stressful time or crisis for you?
4. *Widows and widowers.* Select an older person you know well who has outlived his or her spouse, including yourself if this applies to you, and comment on how well this person has adjusted to living alone. What has been the most difficult adjustment? Has the experience of loss also brought about personal growth?
5. *Successful aging.* Select someone in your family who has reached late adulthood, such as an aunt, uncle, or grandparent. Or perhaps this applies to you. Then comment on how successfully the person has aged. To what extent has the person kept active or become disengaged from his or her environment? Has this person also grown old in his or her own distinctive way? How has your relationship with this person affected your understanding of aging?

Questions for Self-Reflection

1. In what ways have you mellowed with age and experience?
2. Would you agree that leaving home involves more than moving out of the family home?
3. What were your parents like at your age?
4. At what stage of adulthood are you now? Does this differ from your perceived favorite age?
5. Are you aware that the midlife transition doesn't have to be a crisis? What characteristics of middle age make others assume that the transition is really a crisis?
6. Why do older people report feeling younger than they really are?
7. What kind of older people were you familiar with as a child? Did these experiences fashion your stereotypes of the elderly? If not, what did fashion your anticipated trajectory into old age?
8. What would you like to do when you retire? Why?
9. Do you think that our personal traits become more pronounced with age?
10. What do you think it would be like to live in a nursing home?

Chapter Four

Seeking Selfhood

After completing this chapter, you should be able to

4.1 Describe the self-concept.

4.2 List the different processes used to protect the self from harm.

4.3 Discuss why the self-concept is important to personal growth.

4.4 Distinguish between self-image, ideal self, and social self.

4.5 Explain the concept of multiple selves.

4.6 Explain the core tendency toward self-consistency.

4.7 Describe the promise and peril of high self-esteem.

4.8 Distinguish between self-enhancement and self-verification.

4.9 Explain how visualization can help personal growth.

4.10 List ways you may use criticism for personal growth.

4.11 Discuss the importance of greater self-direction and self-acceptance in personal growth.

Shandra worked in sales at an auto dealership. She hated telling people what she did for a living because she felt that selling cars didn't reflect who she was or what she loved to do: You see, Shandra had a passion for writing, not sales. Ever since she was a little girl Shandra loved to put pen to paper. In her teens, she filled up one journal after another with short stories, poetry, and self-reflection. Shandra majored in English in college, and her professors frequently commented on how well she wrote; they even encouraged her to pursue a career as a novelist. So, during her senior year, Shandra began her first manuscript, a mystery. But soon after she graduated college, Shandra found herself tens of thousands of dollars in debt. She needed a job, and she needed one fast. So, Shandra did what she had to do, she "temporarily" gave up pursuing a career in writing and got a job selling cars instead. At that point, "life" continued to get in the way of her desired career: one of her parents died, she moved across the country, got married, had two children in three years, and of course, she still had to pay off those pesky student loans. And time slowly passed her by. But despite being overworked, underpaid, and overwhelmed, Shandra had finally done it: after 10 long years, she'd finished her first manuscript; the mystery she had started so many years ago. Two years, and several rejections and rewrites later, Shandra received a letter telling her that her book was going to be published. While flying to New York to meet with her editor for the first time, the person sitting next to Shandra asked her what she did for a living. Shandra replied proudly, and with a smile on her face, "I'm a writer."

BOX 4–1   **Did you know that …**

- While many people think of low self-esteem as an emotional disorder, it's really a thought-based one.
- When a teen has low self-esteem, he or she may become sexually promiscuous in an attempt to improve it.
- The vast majority of girls (close to 70 percent) feel that they aren't doing as well as they should be in key areas of their lives, such as relationships with friends and family, physical appearance, and school.
- Only 15 percent of girls with high self-esteem talk badly about themselves; that number jumps to 61 percent for teen girls with low self-esteem.
- Only 66 percent of girls with low self-esteem feel that they meet their parents' expectations.

Source: Based on "11 Facts about Teens and Self-Esteem," from DoSomething.org, 2012.

WHAT IS SELF-CONCEPT?

LEARNING OBJECTIVES

4.1 Describe the self-concept.

4.2 List the different processes used to protect the self from harm.

4.3 Discuss why the self-concept is important to personal growth.

Essentially, the **self-concept** is the overall image or awareness we have of ourselves. It includes all those perceptions of "I" and "me," together with the feelings, beliefs, and values associated with them. As such, the self-concept is actually a complex concept made up of a variety of "selves," even though we habitually refer to it in the singular. Think of the self-concept as the "glue" that holds our various experiences, behavior, and feelings together. Ordinarily, we take our self-concept for granted, as when we are engaged in an activity at work or play. At other times, we are very much aware of ourselves, as when we're making an important decision, taking on a heavy responsibility, or are feeling embarrassed. We also may become acutely self-conscious whenever we experience a discrepancy between our self-image and the way we appear to others. Moreover, the self-concept functions as a filter through which everything we see or hear passes and it influences our experiences, so that we typically tend to perceive, judge, and act in ways that are consistent with it (Christensen, Wood, & Barrett, 2003). Table 4–1 contains some of the different types of selves that make up the self-concept.

The self-concept provides us a personal identity or sense of who we are. Even though situations and people around us change, our self-concept reassures us that we are basically the same person we were yesterday. In other words, there is coherence or consistency to our thoughts and actions (Nail, Misak, & Davis, 2004). Some even suggest that the fear of death may not be a fear of suffering or of the unknown, so much as it is the deep fear that our personal identity will be dissolved (Pyszczynski & Cox, 2004). Do you agree with this interpretation?

PROTECTING THE SELF   Our sense of self is so important that we typically resist anyone or anything that challenges it; even responding with aggression, if the threat to the self is deemed great enough (Bushman & Baumeister, 1998). Another way we attempt to protect the sense of self is by engaging in a process called **discounting**, where the *significance of an ability traditionally valued by society is lessened.* For instance, adolescents doing poorly in school may dismiss the importance of academics to their future (Harter, 1987). Additionally, we try to protect the self from damage by seeking out positive information about ourselves from our friends, family members, coworkers, etc. As an example, people blog and post information on social networking sites, such as Facebook, in order to elicit positive comments from others;

Table 4–1	Some Specific Selves That Make Up the Self-Concept of "Selves"
Name	**Description**
Academic Self	Appraisal of our "book smarts"
Artistic Self	Evaluation of our ability to create and evaluate art
Athletic Self	Assessment of our physical capabilities, such as coordination, strength, and endurance
Emotional Self	Estimation of our ability to express, regulate, and interpret emotions
Moral Self	Judgment of our ability to follow standards of morality valued by the self and/or society

This is a just short list of the many different types of selves that exist. What other types can you think of?

"fishing for compliments," if you will. As it turns out, more than 75 percent of the time, posted comments are indeed positive (Valkenburg, Peter, & Schouten, 2006). Finally, we tend to give ourselves the benefit of the doubt. When confronted with information that could have a number of meanings, we generally choose to interpret it in the most positive way we can (Sedikides & Koole, 2004). In other words, most people adopt a **self-serving attributional bias,** defined as *beliefs that glorify the self or conceive of the self as causing the good outcomes that come our way.* For example, we often take personal credit for our successes but blame external causes for our failures.

As you can see, we use many different strategies to protect the sense of self. But do these types of defenses actually *benefit* the self? At first, it appears that they do because they can effectively ward off imminent threats to the self. Unfortunately, such short-term benefits do not always turn into long-term gains. Discounting will not work forever, as most people find it difficult to completely ignore the pressures placed on them by society; fishing for compliments can backfire, resulting in a slew of negative comments; and biased viewpoints and aggressive responding are not conducive to the development of a realistic sense of self. Personal growth requires that we evaluate our strengths, and our weaknesses, open and honestly. It is only through an objective assessment of the self, and thus our self-concept, that we can discover how to grow and develop as a person.

THE COMPONENTS OF THE SELF

LEARNING OBJECTIVES

4.4 Distinguish between self-image, ideal self, and social self.

4.5 Explain the concept of multiple selves.

Earlier, several different *specific* types of selves were identified; at a more general level, however, it is common to identify four kinds of self:

- **Body image,** *the awareness of my body*
- The **self-image,** *the self I see myself to be*
- The **ideal self,** *the self I'd like to be*
- The **social self,** *the ways I feel others see me*

Because body image is discussed in great detail in chapter 5, let's begin here by looking more closely at the self-image.

Self-Image

As noted above, self-image is *the way you see yourself.* It is primarily made up of the many self-perceptions we have acquired growing up and by the way we are currently seen and treated by significant others. Across the formative years, youth tend to internalize what others think of them—their judgments and expectations—and regard the self accordingly. For example, during middle childhood, teasing by family members can lead to a negative self-image, as indicated by low self-esteem and depression (Keery, Boutelle, van den Berg, & Thompson, 2005). Now, imagine the *long-term* impact of enduring parents' negative statements (e.g., "Don't do that, Stupid!" "What's wrong with you?") on a child's self-image. Nevertheless, childhood experiences can be overcome, as we tend to revise our self-images through more recent experience with others, especially with our friends, lovers, teachers, and co-workers. However, even a stranger's opinion can influence us now and then, which not only affects how we currently view ourselves, but our future behavior as well (Murray, 2005). For example, parents will often give in to a tantruming child's demands when waiting in the check-out line at a store in order to avoid nasty looks from others—stares that are essentially telling tell them what bad parents they are because they can't control their child.

Ideal self is the self you would like to become or, in some cases, reflects who you currently are.

Ideal Self

Another aspect of self is the **ideal self,** that is, *the self you would like to be, including your aspirations, moral ideals, and values.* The ideal self can be a reflection of whom we currently are or a portrait of whom we would like to become. However, if the ideal self is quite different from the real self, anxiety and other psychological problems may result. For example, adolescent girls suffering from bulimia nervosa (a psychological disorder characterized by binge eating and purging) tend to have an ideal self that is vastly different (and thinner) from the real self (Sonenklar, 2011).

With experience and maturity, our aspirations should increasingly represent self-chosen goals and values (i.e., self-directedness) that express in a healthy, adult way what we've come to expect of *ourselves.* Consequently, our ideal self may serve as an incentive for us to do our best. If we fail to live up to our ideal self, it is healthy to feel we have a choice either to redouble our efforts to achieve our aspirations or to modify them in the direction of more fruitful goals. Ordinarily, we think of having to change our self-image and behavior to better match our ideals. However, in those instances when our aspirations prove to be excessive or unrealistic, it may be more appropriate for us to modify our ideal self as a way of furthering our growth and self-esteem (Baumgardner & Crothers, 2009).

How would you characterize your own ideal self? Do you tend to be idealistic and rather hard on yourself when you fall short of your aims? Or are you more down-to-earth and practical-minded, shrugging off disappointments with yourself and giving it another try? To check on your perceptions, you might do the exercise on self-image and ideal self in Activity 4–1.

Social Self

The **social self (selves)** is comprised of *the impressions we think others have of us,* which may or may not be an accurate reflection of reality. Take, for example, Ari, who has an inflated sense of self-importance. While working on a group project for an art class, Ari firmly believes that the other group members view him as the most creative contributor to the assignment. In reality, the other group members think of Ari as arrogant, and his ideas as uninspired. Ari is not

ACTIVITY 4–1

SELF-IMAGE AND IDEAL SELF

This is an exercise to measure the correspondence between your self-image and ideal self. Reproduce the box containing items A through P. Then cut out the 16 cards or rectangles as indicated by the lines and put them on a table or desk in random order.

First, you're to get a profile of your self-image, or the self you see yourself to be. To do so, arrange the cards in a line, either from top to bottom or left to right. At one end, place the statement that you think describes you best. Then arrange the remaining cards in order, ranging from the next most true and so forth to the least true at the end. Then record the rank number of each item in the column labeled "self." For instance, if you placed card A in the eighth position write "8" next to card A.

Next, repeat this procedure in regard to your ideal self. That is, arrange the cards in the order that describes the self you'd like to be, ranging from the card that you wish were most true of you at one end to that which is least true of your ideal self at the other end. When you've completed your rankings, record the order of the items or cards in the column labeled "ideal."

When you finish ranking the cards and recording the numbers, consult the scoring key at the end of the chapter.

I'm a likable person A	I have sex appeal I
I'm rather self-centered at times B	I'm an anxious person J
I'm physically attractive C	I have above-average intelligence K
I have a strong need for approval D	I'm shy in groups L
I'm usually a hard worker E	I have a good sense of humor M
I daydream too much F	I'm sometimes dishonest N
I can be assertive when necessary G	I have a good disposition O
I often feel discouraged H	I gossip a lot P

Item	Self	Ideal	Differences
A			
B			
C			
D			
E			
F			
G			
H			
I			
J			
K			
L			
M			
N			
O			
P			
		Sum of differences	

alone in his misguided perceptions, for it is relatively easy to make errors when evaluating how others view us. As an example, we frequently *overestimate how prominent our own behavior, appearance, and emotions are to others;* a phenomenon known as the **spotlight effect**. In other words, we think that people pay a lot more attention to us than they really do (Libby, Eibach, & Gilovich, 2005). Additionally, because we tend to critique ourselves harshly, most individuals expect others to judge them *more harshly* than they really do (Gilovich & Savitsky, 1999). Nevertheless, it is the *perception* of how others view us (and not the reality) that greatly influences the way we see ourselves.

We have many different social selves because we see ourselves somewhat differently with each person we meet. With a stranger, we may be guarded and unsure of ourselves; a bossy, critical employer may make us feel anxious and inferior, but a close friend can makes us feel confident and affectionate. It's not that we're being two-faced or untrue to ourselves. Rather, each of these people brings out a different aspect of self, which in turn helps to shape the way we see ourselves. Because of this we need to ask, "Are there overly critical people who devalue us?" We probably should avoid them. "Are there others who see the best in us?" Perhaps we should seek them out more often. In both instances, we can change the way we see ourselves by modifying the social influences on our lives. It would be foolish to think we can change everything about ourselves in this way or that we can always avoid negative people. But the notion of fluid, changing social selves reminds us that we have more possibilities for change and personal growth than we may be using.

Multiple Selves

As mentioned above, the overall self-concept is an organized cluster of selves, so it would be more accurate to speak of our multiple selves or **self-complexity** (McConnell et al., 2005). Self-complexity is *the extent to which one's self-concept is comprised of many differentiated self-aspects.* As such, the self-concept includes hundreds, perhaps thousands, of self-perceptions with varying degrees of clarity and intensity that we have acquired over a lifetime. For example, Shandra's self-concept included her gender role, her concept of herself as a mother, and her attitudes and values.

Moreover, self-complexity varies from person to person and from culture to culture (Bigler, Neimeyer, & Brown, 2001; Markus & Kitayama, 2003). For example, more so than for most Americans, the self-concepts of the Japanese include a family-oriented self as well as a spiritual self (Miller, 1999). Much of the diversity of the self reflects our social and cultural roles, so that even the normally happy person wears "many masks." However, there is one fairly universal aspect of self, the tendency to evaluate oneself favorably, known as *self-enhancement,* which will be discussed shortly (Sedikides, Gaertner, & Vevea, 2005).

CORE CHARACTERISTICS OF SELF-CONCEPT

LEARNING OBJECTIVES

  4.6 Explain the core tendency toward self-consistency.
  4.7 Describe the promise and peril of high self-esteem.
  4.8 Distinguish between self-enhancement and self-verification.

The **core of the self-concept** are *those aspects of ourselves we regard as very important to us,* such as religious, racial, and ethnic identity, as well as academic abilities and physical attractiveness. Once established the core exhibits a high degree of stability, as seen in the consistent ways we perceive ourselves over time. For example, Shandra was very proud of a core concept dear to her heart—her African-American heritage—and little could shake her pride in her racial identity. In contrast, rather peripheral aspects of the self (e.g., musical tastes, food preferences, clothing style) can, and often do, change rather quickly. In this section, we'll focus on the core tendency of the self-concept to maintain and perpetuate itself. In the next section, we'll look at some of the major ways the cores of the self-concepts can and do change.

Self-Consistency

Self-consistency refers to the *tendency to perceive our experiences in a manner consistent with our self-concept.* Events that are in harmony with our self-concept tend to be perceived accurately and admitted fully into our conscious awareness. As an example, getting an "A" on a test (the event) is easily recalled because it reinforces the idea that one is intelligent (a core self-concept). In contrast, experiences that are *not* consistent with our self-concept are perceived more selectively and sometimes inaccurately. Such experiences are either distorted or kept from awareness. For instance, people will *trivialize threatening information* (e.g., failing a test) *by making the behavior seem less important* (e.g., saying "I don't need this class for my major), a process referred to as **self-immunization**. Similarly, **mnemonic neglect,** which involves *poor recall (or forgetting) of negative feedback that is inconsistent with core aspects of the self-concept* can also occur. Case in point, individuals have difficulty remembering words (e.g., stupid, lazy, outgoing) that are inconsistent with their self-perceptions (e.g., intelligent, active, shy) (Greve & Wentura, 2003).

Self-Esteem

TYPES OF SELF-ESTEEM   One of the most important aspects of the self-concept is **self-esteem—** *the personal evaluation of ourselves and the associated feelings of worth.* Although people customarily speak of self-esteem as a single entity—global esteem—our self-esteem typically clusters into four main types: physical attractiveness, physical abilities, cognitive abilities, and social relationships. We can have high self-esteem in one area (e.g., social relationship), and low self-esteem in another (e.g., cognitive abilities). Thus, our overall self-esteem is more complex than ordinarily portrayed and fluctuates somewhat depending on our experiences (Guindon, 2010). But if self-esteem varies from high to low depending on the type, how is global self-esteem established? As it turns out, it is the area deemed to be the most important to the self that has the greatest influence on global self-esteem (Harter, 1987). Thus, for those that assign physical abilities the greatest worth, global self-esteem will be primarily influenced by physical self-esteem. Likewise, if you value social relationships the most, then your global self-esteem will be heavily influenced by your social self-esteem (DeHart et al., 2004). What type of self-esteem do you value the most?

INFLUENCES ON SELF-ESTEEM   Self-esteem is affected by a variety of influences, ranging from significant childhood experiences to our own standards of self-worth to images in the media. For instance, people with high self-esteem appear to have been raised by parents who were supportive, expressed a lot of affection, and established firm but reasonable rules. Individuals with low self-esteem usually were brought up by parents who relied on parenting styles that were overly strict, overly permissive, or inconsistent (Park, Crocker, & Mickelson, 2004). Here's an example of how media can shape our sense of self: overweight teens in Fiji only began to view their bodies negatively after the introduction of television, and the viewing of shows depicting a culture of thinness (e.g., thin actors, being overweight is portrayed negatively, and heavy individuals are ridiculed) (Becker, Burwell, Gilman, Herzog, & Hamburg, 2002). Moreover, culture can also affect self-esteem; with the self-esteem of people from individualistic cultures being affected by the achievement of personal goals the most, and the self-esteem of those from collectivist cultures being based on objectives related to family and society (Schmitt & Allik, 2005).

Exploration 4.1: Self-Growth

www.selfgrowth.com Interested in higher self-esteem, in fact, higher everything? This site provides much information about self-improvement and personal growth.

Our self-esteem is also influenced by both success and failure, although there is often a low correspondence between people's self-views and their actual performance (Dunning, Heath, & Suls, 2004). Moreover, psychologists once thought that a backlog of stored success enhanced self-esteem and repeated failure undermined it. For example, praising children's intelligence (regardless of performance on assignments) was believed to make children think they were intelligent and, thus, improve their self-esteem. However, this belief was proven wrong. Rather, it is praising children for their *efforts,* more so than for their abilities, which benefits self-esteem and creates in children a desire to take on challenges, even when success is not guaranteed (Dweck, 1999). Finally, it is worth mentioning that the impact of any one achievement (e.g., getting a 95 on a test) on self-esteem often depends on the how we did relative to those around us (e.g., your best friend got a 98). Thus, individuals with similar talents and success may vary in their self-esteem, depending on with whom they compare themselves. Table 4–2 contains characteristics of people with high and low self-esteem.

EFFECTS OF HIGH AND LOW SELF-ESTEEM Most people realize that self-esteem can influence how we feel about ourselves; with high self-esteem resulting in positive feelings and low self-esteem leading to negative ones. However, self-esteem also exerts a powerful influence on people's expectations and judgments as well as on their behavior (Dunning et al., 2004). Here is some evidence: individuals with high self-esteem do better in school, are more likely to persist in the face of failure, more frequently exit bad interpersonal relationships, and perform better on their jobs than individuals with low self-esteem. With regards to well-being, people with high self-esteem are happier than those with low self-esteem (Baumeister, Campbell, Krueger, & Vohs, 2005).

Table 4–2 High and Low Self-Esteem

Signs of High Self-Esteem	*Signs of Low Self-Esteem*
Do you ...	**Do you ...**
like your appearance when you see yourself in the mirror?	avoid viewing yourself in the mirror?
feel comfortable with yourself most of the time?	feel discontented with yourself most of the time?
savor your accomplishments?	brag excessively or apologize about your achievements?
regard your failures as opportunities to learn?	make excuses for your failures?
express your opinions readily?	withhold your views, especially if asked?
listen to what others say, even if you disagree?	try to convince others of your views?
accept compliments graciously?	reject compliments or qualify them?
give credit to others when it's due?	envy others and put them down by sarcasm or gossip?
make realistic demands on yourself ?	expect too much or too little of yourself?
give and receive affection generously?	withhold your affection out of fear of being hurt?

Nevertheless, positive consequences are *not* always associated with high self-esteem, for it can also be related to antisocial behaviors, such as cheating on tests and annoying or interrupting others. Bullies, for example, often possess overly inflated self-esteem. Another downside is that there is little evidence to show that high self-esteem creates better health for the individual. For example, high esteem does not prevent alcohol and drug abuse (Baumeister, Campbell, Krueger, & Vohs, 2003).

MINORITY STRESS AND SELF-ESTEEM   Does **minority stress** —*the psychological and social stress associated minority status*—and noticing differences between the self and members of the majority group place minorities at a disadvantage for self-esteem? In most instances, the answer is "no." For instance, in the United States, the self-esteem of racial minorities is just as high as (or higher than) that of the racial majority (Erol & Orth, 2011). Similar findings have been shown for minorities in other Western countries, such as the Netherlands (Verkuytenm & Thijs, 2004). At times, minorities use self-protective mechanisms for maintaining self-esteem. For example, some minority-group members attribute negative feedback and personal failures to prejudice and discrimination against their group rather than to their own flawed attributes (Major, Kaiser, & McCoy, 2003). In the short-term, this sort of thinking can successfully protect self-esteem from harm. Nevertheless, those who repeatedly perceive themselves to be the victim of discrimination and prejudice cannot avoid having their psychological adjustment or self-concept negatively impacted (Tummala-Narra, Inman, & Ettigi, 2011).

Exploration 4.2: Racial Identity

www.myshoes.com   My Shoes is a support group in cyberspace hosted by a clinical psychologist for multiracial children, adolescents, and adults who grapple with the racial identity issue.

STRIVING FOR SELF-ESTEEM   *How* people strive for self-esteem may be just as important, if not more important, for personal growth and adjustment than *whether* their level of self-esteem is either high or low (Crocker & Park, 2004). Here's why:

- Pursuing self-esteem results in mistakes, failures, threats, and other negative consequences that cause anxiety.
- Anxiety inhibits learning, especially from feedback designed to help the esteem-seeker.
- Autonomy or choice is influenced negatively, too. When people in hot pursuit of self-esteem feel they have no choice but to persist, they experience pressure and tension.
- Pursuing self-esteem also negatively impacts relationships because it focuses the pursuer on the self rather than on others who also want attention.

In the end, seeking self-esteem may cause distress in many areas and consequently affect one's physical and mental health in harmful ways. Interestingly, one "cure" for questing for self-esteem is to turn from self-directedness to other-directedness: seeking goals that are beneficial to others as much as or more than to the self (Crocker & Knight, 2005). Another solution may be to seek a self-directed or self-determined life. Seeking self-created standards rather than pursuing self-esteem reduces defensiveness and other negative consequences associated with striving for self-esteem. In the end, such self-determined standards of value become thoroughly integrated with one's core sense of self (Pyszczynski & Cox, 2004).

Exploration 4.3: Self-Esteem

www.self-esteem-nase.org   The National Association for Self-Esteem provides helpful resources for building self-esteem.

Self-Enhancement and Self-Verification

We receive a great deal of information about how people see us through our interactions with them. As a matter of fact, we often make deliberate attempts to elicit such information, whether through actions or direct questioning, and in the modern era, through the Internet, especially social media. As you can see, some individuals strive for **self-enhancement,** where the *try to get positive feedback that affirms their own ideas about their positive qualities.* Most people prefer and seek out positive feedback about themselves, especially for those attributes that they themselves view as positive (Taylor & Brown, 1994). Along the same line of thinking, people's autobiographical memory induces them to perceive themselves as better and better over time (Ross & Wilson, 2003).

In contrast, other people seek out **self-verification,** where they *attempt to preserve their own images (both positive and negative) of themselves and therefore elicit feedback that verifies or confirms their own self-perceptions (both positive and negative).* Thus, self-verification is important to us, in that it gives us a sense of stability or consistency in an unpredictable world. Also, such confirmation is vital to social interaction because if others see us as we see ourselves, they will have a better idea of how to treat us, what to expect of us, and so forth. Generally, people prefer to hear opinions that are not only positive, but also supportive of their own views of themselves.

However, basing self-worth on external sources (such as social standards) is more related to negative psychological outcomes than basing self-worth on more internal aspects of self, such as being a virtuous person. For instance, investment in gender ideals (e.g., men should be independent, decisive, and emotional stable; women should be caring, supportive, emotionally expressive) negatively affects self-esteem for both men and women (Sanchez & Crocker, 2005). Nevertheless, there are some documented sex differences related to the self. Women report engaging more in self-reflection than men do (Rudman & Goodwin, 2004). Similarly, women possess greater **self-clarity,** *which is the extent to which one's individual self-beliefs are clearly and confidently defined, internally consistent, and stable* (Csank & Conway, 2004). Overall, though, the bulk of the research shows that men's and women's self-esteem levels are not necessarily different (Pierson & Glaeser, 2002).

THE SELF-CONCEPT AND PERSONAL GROWTH

LEARNING OBJECTIVES

  4.9 **Explain how visualization can help personal growth**

  4.10 **List ways you may use criticism for personal growth.**

  4.11 **Discuss the importance of greater self-direction and self-acceptance in personal growth.**

SELF-CONCEPT OVER TIME As mentioned earlier, your self-concept continues to change as you mature and develop. Indeed, there is growing recognition that the cluster of selves comprising the self-concept can and does change to a greater extent than previously realized. Self-esteem, for example, is relatively high in childhood, drops during adolescence (particularly for girls), rises gradually throughout adulthood, and then declines in old age (Robins & Trzesniewski, 2005). These developmental trends appear to hold regardless of ethnicity (Erol & Orth, 2011). Much of the change in our self-concept occurs with experience, but a great deal of change in our self-image comes from adapting to different people and situations (Sanchez & Crocker, 2005). Job changes, new friends, and modifications in responsibilities, like marriage and parenting, all affect the way we see ourselves. Although we retain a stable core of self, the many self-perceptions that make up our overall self-concept are in a state of flux or change and are more readily influenced by current experience than previously thought.

BOX 4–2	Focus on Wellness: Visualizing a "Better You"

To help realize your aim of self-improvement, you might visualize the self or selves you'd like to be. Imagine as vividly as possible how you'll look, how you'll feel, and how you'll act. It also helps to create an image of any **feared self**, that is, *the self that would result if you don't succeed*. Think of the failed attempts to lose weight, the mediocre performances in school and at work, and the disappointments in love. Then visualize a better you; a you created from using different strategies to overcome failure. Self-change is difficult but not impossible. In each instance, vivid mental images of our possible selves may help us to become the person we'd like to be, especially when accompanied by the appropriate efforts (Polivy & Herman, 2000).

The Self You'd Like to Be

Americans spend millions of dollars every year in the hope of improving themselves. They buy self-help books and CDs, and attend workshops designed to make you "a better you." One promising approach to self-improvement, and one that will not cost you a dime, consists of visualizing the person you'd like to become. **Visualization,** also known as **guided imagery,** is *a procedure that helps a person shut off the outside world and bypass the censor we call the brain, enabling the person to see, experience, and learn from an intuitive, feeling, unconscious nature* (Leviton & Leviton, 2004). Visualization has successfully been used to improve performance during sporting activities, reduce perceived levels of stress, improve the immune system, and enhance the comfort of people undergoing medical procedures, such as chemotherapy and wound debridement (Trakhtenberg, 2008). See Box 4–2 to learn a technique to visualize a "better you."

Exploration 4.4: Visualization

www.livestrong.com   A site developed by the Lance Armstrong foundation. Contains lots of health-related information, including exercises in visualization. Search for "guided imagery."

Learning from Criticism

How do you feel when you are criticized? Do you feel angry and rejected? Do you feel resentful, even when you're in the wrong? For most people, the answer to these questions is yes. When people have been asked to finish the statement "When I am criticized … ," typical responses include "I get upset," "I resent it," "I feel she doesn't love me anymore," and "I wonder when the axe will fall." Sound familiar? All too often, as these comments suggest, people feel that criticism is a personal attack that they must defend themselves against at all costs. As a result, they waste a lot of energy worrying about criticism, justifying themselves, and going to great lengths to avoid it. Activity 4–2 can help you identify your own sensitivity to criticism.

ACCEPTING CRITICISM   Accepting criticism can become a valuable means of personal growth. For example, when asked to complete the statement mentioned earlier, some people make more positive responses. Thus, it is possible to learn the art of taking criticism constructively. To accomplish this, try viewing criticism as a valuable source of new information to be evaluated objectively. Each time you're criticized, you don't necessarily have to rush out and change something about yourself. Instead, criticism should be taken as a cue that *may* require action. Consider also how many times a specific criticism is offered. If several people offer the same criticism for the same behavior, there's a good chance that the criticism is valid and should be acted on. Ask yourself too, "How important is this criticism?" The more important the information is to you, the more likely you'll need to do something about it. Also consider the source of the criticism. Often, people feel they're being criticized unfairly, especially if the other person is under a lot of

ACTIVITY 4–2

SENSITIVITY TO CRITICISM

To learn how you respond to criticism, rate each statement below as follows: If you strongly agree, circle SA. If you agree with the statement, circle A. If you disagree, circle D. If you strongly disagree, circle SD.

1. When people point out my mistakes, I feel like they are degrading me. SA A D SD

2. When someone gives me negative feedback, I immediately try to think of examples to prove him/her wrong. SA A D SD

3. I remain positive in the face of failure. SA A D SD

4. I get discouraged when I don't succeed at something right away. SA A D SD

5. I tend to dislike people who tell me how I should do things. SA A D SD

6. It's hard for me to admit to myself when I'm wrong. SA A D SD

7. If someone claims that a task I've completed is unacceptable, I can't help but give him or her a piece of my mind. SA A D SD

8. I tend to dislike people who tell me how I should do things. SA A D SD

9. I get discouraged when someone tells me I haven't done my best. SA A D SD

10. I'm really hard on myself when I fail, dwelling on all the ways I could have done better. SA A D SD

SCORING: For each item score as follows: Strongly Agree = 3, Agree = 2, Disagree = 1, and Strongly Disagree = 0. Total your score. Higher scores may indicate a higher sensitivity to criticism. This scale is an adaption of Atlas's (1994) *Sensitivity to Criticism Scale.* Our version of this scale has not been scientifically validated; please interpret the results with caution.

Source: Based on Sensitivity to Criticism Scale from "Sensitivity to Criticism: A New Measure of Responses to Everyday Criticisms" by Gordon D. Atlas, from *Journal of Psychoeducational Assessment,* September 1994, Volume 12(3).

stress. The more qualified the person is to judge you, the more you should take his or her criticism to heart. Even criticism spoken in frustration or anger may need to be heeded, but take into account the exaggerated emotion of the messenger.

ACTING ON CRITICISM Remember, not all criticisms need to be acted upon. To decide how to respond when criticized, weigh the pros and cons of action and inaction. You should decide whether the benefits that come from acting on the criticism balance or outweigh the effort involved. For example, students who do poorly on tests may wonder whether it's worthwhile to follow the teacher's suggestion to get help in reading comprehension and note-taking skills. On the other hand, if they continue to get low grades, their career goals may be in jeopardy. Put the emotional energy aroused by criticism to work for you, not against you. In addition to interfering with a person's ability to perform well, emotional arousal may also negatively influence self-confidence. Instead, when criticized, try to stay calm. Relax physically. Remind yourself that nobody is trying to hurt you. What this person is saying may be helpful. Then use your emotions as a source of energy to make the necessary changes.

The later stages of changes to self are characterized by greater self-direction and self-acceptance. As people come to accept themselves, they may become more accepting of and accepted by others.

Take positive steps to put the needed changes into action. Don't waste energy defending yourself. Instead, listen carefully to what is being said. Ask for more information. Ask the person for suggested solutions to the criticism. You might ask for this information indirectly, such as, "If you were in my place, what would you do?" Or you might ask, more directly, "What would you like me to do?" People usually criticize something we're doing. But it often comes across as a personal attack because many people do not know how to give criticism constructively. So if someone says, "You're rude and inconsiderate," ask, "In what ways have I been inconsiderate? How would you suggest I behave?" In this way, you'll focus on something tangible that you can do, which in due time may lead to the desired changes in your self-image and reputation.

Greater Self-Direction

Learning how to listen to others so that we'll grow and benefit from their criticism is difficult enough. Learning to listen to ourselves and be true to our own deepest desires and goals can be even more challenging. Carl Rogers (1961) once observed that beneath the bewildering complexity of problems people face—such as trouble with grades, a difficult employer, or indecision about an unsatisfying marriage—lies one central search. Underneath it all, each person, knowingly or unknowingly, is asking, "Who am I, really? How can I get in touch with this real self, underlying all my surface behavior? How can I become myself?" (p. 108).

STAGES IN SELF-DIRECTION   Rogers (1980) found that in the process of becoming a new person the individual's experience of growth follows a general pattern. The first stage of self-revision is usually characterized by a movement away from accepting the criticisms of others and the distorted perceptions of the self that followed. This stage also accounts for the prevalence of complaints and self-disparagement (e.g., "I don't like myself this way") so often seen when making significant changes to the self. The later stages of changes to the self are characterized by greater self-direction and self-acceptance. Most important, as individuals strive to discover

---

Activity 4–3

Self-Affirming Activities

Instructions: *Do one or more of the following activities. When you have a low point in your self-image, pull out the activity and your answers and reread them.*

- Name five of your strengths.
- List five things you admire about yourself.
- What are your five greatest achievements in life so far?
- Describe five ways you can reward yourself for accomplishments.
- Explain five ways you can make yourself laugh.
- What are five things you can do for someone else to make them feel good?
- List five things you do to treat yourself well.
- What five activities have you recently engaged in that gave you joy?

Source: Adapted from "Building Self-Esteem: A Self-Help Guide" by Charled G. Curie and Bernard S. Arons. Substance Abuse & Mental Health Services Administration, n.d.

---

themselves, they become more willing to accept the fact that they are engaged in *a process of becoming.* More specifically, individuals become *more open* to their own experiences. They become *more aware of and comfortable with* the complexity of their feelings. For example, they can experience love and disdain toward the same person. Or they may feel excited and fearful about their new job. Activity 4–3 provides some activities that you can complete to help you appreciate your own openness to experience and complexities.

UNSETTLING NATURE OF PERSONAL GROWTH   As individuals accept themselves more fully, they often become more accepting of others. This is the opposite of **self-alienation,** *which occurs when we fail to acknowledge or accept certain aspects of ourselves. We then feel these qualities are foreign to us and we project them onto others, whom we then dislike.* For example, the man who, while denying his own dependency needs, appears to be strong and self-sufficient may feel contempt for men who allow themselves to be taken care of when weak or ill. As you can see, personal growth may be unsettling at times. It involves moving away from some of the familiar self-images acquired during our formative years. And it involves seeing yourself in new ways, especially as a more self-directed person. Because each of us has different values and goals, there is no detailed guide to assure us that we are doing the right thing. Nevertheless, understanding the general pattern of growth, as prescribed by Rogers, may be helpful. And remember, "The good life is a process, not a state of being. It is a direction, not a destination" (Rogers, 1961, p. 186).

Chapter Summary

WHAT IS SELF-CONCEPT?

4.1 Describe the self-concept.
The self-concept is the overall image or awareness we have of ourselves.

4.2 List the different processes used to protect the self from harm.
Defenses used by the self for protection include: resisting anything that may damage the self,

discounting, seeking out positive information, and giving ourselves the benefit of the doubt.

4.3 Discuss why the self-concept is important to personal growth.

The self-concept exerts a tremendous influence on the way we think and act. As such, personal growth requires that we evaluate the strengths and weaknesses of the self.

THE COMPONENTS OF THE SELF

4.4 Distinguish between self-image, ideal self, and social self.

The four main types of selves are: body image (how we perceive and feel about our body), self-image (the self we see ourselves to be), the ideal self (the self we'd like to be), and the social self (the way we feel others see us).

4.5 Explain the concept of multiple selves.

The self-concept is an organized cluster of selves, typically referred to as self-complexity. The self is comprised of hundreds if not thousands of self-perceptions.

CORE CHARACTERISTICS OF SELF-CONCEPT

4.6 Explain the core tendency toward self-consistency.

Once developed, the self-concept tends to maintain and perpetuate itself as it is. It serves as a filter through which we view our experiences, so that experiences that are not consistent with the self-concept are apt to be distorted or kept out of awareness. Largely because of the self's influence, people generally prefer to hear opinions that support their own views of themselves.

4.7 Describe the promise and peril of high self-esteem.

Self-esteem refers to the personal evaluation of the self and the associated feelings of worth. The promise of self-esteem is that individuals with high self-esteem are happier, do better in school, are more likely to persist in the face of failure, more frequently exit bad interpersonal relationships, and perform better on their jobs than individuals with low self-esteem. Today's psychologists, however, are busy debating the perils of self-esteem, with many psychologists suggesting that the practice of seeking high self-esteem is detrimental to the individual.

4.8 Distinguish between self-enhancement and self-verification.

Self-enhancement refers to the attempt to get positive feedback confirming one's ideas about their positive qualities. In contrast, self-verification involves searching for any type of information (both positive and negative) that confirms one's self-perceptions, even those that are negative.

THE SELF-CONCEPT AND PERSONAL GROWTH

4.9 Explain how visualization can help personal growth.

Visualizing our future possible selves not only helps us to attain them but also aids in our present life adjustment.

4.10 List ways you may use criticism for personal growth.

We may use personal criticism for growth by putting the energy it arouses to work for us rather than against us, thus using it as an opportunity to learn about ourselves and put the needed changes into action.

4.11 Discuss the importance of greater self-direction and self-acceptance in personal growth.

Ultimately, personal growth involves moving away from negative reflected appraisals from others that distort self-perceptions acquired while growing up and moving toward greater self-acceptance and self-direction. Then we become more open to our own experiences and willing to affirm ourselves in a process of becoming.

Scoring Key for the Self-Image and Ideal-Self Exercise

To find the correspondence between your self-image and your ideal self, note the difference in the rank for each card. For example, on card A if you ranked your self-image as 8 and your ideal self as 2, the difference would be 6. For each card, record the *absolute* difference between numbers without regard to pluses or minuses. Then total the numbers in the column of differences. A score in the range of 50 would be about average. A difference lower than 30 indicates a high correspondence between your self-image and your ideal self. A score of more than 80 indicates a rather low correspondence between your self-image and ideal self. A high score doesn't necessarily mean that you have problems, however. Remember, this is a self-activity, not a valid test, so use your results to do some self-reflection and personal growth.

Self-Test

1. Rob made it big in business, owning a chain of fast food restaurants. Rob felt that his success was *only* the result of his hard work; good luck and fortunate timing had nothing to do with it. Rob is demonstrating:
   a. an external locus of control
   b. a self-serving attributional bias
   c. an other-serving attributional bias
   d. low self-esteem

2. Which of the following is not an aspect of the self?
   a. body image
   b. ideal self
   c. natural self
   d. social self
   e. self-image

3. Ginny thinks that other people view her as kind, trusting, and helpful. Ginny's beliefs comprise her:
   a. social self
   b. natural self
   c. body image
   d. egocentric self

4. When the _____ is very different from the _____ anxiety may result.
   a. ideal self; real self
   b. natural self; social self
   c. social self; body image
   d. body image; self-image

5. Julia believes herself to be a dedicated, hard-working individual that can be counted on, especially at her job. So, when she decides to skip work (by calling in sick) in order to attend a concert by Pink, Julia minimizes her absence as a minor inconvenience for her boss. As a result, the perception of her work ethic mentioned above does not change. Julia appears to be engaging in:
   a. mnemonic neglect
   b. social comparison
   c. self-enhancement
   d. self-immunization

6. Jonathan loves social-networking sites, such as Twitter and MySpace. Jonathan's favorite site by far is Facebook, because he loves to read peoples comments about his posts. Recently, Jonathan posted "like this if you think I'm a good friend" in order to confirm his belief that he is in fact a "good friend." Which theory explains Jonathan's behavior?
   a. social comparison theory
   b. self-verification theory
   c. self-clarity theory
   d. self-alienation theory

7. Although Trella avoids criticism like it was the plaque, she does like to hear other people say good things about her personal qualities. Which theory explains why Trella only seeks out positive comments?
   a. self-alienation theory
   b. self-enhancement theory
   c. social comparison theory
   d. self-clarity theory

8. According to Rogers, during the later stages of personal growth, people have a heightened sense of:
   a. fixed personal goals.
   b. self-criticalness.
   c. self-direction and self-acceptance.
   d. future orientation.

9. When Stu walked into crowded room at work the other day he stumbled slightly on a raised piece of carpet. Stu felt as if everyone in the room had seen his misstep (they hadn't) and that a video of it had been posted on Failblog (it wasn't). In reality, Stu was experiencing:
   a. psychological absorption
   b. the spotlight effect
   c. desensitization
   d. self-clarity

10. The most helpful way of handling personal criticism is to regard it as something that:
    a. needs immediate action.
    b. necessitates self-defense.
    c. reflects others' faults.
    d. may require action.

Exercises

1. *Self-image*. This is the self you perceive yourself to be. Using a full 8 1/2- by 11-inch page, draw two concentric circles (a circle within a circle)—the inner circle representing the core of your self-concept and the outer circle the more flexible, changeable selves. Within the inner circle, list six to eight of your most enduring aspects (traits). In the outer circle, list a similar number of aspects of yourself that are more dependent on changing roles and circumstances. How would you describe your overall self-image?

2. *The self you'd like to be.* Among the various possible selves you'd like to be, including any feared self, select one specific image. Visualize it in specific terms as vividly as possible. Write down how you'd look, how you'd feel, and how you'd act. If possible, you might spend several minutes a day for a week daydreaming about your possible self. How did this affect your present self-image and adjustment?

3. *Self-esteem*. Our sense of personal worth fluctuates somewhat from one situation to another. Think of several situations or occasions in which you usually feel good about yourself and exhibit a lot of self-confidence. Then think of several situations in which you feel unsure of yourself and inferior. Can you identify the people or demands that make you feel good

or bad about yourself? What are some practical steps you can take to improve your self-esteem?

4. *Identifying your social selves.* Select five or six people you associate with regularly. Then identify which aspects of yourself are most readily expressed when you're with these people. Jot down some of the shared interests, typical activities, and your feelings and attitudes toward each person. Would you agree that you feel and behave somewhat differently with different people?

5. *How well do you take criticism?* Select an instance when someone criticized you and describe your experience in a page or so. Did you interpret the person's remarks as a personal attack? Or did you try to look beyond the surface of the criticism to what the person was trying to tell you? Looking back, to what extent was this a positive learning experience for you? Jot down some suggestions that will help you to benefit from personal criticism in the future.

Questions for Self-Reflection

1. How would you describe your self-image?
2. Which aspects of your self-concept would you like to change?
3. Do you basically like yourself?
4. Are you more self-confident in some situations than in others?
5. Are you aware of how others see you?
6. When you've accepted something within yourself, are you more accepting of it in others?
7. How well do you take personal criticism?
8. What do you say when complimented by others?
9. How has your self-concept changed since you were a child?
10. Do you tend to trust your own experiences?

Chapter Five

Toward Better Health

*A*manda, in her mid-30s, is employed at a large department store as an artist and designer. When she is at work, she drinks one cup of coffee after another. It seems that Amanda is always behind deadline, so for lunch she typically has her assistant get her something from one of the many fast-food restaurant chains nearby. When she finally goes home to her apartment, Amanda is too tired to fix herself a decent meal, eating whatever happens to be in her fridge or pantry. To deal with stress, Amanda has a drink or two or three or more, depending on the day. Complaining she doesn't have time, Amanda rarely exercises. As a result of her eating and drinking choices, as well as her general lack of exercise, Amanda is overweight. She wears baggy clothes to disguise her expanding figure. Amanda also smokes about a pack of cigarettes a day, a habit she developed in college. Amanda is not now sick and, in fact, feels well enough so that she rarely complains of physical ailments to others. But how healthy is she really? Chances are she could be doing much better. Amanda lacks awareness of what her sedentary and stressful lifestyle is doing to her. She subscribes to the mistaken notion that "not being sick" means she is "well."

BODY IMAGE

LEARNING OBJECTIVES

5.1 Explain the difference between body image and the ideal body.
5.2 Discuss the relationship between media and body image.

How We Feel about Our Bodies

Body image refers to *the mental images, attitudes, and feelings we form of our own bodies.* In terms of its weight, shape, height, and muscularity, people can either be satisfied or dissatisfied with their bodies. Unfortunately, dissatisfaction with one's body starts at an early age, as 55 percent of 8- to 10-year-old girls and 35 percent of same-aged boys are dissatisfied with their bodies. And as youth progress from middle childhood into adolescence, body satisfaction continues its downward trend. By age 17, nearly 80 percent of American girls are unhappy with their bodies. Although body dissatisfaction becomes less important during adulthood, it nonetheless remains relatively stable across the lifespan, a surprising finding in that we might expect it to increase with age. As people grow older, they tend to gain weight, develop wrinkles, and report changes in their hair color and thickness—all of which might actually increase body dissatisfaction (Tiggemann, 2004). It may be that, as we age, our expectations for what makes an "age-appropriate body" also changes. Thus, it is the perceived shape of our bodies, relative to same-aged individuals, that primarily influences how we view and accept ourselves. For example, when thinking about the beauty of their bodies, 50-year olds will most likely compare themselves against other 50-year olds and not against 20-year olds.

BOX 5–1   Did you know that ...

- Today, models weigh 23 percent less than the average woman; that number was 8 percent just 20 years ago.
- In 2007, nearly 12 million cosmetic procedures were performed in America. Of those, close to 91 percent were done on women.
- About 7 percent of high school senior boys have used steroids to increase their muscularity.
- In the United States alone, around 40 billion dollars are spent each year on dieting and diet-related products.
- By the time children are 3 years of age, they have already begun to receive messages from their parents regarding the ideal body.

Media and Body Image

MEDIA PORTRAYALS OF THE BODY   Every society throughout history has had somewhat different ideals of beauty (Brody, 2002). During the seventeenth through nineteenth centuries, artists such as Rubens, Renoir, and Raphael painted women as being plump and curvy. Marilyn Monroe's size 14 physique represented bodily perfection during the 1950s, and a decade later, the model Twiggy and her ultra-thin appearance were considered ideal (Derenne & Beresin, 2006). Today, a beautiful body can take many shapes: waif, curvy, or athletic. In fact, for many women, the combination of being curvaceous and thin (with small waist and hips, and a medium-sized bust) is the ideal. But there is one thing that contemporary "ideal" body shapes have in common: they are definitely not Rubenesque (Derenne & Beresin, 2006).

For both men and women, magazine covers, TV ads, and films bombard us with images that reflect the standard, but often unattainable ideal, of a beautiful and fit body. Magazines tell readers that slim bodies are "well-managed" bodies, reflective of people who are in control of their lives. Readers are also told to how reduce "nasties": areas of fat deposit. Moreover, 15 percent of magazine headlines viewed by young women (e.g., *Seventeen, Teen Vogue*) focus on diet and body image (Davalos, Davalos, & Layton, 2007). Incidentally, online versions of teen magazines provide the following messages: (1) a girl's body can easily "get out of control"; (2) every body part should be perfect; (3) beauty requires physical perfection; and (4) girls' are not OK as they are (Ballentine & Ogle, 2005; Labre & Walsh-Childers, 2003). Over the last three decades, depictions of male bodies have not only become leaner, but also more muscular. Men's magazines promote six-pack abs, perfect pectorals, bulging biceps, and low body fat as representative of the ideal male body. Healthy bodies limited in muscularity are rarely shown. The primary message in men's magazines is that achieving a lean, muscular physical appearance is of the upmost importance (Labre, 2005).

Even dolls present to the world body types that are beyond the reach of many. Consider the following as examples of this: For nearly four decades, Mattel's Barbie (if she were real) was estimated to weigh 110 pounds, with measurements of 39-18-33. Like many celebrities of the 1990s, Barbie's body was reshaped and she now sports measurements of 33-17-30. If alive, GI Joe's 5′ 10″ hyper-muscular body would have an 85-inch chest, 34-inch neck, and 65-inch waist. These numbers nearly double those of the average male physique. Over the last 25 years, action figures, in general, have become leaner and more muscular with the arms, chests, necks, forearms, thighs, and calves increasing in size by 50 to 60 percent (Baghurst, Carlston, Wood, & Wyatt, 2007).

Exploration 5.1: Body Image

www.bodypositive.com   A website dedicated to promoting positive body image, at any weight.

EFFECTS OF MEDIA ON FEMALE BODY IMAGE   Because our society places so much emphasis on physical appearance, it is not surprising that media plays an especially important role in influencing how we feel about our bodies. For girls of all ages, the consumption of content in beauty and fashion magazines, television shows, and movies increases the desire to be thin (Bell, Lawton, & Dittmar, 2007; Want, 2009). For instance, after watching a music video featuring Britney Spears, 10-year-old girls become dissatisfied with their bodies (Mundell, 2002). Interestingly, television exposure in prepubescent girls also predicts a desire to be thin in the *future*, after they "grow up" (Harrison & Hefner, 2006). In addition, across adolescence and young adulthood, greater exposure to mainstream television programming and fashion magazine is associated with poorer body image. However, when women of color watch television shows with primarily minority casts, greater body *satisfaction* (rather than dissatisfaction) is actually seen (Schooler, 2008). Why is this so? The answer may lie in the body types of the actors being watched. Shows with predominantly African-American casts tend to present a wider range of female body types than shows with primarily White characters (Tirodkar & Jain, 2003). Taken together, these findings suggest that media has the potential to both help and hurt body image, depending on the body types being viewed. What types of bodies are portrayed in the media you consume?

EFFECTS OF MEDIA ON MALE BODY IMAGE   Men are affected by media portrayals, too, although the idealized body for men is muscular (V-shaped with large torso and smaller hips) rather than thin (Tylka, 2011). Case in point: images of muscular male models in *Sports Illustrated* make adolescent boys perceive their own bodies more negatively (Farquhar & Wasylkiw, 2007). However, body dissatisfaction in men is not as strong as it is in women; a finding that may result from the current societal double standard whereby women are more likely to be judged by their beauty than men (Green & Pritchard, 2003; Tiggemann, 2004).

THE OBESITY STIGMA   It is also worth noting that overweight people are often portrayed in the media as being selfish, lazy, stupid, ugly, sloppy, and unlikable (Puhl & Latner, 2007). Consider Dudley Dursley, from the *Harry Potter* series, and Augustus Gloop, from *Willy Wonka and the Chocolate Factory*, as examples of this. Both are obese, both are gluttons, and both disregard warnings from adults regarding inappropriate behavior. In addition, the **obesity stigma**, which *refers to the negative attitudes, stereotypes, and discriminatory behavior directed at overweight individuals,* exerts a powerful, and negative, influence on our body image. Mean teasing by others, especially when done by parents, peers, and teachers, makes us feel bad about our bodies (Abramovitz, 2002). It is not surprising then, that individuals who don't fit the ideal body tend to have negative feelings about themselves, making it difficult for them to accept themselves as they are and perhaps, in combination with other factors, develop an eating disorder (Mask & Blanchard, 2011).

Our Ideal Body

Satisfaction with our bodies is greatly influenced by our image of the *ideal* body, that is, *the body we would like to have.* Overall, the closer to the ideal body we are, the less pressure we feel to change. On the other hand, those who are obviously different may feel more pressure to change or hide the disliked parts of their bodies, just as Amanda did in her baggy clothes. We also tend to view our bodies more negatively the further they are away from the ideal (Kelly, Bulik, & Mazzeo, 2011). Moreover, our ideal body is greatly influenced by the particular body ideals prevalent in our culture. For example, in Jamaican society, plumpness is desirable, so although foreign media are available, the desire for plumpness is strong enough to counteract foreign preoccupation with thinness (Smith & Cogswell, 1994). Nevertheless, a constant bombardment of thin images in the media can take its toll on one's body image. In one of the most intriguing studies conducted on body image to date, researchers investigated the influence of the *introduction* of television in Fiji on adolescent girls' body image. Researchers found that in comparison to girls who had less than one month of exposure to television, teenage girls with three years of television exposure showed dramatic increases in dieting (70 percent of the sample) and self-induced vomiting (11 percent of the sample). Of note, prior to the introduction of television, these behaviors were virtually unheard of among Fijian girls (Becker, Burwell, Herzog, Hamburg, & Gilman, 2002).

If you are female, close your eyes and imagine the perfect female body as a man would see it. If you are male, what type of male body do you think your female counterparts prefer? Compare your answers with those of two friends, one female and one male. Did the answers vary by gender? According to research, they should. Perceptions of what the opposite sex finds ideal or attractive differ substantially from what the opposite sex actually finds attractive. This is especially true for women's perceptions of what men want. Women believe that men prefer thin or bony body types, but in actuality, men do not prefer such physical characteristics. Interestingly, men tend to be more in tune with what women find attractive in a man's physique (Bergstrom, Neighbors, & Lewis, 2004).

More than men, women have issues with their body image, in part due to media representations of the ideal women.

HEALTH AND THE MIND–BODY RELATIONSHIP

LEARNING OBJECTIVES

5.3 List the four major areas connecting health and the mind–body relationship.

5.4 Discuss the major health hazards: obesity, smoking, and substance use.

Today, physicians and mental health professionals pay greater attention to the mutual interactions of the mind and body than they did in the past. Thus, to understand health and illness we must consider how biological, psychological, and social factors interact.

Exploration 5.2: Health and Wellness

www.seekwellness.com This site provides lots of tips on all types of health and wellness issues such as fitness, weight control, sexuality, and nutrition.

The Immune System

The **immune system** is *a complex surveillance system, including the brain and various blood cells, that defends our bodies by identifying and destroying various foreign invaders.* In emphasizing the link between psychological factors (e.g., stress) and physical illness, it is important to note that psychological factors do not appear to *cause* illness directly. Rather, such factors seem to weaken the immune system, thereby making us more *vulnerable* to illness. How does this happen? First, in times of stress, psychological processes (e.g., depression) can prevent us from taking positive health-related measures, such as eating well. Moreover, in an attempt to cope with life's difficulties, many people make lifestyle choices that can negatively impact the immune system, such as excessive use of alcohol and drugs. Finally, in stressful situations the body's immune system functions less well. For instance, stress lowers the body's resistance to a variety of physical ailments ranging from herpes viruses to upper respiratory infections (Contrada & Baum, 2011). Box 5–2 discusses the use of acupuncture as a means of bolstering the immune system.

Personality

There is increasing evidence suggesting that we can bolster our resistance to stress and illness by harnessing the powers of the mind—our thoughts, attitudes, and emotions. Psychologists recognize the importance of five traits in their descriptions of individuals' personalities: *openness to experience* (being open-minded about novelty), *conscientiousness* (being careful and hardworking), *agreeableness* (being good-natured), *extroversion* (being friendly), and *emotional stability*

| BOX 5–2 | Focus on Health Care: Acupuncture |

Acupuncture—*the clinical insertion and manipulation of thin needles into specific body sites*—is one of the most popular alternative therapies practiced in the United States, Asia, and Europe. How does acupuncture work? According to traditional Chinese medicine (which dates back over 5000 years), interconnected channels of energy run throughout the body. At times, these channels become blocked (damming up energy meant to nourish surrounding tissues) causing a variety of physical ailments. Acupuncture, because of its precise placement of needles, is thought to undam these energy channels, thus restoring the body's natural flow of energy. Modern Western medicine views acupuncture differently, believing that the needles stimulate the body's natural healing process, causing it to release chemicals that can reduce pain and promote healing. Regardless of which viewpoint you believe, one thing is for certain, acupuncture works. Over and over again, studies have shown that acupuncture can effectively treat pain, release tension and stress, and help the body prevent and treat illness by enhancing the immune system (Kim & Hyunsu, 2011).

(levels of anxiety and reactivity). Researchers have demonstrated associations between openness to experience, extroversion, and conscientiousness with perceptions of being in good health and emotional instability with perceptions of having poor health (Goodwin & Engstron, 2002).

Another personality factor that pertains to our ability to resist illness is self-efficacy. **Self-efficacy** is *the belief in one's capabilities to organize and execute actions required to produce given attainments.* As it turns out, both psychological well-being and physical functioning are enhanced by high self-efficacy. Self-efficacy affects our achievement, our physical and mental health, our career development, and even our voting behavior (Bandura, 1997; Schunk & Pajares, 2009). With regard to wellness, self-efficacy enables us to adopt healthy behaviors (such as physical exercise) and to adhere to programs designed to eliminate unhealthy habits (such as smoking) (Bebetsos, Chroni, & Theodorakis, 2002; Lippke & Ziegelmann, 2006). For those without high self-efficacy health may suffer, for people see little point in trying to change if they do not believe they can succeed.

As you can see, self-efficacy is an important component of our health and well-being. But how can individuals develop or promote high self-efficacy? To do so, individuals must learn to monitor their own behaviors, especially the ones they wish to change. They must set short-range, attainable goals to motivate and direct their own efforts and enlist positive social support from others to help them sustain the efforts needed to succeed. Modeling after successful others also benefits those embarking on healthier lifestyles (Bandura, 1997). For instance, many people report being inspired to lose weight after watching the hit TV series, *The Biggest Loser,* during which some contestants lose well over 100 pounds. Interestingly, self-efficacy appears to function similarly across cultures (Luszczynska, Scholz, & Schwarzer, 2005).

Lifestyle Choices

Lifestyle choices kill more people than any other single factor. As such, a change in lifestyle can be extremely effective in attaining good health (Wing & Raynor, 2006). Three major health hazards directly associated with lifestyle that have the potential to change (difficult though it may be) are obesity, smoking, and substance use.

Obesity has become a national epidemic, which in many cases is preventable.

OBESITY   **Obesity**—*an excessive amount of body fat, usually defined as exceeding the desirable weight for one's height, build, and age*—can be measured in numerous ways, including skin-fold thickness and hydrostatic weighing. However, the most commonly used measurement tool is the body mass index (BMI). BMI is *a measure of total body fat calculated from knowing an individual's height and weight.* Less than 30 percent of all Americans have a healthy BMI, whereas nearly 70 percent of Americans are overweight or obese (Lavie, Milani, & Ventura, 2009). Being overweight or obese is not just a problem for adults either as 14 percent of 2- to 5-year olds, 19 percent of 6- to 11-year-olds, and 17 percent of 12- to 19-year-olds meet the BMI criteria for obesity (Ogden et al., 2006). Worldwide, there are over 155 million obese children and adolescents (or 1 in 10) (WorldHeartFederation.org, 2007). High blood pressure, diabetes, stroke, sleep disorders, cancer, as well as, liver and gall bladder disease are but a few of the many complications resulting from weighing too much. And the more overweight people are, the greater the accompanying health risk. For instance, obese individuals have a 50 to 100 percent increased risk of death from all causes, compared with normal-weight individuals (Mayo Clinic, 2005). In fact, each year in the United States, more than 300,000 deaths are linked to obesity. Use Table 5–1 to assess whether you are at a normal weight, overweight, or obese.

Obesity results from an interaction of physiological and psychological factors. We all know overweight people who eat moderately but remain fat and thin people who eat heartily but remain slender. Compared to people at a healthy weight, obese people are three times more likely to have a family member who is also obese, suggesting that genes play a role in body mass. Although some people have a genetic predisposition to carry more fat, a lot of obesity results from overeating and insufficient exercise (Reifschneider, Hamrick, & Lacey, 2011). There is also a variety of psychological and social factors associated with over eating. For instance, obese people tend to be more responsive to external cues, such as the visibility and availability of food, rather than to the internal cues of hunger; a phenomenon referred to as "eating with your eyes." Some individuals also eat more food when with others, especially others who are fast eaters (American Gastroenterological Association, 2008). The finding that our own eating habits are greatly influenced by those around us can help explain why there is a 57 percent increase in a person becoming obese when one of their friends develops obesity (Christakis & Fowler, 2007).

People who want to lose weight must somehow help their bodies burn more calories than they consume. In fact, to lose one just pound of fat, you must burn around 3500 calories more than what you typically burn each week: a daunting task, for sure, but one that can be accomplished. The two basic ways to do so are to (1) change your diet so that you eat less, especially fewer foods high in fat and (2) exercise more. Remember, the benefits of crash diets are generally short-lived. To make matters worse, strict dieting tends to lower the rate of metabolism, so even though you count calories carefully, you will still not lose weight. It's preferable to follow a reasonable diet aimed at a more modest weight loss—say, 1 pound a week—over a longer period of time, combined with regular exercise (Donnelly et al., 2009).

Perhaps you've heard the myth that exercise is self-defeating because it makes you want to eat more. Actually, exercise not only burns up calories but also increases your metabolic rate, so that even when active people are not exercising, their bodies are burning up calories faster. Exercise during and after dieting is an important predictor of successful long-term weight loss (Wing & Raynor, 2006). And small lifestyle changes, such as watching less television, are also related to maintaining weight loss (Raynor, Phelan, Hill, & Wing, 2006). Perhaps this is because commercials for food stimulate eating in general, and not just the eating of foods seen on TV (Halford et al., 2007). For example, commercials for hamburgers at Red Robin can result in the viewer eating a bowl of potato chips. However, only one in five U.S. adults gets the recommended amount of regular physical activity—50 minutes a week of moderate-intensity aerobic activity (such as brisk walking) or 75 minutes a week of vigorous-intensity aerobic exercise (such as running), or some combination of the two. In addition, for optimal health, you should engage in at least 2 days a week of muscle-strengthening activities (U.S. Department of Health & Human Services, 2005). Do you meet these guidelines?

Table 5–1   Are You at a Healthy Weight?

Locate your height in the left-most column and read across the row to your weight. Follow the column for your weight up to the top row to find your BMI.

Normal Weight (18.5–24.9)

Overweight (25–29.9)

Obesity (≥ 30)

BMI	19	20	21	22	23	24	25	26	27	28	29	30	31	32	33	34	35
Height							**Body Weight in Pounds**										
58" (4'10")	91	96	100	105	110	115	119	124	129	134	138	143	148	153	158	162	167
59" (4'11")	94	99	104	109	114	119	124	128	133	138	143	148	153	158	163	168	173
60" (5')	97	102	107	112	118	123	128	133	138	143	148	153	158	163	168	174	179
61" (5'1")	100	106	111	116	122	127	132	137	143	148	153	158	164	169	174	180	185
62" (5'2")	104	109	115	120	126	131	136	142	147	153	158	164	169	175	180	186	191
63" (5'3")	107	113	118	124	130	135	141	146	152	158	163	169	175	180	186	191	197
64" (5'4")	110	116	122	128	134	140	145	151	157	163	169	174	180	186	192	197	204
65" (5'5")	114	120	126	132	138	144	150	156	162	168	174	180	186	192	198	204	210
66" (5'6")	118	124	130	136	142	148	155	161	167	173	179	186	192	198	204	210	216
67" (5'7")	121	127	134	140	146	153	159	166	172	178	185	191	198	204	211	217	223
68" (5'8")	125	131	138	144	151	158	164	171	177	184	190	197	203	210	216	223	230
69" (5'9")	128	135	142	149	155	162	169	176	182	189	196	203	209	216	223	230	236
70" (5'10")	132	139	146	153	160	167	174	181	188	195	202	209	216	222	229	236	243
71" (5'11")	136	143	150	157	165	172	179	186	193	200	208	215	222	229	236	243	250
72" (6')	140	147	154	162	169	177	184	191	199	206	213	221	228	235	242	250	258
73" (6'1")	144	151	159	166	174	182	189	197	204	212	219	227	235	242	250	257	265
74" (6'2")	148	155	163	171	179	186	194	202	210	218	225	233	241	249	256	264	272
75" (6'3")	152	160	168	176	184	192	200	208	216	224	232	240	248	256	264	272	279
76" (6'4")	156	164	172	180	189	197	205	213	221	230	238	246	254	263	271	279	287

Source: "Body Mass Index," from Centers for Disease Control and Prevention website, 2012.

Weight-loss programs are a big business, generating over $60 billion per year in the United States alone (PRWEB, 2011). If you are thinking of dieting, the guidelines presented in Box 5–3 might help you decide which program to start.

SMOKING   **Tobacco abuse**—*the abuse of tobacco to such an extent that heart, respiratory, and other health-related problems develop*—continues to be a major health hazard

BOX 5–3 **Focus on Health Care: Selecting a Weight-Loss Program**

A responsible and safe weight-loss program should be able to document for you the following five features:

1. ***The Diet Should Be Safe.*** It should include all of the Recommended Daily Allowances (RDAs) for vitamins, minerals, and protein.
2. ***The Weight-Loss Program Should Be Directed Toward a Slow, Steady Weight Loss*** unless your doctor feels your health condition would benefit from more rapid weight loss.
3. ***Check for Health Problems before Starting.*** If you plan to lose more than 15 to 20 pounds, suspect or know you have any health issues, or take medication on a regular basis, you should be evaluated by your doctor before beginning your weight-loss program.
4. ***The Program Should Include Plans for Weight Maintenance after the Weight-Loss Phase is Over.*** It is of little benefit to lose a large amount of weight only to regain it. Weight maintenance is the most difficult part of controlling weight and is not consistently implemented in weight-loss programs. The program you select should include help in permanently changing your dietary habits and level of physical activity to alter a lifestyle that may have contributed to weight gain in the past.
5. ***Know How Much It Might Cost.*** A commercial weight-loss program should provide a detailed statement of fees and costs of additional items such as dietary supplements.

Source: Based on "Choosing a Safe and Successful Weight Loss Program," Weight-control Information Network, National Institute of Diabetes and Digestive and Kidney Diseases, June 2008.

(Ostbyte & Taylor, 2004). An estimated 46 million adults in the United States smoke cigarettes, even though this single behavior will eventually result in death for half of them, and disability for millions of others. Cigarette smoking remains the leading *preventable* cause of death in the United States, resulting in over 440,000 deaths each year (National Center for Chronic Disease Prevention and Health Promotion, 2011). On a more global note, it is estimated that over 1.3 billion people smoke worldwide, with nearly 6 million of these dying annually (World Health Organization, 2011).

Notably, 1 in 5 deaths in the United States are thought to be attributable to smoking. That is more than number of deaths caused by alcohol, homicide, car accidents, illicit drugs, suicide, and AIDS *combined* (Glantz, 2003). There is compelling evidence that cigarette smoking is a major factor in heart disease, emphysema, and other fatal illnesses. In addition, smoking causes many different forms of cancer, including lung cancer and cancers of the mouth, larynx, bladder, and pancreas. Smokers who also drink alcohol magnify their risks of cancer even more because it enhances the carcinogenic effect of tobacco at certain sites of the body, such as the esophagus, mouth, and larynx (National Center for Chronic Disease Prevention and Health Promotion, 2011; Ostbyte & Taylor, 2004).

Greater awareness of the health hazards of smoking has prompted some people to give up the habit. Today, around 19 percent of U.S. adults are smokers. That's down from 22.5 percent in 2002 and 22.8 percent in 2001. At the same time, these gains should not blind us to the fact that a large number of teenagers in middle school (5 percent) and high school (17 percent) are smokers (National Center for Chronic Disease Prevention and Health Promotion, 2011). In fact, 61 percent of cigarette smokers start before the age of 18 (Substance Abuse and Mental Health Services Administration, 2006). That means a large portion of children living today will die prematurely because of the decision they made to smoke in their youth.

Smoking is a difficult habit to break, but the benefits of smoking cessation are substantial (Ostbyte & Taylor, 2004). However, even conservative estimates imply that half or more of those who quit smoking eventually resume the habit. In addition to the psychological dependence on the smoking habit, nicotine is considered to be physically addictive. Consequently, smokers build a tolerance to nicotine and need to smoke a larger number of cigarettes or ones with higher nicotine content to get the same effect. The average smoker smokes 20 to 30 cigarettes a day—one cigarette about every 30 to 40 minutes. And because the biological half-life of nicotine in humans is about 20 to 30 minutes, habitual smokers keep their systems primed with nicotine during most of their waking hours. Withdrawal from habitual smoking and nicotine produces a variety of symptoms, including nervousness, headaches, dizziness, fatigue, insomnia, sweating, cramps, tremors, and heart palpitations.

In recent years, people have begun using nicotine replacement products (such as skin patches, chewing gum, and lozenges) which release nicotine into the body, thereby reducing the physical craving for a smoke. In addition, a variety of psychological and behavioral methods are available. One approach is monitoring stimulus control, in which smokers become aware of the objects, events, people, and situations that trigger their smoking. Then they develop alternative behaviors.

BOX 5–4　Focus on Health care: Tips for Quitting

The following five steps will help you quit and quit for good. You have the best chances of quitting if you use them together.

1. ***Get Ready***
   - Set a quit date.
   - Change your environment.
     1. Get rid of ALL cigarettes and ashtrays in your home, car, and place of work.
     2. Don't let people smoke in your home.
   - Review your past attempts to quit. Think about what worked and what did not.
   - Once you quit, don't smoke—NOT EVEN A PUFF!
2. ***Get Support and Encouragement.*** You have a better chance of being successful if you have help. You can get support in many ways:
   - Tell your family, friends, and co-workers that you are going to quit and want their support. Ask them not to smoke around you or leave cigarettes out.
   - Talk to your health care provider.
3. ***Learn New Skills and Behaviors***
   - Try to distract yourself from urges to smoke. Talk to someone, go for a walk, or get busy with a task.
   - When you first try to quit, change your routine. Use a different route to work. Drink tea instead of coffee. Eat breakfast in a different place.
   - Do something to reduce your stress. Take a hot bath, exercise, or read a book.
   - Plan something enjoyable to do every day.
   - Drink a lot of water and other fluids.
4. ***Get Medication and Use It Correctly.*** Medications, such as Chantix and Zyban, can help you stop smoking and lessen the urge to smoke. Make sure you talk to your health care provider before taking any new medication to discuss potential side effects and drug interactions.
5. ***Be Prepared for Relapse or Difficult Situations.*** Most relapses occur within the first three months after quitting. Don't be discouraged if you start smoking again. Remember, most people try several times before they finally quit. Here are some difficult situations to watch for:
   - ***Alcohol.*** Avoid drinking alcohol. Drinking lowers your chances of success.
   - ***Other Smokers.*** Being around smoking can make you want to smoke.
   - ***Weight Gain.*** Many smokers will gain weight when they quit, usually less than 10 pounds. Eat a healthy diet and stay active.
   - ***Bad Mood or Depression.*** There are a lot of ways to improve your mood other than smoking.

Source: "Five Keys for Quitting Smoking," from Centers for Disease Control and Prevention website, 2012.

For instance, Amanda usually lit a cigarette whenever she ate spicy food. A friend suggested that she begin holding a glass of water in her right hand while eating, thereby breaking the association between spicy food and cigarettes. Generally, when trying to convince yourself or someone else to quit, it's better to emphasize the *positive* aspects of not smoking, such as the desire to take charge of one's life and to maintain physical fitness, rather than the fear of illness. Although most smokers who give up smoking resume the habit within three months to a year, former smokers may increase their chance of success through the support of friends, spouses, or support groups (Thomas et al., 2005). Also, vigorous exercise helps smokers quit and stay smoke free (Marcus, 1999). Box 5–4 provides some tips to quit smoking.

DRINKING   The effects of alcohol consumption range from relatively benign hangovers to serious consequences such as alcohol poisoning and death. In fact, alcohol consumption is thought to cause close to 85,000 deaths annually. Furthermore, people with alcohol-related ailments fill between 25 and 40 percent of all hospital beds in the United States. Also, the more people consume alcohol, the greater the likelihood that they will develop long-term health risks, such as cirrhosis of the liver, pancreatitis, and hemorrhagic stroke. Alcohol intoxication negatively impacts decision-making processes and coordination, and as such, individuals that get drunk are prone to accidents and injury. Case in point, alcohol consumption is involved in nearly two-thirds of all fatal traffic accidents; and nearly 50 percent of all drowning victims are drinking at the time of their deaths. Additionally, alcohol use is associated with risky sexual practices, such as engaging in unprotected intercourse, and increased vulnerability to coercive sexual activity by others (Mokdad, Marks, Stroup, & Gerberding, 2004; U.S. Department of Health and Human Services, 2007).

Each day close to 11,000 adolescents drink alcohol for the first time (SAMHSA, 2006). Approximately one-third adults consume alcohol on occasion, but at least 1 out of 10 is considered a heavy drinker—consuming three or more drinks per day for men; two or more drinks per day for women. On the typical college campus, between 40 and 50 percent of students engage in **binge drinking**—*consuming five or more drinks in a short period of time for men, four or more for women.* Moreover, around 20 percent of college students are considered frequent binge drinkers—binge drinking three or more times in a two-week period (Wechsler & Nelson, 2008). Activity 5–1 can help you assess your own level of drinking.

ILLICIT DRUG USE   Illicit drug use results in around 17,000 deaths each year. Drug overdoses, as well as a reduction in the internal prohibitions that prevent us from engaging in unsafe behaviors (e.g., drugged driving), account for this finding (Mokdad et al., 2004). In addition to the cost of human life, the price tag for drug use is staggering. When productivity losses, health care, and crime enforcement are taken into consideration, the annual cost of illicit drug use is around $200 billion, which is slightly lower than the $235 billion in costs associated with excessive alcohol consumption (Office of National Drug Control Policy, 2004).

Early drug use is associated with higher levels of aggression, poor academic achievement, deviant and/or criminal behavior during adolescence, and continued drug use in adulthood. But does alcohol consumption and marijuana use always *precede* the use harder drugs? See Box 5–5 for a discussion of this important topic. A variety of physical and mental health risks occur with illicit drug use, most of which vary by the type of drug used. Consider the following as just a limited sampling of the array of negative health outcomes associated with illicit drug use: marijuana use can cause memory impairment, respiratory complications, and cancer; inhalants can result in liver, kidney, bone marrow, and brain damage; and cocaine use can lead to seizures, strokes, disturbances in heart rhythm, and paranoia. Individuals using illicit drugs are also more likely than others to suffer from mental illness, such as anxiety disorders and depression. However, it is important to remember that the mentally ill may seek out illicit drugs in an effort to cope with their psychological problems (NIDA, 2007).

ACTIVITY 5–1

ARE YOU DRINKING TOO MUCH?

INSTRUCTIONS: *Indicate the strength of your agreement on a scale of 1 to 7 for the following statements by circling the appropriate number under the statement.*

1. I drink alcohol heavily after a confrontation or argument or because of emotional pain.

Strongly disagree   1   2   3   4   5   6   7   Strongly agree

2. I need more and more alcohol to get the same effect.

Strongly disagree   1   2   3   4   5   6   7   Strongly agree

3. I often remember starting out, beginning to drink, and then drinking more, but that's all I remember.

Strongly disagree   1   2   3   4   5   6   7   Strongly agree

4. I often black out or don't remember what happened when I was drinking.

Strongly disagree   1   2   3   4   5   6   7   Strongly agree

5. Not remembering what I was doing when I was drinking causes me alarm to the point of switching drinks, switching jobs, and switching promises to myself.

Strongly disagree   1   2   3   4   5   6   7   Strongly agree

6. My friends have told me that I lose control when I drink too much alcohol.

Strongly disagree   1   2   3   4   5   6   7   Strongly agree

7. I realize that others are talking about my drinking too much.

Strongly disagree   1   2   3   4   5   6   7   Strongly agree

8. My hands shake in the morning and/or I feel hung over after I have been drinking.

Strongly disagree   1   2   3   4   5   6   7   Strongly agree

9. People seem extremely irritated with me because of my drinking.

Strongly disagree   1   2   3   4   5   6   7   Strongly agree

10. I often drink more than I eat.

Strongly disagree   1   2   3   4   5   6   7   Strongly agree

SCORING: Add up all your points for each statement. The higher the total score, the more likely it is that you have an alcohol abuse problem. If you believe that you do have a problem, find professional help as soon as possible.

Source: Adapted from "Moving Forward with Your Life! Leaving Alcohol and Other Drugs Behind" (DHHS Publication No. (SMA) 93-2000), U.S. Department of Health and Human Services, 1995.

BOX 5–5	Focus on Wellness: The Gateway Drug Hypothesis

Research on adolescents has consistently shown that the use of tobacco and alcohol precedes marijuana use, which in turn occurs prior to the use of illicit drugs, such as hallucinogens, heroin, and cocaine. Some have suggested that tobacco, alcohol, and marijuana are "gateway drugs," implying that experimentation with these substances occurs sequentially across development. Evidence for the gateway hypothesis includes studies that link alcohol and tobacco use with subsequent marijuana use. Also, the association between marijuana and illicit drug use is stronger than the connection between alcohol/tobacco and illicit drug use. Biologically, tobacco, alcohol, and marijuana, as well as the illicit drugs mentioned above, primarily operate on the neurotransmitter dopamine, thus providing a potential physiological mechanism for the gateway hypothesis. Nevertheless, rather than early tobacco, alcohol, and marijuana use *leading* to subsequent and harder drug use, it may simply be that users of alcohol, tobacco, marijuana, and illicit drugs share many of the same characteristics (e.g., personality, emotionality, prevalence of psychopathology) that predispose them to use a *variety* of drugs. Moreover, during adolescence, those who smoke marijuana start hanging out with other drug using peers. Consequently, these relationships, and the culture of drug use that they engender, lead to greater opportunities to use harder drugs (Golub & Johnson, 2002; Hall & Lynskey, 2005).

SUBSTANCE ABUSE   Without question, both alcohol and drug use can be problematic for adolescents and adults alike, causing negative and social consequences. In addition to the medical and psychological issues mentioned above, frequent substance use can turn in to **substance abuse**—*the misuse or dependence on a psychoactive substance.* Currently, over 23 million Americans are substance abusers. Scientists have proposed various explanations of why some individuals become involved with drugs and then escalate to abuse. One explanation points to a biological cause, such as having a family history of drug or alcohol abuse. Others suggest that factors within the family, such as a chaotic home environment, ineffective parenting, and a lack of nurturance cause substance abuse. Another explanation is that abusing drugs can lead to affiliation with drug-abusing peers, which, in turn, exposes the individual to other drugs. Still others point to mental illness, such as depression, as the culprit. In reality, substance abuse can occur as a result of any of the aforementioned explanations, or because of a combination of them; there is no single pathway to substance abuse (National Institute on Drug Abuse, 2009).

Although many programs are available for treating substance abuse, most have a relatively high failure rate, with 40 to 60 percent of participants experiencing a **relapse**—*a return to a previous behavior or state*—in this case, a return to drinking alcohol or using drugs (National Institute on Drug Abuse, 2009). Individuals may not be ready for the complete change in lifestyle demanded by the program, often because of denial on their part, or they may become bored and frustrated with the program or the lifestyle changes demanded by it. A large proportion of people who enter substance abuse treatment programs drop out in the first few weeks only to re-enter at a later date. It is worth noting that relapse remains the rule rather than the exception. The prevalence of relapse has led some therapists to develop relapse-prevention training, which generally is incorporated into the treatment program. Substance abusers are taught how to cope with high-risk situations—for example, coming into contact with acquaintances that are still addicted—and to prevent small lapses from becoming full-blown relapses. Individuals are encouraged to view lapses as temporary setbacks that they can learn from and avoid in the future.

Environmental Issues

Various environments in which we find ourselves are more or less conducive to health problems. If you are thinking that environmental pollutants or contaminants are one of the major sources for health-related problems, you are correct. About 25 percent of Americans live where the standards for air quality are not met (National Center for Health Statistics, 2002). It has long been known that living near polluting industries can affect one's *physical* health, but living near pol-luting industries can also affect *mental* health, resulting in greater levels of anxiety and depres-sion (Downey & Van Willigen, 2005).

Social and psychological environments can be just as toxic. Messages about the popular-ity of drugs have become commonplace. For example, 95 percent of all films depict the use of some unhealthy substance (e.g., cigarettes, alcohol, or drugs), but most do not depict the negative consequences of use (Stern, 2005). Moreover, around 50 percent of G- and PG-rated films and greater than 80 percent of films rated PG-13 tend to depict characters smoking and/or drink-ing (Polansky & Glantz, 2004; Roberts, Henriksen, & Christenson, 1999; Thompson & Yokota, 2004). Importantly, viewing such images has been linked with both smoking behavior and early onset teen drinking (Sargent, Wills, Stoolmiller, Gibson, & Gibbons, 2006; Wills et al., 2007). In addition to traditional screen media, the Internet has become a hotbed of information for alcohol and drug use. For instance, there are many websites devoted to the use of illicit drugs. Although providing warnings about the hazards of using drugs, such sites may in fact become "how-to" guides for drug users, with sections devoted to Q & A (in a blog format) and "past experiences." Of note, some of these sites (Erowid.com, DanceSafe.org) state that they promote "safe" and "responsible" drug use. Many believe, however, that rather than promoting substance use, media should play more of a preventive role by portraying substance use as unacceptable, unglamorous, and dangerous (Weiner, Panton, & Weber, 1999). What do you think?

COPING WITH ILLNESS

LEARNING OBJECTIVES

5.5 Describe the three stages of decision making in seeking medical care.
5.6 Explain why patients do not always comply with medical advice.

Minor health problems are an everyday occurrence, and we usually treat them with a variety of over-the-counter remedies such as aspirin, antihistamines, and stomach medicine. However, if the problem persists, especially when it interferes with our everyday lives, we begin to consider seeing a doctor. Whether we are aware of it or not, such experiences set in motion a decision-making process that includes three stages:

1. *Noticing and interpreting* the seriousness of our symptoms.
2. *Seeking professional help* when needed.
3. *Adhering to the prescribed treatment.*

In this section, we'll look at how people react to symptoms and illnesses at each of these three stages.

Exploration 5.3: Learning about Health and Illness

www.WebMd.com   WebMd contains a wealth of information on all types of health concerns, both physical and psychological.

Noticing and Interpreting Symptoms

Every now and then we all experience a variety of bodily symptoms, including nasal conges-tion, sore muscles, stiff joints, headaches, racing heart, dizziness, and constipation or diarrhea. However, each of us differs somewhat in the tendency to label our body aches and pains as symp-toms of an illness. *People who habitually complain of unfounded ailments or exhibit an undue fear of illness* are often called **hypochondriacs**. Individuals high in hypochondriasis report two or three times as many symptoms as the better-adjusted people. On the other hand, some people tend to underreport their physical symptoms. These people are often **extroverts**, *people who* *tend to be warm, outgoing, and involved in life*, so much so that they don't have time to complain about or notice their ailments.

Psychologists have identified other coping strategies related to health concerns. One strategy is **avoidance.** In this pattern, *the individual minimizes or denies that there are any symptoms to notice.* On the other hand, some individuals actively confront stressors. These individuals use **confrontation** to *note symptoms of an illness are present.* Another means for coping with bad health news is through **downward comparison.** Individuals who choose to do this *compare their own situation to others who are worse off.* For example, Amanda smoked about a pack of cigarettes a day but found herself comparing this habit to that of Virginia, a co-worker who smoked almost two packs a day. Which of the above strategies do you use?

Seeking Help

About the only time it's easy to decide whether to see a doctor is when our symptoms become extreme. However, for non-emergencies, the decision to seek professional help depends on many factors. For instance, if people believe their symptoms have a psychological rather than a physical cause, they are more reluctant to go for help. Also, if their complaints—such as hemorrhoids— are embarrassing to talk about, they may resist treatment. Individuals are also less likely to visit a physician if the ailment seems virus-related or involves the upper half of the body. If people believe the benefits of going to the doctor are not worth the time, trouble, and cost of a visit, especially if the visit is not covered by medical insurance, they may hold back. Furthermore, the dread of a devastating or fateful diagnosis might prevent some from seeking help.

Men and women differ in their readiness to see a doctor. Men seek help less often; on average, they go two or more years without seeing a doctor; a situation that may put them at risk for more fatalities than women (Mansfield, Addis, & Courtenay, 2005). In fact, in comparison to women, men have higher rates of hypertension, ulcers, heart attacks, and cancer, as well as significantly shorter life expectancies. Women generally are more sensitive to changes in their bodies and to pain and, thus, visit physicians more often than men (Barsky, Peekna, & Borus, 2001). It may also be that men are more reluctant to seek professional help because it implies a "weakness" on their part. What do you think?

Adhering to Treatment

Adherence to treatment regimens is *the degree to which a person's behavior (e.g., taking medications, attending treatment sessions, etc.) coincides with medical or health advice* (Raynor, Wing, & Phelan, 2007). Surprisingly, as many as one-half of all adult patients do not follow or complete the treatment prescribed by their doctors (Osterberg & Blaschke, 2005). Interestingly, a patient's personality, gender, and socioeconomic status do not seem to predict accurately who will and will not adhere to treatment plans. People may fail to adhere to the prescribed treatment for many other reasons. A common excuse for failure to adhere is dissatisfaction with the physician. Patients who have a warm relationship with their doctor and are involved in planning the treatment are more apt to comply with the doctor's orders. Another reason patients do not follow the treatment plan is that many of them do not sufficiently understand the nature of their illness or the doctor's instructions. By contrast, when the desired treatment is explained in everyday language with easy-to-follow written instructions, patients are much more likely to comply. Patients' beliefs about a medication also influence adherence, with individuals who worry about drug dependence or long-term side effects least likely to take the medication as prescribed. Overall, patients' reluctance to take medicine appears most related to their fear of medication and their preference to take as little medicine as possible (Pound et al., 2005; Vermeire, Hearnshaw, Van Royen, & Denekens, 2001).

The way the information is presented is important, too. Information can be presented or framed in *negative* (about potential losses or costs) or *positive* ways (about potential gains). A negatively framed message would be something like this: "If you don't stop smoking, you are likely to die at a young age." A positively framed message is "If you stop smoking, you'll feel better and live longer." Some scientists believe that positively framed messages from medical practitioners are best for promoting *preventive* behaviors such as sticking to a healthy diet, whereas negatively framed messages are best for facilitating *detection* behaviors such as noticing pain (van Assema, Martens, Ruiter, & Brug, 2001). However, adherence to treatment regimens is more complicated than the mere type of frame—negative or positive. Factors such as involvement of the patient in a particular medical issue are also important (Donovan & Jalleh, 2000). An example would be a patient with family history of heart disease being more involved than a patient with no such history when listening to a message about the importance of diet and exercise to heart health.

PROMOTING WELLNESS

LEARNING OBJECTIVES

5.7 List several factors related to taking charge of your health.
5.8 Explain why "the food plate" is important to our health.
5.9 Explain what makes a personal fitness program effective.
5.10 Discuss the role of social support in wellness.

Until recently, people in the health care field made little distinction between people who were "not sick" and those who were "healthy" (Friedman, 2005). For all practical purposes, wellness was the absence of sickness. However, in recent years there has been a growing realization that health is considerably more than the absence of a minor or major illness. Today, individuals believe that **wellness** means *the positive ideal of health in which one strives to maintain and improve one's health.* To be healthy is to have the full use of one's body and mind and, despite an occasional bout of illness, to be alert, energetic, and happy to be alive even in old age. As a result, health practitioners and the public alike are beginning to think more in terms of optimum health and wellness.

Optimum health is not something you can get from your doctor, guru, health food store, or wonder supplement. Positive health is something that comes mostly through your *own* efforts, aided by good genes and regular medical care. By viewing your everyday well-being in terms of the positive ideal of health, instead of merely the absence of illness, you may function better and live more enthusiastically than you would have otherwise. Activity 5–2 will help you rate your current health habits.

ACTIVITY 5–2

HOW DO YOUR HEALTH HABITS RATE?

INSTRUCTIONS: *Circle the appropriate number after each of the following statements and add up the numbers to get a total score for each section. Then check the norms at the end to determine what your score means.*

Eating habits:	Almost always	Sometimes	Almost never

1. I eat a variety of foods each day, such as fruits and vegetables, whole-grain breads and cereals, lean meats, dairy products, dry peas and beans, and nuts and seeds.

	4	1	0

2. I limit the amount of fat, saturated fat, and cholesterol I eat (including fat in meats, eggs, butter, cream, shortenings, and organ meats such as liver).

	2	1	0

3. I limit the amount of salt I eat by cooking with only small amounts, not adding salt at the table, and avoiding salty snacks.

	2	1	0

4. I avoid eating too much sugar (especially frequent snacks of sticky candy or soft drinks).

2   1   0

Eating habits score: _____

Exercise/fitness: Almost always Sometimes Almost never

1. I maintain a desired weight, avoiding overweight and underweight.

3   1   0

2. I do vigorous exercises for 15 to 30 minutes at least three times a week (examples include running, swimming, and brisk walking).

3   1   0

3. I do exercises that enhance my muscle tone for 15 to 30 minutes at least three times a week (examples include yoga and calisthenics).

2   1   0

4. I use part of my leisure time participating in individual, family, or team activities that increase my level of fitness (such as gardening, bowling, golf, and baseball).

2   1   0

Exercise/fitness score: _____

Alcohol and drugs: Almost always Sometimes Almost never

1. I avoid drinking alcoholic beverages or I drink no more than one or two drinks a day.

4   1   0

2. I avoid using alcohol or other drugs (especially illegal drugs) as a way of handling stressful situations or the problems in my life.

2   1   0

3. I am careful not to drink alcohol when taking certain medicines (e.g., medicine for sleeping, pain, colds, and allergies).

2   1   0

4. I read and follow the label directions when using prescribed and over-the-counter drugs.

2   1   0

Alcohol and drugs score: _____

What your scores mean:

9–10 Excellent   6–8 Good   3–5 Mediocre   0–2 Poor

Source: Adapted from *Healthsyle: A Self-Test* (DHHS Publication No. (PHS) 81-50155). U.S. Department of Health and Human Services, 1981.

Taking Charge of Your Own Health

Taking charge of your own health generally involves basic changes in how you relate to the medical establishment. In traditional practice, individuals are expected to assume the "good" patient role—being cooperative, undemanding, and unquestioning. Such docile behavior often has a detrimental side effect. Patients are anxious and depressed when they have little control over their treatment. In fact, patients are more likely to adhere to treatment plans when they feel they have control or decision-making power over what happens to them medically (McDonald-Miszczak, Maki, & Gould, 2000). Furthermore, because most patients are often cooperative, doctors underestimate patients' desire for information. On the other hand, people who go to the opposite extreme and adopt a "bad" patient role—complaining and demanding a lot from their doctors—may not fare much better because their aggressive behavior usually alienates medical personnel. Rather, individuals should become *active* participants in their health care in a *collaborative* way, by cooperating with doctors but not surrendering their own rights (*Harvard Health Letter*, January 2006). The aim is to establish a working alliance between doctor and patient, with both working together for the good of the patient. Patients need to know that most doctors are willing to inform them of their medical condition and their options for treatment but that they are expected to take the initiative in asking questions. And doctors need to realize that patients who are informed of their medical problems and given an active role in deciding their course of treatment are more likely to monitor their progress and adhere to the prescribed treatment.

Exploration 5.4: Fitness

www.dietandfitnesstoday.com   This site provides valuable diet and fitness tips.

Key factors in assuming greater personal responsibility for your own health include the following:

- Understanding how your body works
- Knowing how the body and mind interact
- Managing stress effectively
- Developing healthy eating and exercise habits
- Monitoring your health
- Getting periodic medical checkups
- Keeping your own medical records
- Knowing the health risks related to your family history
- Being aware of health hazards in your lifestyle, workplace, and environment
- Being an active participant in your own health care

Each individual or family should have one or more appropriate resources to be used as a guide to self-care and medical matters. Such books contain a great deal of valuable information about the body's functioning, eating and exercise habits for staying well, home health care for minor problems, and how to assess if medical help is needed. The use of the self-diagnosis symptom charts in the American Medical Association's *Family Medical Guide* is especially helpful in determining when to seek medical assistance.

Eating Sensibly

CALORIE CONTROL   An integral part of a health-producing routine is practicing good health habits such as sensible patterns of eating and drinking, keeping physically fit, getting adequate rest, and visiting a physician regularly. Because more people "kill themselves" with a knife and fork than by any other means, one of the best ways to promote good health is to eat sensibly. Eating sensibly involves eating a *reasonable* amount of *healthy* food. The amount of food is often measured in **calories**—*a measurement of energy produced by food when oxidized, or "burned," in the body.* The number of calories needed each day depends on such factors as age, sex, size, and rate of metabolism. A woman in her early 20s with a desk job needs about 2,000 calories a day; a woman with a more active life needs about 2,200 calories. A man with a desk job uses about 2,500 calories; one with a fairly active job, such as a carpenter, needs about 2,800 calories. Men and women who are in strenuous jobs or in athletic training may need anywhere from 3,000 to 4,000 calories a day. Sticking to calorie counts is not easy given that high-calorie, fast-food restaurants are everywhere and portion sizes on U.S. tables and in restaurants are increasing. However, doing so is important to wellness, as appropriate calorie control may postpone age-related declines and delay the onset of late-life diseases such as cancer and heart disease (Lofshult, 2006; Spindler, 2001).

HEALTHY FOOD CHOICES   A well-balanced diet includes adequate amounts of various groups of substances: proteins, carbohydrates, certain fats, vitamins, minerals, and fibers. Individuals vary in their nutritional needs because of factors such as their size, age, sex, and level of physical activity. A handy guide to eating a balanced diet is the recent "food plate" issued by the United States Department of Agriculture. The new guide stresses the importance of grains (at least half of which should be whole grains), vegetables and fruits (half of the plate should contain these), as well as a reduction in the amount on foods containing fat, sugar, and sodium (see Figure 5–1). The new food plate, is just a general representation of good **nutrition**, defined as *a proper, balanced diet that promotes health.* The strength of the new food plate is that you can customize it for your age, sex, and lifestyle by going to the website and indicating your personal characteristics (U.S. Department of Agriculture, 2012). The results will reveal exactly how many servings of or how much of each food group you should consume.

Getting Enough Sleep

Have you ever stayed up all night? Perhaps you've missed several consecutive nights of sleep. The effects of sleep deprivation vary from one person to another, but in general none of them are good. Deprived of sleep, people make more errors on routine tasks, show evidence of impaired memory and thinking, exhibit slower reaction times, and experience reduced alertness (by as much as 32 percent), a stronger desire to sleep, and a tendency to fall asleep easily. Finally, each year driving while drowsy causes 100,000 automobile crashes, 40,000 injuries, and 1,550 fatalities

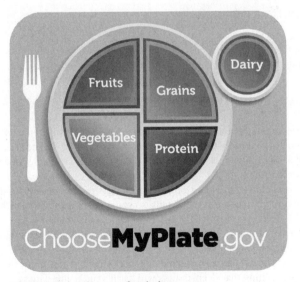

FIGURE 5–1   The new food plate.
Source: ChooseMyPlate.gov

(The National Highway Traffic Safety Administration, 2012). On the bright side, when the sleep deprived finally get a chance to sleep in, the extra time in slumber can help erase any lingering sense of fatigue and mental fuzziness. Of course, the more sleep deprived you are, the more days of sleeping in you'll need to reap these benefits (Banks, Van Dongen, & Dinges, 2010).

Exploration 5.5: Sleep

www.sleepfoundation.org   This site contains valuable information on sleep-related issues, as well as the relationship between sleep and wellness.

Our sleep/wake cycles typically follow a biochemical clock designed to help us conserve energy. Re-establishing our natural sleep cycle is more important than trying to make up all the hours of lost sleep. Although we can accommodate ourselves to a variety of changes such as shift work, jet lag, and all-night study sessions, these adjustments take a toll on our bodies as well as our sense of well-being. Remember, the average person sleeps about seven hours each night, but the need for sleep varies from one person to another. You're probably getting enough sleep if you

1. wake up spontaneously.
2. feel well rested.
3. don't have to struggle through periods of sleepiness during the day.

Perhaps you have difficulty sleeping. Box 5–6 provides tips for falling asleep faster and better.

Keeping Physically Fit

Physical fitness is *our ability to function efficiently and effectively, including both health-related and skill-related fitness components.* When you hear the term "physical fitness," do you imagine some muscular person lifting weights? Or, do you think of people jogging or running along the road? Whatever you imagine, chances are that it represents only part of what is necessary for overall physical fitness. Actually, physical fitness is the *entire* human organism's ability to function efficiently and effectively and therefore to increase life expectancy.

BOX 5–6   **Focus on Wellness: Sleep**

Most of us have trouble falling asleep occasionally. For some, especially older adults, it's a recurring problem. Although there is no magical solution to this age-old complaint, following are some suggestions:

- Go to bed and get up at about the same time each day. Make sure you're allowing enough time for sleep.
- Relax before bedtime. Listen to music or practice yoga. But avoid strenuous exercise.
- Keep your bedroom conducive to sleep. Make sure it's quiet and dark and at a suitable temperature.
- Avoid alcohol and sleeping pills. Although these may put you to sleep sooner, they interfere with your normal sleep cycle.
- Take a lukewarm bath before bed. Hot or cold showers tend to be too stimulating. Sleep is induced when the body's core temperature falls, so you can artificially induce this by taking a warm bath.
- When you're having trouble falling asleep, count sheep or think of something pleasant that will distract you from worrying.
- Take some honey, which releases serotonin, the biochemical that induces sleep and relaxation.
- Don't stay awake fretting that sleeplessness will harm your health.
- If your home remedies don't work, seek professional help at a sleep center.

Staying physically fit is not just a vital part of keeping our bodies functioning efficiently, fitness is also part of our sense of wholeness in that it enhances feelings of mastery and improves our moods.

POSITIVE EFFECTS OF FITNESS   The body responds to physical activity in ways that have important positive effects on the muscular, skeletal, cardiovascular, respiratory, and endocrine systems. These changes are consistent with a number of health benefits, including a reduced risk of premature mortality and reduced risks of coronary heart disease, hypertension, colon cancer, and diabetes mellitus. Regular participation in physical activity also appears to reduce depression and anxiety, improve mood, and enhance ability to perform daily tasks throughout the life span (Centers for Disease Control and Prevention, 2005; Crone, Smith, & Gough, 2005). Despite common knowledge that exercise is healthful, 37 percent of the adult population still engage in no regular physical activity (Fitness.gov, 2012). Moreover, although many people have enthusiastically embarked on vigorous exercise programs at one time or another, most do not sustain their participation. Table 5–2 shows some moderate-intensity activities that will help you stay fit, many of which you may actually enjoy doing. There are few reasons to be completely inactive!

Although generally beneficial, physical activity is not without risk, as injury can occur with excessive amounts of exercise or when suddenly beginning an activity for which the body is not sufficiently prepared. Serious health problems (e.g., heart attack) are less common, occurring primarily among sedentary people with advanced coronary disease who engage in strenuous activity (such as shoveling snow) for which they are not properly conditioned. Sedentary people, especially those with pre-existing health conditions, who wish to increase their physical activity

Table 5–2	Examples of Moderate Amounts of Activity That Will Help You Stay Fit

Common Chores	Sporting Activities
Washing and waxing a car for 45–60 minutes	Playing volleyball for 45–60 minutes
Washing windows or floors for 45–60 minutes	Playing touch football for 45 minutes
Gardening for 30–45 minutes	Walking 1¾ miles in 35 minutes (20 min/mile)
Wheeling self in wheelchair 30–40 minutes	Basketball (shooting baskets) 30 minutes
Pushing a stroller 1½ miles in 30 minutes	Bicycling 5 miles in 30 minutes
Raking leaves for 30 minutes	Dancing fast (social) for 30 minutes
Walking 2 miles in 30 minutes (15 min/mile)	Water aerobics for 30 minutes
Shoveling snow for 15 minutes	Swimming laps for 20 minutes
Stairwalking for 15 minutes	Basketball (playing game) for 15–20 minutes Bicycling 4 miles in 15 minutes Jumping rope for 15 minutes Running 1½ miles in 15 minutes (10 min/mile)

Source: "Guide to Physical Activity," from National Heart, Lung and Blood Institute website, 2012.

should check with their physician first and gradually build up to the desired level of activity (National Center for Chronic Disease Prevention and Health Promotion, 1999).

CHOOSING AN EXERCISE PROGRAM   In selecting your personal exercise program, you may find it helpful to observe the following points:

1. *Identify your personal physical fitness needs.* A good way to do so is to consult someone in the physical education department of your college or a specialist in one of the physical fitness centers in your community.
2. *Select personalized physical exercises to make exercise more enjoyable.* Choose physical activities that are related to your interests, needs, and personality. Choose an activity that feels good to you, regardless of what others do.
3. *Vary your activities.* By varying your activities you can include ones that will develop different aspects of physical fitness. This variation also helps to keep exercise interesting and enjoyable. Usually, changes in the weather and the seasons along with availability of facilities suggest some variation in your exercise program.
4. *Exercise regularly.* It's best to set aside a time and place for your exercise activities, making exercise part of your daily routine. It's also important to perform your exercises to a level that will promote optimal fitness, usually a minimum of 20 to 30 minutes three times a week. For people who are unable to set aside 30 minutes for physical activity, shorter episodes are clearly better than none (National Center for Chronic Disease Prevention and Health Promotion, 1999).
5. *Periodically evaluate and modify your routine.* As time passes, your needs and interests change. Shifts in your work schedule and family responsibilities may also dictate a change in your exercise program. Then, too, your age and overall level of stress should be kept in mind. Listen to your body. Assess how you feel.

Physical fitness is a vital part of the sense of wholeness mentioned earlier, but from all that you have read, it should also be clear that your overall well-being includes other considerations, such as eating habits, work schedules, lifestyles, awareness of health hazards and stress, personal attitudes, and morale.

Finding Social Support

One other means by which we can remain healthy is to *affiliate with others such as friends and family to find comfort and advice,* in other words to seek **social support**. Individuals who are sociable are generally healthier than those without a supportive network of family and friends (Jorm, 2005; Krause, 2006). And when ill, social support can aid recovery. As an example, persons suffering from severe brain trauma rehabilitate better with the love and encouragement of others (Tomberg, Toomela, Pulver, & Tikk, 2005). On the contrary, individuals who are socially isolated are at greater risk for health problems than those who are socially engaged. Some caution is needed here, though, because socializing and seeking social support is not for everyone. In other works, in order to truly benefit from a social support network, one must be *ready* to accept the support of others.

Chapter Summary

BODY IMAGE

5.1 Explain the difference between body image and the ideal body.

Whereas body image refers to the mental image formed and feelings associated with our body, the ideal body refers to the body we would like to have.

5.2 Discuss the relationship between media and body image.

Magazines, TV ads, and movies shower us with images of the human body that for most people are unattainable. As a result of media exposure, there is an increase in women's desire to be thin, and men's need for muscularity. However, the effects of media on women vary by race.

HEALTH AND THE MIND–BODY RELATIONSHIP

5.3 List the four major areas connecting health and the mind–body relationship.

The growing acceptance of mind-body unity suggests that social and psychological factors may play a significant role in almost any physical ailment. The immune system, personality, lifestyle choices, and environmental issues interact to influence the relationship between health, mind, and body.

5.4. Discuss the major health hazards: obesity, smoking, and substance use.

Obesity is associated with an increased risk of illness and death from a variety of causes, including diabetes, high blood pressure, and coronary heart disease. Cigarette smoking is a major factor in heart disease, lung cancer, and emphysema. The effects of alcohol and drug use can be slight or severe. Each year alcohol and drugs cause tens of thousands of deaths, contribute to tens of thousands of car accidents, and put tens of thousands of people in the hospital. When alcohol and drugs are used in excess, substance abuse can follow. Relapse is commonplace for those in substance abuse treatment programs.

COPING WITH ILLNESS

5.5 Describe the three stages of decision making in seeking medical care.

In evaluating the seriousness of our body complaints, we tend to rely on a decision-making process with three stages: (1) noticing and interpreting symptoms, (2) seeking professional help when needed, and (3) adhering to the prescribed treatment.

5.6 Explain why patients do not always comply with medical advice.

As many as half of those who start medical treatments do not complete them. Reasons for noncompliance include: dissatisfaction with the physician, not understanding the nature of their illness or the doctor's instructions, and beliefs (and fears) about the side effects of prescribed medication.

PROMOTING WELLNESS

5.7 List several factors related to taking charge of your health.

Factors related to taking charge of your own health include taking greater personal responsibility, having more collaboration with health care professionals in all matters pertaining to health, learning about your family history, and being an active participant in your own health care.

5.8 Explain why "the food plate" is important to our health.

An integral part of producing a healthy lifestyle is practicing good health habits. Eating sensibly, as prescribed by "the food plate," involves both the amount and the kind of food we eat, including a balanced diet that provides the necessary nutrition and calories for someone of our age, size, and lifestyle.

5.9 Explain what makes a personal fitness program effective.

Keeping physically fit usually involves following a personalized exercise program especially suited to our interests and needs.

5.10 Discuss the role of social support in wellness.

Having a strong social support network can promote health and wellness for those willing to accept the help of others.

Self-Test

1. Which of the following make up a person's body image?
   a. mental images about one's body
   b. feelings about one's body
   c. attitudes about one's body
   d. all of the above

2. Which of the following statements regarding body image is FALSE?
   a. only women are affected by images in the media, men are not affected at all
   b. overweight individuals are often depicted in the media in negative ways
   c. satisfaction (or dissatisfaction) with one's body remains relatively stable over time
   d. culture can influence one's perception of the "ideal body"

3. The negative attitudes, stereotypes, and discriminatory behavior directed at overweight individuals is called _____
   a. a negative body image
   b. the obesity stigma
   c. weight bias beliefs
   d. the thin ideal

4. _____ kills more Americans than any other health-related influence.
   a. environmental hazards
   b. war
   c. disease
   d. lifestyle choices

5. All but one of the following is a stage of decision making when coping with illness. Pick the one that doesn't belong.
   a. creating self-efficacy
   b. noticing and interpreting
   c. seeking professional help
   d. adhering to the prescribed treatment

6. Finding social support
   a. has no effect on health.
   b. has negative effects on health.
   c. has little effect on health.
   d. usually has positive effects on health.

7. Nathaniel decided to start an exercise program and eat a healthier diet. Losing weight proved to be more physically demanding and emotional difficult than he thought it would be. To help himself through this difficult time, Nathaniel went online and joined a discussion group to share his thoughts and feelings with others, as well as to hear how other people cope with this type of lifestyle change. Nathaniel's behavior is an example of:
   a. seeking social support
   b. emotional avoidance
   c. hypochondriasis
   d. relapse

8. Cheryl is concerned that her lack of concentration at work may be due to sleep deprivation. Cheryl realizes that because she _____ she is probably not getting enough sleep.
   a. wakes up spontaneously in the morning
   b. feels well rested throughout the day
   c. struggles with sleepiness during the day
   d. sleeps 7 hours a night

9. Janice is frequently concerned about her health. If she coughs, she thinks she has pneumonia; if she gets a rash, she "knows" it's actually skin cancer; and if she gets an upset stomach she believes that there is something seriously wrong with her digestive system. Because Janice's concerns are unfounded, she is considered to be: _____.
   a. an introvert
   b. an extrovert
   c. a hypochondriac
   d. histrionic

10. When participating in a fitness program, it is helpful to:
    a. vary your activities
    b. identify your personal needs
    c. periodically modify your routine
    d. all of the above

Exercises

1. *Do you practice good eating habits?* Describe your eating habits in terms of the calories consumed each day and a balanced diet. If you're not sure how many calories you consume, keep a daily count for at least three days and take an average. How does your calorie count compare to the average for someone like yourself as indicated in the text? Do you also choose foods from each of the major food areas as described in the chapter?

2. *Describe your personal exercise habits.* How much exercise do you get in the course of your daily activities? Would you agree that everyone needs to be physically active on a regular basis? If you have a personalized exercise program, describe it in a paragraph or two.

3. *Identify your biggest health hazard.* Are you guilty of one of the common health hazards, such as overeating, poor nutrition, smoking, drinking, or drug abuse? If so, what are you doing about it? Try eliminating this hazard for five consecutive days and see if you feel better about yourself and your health. Better yet, try to eliminate it over the long term.

4. *Do you suffer from a chronic ailment?* Do you have to cope with some type of chronic or recurring condition, such as an allergy, asthma, arthritis, hypertension, diabetes, migraine headaches, or ulcers? How well are you managing such ailments? Are you aware of the psychosocial factors that may influence your ailments, such as environmental stress and your emotions? What are you doing to improve your condition? Does this ailment affect your self-esteem?

5. *How much control do you exercise over your health?* Do you believe you can minimize your chances of getting sick by practicing good nutrition, regular exercise, positive attitudes, and stress management? Or, do you feel that coming down with a cold or the flu is mostly a matter of luck?

Questions for Self-Reflection

1. Which part of your body or face has been the most difficult for you to accept?

2. Do you take care of your body?

3. What aspect of your eating habits would you most like to change?

4. Do you enjoy regular, vigorous physical exercise? If not, why not? How could you alter the latter situation?

5. What is your worst health hazard?

6. If you're a smoker, how many times have you tried to quit? What is it that keeps you from quitting permanently?

7. Are you aware that the use of alcohol easily becomes a health hazard? Be honest; do you have a drug or alcohol problem?

8. Do you often find that a cold or flu was preceded by a period of intense emotional stress?

9. Would you agree that a healthy body and a sound mind go together?

10. Do you find that you prefer social support or would you rather cope with your problems alone?

Chapter Six

Taking Charge

LEARNING OBJECTIVES

After completing this chapter, you should be able to

6.1 Define perceived control.

6.2 Summarize the benefits of perceived control.

6.3 Discuss the benefits of learned optimism.

6.4 Explain how learned helplessness and the illusion of control are similar.

6.5 Describe defensive pessimism.

6.6 Identify the stages of decision making.

6.7 List several suggestions for improving decision-making skills.

6.8 Describe the connection between making decisions and personal growth.

S *tan, a 46-year-old married student, was facing an important choice. It seems he had lost his job as a foreman in a steel plant during the past year. Then, after months of unsuccessful job hunting and agonizing over his future, Stan had decided to enroll in college to become an engineer. He worked as a handyman part-time to pay the family bills. Recently and unexpectedly, Stan's former employer called and offered him a chance to return to work. "It's a tempting offer," Stan said to himself. "But I'm not sure I want to go back." Stan acknowledged that by taking back his old job he would be able to support his wife and two small children more adequately. "But then I'd always worry about when the next layoff was coming," he thought. At the same time, Stan was under great stress attending school full-time; he was having a difficult time paying bills, and he was constantly tired. Nor was there any assurance he would get a good job as an engineer once he got his degree. As you can see, Stan is caught in a life dilemma that requires him to take charge, that is, conscientiously make a very important decision.*

PERSONAL CONTROL

LEARNING OBJECTIVES

6.1 **Define perceived control.**
6.2 **Summarize the benefits of perceived control.**
6.3 **Discuss the benefits of learned optimism.**
6.4 **Explain how learned helplessness and the illusion of control are similar.**
6.5 **Describe defensive pessimism.**

At times, many of us feel as if our lives are shaped by forces beyond our control. Powerfully negative events such as terrorist attacks, natural disasters, and oil spills can weaken our resolve, sending us into a tailspin. Questions form in our mind: How will we be able to cope? Can we cope?

> ### BOX 6–1   Did you know that ...

- You're more likely to make bad decisions where your energy is depleted than when it is not.
- Making lots of little unimportant decisions can lead to decision-making fatigue, which makes it harder to make good decisions about important things.
- People spend 3–4 hours each day fighting off temptations.
- Effective habits and good routines conserve energy needed for effective decision making.
- A healthy lifestyle supports good decision making.

Source: Based on "TURN YOUR LIFE AROUND: 14 Ways To Make Better Decisions And Strengthen Your Willpower" by Aimee Groth, from Business Insider website, December 31, 2011.

Does anything I do matter? In such moments, it is well to remember history, which has demonstrated over and over again that what we do *can* matter, even if a large part of society tells us otherwise. The Women's Rights movement of the 1920s, the Civil Rights movement of the 1960s, and the uprisings in Egypt and Libya of the 2010s have clearly established that individuals can effect large-scale social change; and by doing so, help gain greater mastery over their lives. These events didn't just happen by themselves, they happened because someone *believed* that they could.

Explaining Perceived Control

Perceived control refers to *what we think we can control, now and in the future*. Sometimes those beliefs are correct, while at other times, they are not. An example of a correct belief is thinking that by engaging in personal growth you can positively influence your well-being (Baumgardner & Crothers, 2009). In contrast, a mistaken belief is assuming that by not smoking you can *prevent* lung cancer. In reality, being a non-smoker reduces the likelihood of getting cancer, but it can't *prevent* it (because other factors such as genes play a role in its occurrence) (Glantz, 2003). Regardless of whether a belief is mistaken or not, if we *think* that a goal is within reach, we usually surge into action. In these circumstances, we often feel a sense of control or personal mastery over our lives (Jewell & Kidwell, 2005). However, when we *doubt* that a goal is attainable, we are less likely to undertake the actions necessary to achieve it, and thus, we feel that our lives are largely shaped by sources outside our own sphere of influence (Jackson, Weiss, Lundquist, & Soderlind, 2002). As you can see, the decisions we make in our lives are based, in part, on the *perception* of whether we can (or cannot) take charge of the situation. Of note, perceived control is different from **personal control**, which refers to *the influence we actually have over our lives,* such as our choices related to eating habits, music preferences, and clothing style.

SOURCES OF PERCEIVED CONTROL   Psychologists have identified two sources of perceived control. One is an **internal locus of control,** *in which the individual believes he or she has control over life events.* Stan exemplifies this concept, as he believes that if he studies hard and obtains his degree, he and his family will have a better future. The other source of control is **external locus of control,** *in which the individual believes that something outside of the self—such as other individuals, fate, or various external situations—controls life events* (Zuckerman, Knee, Kieffer, & Gagne, 2004). An example of this concept is the belief that no matter what they do, or how hard they try, the Chicago Cubs will never win another World Series because they are cursed (and have been ever since P. K. Wrigley had a goat, and his owner, removed from the stands of Wrigley Field during Game 4 of the 1945 World Series) (CubbiesBaseball.com, 2012).

But does the source of perceived control really matter to well-being? In short, yes! Having an internal locus control is related to a variety of beneficial outcomes, such as higher grades, better performance at work, more effective coping with adversity, bereavement, and trauma, as well as a greater adherence to physical fitness routines and healthier aging (Kormanik & Rocco, 2009; Lachman, Neupert, & Agrigoroaei, 2011). On the other hand, individuals who have an external locus of control are prone to more negative outcomes, such as psychological disorders related to eating, anxiety, and depression (Chapman, Kertz, & Woodruff-Borden, 2009; Sassaroli, Gallucci, & Ruggiero, 2008).

If you currently have an external locus of control but would like to change it, try using the COPE problem solving method discussed in Box 6–2.

Exploration 6.1: Locus of Control

http://www.queendom.com   This site contains a variety of on-line psychological tests, including those related to locus of control. Just do a key word search for the topic you're interested in. Some are even scientifically validated!

BOX 6–2   Focus on Wellness: Developing an Internal Locus of Control

- **C**hallenge yourself to clearly identify your problem, its causes, and the results that you want. Make sure you state the problem clearly and honestly. To help yourself with this step, answer the following questions: What is my problem? What really causes my problem? What results do I want?
- Create a list of **O**ptions for solving, and if possible eliminating, your problem. Assess the advantages and disadvantages of each. Focus on the solutions you can control.
- Make an action **P**lan to solve the problem in a reasonable time frame. Think about what you can do to make the options you listed work.
- **E**valuate the progress you made by answering the following types of questions: Did the plan work? Is the problem still there? Did I give myself enough time to accomplish the plan?

Remember, an internal locus of control doesn't develop overnight. You'll need to work at it, one problem at a time. Eventually, you'll not only learn how to solve individual problems, but you'll also discover that the answer to most difficulties lies within the self, and not with others.

CULTURE AND PERCEIVED CONTROL Interestingly, internalized control is very much a Western notion. In Eastern or collectivist cultures (where interdependence rather than independence is stressed), an external locus of control is more commonplace than an internal one (Grobani, Krauss, Watson, & Le Briton, 2008). For instance, Chinese students are far more likely than American students to attribute school success to luck (Liu & Yussen, 2005). In addition, individuals from Western cultures may prefer and have more experience with primary control,

Protests often provide a sense of control, although those from collective societies may feel uncomfortable expressing such strong individualism.

whereas individuals reared in Asian cultures may prefer and experience secondary control. **Primary control** *refers to actions directed at attempting to change the world to fit one's needs and desires;* **secondary control** *involves the individual utilizing processes directed at making him- or herself fit into the world better.* Some research also indicates age differences in primary and secondary control, with older individuals more likely to use secondary control strategies (Ashman, Shiomura, & Levy, 2006). Given such differences, it appears that for most people, optimal adjustment is achieved *when the amount of actual control matches the desired need for control* (Conway, Vickers, & French, 1992).

The Benefits of Perceived Control

TAKING CHARGE   People who possess a high degree of perceived control tend to exhibit certain characteristics, each of which is related to taking charge of one's life. First and foremost, they are likely to seek knowledge and information about the events that affect their lives (Wang & Wu, 2008). For instance, when facing surgery or a serious illness, patients with a high degree of perceived control are especially likely to seek information about their condition, to ask questions of the doctors and nurses, and to make use of the resources available to them. Second, people high in perceived control are likely to attribute responsibility to themselves and to their abilities and efforts rather than to luck or the environment, at least in regard to desirable outcomes. Third, people high in perceived control are resistant to social influence and are more likely to take part in social action that helps others. Fourth, individuals high in perceived control are strongly achievement-oriented. They appear to work harder at intellectual and performance tasks, and their efforts are rewarded with better grades than those with less perceived control. Finally, in comparison to those with little perceived control, those high in perceived control are more persistent when completing tasks (Jewell & Kidwell, 2005). Can consuming copious amounts of violent media, such as first person shooting video games, help people take charge of their lives? Box 6–3 addresses this very issue.

BOX 6–3   Focus on Wellness: Violent Media and Perceived Control

In his controversial book *Killing Monsters: Why Children Need Fantasy, Super Heroes, and Make-Believe Violence* (2002), Gerard Jones makes the controversial claim that the violent messages found in video games, movies, televisions shows, comic books and music are beneficial to youth, helping them develop perceived control (or as Jones calls it, being strong, powerful, and in control). To support his argument, Jones describes an encounter at a comic book convention with a timid, angry, and slightly depressed teenage girl named Sharon. Jones reports that, while reading comic books about teenage superheroes, Sharon can sense the passion of her favorite characters—a passion that makes them powerful. According to Jones, because Sharon "becomes" the character she is reading about, she too becomes powerful.

Unfortunately, in support of his premise Jones relies heavily on **anecdotal evidence**—*information presented in favor of an argument that is based on casual observations rather than data collected using more objective and scientific methods.* Typically, anecdotal evidence involves the presentation of vividly detailed and emotional stories. And much like horoscopes, the details of anecdotal stories are usually general enough so that a great number of people can relate to some aspect of the account. Most anecdotes are memorable and unilaterally supportive of the argument being presented. Nevertheless, no matter how compelling an anecdote is, it should not be viewed as objective and scientific. Here's why: Anecdotal evidence is often inaccurate because the information reported was not recorded in an objective manner and, therefore, may not reflect what actually happened. Additionally, anecdotal information is subject to bias because the observer's interpretation and reporting of a behavior may be influenced by their own preconceptions notions about it. For example, Sharon may be reporting feeling "powerful" because she wants to be powerful and is, therefore, ignoring the many times in which she felt powerless after reading comic books. Finally, because anecdotes are interesting stories that relay a singular experience, the findings illustrated in those stories may not apply to the public as a whole. To date, there is little evidence to support the contention that reading about, listening to, observing, or controlling violent characters in the virtual world promotes the development of perceived control in the real world (Kirsh, 2012).

PSYCHOLOGICAL ADJUSTMENT   As you might expect, there is a strong relationship between perceived control and psychological adjustment. Individuals high in perceived control tend to be less anxious, better adjusted, and less likely to be classified with psychiatric labels than those with less perceived control. People high in perceived control also use more effective strategies for coping with stress, such as making a plan of action and sticking to it, taking one step at a time, or getting professional help and doing what is recommended (Cooper, Okamura, & McNeil, 1995; Zuckerman et al., 2004). In contrast, people low in perceived control are more apt to use maladaptive strategies, such as wishing the problem would go away, blaming themselves, and seeking relief through overreacting, drinking, or abusing drugs (Aspinwall & Taylor, 1992; Blum, 1998; Jackson et al., 2002). High perceived control also helps to predict who will succeed in overcoming eating disorders and psychological trauma. Finally, people who feel empowered in their personal lives also demonstrate a relatively high level of happiness or subjective well-being (Luszczynska, Benight, & Cieslak, 2009; Mellor et al., 2008).

PERCEIVED CONTROL AND PHYSICAL WELL-BEING   People high in perceived control also are more likely to take steps that will maximize their health and well-being and minimize the risk of illness. These individuals are especially apt to seek information about health maintenance, engage in preventive health practices, adopt more positive attitudes about physical exercise, and participate in physical exercise more regularly (Heth & Somer, 2002). People who believe they are in charge of their lives are likely to refrain from or give up the habit of smoking, to successfully complete weight-reduction programs, and to cooperate with prescribed treatment for medical problems. In regard to substance abuse, perceived self-control is a reliable predictor of who will complete the program and who will drop out (those with low perceived control leaving). Given that perceived control is important to so many facets of life, how much control would you say you have over your personal life? To check on your perception, complete the personal control survey in Activity 6–1.

ACTIVITY 6–1

HOW MUCH PERCEIVED CONTROL DO YOU HAVE?

Instructions: This survey is designed to inspire you to think about how much perceived control you have. For each statement below, circle T for true or F for false as the statement applies to you.

T   F   **1.** I like to put off decisions as long as I can because situations affecting the decision might change without warning.

T   F   **2.** The amount of time I study is unrelated to my grades and whether I leave a favorable impression on my professors.

T   F   **3.** Some people are just born lucky; others are not so lucky and in fact seem to be jinxed.

T   F   **4.** If people like you, they like you. If they don't, they don't, so there is little point in trying to woo them as friends.

T   F   **5.** My health is a matter of how many sick people I am around or whether there is a surge of illness in the community.

T   F   **6.** Whether I take care of it or not, something is bound to go wrong at my home once in a while.

T F **7.** People are born good or bad and rarely change over their life span.

T F **8.** Even if I am in good shape, factors outside of me, such as the weather and others' competitiveness, keep me from performing well in competitive events.

T F **9.** I am rather superstitious; I believe in bad omens (such as black cats) and good-luck charms (such as four-leaf clovers).

T F **10.** There are so many bad drivers on the road that I am bound to be involved in a car accident sooner or later.

T F **11.** If I carefully consider my options for major decisions, I know I can make the correct decision.

T F **12.** When my friends and I disagree, I know that we will still be friends because I can argue my points in a reasonable manner.

T F **13.** If people just keep trying, eventually good things will happen for them.

T F **14.** When I am shopping for a hard-to-find item, my persistence typically pays off and I find what I need.

T F **15.** I believe I have good judgment and that in hard times my common sense will prevail.

T F **16.** I am a firm believer in American resilience; we can overcome negative events such as terrorist attacks.

T F **17.** There are times when I feel really angry when things go wrong, but I know I can control my temper and make things better.

T F **18.** When I meet a stranger, I feel that I can befriend this person if I so desire.

T F **19.** If a crisis occurred, I would be fine because I have the wherewithal to overcome it.

T F **20.** If I found myself at a job that was stressful or unappealing, I would take measures to find another and perhaps better job.

SCORING: Items 1–10 were phrased in the negative, indicating low perceived control. Items 11–20 were phrased in the affirmative, indicating higher levels of perceived control. Fill in the blanks below to determine your perceived level of control.

Total "Fs" or falses for items 1–10 _____
Total "Ts" or trues for items 11–20 _____
Grand Total = _____

INTERPRETATION: The higher your grand total, the more you feel you take charge of your own life. A score of 1–5 suggests that you perceive little or no control over your life; a score of 6–10 indicates that you have some doubts that you possess control; a score of 11–15 signifies you believe you have reasonable control; and a score of 16–20 may demonstrate that you perceive high levels of control over your life. Remember, this scale is designed to stimulate thoughts about the amount of perceived control in your own life, it is not a scientific assessment of it.

Misperception and Maladjustment

Unfortunately, the misperception of personal control usually tends to have negative consequences. For instance, some individuals habitually believe they have even less control over their lives than they really do (Gilbert, Brown, Pinel, & Wilson, 2000), and thus they prematurely surrender potential self-mastery available to them. Others, even in the same situation, may go to the opposite extreme: Believing they exercise greater control than they actually do, they set themselves up for frustration and eventual disappointment. In both cases, as you will see, such mistaken beliefs about personal control lead to maladaptive behavior (Zuckerman et al., 2004).

LEARNED HELPLESSNESS When people repeatedly encounter bad outcomes regardless of what they do, such as losing a job because of layoffs, they tend to experience a diminished sense of personal control, thereby attributing too little control to themselves (Bjornstad, 2006). Martin Seligman (1981), who has studied this problem extensively, refers to this phenomenon as **learned helplessness**—*a maladaptive passivity that frequently follows an individual's experience with uncontrollable events.* Notably, a host of psychological and physical difficulties follow the negative events that occur outside of a person's control, such as unemployment, accidents, illnesses, death of a spouse, terrorism, and victimization (Bargal, Ben-Shakhar, & Shalev, 2007). However, uncontrollable events in themselves do not necessarily produce learned helplessness. The crucial matter consists of *how* people explain these events. To the extent they offer a permanent ("It's going to last forever"), universal ("This screws up everything"), and internal ("It's me") explanation for bad events, people tend to surrender control over their lives prematurely and respond poorly to such events when they occur. Accordingly, learned helplessness is associated with a variety of ills, including depression, academic failure, bureaucratic apathy, and premature death (Bouton, 2007).

ILLUSION OF CONTROL Although some people develop a sense of learned helplessness, others believe that they exercise more control over their lives than they actually do. In some cases, people exaggerate the degree of control they possess when outcomes are positive, perhaps as a way of enhancing their self-regard (Yamaguchi, Gelfand, Ohashi, & Zemba, 2005). In other cases, people subscribe to the **illusion of control,** *believing they exert control over what is really a chance-determined event*—such as winning a lottery. The problem with having an illusion of control is that it can lead to taking unnecessary risks, which may then result in negative consequences. The illusion of control can be quite problematic when gambling or when making decision about health, business, finances, or even personal relationships (Gino, Sharek, & Moore, 2011; Martinez, Le Floch, Gaffié, & Villejoubert, 2011). In the end, it is probably wise to recognize what we can and cannot effectively change or control.

Learned Optimism

Exploration 6.2: Learned Optimism

www.natural-healing-health.com/learnedoptimism.html This website contains information on a variety of health-related topics, including learned optimism.

A helpful way of achieving optimal but realistic perceived control can be seen in what Martin Seligman (1992) calls **learned optimism,** defined as *a learned way of explaining both good and bad life events that in turn enhances our perceived control and adaptive responses to them.* Optimism (often thought of as "seeing the glass half full") relates to control in that the greater control people perceive over future events, the greater their optimism. As mentioned earlier, it is not life events in themselves that overwhelm us. Rather, it is our beliefs and interpretations of them and, in turn, our subsequent responses that most affect our lives. Consequently, in learned optimism, the emphasis is on *interpreting life events in a reasonably accurate way* to enhance our perceived control and, thus, our adaptive responses. This goal is accomplished primarily by modifying our explanatory style, that is, the way we explain life events to ourselves (Jackson et al., 2002).

TEACHING OPTIMISM   Optimism has been linked to a variety of positive outcomes, including better problem solving under stress, better physical health, and overall psychological well-being (Meevissen, Peters, & Alberts, 2011; Sharpe, Martin, & Roth, 2011). But optimism doesn't come naturally to all, and that's where learned optimism comes into play. The term *learned* precedes the word *optimism* because optimism can be taught. Parents can teach their children optimism by instructing them in problem-solving skills and adaptive coping skills and by modeling optimistic thinking for their children (Jackson, Pratt, Hunsberger, & Pancer, 2005; Scheier & Carver, 1993). Moreover, adults can teach themselves to be more optimistic simply by imagining a **best possible self**—thinking about the self in an imaginary future in which everything has turned out in the most optimal way—over a period of weeks (Meevissen et al., 2011). You're never too old to learn, and in the case of learned optimism, it may be to your benefit to do so.

THE RISKS OF LEARNED OPTIMISM   Although there are clear benefits to learned optimism, there is also a danger, namely, that changing beliefs about failure from internal to external ("It wasn't my fault … it was bad luck") will undermine personal responsibility and lead to poor decision making and actions, such as a reduction in health-protective behaviors (Tennen & Affleck, 1987). As a result, it may not be best to change from an internal to external belief in a wholesale manner. That is to say, unconditional optimism should not be blindly applied to all situations. Instead, it is a *flexible* optimism that is more appropriate in some situations than in others (Peterson & Vaidya, 2001). For instance, an optimistic explanatory style tends to be appropriate in the following situations:

- If you're in a situation that involves achievement, such as writing a paper, getting a promotion, or winning a game, it helps to be optimistic. If you're concerned about keeping up your morale or fighting off discouragement and depression, emphasize the positive.
- If you're under chronic stress and your physical health is an issue, an optimistic outlook becomes crucial.
- If you want to lead, inspire others, or gain people's confidence, it's better to use optimism.
- If you are depressed, adopting optimism can help overcome the unwarranted self-blame that accompanies bad events.

However, there are also times when optimism is *not* appropriate.

- If your goal involves planning for a risky and uncertain future, do not use optimism.
- If your goal is to counsel others whose future is dim, do not use optimism initially.
- If you want to appear sympathetic to people's troubles, do not start with optimism, although, once confidence and empathy are established, optimism may help.

The basic guideline for choosing optimism, or not, is to ask what *the cost of failure* is in that particular situation. When the cost of failure is high, optimism is probably the wrong strategy, for example, the partygoer deciding to drive home after drinking too much. When the cost of failure is low, optimism is more appropriate, for example, the sales agent who decides to make one more call at the risk of only losing a little bit of personal time.

Defensive Pessimism

As just mentioned, there are many situations for which optimism is not the best strategy. When this occurs, why not harness the power of negative thinking? That is to say, use **defensive pessimism** which is *characterized by setting unrealistically low expectations and thinking through* *the worst-case outcomes of an upcoming event* (Norem & Cantor, 1986). Examples of defensive pessimism include saying to oneself, "In order to study, I need to think about how unprepared I am;" "I often think about what I need to do to prevent bad things from happening;" and "I frequently find myself thinking about failure." There are three main benefits to defensive pessimism: (1) setting low expectations reduces the sting of failure (if it should occur); (2) thinking about worst-case scenarios allows you to prepare for them in advance; and (3) the potentially debilitating effects of anxiety on task performance are reduced when expectations are low and you have anticipated and prepared for any potential negative event that could happen.

But does defensive pessimism work? In terms of achievement and success, the answer is a resounding, "Yes." In fact, defensive pessimists perform just as well as optimists perform a variety of tasks, including test scores (Martin, Marsh, & Debus, 2001). Moreover, when defensive pessimists are prevented from using their preferred strategy, their performance worsens (Norem, 2002). However, there are emotional and personal costs to defensive pessimism. Frequent users of defensive pessimism experience lower self-esteem, decreased life satisfaction, and higher rates of depression. Moreover, although defensive pessimists harness anxiety for productive purposes, feelings of anxiety still persist (Yamawaki, Tschanz, & Feick, 2004). It appears, then, that defensive pessimism is best used sparingly, and that in the long run, more positive approaches to success should be employed.

DECISION MAKING

LEARNING OBJECTIVES

6.6 Identify the stages of decision making.
6.7 List several suggestions for improving decision-making skills.

As you just learned, a major means of exercising personal control is through the judgments we make—our basic life choices as well as everyday decisions. From the moment we awake until we go to sleep at night, we must choose between the various options presented to us. Fortunately, many of our day-to-day decisions, such as when to get up and what to eat for breakfast, are made with little effort, mostly because of our habits and daily routines. It is mainly when we encounter a new and serious problem or face an important life choice, that we become acutely aware of the need to be decisive. Then we may become so overwhelmed by the alternatives or so caught up in the mental anguish of considering the consequences of our choices that we put off making them (Anderson, 2003). Worse still, we may hastily elect to "get it over with," thereby increasing the risk of an unwanted outcome. In both instances, we lose sight of the overall process of making decisions we can live with.

In this section, you will learn about the process of **decision making**—*the gathering information about relevant alternatives and making an appropriate choice*—along with valuable aids for making sound decisions and acting on them.

Exploration 6.3: Ethical Decisions

www.scu.edu/ethics/practicing/decision/framework.html   This thoughtful site is dedicated to making ethical decisions.

The Process of Decision Making

Psychologists have formulated a system for making *wise* decisions—the kind of decisions we can live with. They recommend that we proceed systematically through several stages:

1. *Rise to the challenge.*   This stage involves you recognizing a problem or challenge for what it is, guarding against such hazards as oversimplifying a complex problem. Key question: "What are the risks of doing nothing, not changing, or not deciding?"

2. ***Search for alternatives.*** This stage requires you to have an attitude of openness and flexibility, with a concern for information about all possible alternatives, obvious or not. Key question: "Have I considered all the alternatives?"
3. ***Evaluate the alternatives.*** You should next evaluate all the options with regard to their practicality and consequences. Here you weigh various risks, costs, and possible gains. Key question: "Which is the best alternative?"
4. ***Make a commitment.*** Ordinarily, it's best for you to choose the alternative that gives you maximum benefits at minimum costs. Yet there's the danger of acting impulsively to "get it over with." Key question: "When do I implement the best alternative and let others know my decision?" After due consideration, you should be able to *act on your decision* at this stage.
5. ***Assess your decision.*** After you have acted on your decision, you can learn about your decision-making ability by assessing the quality, results, and consequences of your decision. Because every decision involves some risk, it is important that you do not overreact with disappointment, criticism, and self-blame. The danger here can be changing your mind prematurely or justifying your choice defensively, thus shutting out valuable feedback.

Critical Elements in Decision Making

There are many factors that directly affect the decisions we make. These critical elements include vigorous information seeking and processing, snap judgments, and reactance. Let's take a look at each.

INFORMATION SEEKING AND PROCESSING   Finding and analyzing information is crucial to deliberate decision making (Hogarth, 2005). However, gathering information takes time and energy, disrupting routines and building tension and conflict, all of which can be unpleasant (Luce, 2005). Consequently, most of us do not seek sufficient information, although we are more willing to look for new information when we expect the benefits of a decision to outweigh the costs. Rather than relying on a single source of information (even if it is Wikipedia), a better idea is to turn to a *variety of resources* (Anastasio, Rose, & Chapman, 1999). Doing so will help you make more realistic and informed decisions. Unfortunately, in making important life choices many of us tend to underestimate the benefits of information gathering and therefore pay a high price for not doing it well or at all. There's nothing more agonizing than discovering a better choice after you've already committed to a less desirable course of action—right?

SNAP JUDGMENTS   In our fast-paced society, we sometimes expect snap judgments and quick action, chiding those who are slow or deliberate when making choices. Similarly, we often use shortcuts in our own decision making, especially when we in a hurry, busy, or tired. Many turn to the media to quickly gather facts. The Internet, for example, has quickly become the number-one source of information (Fox, 2008). Although it can provide valuable content, the Internet (and other types of media) can also offer up inaccurate and/or unrepresentative views of the world (Gray, 2008). Case in point, there are hundreds of websites on the Internet promoting eating disorders (referred to as pro-Ed). Using posted information, message boards and blogs, pro-Ed websites provide users with weight loss tips as well as methods for avoiding detection by health care workers and family (Harper, Sperry, & Thompson, 2008; Wilson, Peebles, & Hardy, 2006). As this example clearly illustrates, gathering information on the Internet can lead to the validation of decisions that are harmful to one's physical and mental health.

Interestingly, rather than making hasty snap judgments, some individuals put off making choices by engaging in a seemingly never-ending search for relevant material (Ferrari & Dovidio, 2000). Although procrastination in the form of thoughtfulness is not so bad, in the long run, the stress it causes can fuel anxiety and other health-related problems (Tice & Baumeister, 1997).

REACTANCE At times decision making is taken out of our hands. When this happens, we often feel uncomfortable because we like to maintain control over our own choices and our own actions. One manipulative strategy that others use to influence our decisions is **reactance**—*an oppositional response that occurs when our personal freedom is restricted.* Reactance occurs when others limit our personal freedoms—and in doing so get us to do what they want us to do rather than what we want (Donnell, Thomas, & Buboltz, 2001). In other words, reactance is experienced when we lose some control over our decision making. Reactance can explain one of the most common findings in media effects research, namely that *warning labels and restrictive age classifications create a desire for the prohibited content in consumers,* commonly referred to as the **forbidden fruit effect** (Bushman & Stack, 1996). For instance, restrictive age labels and violent content warnings increase the attractiveness of violent video games for both children and adolescents (Nije Bijvank, Konijn, Bushman, & Roelofsma, 2009). As you can see, decisions made about which video games to buy and play are clearly influenced by restrictions placed on them by others.

Post-Decision Regret

Another element in decision making of which to be mindful is **post-decision regret,** *the regret that can be experienced shortly after we have finally made a particularly difficult choice or decision.* It is quite normal after you have made a decision to feel that you may have made an incorrect or poor decision and to experience regret (van Harreveld, van der Pligt, & Nordgren, 2008). We all tend to suffer from the "grass is greener on the other side of the fence" phenomenon, but mostly *after* we make a decision. You're not alone if you experience regret after an important decision. Some of the top life-choice decisions about which we experience regret are education, careers, romance, and parenting (Roese & Summerville, 2005).

Regret about decision making may have at least three contributory components:

1. That the outcome is poorer than expected (perhaps because the option you did *not* choose really was better).
2. Self-blame for having made a bad decision.
3. Missed opportunities, especially when the missed opportunity was a *near* miss.

Notably, our *actions* tend to generate more regret in the short term while our *inaction* produces more regret in the long run (Gilovich & Medvec, 1995). Similarly, people usually feel *more* regret because of inaction than from action (Feldman, Miyamoto, & Loftus, 1999). Knowing these parameters may help you avoid or cope better with post-decisional regret when it happens to you.

COGNITIVE DISSONANCE The term *cognitive dissonance* is often the used to describe the *uncomfortable feeling of regret* mentioned above. Most people can live with post-decisional dissonance, especially if they have carefully planned the decision or are well adjusted. Eventually, the dissonance goes away as we discover that we really did make a good decision or that the unselected alternatives really are less desirable. Some individuals cannot live easily with dissonance, so they find ways to make themselves feel better. One method they use is **social comparison**—*the process of using others to compare ourselves to in order to understand who we are relative to them.* Especially in instances of a *bad* decision (or bad performance), individuals prefer to compare themselves to others who have made *worse* decisions (or performed more poorly), thus lessening their feelings of regret (van Harreveld et al., 2008).

Eating ice cream, especially while on a diet, may induce post-decisional regret.

HINDSIGHT BIAS A common, but not always good strategy for reducing post-decision regret is **hindsight bias**—*a biased representation of events or information once they have happened or after the fact.* This is a sort of being-wise-after-the-event, sense-making process that is triggered by surprising or negative events as well as events that inspire "why" questions (as in "Why did that happen?" or "Why did that go wrong?") (Blank, Musch, & Pohl, 2007). When we make a poor decision, we are likely to suffer from biased memory such that we begin to explain what happened in terms of inevitability rather than in terms of the facts. For example, after getting fired for disrespectful treatment of coworkers and supervisors, an employee might say something along the lines of, "I should have never taken this job. Management clearly doesn't appreciate thoughtful comments from front-line workers." Research on hindsight bias indicates the following: (1) everyone experiences it at one

BOX 6–4	Focus on Wellness: Making-up Excuses

"I had too much else to do." "The professor didn't ask fair questions." "It wasn't my fault, it just happened? Sound familiar? It should, for we all make excuses for our failures, misgivings, and bad decisions at one point or another. So, why do so many of us make-up excuses? The answer is pretty straight forward: self-protection. Rather than experiencing the negative thoughts (e.g., I'm a screw-up; I'm not smart), emotions (e.g., guilt), and blows to self-esteem and self-confidence that accompany failure, we make up reasonable excuses for them. Some people, called **self-handicappers**, even *make up excuses before an event* (e.g., "I'm not feeling well") *in order to explain away a potential failure*. In the short term, making-up excuses can make us feel better about ourselves and even motivate us to improve our performance in the future (Schlenker, Pontari, & Christopher, 2001). However, if the excuses are clearly false or occur to often they can negatively impact our self-control, performance, and confidence. Moreover, frequent excuse makers tend to be viewed by others as unreliable, lacking in integrity and self-centered (Baumgardner & Carothers, 2009).

point or another; (2) it is hard to avoid; and (3) it is potentially detrimental because it causes actual memory distortions or worse yet poorer decisions in the future. As you can see, when hindsight bias occurs, excuses follow. Box 6–4 further discusses the causes and consequences of making-up excuses.

Making Better Decisions

Keep in mind that your purpose in making a decision is to bring about desired results and avoid undesirable ones. In this sense, only you can define what constitutes a "good" or "bad" decision. At the same time, your personal traits, such as your attitudes, values, and tolerance for uncertainty, can complicate decision making. With such factors in mind, you can improve your decision-making skills by following these suggestions:

- *Use sounder judgment.* Judgment, the raw material of decision making, involves drawing inferences from data. Many decisions are doomed from the start because of poor judgment, often involving the human tendency to simplify complex matters. You probably should replace simplistic, intuitive strategies with the more "investigational" orientation that guides scientists, asking yourself such questions as these: What are the facts? How representative are they? What do the alternatives look like? How much of what is true is due to situational or chance factors? Sounder judgments may lead to better decisions.
- *Draw up a balance sheet.* This step consists of listing the various advantages and disadvantages of each course of action. A sample balance sheet in Table 6–1 represents Stan's situation before he made his decision. Students like Stan as well as adults of all ages have found that the balance sheet procedure helps them to make a comprehensive appraisal of a situation requiring a decision and promotes contingency planning, that is, figuring out what to do if something in the minus column materializes. People who use this procedure are more likely to stick to their decisions and express fewer regrets about the options not taken.
- *Clarify your values and objectives.* Many conflicts arise from confusion over the values that guided the decision rather than rejection of any alternative decisions. Thus, this step requires personal examination, and once you have clarified your values, they can be translated into tangible objectives that guide your decisions. For example, often vacillating in their decisions, students are sometimes torn between the need to study, work, socialize, and play. Those who have made a clear choice about what they hope to gain from college will be more likely to resolve their daily decisions effectively.

Table 6–1	Stan's Balance Sheet: Attending College	
Projected Consequences	**Positive Anticipations**	**Negative Anticipations**
Tangible gains and losses for me	1. Better job prospects 2. Better income 3. More challenging career	1. Hard courses 2. Financial difficulties 3. Need to start over in new job and career
Positive and negative effects on family	1. Family proud of me 2. Substantial emotional support from family 3. Positive role model for my children	1. Fewer toys and clothes for children 2. Wife will need to work and care for children—more stress for her
Self-approval or disapproval	1. Confidence in mastering challenges 2. Pride in new opportunities	1. Lingering doubts about my academic abilities
Social approval or disapproval	1. Admiration from others for making a midlife change	1. Will be unemployed and perhaps stigmatized due to this

- *Accept reasonable results.* Nothing is as devastating to decision making as the wish for an "ideal" solution. People with perfectionist tendencies are especially susceptible, because constant striving for perfection guarantees failure. It is usually wiser for you to accept the most reasonable results under the circumstances. Among the methods of combating perfectionism—should it be characteristic of you—are recognizing the advantages and disadvantages of perfectionism and comparing how perfectly you did something with how much you enjoyed it. For example, you may feel that you didn't play tennis very well, but you enjoyed the game nevertheless because of the exercise and companionship, so you decide to continue with the sport.

- *Make the best of faulty decisions.* Despite your best efforts, not every decision will turn out to be a wise one. Some common reasons are limitations in circumstances, unforeseen events, and the difficulty of anticipating how differently you'll view things 5, 10, even 20 years down the road. Many people waste time berating themselves or trying to justify their poor decisions. It may be wiser to realize that more often than not people made the best decision possible under the circumstances. It's better to learn from your mistakes and, whenever possible, to modify your decisions to achieve a more desirable result than beat yourself up. If all else fails, take heart in the fact that no one makes perfect decisions. Box 6–5 provides some interesting facts about successful as well as failed decision making.

BOX 6–5   Did you know that ...

- Half the people who make New Year's resolutions give up within three months. Nearly one-quarter give up the first week.
- Those who put their resolutions in writing or reveal them openly are more likely to achieve them.
- It's easier to choose between two desirable outcomes, such as attaining better health or more money, than between two undesirable ones, such as being ill or poor.
- Our decisions are affected by whether the outcome is presented positively or negatively; for example, more people elect to have surgery when told they have a 90 percent chance of living than when told they have a 10 percent chance of dying.

DECISIONS AND PERSONAL GROWTH

LEARNING OBJECTIVES

6.8 Describe the connection between making decisions and personal growth.

Decisions are especially crucial with regard to personal growth. All too often, people become stuck in self-defeating behaviors because they've never made a decision to change their ways. Change may be resisted because of the inertia of past habits, psychological laziness, or simply fear (Anderson, 2003; Blum, 1998). When confronted with the need for change, people sometimes become defensive and resist, although they may promise to change if threatened with the loss of their jobs or their family's love. However, many of those who enter psychotherapy or a treatment program drop out prematurely, mostly because they really haven't made a firm decision to change.

Exploration 6.4: Understanding your Actions

www.mentalhelp.net/poc/center_index.php?id=353&cn=353   Through the use of an online self-help book, this site helps you understand why you behave as you do by examining a variety of topics.

Making New Decisions

A good beginning point for personal growth is to examine the basic decisions underlying your everyday behavior, especially problem behaviors such as habitual procrastination or drinking too much alcohol. However, it is only when a *wish* to change leads to a *decision to change* that we can *really change and grow.* For example, many smokers know about the negative health effects of their smoking habit. They say things such as "I'd like to stop smoking" and "I hope to give it up soon" and "I plan to cut down on my smoking" or "I know it's bad for my family and me." Until they *really decide* to stop smoking and learn how to implement that decision, nothing happens or they try and fail.

So far we have assumed that people will automatically decide to change for the better, but this is not always the case. In some instances, people may become so overwhelmed with the anxiety and risks of change or fear post-decisional regret so much that they decide to remain the way they are, however unsatisfying or painful that may be (Anderson, 2003). Nor can someone be forced into growth, especially by therapists who may be adamant about people living up to their human potential. However well-intentioned such therapists may be, they can make the same mistakes that parents and spouses are prone to make—namely, trying to tell someone else what he or she *ought* to decide. Rather, the therapist's task should be to help the client discover first what he or she wants to do and then help the client make a personal decision to do it. As most of us have discovered, once you know what you want to do and really decide to do it, you're well on your way. You can use Figure 6–1 to help you make your next few important decisions so that you can learn from them.

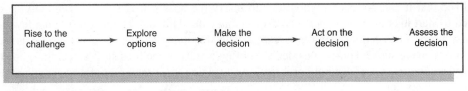

Rise to the challenge → Explore options → Make the decision → Act on the decision → Assess the decision

FIGURE 6–1 Steps in making effective decisions.

We can promote personal growth by seeing our problems in terms of past decisions, examining the consequences of such decisions, and then choosing a more satisfying alternative. In this way, we learn to view our problems and unfulfilled potential more in terms of our decisions than as the result of events and circumstances that simply happen or are beyond our control.

Some Practical Applications

DECISION BY DEFAULT   One of the most common examples of decision making is decision by default—taking the path of least resistance, taking the most familiar path, or taking no action at all (Anderson, 2003; Chapman, 1999). Putting things off, whether temporarily or indefinitely, while itself a decision (Anderson, 2003), nonetheless is a poor decision. A young man whom Stan knew as his teaching assistant in one of his classes was just such an example. This young man was having considerable difficulty completing his doctoral dissertation, partly because of writer's block and partly because of conflicts with his adviser. The young man became so frustrated that he simply turned his efforts elsewhere. He took the part-time teaching assistant job at the university ("while I finish my degree") and spent more time jogging ("to take my mind off my problems"). Several years later, when asked how his degree program was progressing, he said he had finally "decided" to give it up. Actually, he had made that decision earlier on, hadn't he? The failure to make a positive decision often is itself a decision with fateful consequences.

SELF-DEFEATING BEHAVIOR   Overcoming negative, self-defeating behavior usually involves making a positive decision at a basic level of motivation. For example, Stan's sister, Janet, at midlife was bothered by depression and a poor relationship with her work supervisor. She disclosed to Stan that she had spent much time at work complaining and had been especially critical of her boss, often without any apparent reason. During some subsequent counseling, Janet discovered that earlier in her life she had learned to suppress her anger for fear of parental disapproval. She had become a passive "good little girl" but resented those on whom she remained dependent. Gradually, she learned to take more initiative, to show her anger more directly as an expression of her feelings rather than as judgmental remarks that would otherwise put others on the defensive. As Janet became more assertive, she felt less depressed and enjoyed a more satisfying relationship with those in authority.

REVERSING EARLIER DECISIONS   Sometimes it is wise to make a decision that counters or reverses an earlier commitment that has led to undesirable consequences. For example, Stan's brother-in-law was a 45-year-old lawyer who married the daughter of the senior partner in his firm. He admitted to having married out of "mixed motives." That is, although he had been genuinely attracted to his wife, he had also hoped that her "connections" would enhance his career. He soon discovered that conflicts with his father-in-law complicated his life both at work and at home. Consultation with a specialist about his asthma attacks, which seemed worse during joint vacations at his in-laws' summer cottage, suggested that the attacks were brought on by emotional conflicts concerning his in-laws. Gradually, Stan's brother-in-law realized that it had not been a good idea to marry the boss's daughter, so eventually he decided to start his own firm rather than divorce his wife. Although he went through a few lean years, he soon had a flourishing law practice and was much happier in his marriage as well. Failure to make such a courageous decision often results in feelings such as being trapped in one's career, developing drinking problems, or engaging in extramarital affairs and other self-defeating behaviors.

Chapter Summary

PERSONAL CONTROL

6.1 Define perceived control.

Perceived control refers to what we *think* we can control, now and in the future.

6.2 Summarize the benefits of perceived control.

Those high in perceived control benefit in the following ways: (1) they are likely to seek knowledge and information about the events that affect their lives; (2) they are likely to attribute responsibility to themselves and to their abilities; (3) they are resistant to social influence and are more likely to take part in social action that helps others; (4) they are achievement-oriented; and (5) they work harder at and are more persistent about completing tasks. Also, people who are high in realistically perceived control tend to be less anxious and better adjusted.

6.3 Discuss the benefits of learned optimism.

A way to achieve optimal perceived control is through learned optimism—interpreting life events in a reasonably accurate way that enhances our perceived control and, thus, our adaptive response to events.

6.4 Explain how learned helplessness and the illusion of control are similar.

People who underestimate the control they have over their lives sometimes exhibit learned helplessness; those who exaggerate their personal control often exhibit the illusion of control. In both cases, the misperception of control leads to maladaptive behavior.

6.5 Describe defensive pessimism.

Defensive pessimism involves setting unrealistically low expectations and thinking through the worst-case outcomes of an upcoming event. Although there are achievement-related benefits to using defensive mechanism, negative emotional and personal costs are present as well.

DECISION MAKING

6.6 Identify the stages of decision making.

Guidelines for making sound decisions include five stages: Accept the challenge, search for alternatives, evaluate the alternatives, make a commitment, and follow through with the decision.

6.7 List several suggestions for improving decision-making skills.

We may improve our decision-making skills by better judgment, the balance sheet procedure, clarifying our objectives, accepting reasonable results, and making the best of a poor decision. Also, we must repeatedly reaffirm our choice to change by abandoning perfectionism, accepting an occasional failure, picking ourselves up, and continuing our commitment to personal growth.

DECISIONS AND PERSONAL GROWTH

6.8 Describe the connection between making decisions and personal growth.

It is only when a desire to change leads to an actual decision to change that our personal lives begin to improve.

Self-Test

1. Personal control and perceived control are very similar concepts. The biggest difference between the two is that:
    a. personal control refers to what we actually control whereas perceived control refers to what we believe we can control
    b. perceived control refers to what we actually control whereas personal control refers to what we believe we can control
    c. only personal control influences the behaviors we engage in
    d. only perceived control influences the behaviors we engage in

2. The first stage of decision making is to
    a. evaluate the alternatives
    b. rise to the challenge
    c. make a commitment
    d. search for alternatives

3. Following the loss of her teaching position due to layoffs, Adrienne had great difficulty finding a new job. Adrienne felt that no matter what she did, she would probably never find a good job again. Adrienne maladaptive passivity is referred to as:
    a. reactance
    b. the illusion of control
    c. hindsight bias
    d. learned helplessness

4. After years of buying "scratch-off" lottery tickets, Ellen finally won big: a $1000 a month for life! Ellen doesn't think that luck had anything to do with her winning, instead she thinks that the strategy of buying 1 ticket a week and revealing the numbers with her left hand resulted in her lottery win. Ellen's belief that she controlled a random event is called:
   a. learned optimism
   b. secondary control
   c. the illusion of control
   d. reactance

5. Luanne recently decided to go back to college to get a degree in nursing. Two years later, with a degree in hand and a new job starting in just a few days, Luanne reflected on the decision to pursue her new career. Luanne is in which step in the process of decision making?
   a. Rise to the Challenge
   b. Make a Commitment
   c. Assess your Decision
   d. Search for Alternatives

6. After sweltering in the heat, Sue decided that what her family needed was a swimming pool. The day after the pool installation started (and the pool had been half paid for), the heat wave broke, and by the time the pool was finished a period of unseasonably cold weather set in. At this point, Sue began to question her decision to buy a pool. She kept thinking that maybe the money could have been spent on something better (like a new heater). Sue was experiencing:
   a. reactance
   b. post-decision malaise
   c. post-decision regret
   d. learned helplessness

7. Due to the unforeseen selling of his company, Fred lost his job as a project manager. Lacking a steady income, Fred missed several payments on new car, and as a result, the car was repossessed. As he watched the car get towed away, Fred said to himself "I knew that would happen, I should have taken into consideration what I could afford if I lost my job" Despite the fact that Fred could not have predicted getting fired, and that the decision to get a new car was financially sound at the time Fred experienced:
   a. hindsight bias
   b. social comparison
   c. reactance
   d. post-decision malaise

8. Fifteen-year-old Dave was irate. The sequel to his favorite video game, "Mega Manslaughter" was banned from sale in his country, preventing him from buying it. Dave felt as if a personal freedom (the freedom to play any type of video game he wanted to) had been lost: Dave experienced:
   a. learned pessimism
   b. resilience
   c. learned helplessness
   d. reactance

9. Which of the following skills is not used to improve decision making?
   a. make the best of faulty decisions
   b. clarify values and objectives
   c. avoid using balance sheets
   d. accept reasonable results

10. If you really want to experience true change that can lead to interpersonal growth, it is crucial that you:
   a. wish to change.
   b. decide to change
   c. hope to change
   d. none of the above

Exercises

1. *Personal control.* To what extent do you believe you can influence the occurrence of events in your environment that affect your life? In a page or so, discuss the degree of personal control you have over your life, emphasizing *perceived* control or the belief that you can control your life. How does your belief affect specific aspects of your life, such as your goals, work, intimate relationships, fitness, and health?

2. *Stages in decision making.* Review the five stages of decision making discussed in the chapter. Select an important decision you're about to make or one you've already made. Then analyze it in terms of the five stages of the decision-making process. How well did you follow these five stages? What do you find to be the most difficult part of making decisions?

3. *Aids in making decisions.* Reread the section on aids (such as the balance sheet method) to making sounder decisions. Then select one of the poorer decisions you've made and review this decision in light of these aids. What do you think you need to do to make better decisions in the future?

4. *Decision making and personal growth.* Select some aspects of your life, such as a habit or problem behavior, that you would like to change. Do you consider the problem behavior to be partly the result of some other decisions you've made? Have you made a deliberate decision to change your behavior, or do you merely wish to change? What do you need to do to really make the change?

5. *Understanding bad outcomes.* Select a negative event that has happened to you over which you had little control, such as losing your job because of a layoff at work. Did you take an optimistic or pessimistic approach? Would learned optimism have helped you?

Questions for Self-Reflection

1. How much control do you believe you have over your life?
2. Are you inclined to underestimate or overestimate your level of personal control?
3. Do you suffer from the illusion of control when you have little actual control?
4. When there appears to be no choice in a situation, what do you do?
5. How do you go about making important decisions?
6. Do you often "decide" things by not deciding?
7. Are you willing to take calculated risks?
8. What was the best decision you ever made? Why was your decision successful?
9. Is the grass always greener on the other side of the fence for you? Why do you think this is so?
10. How much truth is there in the saying that "life is what happens to us while we're making other plans"?

Chapter Seven

Managing Motives and Emotions

*Q*uincy was one of those students never to be forgotten. A pleasant young man, he sat in the rear of the classroom next to the door. Quincy was cheery, articulate, eager to learn, and unlike many of his classmates, he didn't surf the Internet or text during class. He was well liked by his peers and professors alike. Everyone who knew him realized that golf was Quincy's "reason for being," as he often declared. Quincy hoped to make it as a professional golfer one day, but "just in case," he said, "I'm going to college to obtain an education if my golf career never pays off." Quincy's parents were none too happy about his plans to play sports. Instead, they wanted him to become a doctor—a dream they held for him from the day he was born. While Quincy loved and respected his parents, he could not help but be disappointed that they did not share his enthusiasm for golf.

UNDERSTANDING MOTIVATION

LEARNING OBJECTIVES

7.1 Explain motivation.
7.2 Describe Maslow's hierarchy of needs.
7.3 Discuss the difference between intrinsic and extrinsic motivation.
7.4 List several different ways in which sensation-seeking behavior is manifested.
7.5 Compare achievement motivation in individualistic and collectivist societies.
7.6 Discuss the importance of goals in personal motivation.

Most of us can sympathize with Quincy. Sometimes we eagerly do the task at hand, especially when it will bring us closer to some desired goal, such as becoming a professional golfer. At other times, however, we may feel little or no motivation for what we're supposed to get done. We procrastinate, we make excuses, and we waste precious time. Not surprisingly, many people, such as parents, teachers, and managers in the workplace, are interested in learning how to motivate people. Essentially, **motivation** has to do with *energizing and directing our efforts toward a meaningful goal.*

> **BOX 7–1**   **Did you know that ...**
>
> Each of the following famous motivational quotes are under five words
>
> - Just do it—Nike
> - Git-R-Done—Larry the Cable Guy
> - Just say no—Nancy Reagan
> - There is no tomorrow—Rocky Balboa
> - Carpe Diem (Seize the Day)—Horace
>
> *Sources:* Nancy Reagan; ODES by Horace; ROCKY III. United Artists, 1982.

Understanding Your Needs

Your understanding of motivation may be enhanced by a study of Maslow's (1954) **hierarchy of needs,** which is a growth model of motivation, where **needs** are *tension states that arouse us to seek gratification.* Maslow suggests that our *needs and motives function in a hierarchical manner from the bottom up according to how crucial the need is for survival.* He describes five levels of needs, from lowest to highest, as follows:

1. *Physiological needs*   *include the need for food, sleep, and sex.*
2. *Safety needs*   *include the need for protection from bodily harm and security from threat, as well as the need for order and stability.*
3. *Love and belongingness needs*   *include the need for acceptance, affection, and approval.*
4. *Esteem needs*   *are the need for self-respect and the sense of achievement.*
5. *Self-actualizing needs*   *include a variety of needs, such as the need for autonomy, uniqueness, aliveness, beauty, and justice in our lives.*

Maslow theorized that the lowest level of unmet needs remains the most urgent, thus commanding our attention and efforts. Once a given level of need is satisfied, we become more motivated by the unmet needs at the next higher level (Figure 7–1). To that end, as we satisfy our needs for food and shelter we become more concerned about things such as job security. However, Maslow believed that across all five categories our needs are only partially satisfied. He once estimated that the average person is only 85 percent satisfied in terms of physiological needs, 70 percent in safety needs, 50 percent in love needs, 40 percent in esteem needs, and only 10 percent in self-actualizing needs. As a result, during every moment of every day we are motivated to meet at least some of our needs. Such striving is part and parcel of personal growth (Deci & Moller, 2005).

An important implication of Maslow's growth model of motivation is that we aren't content to achieve a stable, harmonious state. Instead, once we've reached a relative level of satisfaction, biologically and psychologically, we're increasingly motivated by growth needs. This theory helps to explain why successful people are rarely satisfied to rest on their laurels—that is, their previous achievements. They're constantly striving to attain something better. Here's an example: People who are happily retired seldom sit around doing nothing; they're forever developing new interests and deepening their relationships with others. It seems as if we're at our happiest when we're growing and actualizing.

Differences between You and Others

Although each of us desires the creature comforts of food and sleep, as well as higher goals such as success in education or sports, the relative strengths of such motives differ from one person to another (Hinsz & Jundt, 2005). Accordingly, we need to think in terms of the individual's

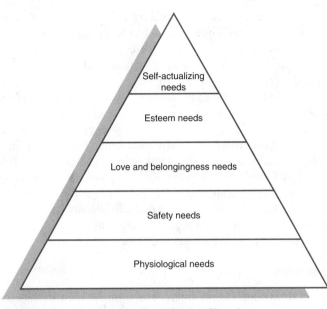

FIGURE 7–1   Maslow's (1954) Hierarchy of Needs.

Source: Figure from MOTIVATION AND PERSONALITY, 3rd edition
by Abraham H. Maslow, Robert D. Frager, and James Fadiman.

personal hierarchy of motives as well as Maslow's generalized pattern. Discovering which motives have top priority for a given person will depend on factors such as inborn dispositions, culture, personal values, gender roles, and past experience. For example, individuals who have been deprived of love and affection as children may be more motivated by the desire for approval than achievement.

Our **motives**—*goal-directed activities that energize and direct behavior*—also change over time depending on the **motive targets** around us—*the people toward whom our attention or motives are directed.* At work you may have a strong motive to compete with your associates. In your leisure hours, you may be more concerned about being accepted by your friends. Then again, at home you may feel inclined toward intimacy and involvement with your lover or spouse. As you can see, our motives are constantly changing throughout the day, as we move from one situation to another and as we encounter various people. Furthermore, motives tend to vary across the life span and by culture, mostly because of experiences and personal growth.

Everyone's Basic Needs

In order to survive, everyone must eat, drink, and avoid extreme pain and injury. Although sex is not essential to our personal survival, it is necessary for the *survival* of the species. Such needs, though shaped by learning in varying degrees, have a clearer *physiological basis.* As a result, they are variously labeled *basic needs,* primary drives, or survival motives (Scioli, Ricci, Nyugen, & Scioli, 2011).

Basic needs are influenced by both biological and environmental influences. For example, eating and drinking behaviors are affected by a part of the brain known as the **hypothalamus** (*a small but important structure at the core of the brain that governs many aspects of behavior, such as eating and hormonal activity*) as well as by a variety of learned influences (Nieuwenhuizen & Rutters, 2008). As an illustration, some of the more common learned cues for eating are the smell, sight, and taste of food. Here's a study that demonstrates the power that visual cues have on the amount of food we consume. Participants were seated at a table and given some soup to eat. Half of those in the study were given normal bowls, the other half were given bowls that automatically refilled themselves from a hole in the bottom of the bowl. Participants with the refilling bowls ate 73 percent more soup than those with normal bowls; interestingly, there were no differences between the two groups in "feeling full." Clearly, our motivation to eat is heavily influenced by the amount of food we see in front of us (Wansink, Painter, & North, 2005).

Culture also plays a large role in learning various eating habits (Guendelman, Cheryan, & Monin, 2011). Most Americans, for example, prefer white eggs to brown ones; the brown ones appear dirty. On the other hand, Russians do not mind eating brown eggs; in fact, most of the eggs they eat have brown shells. Additionally, some individuals learn to use food as a means of relieving emotional stress. Chocolate, ice cream, cookies, pizza, and other "comfort foods" have this in common: They are all calorically dense and contain high amounts of carbohydrates and/or fats. But are such foods really comforting? You probably already know the answer to this: Yes they are! Comfort foods clearly reduce the negatives effects associated with stress, at least in the short term (Ulrich-Lai et al., 2010). What's your favorite comfort food?

Psychosocial Motives

Some psychosocial motives—such as the motives for stimulation, curiosity, and exploration— seem to be largely inborn and are sometimes labeled *stimulus* needs. Others, like *achievement motivation,* are shaped more extensively by psychological, cultural, and social influences. Because of the complexity of human behavior, there is no one authoritative list of our psychological and social motives. Some of these motives are addressed in other chapters, such as our sexual motives, friendship needs, and the need for personal freedom and control. Here, we'll focus on two of the psychosocial motives not covered elsewhere, namely, the need for stimulation and for achievement.

STIMULATION We need both sensory and social stimulation. People deprived of both, for instance, prisoners in solitary confinement and subjects in sensory deprivation experiments, display

Some people enjoy parachuting out of planes or hang-gliding; these individuals are probably high in sensation seeking.

symptoms of stress, including distorted perceptions. They see and hear strange things; they hallucinate, have delusions, and fear losing their sanity. Military personnel in lonely outposts have shown similar reactions, though to a lesser degree (Wallace & Fisher, 2003). Most of us are rarely placed in a situation in which we suffer from extreme sensory or social isolation. But even after several hours of studying alone, you may feel a need to listen to the radio, call someone on the phone, or talk to a friend, mostly for variation in stimulation.

Perhaps you've noticed how some people have a greater need for trying novel experiences and meeting new people. Others prefer more peaceful activities, such as reading or stamp collecting. Such differences in human behavior are due to the relative strength of the **sensation-seeking motive,** defined as *our tendency to seek out stimulating and novel experiences.* Sensation-seeking motive may be partly dependent on biological factors, like brain stimulation and biochemical secretions, so that each of us has an optimal arousal level (Campbell et al., 2010). Whenever we find ourselves in situations that arouse us to a significantly lesser or greater extent than our optimal arousal, we become uncomfortable. If not sufficiently aroused, we seek greater stimulation; if we're overly aroused, we try to reduce the stimulation. Partly because of its biological basis, sensation seeking is at a peak during the college years and tends to diminish with age.

Generally speaking, individuals high in sensation seeking out stimulating experiences (e.g., watching violent movies; Xie & Lee, 2008). They are also more likely to take both positive (e.g., kayaking) and negative risks, such as unprotected sex, reckless driving, and an increased use of alcohol and illicit drugs (Hatfield & Fernandes, 2009; Miller & Quick, 2010). Interestingly, although both men and women can be sensation seekers, men display this characteristic more so than women. This finding occurs, in part, because of men's tendency to easily become bored (Fink, Hamdaoui, Wenig, & Neave, 2010; Hugill, Fink, Neave, Besson, & Bunse, 2011). Differences in sensation seeking may also influence the way we relate to one another. Low-sensation seekers may feel that high-sensation seekers are foolhardy and hungry for attention. In contrast, high-sensation seekers may feel that low-sensation seekers are timid and boring. A scale for you to assess your level of sensation seeking is provided in Activity 7–1.

ACHIEVEMENT Perhaps you've noticed how your friends differ in **achievement motivation**—*the desire to accomplish or master something difficult or challenging as independently and successfully as possible.* Some relish taking on a challenge, and no matter the task, they strive to do their best. Others seem to be happy just getting the job over and done with. Actually, achievement motivation is comprised of several factors, including the **desire for success** or *the urge to succeed,* and the counteracting **fear of failure**—*the fear that we will be humiliated by shortcoming* (Corpus, McClintic-Gilbert, & Hayenga, 2009). Each of us has a different mixture of these tendencies, mostly because of our personal makeup and past experiences (Acharya & Joshi, 2011). As a result, the difficulties of the tasks people choose differ. For example, someone who has a strong desire for success and a low fear of failure is more apt to choose moderately difficult but realistic tasks, thus maximizing their chances of success. Another person with an intense desire for success yet coupled with a high fear of failure will set a much lower goal and perhaps be more anxious about achieving these goals. It is worth noting that achievement motivation remains fairly stable over time (Senko & Harackiewicz, 2005). Achievement motivation affects our cognitions, our health, athletic ability, career functioning, and other activities and behaviors. For example, athletes must learn the required skills for a sport, survive a highly competitive selection process, and then execute their skills perfectly in each game. Any and all of these processes can be affected by a sense of achievement motivation (Gu, Solmon, Zhang, & Xiang, 2011).

Of note, in collective (as compared to individualistic) societies where individual gain is shunned in favor of the collective good, achievement motivation occurs in a different form. Achievement motivation and satisfaction are not derived from personal accomplishment. For example, in Japan, both the young and old tend to view self-promotion quite negatively. Instead, positive feelings about the self come from fulfilling tasks associated with being *inter*dependent with others (Markus & Kitayama, 1991; Matsumoto, 2000).

ACTIVITY 7–1

HOW MUCH STIMULATION DO YOU NEED?

The need for stimulation is related to sensation seeking. Circle which of the two choices for each statement best describes you.

1. I prefer to   A. read a book.   B. do something physically exciting.

2. When driving a car, I generally drive   A. at near the speed limit.   B. over the speed limit.

3. I would like to   A. go to a place I know.   B. visit a foreign country.

4. I would describe myself as   A. an introvert.   B. an extrovert.

5. I like to listen to   A. music I know   B. recently released or new music.

6. As a general theme in my life, I favor   A. risk taking.   B. security.

7. I would describe my best friends as A. quirky.   B. conventional.

8. I often watch   A. adventure movies.   B. romantic movies.

9. When I know water is cold, I   A. jump right in.   B. submerge myself slowly.

10. I think I would   A. like hang-gliding.   B. stay anchored on the ground.

SCORING:

For Items 1–5: Answer "A" indicates low need for stimulation or sensation seeking. Answer "B" indicates a high need for thrill seeking and/or avoidance of boredom. Total number of "Bs" _____

For Items 6–10: Answer "A" indicates a need for thrill seeking or avoidance of boredom. Answer "B" indicates low need for stimulation or for sensation seeking. Total number of "As" _____

Now add your scores from both lines here. _____

Remember, this scale was specially designed for this book, interpret the results with caution. A total composite score of 1–3 indicates a low need for sensation; a score of 4–7 indicates a moderate need for sensation seeking, and a score of 8–10 indicates a high need for sensation seeking. Using your score, think about whether you are prone to taking unnecessary risks, whether your life needs a little more spark, or have you found just the right balance between serenity and thrill seeking.

Personal Motivation

GOAL SETTING   A secret of being an active, motivated person is setting personal goals and then striving hard to reach them. In one sense, goal setting comes naturally in that we tend to be future oriented. Most of us are more concerned about today and tomorrow than yesterday. However, it takes some thought and soul-searching to set personal goals or objectives, which is why a lot of people don't bother to do it. Nevertheless, the risk of not doing it can be costly in terms of wasted time and energy.

There are several types of personal goals:

- *Long-range goals* are concerned with the kind of life you want to live with regard to your career, marriage, and lifestyle. It's wise to keep these goals broad and flexible, especially during your college years.
- *Medium-range goals* cover the next five years or so and include the type of education you're seeking or the next step in your career or family life. You have more control over these goals, so you can tell how well you're progressing toward them and modify them accordingly.
- *Short-range goals* apply from the next month or so up to one year from now. You can set these goals quite realistically and should try hard to achieve them.
- *Mini-goals* cover anything from one day to a month. You have a lot of control over these goals and should make them specific.
- *Micro-goals* cover the next 15 minutes to a few hours. Realistically, these are the only goals over which you have direct control.

As you can guess, the shorter the time span covered, the more control you have over your goals. Remember, it is only through achieving the modest, short-range goals that you'll ever attain your medium- and long-range goals. Too often, people make the mistake of setting grandiose or idealized goals (Kayes, 2005) and then quickly become disillusioned because they're making so little progress toward achieving them. It's far better to set *realistic* but desirable goals and then concentrate on achieving your day-to-day goals; which when accomplished, will make it possible to reach your "dream" goals. Keep in mind that once you've achieved a goal, it's important to set new ones!

INTRINSIC AND EXTRINSIC MOTIVATION   Two important motivational sources, related to goal setting and achievement, are intrinsic and extrinsic motivation. **Intrinsic motivation** concerns *active engagement with tasks that people find interesting and that, in turn, promote growth.* In other words, the aim of intrinsically motivated behavior is not to succeed or to reach some other outcome but rather to engage in an activity naturally and spontaneously. Such behaviors are inherently satisfying to pursue in and of themselves. Alternatively, **extrinsic motivation** is *the desire to engage in an activity because it is a means to an end and not because an individual is following his or her inner interests.* Extrinsically motivated behaviors are not based on an individual's need to feel competent and autonomous but on some external reward or outcome, such as money, fame, or prestige (Deci & Ryan, 2008). Importantly, intrinsic motivation has generally been demonstrated to result in increased satisfaction and enhanced well-being. In contrast, external rewards, surveillance, deadlines, and threats undermine intrinsic motivation and weaken creativity and problem solving. Although extrinsic motivation can result in the successful accomplishment of goals, there is an emotional cost, as well-being is reduced and its polar opposite **ill-being**—*psychological distress, such as anxiety and depression*—is increased (Niemiec, Ryan, & Deci, 2009).

Exploration 7.1: Motivation

www.selfdeterminationtheory.org   This website contains information and self-tests on motivation and personality.

UNDERSTANDING EMOTIONS

LEARNING OBJECTIVES

7.7 List the four components of emotions.

7.8 Explain the difference between primary and secondary emotions.

7.9 Identify two ways to determine if a person is lying.

7.10 Describe methods for managing unproductive emotions.

7.11 List the four components of an "I" message.

7.12 Compare the negative emotions of anxiety, anger, and jealousy.

7.13 Discuss which factors are related or unrelated to happiness.

As the previous section revealed, our motivation is affected by many influences, some of them rather obvious but others less so. One of the most important motivational forces is emotion (Roseman, 2008). When we feel happy, we are eager to continue to feel happy. When we are sad, we are motivated to end the pain as quickly as possible. Here is an interesting example, involving the September 11, 2001, terror attacks on New York and Washington, regarding the grip emotions had over us and their relationship to our motivational state. Dr. Tedd Mitchell (2003) said:

> Conflicting emotions set in: the fear of travel—the defiant need to travel; resignation that another attack was inevitable—and a resolve to prevent an attack no matter what: emotional exhaustion from reliving the event over and over in the media—and an inability to turn off the TV... . Fortunately the negative emotions brought on by the tragedy were counter-balanced by a flood of positive energy. (p. 4)

With the understanding that motivation and emotion are intertwined, let us probe deeper into emotions—what they are and how they are expressed verbally and nonverbally.

What Are Emotions?

Emotions—*complex patterns of change that include physiological arousal, subjective feelings, cognitive processes, and behavioral reactions*—occur in response to situations we perceive to be personally significant. Accordingly, emotions have four components:

1. *Physiological arousal.* Emotions engage the nervous and endocrine (i.e., hormones) systems so that when you're emotionally aroused your body is aroused.

2. *Subjective feelings.* Emotions involve the subjective awareness of "feelings," such as joy, sorrow, anger, disgust, anxiety, and fear.

3. *Cognitive processes.* Emotions include cognitive processes such as memories, perceptions, expectations, and interpretations.

4. *Behavioral reactions.* Emotions consist of behavioral reactions. Facial expressions, gestures, and tone of voice serve to communicate our feelings to others. Cries of distress and running for our lives are also adaptive responses that may enhance our chances for survival.

BOX 7–2 Did you know that ...

- Women try to suppress expression of anger more than men do. Men try to suppress expressions of fear more than women do.
- Starting around age 4, children can mask negative feelings with smiles.
- Culture can influence the ability to recognize emotions. For instance, Americans recognize anger, disgust, fear, and sadness better than Japanese.
- People recognize emotional expressions the best when they are displayed by members of their own cultural group. Accuracy decreases when judging members of other cultures.
- The American A-OK sign is considered an obscene gesture in many European countries.

Source: The Sage Handbook of Nonverbal Communication, edited by Valerie L. Manusov and Miles L. Patterson. Sage Publications, Inc., 2006.

General Categories of Emotions

Psychologists have identified two general categories of emotions: primary and secondary. **Primary (basic) emotions** *refer to the initial and direct emotional response to an experience,* such as being frightened at the sound of thunder or the joy of seeing a loved one. Eight primary emotions have been identified: joy, acceptance, fear, surprise, sadness, disgust, anger, and anticipation. These emotions can be experienced more or less intensely to *create* other emotions. Think about disgust and its complexities, when you are intensely disgusted with someone, you may experience loathing; when you are moderately disgusted, you may feel dislike; and when only mildly disgusted, you may experience mild disapproval (Marzillier & Davey, 2004). Thus, many of our feelings may represent a mixture of various primary emotions and thus defy easy labels.

In contrast, **secondary (complex) emotions** are *emotional experiences that are reflective, involve evaluation of the self, and typically follow primary emotions.* For example, after getting angry (a primary emotion) at your sister, you feel shame (a secondary emotion) because of the amount of anger that you expressed. Three common secondary emotions are shame, guilt, and pride. The negative emotions of shame and guilt follow a failure to meet an internalized social standard; but whereas shame occurs due to a loss of social status, guilt is typically evoked after a moral transgression. By comparison, the positive emotion of pride occurs when internalized social standards are met (Tangney, 1999). Moreover, unlike basic emotions, which appear before a child's first birthday, secondary emotions are not present until the second year of life, accompanying the development of the sense of self (Orth, Robins, & Soto, 2010).

Other models of emotions also exist. For example, when people from various cultures are asked to report their experience of different emotions, they seem to place emotions along two dimensions—*pleasant versus unpleasant* and *intensely versus weakly aroused.* Thus, the emotions of contentment, joy, and love would fall into the category of pleasant or positive emotions, whereas anger, disgust, and sadness fall into the category of unpleasant emotions. On the intensity (arousal) scale, rage is more intense than anger, which in turn is more intense than annoyance. On the other hand, love is more intense than liking (Tsai, Knutson, & Fung, 2006).

Specific Emotions

ANXIETY **Anxiety** is *a vague, unpleasant feeling that serves as an emotional alarm signal, warning us of an impending threat or danger.* In ancient times, anxiety may have been evoked by natural disasters, predators, or inter-clan hostilities; its arousing nature may have been adaptive in that it helped humans survive. Today, our worries tend to be related less to survival and more to everyday frustrations, bureaucracies, personal achievements, and other non-life-threatening issues (Zeidner & Matthews, 2005). Unfortunately, we sometimes feel quite anxious when there is little actual danger, for example, when making a speech or going to the dentist. And as a professor once said, "There is little point to test anxiety; I have yet to see a midterm leap off a desk and viciously attack someone."

When a threat is real (not imagined) and can be pinpointed, such as the fear of failing an examination or visiting a professor's office to request a favor, moderate levels of anxiety may motivate us to take the necessary steps to avoid a gaffe. On the other hand, people who are prone to unusually high, chronic, "free-floating" anxiety tend to overreact to stressful situations, frequently making the situations worse. Furthermore, high levels of anxiety can distort our perception and thinking so much that our performance is impaired. Finally, anxiety siphons off energy by keeping us mobilized for action when none is needed. It makes us tense and tired, thereby robbing us of much of the enjoyment of life (Starcevic, 2005).

You are not alone if you suffer from anxiety, as it is quite common. For instance, somewhere between 20 and 50 percent of adults have math- and computer-related anxieties. Many more adults, 60 percent, suffer from social anxiety or general timidity about social situations. And **evaluation apprehension**—*the fear of others' appraisals of us*—is nearly universal across people of different ages, genders, and cultures (Zeidner & Matthews, 2005). Box 7–3 discusses

BOX 7–3   **Focus on Psychology: Test Anxiety**

How Does Test Anxiety Affect You?

Test anxiety is a familiar problem for many students. Ask yourself this: Does test anxiety help you to learn better or does it interfere with your performance? As it turns out, a lot depends on you *and* on your situation. Typically, the relationship between anxiety and test performance takes the form of an inverted U-curve, as depicted in Figure 7–2. That is, at low levels of anxiety, we remain unmotivated and perform well only on easy tasks. Moderate levels of worry tend to enhance performance (Perkins & Corr, 2005), at least up to a point. But at high levels of anxiety, many people become distracted and overwhelmed, thereby performing more poorly on tests. Recognize, too, that people differ widely on the amount of anxiety needed to perform at peak levels (Zeidner & Matthews, 2005). People with relatively little anxiety often do their best only when challenged, such as in a highly competitive situation. Those with characteristically high levels of anxiety tend to do better, at least on difficult tasks, under conditions of less pressure. Which of these two patterns do you most resemble?

Coping with Test Anxiety

So, how do you cope with test anxiety? First, adaptive coping in exam situations involves a flexible use of multiple coping strategies. In other words, when one strategy does not work, the individual needs to be able to turn to another. Here are a few anxiety-reducing strategies from which to choose. When you find yourself getting anxious during a test, you can employ anxiety-reducing statements ("I know I can do it" and "I'll take one question at a time and do my best on each question"), as they can ease tensions. Additionally, try to avoid negative and self-defeating thoughts (e.g., "I'm going to fail this test" or "All of these questions are too hard"), as they distract you from the primary task of exam taking (Hopko, Crittendon, Grant, & Wilson, 2005). Another effective method for coping with test anxiety is to study hard and learn well (Beilock, Kulp, Holt, & Carr, 2004)—a strategy that increases confidence and thus decreases test anxiety. Helpful study techniques are reviewed in the "How to Study" section (PQ4R) at the beginning of this book.

Second, effective coping strategies should match both the context and the individual. This means that the individual needs to be comfortable with the strategy and also that the strategy should be appropriate to the level of challenge of the examination. Happily, most students cope effectively because they utilize active coping, in which they plan study time and techniques, suppress competing activities (such as socializing with friends), and reframe the stressful event positively (e.g., "A good grade means a higher GPA and perhaps a better job when I graduate") (Macklem, 2008).

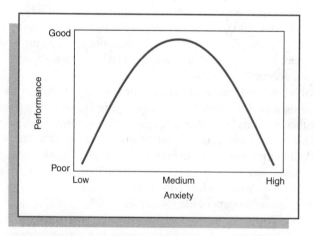

FIGURE 7–2   **The relationship between anxiety and performance.**

a form of evaluation apprehension common on college campuses: test anxiety. You'll also find some helpful hints on coping with it.

ANGER   A basketball coach yells profanities at the referee after a controversial call. A teenage girl screams "I hate you" at her mother who won't let her stay out as late as her friends' parents allow. A red-faced worker slams his fist on the table to make his point during a dispute with his boss. All these people are venting **anger**—*feelings of displeasure or resentment over (perceived) mistreatment.* For decades, psychologists have been investigating whether holding anger in or *venting anger out*—**catharsis**—is the best way to deal with this type of negative emotion. Many of you have grown up with the idea that when you're angry, it's healthy to "get it off your chest" or "let it all hang out." Holding anger in, goes the popular notion, leads to all kinds of problems—high blood pressure, increased risk of heart attacks, depression, and suicide. On the other hand, we have all seen people blowing off steam and who afterward seemed pleased or relieved. So where does the truth lie?

Deciding whether venting anger is healthful or hurtful actually depends on *how* you vent your anger. More often than not, venting anger through action (e.g., hitting a pillow; playing a violent video game) or words (i.e., yelling and screaming) only results in more anger and aggression (Anderson & Bushman, 2002). On the other hand, venting anger through expressive writing can actually help lower blood pressure (McGuire, Greenberg, & Gevirtz, 2005). At times, doing nothing or displacing anger onto a more productive project (e.g., drawing) may be an effective way to manage anger. There is some truth to the notion that people who unduly suppress or hold in their high levels of anger are more prone to high blood pressure, intensification of pain, and heart attacks. Whether held in or exploded, hostility and anger are not beneficial to us. We therefore need to learn to address them better (Burns et al., 2012; Potter-Efron, 2005). Box 7–4 further suggests that school bullies are often depressed and angry and, thus, turn their anger on their victims.

Exploration 7.2: Bullying

www.StopBullying.gov   This websites provides information from various government agencies on how children, parents, educators, and others in the community can prevent or stop bullying.

Anger issues often develop during childhood, as such it's important to understand how to prevent them. Here are some suggestions. First, certain child-rearing practices can go a long way toward preventing inappropriate forms of anger expression. Developmentally appropriate strategies for encouraging children to responsibly handle their anger include modeling by parents of appropriate anger management, avoiding shaming a child's anger, and increasing the child's understanding of anger as well as the sense of control over anger-arousing events (Landy, 2009; Roelofs, Meesters, Ter Huurne, Bamelis, & Muris, 2006). Eliminating exposure to aggressive models also helps (Kirsh, 2012). Parents might want to monitor their child's consumption of media violence. There is much evidence that watching televised violence, playing violent video games, and the like, increases aggressive feelings, aggressive thoughts, aggressive behaviors, and it desensitizes (i.e., violence bothers us less and less) us to its effects (Huesmann, 2007). Parents also need to be cautious about physically punishing their children, especially when the child has a temper tantrum or has acted aggressively toward another. Such parents are modeling the very behavior they are trying to eliminate in their children.

From childhood through adulthood, increasing social support and providing opportunities to discuss negative emotions often improves anger management (Dahlen & Martin, 2005). Moreover, training in social skills is another option. If we don't know how to respond appropriately to others, we sometimes lose our tempers or they lose theirs. Lessons in social skills can also help individuals find alternative solutions to provocations. Such training can be effective, even after a few hours (Martsch, 2005). For other individuals, therapy might be the only answer.

BOX 7–4	Focus on Relationships: Bullying

Bullying is *repeated, unprovoked, harmful actions by one person (or persons) against another.* The *bullying* acts can be physical (e.g., punching or kicking) or psychological (e.g., name-calling or taunting) and can occur in person or *via the Internet,* more commonly referred to as **cyber-bullying** (Stassen Berger, 2007). The following are just a few of the many ways that people can be aggressed against online: receiving frequent negative comments on their profile pages, experiencing taunts or threats, being victims of malicious gossip, having embarrassing pictures or videos posted without consent, and undergoing exclusion (e.g., blocking someone from a buddy list) (Vandebosch & Van Cleemput, 2009; Werner, Bumpus, & Rock, 2010).

Bullying Statistics.   Across the globe, bullying is a common phenomenon of childhood and adolescence. For instance, nearly 50 percent of Chilean and Kenyan 12- to 18-year olds report being bullied. In China, close to 30 percent of adolescents are bullied, and in Ireland around 20 percent of teens experience bullying (Fleming & Jacobsen, 2010; McGuckin, Cummins, & Lewis, 2009). Bullying may be rampant in U.S. schools (Flynt & Morton, 2004). One out of every five children reports being a bully while 25 to 50 percent of children report being the victim of bullying (Flynt & Morton, 2004). Moreover, 20 percent of children and adolescents have been cyber-bullied (Werner et al., 2010). Interestingly, cyber-bullying appears to be a pernicious gift that keeps on giving in that those who are victims of cyber-bullying are themselves 16 times more likely to engage in the same negative practice.

Motives for Bullying.   Bullies have different motives for picking on other children. Some children may bully because they have too high or too low self-esteem (Bullock, 2002). Other children have learned from their parents to hit back or become more aggressive when their self-esteem is threatened. Other bullies taunt and bully because they, themselves, have been bullied. And some studies show that bullies may be depressed. For these children, especially for boys, the most acceptable way to express their misery is to act macho rather than sad (Elias, 1999). Because schools themselves may inspire a "culture of sameness," children and adolescents who are different and do not fit in are often bullied. Youth are bullied because of their race, ethnicity, sexual orientation, because they dress differently, are weaker, smaller, disabled, or more passive (Bullock, 2002). Moreover, the anonymity of the Internet, the absence of contextual cues typically available during offline social interactions (e.g., facial expression, tone of voice), the ability to successfully aggress against individuals who are physically intimidating, and the potential to challenge those high in traditional social power (e.g., popularity) make cyber-bullying appealing to many (Werner et al., 2010).

Gender and Bullying.   Although boys are stereotyped as bullies, girls tend to bully just as much. However, the type of bullying used appears to vary by gender (Hoffman, 2002). Girls are more likely to use gossiping, taunting, glaring, and bad-mouthing (i.e., relational bullying), whereas boys are more likely to use physical forms of aggression (i.e., direct bullying) (James & Owens, 2005; Woods & White, 2005). Interestingly, both males and females tend to be crueler in their bullying to those of the same sex than they are to those of the opposite sex (Ladd, 2005).

The Victims of Bullying.   Victims of bullying may go largely unnoticed by teachers and parents, in part because teasing in childhood is sometimes considered "normal" (Bullock, 2002). However, bullying has serious psychological and social consequences (Nishina, Juvonen, & Witkow, 2005). Depression, low self-esteem, social isolation, behavior problems, and at times suicide are some of the varied effects of bullying (Bauman, 2011; Stassen Berger, 2007). Nevertheless, there are steps that parents and teachers can take to help victims of bullying (Bauman, 2011). The first is to recognize signs of victimization. If a child is experiencing the following, suspect bullying:

- Behavioral changes (e.g., more aggressive or more withdrawn)
- Frequent crying or depression
- Lower self-esteem
- Unexplained injuries
- Academic difficulties not manifested earlier
- Unexplained health problems such as stomach pains or fatigue
- Fear of school or desire to avoid school

After both teachers and parents observe the symptoms, they should talk in private to the children whom they suspect are victims. Second, many schools have instituted bullying prevention programs. Some of these programs include using a peer mediator (someone empowered to intervene in the bullying) or a mentor who can help protect the victim (such as an adult or an older student). Finally, children can be taught not to tolerate bullying but rather to report it to parents, teachers, or other adults. In fact, websites, such as ReportABully.com, are now available for children to report the names of those who have bullied them anonymously (or if they choose they can identify themselves).

Therapy should convey the sense that anger is destructive and that better communication and problem-solving skills, and increased empathy for the target of the anger all reduce anger (DiGuiseppe & Tafrate, 2003).

JEALOUSY   Essentially, **jealousy** is *a complex emotion that occurs when we fear losing a close relationship with another person or have lost it already.* Jealousy is characterized by fear of loss, distrust, anxiety, and anger (Parrott & Smith, 1993). Jealousy is especially apt to occur in romantic and sexual relationships, so that it is popularly known as romantic jealousy. Jealousy can be contrasted with **envy,** *which is distinguished by feelings of inferiority, longing, resentment, and disapproval.* Some situations likely to trigger romantic jealousy are: (1) the person you like goes out with someone else; (2) someone gets closer to a person to whom you are attracted; (3) your lover or spouse tells you how sexy a former boyfriend/girlfriend was; (4) your lover or spouse visits a person he or she used to go out with; (5) you find that your partner is having an affair; and (6) you are the second spouse of your mate and he or she has to pay support to the first spouse.

Of note, jealousy in men and women is activated by different types of situations. Men are more likely to get jealous when their significant other is talking to a potential suitor that is physically imposing. In contrast, women tend to get jealous the most when their partners are interacting with physically attractive or socially powerful rivals (Buunk, Solano, Zurriaga, & González, 2011). Moreover, men are concerned with sexual infidelity while women are upset over emotional betrayals (Fernandez, Vera-Villarroel, Sierra, & Zubeidat, 2007; Schützwohl, 2006). Some people are especially prone to jealousy, such as individuals with low self-esteem, high levels of anxiety, a negative view toward the world, low levels of life satisfaction, little control over their lives, low threshold of emotional arousal, and a greater sensitivity to threatening stimuli in social environments (Guerrero & Andersen, 1998). Those with **pathological (obsessional) jealousy** possess *repeated, and unfounded, suspicion of a partner's fidelity.* These suspicions modify thoughts, feelings, and behaviors. For example, a pathologically jealous person obsessively checks the whereabouts of the object of their affection, argues often with that person about their interactions with others, and makes groundless accusations against that person (Marazziti et al., 2005). Box 7–5 discusses strategies for dealing with jealousy that are predictive of domestic violence.

BOX 7–5	Focus on Relationships: Jealousy and Domestic Violence

There are many different strategies for dealing with jealousy, some of which are predictive of domestic violence. One is *direct guarding,* where the jealous person drops in unexpectedly to see what his significant other is doing. Another is what the researchers call *negative inducement,* as in threatening a romantic partner who has shown attention to another. A third method used to guard against rivals is through *public signals of possession,* such as holding a significant other's hand when potential suitors are around. Yet another approach is *positive inducement,* where help is given to the significant other when distressed. Not surprisingly, the first three tactics are much better predictors of the use of violence toward romantic partners to "keep them in line" than was the last, more positive approach. However, the strongest predictor of all for violence is emotional manipulation that includes pleading that they cannot live without their partner or that they would die if their significant other left. Excessive direct guarding and monopolization of time also predicts violence toward significant others (Shackelford, Goetz, Buss, Euler, & Hoier, 2005).

When jealousy is present, communication between partners varies widely, from face-to-face interactions to avoidance to violence. Some methods of coping with jealousy are productive, such as using apologies, increasing affection, and using reassurances; others are less productive, such as making up excuses, being manipulative or vengeful, and arguing. What perhaps is most important is that the *initial* expression of jealousy strongly influences the trajectory of the rest of the cycle. In other words, positive communications at the onset (such as "I'm sorry I made you feel jealous; I want to reassure you that I love you very much") result in the most positive responses from partners. As expected, initial negative communications (such as "You're just insecure") disintegrate into further negative interactions. Regardless of the strategy used, one thing is for certain, in close relationships jealousy can be an unnecessary and potentially destructive emotion (Wigman, Graham-Kevan, & Archer, 2008).

HAPPINESS **Happiness,** or as psychologists refer to it, **subjective well-being (SWB),** *includes a preponderance of positive thoughts and feelings about one's life.* People high in SWB have a global sense that work, marriage, and other life domains are satisfactory. They experience and report pleasant rather than anxious, angry, or depressive emotions. Happy people are less self-focused, less hostile, and less vulnerable to disease. They are more loving, forgiving, trusting, energetic, decisive, creative, helpful, and sociable than unhappy people (Lyubomirsky, Sheldon, & Schkade, 2005). Study after study shows that happy people have high self-esteem, a sense of personal control and optimism (Cohn, Fredrickson, Brown, Mikels, & Conway, 2009; Diener & Seligman, 2002). In addition, when working or at play, happy people often lose a sense of time and self because they typically find the task at hand both challenging and absorbing (Carr, 2011).

Happiness does not discriminate between genders: Across cultures, both men and women have equal opportunities to find happiness (Michalos, 1991). However, the sources of happiness for each gender often differ, with men's SWB being predicted by self-esteem, and women's happiness resulting from both self-esteem and relationship harmony (Reid, 2004). Aging does not necessarily involve a decline in happiness either (Westerhof & Barrett, 2005). Although there is also only a modest association between wealth and happiness (Fischer, 2008), as Myers and Diener (1995) persuasively state, "[wealth's] absence can breed misery, yet its presence is no guarantee of happiness" (p. 13).

Table 7–1 lists the average level of reported happiness (on a scale of one to ten) and the average number of "happy life years" (which combines life expectancy and time spent happy) across the globe. Do any of the results surprise you?

Across a variety of different cultures, happy people outnumber unhappy people (Shmotkin, 2005). Perhaps this occurs because one of the overarching principles of happiness is a sense of "owning" one's goals, that is, pursuing one's life goals because of an authentic desire to do so. And members of both individualistic and collective cultures experience well-being when they pursue self-chosen goals, although those goals typically differ. In individualistic culture a self-selected goal may be "a better life for myself," while in a collective society a self-selected goal may be "to fit in better." Nonetheless, when an individual's goals is self-chosen, the individual reports higher levels of happiness and well-being than when goals are not self-selected (Sheldon et al., 2004). Everyone, then, has the possibility for happiness. Remember, though being happy has many benefits, the pursuit of happiness, in and of itself, can lead to loneliness and disappointment (Mauss, Tamir, Anderson, & Savino, 2011). Best to let happiness find you (through the pursuit of self-chosen goals), rather than go searching for it.

Exploration 7.3: Happiness

www.authentichappiness.sas.upenn.edu   Dr. Martin Seligman's website for positive psychology. The site contains questionnaires, newsletter articles, and more.

Table 7–1	Happiness throughout the World	
Country	Average Happiness (Scale: 1 to 10)	Happy Life Years (Scale in years: 1 to 100)
Angola	4.3	18
Australia	7.7	63
Canada	7.8	62
China	6.3	46
Costa Rica	8.5	67
Denmark	8.3	65
Guatemala	7.2	50
Haiti	3.9	23
Japan	6.4	54
Mexico	7.9	60
Russia	5.5	36
South Korea	6.0	47
United Kingdom	7.1	56
United States	7.4	58
Zimbabwe	3.0	13

Source: Data compiled from World Database of Happiness website, 2012.

Expressing Emotions

Emotions not only motivate us to do certain things and to approach or avoid particular situations, they also offer a primary means of communicating with others. However, we often assume it is not always safe to share our intimate feelings, even when casually greeting a good friend. How often has someone asked, "Hey, how ya doin'?" and you answered "Great" when you really were feeling glum or overwhelmed by too much to do? Sharing our feelings is risky and makes us vulnerable to the judgments of others. Some people are so afraid of their inner feelings that they're unable to experience, much less express, their deeper emotions, such as in times of great joy or profound sorrow. Others more in touch with their emotions disclose their feelings freely, whether the emotion be anger or love. Whichever way you're inclined, the most important thing is to find that balance of expression and control of feelings with which you and those around you are most comfortable.

Emotional balance is all the more difficult because of some of the individual differences in emotional expressiveness. Women, for example, report sadder responses to negative personal events than do men (Hess et al., 2000). However, women also smile more than men (LaFrance, Hecht, & Paluck, 2003). Moreover, across a wide variety of cultures, men more frequently report power*ful* emotions (e.g., anger, contempt, disgust) while women are more likely to report power*less* feelings (e.g., sadness, fear) (Safdar et al., 2009). Scientists have yet to tease out whether such differences are learned or biological. Other studies indicate that *culture can influence the expressions of emotion* (known as **cultural display rules**). For instance, those from collectivist

Joy is a primary emotion, according to psychologists.

cultures tend to express positive emotions (e.g., happiness) to a lesser extent than those from individualistic cultures. However, those from collectivist cultures are also more likely to mask negative emotions with smiles when they are with others, but not when they are alone (Safdar et al., 2009; Tsai et al., 2006).

Recognizing Emotions

SELF-RECOGNITION OF EMOTION In terms of understanding and recognizing our *own* emotional states, men more so than women ruminate about upsetting events and report more inhibition of hostile feelings (McConatha, Lightner, & Deaner, 1994). Across adulthood, whereas older persons think more about upsetting events than their younger counterparts, they express emotions less frequently than younger individuals. Moreover, contrary to stereotypes, the elderly are still highly capable of experiencing profoundly positive emotions (Carstensen & Charles, 1998).

FACIAL AND BODY EXPRESSIONS The ability to monitor and correctly identify facial expression is a key component of social relationships (Halberstadt, 2003). For instance, the recognition of sadness may evoke comforting behavior and the identification of fear may elicit protection. Conversely, the misidentification of anger may increase the likelihood of a social interaction becoming aggressive. Interestingly, *positive emotions are more quickly identified than* *negative emotions*, a phenomenon known as the **happy-face advantage** (Leppänen, Tenhunen, & Hietanen, 2003). It may be that the distinctiveness of the visual features of happy faces and the relative indistinctness of negative facial expressions accounts for this finding. For years, psychologists have regarded faces as the key to emotional expression (Coulson, 2004). There is little doubt that the face is important, but body postures, vocal changes (e.g., pitch modulation and speed of speech), and hand gestures also signal us as to what others are actually feeling (Azar, 2000; Pell, 2005). Research indicates that deciphering these and other nonverbal information is complicated. For instance, body posture greatly helps us decode anger and sadness but helps little in gauging others' level of disgust (App, McIntosh, Reed, & Hertenstein, 2011).

ISSUES OF DIVERSITY In comparison to men, women decode emotions more accurately (Hoffmann, Kessler, Eppel, Rukavina, & Traue, 2010). Likewise, everyone is a better decoder of emotions expressed by members of their *own* culture, relative to those displayed by people of a different one (Beaupré & Hess, 2005). Perhaps such differences occur because same-race faces and other-race faces activate different parts of the brain (Iidaka, Nogawa, Kansaku, & Sadato, 2008). Moreover, race appears to influence emotion recognition in others. For example, Whites tend to recognize happy faces faster than angry faces, but only if the expressions are made by Whites. In contrast, when the same expressions are displayed by African-Americans, angry faces are recognized faster than happy expressions (Hugenberg, 2005). Additionally, Whites high in prejudice are more likely to categorize racially ambiguous (i.e., biracial) faces as African-American when angry facial expressions are being posed, but not happy ones (Hugenberg & Bodenhausen, 2003).

DETECTING DECEIT Another factor that makes recognition and interpretation of expressed emotions difficult is that some individuals purposely try to deceive us. Identifying deception in others is a difficult task, with the ability to accurately judge whether someone is lying hovering around 50 percent (Bond & DePaulo, 2008). So, how can we detect their dishonesty? One helpful aid is **microexpressions,** or *fleeting facial expressions that last only a fraction of a second* (Ekman, 1985). Microexpressions may be momentary, but they are still detectable by the astute observer (Dimberg, Thunberg, & Elmehed, 2000). Many people try hard to control their outward facial expressions because they believe we think the face is the primary clue to their secrets. Deceivers, however, may blink more or smile more broadly in an effort to mislead and thus can be exposed. In addition, yet another individual hoping to deceive you may express one emotion followed quickly by another, which can indicate that the person is lying (Baron & Byrne, 1997; Porter & ten Brinke, 2008).

Some individuals are so good at monitoring and controlling their faces that their true feelings are difficult to detect. Watching for **body leakage,** *where body postures rather than the face leak the truth,* can be just as revealing of emotional deceit. While individuals are concentrating on monitoring their words and their facial expressions, they attend less to their bodies, which consequently betray their true feelings (Vrij, Granhag, & Porter, 2010). For example, despite the fact that a smile is being expressed, crossing arms with clenched fists is an indicator that beneath their seemingly happy exterior, anger and hostility are present.

Managing Emotions

Because emotions are related to psychological adjustment, it is desirable to manage our feelings well. Learning to express feelings effectively involves a suitable balance between spontaneous expression and deliberate, rational emotional self-regulation. **Emotional self-regulation** refers to *the process by which one inhibits or moderates one's emotional responses in order to remain engaged in thoughtful interaction.* Areas of emotional management needing improvement vary somewhat from one person to another. Some people who are overly emotional and impulsive may blurt out their feelings without much thought; they need to

> ### BOX 7–6 Focus on Relationships: Emotional Intelligence
>
> **Emotional intelligence (EI)** *is the ability to regulate one's own emotions and to be empathic for others' emotions.* Specifically, emotional intelligence is comprised of four abilities, the ability: (1) to detect and decipher emotions in the self or others; (2) to harness emotions to facilitate various cognitive activities such as problem solving; (3) to comprehend emotion language such as slight variations between emotions (e.g., happy versus ecstatic); and (4) to regulate one's own and others' emotions. People with high EI engage in better-quality interactions with their friends and coworkers, as well as possessing better impression management skills (Lopes et al., 2004). Moreover, those high in EI advance their careers even faster than people with high levels of general intelligence (Schutte et al., 2001), and they show better levels of performance under stress than those low in EI (Lyons & Schneider, 2005).

develop better self-control. On the other hand, those who keep their emotions under tight control may need to loosen up to become more aware of their feelings and more comfortable expressing them appropriately to others. Box 7–6 discuses a characteristic of human growth and adaptation that is just as important as (if not more than) cognitive intelligence, namely emotional intelligence.

Exploration 7.4: Emotional Intelligence

www.helpself.com/iq-test.htm Test your emotional IQ at this site. A self-help site with lots of useful information in a variety of areas, including emotional intelligence.

We can become more adept and practiced at managing our emotions by sharing our everyday feelings more readily with family and friends we *trust* and those who can provide *productive* feedback. As you become accustomed to sharing your emotions, you'll get more in touch with your feelings. Then, when you experience an intense emotion, like rage or extreme disgust, you should find it easier to recognize your feelings and be more willing to express them *in appropriate and modulated ways*. That is, engage in emotional self-regulation. When you express your feelings openly *and* in a constructive manner, it helps to clear the air and facilitate communication. Sharing your feelings with a willing person may also help you shed light on your emotions, especially when several come flooding forward at the same time.

COMMUNICATING INTENSE EMOTIONS A technique that is particularly useful for expressing intense emotions, especially negative ones, is the use of an **"I" message** (Gordon & Sands, 1984). Essentially, this message *consists of saying what you honestly feel in a way that encourages others to listen and cooperate.* "I" messages are especially helpful in expressing your feelings about someone whose behavior has become a problem for you. An "I" message consists of four stages:

- First, *describe the other person's objectionable behavior* in specific but nonjudgmental terms. For instance, you might use the phrase "when you fail to return my book on time" instead of "you're irresponsible." Avoid using fuzzy and accusatory responses or guessing the person's motives. Such communication only intensifies the person's resistance to changing the behavior.
- Second, *point out the specific ways in which that person's behavior affects you.* In most instances, people are not deliberately trying to make life miserable for you; they simply

| Table 7–2 | Examples of "I" Messages | | |

Nonjudgmental Description of Person's Behavior	Concrete Effects on Me	My Feelings About It	What I'd Prefer the Person to Do
1. If you don't complete what you promised to do	then I have to do it in addition to my other tasks	and I feel annoyed	I wish you would do what you've promised
2. Each time you criticize my work without telling me what I'm doing wrong	I don't know how to improve it	and I feel frustrated and resentful	Tell me what I'm doing wrong so I can correct what I'm doing wrong
3. When you change your mind at the last minute	it's too late to make other plans	and I feel angry and disappointed	Give me more advance notice when you think things may not work out

aren't aware of the consequences of their actions. Once a person becomes more aware of how the behavior has become a problem for you, they may be willing to modify it.

- Third, *tell the person how you feel about the behavior in a way that "owns" your emotions.* To do this, you should generally start your sentences with the pronoun *I.* Say "I feel hurt" instead of "you hurt me." Avoid projecting your emotions onto the other person.
- Finally, *tell the person what you want done to correct the situation.* For example, if you object to the casual way telephone messages are left for you, you might say something like this: "I don't have the information I need and I feel frustrated when you don't write down my telephone messages. I'd appreciate your writing down my telephone messages."

Initially, "I" messages may seem a bit contrived or stiff. But as you become more experienced in using them you'll feel more comfortable expressing your feelings in this way. Table 7–2 provides more tips on "I" messages.

Emotions and Personal Growth

Emotions are a kind of barometer of our inner world, giving us an intuitive knowledge about ourselves and our involvement with others at the moment. Intense emotions tell us our lives are strongly affected by some person or event and prompt us to act accordingly. On the other hand, when we feel little or no emotion in a given situation, chances are our needs, goals, or values are not affected; that is, we're not "emotionally involved." Perhaps that's why we're constantly asking each other, "How do you feel about this?" or "What's your reaction to that?" Unfortunately, it's not always easy to say, is it? A major reason is that we often have trouble identifying our feelings at the moment, and even more finding the right words to express them (Solomon, 2005). Then, too, our emotions are in a state of constant flux or change so that we may feel pleased one moment and annoyed the next.

Although some theories of emotion emphasize physiological factors such as the central nervous system and the endocrine system, many contemporary theories of emotion now emphasize the role of cognitive factors (Beitel, Ferrer, & Cecero, 2005). An experience arouses our emotions mostly when the individual *appraises the stimuli as having personal significance.* In this view, an emotional experience cannot be understood as something that happens solely in the person or in the brain but more in our relationship to the environment. The particular emotion that is felt depends largely on how we label a given situation, that is, on how we interpret the personal meaning it has for us (Schachter & Singer, 1962). A major implication of the cognitive view of emotions is that each of us has more potential control over our feelings than what was once popularly believed. Whenever we feel angry, jealous, or depressed, we are not simply at the mercy of our momentary feelings (Richards, 2004). Nor should we take our "gut" reactions as infallible, as important as these may be. Instead, it's better to realize that our momentary feelings are partly the result of the way we perceive and respond to an event. Particularly for negative events, it is also important to know that most people fail to understand just how well and how quickly they can cope with them (Wilson & Gilbert, 2005).

Another implication of the cognitive perspective is that interpretation of personal emotions may well underpin psychological adjustment (Bonanno, Papa, Lalande, K., Westphal, M., & Coifman, 2004). Perhaps anxiety over emotional expression creates problems for us, or perhaps we consistently misinterpret our own and others' emotional reactions. As Plutchik states, "Most of us often censor our own thoughts and feelings, and we have learned to be cautious about accepting other people's comments about their feelings" (2001, p. 344). Alternatively, perhaps the ability to use a large repertoire of emotions and call on each when *appropriate* may be the key to healthy adjustment (Bonanno et al., 2004).

Chapter Summary

UNDERSTANDING MOTIVATION

7.1   Explain motivation.

Motivation energizes and directs our efforts toward a meaningful goal.

7.2   Describe Maslow's hierarchy of needs.

At the bottom of the Maslow's hierarchy are basic needs such as the need for food and the need for safety or security. The middle but narrower level involves the need for belonging or the need to fit in and be accepted. At the top levels are self-esteem needs and self-actualizing tendencies, respectively. Self-esteem needs involve the need to feel a sense of self-worth and achievement, whereas self-actualization includes a sense of autonomy and uniqueness. These higher-level needs cannot be met if the lower-level needs are unfulfilled.

7.3   Discuss the difference between intrinsic and extrinsic motivation.

Intrinsic motivation refers to the pursuit of tasks that people find interesting in and of themselves. In contrast, extrinsic motivation is the desire to engage in an activity because of the outcomes associated with it, such as money, prestige, or power.

7.4   List several different ways in which sensation-seeking behavior is manifested.

Sensation seeking refers to our tendency to seek out stimulating and novel experiences, such as going on roller coasters, mountain climbing, driving too fast, and watching horror movies.

7.5   Compare achievement motivation in individualistic and collectivist societies.

Achievement motivation is the desire to accomplish or master something difficult or challenging. In individualistic societies, achievement motivation is derived from personal accomplishment. In collective societies, achievement motivation results from fulfilling tasks associated with being interdependent with others.

7.6   Discuss the importance of goals in personal motivation.

Motivated people set personal goals and then strive to achieve them. There are several types of personal goals: long-range goals, medium-range goals, short-range goals, mini-goals, and micro-goals. You must achieve modest, short-range goals before you can accomplish medium-and long-range goals. Once you've achieved a goal, it's important to set new ones.

UNDERSTANDING EMOTIONS

7.7   List the four components of emotions.

Physiological arousal, subjective feelings, cognitive processes, and behavioral reactions comprise the four components of emotion.

7.8 Explain the difference between primary and secondary emotions.

Primary emotions, such as joy, acceptance, fear, surprise, sadness, disgust, anger, and anticipation, refer to the initial and direct emotional response to an experience. Secondary emotions, such as shame, guilt, and pride, are reflective and involve evaluation of the self.

7.9 Identify two ways to determine if a person is lying.

People frequently try to deceive those around them. To help figure out if someone is lying to you, pay attention to microexpressions and body leakage.

7.10 Describe methods for managing unproductive emotions.

We can learn healthy methods for managing our emotions so that we express them at socially appropriate times and in acceptable intensities and ways. One good method for attaining emotional self-regulation is to raise children to recognize their anger and to manage it when they are young. For adults, sharing emotions and getting in touch with feelings can help control negative emotional expressions.

7.11 List the four components of an "I" message.

The four components of the "I" messages are: (1) describing the other person's objectionable behavior in specific but nonjudgmental terms; (2) pointing out the specific ways in which that person's behavior affects you; (3) telling the person how you feel about the behavior in a way that "owns" your emotions; and (4) telling the person what you want done to correct the situation.

7.12 Compare the negative emotions of anxiety, anger, and jealousy.

Anxiety serves as a useful alarm that warns us of threat. Most causes for anxiety in modern life are less related to survival and more related to dealing with everyday frustrations. Anger refers to feelings of displeasure or resentment over (perceived) mistreatment. Learning to respond in nonhostile ways is therefore important to mental and physical health. Jealousy, which is comprised of loss, distrust, anxiety, and anger, is a complex emotion which occurs when we fear losing a relationship. Many individuals need to learn to cope with jealousy in active and constructive ways where they express their intention of improving the relationships. Extreme forms of jealousy and manipulative strategies can sometimes result in violence against romantic partners.

7.13 Discuss which factors are related or unrelated to happiness.

Happiness (or subjective well-being) refers to a preponderance of positive thoughts and feelings. Happiness is available to everyone regardless of sex, race, or income level. Happy people are less hostile, less vulnerable to disease, and more forgiving, trusting, and energetic than unhappy people. The pursuit of self-chosen goals results in happiness, whereas the pursuit of happiness, in and of itself, often leads to loneliness and disappointment.

Self-Test

1. According to Maslow, _____ needs are usually met first and _____ are typically met last.
   a. self-actualization; physiological
   b. love and belongingness; safety
   c. safety; esteem
   d. physiological; self-actualization
2. Each year, millions of people attempt to find their "soul mates" through Internet dating sights. Under Maslow's hierarchy of needs, each of these people is attempting to fulfill their _____ needs.
   a. belongingness and love
   b. safety
   c. esteem
   d. self-actualization
3. Growing up, Jeff worked as a waiter in a very posh country club. On his last day of work, Jeff told himself that someday he was going to return to this country club as a member. So, he studied hard and eventually became a very well-paid plastic surgeon. Jeff's desire to become a doctor was motivated by:
   a. extrinsic motivation
   b. intrinsic motivation
   c. safety needs
   d. self-actualization
4. Sriram loved riding roller coasters. He especially loved the speed, intense g-forces, and upside down twisty turns. Sriram probably had a very well developed _____ motive.
   a. need for achievement
   b. fear of failure
   c. psychosocial
   d. sensation seeking
5. As the mid-afternoon sunlight streamed through the dining room window, the vast amount of dog hair lying on the floor (which was difficult to see in normal light) became all too visible. Mai Li thought to herself, "That's it! I can't take it

anymore, I'm vacuuming before dinner." What type of motivation goal will help Mai Li clean the dirty floor.
a. micro-goal
b. mini-goal
c. short-range goal
d. medium-range goal

6. _____ refer to the fact that culture can influence the expression of emotion.
a. secondary emotions
b. primary emotions
c. cultural display rules
d. the happy-face advantage

7. After failing a test, Julia was angry at her professor for asking such detailed questions. "It's not fair," she thought. Later that night, as she reflected on how much she had actually studied for the exam, she came to the conclusion that maybe reviewing the material for 1 hour, while watching CSI, and texting, might not have been a good way to study. Soon after, she felt guilty, and vowed to do better on the next exam. Julia's feelings of guilt represent:
a. a basic emotion
b. a secondary emotion
c. emotional self-regulation
d. an "I" message

8. Steve was mad. One of his roommates had eaten his last taquito. Steve tried to "play it cool" around his roommates in order to figure out who the culprit was. Unfortunately, Steve's crossed arms and stiff body alerted his roommates to his true emotions. This example illustrates that Steve experienced:
a. achievement motivation
b. an "I" message
c. a secondary emotion
d. body leakage

9. Right before his big in-class presentation, Paul's girlfriend broke up with him via text message. In order to maintain his composure, Paul suppressed his hurt feelings. Paul behavior is an example of:
a. emotional self-regulation
b. body leakage
c. self-actualization
d. subjective well-being

10. Which of the following is a component of an "I" message?
a. saying exactly how you feel, even if it comes across as judgmental
b. talking about the other person's behavior in general terms, avoiding specifics
c. making it clear that the other person is causing you emotional distress
d. telling the person what you want done to correct the situation

Exercises

1. *Seeking new experiences.* Sometimes the stimulation from new experiences helps to revitalize your motivation and zest for life. You might try several of the following suggestions: Taste a food you've never tried. Take up a new sport or hobby. Invite someone out socially you would like to know better. Attend a workshop or a special course you're interested in. Perhaps you can add other ideas. Try several of these suggestions, and write about your reactions in a page or so. Would you agree that variety is the spice of life?

2. *Assess your achievement motivation.* Look at your achievement motivation in a specific area of your life—a class you're taking, your motivation in school as a whole, your job, or progress toward your career goals. Then answer the following questions:
   • How strongly do you want to succeed?
   • Do you believe your ability is crucial, or is success mostly a matter of luck?
   • How much do you enjoy what you're doing?
   • Do you have the skills needed to succeed? If not, what are you doing about this problem?
   Honest responses to such questions may help you to understand the strength of your achievement motivation and what's needed to increase it.

3. *Share your everyday feelings.* Do you share your feelings as readily as you'd like? If not, you might try this exercise. A good way to begin sharing your feelings is to share some of the safe, everyday feelings. For example, whenever you're especially pleased by something another person has done for you, tell this person how you feel about it. The practice of sharing these safe feelings may help you to become more aware of and comfortable in sharing your deeper feelings.

4. *Practice sending "I" messages.* Think of several situations in which someone else's behavior has become a problem for you. Then write out the appropriate "I" messages under the respective four headings, as explained and illustrated in this chapter. If you feel comfortable doing so, you might try expressing some of these "I" messages in person.

5. *Happiness.* Are you generally a happy person? Why did you come to the answer you did? If yes, what can you do to maintain your current level of well-being? If not, can you think of ways you can improve your general level of happiness?

Chapter Eight

Making and Keeping Friends

*A*fter being the first person in her family to graduate from college, Anita decided to pursue a master's degree. Two years later, she found herself in the position of being a new professor at Ramona Community College. When Anita arrived, Gale was already a professor there. The two women seemingly had nothing in common. Gale was in her 40s, strongly Republican, rather conservative, and mildly spiritual. Anita, on the other hand, was in her late 20s, devoutly religious, and a solid Democrat. Their childhood experiences were also very different. Gale grew up in a middle-class family in Texas, where her father was a journalist and her mother an engineer. Anita, who grew up in Minnesota, had a much more difficult childhood. Anita's father left home when she was very young and her mother needed to work two jobs in order to make ends meet. She had the basic necessities of life, but not much more. Because they were the only two women in the department, Gale decided to informally mentor Anita through her early years as a fledgling professor. That is how their friendship began. Both women soon learned that they did have some common interests. Each enjoyed rhythm and blues, foreign films, and Tex-Mex cuisine. Despite their differences, Gale and Anita eventually became the best of friends.

MEETING PEOPLE

LEARNING OBJECTIVES

8.1 Discuss several factors affecting our attraction to others.
8.2 Explain why people form mistaken impressions.

Do you have at least one good friend with whom to share secrets, troubles, and joy? Each of us needs a deep, caring relationship with one or more special persons, such as a close friend, lover, or spouse. Sharing our deepest thoughts and feelings with an understanding companion who accepts us—despite our faults—is one of life's most satisfying experiences (Steiner, 2002). It makes us feel at home in the world despite the usual ups and downs that occur during our lives. Those who lack close relationships often experience emotional isolation and loneliness, regardless of their other acquaintances. On the other hand, we also need a network of people to fulfill a variety of practical needs (such as moving furniture; shuttling the kids to their events; watering the plants when on vacation) as well as the alleviation of stress through friendly activities, such as watching sports or going to the movies (Fischer, 2011). As you can see, friendships are crucial components to successful adjustment. But how do we go about making friends in the first place?

BOX 8–1   Did you know that . . .

- Children's first friendships form between 18 and 36 months of age.
- At age 3, children start showing a preference for same-sex friendships, a trend which continues throughout childhood and adolescence.
- Intimacy and self-disclosure isn't a very important aspect of friendship until the teen years.
- Having "enemies" during childhood and adolescence is associated with greater levels of loneliness
- The most common reason why parents take their children to see psychologists is because of problems with peers.

Source: Based on "Peer Relationships, Child Development, and Adjustment: A Developmental Psychopathology Perspective" by Jeffrey G. Parker, et al., from *Developmental Psychology: Theory and Mind,* 2nd Edition, edited by Dante Cicchetti and Donald J. Cohen. John Wiley & Sons, 2006.

Are First Impressions Most Important?

The next time you're out in public, take a quick look at someone you don't know. Based on what you see, what can you tell about that person? Are they rich or poor, friendly or mean, arrogant or humble? We can make such judgments because from the moment we meet someone we're busy forming **first impressions** of them (and they of us). *These are the initial impressions we form of others in which we tend to judge them on the basis of very little information.* Forming such impressions seems to be a very natural and inescapable process. Moreover, first impressions can form quickly (in the blink of an eye to be exact) and endure for weeks (Biesanz et al., 2011; Sunnafrank, Ramirez, & Metts, 2004).

All of us do this—form indelible first impressions of other people. Why? One reason has to do with the need for understanding people around us, especially if we think we may have to interact with them in the future. We think forming impressions of others helps us better predict their behavior. Another reason may be social comparison**,** which involves using others as a source of comparison to understand who we are relative to them (e.g., contrasting ourselves with classmates on intelligence). Whatever the reasons, the basic principle of person perception remains the same: We frequently tend to form extensive impressions of others on the basis of very little information (Quinn & Macrae, 2011).

Factors that Influence First Impressions

In terms of making friends, first impressions are of the utmost importance, for subsequent impressions or interactions with others alter our first impressions of them very little (Ybarra, 2001). There are several factors that predictably influence our first impressions of others. Let's take a look at them.

SOCIAL NORMS   In impression formation, we do not treat all information equally. Upon meeting a new person, incoming negative (e.g., impatient, obnoxious) and positive information (e.g., helpful, sweet) is used differently. Negative information is given more weight and is viewed as being more stable. Why? As it turns out, positive behavior is the *expected* social norm. We simply anticipate, and expect, positive behavior from all people. On the other hand, when someone behaves badly, we assume the behavior was done *intentionally,* and thus the person is evaluated as being bad. Because we are unlikely to voluntarily interact further with this type of person, our initial negative impression maintains itself (Denrell, 2005).

PHYSICAL ATTRACTIVENESS   Another person's physical appearance is important in determining our impressions of them, whether they be potential friends or prospective romantic partners. We do, in fact, appear to judge a book by its cover (Olivola & Todorov, 2010). Being pretty or handsome makes a strong first impression on others. Height, weight, sex, facial features, and

BOX 8–2   Focus on Psychology: What Makes Someone Attractive?

Studies show that women are considered beautiful if they have an hourglass shape and a slim waist that is about 70 percent or 80 percent of their hip circumference, full breasts, a symmetrical face, small nose, full lips, and a slight eyebrow arch. The faces of men deemed most attractive are symmetrical with a strong jaw and pronounced eyebrows. Moreover, most people find broad shoulders, a relatively narrow waist, and accompanying V-shaped torso attractive in men (George, Swami, Cornelissen, & Tovee, 2008; Saxton, DeBruine, Jones, Little, & Roberts, 2011). As it turns out, having eye-catching *friends* can also influence how attractive other people find you. On Facebook, profile owners with pictures of good-looking friends posted on their "walls" are rated as more beautiful than those with less attractive friends (Walther, Van Der Heide, Kim, Westerman, & Tong, 2008).

Across cultures, the characteristics of attractive faces are very similar (Langlois et al., 2000). For instance, Americans, Brazilians, and Russians prefer large eyes, small noses, and full lips (Jones, 1995). These generalities are true up to a point. For individuals within various ethnic and racial groups tend to show some degree of ethnocentrism when judging the attractiveness of others. That is, they find members of their own racial/ethnic group more attractive than members of other races and ethnicities (Schooler, Ward, Merriwether, & Caruthers, 2004). At the same time, each of us manages to modify such cultural preferences to fit our significant others, such as a friend, lover, or spouse (Fudge, Knapp, & Theune, 2002). As a result, the better we like someone, the more attractive we find that person to be. Beauty undeniably is in the eye of the beholder. Hence, there are any number of people in the world who would consider each one of us attractive—a good thing for you to keep in mind.

dress all affect our senses and feelings. The more physically attractive someone is, the more positively we judge that person. Attractive people are rated as being more interesting, intelligent, compassionate, sociable, and better adjusted than less attractive people. Not surprisingly, being physical attractive is associated with such diverse accomplishments as earning higher grades, landing better jobs, obtaining faster promotions, being happier, and experiencing less serious psychological problems (Judge, Hurst, & Simon, 2009; Lorenzo, Biesanz, & Human, 2010). In contrast, people we view as physically *un*attractive are typically judged unfavorably. Like beauty, ugliness is in the eye of the beholder. For some, it is a homely face, whereas for others, it is irregular features (such as large noses or discolored skin) that are deemed unattractive (Crandall, 1994). Whatever the case, unattractive people frequently experience discrimination based solely on their looks (Puhl & Latner, 2007). See Box 8–2 for a discussion of issues surrounding physical attractiveness.

Exploration 8.1: Attractiveness

www.faceresearch.org   This website allows you to participate in short experiments looking at the traits that people find attractive in faces and voices.

REPUTATIONS   Reputations can also affect our first impressions of others. Suppose Gale is your friend and says, "I can't wait for you to meet Anita." Even before you meet her, you'll probably find yourself forming a positive image of Anita based on what Gale tells you. Should you later discover Anita has some unfavorable qualities Gale didn't tell you about, chances are you'll give her the benefit of the doubt. Of course, it works the other way, too. If someone says, "I hear that professor named Gale is a terrible teacher," you may find yourself forming a negative impression of her, rightly or wrongly. Such is the power of a reputation (Sleebos, Ellemers, & de Gilder, 2006).

SIMILARITY   One other reason that we initially notice and decide to like others is that they seem similar to us. In particular, people with the same attitudes, social class, ethnicity, and musical tastes are often attracted to one another. Apparently, "birds of a feather [really] do flock together." Interestingly, we may even be genetically hardwired to seek out friends based on resemblances. It is possible that similarities among friends improve group cohesiveness, which ultimately helps the group members prosper (Fowler, Settle, & Christakis, 2011). In addition, hanging out with other people that remind us of ourselves can be self-reinforcing; we like them, so in turn, we like ourselves. And of course, our friends like us for the exact same reasons. Unfortunately, this process occurs even when the similarities between friends involve attitudes and behaviors that are detrimental to our own well-being (such as drug use) or the welfare of others (such as bullying) (Duffy & Nesdale, 2009; Smith, Thurston, & Green, 2011).

In general, people with similar needs and personalities are attracted to each other. Nevertheless, we also become friends with people who are complementary (opposite but compatible) to us, in terms of needs and traits. Actually, the notion of complementarity tends to apply mostly to *specific* traits rather than to the meshing of two personalities as a whole. A talkative person may therefore become attracted to someone who is quiet; a dominant individual might seek out a more dependent partner. Also, complementarity probably isn't important in the early stages of attraction, although it may become more important in a long-term relationship such as marriage. Nevertheless, even among married couples, the weight of evidence seems to favor similarity as most influencing liking (Myers, 1998).

PROPINQUITY   Chances are that at some point in time your friends lived nearby, attended the same school, or worked at the same place. Geographic nearness is especially important in the early stages of attraction, although the Internet is quickly changing this. First, the more you come into contact with people, the more opportunities you have for getting to know them better. This factor is called proximity or **propinquity,** meaning *physical closeness.* Typically, the farther away a person lives or sits (in class, for example), the less likely that person is to become a friend (Smith & Weber, 2005). Being in close proximity also exposes us more to that individual so that we apparently come to know him or her better. It is also true that "the better I know you, the better I know you." In other words, as we become more familiar with someone, we become better judges of that person's facial expressions and other nonverbal cues (Sternglanz & DePaulo, 2004).

There's also a strong association between interaction and liking. That is, "the more I see you, the more I like you." And it works the other way, too: The more you like someone, the more you *want* to socialize with him or her (Vittengl & Holt, 2000). Of course, if you start out disliking someone, then the more you see them, chances are, the more you'll dislike them. In such cases, "familiarity breeds contempt." Still, we tend to emphasize the positive qualities and minimize the negative qualities of people we associate with (Denrell, 2005). Otherwise, we would probably feel that we're stuck with an unpleasant friend, co-worker, or roommate, resulting in the build-up of resentment. Because most social norms imply *cooperative* relationships with others, we make special efforts to get along with people we live or work with; otherwise, life might just become too miserable.

NONVERBAL SIGNALS   Our impressions of others are also shaped by a variety of nonverbal signals (Hugill, Fink, & Neave, 2010). In general, if a new acquaintance's face or gestures remind us of someone else that we know and like, we transfer our positive feelings about the old acquaintance to the new one. On the other hand, we also tend to transfer our negative feelings about a disliked person onto a new acquaintance who reminds us of them (Anderson & Berk, 1998). Additionally, a person's posture and gestures can affect our impressions. Those who stand erect or walk youthfully make a more favorable impression than those who slouch. Also, people who point, glare, and interrupt a lot make a more negative impression than those who are attentive to what we say.

As you might guess, the face plays an especially vital role in our perception of others. As an example, we are favorably impressed with people who smile and look us in the eye. People who make eye contact with us are also apt to be seen as more trustworthy and likable; unless they gaze into our eyes for an uncomfortably long time. Those who avoid our gaze, whether from

| BOX 8–3 | Focus on Communication: Nonverbal Signals |

According to ex-FBI counterintelligence agent Joe Navarro, you can read people's *true* feelings by carefully observing their body positioning and movement. Here is some body language that relates to attraction and friendship (Navarro & Karlins, 2008).

Body Language	Meaning
Leaning away from you	disagreement or discomfort
Squinting or closing eyes with fingers	disbelief or disagreement
Covering of base of neck (front)	emotional discomfort or insecurity
Elbows out, arms bent, hands on hips	dominance or anger
Arms behind the back	stay away
Foot points away during conversation	person wants to leave
Leaning in	comfort, agreement, or liking
Head tilt	comfort, attraction
Eyebrows arch or eyes widen	positive feelings, interest
Feet or legs start wiggling	excitement about what's happening
Crossing of legs while standing	comfort, at ease, positive sentiment
Mirror each other's behavior	attraction

Source: Based on *What Every BODY is Saying* by Joe Navarro and Marvin Karlins. HarperCollins, 2008.

shyness or deceit, may strike us less favorably. In addition, those whose faces appear angular seem to us to be threatening or angry, while those whose faces appear rounded are perceived as happy and likable (Bar & Neta, 2006). See Box 8–3 for a list of nonverbal behaviors and their accompanying meaning.

As mentioned in the previous chapter, some facial expressions are universal (Matsumoto, 2002). In other words, a smiling face in Nigeria communicates joy in much the same way a smiling face communicates joy in Germany. However, there is one culturally based caveat that needs to be taken into consideration: Just as languages and voices contain accents, so, too, do expressions of emotion. Such nonverbal "accents" can even identify the expresser's nationality or culture (Beaupré & Hess, 2005). For example, in Latin America males that are friends will engage in a brief hug (known as abrazo) in which chests touch and arms wrap around the back of the other person (Navarro & Karlins, 2008).

VERBAL SIGNALS There are also dimensions of other people's verbal communication patterns that shape our perceptions of them—not the words and their meanings, but other features of verbal communication, such as the rate of speech, pauses, and pitch. *These unspoken but important features of spoken communications* are called **paralinguistics.** Certain paralinguistic cues, such as gestures—when used without speech, can actually take on the full burden of communication to another person (Goldin-Meadow, 2006). As we're sure many of you have experienced, paralinguistic cues are *absent* when writing e-mails, engaging in online chat, and texting others. As a result, the accuracy and comprehension of electronic messages may be negatively affected (Porter & ten Brinke, 2010). Thus, when you communicate via the Internet or cell phone, it is important to make sure that your word choice clearly relays your intended meaning.

Recently, paralinguistic cues, such as word repeats, speech speed, and nonverbal animation level, have been used to detect deception and lying. For instance, people use fewer words, speak more slowly, and engage in longer pauses between words when lying then when telling the truth (Davis, Markus, Walters, Vorus, & Connors, 2005). There are also verbal and nonverbal communication differences between men and women, which you can read about in Box 8–4. Of note, some of these gender differences may be meaningless, because it is not "men" versus "women" per se, but rather masculinity and femininity (traits available to both men and women) that create such differences (Basow & Rubenfield, 2003).

BOX 8–4	Focus on Communication: When Men and Women Talk to Each Other

When a man and a woman converse with each other …

- Women and men respond similarly to comforting messages that are person-centered (Jones & Burleson, 2003).
- Men have more difficulty interpreting what women are saying than women have interpreting what men are saying (Edwards, 1998).
- In terms of nonverbal communication, women more directly orient their bodies to the speaker and use gaze, while men lean forward and show more postural congruence with the speaker (Guerrero, 1997).
- Women underestimate men's commitment, and men over-perceive women's sexual intent (Haselton, 2003).
- Men do most of the talking, more of the interrupting, and raise fewer topics than women (Atwater, 1992).

Mistaken Impressions

Because of their age difference, Anita initially assumed that Gale would not be interested in being friends. Anita was wrong. But why did she make that assumption in the first place? Anita had fallen prey to a **mistaken impression**—*false or erroneous perceptions of others, of often based on insufficient evidence.* The biggest single reason we misjudge others is the lack information about them. Not that this should be surprising, given our tendency to "size up" people so hastily. When we quickly assess someone, we generally use **heuristics** or *mental shortcuts* for making complex decisions. One such shortcut or heuristic is the **false consensus effect,** *in which we assume others feel as we do* (Wojcieszak & Price, 2009). We might guess, then, that if Anita initially thought that the age difference between her and Gale was too great for friendship, she also falsely assumed that Gale thought the same thing. Likewise, we also form mistaken impressions of others because of false cues generated by stereotypes, positivity and negativity biases, and attributions. Let us take a look at each.

STEREOTYPES   **Stereotypes** are *widespread generalizations that have little, if any, basis in fact and are typically held about groups of people.* Whenever people begin statements with phrases such as "*all* teachers" or "*those people* are all the same," they're slipping into stereotypical thinking. Stereotypes are learned in one of three main ways—by actual contact with an individual from the stereotyped group, by discussing the stereotyped group with others, and by encountering stereotypes in the media (Kirsh, 2010; Ruscher, Cralley, & O'Farrell, 2005). In fact, youth frequently encounter both racial (e.g., minorities are perpetrators of crime) and gender stereotypes (e.g., women are emotional; men are independent and aggressive) in story books, television shows and commercials, as well as in video games (Baker & Raney, 2007; Jansz & Martis, 2007). Some examples of gender stereotypes in the media include the following: Children's picture books depict males as more independent and creative than females; males are rarely shown doing household chores or caring for children (Hamilton, Anderson, Broaddus, & Young, 2006); and commercial advertisements tend to show females, more so than males, engaging in either passive activities (e.g., sitting and talking) or domestic chores (Davis, 2003). Box 8–5 points out some common racial stereotypes in the media.

Research shows that the tendency to stereotype is quite natural and occurs automatically (Lepore & Brown, 2002). Moreover, stereotyping might be our *dominant* response, in both private and public settings (Lambert et al., 2003). Unfortunately, if the stereotype is negative, the biased holder of the stereotype is unlikely to associate further with the target of the bias, thus

BOX 8–5   Focus on Diversity: Racial Stereotypes in the Media

Here are some examples of racial stereotypes in media that youth consume (Kirsh, 2010). As you read the information below, think about this question: How much influence do you think stereotypes in the media have on the beliefs of children and adolescents?

- In children's picture books, African-Americans, Asians, and Latinos are less likely than Whites to be characterized as smart. If a story involves folklore which emphasizes bravery, then the main characters are typically Native American.
- In cartoons, if a character is singing, dancing, or entertaining those around them then they are most likely to be shown as African-American. The race that is least likely to be working is Hispanic.
- In television commercials, athletes and musicians are portrayed by African-Americans the most. It is unusual to find Asians in commercials for anything other than technology products.
- On television shows, African-Americans are dressed more provocatively than other races. They are also more likely to be cast in roles involving the criminal justice system. Hispanics, more so than any other race, play characters that commit crimes or do domestic work.
- In video games, criminals, athletes, thugs, and victims or crime are most often rendered as African-American or Hispanic. Heroes, in contrast, are White.

maintaining the negative stereotype (Sherman, Stroessner, Conrey, & Azam, 2005). Do you use stereotypes? Why? Do you, yourself, sometimes feel misunderstood because of stereotypes? If so, which ones?

POSITIVITY AND NEGATIVITY BIAS   We also tend to label people as globally good or bad because we know they possess (at least) a few good or a few bad characteristics. It's as if the people we enjoy wear a halo over their heads like an angel, and can do no wrong. In other words, the **halo effect** *is inferring uniformly positive traits from the appearance of a few positive traits.* For example, when we regard people as warm and outgoing, we also attribute all sorts of other positive qualities to them, such as being helpful and industriousness. Preschool children even believe that a child that they perceive as nice will also be smart and athletic (Koenig & Jaswal, 2011). Conversely, if we see others as cold and withdrawn, we tend to attribute additional negative qualities to them. Hence, the **devil (horns) effect** means *inferring uniformly negative traits from an appearance of a few negative traits.* In reality, of course, few individuals are all good or all bad. Instead, you should bear in mind that each of us is a complex mixture of traits, some desirable and others not so desirable (Palmer & Loveland, 2008).

ATTRIBUTIONS   Another source of error is that we frequently misjudge people by not taking sufficient account of *situational* influences on their behavior. That is, we make erroneous **attributions** *in which we search for the causes for our own or someone else's behavior.* We assume that people are *always* acting in character (i.e., the behavior is personality based). Consider this, when you see someone drop their coffee, do you think of that person as clumsy or do you attribute the spill to the fact that the coffee was hot? The truth is that people are often constrained by their immediate situations. Nevertheless, *the tendency to overattribute people's behavior to their personalities rather than to their circumstances* is so pervasive and of such importance to social perception that it has been called the **fundamental attribution error**. To avoid misjudging people, we must take account of the powerful and changing influences of their environments. Thus, it is wise to observe someone in a *variety* of different situations *across time* in order to know what that person is really like (Alfano, 2011).

We often form impressions of others based on very little information, for example what kind of car the individual drives.

KEEPING FRIENDS

LEARNING OBJECTIVES

8.3 Discuss how mutual self-disclosure shapes friendships.

8.4 Discuss friendship differences between men and women.

8.5 List several major reasons friendships break-up.

After we have formed our first impressions and decided whether we want to continue the interaction, the more we get to know someone the more likely our relationship will ripen into friendship. **Friendship** can be defined as *the affectionate attachment between two or more people*. We usually think of a friend as someone we've known a long time, which is often true. Yet friendship has more to do with *the quality of the relationship* rather than with the frequency of association. A high-quality friendship is characterized by helping one another, intimacy or the disclosing of secrets, mutual praise for successes, loyalty, and other positive features. Friendships provide warmth and closeness that are often missing in other daily interactions. Close friendships can save us from depression and loneliness and thus enhance our mental and social well-being. Likewise, friendships (including those occurring during childhood and adolescence) can influence overall levels of happiness, self-esteem, and a wide range of attitudes, such as those related to sex, clothing style, music, and alcohol and drug use (Prinstein & Dodge, 2008).

When Friends Get Together

Not surprisingly, one of the most common activities among friends is having an intimate talk (Berndt, 2002). You may call a friend to tell them about an embarrassing incident that happened to you in class. Or your friend may want to talk about the trouble they're having with a significant other. In both instances, sharing your feelings and getting someone else's reaction on the subject may be extremely helpful. Another frequently mentioned activity, especially for men, is doing a favor for a friend. Perhaps you ask to borrow a friend's car. Or your friend may want you to pick them up after work. Asking or doing a favor for someone else presupposes a great deal of trust as well as give-and-take in a relationship, both important qualities of friendship.

SOCIAL SUPPORT AND FRIENDSHIP   As mentioned in the chapter on stress, one of the greatest favors friends can do for each other is to lend a listening ear. This form of social assistance is

Friends often disclose confidential information to each other.

called social support, whereby one individual or group offers comfort and advice to others who use it as a means of coping. Although people who report good general well-being have only a few close friends, they often report high levels of sharing of intimate and personal information with those friends (Reynolds & Repetti, 2006). Sometimes a casual friend becomes a close friend *because* that person listens sympathetically to some personal problem. When faced with a crisis, many people will turn to a friend before talking about it with their families, because a friend may serve as a sounding board and provide needed support without the conflict of kinship loyalties.

Interestingly, the people you turn to for social support differs with increasing age. Young adults are more apt to turn to their peers than their families when in need. In contrast, people who are middle-aged or older are more inclined to seek out members of their families (Steiner, 2001). With a growing population of elderly and the development of adult communities, perhaps future generations of older people will be more peer-oriented (Buys, 2001). Do you have friends you could turn to in a personal crisis? If so, who are they? Remember, though, some personal issues are more properly discussed with a professional than with a friend. In such instances, it's often best to seek out the help of an expert.

Self-Disclosure—Those Little Secrets

As the relationship between two people progresses from strangers to acquaintances to close friends, individuals disclose a greater breadth and depth of information about themselves. In fact, **self-disclosure**—*the sharing of intimate or personal information with others*—is a way to bring us closer to others (Gibbs, Ellison, & Heino, 2006). Self-disclosure can signal commitment and trust between friends because the sharing of secrets makes you vulnerable to that person. As it turns out, self-disclosure, especially of personal secrets, has health benefits (Patterson & Singer, 2007). For instance, writing about positive or traumatic experiences, for as little as two minutes a day, can lead to a dramatic reduction in health-related complaints (Burton & King, 2008).

What is it about self-disclosure that promotes well-being? One notion is that the teller of the secret gains new insights into the secret, and as such, no longer has to expend effort hiding it.

BOX 8–6   Focus on Psychology: Beware the Frenemy

The term *frenemy* is the blending of the words "friend" and "enemy." It should come as no surprise then that a **frenemy** *is a person who acts like a friend, but in reality, has little concern for your personal welfare.* One minute the frenemy is hanging out with you, smiling, and listening to your problems, and the next minute your secrets have become fodder for gossip and posted on Facebook. Here are some situations that can help you identify if your friend is really a "frenemy."

The Frenemy:

- Frequently gives backhanded compliments like, "He seems much nicer than the guys you normally date."
- Belittles the characteristics about yourself that you like the most.
- Makes you look bad or feel awkward in front of others
- Frequently tags bad pictures of you on Facebook.
- Tries to make themselves look good at your expense.
- Ruins positive moments for you by trying to diminish your achievements.
- Gossips about you behind your back.
- Competitively compares their life with yours.

Psychologists refer to the behavior of frenemies as **relational aggression**—*aggressive acts which attempt to hurt another person's social relationships or level of group inclusion.* Although relational aggression leaves no physical marks, marks are left nonetheless, as the part of the brain responsible for experiencing physical pain, the *anterior cingulate,* also registers the effects of social exclusion (Eisenberger, Lieberman, & Williams, 2003). Thus, the old adage "sticks and stones can break my bones, but names will never hurt me" appears to be incorrect. The psychological pain resulting from relational aggression produces real wounds; it is just that those injuries are not visible to the naked eye.

Still, increasingly higher levels of self-disclosure do not always lead to greater intimacy between two people and can sometimes backfire. Ordinarily, the more you disclose about yourself, the more your friend will reciprocate (Morry, 2005). If your friend does not feel sufficiently comfortable or trustful in the relationship, however, they may not reciprocate by telling you intimate details of their life. Unfortunately, knowing intimate details about you would help your friend hold a power advantage in the relationship. Eventually, you'd back off and restrict your communication to more insignificant matters to balance the power. In other instances, someone may share information that presents a conflict in the relationship, so that both partners may retreat to more superficial levels of sharing. Remember, it is important to choose wisely when deciding with whom to share your innermost thoughts and feelings, for your "friend" could actually be a frenemy. Box 8–6 further elaborates upon this theme.

GENDER DIFFERENCES IN SELF-DISCLOSURE   Men and women differ in their willingness to share personal matters face-to-face or even electronically. Pairs of women characteristically engage in more intimate disclosure than do pairs of men. In fact, female–female friendship pairs seem particularly close. Disclosure by men is less reciprocal. That means men disclose less than is disclosed to them, and their disclosures are apt to cover less personal topics such as politics or school. Some psychologists suspect that women use disclosure to enhance interpersonal connectedness, whereas men use disclosure to strive for mastery and power (Fehr, 2004; Suh, Moskowitz, Fournier, & Zuroff, 2004). However, with the diminishment of gender-role stereotypes, we can expect men to engage in more self-disclosure than has been the case in the past. Regardless of gender, those who enjoy high self-esteem not only feel more comfortable sharing personal information about themselves but they also experience greater security in close relationships. Those with low self-esteem are more apt to withhold personal information and thereby fail to learn about themselves through closeness with others.

CULTURAL DIFFERENCES IN SELF-DISCLOSURE There are significant cultural differences in how acceptable self-disclosure is in Eastern and Western societies. Case in point, there is less self-disclosure in Japan and Taiwan than in the United States. In fact, in comparison to people from Asian countries, Americans typically disclose more information on all topics, especially those that are superficial (such as interests, work, and finances). Some suggest that because relationships are more stable in collectivist societies (where the focus in on the larger group) than in individualistic societies (where the focus on the individual), less effort is needed to maintain a relationship in Eastern countries like Japan. As a result, Westerners are required to invest more time and effort into maintaining their relationships than Asians; and one way to accomplish this is through self-disclosure (Kito, 2005; Schug, Yuki, & Maddux, 2010). In addition, Asians seek out social support less often during times of stress than Westerners. In part, these findings occur because Asians are particularly concerned that self-disclosure might ruin existing relationships. Interestingly, relative to Americans, when Asians do receive social support it proves to be less psychologically beneficial to them (Schug et al., 2010).

Gender Differences in Friendship

PLATONIC FRIENDSHIPS Friendship is not necessarily more important to one sex than to the other, but it does tend to have different meanings for men and women. In platonic friendships, intimacy plays a more central role among women friends (Fehr, 2004). Women generally are more physically and emotionally expressive in their friendships than men. Also, as we've already seen, women are more apt to share intimate details about their lives, such as their worries, joys, and secrets. At the same time, women experience greater anxiety over close relationships. Tensions, jealousies, and rejections are more common in friendships between women, whereas men are apt to engage in outright disputes over money, property, and dominance. Usually, men are not as emotionally close in their friendships with other men (Oxley, Dzindolet, & Miller, 2002). Instead, they are more likely than women to seek out a male friend to share in a particular activity, like tennis or hunting, or to ask a favor. Yet, when in the throes of a serious personal problem, men are just as inclined to seek out a close friend. Moreover, when learning how to best attract a mate, heterosexual males and females turn more to opposite-sex friends than to same-sex friends (Benenson & Alavi, 2004).

Worth mentioning is the fact that with changing gender roles, neither the "activity friend" nor the "all-purpose friend" friendship style is distinctively male or female. Women, whose active lives now include everything from working lunches to health-club workouts, are discovering the pleasure of activity friends. And men, realizing the importance of a personal support system, are discovering the value of an all-purpose friend with whom they share their deeper feelings and concerns. Neither friendship style gives an advantage in mental health, achievement, or the enjoyment of life. Nevertheless, most of us are better off with a mixture of both types of male and female friends, as each type brings out and sharpens different aspects of ourselves.

FRIENDS WITH BENEFITS Historically, the presence (or absence) of physical intimacy was used to distinguish friendships from romantic relationships. Sexual activity was thought to primarily occur between romantic partners or between anonymous strangers interested in a short-time liaison (e.g., casual sex). Not so anymore, as a new relational style has been identified: **friends with benefits (FWB)**—*friendships that involve recurrent sexual activity*. FWB relationships have characteristics of both friendships (e.g., support, companionships, non-sexual activities, trust, and understanding) and romantic relationships, namely sexual activity. However, FWB relationships lack the commitments associated with romantic relationships.

Would it surprise you to learn that there are significant gender differences in FWB relationships? Men are more likely than women to (1) have multiple FWB relationships occurring simultaneously and (2) have more past FWB relationships, in general. Likewise, men report that sexual desire is the primary reason for being in such relationships. In contrast, women are more likely than men to report increasing emotional connections as a motivating reason for starting an FWB relationship. Moreover, whereas men hope that there are no future changes in the status of an FWB relationship, women express a greater desire for a relationship change (either to a romantic relationship or platonic friendship). Interestingly, both men and women report that the "friendship" aspect of the relationship is more important than the "benefits" aspect (Lehmiller, Vanderdrift, & Kelly, 2011).

Around 50 percent to 60 percent of college students report being in an FWB relationship (Owen & Fincham, 2011). And although those involved name many benefits of such relationships, such as easy access to sex, boosting sexual confidence and experience, and increased companionship, FWB relationships are not without risk. Friendships can become awkward or ruined, participants can get emotionally hurt, and the risk of getting sexually transmitted infections (STIs) is often underestimated. Despite the fact that sexually exclusivity is not required in FWB relationships, and that nearly 50 percent of those in them have more than one active sex partner, many fail to protect against STIs by using a condom (Weaver, MacKeigan, & MacDonald, 2011).

Of note, even for sexually active adults, most friendships do not turn into an FWB relationship. Here are some reasons that college students give for keeping friendships purely platonic.

- Wanting to safeguard the friendship as a friendship.
- Not being physically attracted to the other person.
- Fearing disapproval from a network of mutual friends.
- Already being committed to a third party.
- Avoiding physical (e.g., STI) and emotional risk that can occur in an FWB relationship.
- Not being ready to be in an FWB relationship.

Staying Friends

"There's no friend like an old friend," goes the time-honored saying. With old friends we can relax and be ourselves without much fear of rejection. We're familiar with each other's mannerisms and make allowances for each other's weaknesses. Staying friends depends more on the special qualities of the relationship and less on the frequency of contact between two people (Bagwell et al., 2005). Most of us have some friends we don't see very often, but we still consider them friends. We may keep in touch by calling occasionally or exchanging cards, letters, or e-mails. Class reunions and vacations also afford opportunities for renewing old ties, as do social networking sites such as Facebook. At the same time, physical separation often exacts a toll on friendships, as when high school best friends attend separate colleges (Oswald & Clark, 2003). When people are asked why friendships *cool off*, the most frequently cited reason is that one person has moved away.

In contrast, the most common reason people give for friendship *break-ups* is life transitions, such as marriage, childbirth, new jobs, and different schedules (Davis, 1996). Not surprisingly, break-ups in friendships are more likely to happen if one person's life undergoes significant change while the other person's does not. Betrayal is another reason that friendships end; in other words, trust is broken (Sheets & Lugar, 2005). **Trust** can be defined as *people's abstract, positive expectations that they can count on friends and partners to care for them and be responsive to their needs, now and in the future.* In some instances, the violation of trust involves minor infringements, such as using a personal item without asking permission. At other times, trust violations involve more serious offenses, such as repeating things said in confidence or making a pass at your significant other. Regardless, when trust is broken the relationship requires a significant amount of repair work if it is to continue. Friendships may also break off because the individuals discover they have very different views on matters that are important to them. Curiously, increasing contact between friends (such as becoming roommates in college) may make them painfully aware of such differences. Despite break-ups, friendship is such a deeply satisfying experience that each of us will continue making new friends throughout life, while at the same time, cherishing the special closeness that comes with a long-lasting friendship.

WHEN IT'S HARD TO MAKE FRIENDS

LEARNING OBJECTIVES:

    8.6 Know how shyness shapes relationships.

    8.7 List the consequences of chronic loneliness.

    8.7 Provide suggestions for someone who is lonely and wants to overcome the loneliness.

As you know, the desire for connectedness and companionship is a fundamental human motive. And while there are many factors that attract us to others, there are also influences that make it difficult for friendships to form. Two such factors are shyness and, what may seem counter intuitive at first, loneliness.

Shyness

"Everyone but me was having such a good time laughing and talking." "Other people were moving around the room greeting old friends and making new ones, and I was stuck up against the wall as if I was super-glued to it." "There I was trying to think of something to say to this woman I hardly knew. She must have felt sorry for me. I couldn't wait until the party was over." Do any of these quotes sound familiar to you? If so, then you might be shy.

Exploration 8.2: Shyness

www.shyness.com   If you are shy or want to research shyness and social anxiety, this is the page for you. There are resources and links to other sites, a shyness questionnaire, and social support for shy people offered on the site.

    Shyness—*the tendency to avoid contact or familiarity with others*—can be characteristic of people of all ages, but especially the young. A large number of people identify themselves as shy (Saunders & Chester, 2008). Case in point, almost half of all Americans report a chronic problem with shyness (Marano, 2005). Similarly, about 80 percent of college students report they have been shy at some point in their lives (Carducci & Zimbardo, 1995). It is now thought that more women suffer from shyness than men (Walsh, 2002). Shyness is typically consistent across situations and over time; in other words, shyness seems to be an enduring personality trait (Crozier, 2005). Shyness means different things for different people and covers a wide range of feelings and behaviors, but overall the experience of shyness (e.g., fear of social rejection and of social incompetence) is essentially the same in most cultures (Jackson, Flaherty, & Kosuth, 2000).

WHAT DOES IT MEAN TO BE SHY?   At one end of the shyness spectrum are those people who are not especially apprehensive about meeting people. When they are alone, it is because they prefer being in nature or working with ideas or things rather than with people. In the middle range are those who are sometimes embarrassed or occasionally lack self-confidence and prefer their own company (Crozier, 2005). Such individuals hesitate to ask for a date or a favor from others. At the other extreme are individuals whose shyness has become a sad form of self-imprisonment. *In its extreme form, shyness is called* **social anxiety** *or* **social phobia** *and may severely interfere with a person's life* (Heiser, Turner, Beidel, & Roberson-Nay, 2009). Some individuals with social phobia turn to alcohol to lubricate their social interactions, that is, they drink to inhibit their shyness (Santesso, Schmidt, & Fox, 2004). For this extreme form of shyness, anti-anxiety medication can be used for treatment (Robinson & Hood, 2007). Other psychological interventions, such as social skills training, may work equally well (Aron, 2010).

CHARACTERISTICS OF SHY PEOPLE   People who are habitually shy are different: They see shyness as something within themselves, that is, as a personal trait (Bruch & Belkin, 2001). However, most dislike being shy, because shyness creates many problems for them: feeling lonely, being overly self-conscious and unassertive, having difficulty making friends, being unable to think clearly in the presence of others, or freezing up in the middle of a conversation (Alfano & Beidel, 2011). Moreover, it is not uncommon for shy people to be depressed and misunderstood by others (Jackson, Weiss, Lundquist, & Soderlind, 2002). They are apt to be regarded as aloof, condescending, emotionally "cold," and egocentric rather than shy. Yet, this is not true in all cultures. In many Asian cultures, for example, reticent individuals are often thought to be more socially sensitive than extroverted individuals and therefore are more accepted by their peers (Sakuragi, 2004).

Where does shyness originate? Although some shyness can be traced to biology, most psychologists assume it is the result of *both* biological and environmental influences (Rubin & Coplan, 2010). Almost all of us tend to be shy in some situations, such as meeting strangers, dealing with people we're physically attracted to, and being in large groups. To learn more about your own shyness level, answer the quiz on shyness found in Activity 8–1, "How Shy Are You?"

SHYNESS AND TECHNOLOGY   The advent of technology in the form of e-mail and voice mail has reduced the need for us to meet face-to-face (Yuen & Lavin, 2004). Some experts claim that these electronic means of communication have the potential to isolate us from others, reduce our social well-being, and increase our isolation (Scealy, Phillips, & Stevenson, 2002). By using the Internet and other less personal means of communication, the opportunities for shy people to practice their face-to-face interpersonal skills are decreased. On the other hand, if face-to-face interaction is so feared that individuals are lonely and isolated from others, technology may afford some opportunities for meeting others (Baker & Oswald, 2010). In fact, shy people tend to use social networking sites, such as Facebook, more than their non-shy counterparts (Orr et al., 2009). The reason is simple, shy individuals find it more comfortable to talk with other online than in person (Ryan & Xenos, 2011). Nevertheless, probably a balance of electronic and interpersonal communication is best for long-term personal growth.

REDUCING SHYNESS   If you or someone you know is shy, rest assured that shyness can be reduced by learning to modify it when it creates problems (Albano & Hayward, 2004). Here's how:

- Strive to reduce the inner monitoring of your own thoughts, feelings, and actions, especially the concern for how people see you and whether they will reject you. Instead, focus on your participation in the activity.
- Identify those aspects of situations that elicit shyness, such as meeting new people, as well as the social skills you may be lacking.
- Develop your social skills, such as how to initiate and carry on a conversation and how to assert yourself. In other words, allow yourself some successes on the interpersonal front.
- Keep in mind that shyness subsides when you step out of your usual identity, as in when you become totally absorbed in something or when you are helping others.
- Try to stop being so self-critical and perfectionistic. If shyness has become too disabling, seek counseling or therapy.

Loneliness

Some people have trouble forming or keeping close friendships, and as a result they experience loneliness—*a subjective state reflecting the fact that the quality and quantity of relationships wanted is lower than the quality and quantity of relationships available.* In essence, when we are lonely we feel an unhappy sense of isolation. We all feel lonely from time to time. And in general, this type of loneliness has no long-term consequences. But when loneliness becomes a way of life, the outcomes associated with it are clearly negative. Chronic loneliness is associated with low self-esteem, depression, anxiety, higher levels of stress, and general feelings of unhappiness (Asher & Paquette, 2003). In addition to these psychological effects, being lonely for long periods of time is also associated with a variety of issues affecting our physical health. Lonely people, for instance,

ACTIVITY 8–1

How Shy Are You?

Instructions: For each of the following statements, indicate your level of agreement on a scale of one (1) = "strongly disagree" to seven (7) "strongly agree."

1. I like to go on blind dates or to go out with someone I hardly know.

   Strongly disagree   1   2   3   4   5   6   7   Strongly agree

2. When I have to give a speech or participate in a debate, I approach the task with confidence.

   Strongly disagree   1   2   3   4   5   6   7   Strongly agree

3. I am assertive enough to stop a stranger on the street and ask what time it is.

   Strongly disagree   1   2   3   4   5   6   7   Strongly agree

4. When there are lots of strangers at a social gathering, I enjoy meeting them.

   Strongly disagree   1   2   3   4   5   6   7   Strongly agree

5. I am not bashful about meeting other people I do not already know.

   Strongly disagree   1   2   3   4   5   6   7   Strongly agree

6. When a small group of people is talking, I am one of the individuals who participates most.

   Strongly disagree   1   2   3   4   5   6   7   Strongly agree

7. I do not mind riding in crowded elevators even if all of us strangers should become trapped together.

   Strongly disagree   1   2   3   4   5   6   7   Strongly agree

8. If I think that my grade is incorrect, I am not timid about approaching the professor.

   Strongly disagree   1   2   3   4   5   6   7   Strongly agree

9. I feel I can readily ask my neighbors or friends for favors.

   Strongly disagree   1   2   3   4   5   6   7   Strongly agree

10. I generally feel comfortable the first day of class regardless of whether I know anyone else in the room.

   Strongly disagree   1   2   3   4   5   6   7   Strongly agree

Scoring: Add up your scores and record the total here: _____

The highest possible score is 70. If you scored at the high end of the scale (i.e., 50–70), you likely have confidence in your social skills and enjoy the company of other people, whether they are friends or strangers. If you scored at the low end of the scale (0–20), you might want to think about how shy you really are and what you can do to overcome shyness if it is a detriment to you. Remember, this scale is not scientific, it is only intended to start you thinking about your own level of comfort around other people.

tend to smoke more, have a more sedentary lifestyle, eat a more unhealthy diet, drink more alcohol, have more difficulty sleeping, and be more obese than those who are socially connected (Cacioppo & Patrick, 2008). Clearly, being lonely can put both our physical and mental health at risk.

Exploration 8.3: Loneliness

www.WebOfLoneliness.com A site that explains what loneliness is, what causes it, and how others have coped. Essays and poems about loneliness are also available.

LONELINESS VERSUS SOLITUDE Do not confuse loneliness with solitude, which is a more objective and, often, a desired state denoting the absence of people. You can feel lonely despite being surrounded by others if you don't feel close to those people. On the other hand, in terms of solitude, you have many friends but deliberately seek brief periods away from them without feeling lonely. It thus appears that loneliness is largely a state of mind that results from the gap between our desire for closeness and the failure to find it (Hawkley, Thisted, & Cacioppo, 2009; Rokach & Neto, 2005).

LONELINESS ACROSS THE LIFESPAN From early childhood to old age, people experience loneliness. Ironically, traditional college students who are surrounded by hundreds, even thousands, of peers suffer more loneliness than any other age group. Having newly loosened ties with parents and high school friends causes college students to actively seek out new relationships. The idealism of youth, plus the desire for intimacy, makes them especially sensitive to the discrepancy between their expectations of closeness and their actual relationships. Moreover, college may be the first time some adolescents are away from their parents (Wiseman, Mayseless, & Sharabany, 2006). Loneliness tends to decline over the years, leveling off throughout middle age, though less so among women than men. Although older adults spend much of their time alone, most of them are less prone to loneliness than popularly depicted; probably because they have learned to put their need for companionship in better perspective. However, loneliness appears to increase again among those in their 80s, reflecting, in part, the greater sense of disengagement from life among those at an advanced age.

CAUSES OF LONELINESS Many factors contribute to loneliness, including those occurring during childhood. Children who are raised by warm and responsive parents are less likely to report loneliness in adulthood than those reared by disagreeable and unhelpful parents. In addition, some of the loneliest adults are those whose parents divorced when they were younger than

Loneliness and solitude are quite different.

6 years old, partly because young children misperceive parental divorce as abandonment. In contrast, people who have lost a parent through death experience no corresponding increase in loneliness; probably because they realize that the loss was not intentional or their fault.

People with low self-esteem tend to experience more loneliness than those with high self-esteem. This occurs, in part, because individuals with low esteem view themselves as unworthy of friendship, which subsequently prevents them from taking the necessary steps to reduce their loneliness. Having poor social skills can also result in loneliness (Efrati-Virtzer & Margalit, 2009). Case in point, children who lack appropriate social skills are rejected by their peers when they are aggressive, withdrawn, or fail to show appropriate responses to others' needs. Unfortunately, rejection from others (in childhood or adulthood) can create a negative cycle in which lonely people avoid interacting with others in order to prevent further rejection. Of course, such avoidance behavior leads to fewer opportunities for human contact, and as a result, loneliness increases (De Bruyn, Cillessen, & Wissink, 2010).

CULTURE AND LONELINESS   Culture affects loneliness, too (Rokach & Neto, 2005). The emphasis on personal fulfillment, often at the expense of stable relationships and commitment to others, is thought to make Americans especially prone to loneliness. Immigrants, and long-term visitors to the United States, are also likely to report heightened feelings of loneliness, especially when the culture of their home country is very different from that experienced in America. For instance when studying in the United States, Canadian students are less apt to be lonely than students from Nigeria. Befriending international students and helping them adjust by assisting them with understanding our culture would be a very kind and considerate thing to do. At the same time, you would have the interesting opportunity to learn more about their culture (Ditommaso, Brannen, & Burgess, 2005).

COPING WITH LONELINESS   How we handle loneliness depends largely on how long we have felt lonely. To ward off the occasional bout of loneliness, it is helpful to read a book, phone an old friend, spend time in nature, play with our pets, or distract ourselves through music, television, and the Internet. However, for chronic cases, the issues become more complex, and how we cope with loneliness depends largely on how we interpret its causes. People who suffer the most from loneliness tend to exaggerate its internal aspects and minimize its external ones. Thus, people who blame their loneliness on their personal inadequacies ("I'm lonely because I'm unlovable" or "My lover and I have split up because I gained too much weight and have no will power") make themselves even more lonely and depressed. Eliminating such negative thoughts can help reduce loneliness.

Additionally, people are more likely to overcome loneliness when they focus on changing the *external, situational* factors that contribute to it. The following quotes illustrate this point, "It's hard to meet people in large classes, so I'll take smaller ones next semester" or "I'll stop working so much and get out and meet more people." Similarly, people who react to chronic loneliness in passive ways—watching television, crying, and sleeping—feel even lonelier. Those who adopt more active or behavioral strategies—writing a letter or calling up an acquaintance—are more likely to alleviate their loneliness. Social skills training can help change behaviors, too (Cook et al., 2008). The best course is to continue developing your interpersonal skills so that you always have access to a broad network of social ties as well as a circle of close friends.

Chapter Summary

MEETING PEOPLE

8.1 Discuss several factors affecting our attraction to others.

We're attracted to people for a variety of reasons, including such factors as familiarity, reputations, physical attractiveness, verbal and nonverbal signals, as well as similarity to us, especially similarity to our attitudes. The more we interact with someone, the more we tend to like that person, unless we discover serious differences or basic incompatibilities. In long-term relationships, however, we're often attracted to someone on the basis of a mixture of similar and complementary needs.

8.2   Explain why people form mistaken impressions.

We tend to form erroneous impressions of others on the basis of information that is influenced by our own stereotypes, biases, and attributions, as well as the physical appearance (especially attractiveness) of others. The failure to account for situational influences on people's behavior also contributes to mistaken impressions.

KEEPING FRIENDS

8.3   Discuss how mutual self-disclosure shapes friendships.

Close friends frequently get together for good talk and companionship, in addition to sharing a variety of other activities. There's a close link between friendship and mutual self-disclosure, so that emotional sharing often strengthens the bond of friendship.

8.4   Discuss friendship differences between men and women.

Intimacy plays a more central role in friendships among women than men. Women generally are more physically and emotionally expressive and engage in more self-disclosure than men. Women, more so than men, are likely to experience negative emotions, such as, anxiety and jealousy, in their relationships. Men are more likely than women to have had a past FWB relationship, and to have multiple FWB relationships occurring simultaneously.

8.5   List several major reasons friendships break-up.

Moving away, life transitions, differing viewpoints, and feeling betrayed are the most common reasons for friendships break-ups.

WHEN IT'S HARD TO MAKE FRIENDS

8.6   Know how shyness shapes relationships.

Shy people have difficulty making friends because it is hard for them to introduce themselves to others and because they are often unable to think clearly during a conversation. Also, shy people tend to be misperceived as aloof and disinterested, largely because of their silence and lack of eye contact. The use of technology can help shy people connect with others. Shyness can be overcome, but it takes work.

8.7   List the consequences of chronic loneliness.

Loneliness is a state of mind that results from the gap between our desire for closeness and the failure to find it. Chronic loneliness is associated with psychological effects, such as low self-esteem, depression, anxiety, higher levels of stress, and general feelings of unhappiness, as well as poor health habits, such as eating poorly, drinking too much, and not getting enough exercise.

8.8   Provide suggestions for someone who is lonely and wants to overcome the loneliness.

Those who cope best with loneliness avoid blaming their lack of friends solely on personal inadequacies. Changing negative thoughts to positive ones can help accomplish this. Learning social skills can help people make new friends, thus reducing feelings of loneliness. Finally, people are likely to overcome loneliness when they address the situational factors (e.g., not around people very often) that contribute to it.

Self-Test

1. The first time Joe met his fiancée Julie's parents, he accidently insulted them by making a joke about their taste in furniture. According to what we know about first impressions, which of the following is true?
   a. Joe shouldn't worry, first impressions usually don't last more than a day or two
   b. Joe shouldn't worry, Joe's "bad behavior" was probably viewed as unintentional
   c. Joe should worry a lot, his "bad behavior" was probably viewed as intentional
   d. Joe should worry a lot, once an impression is made, it can never be changed

2. Joe first met Julie at the local bait and tackle shop. It turns out they both lived within three miles of the best fishing hole in the county. Based on the above information only, which of the following aspects of attraction was at play?
   a. propinquity
   b. physical attractiveness
   c. reputations
   d. remoteness

3. Julie figured out that Joe "like-liked" her after she noticed the following paralinguistic cue.
   a. Joe wrote her a poem
   b. The speed at which Joe talked and the pitch in his voice changed when he talked to her, in comparison to her friends
   c. Joe bought her flowers, roses in fact
   d. Joe texted her 54 times in one day

4. Although Joe's attraction to Julie was almost instantaneous, Julie's was not. In fact, Julie didn't want to go out with Joe the first time he asked her. Her rejection greatly surprised him as he thought that she liked him and much as he liked her. This scenario best illustrates the phenomenon known as:
   a. the relationship algorithm
   b. propinquity
   c. the Venus-Mars interaction effect
   d. the false consensus effect

5. As mentioned above, Joe insulted Julie's parents the first time he met them. "That one's a bad seed, I don't see anything good about him" said Julie's father. Which of the following

can best explain why Julie's father had such a negative view about Joe, based on just a few personality traits?
  a. the devil effect   b. the heuristic effect
  c. the halo effect   d. the matching hypothesis

6. On their first date, Joe took Julie to see a movie. Joe was so focused on Julie that he didn't realize that he "cut" into the line to get pop-corn. Unfortunately for Joe, one of Julie's cousin's, Jessica was in line at the time. "Yep, Uncle was right, that Joe is a nogoodnik." Jessica over-attributed Joe's behavior to a flawed personality rather than to the circumstances of being distracted by Julie. Jessica's thinking illustrates the:
  a. fundamental attribution error
  b. halo effect
  c. heuristic effect
  d. ambiguous situation effect

7. Prior to dating Julie, Joe went out on one date with a woman named Jill. There wasn't a second date, because while at dinner on their first night out Jill told Joe too much intimate information about her past boyfriends, personal flaws, and sexual history. Jill engaged in so much _____ that it scared Joe away.
  a. attributional sharing   b. self-disclosure
  c. social support   d. paralinguistic activity

8. While in college Joe had a sexual relationship with one of his good friends from high-school. Their relationship remained platonic throughout college, and they never thought of themselves as a couple. This type of relationship is called:
  a. friends with benefits   b. romantic
  c. casual sex   d. parasocial

9. One of Julie's best friends, Marcia, loved nothing more than to drive a golf-cart around the local golf course by herself. She relished the peace and quiet of her time alone, especially since her coworkers, Julie included, were quite boisterous. Based on this information one could conclude that Marcia was experiencing _____.
  a. loneliness   b. solitude
  c. social anxiety   d. social phobia

10. At first, Joe didn't know what to think about Julie's rather shy coworker Donna. Research would suggest that the more Joe became familiar with Donna, the more he would _____ her.
  a. like   b. dislike
  c. become more critical of d. become more envious of

Exercises

1. *First impressions.* Look around in your classes and select someone you haven't met. Jot down your impressions of this person. Then make it a point to introduce yourself and become better acquainted. To what extent was your initial impression accurate or inaccurate? What steps can you take to improve your accuracy next time you meet a stranger?

2. *Write a personal ad about yourself.* Suppose you were writing a personal ad for the classified section devoted to finding new friends (not romantic or sexual partners). How would you describe yourself? How would you describe the type of person you're looking for? Write a paragraph about why you gave those particular descriptions.

3. *Self-disclosure.* Write a paragraph or two including your thoughts on the following matters: How comfortable do you feel sharing personal information with friends? With whom do you share the most? Which topics do you share? If married, do you share more with your spouse or with your friends? Are the friends to whom you disclose same-sex or opposite-sex? Would you agree that the rewards of mutual self-disclosure outweigh the risks?

4. *Social support.* To whom can you turn? If you were experiencing a personal crisis, to whom would you turn for help—your family or friends? Which person would you seek out first? Explain the reasons for your answers. If you do not have good social support, how can you cultivate some friends to whom to disclose?

5. *Intimacy and growth.* Think of a close friendship or love relationship. Then describe your relationship in a page or so, including your thoughts on the following points: Do you both maintain other friendships? If lovers, are you also friends? Can each of you experience closeness without giving up your individuality? To what extent does this relationship encourage each of you to grow as a person?

Questions for Self-Reflection

1. How much do you judge by first impressions? Are they accurate?

2. Do you make a good first impression on others? If not, how can you correct this?

3. Are you ever bothered by shyness? Loneliness? How can you overcome each?

4. Do you usually find that the more you know someone, the better you like the person?

5. How important are good looks to you in being attracted to someone of the opposite sex?

6. Do some of your friends have interests and personalities quite different from yours?

7. Who is your best friend? With which people do you feel most comfortable sharing secrets?

8. Do you have a close friend of the opposite sex? Do you have a close friend of the same sex? If you have both, how are these two friends similar? How are they different?

9. Have you ever been betrayed by a close friend? How did you react?

10. Have you ever befriended another person from a different country? How was that person's culture similar to yours? How was it different?

Chapter Nine

Groups: Belonging, Following, and Leading

9.1 Name and describe various types of groups.

9.2 Differentiate discrimination, prejudice, and stereotyping.

9.3 Discuss how groups form.

9.4 Provide reasons to explain why people join groups.

9.5 Describe how groups communicate.

9.6 Explain how the size of a group can affect its functioning.

9.7 Compare three types of social influence: conformity, compliance, and obedience.

9.8 Understand social loafing and group polarization.

9.9 Explain groupthink.

9.10 Discuss some ways to prevent groupthink.

9.11 Explain how conflict can be both good and bad.

9.12 Discuss conflict management.

9.13 Describe how individuals become leaders.

9.14 Explain various types of leadership styles and traits.

Roy grew up in the cornfields of Iowa. His father, Harry, inherited the family farm and soon married Sara, Roy's mother. Sara and Harry were excited and proud the day their baby boy was born. Sara and Harry developed great plans for their child from the moment of his arrival. They pushed hard for Roy to achieve in school. Although Roy was resistant at first, much like any child who enjoyed playing rather than studying, he soon settled into his studies and was near the top of his class. During his senior year in high school, Roy became class president and organized a student-led rally in the support of small family-owned farms, like his parents. Upon graduation, Roy was accepted to a large university in the Midwest and even landed a good scholarship. Not only did Roy's academic success continue while pursuing his bachelor's degree, but so did his desire to take on leadership responsibilities. He quickly became involved in the local "Occupy Wall Street" protest taking place on his campus. By the time Roy graduated, he was the leader of the local chapter, responsible for planning protests and recruiting new members. Under Roy's leadership, the group flourished, nearly doubling in size.

Groups affect us daily, and in a myriad of ways. Understanding how groups form and function, comprehending why people join and lead groups, recognizing detrimental group processes when they first develop, and knowing how to correct dysfunctional group behaviors are valuable coping skills and are necessary to personal growth and interpersonal relationships.

KINDS OF GROUPS

LEARNING OBJECTIVES

9.1 Name and describe various types of groups.
9.2 Differentiate discrimination, prejudice, and stereotyping.

Groups are all around us. Everywhere we look we see people in groups. Here are just but a few examples: People congregate in their places of worship, families eat together in restaurants, and college classrooms are filled to the brim with eager students. Everywhere—groups. There are many different kinds of groups, each with its own unique characteristics, but in general, most groups we come into contact with on a daily basis fall into one of two types: primary and secondary.

BOX 9–1   Did you know that . . .

The five characteristics of great leaders in business are:

- Have a vision for the future
- Are passionate about what they do
- Are great decision makers
- Know how to be team builders
- Have character

Source: Based on "5 Key Traits of Great Leaders" by Patty Vogan, from Entrepreneur website, April 17, 2006.

Favored Groups—Primary Groups

Perhaps the most important type of group in your life is your **primary group.** *This group is important because it is small, intimate, and interacts face-to-face.* Primary groups have much influence on us, affecting among other things our attitudes, behaviors, emotions, beliefs, and thought processes. Case in point, parents instill in their children the same values, dreams, and culture as their own. And as a result, children often adopt their parents' religion, political views, and other likes and dislikes (DeHart, Sroufe, & Cooper, 2004; Lauglo, 2011). Here's an example involving a primary group that you might find personally relevant: College roommates begin to use similar words and phrases the longer they live together (Pardo, Gibbons, Suppes, & Krauss, 2012). Simply put, primary groups impact virtually every area of a person's life, and therefore, can be a major influence (either positively or negatively) on psychological adjustment and personal growth.

Bigger Than Both of Us—Secondary Groups

Another type of group is a **secondary group.** *These groups are usually larger than primary groups, have a formal or contractual reason for coming together, often disband when the reason for their existence ends, and are less likely to engage in regular face-to-face interaction.* An example of this type of group would be the class for which you are reading this book. The class has a formal reason for coming together (to learn about adjustment and personal growth) and may have limited to no face-to-face interaction (e.g., small group and class discussions). Other examples would be a church congregation or a social organization such as the psychology club. Secondary groups, then, often configure in an audience. Box 9–2 discusses other groups that involve large numbers of people, namely collectives and flash mobs.

BOX 9–2   Focus on Communication: Collectives

You may have read about stampedes of people and riots in the streets during or following major sporting events. Fans clashing at rock concerts offer another example. What to each of these events have in common? They all involved **collectives,** *groups which tend to be very large and are less likely to have a true leader or clear rules* (compared with primary and secondary groups). Collectives often form and disband for no readily apparent reasons. Because collectives are large and without clear-cut rules, they can often be disorderly. Case in point, following the Vancouver Canucks loss to the Boston Bruins in the 2011 NHL Stanley Cup finals, upset Canuck fans took to the streets, setting cars on fire, looting, and destroying millions of dollars in property (CBC News, 2011).

   Of note, collectives are different from **flash mobs**—*in which social media is used to organize the appearance, and accompanying performance, of a group of strangers.* Here's an example: As a result of a postings on Facebook and Twitter, a larger number of freshman show up at noon in the college quad to dance to The Village People's hit *YMCA.* Unlike collectives, flash mobs have a leader of sorts (the organizer) and are typically meant to be entertaining.

Exploration 9.1: Flash Mobs

www.socialtimes.com   This website offers a list of some of the best flash mobs available for viewing on the Internet.

"Us" Versus "Them"—In-Groups and Out-Groups

There are two other very important groups that influence you. One is *the group with which you identify*—the **in-group.** Then there is everyone else, the **out-group**—*the group that we perceive as being different from (outside of) your own group.* In-group/out-group perceptions can develop based on a variety of characteristics, including ethnicity, gender, age, religion, occupation, attitudes, athletic prowess, academic ability, and income level (Halevy, Bornstein, & Sagiv, 2008). In other words, we have a natural tendency to classify the people around us (even when we are among strangers) into two groups: *us* and *them.* Not only that, but we tend to view *us* more positively than *them*; further believing that (1) all out-group members are alike and (2) out-group members have many undesirable characteristics, such as being lazy, stupid, or untrustworthy (Ratliff & Nosek, 2011).

Exploration 9.2: Prejudice

www.understandingprejudice.org   A website dedicated to understanding of the causes and consequences of prejudice.

PREJUDICE, DISCRIMINATION, AND STEREOTYPING   What is most important about the distinctions we make between our own group and the out-group is that these differentiations often result in prejudiced attitudes and negative behaviors against others (Carnaghi & Maass, 2007). **Prejudice** is *an unfair, often negative attitude toward another person or group based solely on group membership.* The distinction can be based on barely visible differences such as skin tone shades. For example, individuals having darker skin experience more prejudice than individuals of the same race with lighter skin (Brown, 2004). Prejudice is sometimes accompanied by behaviors that discriminate against or treat the out-group worse than our own group. *Applying unfair or negative treatment to groups on the basis of such features as age, sex, or race* is called **discrimination.** Although the two usually occur together, prejudice can occur without discrimination and discrimination can occur without prejudice. For example, a restaurant owner could harbor negative attitudes toward Native Americans but still serve them food because of laws against discrimination. Prejudice can also prompt stereotypes, or widespread generalizations about people (based solely on their group membership) that have little if any basis in fact (Dovidio, Glick, & Rudman, 2005). Being either positive or negative, stereotypes relay a simplified view of others that typically center on a limited number of characteristics. Stereotypes create biased expectations for what others should look like and how they should think, feel, and act. Table 9–1 points out some common racial stereotypes. How many of these characterize your own beliefs?

CAUSES AND CONSEQUENCES OF IN-GROUP/OUT-GROUP BIAS   Psychologists are concerned about prejudice, discrimination, and stereotypes because they invariably lead to negative and unfair evaluations of others (Carnaghi & Maass, 2007). Prejudice and its correlates produce stress in those who experience it and may cause damage to their self-esteem (Platow, Byrne, & Ryan, 2005). Interestingly, one reason people hold prejudices is that they seek to enhance their own self-esteem by viewing themselves, and other members of the in-group, as superior to those in the out-group (Major & Eccleston, 2005). Nevertheless, in-groups can still be hard on their own members, especially when one deviates from or disagrees with the group (Conway & Schaller, 2005). The

Table 9–1	Racial Stereotypes		
African American	**Asian**	**Latino**	**Native American**
Athletic	Compliant	Drug Dealer	Alcoholic
Criminal	Humble	Illegal Immigrant	Brave
Poor	Model Minority	Low Status Jobs	Lazy
Rhythmical/Musical	Smart	Uneducated	Spiritual
Unintelligent	Wealthy	Very Religious	Wild

overarching message you should take away from this information is that group dynamics can be harsh and unpleasant, but they need not be. For example, while *intergroup* contact is not always successful at breaking down stereotypes, prejudice, and in-group–out-group barriers, some research shows that it does work (Neili, 2008; Pettigrew & Tropp, 2008).

CULTURAL DIFFERENCES Another significant point about in-groups and out-groups is that their importance varies by culture (Hornsey & Jetten, 2005). People from individualistic cultures value individual gains (needs, wants, and autonomy) over those of the group. As a result, those from individualistic cultures are less likely than people from collectivist cultures to become emotionally attached to any one particular group. Rather, they join and leave groups based on rewards gained or lost. Accordingly, it should come as no surprise that those from individualistic cultures join a greater variety of groups, relative to those in collectivist cultures. In collectivist cultures, where collective or societal gain is cherished over individual advancement, people have fewer in-groups, so they are more attached to the groups of which they are members. Here, survival of the group is more dependent on the effective functioning of the group as a whole rather than that of individuals. Moreover, whereas members of collective societies self-enhance (i.e., feel good about themselves and increase self-esteem) based on loyalty to the group, those from individualistic cultures self-enhance on independence (from the group) dimensions. Finally, in collectivistic cultures, individuals seeking harmony are more likely to take a middling approach to volatile group-based issues. In contrast, those from individualistic cultures are far more expressive of their own independent views (Johnson, Kulesa, Cho, & Shavitt, 2005).

CREATING AND JOINING GROUPS

LEARNING OBJECTIVES

9.3 Discuss how groups form.

9.4 Provide reasons to explain why people join groups.

Think about a fairly new group that you recently joined. How and why did the group form? Did the group evolve or change from its original intent or purpose? Why did you join it in the first place? Although the specifics of your responses may differ from the person next to you in class, in general, the answers you both give are probably quite similar. Let's see why.

How Do Groups Form?

FORMING Much like people, groups change over time. *The initial stage in group development* is **forming** *where individuals come together to form the group.* In the forming stage, members sometimes do not know each other as well as they will later in the developmental process; they are simply coming together as a group. If enough differences exist, friction can build and squabbles between group members can happen. Initially, though, most group members step forward with their best and most cooperative foot as the group forms and people (sometimes secretly) jockey for positions.

STORMING   When group members learn more about each other's attitudes and predilections, differences among individuals lead to *the second stage,* **storming**. In this stage, which can follow quickly on the heels of the first, *individuals disagree or often openly conflict when they learn each other's opinions.* For many groups, this stage is a troublesome one. Members may decide too much friction exists and leave the group. Other members may decide that it is best to remain passive rather than be pulled into the fray; and others are so vociferous and aggressive about promoting their agendas that the remaining members intensely dislike them. At this point it may seem that the group will never start functioning. If group members recognize that this is a normal group stage, however, they can move beyond their differences to the next, more productive stage. As with personal growth, group growth can develop via adversity.

NORMING   When roles become more sharply defined; when groups finally come to terms with how they will function; and when rules by which they will function become clearer, the group is said to be **norming**. That is, through discourse and debate *the group eventually comes to consensus about the rules under which it will operate.* As just mentioned, roles start to emerge in the storming and norming stages. A **role** is *a set of rules that defines how an individual in a particular post in a group will behave.* Also, and as mentioned previously, each group develops its own idiosyncratic **norms**—*standards or unwritten rules by which it will function and by which it will exert pressure on nonconforming members.*

PERFORMING   Once a group has formed, has worked through its initial disagreements, and has developed norms, the group is ready to function well. **Performing** *is the final stage of group development. It is during this stage that the group functions better and actually performs its business,* whether it is organizing a fundraiser or developing a strategic plan for a work team. Once this developmental pattern has been played out by a group, new issues can arise or new members can be added. The group then cycles through these stages again (see Figure 9–1; Tuckman, 1965).

Why Join a Group?

AFFILIATION   What makes you join some clubs, teams, or committees but resist pressure to join others? First, it is important to realize that our awareness of others and our social interactions have biological underpinnings. That is to say, we appear to be genetically hardwired to seek out others for affiliation (Chen, 2009). Beyond biology, social psychologists have identified a multitude of reasons to explain why people join groups. People sometimes connect with groups because groups offer opportunities not available to us as individuals, such as the chance to **affiliate,** *to be with others who are similar to us or whom we like.* For instance, synagogues, churches,

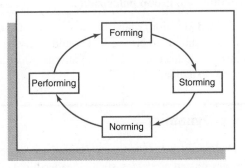

FIGURE 9–1   The cycle of group formation.

and mosques provide more than just religious support; they also offer the chance to socialize with members of the same faith.

INFORMATION AND UNDERSTANDING   Moreover, groups to which we belong can keep us informed about important as well as mundane issues and provide us information we might not otherwise possess. Groups, however, offer us more than mere facts. Groups help us *understand* whether we harbor attitudes that represent a minority or majority position. Groups also help us figure out our position in the social order. For example, when you receive examinations back in a college class, you may think that a score of 37 is terrible until you see that the classmates around you received 25, 19, and 32. *Groups, then, allow us to compare ourselves to others and understand who we are relative to them*, a process referred to as **social comparison.** We generally select another person with whom to compare ourselves based on that person's expertise, similarity to us, and previous level of agreement (Stapel & Johnson, 2007).

SOCIAL SUPPORT   Providing opportunities for social support is a very important function of groups. You may recall that social support is a process whereby one individual or group offers psychological and sometimes physical aid to another individual or group. Primary groups, especially of friends and family, can offer us much-needed social support. When something goes wrong in our lives, when we have difficult decisions to make, or conversely, when something wondrous occurs, groups can give us a needed boost, providing affection, sympathy, a friendly face to look at, and so on. As you can see, groups offer up support that has the potential to promote our own personal growth, adjustment, and mental health (Masood, Okazaki, & Takeuchi, 2009).

POWER   Groups also give us more collective power. There may be needs we have that we simply cannot meet alone. Labor unions offer an example. Unions, which have collective power, can negotiate better raises and working conditions than any individual member can. Alliances and coalitions can better lobby governments for needed legislation. And student groups, such as your student government, possess consolidated power compared to each individual student. The student government with the force of hundreds or thousands of students behind it can better approach the administration to advance student causes, such as assistance for commuting students. Thus, when in a group, people come to realize their collective power and ability to influence others.

WHAT GOES ON IN GROUPS?

LEARNING OBJECTIVES

9.5 **Describe how groups communicate.**

9.6 **Explain how the size of a group can affect its functioning.**

9.7 **Compare three types of social influence: conformity, compliance, and obedience.**

9.8 **Understand social loafing and group polarization.**

You have already been introduced to major group practices, such as the development of roles and norms. There are other processes unique to groups that would rarely be discussed with regard to an individual. These processes include communication patterns, social influence, social loafing, and group polarization. Each is examined next.

Exploration 9.3: Group Dynamics

facultystaff.richmond.edu/~dforsyth/gd   This group dynamics resource page has links to information about a variety of group-related processes, such as leadership, group influence, and power.

What Did You Say?—Communication Patterns

One of the most important group processes is intra-group (i.e., within group) communication. Communication within a group allows group members to coordinate their actions, share information, and express emotions and ideas—all of which are essential to decision making and performance.

NETWORKS There are two main types of communication networks: centralized and decentralized (Brown & Miller, 2000). In **centralized communication networks**, *one or two individuals control the flow of information.* One such network is the wheel, in which the flow of information (and decisions) comes from a centralized source (i.e., the leader), and not from other group members. The leader makes all of the decisions and decides who gets what information. The wheel is similar to a university, where all department chairs report to a dean or vice president who makes final funding, personnel, and other decisions. Centralized networks can be contrasted to **decentralized communication networks** in which *individuals can communicate relatively freely with one another.* Rumors that pass from one person to another, then to yet another, and back to the original source offer an example of the circle. Of course, there are other centralized and decentralized systems. Can you think examples for the different types of communication networks represented in Figure 9–2?

Centralized and decentralized networks result in different types of performance (e.g., how many widgets are made, how long the group meets, how good the decisions are). For simple tasks (or simple decisions), centralized networks work the best; they are much more efficient and effective than decentralized networks. However, when tasks are complicated or decisions require complex input and deliberation, decentralized networks produced better outcomes (Sharma & Sharma, 2010).

GROUP SIZE Another factor that affects the quality of group communication is the *size* of the group. Of course, groups vary in their size depending on the situation. For example, juries are usually comprised of 12 individuals; university academic departments can be as small as two people or as large as 60; and the U.S. House of Representatives has 435 voting members. In comparison to smaller groups, larger groups are perceived by its members to be more competitive, less unified, and more argumentative. Moreover, group satisfaction among members decreases as groups become larger. In terms of productivity, very large groups are usually not as successful as smaller groups of three to eight members (Wheelan, 2009). Although groups with many members have more resources available, the number of ideas generated is not directly proportionate to group size. Curiously, as the size of the group increases, the number of ideas generated increases at a slower rate.

Communication style and effectiveness also differ by group size. In small groups, group discussions actually appear to be interactive dialogues or conversations. In larger groups, the discourse resembles a monologue in which a few individuals dominate or speak sequentially (Fay, Garrod, & Carletta, 2000). Interactions and communications are also more likely to be formalized in a larger

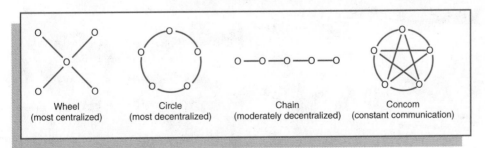

Wheel	Circle	Chain	Concom
(most centralized)	(most decentralized)	(moderately decentralized)	(constant communication)

FIGURE 9–2 Examples of various communication networks. "O" represents an individual, and the lines represent the communication links between individuals.

group. For instance, large groups, such as the United States Congress, are more likely to set agendas and to follow Roberts' Rules of Order to control discussions. Overall, group discussion is less satisfying in larger groups than in smaller ones.

ELECTRONIC COMMUNICATION As our world turns more to electronic forms of communication (such as e-mail, texts, tweets, Facebook, blogs, etc.) it will be interesting to verify whether the principles just described still hold true. One of the benefits of electronic communication is that it affords those that are shy, or have difficulty turning their thoughts into words, the opportunity to become active participants in the group, rather than passive observers. Nevertheless, compared to face-to-face communication where nonverbal cues enhance interpersonal understanding, in electronic communication the opportunity for miscommunication is increased (Workman, 2007). As an example, e-mail users are largely unaware of these limitations; they know what they intend to communicate, so they assume that their audience does as well (Kruger et al., 2005). Text messaging may prove even more troublesome because texts involve truncated or abbreviated messages. There are other problems with electronic communication. Trust, for example, is greater in face-to-face interactions than in electronic meetings (Wilson, Straus, & McEvily, 2006). And of course, many of us know all too well the dangers of hitting "replay all" instead of "reply" when sending out an angry electronic missive, gossiping, or writing something inappropriate about another group member.

On the bright side, status inequalities are reduced with electronic participation (Dubrovsky, Kiesler, & Sethna, 1991). This is important because in face-to-face groups, often the highest status members do the most communicating. With electronic communication, each group member has a greater likelihood of participating. Given this, the group has a better chance of maximizing the potential of all its members. Moreover, electronic communication, especially at workplaces, is more task-oriented and more efficient than face-to-face meetings (Lantz, 2001). However, this effect requires that group members do not miss the socializing aspects of work, such as "schmoozing" (i.e., establishing rapport by sharing personal information) (Morris, Nadler, Kurtzberg, &Thompson, 2002). Electronic communication also enables its users to expand their

Compared to face-to-face communication, electronic communication may result in more miscommunication because it lacks subtle cues such as facial expressions.

group's size and influence and to heighten the number of social contacts. Cyberspace can also help build community spirit as well as provide both emotional and tangible support to its users (Drentea & Moren-Cross, 2005).

You Want Me to Do What?—Social Influence

Social influence involves *efforts on the part of one person to alter the behavior or attitudes of one or more others.* For instance, advertisements on TV are meant to influence your opinions about specific goods, so when you're at the store you'll buy the advertised product, instead of one of its competitors. (See Box 9–3 for a discussion of some techniques that advertisers use to influence consumer behavior.) Social influence can affect us in a variety of ways. We can

---

BOX 9–3   Focus on Psychology: Advertising and You

Traditional Advertising

Movie stars, musicians, professional athletes, and other celebrities are frequently used to advertise products. Endorsements by cartoon characters, such as Dora the Explorer, fit in this category as well. Advertisers believe that positive attitudes towards celebrities are transferred to the products they are endorsing. Another technique to sway the behaviors of consumers is the use of premium prizes, which are objects given away for free with the purchase of a specified product. For instance, *McDonald's* "Happy Meals" typically include a toy as the premium prize. Additionally, through animation, special effects, and misleading statements (e.g., "the best"), advertisers deceive the consumer into thinking that the advertised product offers more excitement, fun, ways of playing with it, etc., than it does in reality.

 Advertisers will use every trick they know to influence the behavior of consumers, including creating an appealing "look." For example, a fun-looking, colorful package is thought to grab the attention of children, increasing the likelihood that they will ask their parents to buy it for them at the point-of-sale. In addition, branded characters/mascots, like the *Tony the Tiger*, frequently appear on packages in an attempt to sway consumers' choices (Palmer & Carpenter, 2006). Advertisers are also increasingly using co-branding to promote toys, food, and the like. **Co-branding** is the *advertising technique in which two companies work together to cross-promote products or services.* A popular co-branding technique is to adorn the packaging of food products with popular cartoon and movie character, such as *SpongeBob Squarepants Macaroni `n' Cheese* (Batada & Wootan, 2007).

Modern Advertising

Advergames, which combine advertisement and entertainment, are web-based games that incorporate the product brand and/or brand character into the game itself. Rather than providing stand-alone games, some websites create a virtual world for consumers to explore. One such website, *Happymeal.com* (which is operated by McDonald's) allows the user to play games and watch videos. Of course, McDonald logos are found throughout this virtual community. Moreover, advergames make use of *viral advertising* to promote products. **Viral advertising** is *a marketing technique in which advertisers rely on pre-existing social networks (e.g., blogs, e-mail, etc.) to promote products by encouraging users to voluntarily pass along web links, video clips, Flash games, etc.*

The Importance of Brand Awareness

Remember, brand awareness at a young age has the potential to turn into consumer behavior years later. As such, some "adult-oriented" advertisements appear to be designed to attract the attention of a younger audience. For instance, one of the primary goals of cigarette advertising is to attract smokers *before* they start smoking. Because TV commercials for cigarettes were banned in 1971, *R. J. Reynolds* shifted their advertising dollars from television to magazines and billboards, promoting their product with the cartoon-like character *Old Joe Camel*. By 1991, 30 percent of 3-year olds and 91 percent of 6-year olds correctly associated *Old Joe the Camel* with cigarettes (Fischer, Schwart, Richards, Goldstein, & Rojas, 1991). What advertisements do you remember from your childhood? How many were for products meant for adults? The answer may surprise you.

publicly go along with others but refuse to change our private beliefs. An example of this would be that you are seated in the snack bar between classes and three friends all declare that they are voting for a political candidate whom you detest. Because you are in a hurry to make your next class and you do not want to enter into a debate with them, you slowly nod your head in agreement. Another level of social influence is when you behave like or are influenced by others because you are attracted to them. Very often when you begin to steadily date someone, you adopt the new date's tastes for food and music. If you and your date then part company, you return to your own tastes in cuisine and melody. The third level is one where someone has truly influenced you so much that you change forever. At this level, an individual or group convinces you that you should adopt their ideas, behaviors, and tastes. How and why do people gain influence over others? Three processes—conformity, compliance, and obedience—shed light on the mechanisms (Mason, Conrey, & Smith, 2007).

CONFORMITY   **Conformity** is a *change in behavior due to the real or imagined influence (pressure) of other people.* For example, in an attempt to "fit in" many teens will imitate the clothing style of their peers, such as wearing baggy pants or belly shirts. Of course, no one issued official orders proclaiming that youth needed to wear these types of clothing; there was just subtle peer pressure to do so. Conformity has been examined for over 60 years, starting with the seminal work of Solomon Asch (1951). In his experiment, a single subject entered a testing room and sat down next to "participants" who had supposedly arrived earlier. In reality, the other "participants" were **confederates** or *agents of the experimenter who were told in advance how to behave.* The subject and confederates were asked to judge a "standard" line (X) with a series of comparison lines (A, B, C) to determine which line these three lines was closest in length to the standard (see Figure 9–3). At first, confederates matched the lines correctly, but then confederates gave the same, but obviously wrong, answer. Much to his surprise, Asch found that many subjects conformed to the apparently wrong answer. Asch concluded that the tendency to conform in our society is strong, even on obviously easy tasks; and even when no one forces conformity. Since Asch's initial research, scientists have discovered different factors that enhance or reduce conformity. Here's what they found: We are most likely to conform when our responses are public and face-to-face; when we want to be accepted by the group; when agreeing seems easier than disagreeing; and when the proportion of other conformists is high (Bond, 2005; Coultas, 2004).

It is also important to comment on individual and cultural differences in conformity. Despite Asch's results, many Americans espouse independence and autonomy, and as a result shun conformity. Cultures that emphasize **interdependence** (*mutual dependence among individuals in a given group or society*) also exist. Many of these are collectivist societies. Conformity

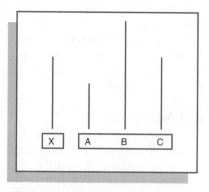

FIGURE 9–3   Asch's line experiment.
In Asch's line experiment, confederates said line X was the same length as a clearly incorrect comparison line, such as line B. Would you say the correct answer (C), or conform to the group?

and harmony is an integral part of the social fabric of these cultures (Johnson et al., 2005). Some examples of more interdependent cultures (where conformity to group norms is *expected*) are the Zimbabwean and Lebanese societies (Smith & Bond, 1993). On the other hand, research is now pointing out the fact that some collective cultures are not as conformist as we expected (Takano & Sogon, 2008). Perhaps as cultures have come into contact with each other, distinctions between collective and individualistic societies are disappearing. With regard to gender, research on over 70 different cultures has consistently shown that men and women conform with the same degree of frequency (Schwartz & Rubel, 2005).

COMPLIANCE **Compliance** may be defined as a *change in behavior in response to a direct request from another person to do so.* Compliance, like conformity, is an everyday phenomenon. Examples include, quieting down at the request of a professor; coming to the dinner table when called to do so; and refraining from talking on a cell phone during a movie. Note that we sometimes comply publicly but disagree with the request privately, just as is true for conformity. There are conditions under which we are more or less likely to comply. In many societies, the United States included, a norm of reciprocity is common (Park & Antonioni, 2007). This unwritten rule guides reciprocal behavior related to the granting of favors. If someone does you a favor, you feel compelled to return (reciprocate) the favor. A more manipulative way to induce compliance is through **ingratiation,** which involves *managing the impressions you leave on others so that they will like you more and comply with your requests.* Flattery is a form of ingratiation, as is imitating the attitudes, preferences, and behaviors of others (Robinson, Tobias, Shaw, Freeman, & Higgs, 2011).

Sometimes, a two-step approach to compliance increases the likelihood of its success. In the **door-in-the-face effect**, *the requester first issues a large, unreasonable request. When the respondent answers "no," the requester makes the truly desired but smaller and more reasonable demand.* Not wanting to appear difficult or stubborn, the respondent often answers "yes" to the second, smaller request (Cialdini & Goldstein, 2004). For example, a rather calculating friend may ask to borrow your new, expensive car to impress his new date. Not having driven the car much yourself, you quickly answer "no." The friend then asks to borrow $15 for the same date, to which you more readily agree.

OBEDIENCE **Obedience** involves *following a direct order or command.* The command typically comes from someone who has the capacity to enforce the order if it is not followed (Burger, Girgis, & Manning, 2011). In 1974, Stanley Milgram published his dramatic *Obedience to Authority.* In it, he details a series of studies on obedience to authority figures that rattled the psychological world. Imagine that you are in Milgram's experiment. You are led to a room and introduced to Mr. Wallace, a kindly older man who is to be the learner in the study. You are going to be the teacher. Mr. Wallace is to learn a list of words. Each time he errs, you are to give him an electric shock that you are both told will be painful but will cause no permanent tissue damage. For each error, you are to increase the level of shock by one increment. The first level is 15 volts and labeled "slight shock." The last is 450 volts and labeled only with "XXX"—to designate its dangerous nature. As the teacher you are not aware that the experiment is fixed such that you are not really administering shocks and that Mr. Wallace is really a confederate.

As you proceed up the shock generator, you hear Mr. Wallace's groans. Eventually, Mr. Wallace refuses to continue and states that he has a heart problem. Each time you query the experimenter (the authority figure) about Mr. Wallace's condition, the experimenter urges you to continue. The experimenter reminds you that although the shocks may be painful, they cause no permanent damage. The experimenter then orders you to go on. During the final stage of the experiment, Mr. Wallace becomes silent; and yet, you are asked to shock him one more time and at the highest level! The most dramatic and disconcerting part of these studies is that 65 percent of subjects went all the way up the shock generator at the urging of the experimenter. Milgram's findings suggest that within each of us there is the capacity to harm another; and all that needs to

Imagine being the only bicyclist without a basket; you'd be a nonconformist.

happen for this to occur is for someone to tell us that we *must* do so. What would you do if you were a participant in Milgram's study?

Let the Other Guy Do It—Social Loafing

Have you ever "goofed off" in a group? If you haven't, have you observed others "not holding up their end of the deal"? Another process that occurs in groups is **social loafing** *in which individuals contribute less to a group effort than they would contribute to an individual effort.* For example, if individuals are asked one at a time to paint a mural or to clap for an athlete, they put more effort into the performance alone than they would if asked to perform as a group. In fact, the larger the group, the less individual effort everyone puts into his or her performance (Kayes, Kayes, & Kolb, 2005). Of note, there are cultural differences in the prevalence of social loafing. In individualistic societies, people are expected to be independent and autonomous, so they contribute less to group efforts. In more collective societies in which group effort is valued, social loafing is less likely to occur (Hong, Wyer, & Fong, 2008).

As many of you know, it's not fair for a slacker to get the same grade on a group project as those putting forth significant effort. Fortunately, there are ways to reduce the likelihood of social loafing occurring. When people believe their performance will be individually evaluated; when the task is important or meaningful; when failure is possible if social loafing occurs; and when individual members value the group, social loafing is minimized (Pearsall, Christian, & Ellis, 2010).

All in Favor Say "Aye"—Group Polarization

Surely you have worked in groups that make decisions requiring consensus or unanimity. Interestingly, the decisions of the individual can become more extreme when part of a group. At times, *groups coming to consensus make riskier decisions than individuals,* an event known as the **risky shift.** For instance, the likelihood of administering an experimental drug to a patient increases

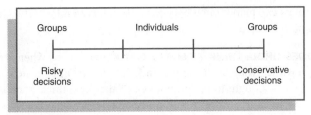

FIGURE 9–4   The group polarization effect.   Groups often make more extreme decisions (conservative or risky) than individuals.

when the determination to do so is made by a committee, in comparison to when the same decision is made by a single person. At other times, groups coming to consensus make more cautious decisions than individuals. The phenomenon whereby *individuals in a group make either more conservative or riskier decisions than when alone* is referred to as the **group polarization effect**, as depicted in Figure 9–4. It should come as no surprise to learn that when group polarization occurs, viewpoints and attitudes corresponding to the more extreme decision become more extreme themselves (Palmer & Loveland, 2008). For example, those who are only slightly in favor of using experimental medications to treat incurable diseases become staunch supporters of this viewpoint after being part of a committee that decided to administer a controversial drug to a dying patient.

Group polarization occurs, in part, because *people in groups feel less individual responsibility for the outcome of their decisions,* in a process known as **responsibility diffusion.** Additionally, people in groups become increasingly confident in their decisions because, through discussion, viewpoints consistent with their own are repeatedly being stated, thus strengthening the belief that they are correct. Interestingly, another factor that predicts whether individuals in a group will press for caution or for risk is culture. In African cultures, for example, caution is valued over risk. In the United States, risk and bravado are valued over caution (Gologor, 1977). Given that you, too, spend so much time in groups, you need to be aware of these effects so that you can override their consequences and make the best possible decisions.

WHEN GROUPS GO WRONG

LEARNING OBJECTIVES

9.9 Explain Groupthink.

9.10 Discuss some ways to prevent groupthink.

9.11 Explain how conflict can be both good and bad.

9.12 Discuss conflict management.

Just because everyone in a group thinks an idea is a good one doesn't mean that it actually is. Case in point, in 1961 the newly formed Kennedy administration went ahead with a plan to support a group of Cuban exiles' attempt to invade their homeland at the Bay of Pigs and overthrow Fidel Castro. Three days after the attack began the defeat of the rebel forces was complete. How could President Kennedy make such a clearly bad decision to support a rag-tag attempt to overthrow a foreign government? The concept of groupthink has been credited as being one of the major reasons for the Kennedy administration's confidence in the success of their plan and lack of foresight is discussing the likelihood of its failure (Janis, 1982).

Groupthink

Groupthink is *the tendency for groups to reach a consensus prematurely because the desire for harmony overrides the process of critical thinking and the search for the best decision.* Groupthink occurs when a group becomes more concerned with maintaining consensus and cohesion than with developing good ideas. Remember, when groupthink *is not* present, well-functioning groups can make sound decisions. With that in mind, let us look at how group-think develops and how it can be prevented.

HOW AND WHY DOES GROUPTHINK OCCUR?   Groupthink begins when a group is close-knit and the members view the group as attractive. In fact, cohesiveness or how close group members are to one another is thought to underlie much of the groupthink phenomenon. Moreover, the group typically operates in isolation with a decisive leader who controls the discussion or promotes their own agenda (Ahlfinger & Esser, 2001; Henningsen, Henningsen, Eden, & Cruz, 2006). Another symptom of this phenomenon is the **illusion of invulnerability.** The group is so close-knit and in agreement that *the members believe they are invincible; they can do no wrong.* This occurs because no one in the group wants to dissent and break the cohesiveness. In fact, dissenters are quickly dismissed or pressured to conform to the group's sentiments. *The individuals who take it upon themselves to censor dissenters* are labeled **mindguards.** Because of mindguards, dissension ceases and the group comes to think that it is unanimous and morally correct. What makes the process of unanimity and self-righteousness likely is that the group also stereotypes the out-group (the opposition). Members may denigrate the out-group as lazy, stupid, or incapable. Other indicators that group think is occurring are as follows:

The group:

- discusses only one or two ideas.
- fails to survey all possible alternative solutions.
- commits the blunder of not looking at all possible risks.
- avoids discussing the downside of its chosen alternative.
- never develops any contingency plans in case something goes wrong.

PREVENTING GROUPTHINK   Fortunately, groupthink can be averted. One means to prevent it is to promote open inquiry and skepticism. Perhaps the group can appoint an official devil's advo-cate, or the group leader can invite criticism and open debate about each alternative. To ensure that a number of alternatives are generated, subgroups can be formed. Each subgroup should pro-duce its own solutions; and consequently, several alternatives result. Once an alternative has been selected, a second-chance meeting should occur. In this way, the group has the opportunity to rethink its position and to express any remaining doubts. The leader should also refrain from ex-pressing his or her opinion at the outset so as to foster the generation of options. One last recom-mendation is to call on outside experts so that the group does not remain isolated and decisions can be made by better-informed group members. You should fill out the information requested in Activity 9–1 to see whether you recently have been subjected to groupthink.

A Little Shove Goes a Long Way—Group Conflict

When you enthusiastically join a group, you hope that the group is free of conflict. However, whether at work or as part of committee, social organization, or team, each of us can recall in-stances of within-group (e.g., disagreements over a course of action; power struggles; arguments between employees) and between-group (e.g., feuds among competing companies; negotiations between employers and employees) conflict. Although the term "conflict" is frequently associ-ated with adverse situations, conflict need not always be problematic. In fact, some conflict can be beneficial to the group (De Dreu, 2005).

THE UPSIDE AND DOWNSIDE OF CONFLICT   Conflict need not always be bad, in fact, it has an upside. Conflict can be useful in terms of testing and assessing ourselves, others, and the issues facing us. Conflict challenges us to develop creative responses and solutions. Conflict can also result in much positive social change. Witness, for example, how the civil unrest of the 1950s and 1960s resulted in advances for African-Americans and other people of color. Moreover, con-flict with a second group can sometimes increase cohesiveness within a group as people band together to face their common "enemy." Conflict, then, is not always bad.

ACTIVITY 9–1

GROUPTHINK—HAS IT HAPPENED TO YOU?

INSTRUCTIONS: *Think about a group situation you were in where the group made an important decision. Using the following true (T) or false (F) scale, indicate whether the following statements describe the situation.*

1. Early in our deliberations, the group leader announced his or her preferences.   T   F

2. Our group was particularly friendly and close-knit.   T   F

3. The group was not very tolerant of dissent or disagreement.   T   F

4. Once we understood the issue, we developed our ideas quickly.   T   F

5. I don't think the group ever recognized the ramifications of its final decision.   T   F

6. The group did not generate ideas in case things went wrong after our decision was implemented.   T   F

7. Our group was a bit self-righteous during our deliberations.   T   F

8. People outside the group were ignored or even made fun of.   T   F

9. Once we decided what we wanted to do, we quickly went off topic and chatted about personal issues.   T   F

10. The group looked unanimous, but I think some people privately disagreed.   T   F

SCORING: Count up the number of Ts. The higher the number, the more likely your group suffered from groupthink. Now examine how good your decision was. Did it work? Were others outside of the group pleased with the decision? Did anything go wrong during implementation or afterward? If your group was fraught with groupthink as indicated by your score (a high number of "trues"), then your answers should indicate the final decision was rather poor. Was it? If yes, what would you do differently next time?

Nevertheless, conflict does have its downside. Conflicts typically are the result of complex mixed-motives where a number of divergent intentions fuel the clash (e.g., "Even if I lose, I want to keep my opponent from gaining too much"). For instance, individuals and groups generally want more than just to win the conflict. Sometimes they also hope to inflict revenge, humiliation, or punishment to make the other side suffer a greater loss than they themselves have. Another major problem with conflict is that it sometimes seems to escalate out of control. In other words, a little shove really does go a long way (Kennedy & Pronin, 2008).

WHY DO CONFLICTS OCCUR?   Many factors contribute to the development of conflicts and/or their escalation. Threats are one such factor. When one group or party threatens another, the other side often responds with a like threat. For example, in international conflict, if one country threatens invasion, the threatened country often responds with a counterattack or at least a threat of retaliation (Huntington, 1999). Moreover, differences in strongly held but incompatible beliefs and ideals can spawn conflict (Chrobot-Mason, Ruderman, Weber, Ohlott, & Dalton, 2007). Another reason conflict escalates is that once we are committed to a position we tend to devote time and energy to maintaining that position, rather than to investigating alternatives (Cardona-Coll, 2003). In such instances, people do not seem to be able to cut their losses things go wrong. *This process* *of throwing more time, energy, or money into a bad situation* is called **entrapment**. Entrapment occurs when commitments to a failing course of action are increased to justify investments already made. Entrapment contributes to conflict escalation by motivating the losers to keep trying to win.

Our biases toward others, such as stereotypes and prejudice, also fuel conflict escalation (Ledgerwood & Chaiken, 2007). Such perceptions divide conflicting groups into "us" versus "them." The fundamental attribution error in part accounts for this division. When you fall prey to the fundamental attribution error, you overattribute other people's behaviors to personality (traits) rather than to situations. In the case of conflict, negative behaviors are viewed as long-term characteristics of the individual. And once a negative image is established, a self-fulfilling prophecy often sustains it. The **self-fulfilling prophecy** *occurs when people's expectations become a reality by virtue of their own behavior.* For example, if we expect someone to be impolite, we may treat them in such a way (such as being rude ourselves) that elicits discourtesy.

CULTURE AND CONFLICT   Psychologists, sociologists, and anthropologists have noted that different cultures manage conflict differently (Cushner, 2005). Recall that collectivist societies value group efforts over individual efforts, but the converse is true for individualistic cultures. Such differences become apparent when looking at the role of face-saving in conflict negotiations. **Face-saving** *relates to saving one's own or someone else's image.* In collectivistic cultures, opponents purposely try to avoid humiliating or conflicting with others. In individualistic societies, individuals are more concerned with saving their *own* images, and as a result of this belief, they will debase or denigrate their opponent (Ulijn, Rutkowski, Kumar, & Zhu, 2005). Furthermore, those from individualistic cultures use dominance as a style of negotiating, whereas individuals from collective cultures are more likely to use integrative solutions, which you will read about momentarily (Oetzel & Ting-Toomey, 2003).

CONFLICT MANAGEMENT   At times, a resolution to a conflict, in which both parties agree upon a solution to their differences, cannot be found. In situations such as these, at best, the conflict can be *managed*, that is, contained or kept from escalating. Because most conflicts are mixed-motive conflicts, it is not always true that when one side loses, the other must win. Groups and individuals in conflict can look for integrative solutions. **Integrative solutions** are *those that take into account the needs of both sides such that both sides can win something.* At first, it may sound as if integrative solutions involve compromise. In compromise, though, each side must also lose a little to win a little. Integrative solutions go *beyond* compromise.

Charles Osgood (1962) introduced a negotiating technique designed to end or lower the level of conflict. The technique is known as **GRIT,** or **graduated and reciprocated initiatives in tension reduction.** With this technique, *each side gradually concedes something to the other side.* For example, in international conflict, one side might concede a small piece of disputed territory. Because of the norm of reciprocity, pressure exists on the other side to give something up as well (Park & Antonioni, 2007), perhaps a partial troop withdrawal. Often these concessions are made *public* so as to keep pressure to reciprocate on both sides. The key here, then, is *communication with the public* as well as with the opposition. There is always a danger with GRIT that one side will not reciprocate and in fact take advantage of the other, conceding side. Should this happen, the side that made the concession needs to respond with a like competitive action so that the opposition knows that they will not be taken advantage of.

Another way to promote conflict management and resolution involves the intervention of a third party (Arnold, 2007). Third parties are usually mediators or arbitrators. **Mediators** are *neutral third parties who intervene in conflict and who help the two disputing parties come to common agreements via communication, creative problem solving, and other techniques.* **Arbitrators** are similar to mediators in that they are *neutral third parties who, using the same techniques, assist the parties with the conflict, hope that the parties can resolve their differences, but if they cannot, render a binding decision upon the parties.* Every state in the United States houses mediation or neighborhood justice centers as alternatives to the courts (McGillis, 1997). The typical case is a two-party dispute over property, but some centers handle felonies such as rape where the rapist and victim meet face-to-face. Mediators and arbitrators are used in many different arenas to facilitate the resolution of conflict. In fact, mediators have successfully resolved conflicts involving international, environmental, business, family, and neighborhood disputes (Moritsugu, Wong, & Duffy, 2010).

GROUP LEADERSHIP

LEARNING OBJECTIVES

9.13 Describe how individuals become leaders.

9.14 Explain various types of leadership styles and traits.

Have you ever led a group? Do you think you have leadership qualities? Or would you rather sit back silently and let someone else have the limelight? By reading the next passages, you should understand yourself better as well as the challenges facing all leaders of groups.

In almost all groups, someone rises as leader. Committees elect their leaders; corporations retain CEOs appointed by the board of directors; some countries are governed by a self-appointed dictator while others have hereditary rulers or elected officials. Leaders are vitally important because groups with leaders typically outperform groups without them (De-Souza & Klein, 1995). How do leaders emerge and what qualities make for good leadership? The answers to these questions are difficult because each situation is so different from the next. To start, let us first examine theories about the origins of leaders.

Exploration 9.4: Leadership

www.whatmakesagoodleader.com   This website provides free how-to guides on leadership- and management-related issues.

The "Great Man" Theory

Do people possess certain traits at birth that set them on the path to leadership? The earliest theory of leadership was the **"great man" theory** (Mayseless & Popper, 2007). The theory predated feminism so the term "man" was used. This theory suggests that *great leaders are born with a certain common set of traits.* If an individual possesses these traits, such as good public speaking skills or high intelligence, then that person will become a leader and be capable of leading in a variety of situations. If not, the individual is out of luck. Researchers thus assumed that they ought to be able to assess great leaders and find common characteristics or traits (Zaccaro, 2007). Unfortunately for the "great man" theory, but good for most of us, there is little research to support it. For instance, one study found that the only common characteristics of the presidents of the United States were that they come from small families and were tall (Simonton, 1987). As a result of findings like these, the "great man" theory was essentially abandoned in favor of other notions of leadership.

Situational Explanations of Leadership

Other explanations for the emergence of leaders involve the situation people find themselves in. In other words, perhaps being in the right place at the right time means that you are likely to become a leader (Vroom & Jago, 2007). Here's an example: A tour group is visiting France. Only one person in the group speaks French. This person interprets and translates for everyone else in the group, and thus becomes the de facto leader. According to this notion of leadership, the situation creates the leader.

Contingency Theory

Some of the most popular theories of leadership are those that combine personal factors with situational factors. In other words, these theories suggest that you have to have the right leadership qualities for *that particular* situation (Zaccaro, 2007). Then and only then will you be an effective leader. One such theory is **contingency theory of leadership.** *The theory identifies two attributes or styles of leaders known as people-oriented or task-oriented, which are effective at leading in different situations.* **People- or relationship-oriented leaders** *concern themselves with members' feelings and relationships.* In contrast, **task-oriented leaders** *are primarily concerned with getting the job done well and in a timely fashion.* That is, they initiate structures that allow tasks to get done (van Emmerick, Euwema, & Wendt, 2008). Interestingly, people-oriented leader see the good in their coworkers, even if they are not well liked and not as productive as they could be. In contrast, the task leader, interested more in performance than people, has stronger negative feelings toward coworkers who do not do their jobs well (Kaplan & Kaiser, 2003). Activity 9–2 presents a scale to help you figure out your own leadership style.

Situations in which the task to be done is clear and members of the group have good relationships are referred to as *high control situations.* In contrast, vague tasks and poor relationships among group members create *low control situations. Medium control situations* fall in between high and low control situations in terms of task direction and group relationships. Interestingly, task-oriented leaders are most effective in either high or low control situations. On the other hand, people-oriented leaders are most effective in medium control situations (Morris, Brotheridge, & Urbanski, 2005). As you can see, one style alone does not produce effective leadership across all situations, as suggested by the "great man" theory. A better theory might be one that emphasizes the balance between task- and people-oriented styles matched to appropriate situations (Kaplan & Kaiser, 2003).

Contemporary Theories

EMOTIONALLY INTELLIGENT LEADERS   Although the leadership style should match the situation, there are some traits that increase the likelihood that one could become an effective leader. One such trait is emotional intelligence (EI). As you recall, EI is the ability to regulate one's own emotions and to be empathic for others' emotions. Leaders high in EI are self-aware, have exceptionally good interpersonal skills, demonstrate self-control and social awareness, and know how to manage interpersonal relationships (e.g., possess good conflict management skills) (Dearborn, 2002). Leaders with EI are also confident without being arrogant. These traits make the person with EI very popular with others. In fact, EI is twice as important as any other personal characteristic (e.g., possession of technical skills) for predicting who will achieve the highest roles in organizations (Goldman, 2005). Moreover, leaders high in EI perform their jobs better than their low-EI counterparts (Koman & Wolff, 2008).

CHARISMATIC LEADERS   Emotionally intelligent leaders may share some traits with another type of leader—**the charismatic leader** who *inspires social change, is visionary, and appeals to followers' self-concepts and values* (Bedell-Avers, Hunter, & Mumford, 2008). The charismatic leader often guides followers to solutions that alleviate the problems they face. Typically, charismatic leaders "run the show," that is they are singularly responsible for relaying their vision to others, and for getting followers to agree and commit to that vision. However, the "vision" of charismatic leaders does not necessarily have to serve the greater good. For instance, cult heads Jim Jones and Charles Manson exemplify this leadership style. Given that the followers of Jim Jones committed mass suicide, and that those in the Manson "family" committed murder, being overly dependent on a charismatic leader to make decisions for you, and blindly following their vision, can be quite problematic (Mayseless & Popper, 2007).

TRANSFORMATIONAL LEADERS   Similar to charismatic leaders, **transformational leaders** *stimulate interest among colleagues and followers to view their work from a new perspective. The leader does this by generating awareness of the mission or vision of the organization and helps members to look beyond their own interests.* However, in contrast to charismatic leaders,

ACTIVITY 9–2

WHAT TYPE OF LEADER ARE YOU?

INSTRUCTIONS: *Rate your least favorite classmate on the following dimensions by placing an "X" in the appropriate space. First impressions are best.*

Friendly	___ ___ ___ ___ ___ ___ ___	Unfriendly
Cold	___ ___ ___ ___ ___ ___ ___	Warm
Strong	___ ___ ___ ___ ___ ___ ___	Weak
Honest	___ ___ ___ ___ ___ ___ ___	Dishonest
Active	___ ___ ___ ___ ___ ___ ___	Passive
Bad	___ ___ ___ ___ ___ ___ ___	Good
Intelligent	___ ___ ___ ___ ___ ___ ___	Unintelligent
Closed-minded	___ ___ ___ ___ ___ ___ ___	Open-minded

Now rate your most favorite classmate on the following scale by placing an X in the appropriate space. First impressions are best. Try not to let your ratings of the least favorite classmate influence these ratings (i.e., don't use comparisons).

Friendly	___ ___ ___ ___ ___ ___ ___	Unfriendly
Cold	___ ___ ___ ___ ___ ___ ___	Warm
Strong	___ ___ ___ ___ ___ ___ ___	Weak
Honest	___ ___ ___ ___ ___ ___ ___	Dishonest
Active	___ ___ ___ ___ ___ ___ ___	Passive
Bad	___ ___ ___ ___ ___ ___ ___	Good
Intelligent	___ ___ ___ ___ ___ ___ ___	Unintelligent
Closed-minded	___ ___ ___ ___ ___ ___ ___	Open-minded

Look at how close the Xs are for each designated classmate. Were your ratings for least favorite classmate similar to the ratings for your most favorite classmate? In other words, were the Xs located in about the same position on the scales? If yes, then you possess a person-oriented leadership style. If they are farther apart (at opposite ends of each scale), then you may possess a task-oriented leadership style. This scale is designed to assist you in thinking about your own personal style of leadership. Remember that both styles have their advantages. Good leaders learn to adopt each style when the situation dictates.

transformational leaders are characterized by power sharing, openness to the opinion of others, and a give and take relationship with followers. Such leaders raise their supporters to a higher level of morality and motivation by inspiring them to work toward the greater good or shared goals (Nielsen, Randall, Yarker, & Brenner, 2008). Examples include Mahatma Gandhi and Martin Luther King Jr. whose leadership styles lead to significant social change in the India and the United States, respectively.

Gender and Leadership

As you can tell from the dated name of the "great man" theory, interest in women as leaders has developed only recently, in part because of the feminist movement and in part because there are now more women involved in leadership roles, such as Hillary Clinton. In 1976, 21 percent of all managers were women; by 1999 the percentage had increased to 46 (Powell, Butterfield, & Parent, 2002). Today, about half of all managers are women (U.S. Department of Labor, 2012). Researchers examining acceptance of women as leaders have found that while people today place less emphasis on masculine traits for leaders, a good leader is still perceived more often as masculine than feminine (Hogue & Lord, 2007; Sczesny, Bosak, Neff, & Schyns, 2004). Perhaps because of this, women are not as likely as men to become leaders and when they do lead, they are still not as well received as men (Ayman, Korabik, & Morris, 2009; Ritter & Yoder, 2004).

Women leaders tend to consult more with subordinates, that is, to be more democratic, utilize larger social networks, and share more information and power with colleagues than do men (Helgeson, 1990). This probably explains why women leaders are viewed as being more people-oriented than male leaders. Nevertheless, objective data indicates that women are every bit as task-oriented as men, even though they might not be perceived as such (Eagly, 2007). Gender stereotypes appear to partially influence the perception of leaders, with women being viewed as most effective when their roles are defined in both feminine (e.g., sensitivity) and masculine terms (e.g., strength). For men to be considered effective leaders, however, they need only demonstrate masculine traits, such as strength (Johnson, Murphy, Zewdie, & Reichard, 2008).

If women are equally as effective as men why are there so few women leaders? Several factors help explain this societal phenomenon. First, women leaders tend to be evaluated slightly less positively and have more negative affect directed at them than men; especially when men are doing the evaluating (Koch, 2005). Another reason fewer women achieve top leadership positions may be that because of societal pressure they are more conflicted about mixing career and family. For example, although most women work outside the home, it is still relatively common to see television portray women as homemakers (Kirsh, 2010) and not in leadership roles (Lauzen & Dozier, 2005). A final reason is that *women are more likely than men to be placed in precarious leadership positions*, known as the **glass cliff**. This means women may be set up for failure as leaders more often than are men (Ryan, Haslam, & Postmes, 2007).

Many Asian societies are high-power-distance cultures where followers accept that leaders have more authority than they do.

Culture and Leadership

The literature on culture and leadership is ever increasing; first, because the U.S. workforce is diversifying, and second, because different leadership expectations and styles are firmly ensconced in other cultures. Just as important is the fact that many U.S., Canadian, and other companies have "gone global," with offices or factories scattered around the world (Chrobot-Mason, Ruderman, Weber, Ohlott, & Dalton, 2007).

One extremely important dimension of leader or managerial style that differs across cultures is **power distance,** which is *the idea that people in groups accept the concept that people in an organization rightfully have different levels of power and authority* (MacNab & Associates, 2007). In a high-power-distance culture, the leader makes decisions because they have the authority to do so. That is, the subordinates accept large distances in the distribution of power and expect leaders to behave autocratically, be somewhat paternalistic, be subject to different rules than subordinates, and enjoy privileges not available to subordinates. In other words, the managers or leaders are not psychologically close to their subordinates. Examples of high-power-distance cultures are Mexico and India. In medium-power-distance cultures such as the United States, Canada, and Italy, subordinates expect to be consulted but will sometimes accept autocratic behavior. Subordinates also expect rules and policies to apply to all; however, they will accept some status differences between superiors and subordinates. In low-power-distance cultures, subordinates expect to be consulted on most issues, prefer a participatory and democratic style of leadership, and often rebel if superiors appear to be stepping outside their authority or possess status symbols. Rules are seen as applicable to all. Examples of such cultures are those of Denmark and Israel.

Chapter Summary

KINDS OF GROUPS

9.1 Name and describe various types of groups.
Primary groups consist of the small, close-knit, face-to-face groups formed by family or friends. Secondary groups are larger and less intimate, whereas collectives are very large. We usually also distinguish our own group, or in-group, from other outside groups, or out-groups. In-groups are our reference points for our feelings about ourselves.

9.2 Differentiate discrimination, prejudice, and stereotyping.
Prejudice is an unfair, often negative attitude toward another person or group based solely on group membership. Discrimination occurs whenever we apply unfair or negative treatment to groups on the basis of such features as age, sex, or race. Stereotypes, which can be either positive or negative, are widespread generalizations about people (based solely on their group membership) that have little if any basis in fact.

CREATING AND JOINING GROUPS

9.3 Discuss how groups form.
Groups go through a developmental process. First, groups come together in the forming stage and then usually move quickly to the storming stage when friction exists. Once the storming is over, the group agrees on norms or rules by which it functions and then moves to the performing or productive stage. Groups sometimes slide back to one of these stages and the process recycles.

9.4 Provide reasons to explain why people join groups.
Individuals join groups for a variety of reasons. One reason is that groups furnish us with the opportunity to affiliate or to be with similar others; groups also provide us with social support or psychological aid. Groups, too, often possess more information and more collective power than a single individual would.

WHAT GOES ON IN GROUPS?

9.5 Describe how groups communicate.
Groups typically communicate in one of two ways. In a centralized communication networks, one or two individuals control the flow of information. In contrast, in a decentralized communication networks individuals can communicate relatively freely with one another.

9.6 Explain how the size of a group can affect its functioning.
Larger groups are less productive, more competitive, less unified, and more argumentative than smaller groups. As group membership increases, the satisfaction of individual members often go down and the number of ideas generated slows.

9.7   Compare three types of social influence: conformity, compliance, and obedience.

Whereas conformity refers to a change in behavior due to the real or imagined influence (pressure) of other people, compliance is as a change in behavior in response to a direct request from another person to do so. In contrast, obedience involves following a direct order or command.

9.8   Understand social loafing and group polarization.

Some individuals feel they do not have to work as hard in a group, in which their individual efforts are less likely to be noticed, a phenomenon known as social loafing. Groups often become polarized in their decision making, whereby groups make more extreme decisions than individuals. This is known as the group polarization effect.

WHEN GROUPS GO WRONG

9.9   Explain groupthink.

Groupthink occurs when groups value cohesiveness or "sticking together" over sound decision making. Groupthink can result in disastrous decisions.

9.10   Discuss some ways to prevent groupthink.

Techniques used to prevent groupthink include promoting open inquiry and skepticism; creating subgroups to generate alternatives; having multiple meeting to address different positions and to express any remaining doubts; and calling on outside experts so that the group does not remain isolated.

9.11   Explain how conflict can be both good and bad.

On the positive side, conflict challenges us to develop creative responses and solutions. At times, conflict can increase group cohesiveness. Although conflict is not always bad, conflict can sometimes keep a group from performing well. Moreover, conflict can escalate differences between group members, and if not dealt with appropriately, get out of control.

9.12   Discuss conflict management.

When solutions to a conflict cannot be found, it is best to try to manage the situations through integrative solutions or third-party interventions. Doing so may provide the opportunity for the parties in conflict to come to some mutual understanding.

GROUP LEADERSHIP

9.13   Describe how individuals become leaders.

Psychologists are unsure exactly why someone in a group emerges as leader. Traits, the situation (i.e., someone being in the right place at the right time), or some combination of the two may account for leader evolution. Several theories have attempted to explain why people emerge or are effective as leaders, but no one theory to date has successfully explained this phenomenon.

9.14   Explain various types of leadership styles and traits.

There are two main types of leadership styles—person-centered, in which the leader attends to group members' feelings and relationships, and task-centered, in which the leader is concerned about success and about meeting goals. The effectiveness of the group is dependent or contingent on leader style and the quality of the situation in which the group finds itself.

Self-Test

1. Which of the following would not be considered a primary group.
   a. tour group of Geneseo
   b. family members
   c. suitemates
   d. life-long friends
2. After winning a national title in basketball, thousands of fans spontaneously poured onto the streets. Cars were overturned, trash was set on fire, and windows were smashed. What type of group caused these antisocial behaviors?
   a. collective
   b. secondary group
   c. primary group
   d. flash mob
3. Brianne was an active member in community theatre. Which of the following people would most-likely be part of Brianne's in-group?
   a. Luanne, a bookworm
   b. Suzanne, a theatre major
   c. Carieann, a track star
   d. Rheann, a historian
4. Which of the following is associated with categorizing others as being members of an out-group?
   a. stereotypes
   b. prejudice
   c. discrimination
   d. all of the above
5. According to Dr. Seuss, Star-Bellied Sneetches refuse to let Plain-Bellied Sneetches play ball with them. This example illustrates:
   a. stereotypes
   b. prejudice
   c. discrimination
   d. storming
6. Adam and Danny decided to create a tournament for players of the fantasy card game *Magic: The Gathering*. During the first few meetings, the 10 members of the organizing

committee hashed out the rules and by-laws of the group. Which stage of group formation does this scenario illustrate?

a. forming
b. storming
c. norming
d. performing

7. Lilly, Rose, Petunia, and Daisy each think that Ms. Flowers may be a slightly better teacher than Mr. Blossom. After discussing their individual opinions together, they now all believe that Ms. Flowers is clearly a much better teacher than Mr. Blossom. This scenario provides an example of:

a. group polarization
b. obedience
c. social loafing
d. door-in-the-face effect

8. Larry the Cable Guy is fond of saying "Git-r-done!" Based on this catch phrase alone, if Larry was a leader of a group, what type of leader would he be?

a. transformational leader
b. people-related leader
c. task-oriented leader
d. charismatic leader

9. Rick and Fred had been good friends for years. Both worked as masons in the local paving company. When Fred was offered a supervisor role in the company, Rick told him "You know, if you take this job we can't hang out together anymore." Rick's belief that managers and subordinate employees can't be friends is a result of the concept known as:

a. power distance
b. glass cliff
c. illusion of invulnerability
d. mind guards

10. InGen, a biotech firm, discovered that by splicing frog DNA with dinosaur DNA, extinct dinosaurs could be brought back to life. Company leaders got together to discuss how to make a profit from such an expensive endeavor. Based on their discussions, it was decided that a dinosaur theme park with real dinosaurs would attract millions of families each year; generating hundreds of millions of dollars in profit. Not a single company leader discussed the ethics of the project or the potential dangers of it (like a dinosaur gets loose and eats the tourists). _____ can explain why InGen decided to go ahead with the project, without doing a critical analysis of its dangers or morality.

a. obedience
b. group think
c. power distance
d. glass cliff

Exercises

1. *Kinds of groups.* Think about the primary and secondary groups to which you belong. Do the characteristics of your groups fit the descriptions in the book? If not, why not?

2. *New groups.* Watch a newly forming committee or some other group. Did the group go through the stages of group development as outlined in this chapter?

3. *Why join groups?* Ask a number of people why they join the groups they choose. Do the reasons conform to those cited in the book? Are they different from your reasons?

4. *Group consensus.* Observe a group coming to consensus about some issue. Do you see any signs of groupthink? How could or did the group have avoided this phenomenon?

5. *Leadership.* For the groups of which you are a member, think about how the leader was selected. Can you add anything to the literature on leader emergence based on your experience? How well does your experience fit any of the theories presented?

Questions for Self-Reflection

1. Why did you join the groups you did? Why did you leave any of the groups?

2. Who are the members of your in-group? Do you think that your in-group will remain the same over a lifetime? Why or why not?

3. Be honest—are there out-groups in your life? Who are the members? Would it be better for you and for them if they weren't in your out-group? How can you overcome stereotyping this group or conflicting with its members?

4. When groups are storming, have you contributed to the storming or tried to move the group toward norming and performing? What were your motives for doing what you did? Did others resist you? Why?

5. Are you as likely to offer social support to someone in need as others are to offer you support?

6. What do you enjoy more—face-to-face communication with others or electronic (phone, e-mail, etc.) communication? Why?

7. Are you a conformist or a nonconformist? Is one better than the other for you given your life circumstances? Could you change strategy if you wanted to?

8. Do you do your fair share of work in the groups of which you are a member? Why or why not? Do you think you need to change your contribution level?

9. Are you a leader of any groups? If you are a leader, why? If you do not lead any groups, why not? Are you more comfortable being a leader or a follower? Why?

10. Reflect on your life; have you experienced groupthink? What were the results of the groupthink process? Can you reverse any of the poor decisions?

Chapter Ten

At Work and Play

Kristin was thrilled. After working hard in college for four years she had finally earned her diploma. She was ready for the next big step in her life: employment in her chosen career! Kristin had graduated with a psychology major with a business minor and had hoped to work in a big company in human resources. The week following graduation, Kristen gave her résumé and cover letter to over 45 different businesses. Unfortunately, nothing happened: The phone never rang; she didn't receive a single e-mail; and no one asked for an interview. Kristin was disheartened. She finally landed a job waiting tables at the local country club, though, she was determined that waitressing was only a means to pay off her student loans until something better came along. Several months, and about 150 job applications later, a large department store requested an interview. The store was interested in Kristin because she had completed an internship in human resources at a smaller store near her university. Kristin nailed the interview and landed the job. She thought, "It's a good thing I had those mock interviews in college, I think that's what made the difference." Like so many people in today's workforce, all Kristen needed was a chance. The hard part was placing herself in a position to get one.

AT WORK

LEARNING OBJECTIVES

10.1 Discuss the process of identifying a compatible career.
10.2 Explain key issues surrounding career decision making and finding a job.
10.3 Identify occupations with the greatest employment growth as well as those predicted to decline.
10.4 Know the relationship between education, employment, and income.
10.5 Discuss factors that contribute to job satisfaction (or lack thereof).
10.6 Identify several major issues related to cultural diversity and gender in the workplace.

Kristin's experience illustrates some of the promises and perils of finding your own niche in the **workplace**—*the place of paid employment outside the home.* On the minus side, you can see that no matter how well educated you are, you can still end up without a job. And a major reason for unemployment is often the lack of a good system for matching people with careers and jobs. As a result, millions of people are either unemployed or **underemployed**—*working in a job beneath their abilities or education.* On the plus side, Kristin's success story shows what you can

BOX 10–1 | Did you know that . . .

. . . . the top five activities done each weekday for full-time college students are:

- Sleeping (8.3 hours)
- Leisure and Sports (3.6 hours)
- Educational Activities (3.3 hours)
- Work (3.0 hours)
- Activities not listed on survey (2.5 hours)

Source: United States Department of Labor website, 2012.

do when you take the initiative and make the most of your opportunities. Notice that in choosing her **career**—*one's purposeful life pattern of work, as seen in the sequence of jobs held throughout one's life*—Kristin needed to take stock of what she had to offer and what she really wanted. One of the keys to Kristin's success was her eventual emphasis on a positive, take-charge attitude. All of these points are relevant for our own lives because we, too, face the challenges of choosing a compatible career and finding a job that uses our talents. Complete Activity 10–1 to learn about myths associated with making career decisions.

Taking Stock of Yourself

When choosing a career goal, it's best to begin by taking stock of yourself. Such self-assessments should include a consideration of your interests, abilities, personality, and personal values

---

ACTIVITY 10–1

CAREER MYTH BUSTER

Below are nine statements related to choosing a career. One or more of these is a myth. Your task is to differentiate fiction from reality? Circle your answers.

1. Figuring out what your career should be is easy to do.	Myth	Reality
2. If you're not sure what career best suits you, go to a career counselor and they'll tell you what career is best for you.	Myth	Reality
3. It's impossible to turn a hobby into a career.	Myth	Reality
4. If you're not sure what to do with your life, choose a career from the "Best Careers" list.	Myth	Reality
5. More money equals more happiness.	Myth	Reality
6. I better choose my career wisely as I won't be able to change it after I get started.	Myth	Reality
7. My best friends love their careers. I should do what they do.	Myth	Reality
8. Once I pick a career, the hard work is over.	Myth	Reality
9. Never change careers. Any skills you have learned will go to waste.	Myth	Reality

Answers: They're all myths. Read the chapter to find out why.

Source: Based on "Ten Myths About Choosing a Career" by Dawn Rosenberg McKay, from About.com, 2012.

(Bolles, 2011). If done well, taking stock will not only help you choose a career, but also help you begin (or continue) your journey of personal growth and fulfillment, for self-reflection is a necessary component of both.

FINDING YOUR INTERESTS   What are your interests? Which school subjects do you like the most? The least? Which hobbies do you enjoy? Which recreational and sports activities do you play or follow? In each case, try to determine what it is that most interests you; whether it's the activity itself or the people you're doing it with. Generally, the intrinsic or *internal enjoyment* of the activity is one of your best guides to the choice of a career. If you can match your interests with your skill-set, then the likelihood of being satisfied in your chosen career increases.

Exploration 10.1: Internships and Jobs for College Students

www.collegerecruiter.com   Find internships while still in school and jobs once you've graduated.

CLASSIFYING YOUR SKILLS   What are you good at? People often balk at this question. They say, "I haven't done anything but go to school" or "I've been busy raising three kids." The implication of such remarks is that these people don't have any marketable skills. A **skill** *is the ability to perform a task well. It is usually developed over time through training or experience.* But when people are confronted with a checklist of things they can do, the picture brightens. For example, a parent who has organized a cooperative day care, planned field trips for children, and managed the family budget has had considerable experience with management skills, a very important ability for a variety of jobs. When classifying your skills, remember to include your hobbies, as many require specific abilities that may be valuable to an employer (McKay, 2012).

Of note, occupations are classified based on how frequently different types of skills (e.g., artistic, communication, interpersonal, managerial, mathematical, mechanical, and scientific; see Box 10–2 for a description of each) are used and by what level of skill is usually needed. One way to identify your own skills is to reflect upon your achievements, including those in school or elsewhere. Select several accomplishments in each of the five-year periods of your life since adolescence. What do these successes have in common? What characteristics do they *not* share?

BOX 10–2   What Skills Do You Possess?

Occupations required a variety of different skills. Some of the most common ones—artistic, communication, computer, interpersonal, managerial, mathematical, mechanical, and scientific—are described here.

Artistic Skills

Occupations that require artistic skills tap workers' sense of what is beautiful or well designed. The level of creativity needed may depend on how structured an occupation is. Workers in occupations that identify art as being somewhat important use artistic creativity occasionally or use artistic originality within precise guidelines. Highly artistic occupations are most likely to require a great deal of independent composition, production, or performance.

Communication Skills

Nearly all workers need communication skills. Occupations in which basic communication skills are required involve speaking and writing clearly, reading, and giving descriptions or instructions. Occupations in which communication skills are somewhat important require persuasive communication, the use of technical jargon, or writing reports or other documents. Occupations that require the highest level of communication skills use vocabulary appropriate for complicated subjects, explain complicated subjects orally and in writing, and include communication as a primary component of the work.

Computer Skills

In today's technological world, more than half of all jobs require the use of a computer. Jobs in information technology (IT) require an understanding of operating systems, computer languages and scripts, software programming, hardware configuration and maintenance, and system analysis. Even outside of the IT field, computer literacy is required for variety of tasks, including application processes, work scheduling, managing benefits, staff training, and internal communications. Moreover, a basic understanding of word processing, graphics, multimedia, and spreadsheet programs is a requirement for many jobs.

Interpersonal Skills

Interpersonal skills refer to workers' ability to interact effectively with other people and to be persuasive. The level of interpersonal skills required in each occupation is based on workers' frequency of contact with the public, other employees, or clients. Beyond dealing with people courteously, workers in occupations that place some importance on interpersonal skills need an ability to sell products, ideas, or services in a convincing manner. Occupations in which interpersonal skills are of high importance might draw on the ability to analyze and solve workplace conflicts.

Managerial Skills

Managerial skills include the ability to organize, direct, and instruct other workers. Many occupations do not require managing others. But in occupations in which these skills are of some importance, workers should be able to motivate and inspire individuals or teams. When managerial skills are essential in an occupation, workers must be able to guide others and to accept responsibility for others' work and actions.

Mathematics Skills

Mathematics skills refer to more advanced ability than the core math skills required in nearly all jobs. Occupations in which basic math is needed require that workers be comfortable using numbers and performing arithmetic; some workers in the occupation might use a higher level of skills—for example, to draft a budget—but these skills are not essential across the occupation. In occupations in which math skills are somewhat important, quick calculations and number analysis are often required; these occupations might also involve a working knowledge of complex mathematical theorems, such as algebra, geometry, or statistics. High-level importance is indicated when many workers use algebra, geometry, or statistics frequently or when mathematical decision making is a primary responsibility of most workers; these occupations might also require study of both linear algebra or calculus and advanced statistics.

Mechanical Skills

Mechanical skills include a broad range of abilities, such as installation, maintenance, troubleshooting, and quality control analysis. Occupations in which these skills are somewhat important might require basic mechanical ability, such as an understanding of the relationship between moving parts. Higher-level mechanical skills may require knowledge of operations as well as an ability to diagnose and repair failures of equipment, machines, or systems.

Science Skills

When basic science skills are often needed in an occupation, workers must have an ability to apply some scientific theories and to communicate about science at a basic level. When science skills are deemed somewhat important in an occupation, workers need a theoretical knowledge of the principles of life and physical sciences, including biology, ecology, chemistry, and physics; or, they might need to communicate with science experts. In-depth practical knowledge often is required in highly scientific occupations, particularly in those related to scientific research and development; workers in these occupations almost always study science in college.

Source: Adapted from "Matching Yourself with the World of Work: 2004" by Henry T. Kasper OCCUPATIONAL OUTLOOK QUARTERLY, Fall 2004, Volume 48(3). Bureau of Labor Statistics, U.S. Department of Labor.

What can you learn about your goals and skills from your achievements? Career centers on your college campus can also help you identify your skill-set. In the end, you should know the skills you have and understand how they could be transferable to a job. You'll be asked about your skills at job interviews, so it's best if you can state this information freely and confidently ahead of time (Schein, 2006).

PERSONALITY MATTERS   Your personality also offers valuable clues for choosing a compatible career. Each of us possess a unique combination of traits, needs, and motives that make some work environments more compatible for us than others. For example, a social person may be good at sales; a meticulous person could excel as an accountant; a creative person might decide to become a graphic artist; and a person who likes being alone might start their own small business. It's also important to know how well you handle pressure, as some jobs are more stressful than others. Try to find a career well-matched with your personality; if not, you'll have more difficulties on the job than just the work you're tasked to complete.

KNOW YOUR VALUES   Your values are also an important consideration when choosing a career, especially your **work values**—*what brings you the most enjoyment or satisfaction in a career or job.* For some, the bottom line is all that matters, whereas for others, giving back to the community and "making a difference" is the most important thing. You'll need to consider your work-life balance, and how much money you want to make, as well. There may come a time when you have to choose between a high-paying job that will keep you away from your family and a lower-paying job that won't. All too often, we take our work values for granted, only becoming acutely aware of them when faced with job dissatisfaction, job changes, or completing a job-related task that we feel uncomfortable with. However, the sooner we clarify our work values, the easier it will be to make a satisfying decision regarding a career or job (Martini & Reed, 2010).

Identifying Compatible Careers

Once you have a better understanding of your interests and abilities, you're ready to match yourself with a compatible career. In identifying compatible careers, it's often advisable to talk over your plans with an interested teacher, school counselor, mentor, career services professional, or someone in your field of interest. Remember, though, no one can *tell* you what career you should choose; it's a decision that only you can make. Additionally, don't wait until you are looking for a job to assess your strengths and values; working with career centers while you are a freshman or sophomore can be an invaluable guide to planning your education before you graduate or hit the job market.

OCCUPATIONAL OUTLOOK HANDBOOK   Choosing among the more than 20,000 different career possibilities can be a formidable task. Fortunately, there are many helpful resources such as the *Occupational Outlook Handbook* (OOH) published by the Bureau of Labor Statistics. This handbook contains more than 20 basic career groups, each with dozens of related **occupations**—*the activities and responsibilities necessary to perform given work tasks in a particular line of work.* For example, health-related occupations include physicians, physician's assistants, registered nurses, medical technicians, and the like. For each career, the handbook provides information on the type of work involved, places of employment, entrance requirements, working conditions, and employment outlook. The OOH also has an introductory section with helpful information on such topics as how to find a job and employment opportunities. The OOH, revised every two years, is available in most libraries and job counseling centers or can also be found online at http://www.bls.gov. In addition, the book provides job search tips and links to information about the job market in each state.

CAREER PLANNING INVENTORIES   As mentioned above, professionals can successfully assist people with their career planning. They also have access to a wide assortment of psychological inventories for this purpose. One popular measure, the *Strong Interest Inventory*, has been shown to be very effective in dealing with the complexities of career interests (Bailey, Larson, Borgen, & Gasser, 2008). Using this inventory, you indicate your preferences (like, dislike, or indifferent) for various careers, school subjects, activities, amusements, and types of people. The inventory will also ask you to provide some personal characteristics. Computer-scored printouts organize the results around six basic categories, which are briefly described here:

- Realistic—practical, stable, persistent (example: engineer)
- Investigative—task-oriented, introspective, and independent (example: biologist)
- Artistic—creative, impulsive, and expressive (example: musician)
- Social—sociable, responsible, and humanistic (example: social worker)
- Enterprising—aggressive, confident, and energetic (example: stockbroker)
- Conventional—predictable, conforming, conscientious, and obedient (example: accountant)

The results of the *Strong Interest Inventory* include information on general career themes, basic interests, and specific careers with which you are most compatible. Discussion of the results with a counselor usually provides valuable leads to the most compatible careers for you. To help you prepare to see a career counselor, think about which of these descriptors best fits you. Which others come close to describing you, and which do not describe you at all?

Such inventories may furnish valuable leads to finding compatible careers tailored to the specific interests of the individual. Nevertheless, an important question to ask yourself is this: "Just how helpful are these inventories?" A lot depends on how they are used. If you take them in hopes that they'll tell you which career you should choose—a common misunderstanding— you'll probably be disappointed. Nor will the results predict how successful or happy you'll be in a given career, inasmuch as these factors depend on your abilities, personal motivation, and so on. Instead, these inventories are best used as an aid in making an *informed career choice* (Smith & Campbell, 2009). Of note, those who choose careers very similar to their career profiles tend to remain in their careers for long periods of time, whereas those who enter careers highly dissimilar to their profiles tend to drop out of them (Hansen & Dik, 2005). When you consider all the time and money invested in preparing for a career, this information can be extremely helpful to you.

Arriving at Your Career Decision

If you're like most people, you'll end up with not just one but a number of potentially compatible careers. Ultimately, you must make a decision about which is the best career for you. However, there are three things you'll need to consider before gaining suitable employment: career growth, potential pitfalls, and job preparation. Each is addressed in turn.

CAREER GROWTH How promising your job is often depends on the outlook for your field. To help you make an informed career choice, the Bureau of Labor Statistics periodically makes employment projections for a variety of careers. Because such estimates, by their nature, are somewhat imprecise, you should not use them as the sole basis for a career decision. Rather, they can help you assess future opportunities in the careers that interest you.

Currently, the unemployment rate in the United States is hovering around 8.5 percent. However, higher levels of education are associated with lower rates of unemployment. For instance, the unemployment rate of individuals without a high school diploma (14.9%) is more than three times that of those holding a bachelor's, master's, or doctoral degree (4.7%) and more than two times the rate of unemployment for those holding an associate degree (7.0%). Nevertheless, there are jobs out there. As projected through 2018 by the U.S. Department of Labor, total employment is expected to increase by slightly over 1 percent per year; adding more than 15 million jobs total. The professional (doctors, lawyers, etc.), service (finance, real estate, health care, communication, data processing, etc.), and construction sectors are expected to dominate employment growth. In contrast, farming (including fishing and forestry) and production services

Table 10–1	Employment Projections for 2018
Occupational Group	**Percent Change from 2008 to 2018**
Professional	16.8%
Service	13.8%
Construction and Extraction	13.0%
Management, Business, and Financial	10.6%
Installation, Maintenance, and Repair	7.6%
Office and Administrative Support	7.6%
Sales	6.2%
Transportation and Material Moving	4.0%
Farming, Fishing, and Forestry	−0.9%
Production	−3.5%

Source: Data from "Industry Employment and Output Projections to 2020" by Richard Henderson, from MONTHLY LABOR REVIEW, January 2012, Volume 135(1). Bureau of Labor Statistics, U.S. Department of Labor.

(e.g., assemblers, fabricators, food processors, metal workers, etc.) are expected to decline the most (U.S. Department of Labor, 2012). Table 10–1 provides you more detail on the changing employment sector.

PITFALLS TO AVOID   In the process of deciding on a career, you should guard against certain pitfalls. One is the accidental choice, which consists of choosing a career mostly because of attraction to one's first job. People who fall into this trap may discover later, to their regret, that they would have been happier or more successful in another line of work. Another pitfall is the choice of a career or job because of its external trappings, such as money, prestige, power, or security. In the long run, it's better to choose a work activity that is enjoyable in itself, as long as the financial rewards are adequate. An additional major mistake is not exploring your career options sufficiently. You must take the initiative and engage in an *active* process of finding a compatible career, as already discussed. In the end, you need to choose a career but be willing to modify that choice in light of your subsequent experiences and personal growth.

PREPARING FOR YOUR CAREER   Once you've determined your career goal, you'll need to know how to prepare for it. As you might expect, there are many ways to do this. Some careers are entered through an apprenticeship, vocational-technical school, or on-the-job training program. Other careers require a two- or four-year college degree, with many professions such as clinical psychology, medicine, and law also necessitating an advanced degree and supervised training. In addition, a state license or some type of certification is needed for a variety of careers, such as the professions previously mentioned, as well as occupations in teaching, accounting, and nursing. Because you are already enrolled in some sort of post–high school education, you may have begun the appropriate education for your career. On the other hand, others of you may not have arrived at a firm career goal. But in either case, an integral part of career planning is finding out the appropriate educational requirements for your chosen career.

One of the attractions of a college education is that it provides an in-road to higher status and better-paying careers. College graduates continue to have higher lifetime earnings and lower unemployment rates than high school graduates, as shown in Table 10–2. For instance, people

Table 10–2	Education and Pay: The Better the Education, the Better the Pay

Earnings in 2010, based on education level, for people aged 25–64.

Education Level	Average Salary ($)
No high school diploma	27,470
High school diploma	34,197
Some college, no degree	40,556
Associate degree	44,086
Bachelor's degree	57,026
Master's degree	69,958
Doctoral degree	88,867
Professional degree	103,411

Source: Data from Table 1 of "Education and Synthetic Work-Life Earnings Estimates" (ACS-14) by Tiffany Julian and Robert Kominsky. U.S. Census Bureau, September 2011.

with a four-year college degree earn substantially more than high school graduates of the same age. Those with graduate or professional degrees enjoy an even greater advantage. Of course, people's salaries vary considerably depending on many factors, such as the field of study, actual position held, and geographic location. Given the rapid changes in the job market, and the fact that one in nine persons changes careers every year, some of the most valuable but often overlooked advantages of a college education are the abilities for critical thinking, appreciation of lifelong learning, and enhanced adaptation to continuing change.

Landing a Job

Two additional hurdles you'll need to go through on your way to landing your first full-time professional position are the job search process and the job interview. It is never too early to start preparing yourself.

THE JOB SEARCH   Although not exhaustive, here is a list of possible places to search for a position:

- Apply in person or walk in the door with your résumé.
- Search Internet job sites such as Monster.com.
- Use an employment agency or recruiter that hires individuals for companies.
- Find a position through the university or college career service center.
- Look in professional journals and newsletters or attend professional conferences.
- Visit job fairs or other venues where jobs are posted.

As it turns out, many jobs are never advertised. To land one of these, you'll need to utilize a **networking** strategy—*using personal contacts to establish career opportunities.* Talk with alumni from your campus, neighbors, volunteer or internship supervisors, and other people you know (including family and friends) and tell them that you're on the job market. You might think that this provides you with an unfair advantage over any other candidates—which it might. This is, however, a perfectly acceptable and ethical technique, especially given that up to half of all position openings are unadvertised. Remember, if people don't know you're looking for work, it becomes really difficult to land a job through networking. To expand your network, consider joining a group or two at your college, in your community, or even an organization in your chosen profession. Don't forget to use technology to your advantage. You can also use online professional networks, such as LinkedIn, to find out about potential job openings. And remember, virtually every single one of your "friends" on Facebook or followers on Twitter may know about an unadvertised employment opportunity.

Exploration 10.2: Networking

www.linkedin.com   Join the world's largest professional network. You can post a work-related profile, network with others, and search for jobs.

THE JOB INTERVIEW   Securing a job usually involves one or more formal interviews. Some of these interviews occur in face-to-face interactions while others involve **e-recruiting,** in which *job candidates are screened by phone, video, or computer* (Russell, 2007). Whether in-person or online, your major goal is to convince the employer that you are the person for the job, that is, that you have the necessary qualifications and personal qualities and would fit into the organization. To do this, you'll need to create a favorable impression. Here's how: Be confident and ambitious, emphasizing your strengths. If asked about your weaknesses, admit a minor one such as "At times I'm too conscientious." Also, it's generally best not to furnish more information than requested by the employer. Finally, a crucial part of a successful job interview is preparing for the interview. See Box 10–3 for some helpful information.

Changing Jobs or Careers

STATISTICS ON JOB CHANGE   People are changing jobs more frequently than in the past. The time a worker keeps a job has steadily declined, and the typical U.S. worker has more jobs (or employers) in his or her lifetime than workers during the 1950s. The typical pattern is that an individual tends to hold several brief jobs in the first few years after graduation, then settles into a position that lasts several years. Workers in their 30s who stay with the same employer for five years or more are likely to remain in that job for a long time. As men and women get older, they make fewer job changes. By the age of 40, workers will make about two more job changes; at 50, only one more. Few people change jobs in their 60s, and most of them are probably moving

Manufacturing jobs are declining while service sector positions are increasing.

| BOX 10–3 | Focus on Communication: Interview Tips |

To help make a great impression on a job interview consider the following tips:

Preparation:
- Learn about the organization.
- Have a specific job or jobs in mind.
- Review your qualifications for the job.
- Prepare answers to broad questions about yourself.
- Review your résumé.
- Practice an interview with a friend or relative.
- Arrive before the scheduled time of your interview.

Personal appearance:
- Be well groomed.
- Dress appropriately.
- Do not chew gum or smoke.

The interview:
- Relax and answer each question concisely.
- Respond promptly.
- Use good manners.
- Learn the name of your interviewer and greet him or her with a firm handshake.
- Use proper English—avoid slang.
- Be cooperative and enthusiastic.
- Use body language to show interest.
- Ask questions about the position and the organization, but avoid questions whose answers can easily be found on the company website. Also avoid asking questions about salary and benefits unless a job offer is made.
- Thank the interviewer when you leave and, as a follow-up, in writing.

Information to bring to an interview:
- Résumé. Although not all employers require applicants to bring a résumé, you should be able to furnish the interviewer information about your education, training, and previous employment.
- References. Employers typically require three references. Get permission before using anyone as a reference. Make sure that this person will give you a good reference. Try to avoid using relatives as references.
- Transcripts. Employers may require an official copy of transcripts to verify grades, coursework, dates of attendance, and highest grade completed or degree awarded.

Source: Based on "Occupational Outlook Handbook," from Bureau of Labor Statistics website.

into second careers because of retirement. At the same time, there are exceptions to this pattern. A small number of workers exhibit extremely stable job patterns throughout their careers. Others change jobs every few years until they reach retirement.

Exploration 10.3: Building a Career

www.careerbuilder.com Another site that can help you find jobs and information about work. After posting your resume, job recommendations will be sent to you.

CAREER GOALS   Looking over the job projections and alternative career patterns may start you thinking about your own career goal. Perhaps you already have a firm career direction and are busily preparing for it. Someone else may have doubts or reservations. Either way, remember that it's perfectly natural to modify your career goal with experience and with greater knowledge of career opportunities. People are often reluctant to change their career goals for many reasons. Sometimes they would rather keep to their original goal than risk disappointing their parents, spouses, or peers. They forget they are choosing for *themselves*—not for anyone else. People also fear that switching career goals may be regarded as an admission of failure, but to continue in a direction you have misgivings about will only make matters worse. Then, too, individuals may overestimate the price of changing career goals. After gathering all the facts, you may find that the penalties are not as great as expected. The longer you delay changing career goals or careers, the more difficult it is. More often than not, the positive gains outweigh the costs.

Exploration 10.4: Career Change

www.careercast.com   This site contains lots of useful information on career building, from preparing to find your first job to mid-career changes in jobs.

JOB SATISFACTION   A primary reason for staying in a career or finding a new one is **job satisfaction,** defined as *people's feelings about different aspects of their jobs; how well one likes a given job, depending on such factors as pay and coworkers.* Beyond influencing career decisions, those with job satisfaction feel less stressed, are less susceptible to stress-related illnesses, visit the doctor less frequently, and live longer than those who are dissatisfied in their jobs (Warr & Clapperton, 2010). As you can see, job dissatisfaction can negatively affect physical health and be an impediment to personal growth.

Despite all the griping you hear on the job (perhaps including your own choice comments) nearly 9 out of 10 Americans are satisfied with their jobs (Petrecca, 2009). Nevertheless, there are differences in job satisfaction, with the amount of education attained being a significant predictor. Specifically, college-educated workers, especially those in the professions and executive positions, are generally more satisfied with their jobs than those whose education stopped prior to or after receiving their high school diplomas. Workers in unskilled and service jobs tend to be less satisfied. Sales personnel also tend to fall below the norm in job satisfaction, despite being fairly well compensated (Baum, Ma, & Payea, 2010; Mohr & Zoghi, 2006).

Satisfaction on the job depends heavily on the work activity itself. People generally prefer work that involves contact with others, is interesting, offers the opportunity to learn new skills, and allows them some independence (Mohr & Zoghi, 2006). In addition to a rewarding job, workers generally prefer having a job that provides for advancement, job security, and good working hours. They also want friendly, cooperative coworkers and considerate supervisors. Workers also experience less stress at work when they are allowed some control or can make decisions on their own (Spector, 2002). To the surprise of many, the highest paying jobs do not necessarily result in higher job satisfaction (Iyengar, Wells, & Schwartz, 2006). In particular, workers are frequently concerned with their pay *relative* to those around them, with greater job satisfaction associated with a higher pay ranking (Brown, Gardner, Oswald, & Qian, 2008). However, for the majority of people in the middle and working classes pay is a very important part of job satisfaction. Job satisfaction is also governed to a great extent by the working conditions of the job. The better the working condition are (perks, on-site day care, quality of their environment, etc.), the greater the job satisfaction. Box 10–4 discusses the role of technology (an important aspect of the working conditions for many) in job satisfaction.

Many other variables affect satisfaction on the job. Age and years on the job continue to be important considerations. Recent graduates initially enjoy high job satisfaction. As soon as the novelty of the work wears off and reality sets in, job satisfaction can drop sharply. After five years on the job, satisfaction tends to rise steadily with age and years on the job. Major reasons include greater job security and better pay as well as more realistic expectations. The rising level of education among younger workers helps account for the relative dissatisfaction among younger, better-educated workers. The major exception is for workers with professional and graduate

| BOX 10–4 | Focus on the Workplace: Technology and Job Satisfaction |

The addition of technology into American work sites is affecting how people work and whether they are satisfied with their jobs. Computers, electronic organizers, smartphones, voice mail, and teleconferencing are but a few of the innovations. Given our hi-tech world, most workers immersed in technology are more satisfied with their jobs than those without such access (Akkirman & Harris, 2005). Nevertheless, there are both positive and negative aspects of a technological "workplace." For example, instant messaging can both enhance collaboration among employees spread out geographically as well as causing workers to miss the richness of face-to-face communication. Even though instant messaging can increase feelings of privacy at work, employees tend to find them distracting, and a hindrance to job production (Cameron & Webster, 2004). Moreover, chain e-mails, joke e-mails, and other objectionable forms of communication are proliferating in the workplace, making people feel uncomfortable and/or disrupting productivity (Whitty & Carr, 2006).

Some employees are even being fired because they spend *too much* time playing with technology, a behavior known as **cyberslacking**—*the overuse of the Internet in the workplace for purposes other than work.* Examples of cyberslacking include shopping for gifts online, playing solitaire on your computer, and perusing or updating non-business-related Facebook and Twitter accounts. Given that cyberslacking costs businesses billions of dollars in lost productivity each year, many employers now monitor their employees' online behavior. In fact, some employers even prevent access to certain Internet sites, with Facebook, Youtube, and Twitter being blocked the most (OpenDNS, 2011).

In addition to the technological advances mentioned above, millions of employees are using technology to perform *either periodic or regular work for one's employer at home or another remote location*, a phenomenon known as **telework.** Currently there are close to 26 million full- and part-time teleworkers in the United States. For both employers and employees, the ability to telework, rather than physically commute to the workplace, is viewed as a perk. As such, those who telework tend to be more satisfied with their jobs than those who physically go to the office (World at Work, 2011).

degrees, such as doctors and lawyers, who generally are happy in their work. However, unlike blue-collar workers, who reach a plateau in earnings relatively early, college-educated workers generally reap the rewards of greater education in the later years of their careers. Another important factor related to job satisfaction and career change is burnout. Box 10–5 explains some of the issues surrounding it.

Work Issues Related to Culture and Gender

CULTURAL DIVERSITY AT WORK   Throughout this book, we have made the distinction between two general types of cultures—*collectivistic* and *individualistic*—so we will use this distinction again to explain differences in work behaviors. In individualized cultures like the mainstream United States, people have an easier time distinguishing between work time and personal time and also between work activities and social activities. In such cultures, initiative, challenge, and freedom on the job are valued and encouraged. On the other hand, in collectivistic societies, people view their work groups and work organizations as fundamental parts of themselves (like families), so the bonds between individuals and organizations are stronger. Work is also seen as the fulfillment of an obligation to a larger group (e.g., to family or to society) rather than as a means to accumulate money. Organizations in collectivistic societies are considered morally responsible for the welfare of their employees and are expected to care for them across their life spans (Matsumoto, 2003).

The rise of the "global economy" has resulted in the internationalization of many North American businesses. As such, a working understanding of cultural similarities and differences becomes a key component to a business' success. This means it will be wise for you to understand others' work habits and work values. One of the best ways to do this is to get first-hand experience with the culture you'll be working in (Schuler, 2003). Remember, failing to

BOX 10–5   Focus on the Workplace: Job Burnout

The Defining Features of Job Burnout.

Burnout is *a psychological syndrome of emotional exhaustion, depersonalization, and reduced personal accomplishment that occurs among individuals, especially those who do "people work."* Emotional exhaustion is the primary symptom or characteristic of burnout. Causes of emotional exhaustion include a steady stream of problematic clients, long work hours, too much responsibility, and a myriad of other factors. Depersonalization means that clients, customers, or others with whom the burned-out individual comes in contact are not seen as particularly human anymore; they are numbers or faceless souls. The burned-out employee interacts with them in a detached, impersonal, and cynical manner. Finally, the sufferer's performance may decline or the individual may feel that they no longer make a difference—no matter how well or how many hours the individual works. Human service workers are probably most affected by burnout, although those in other occupations certainly are eligible as well. Teachers, nurses, police, and social workers are good examples of people prone to burnout (Peisah, Latif, Wilhelm, & Williams, 2009).

Men and women are equally likely to burn out, although women's health may suffer more from job stress. In addition, those who are unmarried are more prone to it (Toker, Shirom, Shapira, Berliner, & Melamed, 2005). Low levels of hardiness, poor self-esteem, emotional instability, an external locus of control (e.g., being controlled by forces beyond the individual), and an avoidant coping style typically constitute the profile of a stress-prone or burned-out individual (Wierda-Boer, Gerris, & Vermulst, 2009). We should not forget, however, that certain job characteristics can also contribute to burnout and job fatigue, namely time pressures, role ambiguity, long working hours, low control over the work, and so forth (Sonnentag & Zijlstra, 2006).

What to Do When You Are Burned-Out

The best way to avoid burnout is to prevent it in the first place. Before you take a job, consider whether you and the job are a good fit. If the job requires you to report early to work, are you an early riser? If you like being creative on the job, is there room for creativity in the day-to-day routine of the job? If you are a social butterfly, does the position provide you possibilities for interacting with customers and coworkers? If the job requires public speaking, are you frightened to get up in front of a large audience? Consider all aspects of the position as well as your personality and preferred work environment. Don't take the job if it isn't a good match.

If you find yourself victimized by burnout, you can still escape some of its consequences. One of the most important ways to reduce the effects of burnout is to have a good social support system. Perhaps coworkers feel the same way you do but cope better; talk to them and see what helps them. Family members who know about your work may also offer a sympathetic ear and some good advice for how to deal with burnout. A good sense of humor and the ability to have fun can also help you better manage this type of job stress. Be sure that you allow for leisure time off the job, too. Try not to come home from work so exhausted that you can't do a few fun things after work (Leiter & Maslach, 2005).

You might also think about how you do your job. Are there positive aspects you could focus on more? Why did you take the position in the first place? Perhaps you can realign your work values with the initial aspects of the job that interested or excited you. Perhaps you or your supervisor can think of ways to expand your job to include elements that make the job more exciting or more rewarding. Maybe there are new skills you can learn or utilize, too. Finally, as can any other type of stress, burnout can cause physical and mental health problems, so it is best to confront it when it happens (Eriksson, Starrin, & Janson, 2008). If burnout becomes too intense and too much for you to handle, perhaps it is time to do another self-assessment and find a new job in a different company or even a new occupation. Don't let burnout get the best of you.

---

understand the language and culture of another country can affect the bottom line. See Table 10–3 for a listing of some expensive cross-cultural business blunders.

GENDER AND WORK   Currently, women comprise 49 percent of the workforce. Nonetheless, there is still *inequity between men and women in terms of their pay,* which is often referred

Table 10–3	Cross-Cultural Blunders in Business
What Went On	**Why It's a Cross-Cultural Blunder**
Advertisements involving cute animals aired in Islamic and Southeast Asian countries.	In these cultures, animals are considered unclean and/or low life-forms. Sales were hurt.
The "OK" finger sign was printed on catalogues in Latin America.	In Latin America, this sign is considered to be an obscene gesture. The catalogues had to be reprinted.
To commemorate the beginning of new flight service to Hong Kong, an airline handed out white carnations to the passengers.	For many Asians, white flowers are symbolic of bad luck and death. They switched to red carnations.
Golf balls packaged in fours were put on sale in Japan.	The Japanese pronunciation of "four" is similar to the word for "death." People avoid buying products packaged in fours.
Pepsi used the tagline "Come alive with Pepsi" in their ad campaign in Taiwan.	The translation into Chinese ended up saying "Pepsi brings your ancestors back from the dead."

Source: Based on Cross Cultural Blunders," from Kwintessential website, 2012.

to as an **earnings gap**. In 2010, women's pay was 81 percent of men's (U.S. Department of Labor, 2012). A major reason for the earnings gap is that many women enter lower-paying service jobs such as secretarial positions. Until recently, most women have been crowded into less than 10 percent of the Labor Department's job categories. Women are overrepresented in careers such as secretaries, nurses, and librarians; they are underrepresented in careers such as engineers, dentists, and physicians. Another reason for the discrepancy in pay between the sexes is that women workers have had less education and work experience, but this factor, too, is changing. Entering college classes now contain slightly more women than men (Mather & Adams, 2007). Although the proportion of women in the traditional male careers remains small, the rate of increase has been dramatic. Compared to the past, there are now more women physicians, more women in the life sciences and physical sciences, and more women engineers, lawyers, professors, and judges. Nevertheless, ambitious women often feel that their careers are hindered by a glass ceiling. Although they can see through it, they can't pass beyond this invisible barrier, mostly because of stereotyped attitudes and expectations in the workplace (Ortiz & Roscigno, 2009). For example, a smaller percentage of the *top* management jobs are held by women than men. Similarly, women who are promoted into better managerial positions are likely to have salaries that lag behind those of their male colleagues. Box 10–6 discusses sexual harassment in the workplace—an unfortunate, yet pervasive situation that is faced by women more so than men.

AT PLAY

LEARNING OBJECTIVES

10.7 Understand why leisure is important to personal growth.
10.8 Explain positive use of leisure.
10.9 Know why most American don't use up all of their vacation time.
10.10 Discuss changes in the amount of leisure time across adulthood.

No matter how much you like your job, it's important to have sufficient time off to do many of the other things you enjoy in life. In other words, **leisure**—*time free from work or duty that may be spent in recreational activities of one's choice*—is as important as work. Leisure activities

BOX 10–6   Focus on the Workplace: Sexual Harassment

Just What Is Sexual Harassment?

Sexual harassment refers to *any unwanted attention of a sexual nature occurring in the workplace that interferes with a person's ability to work.* It includes, but is not limited to, unwelcome sexual advances, physical contact, offensive language, and threats of punishment for rejection of these acts. Sexual harassment in the workplace takes many forms. A familiar practice is directing catcalls, whistles, and demeaning words such as "doll" at women. Another one is recurring, offensive flirtation. Although most sexual harassment is verbal, physical patting, pawing, or sexual advances are not uncommon. Instances of sexual harassment still abound in many places and create double jeopardy (prejudice and harassment) for minority women (Buchanan & Fitzgerald, 2008).

In order to reduce such instances, the Equal Employment Opportunity Commission (EEOC) has issued guidelines for preventing sexual harassment. These guidelines suggest that employers should raise the consciousness of employees about the subject of sexual harassment, express strong disapproval of such behavior, inform all workers of their right to raise the specter of sexual harassment, explain the appropriate procedures for making a complaint, and sensitize everyone concerned. Yet, soliciting sexual favors for promotion at work is still cited in lawsuits against large companies. And despite the efforts of the EEOC, in 2011 alone, more than 11,000 charges of sexual harassment were filed against coworkers; 84 percent involved female victims (EEOC, 2012).

Coping with Sexual Harassment on the Job

Although each situation is different, some suggested strategies are usually helpful in dealing with sexual harassment on the job.

1. Make it clear when you disapprove. Say directly but tactfully something such as, "I find that remark offensive."
2. Jot down the time, place, and manner of such incidents. Who are the biggest offenders? Under what circumstances did the offensive events occur?
3. Talk about the incident to other workers. Find out how many other women (or in some instances, men) have been harassed.
4. Take positive steps in raising the awareness of male workers. Report offensive incidents to supervisors. Discuss problems of sexual harassment at staff meetings. Encourage workshops on the subject.

If necessary, make an official complaint to your employer, either orally or in writing, depending on the situation. As a last resort, contact federal agencies, like the EEOC.

---

help us cope better with negative life events, assist us in our overall adjustment, and improve our sleep and overall physical health (Spiers & Walker, 2009).

Despite the importance of leisure to our well-being, many of us feel that they are working more and playing less—a perception based on reality. Currently, Americans spend about 4.67 hours per weekday and 6.4 hours on weekends engaging in leisure (including sports). However, since 2004, the amount of leisure time available to the average person has dropped by about a half hour per day (BLS, 2012).

Economic factors seem to be driving down the amount of available leisure time. For instance, because businesses and other organizations employ fewer workers, additional responsibilities fall upon those currently on the job. Ironically, the most affluent sectors of society—college graduates, professionals, and those with incomes of $50,000 or more—work the longest hours and have the least time for leisure. For instance, people who never went to college engage in one more hour of leisure activities per day than those with a bachelor's degree (or higher) (BLS, 2012). Moreover, although women in dual-income families work almost the same number of hours as their husbands, they experience a smaller amount leisure time (about 1 hour less per day). This isn't too surprising given that women do more chores at home than men—a phenomenon commonly referred to as the "second shift" (Sinno & Killen, 2011).

The distinction between work and leisure is delicate. Does this man work on a farm or keep horses as a hobby? Either involves a lot of effort.

These data run counter to predictions made 25 years ago, when it was assumed that automation and technology would shorten the work week and give us more leisure time (Whitty & Carr, 2006). Actually, the opposite has occurred, perhaps because work often *spills over* into leisure time (Hilbrecht, Shaw, Johnson, & Andrey, 2008). Here's an example: Many people who go on vacation take work with them, check in with the office, or at the very least read and respond to work-related e-mail. Another factor that contributes to the seeming compression of leisure time is that more and more people are working from home; they use computers or other electronic methods for connecting to their workplace, so the distinction between work and home is blurring (Kirk & Belovics, 2006).

What Is Leisure?

There are many things we do outside of work that are anything but leisure, for example, cleaning up after meals, dusting our homes, studying, and visiting the dentist. Such activities are usually labeled **maintenance activities,** *nonleisure and nonwork time spent in activities necessary for the maintenance of life.* In contrast, leisure has to do with the way we use our free time, our motivation for doing it, the meaning it has for us, and how it affects our lives. From an adjustment perspective, the purpose of leisure is the cultivation of the self and the pursuit of the higher things of life. Playing a musical instrument primarily for the enjoyment of it or bicycling for pleasure are examples of **unconditional leisure;** these are *activities freely chosen, excluding work and maintenance activities.* People who have a satisfying leisure life often find they must acquire certain skills or frequently practice the activity to maintain their current level of performance. At the same time, individuals who are highly competitive or perfectionistic may become so concerned about their performance that the pleasure in their leisure activities is lost. True leisure, then, is considered something we do primarily for the enjoyment we get out of it (Buettner, Shattell, & Reber, 2011).

Using Leisure Positively

THE POSITIVE USE OF LEISURE   By the time people have arrived home after a hard day's work and eaten dinner, they're often too tired to do anything else. When asked about their favorite way to spend an evening, the majority says watching television. Adults now watch television between four and six hours a day, most of it in the evening. Although people watch television primarily for entertainment and to a lesser extent for the news, watching television is also a time to relax and unwind, or to recuperate, which is mostly a *maintenance activity*, as described earlier. The same goes for surfing the Internet or updating your Facebook status. The ease with which someone may push a button (or click a mouse) and be entertained for hours on end remains a great temptation. At the same time, individuals who have curtailed their media habits are usually amazed at how many other interesting things there are to do in life (Blackshaw, 2010).

The *positive* use of leisure requires a certain degree of choice. Ideally, you should select activities that are compatible with your interests and lifestyle rather than simply doing whatever is convenient at the time or what your friends want to do. To enjoy an activity to the fullest, you usually have to acquire the necessary skills. You must also budget your time and money to keep up the activity. For example, people who take pride in their tennis game tend to play regularly and probably derive greater satisfaction than those who play only on occasion. If learning the skills and budgeting time and money are too stressful for you, perhaps you should switch to another form of leisure activity. Leisure activities can become stressful, and when they do, the possibility of positive leisure use diminishes (Hébert, 2005).

VACATIONS   A favorite form of leisure is taking a vacation. Most people feel little or no guilt taking time off from work for a vacation; they believe they have earned it. When asked the main reasons for taking a vacation, their responses reflect a variety of motives. The most common motive is to relax. Other motives are intellectual stimulation, family togetherness, adventure, self-discovery, and escape. After the vacation, most people are glad to be back home and look forward to returning to work. Only a few feel depressed at facing the familiar routine. Many Americans feel that work is more important than leisure, and they seek not so much a leisure-filled life as a better balance of the two. Furthermore, the advent of more flexible work schedules enables people to take long weekends, which promise to make short vacations a regular event rather than a once-a-year affair (Kühnel & Sonnentag, 2011).

About half of all American workers take some type of vacation each year, typically lasting for one or two weeks. However, Americans frequently do *not* use up all of the vacation time that they have earned; leaving about half of them unused annually. So, why don't people use all of the vacation time that they are entitled to? As you might well guess, the primary reason is that people are fearful about losing their jobs. They are concerned that by going on a vacation they may miss something important or fall behind in their work (Mayerowitz, 2010; Yancy, 2011). Although there are no legal requirements for the length of vacations in the United States, other countries have such mandates. Table 10–4 lists some annual minimum vacation days found in selected countries.

Leisure across Adulthood

The amount of leisure time available to adults changes over time. In general, leisure time decreases from early adulthood to middle adulthood, then increases once again (see Table 10–5). Moreover, leisure becomes increasingly important from midlife on because of all the changes in people's lives. By this time, people are reassessing their needs and values and what they want out of life. Also, people of this age tend to have more job security, more discretionary income, more free time, and more paid vacation time than younger adults. And by this time in life, most adults are unlikely to be caring for younger children. That fact alone adds about an hour of extra of leisure time per day (BLS, 2012). For many, this may be the first time they've been able to follow their own inclinations without having to worry about the productivity of their efforts.

Table 10–4	Annual Minimum Vacation Days Worldwide
Country	**Number of Vacation Days**
Austria	35
Belgium	20
Chile	15
Croatia	18
Germany	24
Norway	25
Ireland	20
Japan	18
Spain	30
United Kingdom	20

Source: Data from NationMaster.com, 2012.

Now they can take up interests and express abilities not previously used in career and family responsibilities. In short, with increasing age leisure becomes a means of personal growth (Chen & Fu, 2008).

Constructive leisure activities are also an important way to prepare for retirement. People who have developed rewarding leisure activities as well as a network of social and family relationships are more able to make the crucial shift from full-time work to a satisfying retirement. A common and very constructive leisure activity is performing volunteer work. You can read more about volunteering in Box 10–7.

Exploration 10.5: Volunteering

www.volunteermatch.org   At this site, you can search by zip code and interest area (such as emergency services, animal care, arts and culture, religion, etc.).

Table 10–5	Hours of Leisure per day during Adulthood
Age	**Hours Per Day Spent in Leisure**
20–24	5.3
25–34	4.4
35–44	4.2
45–54	4.7
55–64	5.2
65–74	6.9
75 and over	7.7

You don't have to wait to retire or be elderly to jump on the volunteer wagon. You can join over 62 million Americans, who volunteer a combined total of 8.1 billion hours of their time worth an estimated $173 billion, now (VolunteeringinAmerica.gov, 2012). All types of people volunteer, although middle-aged persons, those who are married, the employed, and people with a bachelor's degree (or higher) volunteer the most. Volunteers spend an average of about 52 hours a year volunteering at a variety of educational, religious, and community service-based organizations. Volunteers complete a wide range of tasks for their organizations, such as fund-raising, food service, general labor, transportation, and teaching. These individuals either step forward of their own initiative or are asked by the organization to participate (BLS, 2012).

Volunteering not only gives back to your community or organization for everything it has done for you, it also provides free on-the-job training, helps you explore possible careers, builds your résumé, and establishes networking connections (and perhaps letters of recommendation). And a recent survey of volunteers also found that volunteer work was directly linked to career advancement because volunteers learned leadership skills, developed confidence, practiced interpersonal cooperation, and enhanced communication skills while they volunteered (Women's Way, 2006). To find volunteer opportunities, contact your college's volunteer office or the local Chamber of Commerce. And of course, you can always search online. One final thing, volunteering may be good for you! Research has shown that volunteering among the elderly is associated with reduced mortality, fewer health problems, and less depression (Ayalon, 2008).

Chapter Summary

AT WORK

10.1 Discuss the process of identifying a compatible career.

In choosing a career goal, it's best to begin by taking stock of yourself, including your interests, abilities, personality, and work values. Then you're ready to explore the career options. There are many helpful resources such as the *Occupational Outlook Handbook* (OOH) published by the Bureau of Labor Statistics. In addition, inventories available at career centers may help to identify the most compatible careers.

10.2 Explain key issues surrounding career decision making and finding a job.

It's best to keep your career goal somewhat flexible and to be willing to modify it in light of subsequent experience, especially while you are in college. Nevertheless, three things you'll need to consider before gaining suitable employment are potential pitfalls, job preparation, and the job search process. You should also be aware of certain difficulties in decision making, such as arriving at a career goal prematurely. You'll also need to identify (and successfully obtain) the required training and/or education that is needed for your chosen career. Although there are a variety of ways to search for employment, networking is one of the best ways to find a job. Knowing how to conduct yourself in an interview is crucial to finding gainful employment.

10.3 Identify occupations with the greatest employment growth as well as those predicted to decline.

The professional, service, and construction sector are expected to dominate employment growth. In contrast, farming and production services are expected to show the greatest declines.

10.4 Know the relationship between education, employment, and income.

Because jobs for college-educated workers will grow faster than average, college graduates will continue to have higher rates of employment and incomes. In contrast, people with less than a high school education will find it difficult to get good jobs with good pay and chances for advancement.

10.5 Discuss factors that contribute to job satisfaction (or lack thereof).

Satisfaction on the job depends heavily on how interesting and meaningful the work activity itself is, as well as the conditions on the job. People want opportunities for advancement as well as considerate and cooperative coworkers. Technology affects different employees in different ways—sometimes increasing or decreasing job satisfaction. Pay has become an increasingly important part of job satisfaction. Age, years on the job, and burnout also influences job satisfaction.

10.6 Identify several major issues related to cultural diversity and gender in the workplace.

A working understanding of cultural similarities and differences has become a key component to a business' success. In individualistic cultures initiative, challenge, and freedom on the job are valued and encouraged. In collectivistic societies, people view their work groups and work organizations as fundamental parts of themselves, so the bonds between individuals and organizations are stronger. Among the many issues surrounding gender are the earnings gap between the sexes, opportunities for advancement, and sexual harassment.

AT PLAY

10.7 Understand why leisure is important to personal growth.

No matter how much you like your job, it's important to have time off for other things you enjoy. Leisure activities help us cope better with negative life events, assist us in our overall adjustment, and improve our sleep and overall physical well-being.

10.8 Explain positive use of leisure.

The positive use of leisure becomes increasingly important from midlife on as we reassess what we want out of life. Ideally, you should select activities that are compatible with your interests and lifestyle rather than simply doing whatever is convenient at the time or what your friends want to do. Volunteer work is a valuable and common form of leisure activity.

10.9 Know why most American don't use up all of their vacation time.

Concerns about job security and falling behind on their work explain why nearly half of all Americans do not use up all of their vacation time.

10.10 Discuss changes in the amount of leisure time across adulthood.

In general, leisure time decreases from early adulthood to middle adulthood, followed by decade's worth of increases. Older Americans spend almost three more hours a day in leisure activities in comparison to young adults.

Self-Test

1. As a result of downsizing, Shannon lost her upper-management position in a computer software company. In order to make ends meet, Shannon took a job as a tech-support consultant for the local computer store (which does not make use of her managerial abilities). The scenario is an example of:
    a. over-employment
    b. parallel employment
    c. under-employment
    d. translational employment

2. Which of the following statements about the relationship between education and pay is true?
    a. typically, as the level of education increases, so too does the pay
    b. there is no relationship between education level and pay
    c. on average, high school graduates make just as much money as college graduates
    d. financially, there is no benefit to finishing high school

3. In order to find a job in video game engineering George decides to try networking. Which of the following activities should George do?
    a. post his resume on Monster.com
    b. contact alumni of his college who work in similar field
    c. search the classified ads in the newspaper
    d. stop by video game software companies and ask to speak with human resources

4. After a decade of working as a high school counselor Ruthy began to care less and less about her student's problems. And each workday seemed to leave her more emotionally drained than the previous one. Ruthy was experiencing:
    a. self-actualization
    b. school phobia

    c. job satisfaction
    d. burnout

5. Jeff was successful in business, rising to become a vice-president in less than 10 years. Jeff found the work to be rewarding and the hours manageable. In terms of salary, he made $250,000 a year, which was $10,000 less than other vice-presidents in the company. Which of the following statements regarding Jeff's job satisfaction could be true?
    a. Jeff had poor job satisfaction because his pay was lower than his colleagues
    b. Jeff made enough money to guarantee a high degree of job satisfaction
    c. Jeff had high job satisfaction because pay does not influence job satisfaction
    d. none of the above

6. Nancy spends 3 hours each day going back and forth to work. Her company just installed some new technology that will allow Nancy to work from home several days a week. Nancy is one of the growing number of people whose work includes:
    a. telework
    b. web-commuting
    c. cyber-commuting
    d. Internet-commuting

7. Eric worked the midnight shift at a department store as a security guard. According to Eric, "Nothing interesting ever happens," so he spent most of his time looking up sites on the Internet. Eric was engaging in:
    a. cyberslacking
    b. teleslacking
    c. web-slacking
    d. pc-slacking

8. Although Sadie enjoyed her work, she was less enthusiastic about her coworkers. The constant sexual jokes, comments about her looks, and propositions for sex resulted in Sadie seeking employment elsewhere and suing the company that she once respected. Sadie was a victim of:
   a. stalking
   b. physical harassment
   c. sexual harassment
   d. sexual terrorism

9. Prior to leaving the company, Sadie attempted to cope with the sexual harassment she was experiencing. Which of the following did Sadie do?
   a. make it clear she disapproved
   b. document her experiences

   c. raise the awareness of coworkers as to what sexual harassment is
   d. all of the above

10. After a long day of writing test question for a Psychology of Adjustment book, Steve wanted nothing more than to relax and read a good zombie apocalypse novel. But before he could begin reading, Steve needed to cook dinner, do some laundry, and attempt to get his kids to do some chores. In other words, Steve needed to complete some _____ activities.
    a. unconditional leisure
    b. maintenance
    c. preservation
    d. upkeep

Exercises

1. *Explore your career interests.* Make an extensive list of all the activities you've enjoyed, including school courses, extracurricular activities, full- and part-time jobs, hobbies, and sports. Then select a dozen of the most satisfying activities and rank them from the most enjoyable down. Ask yourself what made each activity satisfying. Was it the activity itself? Or was it mostly the people you did it with or the recognition or money involved? Activities that are intrinsically enjoyable are usually the best indications of the types of careers you'll enjoy.

2. *Identify compatible careers.* Go to your campus career development center or career guidance center and take some type of career inventory, such as *Holland's Self-Directed Search*, or one that requires professional supervision, such as the *Strong Interest Inventory*. Then review the results with a trained counselor.

3. *Become better informed about your career goal.* How much do you know about your chosen career? You might find it

helpful to look up some basic information about it in a resource such as the *Occupational Outlook Handbook*. Look up your chosen career or one you're interested in. Then write down information on the following: (1) description of the work, (2) typical places of employment, (3) educational and entry requirements, and (4) employment outlook. This exercise should give you a more realistic view of your career goal and how to prepare for it.

4. *Favorite leisure activities.* What do you like to do in your leisure time? Do you have enough time for play and leisure? Do you like solitary or social leisure activities? What can you learn about yourself given your analysis of leisure time?

5. *Think about your work and leisure cycles.* In what ways would you like to change your patterns of work and play? How would you keep your patterns the same? Why?

Questions for Self-Reflection

1. Do you have a specific career goal?
2. If not, are you actively engaged in choosing a career—or are you "waiting for things to just happen"?
3. Do you believe that hard work eventually pays off?
4. What are the three most important things you look for in a job?
5. If you won a million dollars in the state lottery, would you continue to work? Why or why not?
6. What is the projected outlook for your chosen career?

7. If you were to change careers, what would your alternate career choice be?
8. Have you ever been unemployed? What did it feel like? How did you overcome these feelings?
9. What is the most important thing you've learned from part-time jobs?
10. What is your favorite leisure activity?

Chapter Eleven

Sexuality

*A*fter taking a test during their evening Eastern Philosophy and Religion class, Carol and Kim stood in the hallway discussing some of the questions. Both felt tense, and both agreed they needed some time to unwind. They decided to visit a café near the campus. Because the café was crowded, they had to share a table with two male students, Jeff and Bob, whom they didn't know. Striking up a conversation, they soon discovered several areas of mutual interest. Carol found that Jeff was also an English major and shared her career aspirations with him. Kim soon discovered that she and Bob, Jeff's friend, liked the same musical groups. Initially, the four of them enjoyed talking and interacting. However, as the evening wore on, the men began drinking too much beer and telling sordid jokes. The women felt very uncomfortable. Furthermore, Carol and Kim became aware that what they intended as friendliness was being perceived by the men as a sexual invitation. Sensing that an awkward situation was imminent, the women excused themselves and left.

SEXUALITY AND SHARED PARTNERSHIPS

LEARNING OBJECTIVES

11.1 **Explain how gender stereotypes and the media influence sexuality.**
11.2 **Recognize the importance of sexual communication for a mutually satisfying sex life.**

Beliefs about Sexuality

Today, men and women are discovering that they cannot achieve true sexual satisfaction until they realize that sex is not something one partner *does to* or *for* another. Instead, sex is something that partners do together, *as equals*. If one partner is critical, unresponsive, or at best passive, the emotional vitality of the couple's sex life steadily weakens and eventually withers away. In contrast, when both partners are actively involved and when each person spontaneously communicates feelings, the other person's excitement and responsiveness are heightened. Thus, the quality of a couple's sex life, along with their overall relationship, is greatly enriched by a fully shared partnership (Greene & Faulkner, 2005).

GENDER STEREOTYPES AND SEXUALITY The experience of Kim, Carol, Jeff, and Bob demonstrates how an individual's approach to sexual satisfaction can be hampered by

BOX 11–1	Did you know that . . .

- Many older adults continue to have active pleasurable sex lives, reporting a range of different behaviors and partner types, however adults over the age of 40 have the lowest rates of condom use.
- There is enormous variability in the sexual repertoires of U.S. adults, with more than 40 combinations of sexual activity described at adults' most recent sexual event.
- About 85% of men report that their partner had an orgasm at the most recent sexual event; this compares to the 64% of women who report having had an orgasm at their most recent sexual event.
- Men are more likely to orgasm when sex includes vaginal intercourse; women are more likely to orgasm when they engage in a variety of sex acts and when oral sex or vaginal intercourse is included.
- Adults using a condom for intercourse were just as likely to rate the sexual extent positively in terms of arousal, pleasure and orgasm than when having intercourse without one.

Source: Center for Sexual Health Promotion. (2012). National survey of sexual health and behavior. Retrieved July 7, 2012, from http://www.nationalsexstudy.indiana.edu/.

gender stereotypes—*widespread generalities about the characteristics and behaviors of men and women that exaggerate the differences between the sexes*—thereby setting the stage for misunderstanding and frustration. For example, there's a long-standing belief that men enjoy sex more than women do. Although this stereotype is beginning to diminish as younger generations are socialized differently, there is ample evidence that men and women still subscribe to it in varying degrees (Regan & Atkins, 2006). Another commonly held stereotype is that whereas women fantasize about having sex with familiar partners, men picture themselves having sex with strangers. In general, men's attitudes are stereotyped to be more permissive and promiscuous than women's when it comes to sex. As a result of these stereotypes, men may regard women as sexual challenges or objects to be obtained. In contrast, having been taught that men are lustful creatures with "sex on the brain," women might feel they must assume the role of a "controller," regulating the pace of sexual encounters, at the expenses of their own personal satisfaction. As you can see, gender stereotypes make it difficult to achieve a fully shared partnership because partners are not viewed, nor subsequently treated, as equals.

Nevertheless, there are some real differences between men and women when it comes to sex. For example, women (more than men) tend to "romanticize" or feel that love ought to play an important role in sexuality (Regan, Durvasula, Howell, Ureño, & Rea, 2004). Women are also more likely than men to state that sex should only occur in *committed* relationships. In contrast, men are more likely to endorse *casual* sex (McCabe, 2005). Moreover, men do report greater sexual desire than women. On a more negative note, men also tend to be more sexually aggressive and sexually coercive than women (Chung, 2005; Katz & Myhr, 2008). And as Carol and Kim found out, men are more likely than women to misinterpret friendly behaviors as sexual overtures (Lindgren, Parkhill, George, & Hendershot, 2008).

MEDIA AND SEXUALITY   In addition to gender stereotypes, sexuality is also influenced by the sexual content of magazines, television/movies, music, video games, and other forms of media. Exposure to sexual media is of special concern during the teen years, when adolescents' sexuality is just beginning to blossom (Eggermont, 2005). In fact, many adolescents consume media to help them understand the new sexual landscape before them (Kim et al., 2006). Here are just a few examples of the sexual media that youth *under the age of 18* are exposed to:

- Sex and romance are the most frequently written about topic in magazines read by teenage girls; with nearly one-fifth of headlines focused on issues of sexuality (Davalos, Davalos, & Layton, 2007).
- When women are on the cover of *Rolling Stone* magazine they are presented in a sexualized manner—such as being in a provocative position while nude with a sexually charged

Sexuality is a frequent issue in the media and in marketing promotions, which serve to promote gender role stereotyping.

label printed next to their picture—83 percent of the time. Only 17 percent of men are shown in this way (Hatton & Trautner, 2011).

- Magazines directed at men and teens present women as sex objects more so than any other type of non-pornographic magazine (Stankiewicz & Rosselli, 2008).
- Between 44 and 81 percent of music videos show men and women in revealing clothing, depict scenes involving sexual innuendo, and provide indications that sexual behavior has or is about to take place (Zurbriggen et al., 2007).
- Seventy percent of the top 20 shows popular with adolescents average nearly seven scenes of sexual content per hour (Eyal, Kunkel, Biely, & Finnerty, 2007).
- Thirty-eight percent of 16- to 17-year-olds reported successfully seeking out online sexually explicit content (Wolak, Mitchell, & Finkelhor, 2007).
- Exposure to Internet pornography is associated with more sexually permissive attitudes and behaviors (Lo & Wei, 2005).

Exploration 11.1: Sexuality

www.siecus.org   The Sexuality Information and Education Council of the United States (SIECUS) is a national, nonprofit organization that affirms sexuality as a natural and healthy part of living.

So, just what are teens learning from these sources of sexual information? Although frequently mentioning the importance of "safe sex," the media tend to characterize sex as a casual, fun, natural, and an overall positive activity (Epstein & Ward, 2008). However, conflicting messages are also given. For women, sexuality is shown to be controlled, discrete, restricted, and responsible; for men, an active sex life is viewed as acceptable and even encouraged (Ward, 2003). As you can see, the media frequently portrays sexuality in a manner consistent with the gender stereotypes mentioned above.

Here's a sobering finding: Across adolescence, youth report learning more about sexuality from media than from their parents—a finding that conflicts with parental desires to be the primary source of sexual information (Lagus, Bernat, Bearinger, Resnick, & Eisenberg, 2011; Somers & Surmann, 2004). For many teens, the sexual messages provided by the media may be having an effect, as 34 percent of ninth graders, 43 percent of tenth graders, 51 percent of eleventh graders, and 63 percent of twelfth graders report having sexual intercourse at least once. Surprising to many is the fact that more than 50 percent of adolescents have engaged in oral sex by the time they graduate high school. And around 10 percent of adolescents and young adults report **sexting**—*sending sexually explicit messages or photos via electronic communication* (Kaiser Family Foundation, 2011). Furthermore, youth with a heavy sexual media diet are more likely to engage in sexual intercourse and partake in non-coital sexual activity (e.g., genital touching) than youth consuming little media (Collins et al., 2004). Thus, media portrayals of sex appear to influence the decisions teens make, in their personal lives, regarding the appropriateness of engaging in different types of sexual activities (Collins, Martino, Elliott, & Miu, 2011).

Sexual Communication

One of the most astounding things about sexual behavior, at any age, is the reluctance of most people to talk about sex with their lovers or spouses. It's as if talking about sex would spoil the spontaneity—which might be only partly true. A lot depends on how you talk about your sex life. Frequently, people don't have the foggiest notion of their partner's sexual likes or dislikes. Consequently, well-intentioned caresses are not fully appreciated because they're either too heavy-handed, too quick, or too far off the mark—all matters that could be easily corrected by a few words murmured at the right time. However, it's best to avoid discussing sex in a calculating or clinical way. Likewise, it might be best if couples avoid talking about sex immediately before or after, lest it put their partner on the defensive (McCarthy & McCarthy, 2009).

HOW TO TALK ABOUT SEX The most important part of sexual communication is the attitude you and your partner have toward each other. Especially crucial is the sense of trust and mutual empathy—the sense that each cares for the other and knows this feeling is reciprocated (Holmberg & Blair, 2009). A lot depends on the spirit and tone of voice in which you say something and your partner's willingness to discuss it in good faith. For instance, in making a request, you might say something like "I'd prefer doing something together before we have sex, such as taking a walk." You may also want to ask a yes-or-no question, such as "Did you enjoy that?" Or you could ask an open-ended question, such as "What part of our sexual relationship would you most like to improve?" Some individuals prefer either-or questions such as "Do you want to talk about this now or at a later time?" Open-ended and either-or questions encourage more participation from your partner than simple yes-or-no questions. It's also important to use questions selectively and, of course, *really* listen to what your partner is saying to you. When you feel you must criticize, express your remarks in a non-judgmental way—using "I" messages, as discussed in the chapter on emotions and motivation (Chapter 7). Whenever possible, demonstrate what you mean. If one person feels a partner has been too frenetic during foreplay, he or she might place one hand on the partner's and demonstrate a slower method, saying, "This is what I prefer." When receiving criticism, try not to overreact. Look beyond the words to what your partner is trying to tell you. Remember, often, the goal of sexual criticism is to enhance both partners' sexual satisfaction, with the end result being a fully shared partnership.

HOW NOT TO TALK ABOUT SEX   Giving and receiving criticism regarding sexuality is a touchy but important matter. In fact, some highly destructive patterns have been identified (Gottman & Carrere, 2000). One pattern is **criticism** *that entails attacking the partner's character,* for example, calling the partner "selfish." Another pattern is **contempt,** *in which insults are used to denigrate the partner's sexuality.* A third damaging type of communication is **defensiveness,** *in which we make excuses or refuse to take responsibility for our sexuality or use some other self-protective defense.* Finally, withdrawal is lethal to sexual relationships. In **withdrawal,** *we ignore our partners by watching TV or turning our backs on them.* When you feel the urge to criticize, ask yourself, "What's the reason for my saying this?" If there's no good reason, perhaps it's better *not* to say it. To assess your own level of communication in intimate relationships, you and your partner should complete Activity 11–1 and then discuss the results.

Initiating and Refusing Sex

Nowhere is sexual communication put to the test more than in initiating and refusing sex (Bevan, 2003). Some people don't communicate very well in this area and expect their partners to be mind readers. Others have developed nonverbal cues or elaborate rituals to signal their interest in sex. For example, one of Carol's friends once said to her, "When John gets out the good wine and suggests we cuddle up and watch a movie, I know what he's *really* thinking." Men have traditionally taken the initiative in sexual intercourse, but nowadays men and women are moving away from such restricted notions of what "men must do" or what "women must not do" (Wilde & Diekman, 2005). The more couples can initiate and refuse sex on an equal basis, however, the more satisfied they are with their sex lives. Not surprisingly, they also engage in sex more frequently than other couples (Crooks & Bauer, 2008).

Finally, it is not just our sexual desires that we need to communicate to our partners; we also need to discuss with our partners their and our sexual histories. Few people are comfortable asking partners, both romantic partners and relative strangers, if they have been exposed to sexually transmitted diseases or whether they use contraception (Ryan, Franzetta, Manlove, & Holcombe, 2007). But these are *very important* aspects of human sexuality, so broaching the subject with our partners is a must. It is worth noting that individuals who raise this topic with their prospective sexual partners also tend to use contraception, are less likely to use drugs and alcohol, and are more likely to believe in committed relationships (Moore & Davidson, 2000).

SEXUAL RESPONSIVENESS

LEARNING OBJECTIVES

11.3 List the phases in the human sexual response cycle.
11.4 Identify gender differences in sexual responsiveness.

A week or so after their initial meeting Carol ran into Jeff in the Student Union. Jeff apologized for his previous drunken behavior and started talking to Carol about college life. They soon found out that they went to high schools in the same city and that they both enjoy basketball and trying new foods. After dining at a Thai restaurant and spending the night talking, Jeff and Carol agreed to go out on an "official" date. Eventually, their dating led to a sexual relationship.

The Sexual Response Cycle

Despite people's reluctance to discuss their sex lives, researchers have been able to better understand human sexuality due to the pioneering work of William Masters and Virginia Johnson (1966, 1979). Through an extensive series of interviews and controlled observations of volunteers masturbating and engaging in **sexual intercourse** (here defined as *penetration of the vagina by the penis*), Masters and Johnson identified *the basic sexual response patterns of men and women.* These patterns consist of certain common physiological changes that occur in a

ACTIVITY 11–1

HOW WELL DO YOU AND YOUR PARTNER COMMUNICATE SEXUAL FEELINGS?

This exercise is designed to give you some indication of your own level of communication in close relationships. With your partner or significant other in mind, respond to each of the following questions by answering true (T) or false (F) in the blank.

_____ **1.** I readily tell my partner my wishes and needs.

_____ **2.** My significant other knows my favorite foods, television shows, and hobbies.

_____ **3.** My partner and I calmly discuss financial problems.

_____ **4.** My partner and I are able to give each other criticism without becoming angry.

_____ **5.** My companion and I are able to understand each other even without speaking.

_____ **6.** We discuss with sensitivity and sympathy one another's problems at work.

_____ **7.** If my partner does something I do not like, I can straightforwardly tell him or her.

_____ **8.** When we fight, our fights are problem focused and of short duration.

_____ **9.** My significant other enjoys my sense of humor, even if he or she is the target of it.

_____ **10.** My partner and I know each other's sexual desires and preferences.

_____ **11.** When my companion tells me a secret, it remains a secret with me.

_____ **12.** My partner and I rarely lie to each other about anything.

_____ **13.** If my partner makes me jealous, I express my jealousy in productive ways.

_____ **14.** My significant other and I pretty much agree on the types of people we both like.

_____ **15.** I provide feedback to my partner without hurting his or her self-esteem.

_____ **16.** We regularly and calmly disclose personal information to each other.

_____ **17.** I easily communicate with my partner when he or she has had a bad day.

_____ **18.** My partner and I frequently and effortlessly make joint decisions.

_____ **19.** I am just as happy to be a follower as a leader where my companion is concerned.

_____ **20.** My significant other and I don't have to "give in" to each other to keep the peace.

SCORING: Add up the number of "true" or Ts. The higher your score, the better your communication skills with your partner appear to be. If you had a low score (for example, below 7), you don't necessarily have poor communication skills. You might, however, want to sit down with your partner and discuss whether there are better ways to communicate with each other. Remember, this survey was designed specifically for your own self-understanding. It has not been scientifically validated.

predictable sequence and are collectively labeled the **sexual response cycle.** What follows is a modified version of the cycle, incorporating some of the recent changes suggested by other authorities in the field. We'll describe five phases of the sexual response cycle: (1) transition, (2) excitement, (3) plateau, (4) orgasm, and (5) resolution.

TRANSITION (OR DESIRE)   In the sexual response cycle, **transition** is *the gradual shift from a nonsexual to a sexual state of being and includes the awakening of sexual desire and a readiness for sexual arousal.* We're all familiar with the importance of "getting ready" for a special evening out. The same is true with sex. Although individuals vary widely in regard to what puts them in the mood for sex, certain activities commonly facilitate the transition. Some people enjoy a relaxed, candle-lit meal; others may prefer dancing, listening to certain music, or watching a romantic or erotic movie. Touching, massage, and relaxing in hot water are also favorite ways to get into the mood for sex. However, men, more so than women, tend to be impatient and less in tune or interested in the need for transition. Many women prefer a more gradual transition, accompanied by emotional sharing and tender caressing and kissing. Some partners like to use erotic materials to stimulate each other. Interestingly, most of the erotica produced in the United States is designed to stimulate sexual interest in men, not women (Attwood, 2005). This may be because men find visual images more sexually arousing than do women (Canli & Gabrieli, 2004).

EXCITEMENT   *Sexual arousal,* or excitement, involves a combination of mental and sensory stimulation. **Excitement** means that *sexual arousal causes increased muscle tension, engorgement of the genitals with blood, and increased heart rate.* Each partner's anticipation of sex is an important part of getting in the mood. Sexual desire is also heightened through the stimulation of the senses: sights, sounds, the sense of smell, and even taste combine to heighten excitement. Mutual caressing of various parts of the body, especially the erogenous zones, almost always intensifies sexual arousal, even when sexual desire is initially low in one partner. It is during this stage that the man's penis becomes erect and the woman also experiences arousal (or engorgement with blood) of her sex organs. The length of this stage varies greatly among individuals and couples.

Sexual arousal also depends greatly on psychological changes in the central nervous system, such as thoughts and feelings about a specific partner or the sexual act (Toates, 2009). Many people become aroused more readily through erotic fantasies. For some, fantasy provides an initial boost to sexual arousal, whereas for others, an orgasm can't be experienced without it. Erotic fantasy serves a variety of functions, ranging from the reduction of anxiety to the focusing of our thoughts and feelings. Sexual fantasies are especially helpful in counteracting boredom, a common obstacle in long-term relationships such as marriage. Common fantasies include reliving a past sexual experience or having sex with a famous partner (Kahr, 2008; Meana & Nunnink, 2006).

There are some gender differences in fantasies. Men fantasize about women's bodies, physical appearance, and sexual activity, whereas women fantasize about their own attractiveness to men. Men are likely to fantasize about being dominant and women fantasize about the emotional or romantic context of the sexual activity. Men and women, though, seem equally likely to fantasize (Canli & Gabrieli, 2004; Zurbriggen & Yost, 2004). Interestingly, research on the fantasies of gay men and lesbians has found similar gender effects, except that the fantasized partner is usually of the same sex (Chivers, Rieger, Latty, & Bailey, 2004). As revealed, men and women are often aroused by different stimuli, thereby setting the stage for misunderstanding between the sexes. At the same time, *individual* differences tend to outweigh *gender* differences, so that each person needs to be appreciated in terms of his or her own preferences.

PLATEAU   The **plateau** phase *occurs just before orgasm; in this phase, sexual arousal becomes more pronounced.* It is usually quite brief, lasting anywhere from a few seconds to several minutes. It's difficult to define the onset of this phase because there is no clear outward sign, such as erection of the man's penis or lubrication of the woman's vagina. Actually, the usual signs of sexual arousal become more pronounced as the individuals approach orgasm. The heart beats faster and breathing grows more rapid. Increasing muscle tension and blood pressure lead to engorgement of the sex organs, promoting the partner's readiness for orgasm. Men rarely lose their erection at this phase. Women also experience a marked increase in the swelling of the outer third of the vagina, making stimulation even more pleasurable. At this point, the partner who is moving faster toward orgasm, often the man, may need to slow down or vary the stimulation from time to time so that both partners can reach orgasm at the same time, if they so desire.

ORGASM   **Orgasm** is *the climax of sexual excitement that is pleasurable and releases tension.* As this climax of sexual excitement approaches, the partners may sense that orgasm is inevitable. Men usually realize orgasm accompanied by tingling muscle spasms throughout the body and perhaps uncontrollable cries and moans. However, women may arrive at the heightened sexual tension of the plateau phase without necessarily experiencing orgasm. This is sometimes the case during penile–vaginal intercourse when the man reaches orgasm first or when he replaces manual or oral stimulation with penetration as the female approaches orgasm. During orgasm, muscles in and around the man's penis contract rhythmically, causing the forcible ejaculation of semen. Similarly, the outer third of the woman's vagina contracts rhythmically along with the pulsation of her uterus. For both sexes, the first few contractions are the most intense and pleasurable, followed by weaker and slower contractions. Individuals of both sexes vary considerably in their subjective reports of orgasm.

RESOLUTION   When no further stimulation occurs, orgasm is immediately followed by the **resolution phase,** where *the body returns to its normal, nonexcited phase.* Heart rate, blood pressure, and breathing quickly subside. Muscle tension usually dissipates within 5 minutes after orgasm. Men lose about 50 percent of their erection within a minute or so after orgasm, and the remainder in the next several minutes. Men also enter into a **refractory period**—*a time when added stimulation will not result in orgasm.* The length of time varies widely, from a few minutes to several days, depending on such factors as the man's age, health, and frequency of previous sexual activity as well as his sexual desire for his partner. Women experience no equivalent refractory period. Most women are physically capable of another orgasm, though they may not desire it or experience it. Women who have not experienced orgasm after high levels of arousal usually experience a slow resolution. However, when both partners have attained orgasm, they generally find this a pleasant and relaxed time.

Gender Differences in Sexual Responsiveness

SEXUAL AROUSAL   In addition to the refractory period in males, there are some important variations between men's and women's experience of sex. First, there are marked differences in sexual arousal in men and women; some of which have already been noted. Another major gender difference is that the areas of the brain related to sexual arousal, such as the amygdala and hypothalamus, are more strongly activated in men than women when viewing erotic images (Canli & Gabrieli, 2004). Moreover, when viewing sexual material, men respond to the sexual attractiveness of the female participants and to watching as an observer or imagining oneself as a participant. Women, on the other hand, tend to respond more exclusively to imaging themselves as a participant (Meana & Nunnink, 2006).

Much of the difference in sexual activity between the sexes may be due to cultural factors, especially those that restrict women's sexuality more than men's. One of the clearest examples is the double standard in sex, which implies that the same sexual behavior is evaluated differently, depending on whether a man or a woman engages in it. At the same time, there are other factors not easily classified as biological or cultural that may contribute to the differences in sexual arousal between men and women. For instance, when asked, "What has prevented you from freely expressing your sexuality?" women are more likely than men to report being affected by fear of pregnancy, guilt, lack of desire, and social disapproval. The fact that women can become pregnant and men do not remains a factor even in this era of more effective contraceptives.

CHANGES ACROSS THE LIFESPAN The differences between male and female sexuality tend to change across the life span (SIECUS, 2002). The teenage male's sexuality is very intense and almost exclusively genitally focused. But as he ages, his refractory period becomes longer, he becomes satisfied with fewer orgasms a week, and his focus of sexuality is not so completely genital. Sex becomes a more sensuously diffuse experience, including a greater emotional component in relation to his partner. In women, the process is often quite different, as their sexual awakening tends to occur much later. While they are in their teens and 20s, their arousal and orgasmic response may be slow and inconsistent. However, by the time they reach their 30s, women's sexual responsivity has become quicker and more intense, especially among sexually experienced women. In sum, men seem to begin with an intense, genitally focused sexuality and only later develop an appreciation for the sensuous and emotional aspects of sex. In contrast, women have an earlier awareness of the sensuous and emotional aspects of sex and tend to develop the capacity for intense genital response later. This explains why women find their sex lives increasingly satisfying after age 40 (Hyde & DeLameter, 1997; Yoquinto, 2012).

ORGASMIC VARIATION Another major difference between the sexes is the greater orgasmic variation among women compared to men, both in the physiology of orgasm and in the individual's subjective awareness of sexual climax. As it turns out, there are three basic patterns of the sexual response cycle in women, though only one for men (Masters, Johnson, & Kolodny, 1988).

- One pattern resembles the male pattern (mentioned above) and differs mainly in the woman's capacity for additional orgasms.
- A second shows a prolonged, fluctuating plateau phase, with small surges toward orgasm, followed by a gradual resolution. This is sometimes referred to as "skimming" because of the lack of a single, intense climax and is most often reported by young or sexually inexperienced women.
- Another pattern shows a rapid rise in sexual excitement leading to a single, intense orgasm and quick resolution.

Although men exhibit fewer variations, it would be a mistake to assume that all men experience the sexual response cycle in the same way. Some men have reported extended periods of intense sexual stimulation before reaching orgasm. Others have experienced several mild sexual climaxes, finally leading to an expulsion of semen. Still others have prolonged pelvic contractions after ejaculation. A marked difference between the sexes is **multiple orgasms**—*two or more sexual climaxes within a short period of time*—with women more likely to have multiple orgasms. Although it is not uncommon for women to have several orgasms in quick succession, multiple orgasms are the exception rather than the rule for men. Multiple orgasms, though, are best seen as a potential area to be explored by some rather than an ultimate goal for all.

Love and Sex

So far we've been emphasizing the physical aspects of sex. What about the attitudes and relationships between the partners? Let's say Carol and Kim had become sexually involved with Jeff and Bob the first night they met, would they have experienced guilt and shame? Would they find themselves more attracted to the men? Healthy, guilt-free people can function well sexually and derive pleasure from sex without being in love. Masters and Johnson observed that there is nothing inherently "bad" about sex without love, especially if both parties consent. Under certain circumstances, for some people, sex without love may be enjoyable in its own right (Masters, Johnson, & Kolodny, 1995). However, in reality a great deal depends on the individuals involved, especially their value systems. For example, Carol did not want to have sex with Jeff the first few nights she dated him. Rather, she wanted to get to know him better and feel that he acknowledged some commitment toward her before even thinking of having sex with him. Another woman might have reacted quite differently and have seen the opportunity for sex on the first date to be an exciting adventure or a way to feel closer to her date.

Love and commitment
enrich sexuality.

It is worth emphasizing that *love can enrich sex,* especially in a long-term relationship such as marriage. The affection and commitment two people enjoy in their relationship can enhance their overall pleasure, compensating somewhat for the loss of sensual excitement that can occur after years in a committed relationship. In contrast, couples that have sex mechanically, especially when one or both partners have little or no affection for the other, soon discover that sex itself is no longer satisfying (Granvold, 2001).

Romantic love, *which consists of intimacy or closeness and passion,* may lead to satisfying sex, at least for a while, although the satisfaction may soon diminish as romantic ardor cools. In contrast, for couples in a long-term relationship, romantic love often matures into **companionate love,** *a kind of loving but practical relationship based primarily on emotional closeness and commitment rather than physical, sexual intimacy.* Indeed, many therapists have worked with hundreds of couples with a loving, committed relationship (companionate love) whose sex life is disappointing. In the United States at least, the ideal type of love remains that of **consummate love,** *a complete and balanced love characterized by emotional closeness, sexual intimacy, and commitment between the partners.* Of note, for most couples, a good sex life and marital happiness go hand-in-hand. Love not only strengthens the closeness and commitment between partners but also engenders better sex. It is no coincidence that most couples refer to sexual intercourse as "making love."

Exploration 11.2: Sexual Orientation

Thetaskforce.org   A good place to find information on gay and lesbian issues.

SEXUAL ORIENTATION

11.5 Discuss different types of sexual orientation.
11.6 Describe the short-term and long-term consequences of coming out.
11.7 Explain what sexual prejudice is and the behaviors associated with it.

BOX 11–2   Focus on Diversity: Transgendered Persons

In 2011, Chaz Bono appeared on the popular TV show *Dancing with the Stars,* bringing the issue of gender-identity, transgendered persons, and gender-reassignment surgery to the national stage. **Gender identity** refers to *self-identification as male or female.* For most people, gender identity and anatomical sex are compatible. But for some (and the exact numbers are unknown), gender identity and the corresponding sexual anatomy are mismatched. Hence the term **transgendered persons**— *one's sense of maleness or femaleness is inconsistent with their anatomical sex.* In essence, transgendered people feel as if they were born with the wrong sexual anatomy. To rectify this situation, and make their bodies more consistent with their gender identity, many transgendered persons undergo hormone replacement therapy (HRT) and gender reassignment surgery. Female-to-male HRT, which involves the administration of androgens (e.g., testosterone), results in numerous body changes, including deepening of the voice, facial hair growth, and increasing muscle mass. Male-to-female HRT, which utilizes estrogens, also results in significant changes to the body, including breast development, reduction in body hair and muscle development, and thinning of the skin. Gender reassignment surgery can further change the outward appearance of the transgendered individual by surgically altering their genitalia to match their gender identity. However, even before these biological changes are made, transgendered persons feel most comfortable with themselves when they assume the **gender roles**—*social and cultural expectations about what is appropriate for males and females*—and outward appearance (e.g., clothing, hair style, etc.) of the gender with which they identify. Because gender identity and sexual orientation are different, transgendered persons can be heterosexual, homosexual, or bisexual (Israel & Tarver, 2001; Samons, 2009).

Of note, transgendered people are born with a complete, and intact, set of genitalia, unlike **intersexed persons** who *are born with chromosomal or hormonal birth defects so that they do not readily fit into "male" or "female" categories.* For example, an XY intersexed person has the chromosomal make-up of a man, but external genitalia that range from entirely female to incompletely formed as male (Allen, 2009).

Variations in Sexual Orientation

Sexual orientation is *a component of sexuality and is characterized by enduring emotional, romantic, or sexual attraction to a particular gender.* The three main sexual orientations include **heterosexuality,** *which involves attraction to someone of the opposite sex*; **homosexuality,** *which involves attraction to someone of the same sex*; and **bisexuality,** *which involves attraction to members of either sex.* Interestingly, researchers have also discovered that some people's sexual orientation is fluid; that is, they go from bisexuality to homosexuality or heterosexuality to homosexuality as they develop (Rosario, Schrimshaw, Hunter, & Braun, 2006). Box 11–2 discusses transgender, which is often thought of as a variation in sexual orientation, but in reality is a form of gender identity.

Coming Out

Coming out occurs *when an individual accepts his or her sexual orientation as homosexual (or bisexual) and then tells others.* Coming out involves many processes for the lesbian, gay, and bisexual (LGB) individual (as well as for others who are told), including but not limited to challenging one's own beliefs and self-concept, managing conflicts differently, changing established relationships with other people, and asking questions of the self and others (Broad, 2011; Goldman, 2008).

SHORT-TERM EFFECTS RELATED TO COMING OUT Discovering that one's sexual orientation is not heterosexual—the predominant orientation in our society—can be distressing because of societal stigmas and prejudices against homosexuality (Wilson, Zeng, & Blackburn, 2011). In fact, disclosure of homosexual orientation to friends and family is the second most significant life stressor for homosexuals, with the most significant being initial discovery of their own homoerotic attractions (D'Augelli, Hershberger, & Pilkingston, 1998). One reason disclosure surrounding sexual orientation is difficult is because unlike other marginalized groups (e.g., racial minorities), most young homosexuals (and bisexuals for that matter) are not raised in a community of similar others (Rosario et al., 2006).

When family and friends are supportive, LGB individuals cope much better with the coming out revelation (Willoughby, Malik, & Lindahl, 2006). Gay men, however, seem to be more estranged from their families (especially their fathers) than heterosexual men and lesbians (Bobrow & Bailey, 2001). However, gay men and lesbians report that their intimate relationships with their partners are not very much affected by parental disapproval (LaSala, 2002). When families do not accept or support their LGB family member, involvement in the gay and lesbian community and support at school can help diminish psychological distress (Lasser, Tharinger, & Cloth, 2006).

LONG-TERM EFFECTS RELATED TO COMING OUT   Although most LGB are well adjusted after coming out, LGB individuals report more suicidal ideation, suicide attempts, self-injurious behavior, drug use, and use of therapeutic interventions than heterosexuals do. This may occur because societal stigma against homosexuality, along with being a victim of sexual prejudice, contribute to depression and other mental disorders (Balsam, Beauchaine, Mickey, & Rothblum, 2005; Rosario, Schrimshaw, & Hunter, 2009). However, in agreement with the Public Service Announcements targeting LGB youth, research does indeed indicate that "it gets better." With time, and the support of friends and family, self-esteem rises (Ryan, Russell, Huebner, Diaz, & Sanchez, 2010). Though societal views towards the LGB community, and the associated stress, still place individuals' self-esteem at risk during adulthood (Spencer & Patrick, 2009).

Exploration 11.3: Helping LGBT Youth

www.itgetsbetter.org   The website offers insight and support to LGBT youth experiencing minority stress.

Sexual Prejudice

Sexual prejudice refers to *all the negative attitudes based on sexual orientation, whether the target is homosexual, bisexual, or heterosexual.* Individuals who are sexually prejudiced against those in the LGB community are called **homophobic**, that is they are *afraid of homosexuals or hold negative attitudes toward homosexuals* for various reasons. Sexual prejudice has declined somewhat over the last two decades. In the 1970s and 1980s, two-thirds of surveyed Americans said that homosexuality was "always wrong." Today, 52 percent of Americans view homosexuality as "morally acceptable" (Saad, 2010). And the success of television shows with LGB characters, such as *Glee, Gossip Girl, Modern Family, Pretty Little Liars, and Will and Grace,* gives testament to the growing acceptability of sexual orientations other than heterosexuality.

Nevertheless, sexual prejudice abounds, especially among teens: 93 percent of youth report hearing derogatory words about sexual orientation; 78 percent of LGB teens are bullied because of their sexual orientation; and the group of teens that is most likely to be bullied are those who are LGB or *thought* to be LGB (Riese, 2012). Moreover, only six states, and the District of Columbia, allow same-sex marriage. And in 2010 around 19 percent of **hate crimes**—*crimes motivated by biases based on race, religion, sexual orientation, ethnicity/national origin, and disability*—involved a sexual-orientation bias (FBI, 2012). Sexual prejudice is more likely to be manifested in individuals who do not personally know or think they know any homosexuals, in very religious individuals, and those who possess anxiety about gender roles (Green, 2005). Andrew Sullivan (2003) says, "Every day, if you're a gay person, you see amazing advances and terrifying setbacks. . . . Wal-Mart set rules . . . to protect its gay employees from discrimination [but] the Vatican comes out and announces that granting legal recognition to gay spouses will destroy the family and society" (p. 35).

PRACTICAL ISSUES

LEARNING OBJECTIVES

11.8 Identify various sexual dysfunctions in both sexes.

11.9 Explain why people choose different forms of birth control.

11.10 Explain the difference between bacterial and viral STIs.

11.11 Understand various aspects of sexual abuse of children.

11.12 Describe the effects of sexual assault on victims.

The emphasis on sexual fulfillment in recent years has had some beneficial effects. Today, there appears to be more objective information about sex, increased sexual communication between partners, and less anxiety and guilt over harmless sexual practices such as masturbation. At the same time, such changes have been accompanied by new anxieties. Many sexually normal men worry about their sexual performance. A woman who is not orgasmic may suffer the same loss of self-esteem as the man who has a fairly flaccid erection. Then, too, the increasing sexual activity outside of marriage today has accentuated the perennial problems of birth control, unwanted pregnancies, and sexually transmitted diseases. Most disturbing of all is the occurrence of sexual victimization in our society.

Sexual Dysfunctions

Even sexually experienced couples discover that each time they engage in sex, it is different. Sometimes sex is highly pleasurable for both partners; at other times it is less satisfying for one or both of them. Such occasional problems are usually not serious; they often are caused by fatigue or stress. Moreover, alcohol consumption and certain antidepressants can interfere with sexual activity (Haberfellner, 2007; Johnson, Phelps, & Cottler, 2004). When sexual setbacks persist, or become distressing to the individual (such that they cannot enjoy sex), the difficulties can be classified as **sexual dysfunctions**—*persistent problems that prevent an individual from engaging in or enjoying sexual intercourse.* Sexual dysfunctions may be grouped according to the phase of the sexual response cycle in which they occur. They include difficulties of desire, arousal, and orgasm. Each is addressed in turn.

DYSFUNCTIONS OF DESIRE **Hypoactive sexual desire,** sometimes called **inhibited sexual desire,** refers to a *lack of interest in sex.* There is a higher incidence of this disorder in women than in men (Heiman, 2008). In some instances, the lack of desire may be a psychological response resulting from emotional (e.g., fear of intimacy; life stress), relationship (e.g., excessive conflict), and/or sexual difficulties (e.g., boredom, proficiency) with their partners. It is also important to realize that the issue of low sexual desire often stems from the fact that one partner simply has a higher level of desire than the other, and as a result, defines the partner with lower desire as having a disorder. Emphasis should not necessarily be placed solely on the psychological causes of this disorder because the source can also be physiological. For example, in women who have experienced menopause, low estrogen levels, or lack of vaginal lubrication can reduce sexual feelings or make sex painful. Similarly, decreasing levels of testosterone can diminish sexual desire in men (Advani, 2011; Dennerstein & Hayes, 2005).

Aversion to sex refers to *anxiety, disgust, repulsion, and other negative emotions toward sex.* Although both men and women experience sexual aversion, it is more common among women. Individuals who are repelled by sex often have a history of childhood sexual abuse, such as incest, or have been victims of sexual assault. In some instances, such individuals have been subject to constant pressuring or bargaining for sex in a relationship. Repeated but unsuccessful attempts to please a sexual partner may eventually lead to the avoidance of sex. Finally, anxiety about conflicts in one's sexual identity or orientation may also create fear of sex (Masters et al., 1995).

DYSFUNCTIONS OF AROUSAL   Another type of sexual dysfunction is **inhibited sexual arousal,** which is *insufficient sexual arousal.* This disorder occurs most as **erectile inhibition** (*impotency*) and **inhibited vaginal lubrication** (*when insufficient vasocongestion and insufficient lubrication occur in women*). Men who suffer from inhibited sexual arousal usually have **secondary erectile inhibition**—that is, *they've previously experienced erections but are consistently unable to have an erection of sufficient firmness for penetration.* Most men have occasional difficulties with erections, usually because of fatigue or stress. But sometimes these experiences may generate such concern and anxiety that they develop into a chronic pattern. The man's anxiety assumes the form of a "spectator's role." That is, instead of relaxing and letting his erection occur spontaneously, he watches and judges his own performance. Thus, his self-critical attitude and tenseness contribute to the erectile problem. Physiological factors related to erectile inhibition include severe diabetes and the effect of certain drugs (such as narcotics and amphetamines), alcohol, and prescribed medications. As you recall from the chapter on aging (Chapter 3), Viagra and other medications are designed to help alleviate some of this sexual dysfunction (Decaluwé, Pauwels, Verpoest, & Van de Voorde, 2011).

Inhibited vaginal lubrication in the woman is similar to the man's lack of erection because in both cases *insufficient vasocongestion occurs.* Normally, during sexual stimulation the congestion of blood vessels causes the vaginal walls to secrete droplets of fluid, which eventually form a shiny film on the walls of the vagina. At times, this lack of lubrication is caused by insufficient stimulation or prolonged intercourse. In such instances, increased stimulation of the woman's clitoris or other parts of her body may help to increase vaginal lubrication, as can adding small amounts of vaginal jelly or cream containing estradiol (by prescription from a physician).

DYSFUNCTIONS OF ORGASM   The most common difficulty of the orgasmic phase in the sexual response cycle is **premature** (*early orgasm in a man*) or **retarded ejaculation** (*the delay or absence of orgasm in a man*) and *delay or absence of orgasm (for the woman)*, known as **female orgasmic disorder.** Premature ejaculation consists of experiencing orgasm so quickly that the man's enjoyment of sex is significantly lessened or his partner is not contented. It is a common problem for men; as many as half of the cases may be due to organic factors. Fortunately, this condition is readily treatable through such measures as the stop-start technique in which the man, usually with the aid of his partner, practices recognizing the sensations of impending orgasm and momentarily stops stimulation until he gradually learns to delay ejaculation (Wincze, 2009).

The most common problems for women are slowness or inability to experience orgasm. Women who have never experienced orgasm sometimes lack knowledge of their own sexual response cycle, something that is often learned by other women through masturbation. These women may become orgasmic by minimizing their inhibitions and by maximizing their sexual stimulation through self-pleasure. A more common issue is slowness or failure to climax through intercourse with a partner. This problem is not surprising, considering that orgasm is usually triggered through sensory stimulation of the clitoral area, which is accomplished only indirectly during intercourse. Consequently, only about one-half of women experience orgasm regularly through intercourse (Masters et al., 1995).

There are many more women who need direct clitoral stimulation, either by manual or oral stimulation or who prefer self-stimulation, in addition to the penile–vaginal thrusting during intercourse to reach climax. In such instance, a more indirect, playful approach, which may include caressing one side of the clitoral shaft or use of an indirect, circular motion of the whole clitoral area, can be helpful. Keep in mind that even healthy, sexually experienced women do not always reach orgasm, either because of fatigue or temporary, situational factors.

Exploration 11.4: Safe Sex

www.sexuality.org   A place to find quality information about safe sex. There is some fairly explicit information here, but it is presented in a no-nonsense style.

Contraception

The availability and use of reliable birth control and contraceptive methods has become increasingly important in recent years for a variety of reasons, including the fact that half of all pregnancies are unplanned (Guttmacher Institute, 2004) and because of the deadly AIDS epidemic. U.S. women are not particularly happy with the contraceptive choices available to them. Nor are they pleased that the burden of birth control typically falls on them. Most women have tried several contraceptive methods in the search for one that suits them best, but they feel that every method requires tradeoffs among safety, convenience, and effectiveness. The effectiveness of the various contraceptives, along with their general type and a brief description, are shown in Table 11–1.

Table 11–1	Comparative Effectiveness of Birth-Control Methods		
Contraceptive Type	**Definition**	**Type**	**Failure Rate**
Birth-Control Pill (Oral Contraceptive)	A hormonal pill taken daily to prevent ovulation or fertilization.	Hormonal	1–9%
Implants	Small capsules inserted into the arm that release hormones to prevent ovulation.	Hormonal	<1%
Injection	An injection of a hormone that prevents ovulation.	Hormonal	1–6%
Emergency Contraception	An emergency, high dose of birth-control pills taken within 5 days of unprotected sex. Failure rate varies depending upon when pill is taken.	Hormonal	5–11%
IUD	A T-shaped, plastic device placed inside the uterus that contains copper or hormones.	Hormonal	<1%
Male Condom	A thin, latex or polyurethane sheath that covers the penis.	Barrier	2–18%
Female Condom	A polyurethane sheath or pouch that lines the vagina.	Barrier	5–21%
Cervical Cap	A small rubber or plastic cup that fits over the cervix	Barrier	6–16%
Diaphragm	A round rubber dome inserted inside the vagina to cover the cervix.	Barrier	6–16%
Spermicide	A cream, foam, jelly, or insert that kills sperm.	Barrier	18–28%
Natural Family Planning	Avoiding sexual intercourse near the time of ovulation, when pregnancy is most likely to occur.	Other	4–25%

Source: Data from "Contraception," from Centers for Disease Control and Prevention website, 2012.

Typically, condoms and birth-control pills are most popular among people in their teens and 20s. It is important for couples to choose the method of protection that suits them best.

Remember, shared responsibility for contraception can enhance a relationship. When one partner takes an active interest in contraception, the other is less likely to feel resentment over assuming all the responsibility. Men and women can share responsibility for contraception in several ways. An important step is discussing the matter of protection or prevention before first engaging in intercourse. Unfortunately, this initial step is rarely taken, mostly because of the fear of spoiling the spontaneity of sex.

Exploration 11.5: Sex Degrees of Separation

calculators.lloydspharmacy.com/SexDegrees/   This calculator link allows you to determine the number of both *direct* and *indirect* sexual partners you have had in your life (going back six degrees of separation). You may be surprised at how high your number goes!

Sexually Transmitted Infections

As sex educators are often fond of saying, "You are having sex with everyone your sex partner has had sex with," the gist of which is that you need to know your sex partner's or partners' histories. **Sexually transmitted infections (STIs)** (also called sexually transmitted diseases or STDs) are *infections that are primarily transmitted through sexual interaction.* Each year, more than 19 million Americans contract a *new* STI (CDC, 2011). Although many of these infections can be treated successfully, STIs are on the rise because of increased sexual activity and a tendency to have more than one sexual partner, especially during one's youth. The occurrence of STIs is highest among those in the 20- to 24-year-old group, with the next highest incidence among those in the 15- to 19-year-old group and then among the 25- to 29-year olds. Those age groups represent many traditional college students or recent college graduates. Of note, the rates of many STIs (including chlamydia, gonorrhea, syphilis, and HIV) have doubled in the past decade for older Americans (50 and up). Treatments for erectile dysfunction, a reduction in vaginal lubrication (which increases the likelihood of infection), longer lives, the failure of doctors to talk with their older patients about their sexual health, and a relatively high divorce rate (resulting in more sex partners across the lifespan) are credited as being responsible for this uptick (Gann, 2012).

BACTERIAL STIs   Bacterial STIs are caused by a variety of different bacteria, and as such, each can be effectively treated with a course of antibiotics. If caught quickly enough, the long-term health of those contracting a bacterial STI is not usually placed in jeopardy. However, if left untreated serious consequences can arise (CDC, 2011). Three common bacterial STIs are gonorrhea, chlamydia, and syphilis. Let's take a look at each.

Gonorrhea is a *common sexually transmitted bacterial infection that sometimes produces a cloudy, smelly discharge and a burning sensation upon urination.* There are over 300,000 new cases reported each year (CDC, 2011). Untreated gonorrhea is the single most common cause of sterility among men. Women with untreated gonorrhea may experience inflammation of the fallopian tubes, infertility, birth malformations, or menstrual disorders. **Chlamydia**—*a bacterium that is spread by sexual contact and that affects both males and females*—has rapidly become one of the most common sexually transmitted diseases and continues to be widespread. As many as 1.3 million Americans may be infected each year (CDC, 2011). An estimated 10 percent of all college students are affected by this disease. Men who contract the infection have symptoms similar to gonorrhea, such as a discharge from the penis and a mild burning sensation during urination. Women with chlamydia infections show little or no symptoms and are often unaware of the disease until they are informed by an infected partner. If left untreated in women, Chlamydia may result in cervical inflammation or pelvic inflammatory disease and, if a woman is pregnant, it may cause eye damage to infants at birth. In men, it may spread to the prostate.

Syphilis *is caused by a spiral-shaped bacterium, or spirochete.* Fewer than 14,000 new cases of syphilis are recorded each year (CDC, 2011). The early signs of syphilis are painless sores at the place of sexual contact, usually the man's penis and the inner walls of the woman's vagina or cervix. Although the sores usually disappear within a month or two, in later stages, a skin rash and other sores may appear, along with sores on other parts of the body. These symptoms eventually disappear, but if the disease is left untreated, it may progress to an advanced stage, causing brain damage, heart failure, blindness, or paralysis.

VIRAL STIs In contrast to bacterial STIs, which can be cured, viral STIs have no cure. And in most instances, the person continues to be contagious throughout their lifetime. Current treatment consists of the drugs that reduce discomfort and assist healing during an outbreak.

Genital herpes is *one of several herpes viral infections (herpes simplex virus) that are primarily transmitted through sexual contact.* It has increased dramatically in recent years, with over 45 million (or 1 out of 6) Americans currently infected (CDC, 2011). Symptoms usually appear within several days after sexual contact with an infected partner: one or more small, red, painful bumps (papules) in the genital area, such as on the man's penis and the woman's labia and inner vaginal walls. These bumps change into blisters, which eventually rupture into painful open sores. In addition to the periodic discomfort, genital herpes can have serious complications, such as cervical cancer.

Genital human papillomavirus (HPV), for which there are 40 different types, *infect the genital areas of men and women, and over time can result in the eruption of painless warts.* Currently, around 20 million Americans have HPV, with around 6 million new cases developing each year; and the virus is so commonplace that nearly 50 percent of sexually active individuals will have it at some point in their lives. Unlike many other viral STIs, the body develops immunity to HPV in 90 percent of cases; and the person remains symptom free. It's the unlucky 10 percent that develop warts on their genitals. HPV also places individuals at risk for a variety of cancers, such as cervical, penis, and anal cancer. The vaccine Gardasil can protect sexually active people from most types of genital warts (CDC, 2011).

Compared to other STIs, **AIDS** (*acquired immune deficiency syndrome, which is caused by a virus known as HIV and transmitted primarily through body fluids*) is a fairly new disease. Nevertheless, it has achieved national and worldwide prominence in recent years because of its growing threat. Also in comparison to other STIs, AIDS is far more deadly. Recent statistics indicate that more than 1.2 million persons in the United States have been diagnosed with the AIDS virus, and that 1 out of 5 doesn't even know that they are infected. About 50,000 new cases of HIV occur each year. Since 2008, more than 16,000 people have died from the disease (CDC, 2011). Knowing about AIDS, then, might literally save your life. To test your knowledge, take the AIDS Quiz in Activity 11–2.

People who are initially infected generally show no symptoms and have no antibodies to the disease, so blood tests may come back negative. Individuals can carry this disease and be asymptomatic for long periods of time, years in fact. Because the AIDS virus destroys the T-helper cells in the body's immune system, infections that would ordinarily be less harmful to a person with a normal immune system can produce devastating, ultimately lethal diseases in the person with AIDS—for example, a common cold. This is often when it becomes apparent that the individual has AIDS. By this time it may be too late for the infected individual's sex partners; they may have already contracted the illness.

Although AIDS or HIV is classified as a sexually transmitted disease, it is communicated through blood or blood products containing the virus. As such, AIDS can be transmitted in ways other than sexual activity, such as sharing needles. Infection with other STIs increases the transmission probability for HIV. By all indications, HIV does not readily penetrate intact body surfaces, so there is little danger of getting it through a kiss, a sneeze, a handshake, or a toilet seat. Instead, HIV is acquired by direct exposure of one's bloodstream to the virus, which is carried by body fluids—notably blood and semen. Of note, the risk of catching AIDS through blood transfusions has diminished considerably because of more careful screening of blood donors and programs for intravenous drug users. The stereotype in the United States is that HIV or AIDS is a gay man's disease. However, HIV can also be transmitted through vaginal intercourse, from men to women or, less commonly, from women to men. Gay men represent the largest group

---

ACTIVITY 11–2

AIDS QUIZ

Which of the following statements are true?

1. You can tell by looking that someone has the AIDS virus.

2. People cannot become infected with the HIV virus by donating blood.

3. The AIDS virus can enter the body through the vagina, penis, rectum, or mouth.

4. It's possible to get the AIDS virus from hugging, kissing, or a toilet seat.

5. Condoms are an effective but not a fool proof way to prevent the spread of the AIDS virus.

6. The AIDS virus may live in the human body for years before symptoms actually appear.

7. The AIDS virus may be spread through sneezing and coughing.

8. Any unprotected person can become infected with the AIDS virus through sexual intercourse.

9. If you think you've been exposed to the AIDS virus, you should get an AIDS test.

10. Presently, there is no cure for AIDS.

Answers: Numbers 1, 4, and 7 are false. The others are true.

Source: Based on "Understanding Aids" (HHS Publication No. 88-8404.) U.S. Department of Health and Human Services, 1988.

---

living with AIDS (49 percent of all AIDS patients) followed by heterosexuals (28 percent), and intravenous drug users (17 percent) (CDC, 2011).

No single pattern of symptoms fits all cases of AIDS. Some common symptoms include a progressive, unexplained weight loss; persistent fever (often accompanied by night sweats); swollen lymph nodes in the neck, armpits, and groin; reddish purple spots on the skin; chronic fatigue; and unexplained diarrhea or bloody stools. Symptoms may remain unchanged for months or may be quickly followed by additional infections. People afflicted with AIDS tend to have one overwhelming infection after another until their immune system gives out. AIDS in the past was usually fatal, though with today's modern cocktails of medication some individuals are surviving much longer. People can reduce their risk for AIDS by following some practical guidelines, such as using latex condoms, avoiding anal sex, avoiding oral contact with semen, and asking sex partners about their sexual histories.

Sexual Victimization

Another issue that attracts public concern is **sexual victimization,** which *occurs when a person is coerced to engage in sexual acts under duress or force.* Sexual victimization may take many forms, ranging from the sexual abuse of a child by a parent, relative, or family friend to an adult who feels coerced to engage in offensive sexual acts by his or her partner. In this section, we'll focus on three particularly exploitative forms of sexual victimization: sexual abuse of children, child pornography, and sexual assault.

SEXUAL ABUSE OF CHILDREN   Approximately 64,000 children are victims of sexual abuse every year (U.S. Department of Health and Human Services, 2011). Most often the abuser is a family member, close relative, or friend—usually a man. Women can also sexually abuse children, and their abuse can be just as severe. Not uncommonly, the abuser has been a victim of sexual abuse as a child. In many instances, sexual abuse is not limited to a single episode and may not involve physical force. Sexual interactions generally consist of touching and fondling the genitals of the child, though some child molesters may engage in intercourse. Sexual abuse is most likely to involve prepubescent children between 9 and 12 years of age (Orange & Brodwin, 2005; Prentky, Knight, & Lee, 2006).

The immediate effects of child sexual abuse include increased anxiety, anger, eating or sleep disturbances, guilt, withdrawal, and other psychological problems of adjustment. Abused children are sometimes preoccupied with sex, as seen in an unusual interest in the sex organs, sex play, and nudity. They're also likely to exhibit a host of physical complaints, such as rashes, headaches, and vomiting, all without medical explanation. The child's emotional trauma can be magnified when parents overreact to the discovery of sexual abuse. It is important, however, that parents show sufficient concern, such as making certain the child is not left alone with the suspected abuser as well as reporting incidents of sexual abuse to the police. Above all, the child needs to know that the parents will protect the child from other abuse and that the parents still love the child (Colarusso, 2010).

In adulthood, even when there are no serious psychological problems, victims of sexual abuse often have other problems, such as difficulty becoming sexually aroused or compulsively engaging in sex. Also, abused women may feel isolated and distrustful of men. They're likely to feel anxious, depressed, and guilt-ridden. One of the most disturbing findings is the effect childhood sexual abuse has on the next generation. Boys who are abused are at increased risk of becoming child molesters themselves, and girls are more likely to produce children who are abused. Fortunately, most victims of childhood sexual abuse can benefit from psychotherapy (Jung & Steil, 2012).

CHILD PORNOGRAPHY   **Child pornography** is *a visual depiction of a minor engaging in sexually explicit conduct, especially one lacking serious literary, artistic, political, or scientific value.* Child pornography—in fact, all pornography—has been around for centuries. However, the Internet has greatly increased the possibility that more and more people have access to it despite the fact that *all* states have laws against it. Most children depicted in pornography are girls between the ages of 6 and 12. The main exploiters or consumers of child pornography are White, unmarried men older than 25 years of age, although individuals attracted to child pornography come from all economic and educational levels and all types of communities. Some, but not all, consumers have criminal histories and are socially isolated (National Center for Missing and Exploited Children, 2006).

Children engaged in these activities are altered forever, not just by the exploitation but also by the fact that the pornographer, using modern technology, can keep reproducing the images of the child over and over again. The pornographer can also use these images to blackmail the child into silence. These children not only suffer physical trauma such as bruising and STIs but also experience depression, withdrawal, anger, and mental disorders. These effects can linger into adulthood if left untreated (National Center for Missing and Exploited Children, 2006).

SEXUAL ASSAULT   **Sexual assault**—*unwanted sexual activity, including the touching of body parts as well as oral, anal, and vaginal sex under conditions of actual or threatened force*—has long been a problem in American society. Each year, more than 213,000 people are sexually assaulted. That averages out to about one sexual assault every two minutes. Although the sexual assault of males has increased in recent years, the overwhelming majority of sexual assaults involve male assailants and female victims. One of the most disturbing findings is that around 44 percent of all sexual assault victims are younger than 18 at the time of the attack. Equally unsettling is the fact that only 40 percent of sexual assaults are ever reported to the police. Contrary to popular myth that strangers hiding in bushes commit sexual assaults, nearly two-thirds of sexual assaults are committed by *someone known to the victim* (Rape, Abuse, & Incest National Network, 2012). On college campuses, it is estimated that between 20–25 percent of women and 6 percent of men will experience attempted or completed rape while pursuing their degree (Carr, 2005; Krebs, Lindquist, Warner, Fisher, & Martin, 2007). Box 11–3 discusses other misconceptions or myths about sexual assault.

BOX 11–3	Focus on Psychology: Myths about Sexual Assault

Myth 1:

Victims provoke sexual assaults when they dress provocatively or act in a promiscuous manner.

Fact: Sexual assaults are crimes of violence and control that stem from a person's determination to exercise power over another. Neither provocative dress nor promiscuous behavior is an invitation for unwanted sexual activity.

Myth 2:

If a person goes to someone's room or house or goes to a bar, she assumes the risk of sexual assault. If something happens later, she can't claim that she was sexually assaulted because she should have known not to go to those places.

Fact: This "assumption of risk" wrongfully places the responsibility of the offender's actions on the victim. Even if a person went voluntarily to someone's residence or room and consented to engage in some sexual activity, it does not serve as a blanket consent for *all* sexual activity. When someone says "No" or "Stop," that means STOP. Sexual activity forced upon another without consent is sexual assault.

Myth 3:

It's not sexual assault if it happens after drinking or taking drugs.

Fact: Being under the influence of alcohol or drugs is not an invitation for non-consensual sexual activity. A person under the influence of drugs or alcohol *does not cause* others to assault her; *others choose* to take advantage of the situation and sexually assault her because she is in a vulnerable position. Many state laws hold that a person who is cognitively impaired due to the influence of drugs or alcohol is *not able to consent* to sexual activity.

Myth 4:

Sexual assault can be avoided if women avoid dark alleys or other "dangerous" places where strangers might be hiding or lurking.

Fact: Sexual assault can occur at any time, in many places, to anyone. According to a report based on FBI data, almost 70 percent of sexual assaults reported to law enforcement occurred in the residence of the victim, the offender, or another individual.

Myth 5:

A person who has really been sexually assaulted will be hysterical.

Fact: Victims of sexual violence exhibit a spectrum of responses to the assault, which can include calm, hysteria, withdrawal, anger, apathy, denial, and shock. Being sexually assaulted is a very traumatic experience. Reactions to the assault and the length of time needed to process through the experience vary with each person.

Myth 6:

All sexual assault victims will report the crime immediately to the police. If they do not report it or delay in reporting it, then they must have changed their minds after it happened, wanted revenge, or didn't want to look like they were sexually active.

Fact: There are many reasons why a sexual assault victim may not report the assault to the police. It is not easy to talk about being sexually assaulted. The experience of retelling what happened may cause the person to relive the trauma. Other reasons for not immediately reporting the assault or not reporting it at all include fear of retaliation by the offender, fear of not being believed, fear of being blamed for the assault, fear of being "re-victimized" if the case goes through the criminal justice system, belief that the offender will not be held accountable, wanting to forget the assault ever happened, not recognizing that what happened was sexual assault, shame, and/or shock. In fact, reporting a sexual assault incident to the police is the exception and not the norm. Victims can report a sexual assault to criminal justice authorities at any time so long as the incident is reported within the jurisdiction's statute of limitations.

Myth 7:

Only young, pretty women are assaulted.

(Continued)

BOX 11–3   *(Continued)*

Fact: The belief that only young, pretty women are sexually assaulted stems from the myth that sexual assault is based on sex and physical attraction. Sexual assault is *a crime of power and control* and offenders often choose people whom they perceive as most vulnerable to attack or over whom they believe they can assert power. Sexual assault victims come from all walks of life.

Myth 8:

It's only sexual assault if the victim puts up a fight and resists.

Fact: Many states do not require a victim to resist in order to charge the offender with sexual assault. In addition, there are many reasons why a victim of sexual assault would not fight or resist her attacker. She may feel that fighting or resisting will make her attacker angry, resulting in more severe injury. She may not fight or resist as a coping mechanism for dealing with the trauma of being sexually assaulted.

Myth 9:

Someone can only be sexually assaulted if a weapon was involved.

Fact: In many cases of sexual assault, a weapon is not involved. The offender often uses physical strength, physical violence, intimidation, threats, or a combination of these tactics to overpower the victim. As pointed out above, most sexual assaults are perpetrated by someone known to the victim. An offender often uses the victim's trust developed through their relationship to create an opportunity to commit the sexual assault.

Myth 10:

Sexual assault is mostly an interracial crime.

Fact: The vast majority of violent crimes, which include sexual assaults, are intraracial, meaning the victim and offender are of the same race. This is not true, however, for Native women, as approximately 8 in 10 sexual assaults are perpetrated by Whites. Native women also experience a higher rate of sexual assault victimization than any other race.

Source: Adapted from "Myths and Facts about Sexual Violence," U.S. Department of Justice, Office of Violence Against Women, 2006.

Sexual assault usually has a devastating effect on the victim's mental health. Almost one-third of all sexual assault victims develop sexual assault-related posttraumatic stress disorder sometime during their lives, which in turn, dramatically increases the victim's risk for major alcohol and drug abuse problems. Sexual assault survivors may experience a variety of emotional repercussions in two phases. The acute phase begins immediately after the assault and may continue for hours, days, or weeks. During the first few hours after being assaulted, the woman may react in an expressive manner—crying and being very upset. Or in some instances, a woman may maintain a controlled, subdued manner and only later become aware of her feelings. Victims commonly report anxiety, shame, anger, guilt, self-blame, and a sense of powerlessness. Physical symptoms include headaches, nausea, premenstrual disturbance, and pain syndromes.

Nervousness and fear may continue into the second, reorganization phase, which may last for years. Women often fear retaliation by their assaulter. They might also harbor negative feelings about sex. Some rape victims greatly reduce the frequency of their sexual activity or discover that they have sexual disorders. Sexual assault, therefore, is usually a very traumatic experience that interferes more with the psychological aspects of sexual activity than the physiological response. Fortunately, the passage of time, combined with gentle support from others and psychotherapy, can help to alleviate the negative effects of sexual assault for many victims. Furthermore, improvements in the police and court systems (such as being more sensitive to and supportive of sexual assault victims), along with the establishment of sexual assault advocate programs has (1) increased the likelihood that victims will report crimes to the proper authorities and (2) helped sexual assault victims make an effective recovery (RAINN, 2012).

Chapter Summary

SEXUALITY AND SHARED PARTNERSHIPS

11.1   Explain how gender stereotypes and the media influence sexuality.

Gender stereotypes and media portrayals of men's and women's sexual behaviors and attitudes can influence real-life interactions between genders before, during, and after sexual activity.

11.2   Recognize the importance of sexual communication for a mutually satisfying sex life.

Sexual intercourse is understood as something partners do together as equal participants. Personal communication about sexual matters tends to be more effective when partners express themselves clearly and listen to each other. Nowhere is sexual communication put to the test more than in initiating and refusing sex. Although the more emotionally expressive partner tends to initiate sex most of the time, couples whose partners share the initiator and refuser roles equally tend to have more satisfactory sex lives than other couples.

SEXUAL RESPONSIVENESS

11.3   List the phases in the human sexual response cycle.

There are five phases of the sexual response cycle: transition, excitement, plateau, orgasm, and resolution.

11.4   Identify gender differences in sexual responsiveness.

A major difference between the sexes is the greater variation among women in the physiology and subjective awareness of orgasm, especially in the woman's ability to have several orgasms in quick succession. At the same time, individual differences tend to outweigh gender differences, so that each person needs to be understood and appreciated in terms of personal preferences.

SEXUAL ORIENTATION

11.5   Discuss different types of sexual orientation.

There are three main types of sexual orientation: heterosexual, homosexual, and bisexual.

11.6   Describe the short-term and long-term consequences of coming out.

Coming out is one of the most stressful experiences an LGB person experiences in their lifetime. This stress can be reduced when in the company of supportive others, especially family and friends. In the long term, most LGB people are well adjusted; however, stigmas

against homosexuality along with sexual prejudice can lead to significant mental health issues.

11.7   Explain what sexual prejudice is and the behaviors associated with it.

Sexual prejudice refers to the negative attitudes towards others based on sexual orientation. Homophobia (or sexual prejudice focused on LGB persons) is linked with bullying and hate crimes.

PRACTICAL ISSUES

11.8   Identify various sexual dysfunctions in both sexes.

Common sexual dysfunctions include the lack of sexual desire, erectile inhibition, and premature ejaculation in men, and inhibited vaginal lubrication and female orgasmic disorder in women.

11.9   Explain why people choose different forms of birth control.

Each method of birth control has its advantages and disadvantages, with the final choice often involving a trade-off among safety, convenience, and effectiveness.

11.10   Explain the difference between bacterial and viral STIs.

Bacterial STIs, such as chlamydia, gonorrhea, and syphilis, are curable and if caught earlier enough have little or no long-term consequences for the infected. Viral STIs, such as genital herpes and HIV, have no cure and the person continues to be contagious throughout their lifetime.

11.11   Understand various aspects of sexual abuse of children.

Most children are sexually abused by a family member, close relative, or friend—usually a man. Sexual interactions generally consist of touching and fondling the genitals of prepubescent children, though some sexual predators engage in intercourse. Without psychotherapy, significant short-term and long-term mental health problems are likely to occur. Similar negative outcomes follow children victimized by child pornography.

11.12   Describe the effects of sexual assault on victims.

Sexual assault can have a devastating effect on the victim's mental health, leading to posttraumatic stress disorder, depression, sexual dysfunction as well as drug and alcohol addiction. However, psychotherapy can help survivors recover.

Self-Test

1. Research on the effects of consuming sexual media indicates that:
   a. teens' sexual attitudes and behavior are unaffected by it
   b. teens learn more about sex from their parents than from the media
   c. media can influence the sexual decisions of teens
   d. media rarely portrays male and female sexuality in stereotyped ways

2. Lately, whenever Brittany attempts to seduce her husband, Kevin in bed, he simply rolls over and pretends to be asleep. Based on this information, what pattern of sexual communication pattern is Kevin engaging in?
   a. defensiveness   b. contempt
   c. criticism   d. withdrawal

3. The phase of the sexual response cycle characterized by an increase sexual arousal right before orgasm is referred to as:
   a. transition   b. plateau
   c. resolution   d. excitement

4. When June thought about whom she wanted to be in a romantic relationship with, she realized that she was equally attracted to both males and females. June's sexual orientation is classified as:
   a. homosexual   b. bisexual
   c. heterosexual   d. transsexual

5. Certain countries, such as Cameroon and Estonia, do not allow homosexual couples to adopt children from orphanages. This is an example of the concept known as:
   a. sexual prejudice   b. translational bias
   c. sexual orientation bias d. heterophilic prejudice

6. Nancy and Sid could not get enough of each other. They did everything together, and loved it. One could describe their relationship was intensely passionate. Nancy and Sid are displaying what type of love?
   a. companionate   b. consummate
   c. romantic   d. practical

7. Lanni used to look forward to and enjoy sexual relations with her husband. Now, she has little interest in sex, has difficulty getting sexually aroused, and finds it nearly impossible to orgasm. Lanni is suffering from:
   a. hypoactive sexual desire b. hyperactive sexual desire
   c. sexual aversion   d. paraphilia

8. A week or so after having unprotected sex for the first (and last) time, Jason discovered that he had small, red, painful bumps on his penis. Jason appears to be suffering from:
   a. Syphilis   b. Gonorrhea
   c. Genital Herpes   d. Chlamydia

9. Which of the following is (are) considered to be a type of sexual victimization?
   a. child pornography   b. sexual assault
   c. sexual abuse of children d. all of the above

10. Which of the following statements about sexual assault is true?
   a. It's not sexual assault if it happens after drinking or taking drugs.
   b. Victims do not provoke sexual assaults when they dress provocatively or act in a promiscuous manner.
   c. Sexual assault can be avoided if women avoid dark alleys or other "dangerous" places where strangers might be hiding or lurking.
   d. It's only sexual assault if the victim puts up a fight and resists.

Exercises

1. *Sexual communication.* What has been the most difficult part of sexual communication for you? Have you discovered your partner's sexual likes and dislikes? Do you have difficulty initiating sex? How well can you refuse an unwanted sexual invitation or accept rejection?

2. *How important is love for sex?* Do you feel two people can enjoy sex without being in love? Or do you feel people must be in love to have good sex? Write a short paragraph explaining your views about sex and love.

3. *Sharing sexual fantasies.* If you're married or sexually active in a secure relationship, share some of your sexual fantasies with your partner. Such sharing is usually more helpful when it is mutual. It may be wise to begin with mild fantasies that can help desensitize fears and embarrassment and enable you to judge the impact of such sharing on your partner as well as yourself. It's also best to avoid sharing fantasies that would shock your partner or threaten the relationship.

4. *Shared responsibility for contraception.* How do you feel about men sharing the responsibility for birth control? What are some of the pros and cons? Does it present any special problems for the woman?

5. *Sexual victimization.* Suppose you were asked to suggest ways to decrease the incidence of sexual victimization, for example, childhood sexual abuse and rape, in our society. Write a page or more describing the changes you would propose.

Questions for Self-Reflection

1. When was the last time you read a book about sex by a recognized authority in the field?

2. How well do you and your partner communicate about sex? How can you improve your communications?

3. Do you and your partner share the initiative for sex? Or does one of you usually initiate sex?

4. Must physical hugging and touching always lead to sexual intercourse?

5. Are you aware of what is sexually arousing for your partner?

6. Do you and your partner agree about the relationship between sex and love?

7. Are you aware that an occasional sexual dysfunction may be due to emotional stress that particular day?

8. How safe is your method of contraception? Does your partner share your concerns about contraception?

9. Can you recognize the symptoms of prevalent STIs?

10. Why is it important to talk with you sex partner about their sexual history?

Chapter Twelve

Love and Commitment

*J*ack and Diane, both in their early 20s, have been dating for over three years. When they first met in college, Jack was living alone and Diane was renting an apartment with her best friend from high school. But Jack and Diane soon realized that if they shared an apartment they could spend more time with each other and save money. Both would like a close, rewarding relationship, in which they're best friends as well as lovers, but they're having some difficulty achieving it. Diane feels that Jack is preoccupied with his part-time parts sales job and that when they are together, all he wants to do is watch sports on television. Jack argues that he is too tired to go to a movie or to dinner after attending classes, studying, and working. Even when they're together, Diane says Jack doesn't share his feelings with her. This trait has become especially troublesome when he's moody and won't explain why. In Jack's view, Diane doesn't understand that this is a critical stage in his plans to become a small business owner and that Diane is more concerned about getting married than about him and their careers. Also, Jack feels Diane is too possessive at times, for example, her recent jealousy over his casual friendship with a woman in his marketing class. Jack readily admits that talk of marriage at this point in his life makes him feel "trapped." Diane believes that Jack's feelings have been shaped, at least in part, by his parents' recent, messy divorce. Consequently, she worries about how committed Jack is to their relationship and about their future together.

LOVE IS A MANY SPLENDORED (AND DEFINED) THING

LEARNING OBJECTIVES

12.1 Describe the triangular theory of love.
12.2 Compare love with friendship.
12.3 Explain how attachment style influences relationships.

For centuries, love has been expressed in rhyme, verse, and song; philosophers have debated its meaning; countless wars have been fought over it; religions have been based on it; flowers have

---

BOX 12–1 **Did you know that …**

- Scientists suggest that most people will fall in love approximately seven times before marriage
- Getting dumped often leads to "frustration attraction," which causes an individual to love the one who dumped him or her even more
- On average, men around the world marry women who are three years younger than themselves. In the United States, men who remarry usually choose a wife five years younger; if they wed a third time, they often marry someone eight years younger than themselves.
- When someone looks at a new love, the neural circuits that are usually associated with social judgment are suppressed
- Mystery or "the chase" is often a critical element in romantic love. Sometimes called the "Romeo and Juliet effect," a situation with challenges or obstructions is likely to intensify one's passion for a loved one.

Source: RandomHistory.com

---

been grown for it; babies have been made because of it; and millions of pounds of chocolate and ice cream have been eaten when we fail to attain it. As the saying goes, **love**—*deep and tender feelings of affection for or attachment to one or more persons*—indeed appears to "makes the world go round." We are surrounded by love. There is love between a parent and child; there is love between friends; and there is love between people and their pets. Here, we focus on a different kind of love, the love found in intimate relationships. And as it turns out, there are many different kinds of this type of love as well.

The Many Definitions of Love

TRIANGULAR THEORY OF LOVE   Rather than viewing love as a single entity, the **triangular theory of love** suggests that *love has three components, intimacy, passion, and commitment* (Sternberg, 2004).

Intimacy is *an emotional aspect of love and includes closeness, sharing, communication, and support.* Think of it as the "friendship" component of love. Intimacy tends to develop slowly in the beginning and then progress more steadily until it levels off. An apparent lack of intimacy, or the waning of intimacy, may mean that the relationship is dying. At times, intimacy is not only present but also taken for granted, requiring some disruption (such as a family crisis or separation) to make people more aware of how close they really are.

Passion, *which is an emotional and motivational aspect of love, involves physiological arousal and an intense desire to be united with the loved one.* Passion can be thought of as an "energizing force" that leads to feelings of euphoria and infatuation, as well as physical attraction and sexual arousal. Unlike intimacy, passion blossoms quickly. But after a while it dissipates, so that increased exposure to the person no longer brings the arousal, euphoria, etc., that it once did. When we are passionate, and experience the intensity associated with it, we're initially blind to each other's foibles and faults. Of course, when this element of love eventually fades those same foibles and faults become incredibly irritating (Neff & Karney, 2005).

Commitment—*the cognitive aspect of love, which includes both the short-term affirmation of your love for the person and the long-term commitment to maintain that love*—usually develops in a more straightforward manner than does intimacy or passion. Commitment is what makes a relationship a "partnership" and it begins with the decision to become a couple. In long-lasting relationships, commitment increases gradually at first and then more rapidly. As the relationship continues, commitment levels off. If the relationship begins to weaken, the level of commitment will also decline. And if the relationship falls apart, commitment falls back to zero.

According to the triangular theory of love, different types of love can be created by combining the elements of love: intimacy, passion, and commitment. For example, companionate

Table 12–1	Love Types based on the Elements of Sternberg's Triangular Theory	
Type of Love	**Elements Present**	**Key Characteristics**
Liking	Intimacy	A close emotional bond where the couple shares their innermost thoughts and feelings with one another. Passion and commitment are lacking.
Infatuation	Passion	Often thought of as "love at first sight," this type of love is defined by its passion, but little else. It can come and go quickly.
Empty	Commitment	The couple decides to begin or maintain a relationship for better or worse, in good times and in bad, till death parts them. The relationship lacks both intimacy and passion.
Romantic	Intimacy + Passion	Intimacy and passion without a sense of commitment. An intense form of love that lasts only for a short while.
Fatuous	Passion + Commitment	An extremely passionate relationship where those involved quickly move-in together or get married. It's the love that keeps drive-through Chapels in Las Vegas open for business.
Companionate	Intimacy + Commitment	A deep abiding sense of intimacy along with a strong sense of commitment. This love often manifests itself in long-term relationships, where a once fiery passion has burned out.
Consummate	Intimacy + Passion + Commitment	This love has it all: intimacy, passion, plus a strong commitment to one another. It is the "ideal" love, though it is both difficult to attain and maintain.

love is based primarily on intimacy and commitment rather than passion. This is a practical kind of love that involves trust, caring, and tolerance for the partner's flaws. In contrast, romantic love is characterized by intimacy and intense passion, without a sense of a long-term commitment. Of note, the absence of all three components of love is referred to as nonlove. Many of our relationships with coworkers, teachers, neighbors, people we sit next to on an airplane, etc., can be characterized in this way. Table 12–1 illustrates the seven types of love that can be created by combining intimacy, passion, and commitment. See Figure 12–1 as well.

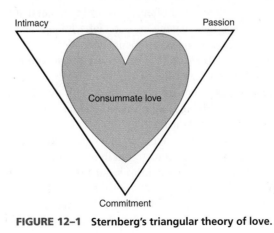

FIGURE 12–1 Sternberg's triangular theory of love.

Love and Friendship

As you might have noticed, intimate relationships and friendships overlap to a considerable extent. Both lovers and friends initially seek out others who are similar to themselves (Lucas et al., 2004). Both types of couples enjoy each other's company, despite occasional disappointments. Individuals in both types of relationships generally accept each other as they are, without trying to make their partner over into a different person. We apparently want friends and lovers who can validate our self-concept (Murray, Holmes, & Griffin, 2000). Both friends and lovers know they can count on each other in times of need. Also, they can confide in each other without fear of betrayal. Friends and lovers understand each other and make allowances when the other person occasionally acts in an unexpected or annoying manner. Finally, we want the same personal characteristics in friends and lovers—warmth, kindness, openness, acceptance, respect, trust, and understanding—but we prefer *higher* levels of these attributes in our lovers than in our friends (Beste, Bergner, & Nauta, 2003).

At the same time, love relationships are distinctively different from friendships. Essentially, it appears that love heightens the potential for both positive and negative aspects of close relationships, making love relationships not only more rewarding but also more frustrating. Typically, love relationships, but not friendships, are characterized by a fascination and preoccupation with their partners in an exclusive sexual relationship (Lucas et al., 2004). There is also intense caring for each other in love relationships, even more so than in friendships; for example, being an advocate for a lover and giving more of oneself. However, because of the greater exclusiveness and emotional involvement between them, lovers also experience greater conflict, distress, and mutual criticism in their relationships than do friends (Rogge, Bradbury, Hahlweg, Engl, & Thurmaier, 2006).

Love and Attachment

Interestingly, the way people approach close relationships as adults, as well as their view of love in general, can be a reflection of early childhood experiences. More specifically, childhood attachment to parents appears to influence adult attachment style to romantic partners (Kanemasa & Daibo, 2003). **Attachment style,** which means *our typical style of becoming involved with others*, can be divided into three main types—secure, avoidant, and anxious (Hazan & Shaver, 1994).

Securely attached people *believe it's easy to get close to others, and they report happy and trusting love relationships.* As adults, these individuals demonstrate relatively positive images of romantic love and value the importance of relationships. Secure adults are loving, dependable, and comfortable with intimacy. They readily share their emotions with others, communicate effectively, and are sensitive to their partner's needs. Not surprisingly, their romances last the longest and end in divorce least often. Many of them feel that romantic love never fades. People in this group also see their parents as especially loving, responsive, and warm. A little over 50 percent of adults manifest this attachment style.

Those with **avoidant attachments** *feel uneasy when people get too close to them,* as closeness in a relationship is interpreted as emotional suffocation and/or the stripping away of independence. Because they fear intimacy, those with avoidant attachments have trouble trusting and depending on others and are prone to jealousy. In general, avoidant adults have difficulty sharing and expressing their feelings. They hold a cynical picture of love, believing that the head-over-heels romantic love depicted in movies and novels does not exist in real life. Instead, they feel it is rare to find someone to fall in love with, and even then, they believe that romantic love seldom lasts. They also tend to regard romantic relationships as unimportant. Avoidant adults generally rate their parents rather harshly, seeing their mothers as not very likable, if not rejecting, and their fathers as uncaring. About 25 percent of adults approach relationships in this way.

The third group, called **anxious,** *includes people who desire a high level of closeness* that many partners don't seem willing to give. Although they desire intimacy, anxious adults tend to view relationship as fragile. They also worry a lot about loved ones leaving them; especially if they don't call when they said they would, arrive home late from work without explanation, forget their anniversary, or just about any situation that could be interpreted as a sign of impending relationship failure. Accordingly, these people experience emotional extremes as well as jealousy in their relationships. They find it easy to "fall in love" but difficult to find "true love." They generally give more mixed reports about their parents, relaying both extremely positive and extremely negative characteristics. Approximately 25 percent of adults are anxious in their relationships (Crittenden & Landini, 2011).

FINDING LOVE

LEARNING OBJECTIVES

12.4 Discuss the effectiveness of using the Internet to find love.

12.5 Explain the benefits and draw backs of self-disclosure at the beginning of relationships.

There are many different ways to find love. You can stumble on that special someone in a classroom, at a café, in a bar, or just about anywhere other people are present. Some even discover, that over time, a platonic relationship can blossom into something more. And of course, a friend or parent can intervene on your behalf; setting you up on a blind date, and in some cultures arranging a marriage for you. Such chance meetings and third party interventions have been around for centuries (Coontz, 2005). However, in today's modern age, the Internet provides an increasingly useful (and used) avenue for finding one's "soul mate." Currently, around 20 percent of Americans report meeting their partners online, a number that has been increasing in recent years, and will continue to do so for years to come (Rosenfeld & Thomas, 2010).

ONLINE DATING The opportunities for online social dating are vast, with nearly 2 billion people in the world online and able to connect with for a potential romance (Finkel, Eastwick, Karney, Reis, & Sprecher, in press). Not surprisingly, online dating is a booming business. Globally, revenues from Internet dating are over one billion dollars annually (Visualeconomics.com, 2011). Moreover, the number of personal ads on the Internet has more than tripled in recent years, with the leading website, *Match.com,* claiming to have a 154 percent growth, with over 100 million members since 2000 and 15 million current members (Hethcock, 2011; PR Newswire, 2009). If you choose to seek out partners on the Internet, here are some useful guidelines you can follow to keep yourself safe and to improve your chances of finding a high-quality relationship (Onguardonline.gov, 2012):

- Think about how different sites work before deciding to join a site. Some sites will allow only a defined community of users to access posted content; others allow anyone and everyone to view postings.
- Think about keeping some control over the information you post. Consider restricting access to your page to a select group of people.
- Keep your information to yourself. Don't post your full name, Social Security number, address, phone number, or bank and credit card account numbers—and don't post other people's information, either. Be cautious about posting information that could be used to identify you or locate you offline. This would include the name of your school, where you work, or where you hang out.
- Make sure your screen name doesn't say too much about you. Don't use your name, your age, or your hometown. Even if you think your screen name makes you anonymous, it doesn't take a genius to combine clues to figure out who you are and where you can be found.

- Post only information that you are comfortable with others seeing—and knowing—about you. Many people can see your page, including your parents, teachers, the police, the college, or an employer.
- Remember that once you post information online, you can't take it back. Even if you delete the information from a site, older versions exist on some people's computers.
- Consider not posting your photo. It can be altered and broadcast in ways you may not be happy about. If you do post one, ask yourself whether it's one your mother would display in the living room.
- Flirting with strangers online could have serious consequences. Because some people lie about who they really are, you never really know who you're dealing with.
- Be wary if a new online friend wants to meet you in person. Before you decide to meet someone, do your research: Ask whether any of your friends know the person, and see what background you can dig up through online search engines. If you decide to meet, do so in a public place, during the day, and with friends you trust nearby. Tell a responsible person where you're going and when you expect to be back.
- Trust your gut if you have suspicions. If you feel threatened by someone or uncomfortable because of something online, tell someone you trust and report it to the police and the social networking site.

As Box 12–2 reveals, there are a variety of different online dating services to choose from, many of which target their clientele by race, religion, sexual orientation, and even dietary preferences. Of note, not all individuals posting personal ads on the Internet are interested in long-term relationships. The proliferation of "adult"-oriented websites geared toward short-term liaisons, such as *AdultFriendFinder.com* and *AshleyMadison.com,* attest to this fact.

In comparison to off-line (i.e., old fashioned) dating, online dating services provide their clients with a combination of three things: (1) access to thousands of people interested in

---

BOX 12–2   **Focus on Relationships: Internet Dating**

Internet Dating Sites for Those Seeking Long-Term Relationships

Name	Targeted Clientele
AsianDating.com	Asian Singles
BlackSingles.com	African-American Singles
ChristianMingle.com	Christian Singles
eHarmony.com	All Singles
IndianDating.com	Indian Singles
InterracialSingles.com	Singles seeking interracial relationships
JDate.com	Jewish Singles
LatinoPeopleMeet.com	Latino Singles
Match.com	All Singles
Muslima.com	Muslim Singles
PrideDating.com	Gay, Lesbian, and Transgendered Singles
VeganDatingService.com	Single vegans
VeggieDate.com	Single vegetarians

Source: "Do You Know Who Your Kids Are Talking To?: Safety Tips for Social Networking Online," Federal Trade Commission website, May 9, 2006.

romance; (2) 24-hour communication services between potential partners via e-mail, chat, instant messaging, and streaming video; and (3) matchmaking services in which "compatible" romantic partners are identified, usually by a computer. The first two items in the list have been validated by research, though it should be known that some online dating services have been accused of overestimating their true number of members by including cancelled subscribers, duplicate members, and fake profiles in their statistics (Hethcock, 2011). But just how good are those computer matchmakers that so many different dating services boast about? As it turns out, it is not very good; in fact, they are no better at producing successful long-term relationships than traditional ways of meeting people, like those mentioned above. Here's why: Computers use matching algorithms based on areas of current areas of similarity and complementarities, but fail to take into consideration areas more important to the success or failure of a long-term relationship, such as the growth and change of partners over time, the presence of challenging life circumstances, individual coping capabilities, and relationship dynamics (Finkel et al., 2012).

THE IMPORTANCE OF SELF-DISCLOSURE   **Self-disclosure** is *the sharing of intimate or personal information with another*. Whether off-line or online, those who are seeking a partner to grow old with tend to be more honest, disclose more, and make their disclosures more consciously and intentionally than those not interested in enduring relationships. In terms of effectiveness, positive self-disclosure appears to be the most effective. When high disclosure is present, high relationship esteem (i.e., confidence in the partner) and good relationship quality develop. Similarly, those who disclose a lot of personal information *over time* are more likely to find relationship success as well as learn pertinent information about their prospective partners. Perhaps this occurs due to the norm of reciprocity—defined as an unwritten rule that guides reciprocal behavior related to the granting of favors. On the other hand, self-disclosure carries the risks of rejection due to a particular disclosure and of ensuing insecurity. In order to feel secure in a relationship, people need to believe that their partners see qualities in them that merit attention, nurturance, and care (Murray, 2005). When one partner of a couple feels threatened and rejected, their self-esteem may lessen, which subsequently diminishes closeness in the relationship.

Interestingly, while the vast majority of individuals feel that they are honest about their own self-disclosures, they feel that others tend to misrepresent themselves or at very least engage in selective self-presentation (Gibbs, Ellison, & Heino, 2006). In fact, people do misrepresent themselves, and for a good reason: When it comes to *establishing* a relationship, complete and total honesty does not always appear to be the best policy. Shortly after meeting someone, greater honesty can actually have a *detrimental* effect on the *establishment* of a relationship, especially when revealing too many personal flaws too soon. In other words, when starting to see someone, it's best to not provide your date with an extensive list of your awkward personal issues. Nevertheless, those little personal flaws that you hide at the start of a relationship can (and probably will) become problematic later on. Ultimately, whether conscious or not, self-disclosure will happen. So, as your relationship develops, you should be prepared to discuss your problematic personal issues with your partner. Doing so can lead to relationship esteem now and prevent heartache later.

MARRIAGE AND OTHER COMMITTED RELATIONSHIPS

LEARNING OBJECTIVES

12.6 Explain the cohabitation effect.
12.7 Describe recent trends in marriage rates.
12.8 Discuss why people get married.

Once a couple has formed, the individuals often indicate their commitment to each other by living together (cohabitation) or becoming engaged and later married. In both cases, they often are committed to each other exclusively. Let's look at each of these states in more detail.

Cohabitation

Although people of varying ages and prior marital statuses engage in **cohabitation** or *the practice of unmarried persons living together, sharing bed and board,* the largest proportion are between 20- and 40-years-of-age. Indeed, the cohabitation rate of 30- to 40-year olds has more than doubled in the past two decades, from 3 percent in 1995 to 7 percent today (Fry, 2011). Currently, close to 8 million couples in committed relationships live together, up from 3.2 million in 1990, with economics driving this increase (it's cheaper for two people to live together than apart) (Census.gov, 2012). However, it is worth noting that some couples simply drift into this type of arrangement; living together but keeping a place of their own (Peterson, 2002).

In addition to financial reasons, some couples cohabitate in an attempt to create a "trial" marriage of sorts. In fact nearly 70 percent of couples live together prior to marriage (Manning, 2010). And couples who cohabitate often experience greater intimacy than other dating couples of their age, at least in the short run. Moreover, young couples today view living together as a way to protect against divorce (and not simply an alternative to marriage) (Swanbrow, 2009). Unfortunately, such trials seem to be ineffective because couples that live together prior to marriage are more likely to get divorced than those that don't. This phenomenon has been referred to as the **cohabitation effect** (Guzzo, 2009), *where couples that cohabit first have greater marital instability than couples that do not cohabit.* However, other factors, such as length of the cohabitation, reasons for cohabiting (e.g., a test of compatibility before marriage), and problem-solving ability, appear to be stronger predictors of marital instability (Cohan & Kleinbaum, 2002). Many cohabiting couples can and do go on to successful marriages (Phillips & Sweeney, 2005).

Marriage

Marriage is *the state of being married, usually the legal union of two people.* Currently, marriage (as an institution) is being challenged by alternative arrangements such as cohabitation and single person households. In fact, marriage in the United States is at 50-year all time low, with around 51 percent of adults currently married. Nevertheless, marriage hasn't gone completely out of style. Most people in the United States still want to marry; and approximately 72 percent have been married at least once (Cohen, 2011). There are numerous benefits to marriage, such as the legitimization of a couple; the security associated with being in a long-term relationship; the emotional benefits of intimacy and a shared partnership; regular access to sex; and support for childrearing. What other advantages can you think of?

Today, couples in nearly all regions of the world tend to wait a bit longer to marry, with the typical age of a first marriage rising slightly each year. Consequently, many people marry during their 20s and 30s. In fact, the median age for first time marriages has never been higher: 26.5 years for brides and 28.7 for grooms. Perhaps this is a positive trend, because the older people are when they marry, the longer the marriage tends to lasts. The reasons for getting married later in life are many and varied, but a rise in education and economic modernization are thought to partially explain this trend (Cohen, 2011). To test your attitudes about marriage, take the Marital Myths Quiz provided in Activity 12–1.

LOVE AND MARRIAGE   Many people tend to marry or make commitments to significant others out of mixed (multiple negative and positive) motives, many of them unclear even to themselves. The tradition of marriage, along with the social, legal, and especially economic advantages of marriage, plays a larger role than is commonly realized (Smock, Manning, & Porter, 2005). When asked, though, most Americans characteristically say they marry because they are in love. Now that marriage is no longer necessary for economic survival, the satisfaction of sexual desire, or, for that matter, the rearing of children, love has become the major rationale for getting and staying married. Even upper-class couples and royalty, who have traditionally married for social reasons, now prefer marriages based on love.

ACTIVITY 12–1

MARITAL MYTHS

INSTRUCTIONS: *Some truisms about marriage follow. Indicate which of them you think are true (T) and which are false (F). Then check your responses by consulting the correct answers at the end of the chapter.*

1. More than 7 out of 10 Americans eventually marry.   T   F

2. Partners who live together before marriage are less apt to get
  divorced than those who did not do so.   T   F

3. Marriage should always be a 50–50 partnership.   T   F

4. Husbands and wives should be best friends.   T   F

5. Differences and incompatibilities between partners are the major
  causes of marital dissatisfaction.   T   F

6. Married people are happier and healthier than single individuals.   T   F

7. Most divorces are initiated by women.   T   F

8. Extramarital affairs will destroy a marriage.   T   F

9. Children are damaged more by a legal divorce than by remaining
  in an intact but unhappy home.   T   F

10. Married people tend to live longer than unmarried people.   T   F

Most American couples believe in **voluntary marriage**—*ones based on the assumption that two people will remain married only as long as they are in love.* When they are no longer in love, it's mutually understood they will separate. When people marry or commit to a significant other on the basis of romantic love—with its emphasis on emotional and physical intimacy—it's no surprise so many relationships and marriages fail; that is, if the love diminishes, the marriage fails. On the other hand, the longer a couple lives together, especially in a satisfying, committed relationship, the more both partners come to value companionate love, with a greater emphasis on personal intimacy and commitment than physical attraction.

DIVERSITY, LOVE, AND MARRIAGE   For the most part, people tend to marry or commit to partners of similar age, education, ethnic or social background, race, and religion. Much of this tendency reflects the ways we have been socialized as well as the opportunities for meeting people, with physical proximity increasing the chances for attraction. As our society becomes more mobile and diverse, however, people are marrying or committing to others who cross many of these familiar boundaries, because factors such as similar values, rather than similar demographics, play a more important role in today's world. As evidence, consider this fact: Nearly 15 percent of recent marriages occurred between partners of different races or ethnicities; more than doubling the number of intermarriages occurring in 1980 (6.7%) (Wang, 2012). According to Matsumoto (2000), these diverse marriages (e.g., intercultural marriages) are especially prone to conflicts about love and intimacy. However, such marriages are *not* more divorce prone.

Although cultural and religious backgrounds can influence the wedding ceremony, love is still the primary reason individuals choose to marry in America.

Although love is a universal phenomenon, its importance in helping us select appropriate others to commit or marry varies by culture. In general, those from individualistic cultures place more emphasis on love as a basis for establishing a marriage than people from collectivistic societies. For example, in selecting marriage partners, individuals from the United States assigned the highest worth to love, whereas those from India emphasized love the least (Levine, Sato, Hashimoto, & Verma, 1995). In such cultures, rather than marrying the loved person or romantic partner, couples *learn* to love each other after they marry (Matsumoto, 2000). Interestingly, countries that do not emphasize romance in mate selection have lower divorce rates. Does this finding surprising you?

ADJUSTING TO INTIMATE RELATIONSHIPS

LEARNING OBJECTIVES

12.9 List the various adjustments that occur during the course of committed relationships.

12.10 Compare the characteristics of successful and unsuccessful marriages.

12.11 Describe ways to improve the quality of existing relationships.

12.12 Discuss sexual changes that often occur in relationships over time.

Whether couples achieve a lasting, happy relationship depends to a large extent on what happens *after* they marry or commit to one another in some other way—over and above how well matched they are in such matters as compatibility. **Couple adjustment** means *the changes and adjustments in a couple's relationship during the course of their committed or married life.* Of great importance to couple adjustment is each partner's flexibility and willingness to transform, especially in our rapidly changing society. At times this can be difficult. Not surprising, during the first year of marriage, it is not unusual for new couples to have frequent arguments (Sullivan, Pasch, Johnson, & Bradbury, 2010). A major difference between today's couples and those of the past is the lack of clearly defined roles for each partner. The changing nature of gender roles creates problems for all types of couples as they settle down to live together. Even the most mundane tasks may become a problem. Who cooks? Who takes out the trash? Who pays the bills? Getting along in a committed relationship, though, involves the larger questions of authority, fairness, power sharing, and fulfillment of needs.

Attitude Adjustment

What keeps love alive? Becoming more attitudinally similar is one factor (Kalmijn, 2005). When a couple's attitudes are measured early in their relationships, the partners' attitudes may differ. However, with the passage of time there is attitude alignment, wherein their attitudes become more similar and, thus, less likely to cause arguments. An example of this is where the couple initially disagrees about methods of birth control (e.g., he wants her to use birth-control pills; she fears side effects and wants him to use condoms, which he hates). Later in the relationship, there may be more attitudinal similarity, with partners settling on a third type of birth control.

Sharing Responsibilities

Partners are sharing responsibilities to a greater degree today than in the past. As a result, the respective role expectations between partners, especially married couples, are becoming more flexible and functional. More women, for example, are sharing the provider role by working outside the home; and men are expected to provide greater emotional support in the relationship, including help with child rearing. Decision making has also become more democratic, especially among dual-income couples.

Although egalitarian relationships seem to be the ideal, one difficulty that comes with the increased sharing of responsibilities is the issue of fairness. If women do work outside of the home, does this mean that they will do fewer chores or that their mates will assist with housework? Several studies demonstrate that women still do more housework than men even when the women work outside of the home (i.e., the second shift) (Sayer, 2005). Consequently, when the woman serves in other multiple roles, such as child or parent care provider, and is also employed, she might well feel exhausted (Streich, Casper, & Salvaggio, 2008). Research has shown that when husbands increase their share of the housework, marital quality improves for women but not for men (Amato, Johnson, Booth, & Rogers, 2003). Interestingly, relative to heterosexual couples, gay partners tended to assign household labor more fairly, resolve conflicts more constructively, and experience a more equal level of satisfaction with the relationship (Dunne, 2000; Kurdek, 2005).

Communication and Conflict

On-going changes in responsibilities make communication and conflict management even more important in committed relationships. Although virtually all couples argue at some point during their relationship, the priorities of particular problems vary from couple to couple. For instance, many couples feel conflicts over money are one of their leading problems. Some regard sexual incompatibilities as the major problem. Other couples complain of unrealistic expectations, lack of affection, and power struggles. Additional problems include issues related to child rearing, such as disciplinary style and basic childcare. Moreover, with the birth of a child comes a decline in passionate love and an increase in marital dissatisfaction (Puterbaugh, 2005). Other issues that create conflict are in-laws, romantic or sexual affairs,

FIGURE 12–2
Communications and attributions are different in happy and unhappy couples.

drug use, problematic drinking, money spending, and jealousy. However, the most common problem (appearing at the top or next to the top of almost every list) is difficulty in communication (Murray& Holmes, 2011). Again and again, those in committed relationships complain, "We just can't talk to each other?"

Why can't couples communicate? They usually communicate very well with their friends and siblings. Of course, partners do talk to each other all the time. They say such things as "What are we having for dinner?" and "I'll be home later than usual tonight." This type of surface level communication is easy enough. In contrast, failures in communication tend to occur at a deeper level involving the sharing of feelings, expectations, intentions, and personal needs. It's in these areas that partners have trouble getting through to each other. In most instances, both partners long for intimacy and tenderness. The price of being open, however, may be vulnerability. Settling into a kind of guarded communication, each partner may tend to hold back. Difficulties in communication are further compounded as couples try to mesh their lives more closely. As they become involved with each other, some areas of disagreement are inevitable. As couples struggle to resolve their disagreements, the sparks can fly. Interestingly, anger is not always the most destructive emotion in marriage, since both happy and unhappy couples fight.

FACTORS THAT PLACE A MARRIAGE IN JEOPARDY Couples on track for divorce start an argument by sending out hostile vibes through their tone of voice, facial gestures, and what they say. The biggest problems occur when the woman brings up an issue "harshly" and critically, and the man responds with great negativity. Because women initiate discussions about relationship issues about 80 percent of the time, this type of dynamic can quickly, and negatively, affect the relationship (Peterson, 1999).

Moreover, there are certain emotions and styles of interaction that prove toxic for marriages (Gottman, 2012):

- *Criticism*—stating complaints in terms of a defect in the partner's personality (e.g., You're so self-centered)
- *Contempt*—making yourself seem superior to your partner (e.g., You're so dumb!)
- *Defensiveness*—self-protection, often in the form of presenting oneself as an innocent victim (e.g., It's not my fault that … It's yours!)
- *Stonewalling*—emotional withdrawal from the situation (e.g., letting your partner speak, but not really listening to them)

The presence of these "Four Horsemen of the Apocalypse" (as Gottman calls them), if left unrepaired, signal that the dissolution of the relationship is ahead; usually within six years (Gottman, 2012). Box 12–3 discusses another but more troubling type of conflict-laden relationship: partner abuse.

BOX 12–3   Focus on Relationships: Partner Abuse

Battering is *a pattern of behavior used to establish power and control over another person through fear and intimidation, often including the threat or use of violence. Battering happens when one person believes he or she is entitled to control another.* Despite better education and more laws, one in four U.S. women is estimated to experience domestic violence in her lifetime. Although men can be victims of domestic violence, women comprise 85 percent of all victims (National Coalition Against Domestic Violence [NCADV], 2012). Intimate partner violence also makes up about 20 percent of all nonfatal violent crimes experienced by women (Rennison, 2003). Over half of all women and one-third of all men murdered are killed by their significant others (Kessler, Molnar, Feurer, & Applebaum, 2001). Across cultures, the most common abusive situation involves a man and a woman, with the woman as the victim (Kim, Park, & Emery, 2009). This situation, in which a man is abusive toward a woman, results in the most negative consequences of all, such as serious physical injury and death (Russo, 2008).

Why Do Men Become Batterers?

Many theories have been developed to explain why some men use violence against their partners. These theories include family dysfunction, inadequate communication skills, provocation by women, stress, chemical dependency, lack of spirituality, and economic hardship. While such issues may be associated with battering of women, they are not the *true* causes. Why? Removing these associated factors will not end men's violence against women. The batterer begins and continues his behavior because violence is an effective method for gaining and keeping control over another person; and he unfortunately does not usually suffer adverse consequences as a result of his behavior. Risk factors that predict violence against a partner include unemployment, drug use, having witnessed similar violence as a child, low income, and low educational levels, especially for male abusers. Very few of these men are truly antisocial, but most lack good communication skills and have a high need to control and overpower their partners (Ehrensaft, 2009).

The Profile of a Batterer

Many theories have been developed to explain why some men use violence against their partners. These theories include family dysfunction, inadequate communication skills, provocation by women, stress, chemical dependency, lack of spirituality, and economic hardship. While such issues may be associated

(*Continued*)

BOX 12–3   *(Continued)*

with battering of women, they are not the *true* causes. Why? Removing these associated factors will not end men's violence against women. The batterer begins and continues his behavior because violence is an effective method for gaining and keeping control over another person; and he unfortunately does not usually suffer adverse consequences as a result of his behavior. Risk factors that predict violence against a partner include unemployment, drug use, having witnessed similar violence as a child, low income, and low educational levels, especially for male abusers. Very few of these men are truly antisocial, but most lack good communication skills and have a high need to control and overpower their partners (Ehrensaft, 2009).

Abusive partners frequently minimize or deny what they have done and frequently blame the victim. Much of the violence occurs in a predictable cycle or pattern, too. First is *the stage of escalation or tension building,* which many victims learn to recognize and thus try to avoid with such techniques as sidestepping certain topics or avoiding various conversations. The second stage in the cycle of violence is *the actual violence,* which is often explosive. The third stage, strangely enough, *involves the abuser begging for forgiveness,* offering love and promises never to batter again (O'Leary & Woodin, 2009).

The Effects of Being Battered

The victims of partner abuse find extricating themselves from such relationships difficult, especially if they are financially dependent on the abuser (Fleury-Steiner, Bybee, Sullivan, Belknap, & Melton, 2006). Besides the horror of the physical bruises, victims often suffer loss of self-esteem, repeated threats of violence, debilitating depression, and stalking if an escape to safety is attempted. Given these, many victims find leaving the abuser to be impossible. Historically, violence against women has not been treated as a "real" crime. Thankfully, today assault, battering, and domestic violence are generally considered crimes. In recognition of this cycle and that victims are unable to escape, some states have passed laws mandating the arrest of batterers. Police, however, sometimes have little training in such matters or find domestic disputes unglamorous or downright dangerous (Moritsugu, Wong, & Duffy, 2010). There is increasing evidence, though, that battering or domestic violence is being taken more seriously by the justice system, with increased rates of police notification, arrest, and judicial involvement (Cho & Wilke, 2005).

Who Can You Call for Help?

If you are a victim or know a victim of partner violence, you can receive referral and support information by calling the National Victim Center (800-FYI-Call); there is also a website for more information: www.ncvc.org. Other resources include the National Coalition Against Domestic Violence (NCADV) at www.ncadv.org and The National Domestic Violence Hotline: 1-800-799-7233.

FACTORS THAT LEAD TO SUCCESSFUL MARRIAGES   Until recently, marital "success" meant longevity, that is, how long the marriage lasted. However, the changes in values in recent years have shifted the emphasis to the *quality* of the marital relationship rather than its duration. Today, success in marriage is interpreted more in terms of **marital satisfaction**—*the sense of gratification and contentment in a marriage*—especially in the relationship aspects of marriage, such as mature love, intimacy, and companionship.

What characterizes long-term, satisfactory marriages? The ability to solve problems together seems paramount. This factor is mentioned by over two-thirds of the highly satisfied couples but by only one-third of the unsatisfied ones. Second, when asked specifically to cite the factors they believe contribute to the longevity of their relationship, almost half of the satisfied couples say they "have fun" together and cherish such experiences. Yet fun, humor, and playfulness are not even mentioned by mildly satisfied couples (or unsatisfied ones, for that matter). It's not to suggest that there is no discord in successful marriages; after all even happy couples argue. But when they do, they use five times more positive than negative behaviors (Fincham, 2003). For example, when the wife is angry, the husband might inject a humorous comment into one of his responses. Such playfulness helps to reduce emotional tension caused by the conflict. Happy couples also accept the fact that they will have differences with which they will always have to cope. For instance, one partner might not be very talkative, while the other partner prefers to engage in extensive conversations. Thus, the ability to tolerate these types of inevitable differences leads to happier marriages.

One of the strongest predictors of marital success is **affective affirmation**—*the communication of loving, accepting attitudes or the unconditional approval of one's mate*. Other factors found to contribute to long and happy relationships include empathic ability for understanding a partner's feelings, a good balance of time spent together and separately, a satisfying sexual relationship, and mutual willingness to make adjustments to each other (Schwartz, 2002). Moreover, when something bad happens we can attribute the cause to the person, such as blaming traits, or to something external, such as to fate or to the situation. Couples who are happy tend to make relationship-enhancing attributions for the partner's behaviors. Couples who are unhappy tend to make distress-enhancing attributions (Gordon, Friedman, Miller, & Gaertner, 2005). Thus, although attributions play a large role in causing and maintaining relationship distress, they can also play a role in relationship happiness. Table 12–2 provides a couple of examples of these attributional styles.

Making the Relationship Better

One of the best ways to make a relationship better is to avoid having it go bad in the first place. Indeed, some marital conflict programs occur even *before* a couple marries (Halford, O'Donnell, Lizzio, & Wilson, 2006). In fact, premarital education results in higher levels of satisfaction, better commitment to marriage, lower levels of conflict, and reduced chances of divorce (Stanley, Amato, Johnson, & Markman, 2006). Remember, though, conflict is not all bad; and it eventually will happen. Indeed, conflict is an inevitable part of vital, close relationships; it may help individuals learn more about themselves and each other and may deepen their relationship. Stated a different way, marital discord can be a growth experience.

TIPS TO IMPROVE RELATIONSHIPS   One way to improve a relationship is to thwart the "Four Horsemen" mentioned above. Instead of using criticism, learn to "complain without blame;" rather than becoming defensive, take responsibility for your actions; turn contempt into a culture of appreciation; and avoid stonewalling by learning to self-sooth (Gottman, 2012). Here are some additional relationship tips by John Gottman (2012):

- Seek help early on. Don't wait until the problem has gotten so bad that it may be impossible to repair.
- Don't say every critical thing that comes to mind, especially on touchy subjects.

Table 12–2	An Example of Attributions of Happy and Unhappy Couples	
	In *Happy* Couples the Wife Says:	In *Unhappy* Couples the Wife Says:
Positive event: The husband remembers his wife's birthday with a present.	"He's so sweet; he never forgets my birthday."	"Hah, he's up to something; he never gives me gifts unless he wants something from me, like forgiveness."
Negative event: The husband forgets his wife's birthday.	"He hardly ever forgets; he must be having a hard week at work."	"That's just like him to forget; he never remembers events important to me."

- Bring up problematic topics gently and without blame; avoid starting discussion with critical and/or contemptuous remarks.
- Be willing to accept influence from your significant other. Typically, men need to improve in this skill more so than women.
- Don't accept hurtful behavior from your partner, expect better of them.
- Learn how to exit an argument without hurting the other person.
- Engender a rich climate of positivity; avoid focusing on the negative.

Exploration 12.1: Couples Therapy

www.aamft.org   This site is supported by the American Association of Marriage and Family Therapists. It contains referral information for marriage and family therapists as well as general information on issues related to marriage and the family.

COUPLES THERAPY   For those couples that cannot alter their relationship on their own, couples therapy might be a viable solution (Wood, Crane, Schaalje, & Law, 2005). Of the most effective therapies for relationship problems is **emotion-focused therapy** (**EFT**)—*a cognitive therapy that provides a technique for changing basic thought and emotional patterns.* The goal of EFT is to help partners feel securely connected by fostering feelings of safety, accessibility, and responsiveness. Couples are usually taught active listening, where one partner can paraphrase what the other has said, in order to encourage a better relational environment between them. Once the feelings of security and receptiveness develop, couples can better process and send clear messages to each other, see each other's perspective, and do collaborative problem solving (Johnson & Patz, 2003). The success rate for this form of therapy is high, somewhere around 70 to 75 percent. Although couples therapy cannot redeem all marriages, couples of younger ages, lower levels of depression, flexibility regarding gender roles, and egalitarian attitudes leave therapy the most satisfied (Fincham, 2003; Underwood, 2002).

Sexuality

Partners, such as newlyweds, bring greater sexual knowledge and experience to their marriages today than in previous decades, but they're also more likely to judge their sex lives by higher standards. Couples today are engaging in sexual intercourse more frequently than couples did in the past, with an average of two to three times a week for couples in their 20s and 30s. They're also open to a wider array of sexual practices, use a greater variety of sexual positions, and engage in sex for a longer time (Smith, 2003; Parker-Hope, 2009). However, the longer couples—unmarried and married alike—live together, the less frequently they have sexual intercourse (Brewis & Meyer, 2005). Reasons usually cited include the lack of time or physical energy. Perhaps a more important factor is the decline of sexual ardor because the partners have become "accustomed to each other." The decrease in physical vigor associated with aging is also a related factor, especially among couples in middle and late adulthood. Couples with children also complain about the lack of privacy. Actually, the longer couples are married, the more attention they pay to the *quality* of sex rather than to its frequency. For most couples, a good sex life and a happy relationship go together.

Most couples aspire to the ideal of sexual monogamy, regardless of whether they adhere to it. But when asked if they've ever had sex outside of marriage, it's a different story. Today, researchers estimate that between 20 to 50 percent of U.S. women and 30 to 60 percent of U.S. men have engaged in extramarital sex (Vangelisti & Gerstenberger, 2004). Another 74 percent of men and 68 percent of women say they would have an affair if they knew they wouldn't get caught. Infidelity is both a cause and consequence of poor marital quality. However, the effects of infidelity on the marriage vary from couple to couple. As mentioned in the marital myth quiz presented above, extramarital affairs can destroy some marriages, rejuvenate others, or make no difference all. A lot depends on how both partners feel about the extramarital affair and whether they can effectively resolve the old relationship issues that contributed to its occurrence (if any) as well as the new ones resulting from it (Previti & Amato, 2004).

Exploration 12.2: Infidelity

www.affairrecovery.com   A site dedicated to helping people recover from extramarital affairs. You can find both free and fee-based content.

DIVORCE AND ITS CONSEQUENCES

LEARNING OBJECTIVES

12.13 Describe various aspects of the divorce experience.
12.14 Discuss the challenges faced by blended families.

Divorce—*the legal dissolution of marriage*—among Americans has more than doubled in the past 40 years, with approximately 4 out of every 10 marriages now ending in divorce. Each year over 1 million couples get divorced, most of them within the first seven years of marriage (Gottman, 2012). Twenty percent of first marriages end within five years and 33 percent of first marriages end within 10 years (Maher, 2003). These data mean that by age 18, 40 percent of U.S. children will have experienced parental divorce (Greene, Anderson, Doyle, & Riedelbach, 2006).

Why the dramatic rise in the divorce rate in the United States? Many different reasons have been forwarded, including: (1) the lack of preparation for marriage; (2) the increasing financial independence of women; (3) the fading of religious values; and (4) the ability to find new emotional and/or sexual partners through the Internet. Moreover, a major factor has been the gradual shift away from the traditional notion that "marriage is forever" to the idea that the primary goal of marriage is happiness and fulfillment. This shift in values has also been accompanied by changes in the laws that make it easier for couples to get divorced (Kneip & Bauer, 2009).

Exploration 12.3: Divorce

www.divorcecentral.com   This site is for individuals contemplating or experiencing divorce. Laws are available by state as well as chat lines and other supports.

The Divorce Experience

The decision to divorce usually comes after a long period of mutual alienation, often accompanied by a separation, in which both partners suffer from damaged self-esteem, hurt, and loneliness. In some instances, the estranged couple may have sought help from professionals, such as couples counselors and family therapists. As is true for dating relationships, in heterosexual relationships women are more likely to initiate the breakup than men (Helgeson, 1994). In fact, women make more specific plans and are more likely to implement their plans for divorce. Women also think more about divorce and talk to their friends during the decision-making process (Crane, Soderquist, & Gardner, 1995).

THE EFFECTS OF DIVORCE ON THE COUPLE   No matter how good or bad the relationship has been, the process of getting divorced is almost always painful (Hendrick, 2006), especially for those who did not initiate the legal dissolution of the marriage (Baum, 2007). Divorce (as well as the end of committed relationships) is a complex experience because so many things are happening at once. The partners tend to withdraw emotionally from each other or coexist with a great deal of mutual antagonism (Perilloux & Buss, 2008). The legal aspects of the breakup are not only expensive but emotionally draining as well, for they frequently involve the settlement of property, money, and child custody/visitation issues. Of note, men typically come out of a breakup with only moderate financial declines while for women financial hardship is more commonplace, especially for those who spent the majority of the marriage as a homemaker (Avellar & Smock, 2005).

Disapproval and rejection by friends, family members, and coworkers can also be distressing. Separating oneself from the influence of a former partner and becoming an autonomous social being again can be difficult. Many find it hard to re-enter the world of dating and to set up and support independent households. Although these changes may be quite intimidating and draining at first, they also offer the individual an opportunity to experience personal growth (Barber, 2006). Nevertheless, it takes most people two or three years to recover fully from the distress of a divorce, and many do not recover completely (Lucas, 2005). The increasing number of support groups available for divorced people helps to alleviate much of the loneliness and emotional pain that inevitably accompany divorce.

Becoming a Single Parent

A divorce involving parents can be particularly painful for the parents *and* for the children (Wallerstein & Lewis, 2005). The courts tend to follow the principle of "the best interests of the child," which traditionally meant that custody was given to the primary nurturer, the wife. Today, there is a tendency to award **joint or shared custody** (*which usually means joint decision making about the child's care*) and in some cases to award custody solely to the father. The partner who is not granted residential custody of the children (i.e., the parent with whom the child does not reside) is usually granted certain visitation rights (Rohrbaugh, 2008). Of note, grandparents also suffer when their adult children divorce, because they may not be able to see their grandchildren as frequently as before or at all (Drew & Silverstein, 2007).

THE EFFECTS OF DIVORCE ON CHILDREN How children are affected by their parents' breakup varies considerably, depending on such factors as the intensity of the parental conflict, the child's personality, the age and sex of the child, whether the child is uprooted from familiar friends in the process, and the custodial parent–child relationship. Divorce typically provides children with a double dose of stress. Immediately after their parents' divorce, many children feel resentful and depressed (Maher, 2003). Older children and adolescents are especially apt to exhibit heightened aggression. However, within a few years, most children do adjust to the new living arrangements. Then, about three to five years after the divorce, there may be a second dose of stress associated with either parent's remarriage (Dunn, O'Connor, & Cheng, 2005). Because most divorced mothers and fathers remarry, many children of divorce gain a stepparent. The stepparent's intrusion into the home may initially be an unwelcome event, disrupting the single parent's relationship with his or her children. All of this turmoil necessitates another period of readjustment. Although some argue that *divorce* makes children vulnerable to depression and other psychological disorders, in actuality, it is high levels of parental discord (before, during, and after the divorce) that negatively influences children's adjustment the most (Bing, Nelson, & Wesolowski, 2009). Importantly, help is available for children adversely impacted by divorce. In fact, there are many successful programs designed to assist children to cope better with the myriad of stressors associated with family dissolution. One such program is Pedro-Carroll's (2005) *Children of Divorce Intervention Program.*

Remarriage

Despite the painful experience of divorce, most divorced people remarry—one-fourth within one year of their divorce. And about 20 percent of all marriages involve a second marriage for at least one of the partners (Bernstein, 2011; Maher, 2003). In most instances, a divorced person marries another divorced person, probably because they share similar experiences or are of the same age. Then, too, participation in various support groups that have been recently formed, such as Parent. Without Partners, increases the likelihood of meeting and marrying someone like themselves.

Exploration 12.4: Remarriage

www.idotaketwo.com   A website for those considering remarriage with helpful advice on blended families, second weddings, prenuptial agreements, financial planning, etc.

DIVORCE AFTER REMARRIAGE   You might ask, "How successful are remarriages?" To be frank, it's difficult to answer because the record is mixed. Statistically, 65 percent of remarriages end in divorce (far greater than the 43 percent occurring for first marriages). You should be aware, however, that there are a small number of "repeaters," who marry and divorce several times, thus inflating the overall divorce figures for remarriages. Many second marriages are successful both in terms of marital happiness and longevity. Partners in a second marriage often benefit from their mistakes in an earlier marriage. They know full well the value of give-and-take in a close relationship like marriage. Age and maturity also help. Most of all, remarried people usually realize the value of commitment and thus work harder at their second marriage. When the divorce repeaters are removed from consideration, the outlook for second marriages may be better than previously thought as at least 6 out of 10 remarriages last (Bernstein, 2011).

BLENDED FAMILIES   *Families that involve the children from a previous marriage of one spouse or both are called* **blended families.** Remarriages involving children pose special demands on the adults as well as the children. Many find that a new marriage and a ready-made family can be taxing, especially because partners tend to have little child-free time to build mutual understanding and acceptance of each other (Pacey, 2005). When partners perceive that stepchildren cause family problems, they report more marital unhappiness and more thoughts about divorce in their remarriages (Knox & Zusman, 2001). When the children are young, the stepparent has more opportunity to develop rapport and trust with the children, but when adolescents are involved, it's more difficult for everyone. If the new partner too quickly assumes parental authority, especially in matters of discipline, the children may be resentful. Both parents must make allowances for the children's initial suspicion and resistance. Part of the problem is that the role of stepparent is not well defined. This issue is often compounded by the child's continued interaction with the remaining biological parent. When both parents in the home develop a good working relationship, talking things out and cooperating on parental issues, stepparent families can do at least as well as intact families, if not better, in many cases (Bjornsen, 2005).

Chapter Summary

LOVE IS A MANY SPLENDORED (AND DEFINED) THING

12.1   Describe the triangular theory of love.
According to the triangular theory of love, intimacy, passion, and commitment comprise the core elements of love. Different combinations of these elements results in a different types of love.

12.2   Compare love with friendship.
There are many similarities between friends and lovers, including enjoying each other's company, accepting each other as they are, counting on each other in times of need, and having interactions that are warm, caring, and understanding. Differences between love relationships and friendships are as follows: love relationships are often more rewarding and more frustrating than friendships; typically lovers engage in sexual activity, whereas friends do not; and there is greater conflict, distress, and mutual criticism in love relationships compared to friendships.

12.3   Explain how attachment style influences relationships.

Attachment style refers to our typical style of becoming involved with others. Securely attached people believe it's easy to get close to others, and they report happy and trusting love relationships. Those with avoidant attachments feel uneasy when people get too close to them and people with anxious-ambivalent attachments desire a level of closeness that many partners don't seem willing to give.

FINDING LOVE

12.4   Discuss the effectiveness of using the Internet to find love.

Online dating provides individuals with millions, if not billions, of potential mates to choose from. Although online dating has many advantages over traditional ways of finding love, automated matchmaking services provided by websites do not appear to be effective at establishing long-term relationships.

12.5   Explain the benefits and draw backs of self-disclosure at the beginning of relationships.

Although self-disclosure can help establish a relationship and prompt reciprocal sharing from others, excessive disclosure at the start of a relationships can scare people away.

MARRIAGE AND OTHER COMMITTED RELATIONSHIPS

12.6   Explain the cohabitation effect.

Couples who live together before marriage may enjoy greater intimacy than other dating couples; this type of union is known as cohabitation. The cohabitation effect refers to the fact that marriages after cohabitation are not as likely to last as long as other marriages.

12.7   Describe recent trends in marriage rates.

Marriage in the United States is at 50-year all time low, with around 51 percent of adults currently married. Nevertheless, most people in the United States still want to marry; and approximately 72 percent have been married at least once. People are waiting longer to get married. The median age for first time marriages is 26.5 years for brides and 28.7 for grooms.

12.8   Discuss why people get married.

People get married for a variety of reasons, such as the legitimization of a couple; the security associated with being in a long-term relationship; the emotional benefits of intimacy and a shared partnership; regular access to sex; and support for child rearing.

ADJUSTING TO INTIMATE RELATIONSHIPS

12.9   List the various adjustments that occur during the course of committed relationships.

Couple adjustment means the changes and adjustments in a couple's relationship during the course of their committed or married life. Over time, couples experience adjustments in attitudes, the sharing of responsibilities, and in communication style.

12.10   Compare the characteristics of successful and unsuccessful marriages.

Unsuccessful marriages are characterized by a communication style filled with contempt, criticism, defensiveness, and stonewalling. Those in successful marriages know how to solve problems effectively, use more positive behaviors than negative behaviors, engage in affective affirmation, and avoid using the "Four Horsemen of the Apocalypse."

12.11   Describe ways to improve the quality of existing relationships.

Do the following to help improve the quality of a relationship: (1) seek help early; (2) don't say every critical thing that comes to mind; (3) bring up problematic topics gently and without blame; (4) be willing to accept influence from your significant other; (5) don't accept hurtful behavior from your partner; (6) learn how to exit an argument without hurting the other person; and (7) engender a rich climate of positivity.

12.12   Discuss sexual changes that often occur in relationships over time.

A satisfying sex life is also an important part of a committed relationship, with a strong association between a satisfying sex life and satisfaction with the relationship itself. Although the average committed relationship tends to devitalize over time, partners who remain open to each other and continue growing in their relationship report increasing happiness.

DIVORCE AND ITS CONSEQUENCES

12.13   Describe various aspects of the divorce experience.

The divorce rate has more than doubled in the past few decades, with about four out of every ten marriages now ending in divorce. Getting a divorce or breaking up a long-term committed relationship involves overlapping and painful experiences, including the emotional, legal, economic, parental, and community aspects. How children are affected by divorce depends on a variety of factors, such as the age and sex of the child and custody arrangements.

12.14 Discuss the challenges faced by blended families.
Blended families, that is remarriages involving children from previous relationships, pose special demands on the adults as well as the children. Difficulties include: having little child-free time to build mutual understanding and acceptance of each other; problems in the development of rapport and trust with the children; children becoming resentful of directives given by stepparents; and a poorly defined role for the stepparent.

Scoring Key for the Marital Myths Quiz

1. *True.* More than 7 out of 10 Americans eventually marry, most of them in their 20s and 30s.

2. *False.* As discussed in the text, couples that live together before marriage may be more apt to divorce than other couples, mostly because of the attitudes and values they bring to the marriage. Newer studies, however, are indicating that these findings may be changing.

3. *False.* Changing circumstances often trigger differing ratios of input between partners. For instance, a 30–70 ratio of husband to wife might be characteristic of a newly married couple in which the man is busy starting a new business, though the ratio might well be reversed (70–30) later in the marriage if the wife works and assumes more responsibilities at home because her husband has a life-threatening illness.

4. *True.* This factor is mostly true in that love and friendship are overlapping relationships. Sexuality adds a special dimension to marriage and love relationships that is not found in friendships.

5. *False.* It is the lack of high-quality communication in discussing their differences rather than the differences themselves that is a major cause of marital dissatisfaction.

6. *True.* Studies show that married individuals report being healthier and happier than single individuals.

7. *True.* In contrast to the past, most divorces are now initiated by women. One reason may be women's greater concern with the quality of the marriage relationship, with divorcing women reporting more dissatisfaction with their marriages than divorcing men.

8. *False.* This factor varies. Extramarital affairs may rejuvenate some marriages, make no difference to others, and prove downright destructive to still others. A lot depends on how both partners deal with an extramarital affair.

9. *False.* Although studies vary, there is mounting evidence that children are damaged more by the conflict-ridden atmosphere of an intact home, especially when it is long-standing, than by the legal divorce itself.

10. *True.* On the average, married people, not simply happily married couples, live longer than unmarried people. One reason may be the need to look after someone else; another may be the emotional support people receive from their partners.

Self-Test

1. Sam started online dating about a year ago. At first, Sam had difficulty getting others to tell him more about themselves than what was listed on their profiles. Then Sam discovered that the more he revealed about himself when engaging in online chat, the more he learned about his potential dates. This example illustrates the concept known as:
   a. self-disclosure paradox
   b. mutuality benefit
   c. norm of reciprocity
   d. benefit exchange

2. Which of the following is not considered to be part of the triangular theory of love?
   a. commitment
   b. companionship
   c. passion
   d. intimacy

3. After watching a romantic comedy with a friend, Tamera said, "That movie was so fake, there is no way that a rich guy will fall in love with a prostitute. And besides, no one really falls head-over-heals in love like that. Besides, relationships are so over-rated. Tamera's view on love are consistent with what type of attachment style?
   a. avoidant
   b. secure
   c. anxious
   d. disorganized

4. Research have identified (or profiled) the characteristics of a batterer. Which of the following should not be considered part of that profile?
   a. Batterers have high self-esteem and feel powerful and effective in the world.
   b. Batterers objectify women. Overall, they see women as property or sexual objects.
   c. Batterers externalize the causes of their behavior and blame their violence on circumstances
   d. Batterers may be pleasant and charming between periods of violence and are often seen as "nice guys" to outsiders.

5. Charles and Diana decided to live together for a year prior to getting married. Once married, the relationship quickly faltered, ending in divorce. This scenario illustrates the phenomenon known as:
   a. post-marriage malaise
   b. the cohabitation effect
   c. the bystander effect
   d. the devil effect

6. According to the concept known as _____, most marriages will change and require modifications over the course of a long-term relationship.
   a. couple adjustment
   b. distancing
   c. mediation
   d. couple attunement

7. Lil and Devon are *happily* married. So it was a bit of a surprise that Devon completely forgot about their 10th wedding anniversary. According to research, which of the following statements would Lil most likely make about Devon's failed memory?
   a. "I'm thinking Devon may be having an affair."
   b. "Poor guy, he's been so stressed at his job lately. He can't focus on anything but work."
   c. "That's it, I'm out of here"
   d. "He didn't forget his anniversary with his first wife, he must not love me as much."

8. Carrie felt that her marriage was unbalanced. She earned most of the money, worked more hours than her husband, while at the same time taking on more household responsibilities. Her husband Earnie completely disagreed with Carrie's viewpoint. What type of couples therapy would be helpful in repairing their relationship?
   a. rationale cognitive therapy
   b. facilitator based therapy
   c. emotion-focused therapy
   d. implementer therapy

9. With regard to relationship infidelity, which of the following statements is (are) true?
   a. extramarital sex can be a cause of a poor marriage
   b. extramarital sex can be a consequence of a poor marriage
   c. less than 15% of men and women have had engaged in extramarital sex
   d. a and b are both true

10. Joni and Antony were recently married. It was Joni's first marriage and Antony's second. In addition to the children Antony sired during his first marriage, he and Joni had two more together. Based on this information which of the following terms best describe Joni and Antony's family?
    a. blended family
    b. mixed family
    c. melded family
    d. amalgamated family

Exercises

1. *Qualities desired in a significant other.* Make a list of some personal qualities you would like in a significant other. You might list a dozen such qualities, then go back and check the three most important ones. Write a short paragraph telling why these three qualities are the most important. You might do the same for personal qualities you would *not* like in a partner. Again, list a dozen such qualities and check the three most important ones. Why do you think these qualities are undesirable?

2. *Qualities you offer to a prospective significant other.* Make a list of the major personal strengths and weaknesses you would bring to a committed relationship. What are the three most desirable qualities you have to offer? What are some of your less desirable qualities that might affect the marriage? If you are already committed to someone or if you are married, you might ask your partner to add to your list. Try to list more desirable qualities than undesirable ones.

3. *The marriage relationship.* If you are going steady, engaged, living with someone, or married, describe the type of relationship you have with your partner. Are you also friends? Do you and your partner return each other's love? Or is one of you more emotionally involved in the relationship than the other? To what extent are both of you relationship-oriented?

4. *Adjustment.* If you're living with someone or married, what has been your major adjustment in learning to live together? Has it involved learning how to communicate and handle conflict? Or has it had to do with specific problems involving money, house chores, or sex? Select one or two of the most difficult adjustments you've had in your current relationship, and write a page or so about it. Is there anything you learned in this chapter that can help you better adjust?

5. *Cohabitation.* If you are currently living with a significant other or have had such an experience, write a page or so telling what you learned from this experience. To what extent is your experience similar to that of cohabiting couples described in this chapter? Did cohabitation include serious plans for marriage? What are some of the values of cohabitation? The hazards? Would you recommend this experience to others?

Questions for Self-Reflection

1. Can you be in love with more than one person at a time?
2. How can you tell whether your partner loves you?

3. Are you and your partner equally emotionally involved in your relationship?

Chapter Thirteen

Stress!

After a frustrating 30-minute delay on the expressway, punctuated by honking horns and waving fingers, Nate arrives at the office late. He is told the boss wants to see him right away. "I wonder what that's about?" Nate muses to himself, as he takes off his coat and heads upstairs. He's ushered inside the boss's office, only to find the boss pacing back and forth. The boss is furious. The big deal they were counting on with a major corporation has just fallen through. The boss makes it clear that if Nate values his job he'd better have a good explanation. Nate gropes for words. "Frankly, I'm stunned. I can't imagine what happened," he says. "Let me call and talk to the people over there and find out the story." Nate's boss continues making accusations about Nate's incompetence and his uncertain future with the company. Eventually, Nate feels enraged at being treated this way. He is tempted to yell back at his boss but knows this is neither a mature nor productive response. Instead, he returns to his office to cool off. His stomach churning, his neck muscles tense, and his blood pressure rising, he sits down at his desk. He reaches for a Maalox and a bottle of aspirin.

OH NO!—UNDERSTANDING STRESS

LEARNING OBJECTIVES

13.1 **Explain the concept of stress.**
13.2 **Identify Selye's four variations of stress.**
13.3 **Describe the major causes of stress.**
13.4 **Discuss the unique aspects of college that can be stressful.**

As Nate can tell you, stress takes a heavy toll on workers, causing absenteeism, decreasing productivity, and increasing medical expenses, all of which are estimated to cost businesses over $350 billion a year (Stambor, 2006). Stress manifests itself in a variety of ways. The most common sign of stress is increased nervousness, anxiety, and tension. Many experience headaches, fatigue, or depression; and others say their stress shows up as anger and irritability (Monroe & Reid, 2009). Other symptoms of stress include muscle aches, stomachaches, an overall feeling of being upset, insomnia, loss of sleep, compulsive eating or loss of appetite, a feeling of frustration, crying, yelling, and screaming. Many of these symptoms are part of the body's physiological stress response—automatic, built-in reactions over which we have little control. However, stress-related symptoms can also occur because of our psychological reactions to events that are

---

BOX 13–1 **Did you know that the following can help you manage stress through self-care?**

- Avoid drugs and alcohol
- Find support
- Connect socially
- Take care of yourself
- Stay active

Source: "Managing Stress," from Centers for Disease and Control website, 2012.

---

more dependent on the way we *perceive* the world, and our capacity for dealing with it, rather than to the actual stressor.

Regardless of its cause, stress has a major impact on our health, contributing either directly or indirectly, to coronary heart disease, cancer, lung ailments, accidental injuries, cirrhosis of the liver, and suicide (Monroe, 2008)—six of the leading causes of death in the United States. Just like Nate, most of us experience "high stress" at one time or another. Many report that they feel "great stress" at least once or twice a week or live with high stress every day. Clearly, stress can be an impediment to adjustment and growth. In the current chapter, the causes and consequences of stress will be identified, and then the ways to effectively manage it will be presented. Table 13–1 presents other statistics on stress so that you can judge for yourself how large a problem stress is for modern life.

Conceptualizing Stress

THE COMPONENTS OF STRESS Although we experience it all of the time, the concept of stress is somewhat difficult to define; partly because it means different things to different people. Nevertheless, most agree that the experience of stress has three components: (1) the triggering event; (2) the perception of the event as stressful; and (3) the nature and degree of reaction to the event. First, the triggers of stress are called **stressors**—*events in the environment, our body, or our mind that evoke stress,* such as a highly competitive work environment, college roommate conflicts, or worries about appearance. Second, most events are neither good nor bad; it's our perception of them as stressful that matters. For instance, while one person may find an upcoming test overwhelming, another may find the exam to be of no concern. Third, it is our response to an event that really characterizes the experience of **stress**—*a reaction to events that disturb equilibrium or exceed coping abilities.* When events disrupt our usual level of functioning and require us to make an *extra effort* to re-establish our equilibrium, we experience stress.

Table 13–1 **Statistics on Stress**

- Over half of Americans view job stress as a major problem in their lives.
- One-fourth of American workers say their stress is so severe that they feel a "nervous breakdown" is imminent.
- More than three out of every five doctor's office visits are for stress-related problems.
- Up to 90 percent of reported illnesses and disease may be stress-related.
- More women than men report feeling super-stressed, including 23 percent of female (as opposed to 19 percent of male) executives and professionals. In college, about 38 percent of women as compared to 20 percent of men report high stress levels.
- Young people are more affected by stress; 75 percent of 18- to 24-year olds have suffered from stress at work.

TYPES OF STRESS   We should be careful not to equate stress solely with distress, as it can have beneficial effects in some cases (Reynolds & Turner, 2008). In fact, four basic variations of stress have been identified: distress, eustress, hyperstress, and hypostress (Selye, 1991). *When events have a harmful effect,* stress is labeled **distress.** For around 70 percent of Americans, the three most frequently mentioned sources of distress are money, the economy, and work. In addition, around half of Americans experience significant distress from relationships, personal responsibilities, health concerns, and housing costs (American Psychological Association, 2010). **Eustress** *refers to events that are stimulating, motivational, or result in personal growth,* such as beginning a new job, getting married, or taking up an exciting sport such as skydiving. **Hyperstress,** or *excessive stress,* usually occurs when events, including positive ones, pile up and stretch the limits of our adaptability. For example, individuals who are already under stress at work and home may experience hyperstress after experiencing a traumatic event such as a car crash. **Hypostress,** or *insufficient stress,* is apt to occur when we lack stimulation, such as working a monotonous job. Moreover, at times bored people resort to sensation-seeking behaviors mentioned elsewhere in the book, such as experimenting with drugs or taking unnecessary financial, personal, or recreational risks.

Of note, stress is often thought of in terms of how long it lasts and how often it occurs. Based on these time-related factors, two different types of stress have been identified: acute and chronic. Whereas **acute stress** *is a momentary response to imminent threat and is relieved when the threat is over,* **chronic stress** refers to *experiencing a long-term, on-going stressor.* Case in point, the boss's surprisingly angry outburst at Nate would elicit acute stress, while Nate's long and arduous daily drive to and from work would cause chronic stress.

Major Causes of Stress

Although we each experience stress somewhat differently, there are some common categories of events that cause most of us to feel stressed at some point or another: life changes, daily hassles, catastrophic events, and economic and social conditions. Before reading the next section on each of these major causes of stress, ask yourself this: "What stresses you out?"

LIFE CHANGES   Besides being stressful, what do getting married, losing a job, having a parent die, and beginning college all have in common? Each of these events represent *a significant*

Scientists do not yet know which theory about the causes of stress is correct; the theory about major life stressors (such as a natural disaster) or the theory about daily hassles (such as not being able to find your car in a parking lot).

change in a person's life—referred to by psychologists as a **life change.** Regardless of whether it is positive or negative, a life change can happen at any point during the lifespan (though they may be more common at some ages than others) and can be predictable (as in a wedding following a long engagement) or unexpected (like the death of a loved one) (Holmes & Rahe, 1967). More often than not, life changes produce acute stress.

While experiencing a single life change can be stressful, most times we can effectively handle it without consequence. However, when there are a number of life changes occurring at the same time, the amount of readjustment required to cope may become overwhelming; and as a result, our health and well-being may suffer. Accordingly, the combined stress of life events has been related to a variety of **stress-related illnesses**—*illnesses affected by our emotions, lifestyles, or environment*—such as sudden cardiac death, stroke, diabetes and other chronic illnesses, depression, complications of pregnancy and birth, everyday colds, flare-up of multiple sclerosis, and many other physical problems (Contrada & Baum, 2011).

Despite its usefulness, the life-events approach to stress has several limitations. First, the particular events considered stressful may not be equally relevant for all groups of people. For examples, divorce is not an issue that most teenagers or the elderly, for that matter, typically encounter. Second, the life-events approach does not take into account how individuals perceive a given change, much less how well they adapt to it. Third, because the life-events approach is built around infrequent, but significant change, it fails to include a great deal of stress that comes with chronic or repeated conditions, such as a boring job or a long-lasting unsatisfying marriage. Finally, it leaves out the "little things" in everyday life that often get to us, such as losing your car keys or snapping a shoelace when you're in a rush in the morning (Monroe, 2008).

DAILY HASSLES For many people, it's not the major life events that cause them angst, rather it's the petty annoyances that surround them every day—the smelly roommate who won't shower, the toilets that needs cleaning, and the dirty laundry that keeps piling up are just a few examples. Such *everyday difficulties that cause stress* are called **daily hassles**. Of note, people vary considerably in terms of what bothers them (Almeida, 2005). Among traditional college students, the most commonly reported hassles are anxiety over tests and grades. Middle-aged people are bothered more by worries over health and money. Professional people feel they have too much to do and not enough time to do it; and they have difficulty relaxing. Daily hassles common to all groups are misplacing or losing things, worrying over physical appearance, and having too many things to do (Kieffer, Cronin, & Gawet, 2006). As it turns out, the cumulative effect of daily hassles on stress is powerful, affecting both psychological and physical health; with people who suffer chronic, intense hassles having the poorest health; for example, an increased likelihood of depression (Lazarus, 1993; McIntosh, Gillanders, & Rodgers, 2010).

CATASTROPHIC EVENTS When *the same life change happens to many people at the same time, disrupting lives and causing death and destruction*, it rises to the level of a **catastrophic event**. Examples include natural disasters, pandemics, and terrorist attacks. Mass tragedies can affect us in many ways: physically, emotionally, and mentally. They can make people feel angry, enraged, confused, sad, anxious, tired, or even guilty. Case in point, after being involved in a catastrophic incident resulting in multiple deaths, those who lived may experience **survivor guilt**—*feeling guilty simply because they are still alive while others are not*. No one who sees or hears about a catastrophic tragedy is untouched by it—and in an era of instant mass communications, the number of people exposed to such trauma in one way or another is significant. For instance, the repeated viewing of graphic images associated with the events of September 11, 2001, has caused fear and anxiety in many youthful viewers (Saylor, Cowart, Lipovsky, Jackson, & Finch, 2003).

Catastrophic events, whether experienced in person or seen in the media, will affect most of us negatively; but those effects will eventually fade over time. For some, however, such feelings may not go away on their own, and alcohol and drug use may follow in a misguided attempt to cope with these feelings (Keyes, Hatzenbuehler, & Hasin, 2011). For others, the stress associated with living through a tragedy is so great that severe depression ensues. Consider this, five years after Hurricane Katrina devastated New Orleans, the suicide rate was still more than double of what it was prior to the levees breaking (Spiegel, 2010).

As the anniversary of a disaster or traumatic event approaches, many survivors report a return of restlessness and fear. The psychological literature calls it the **anniversary reaction** and defines it as *an individual's response to unresolved grief resulting from significant losses.* The anniversary reaction can involve several days or even weeks of anxiety, anger, nightmares, flashbacks, depression, or fear. However, not all survivors of a disaster or traumatic events experience an anniversary reaction. On a more positive note, the anniversary of a disaster or traumatic event can also provide an opportunity for emotional healing. Individuals can make significant progress in working through the natural grieving process by acknowledging the emotions and issues that surface during their anniversary reaction. These feelings and issues can help individuals develop perspective on the event and figure out where it fits in their hearts, minds, and lives (Holland & Neimeyer, 2010).

ECONOMIC AND SOCIAL CONDITIONS The current economic situation in the United States is brutal, with slightly over 46 million Americans in poverty, the largest number in 52 years (U.S. Bureau of the Census, 2012). Globally, it is estimated that more than 1.4 billion people are impoverished, living on $1.25 each day or less (Worldhunger.org, 2012). In addition to causing a number of physical ailments (such as malnutrition), the negative effects of poverty on psychological well-being cannot be understated, especially for those with families. For both children and adults alike, the stress of poverty is associated with increased levels of psychopathology, such as anxiety and depression. Within the family system, poverty also causes parenting to suffer and inter-parental conflicts to increase (Wadsworth, Raviv, Santiago, & Etter, 2011).

Beyond poverty, there are other social conditions that cause stress: discrimination and prejudice among them (Thompson, 2002). For instance, ethnic minorities encountering discrimination experience more stress and are more likely to attempt suicide than those without such experiences (Cassidy, O'Connor, Howe, & Warden, 2004; Gomez, Miranda, & Polanco, 2011). Ethnic minorities may also face **acculturative stress**—*the stress related to the process of adapting to the beliefs, languages, practices, and values of a dominant culture.* Although acculturative stress frequently affects first-generation immigrants shortly arriving in their new country it can also impact their progeny years later. For example, the children of immigrants may feel caught between the values of their parents and those of their peers; resulting in family conflict and tension (Ahmed, Kia-Keating, & Tsai, 2011).

ADDITIONAL FACTORS Here are some additional factors that contribute, alone or in combination, to our experience of stress (Scott, Jackson, & Bergeman, 2011).

- *Physical stressors* such as too much to do or too many demands on our time and attention.
- *Lack of control* over decisions and demands in our personal life or our work life.
- *Unpredictability* of events that therefore find us unprepared to cope with them.
- *Lack of social support* from friends and family.
- *Poor interpersonal relations* with family members, friends, or coworkers.
- *Role conflict* in which one role (e.g., a job) conflicts with another role (e.g., being a readily available parent).
- *Career concerns* including finding a job, receiving a promotion, and being unemployed.
- *Unpleasant or dangerous physical conditions* such as a noisy work environment.

Clearly, this list is not exhaustive, and we're sure you could come up with other stress-inducing situations very easily. But as you can see, the potential for stress is everywhere, including college.

Stress in College

As most of you are all too well aware, the pursuit of higher education comes with a great deal of stress. College students, especially in their first year, are exposed to new social norms and customs, different peer groups, work overload, a change in lifestyle, as well as more demands placed on their time and their self-control (Guo, Wang, Johnson, & Diaz, 2011; Singh & Upadhyay, 2008). As a result of these changes, the transition to college is particularly difficult, with a large number of freshmen reporting overwhelming stress. However, college alone, no matter what year a student is in, stimulates additional stress; especially if the student has work-related responsibilities in addition to their academic ones (Pritchard & Wilson, 2006). Currently, around 37 percent of students work full-time while attending college; a decade ago that number was 25 percent (Bureau of Labor Statistics, 2011; *Techniques*, 2000). And correspondingly, stress levels have increased over the same 10-year period (Huang, 2011). It is also worth noting that college women report more stress than college men (Darling, McWey, Howard, & Olmstead, 2007).

Exploration 13.1: Stress and You

healthfinder.gov   A website devoted to helping people learn about mental health issues, including stress.

The stress of college, resulting from financial, academic, and social pressures, has been associated with a variety of negative behaviors, including increases in "energy" drink and junk food consumption, smoking, and alcohol and drug use. Declines in healthy eating habits, fitness, and other positive health behaviors, such as vitamin taking, are also well documented. Additionally, stressed students are significantly less pleased with their grade-point averages and their health. It is unclear whether high levels of stress produce lower grades and poor health or whether poor levels of academic performance and fitness result in added stress (Economos, Hildebrandt, & Hyatt, 2008; Pettit & DeBarr, 2011). Not surprisingly, high levels of college-related stress also have a harmful impact on mental health; with anxiety, depression, eating disorders, and suicide as potential consequences (Singh & Joshi, 2008; Sulkowski, Dempsey, & Dempsey, 2011).

Faculty (who frequently function as teachers, mentors, and academic advisors) often have a difficult time gauging how much stress their students are under (Misra, McKean, West, & Russo, 2000). Thus, your professors, no matter how well intentioned, might not be the best first line of defense for recognizing and reducing college-related stress. On the other hand, many college campuses offer counseling services for their students as well as workshops on stress reduction, study habits, and career counseling. Others provide support groups for common disorders that accompany stress, such as eating disorders or depression. Do you know what services your campus has available? Perhaps you need to explore them for yourself or someone close to you?

YIKES!—REACTIONS TO STRESS

LEARNING OBJECTIVES

13.5 Explain the general adaptation syndrome.

13.6 Explain the connection between stress and defense mechanisms.

13.7 Discuss how reactions to stress can differ.

13.8 Compare psychological hardiness and resilience.

Our reaction to stressful events takes four primary forms: *emotional, behavioral, cognitive, and physiological*. An emotional reaction to stress refers to the feelings that a stressor evokes; and those emotions can be either positive (e.g., excited, energized) or negative (e.g., anxious, fearful). What we do following a stressful event comprise our behavioral reactions. These behaviors can be beneficial to us (e.g., study harder, go to therapy) or detrimental to our well-being (e.g., drink and use drugs; give up hope). The cognitive aspect of stress is concerned with how we think about the stressor, in terms of its severity, how long it will last, the perceived ease of coping with it, and the likelihood of it occurring again. Collectively, the emotional, behavioral, and cognitive reactions to stress are referred as psychological reactions. Finally, our physiological reactions to stress include changes in hormones (such as adrenaline), brain activity, and basic functions related to survival, such as heart rate, respiration, and blood pressure (Monroe, 2008).

Physiological Stress Reactions

GENERAL ADAPTATION SYNDROME   Hans Selye (1991), a pioneer in the study of how stress affects the body, maintains that in addition to the body's specific responses to a particular stressor (e.g., sweating in response to heat), there *also is a characteristic pattern of nonspecific physiological mechanisms that are activated in response to almost any stressor.* Selye called this pattern the **general adaptation syndrome (GAS).** It *consists of three progressive stages: the alarm reaction, the stage of resistance, and the stage of exhaustion.*

(1) ALARM REACTION   *The initial emergency response to stress-provoking agents is known as the* **alarm reaction.** The alarm reaction consists of the body' initial mobilization of resources that produce similar symptoms regardless of the type of stressor, be it physical (e.g., lifting heavy boxes; being attacked) or psychological (e.g., taking a test; giving a speech). For this reason, people experiencing alarm reaction often complain of common symptoms such as headache, aching muscles and joints, loss of appetite, and a generally tired feeling.

During the alarm stage, the presentation of a stressor can evoke a **fight-or-flight response. Fight,** of course, means *confronting the stressor*, and **flight** means *fleeing from the stressor.* When the stressor is insurmountable, we flee; when it is capable of being vanquished, we often fight it. This stress response starts in the brain when a stressor is perceived; the brain then signals the rest of the body to prepare to fight or to flee. For example, blood flow to our muscles increases, we sweat, and our heart begins to quicken as does our breathing. When the stressor disappears or subsides, so too, do many of the physiological responses to stress; the body relaxes and fight-or-flight responses are no longer present.

(2) RESISTANCE   If our exposure to stressful situations continues, the alarm reaction is followed by the **stage of resistance,** in which *the human organism develops an increased resistance to the stressor.* The symptoms of the alarm stage disappear, and body defenses rise above their normal level to cope with the continued stress. Thus, the goal of this stage is to return the body to normal functioning. If the stressor is effectively dealt with, then this stage becomes one of recovery and renewal; though the body's overall defenses will be compromised for a while. On the other hand, if the stress response is activated too often or turned on for too long, resources become depleted, and the body's responses to stress can actually turn against itself; the stage of exhaustion has been reached.

(3) EXHAUSTION   During the **stage of exhaustion** *body defenses break down and adaptation energy runs out, making the body vulnerable to illness.* Indeed, research on stress and health confirms that chronic stress makes us more susceptible to viruses—not just colds but HIV, which causes AIDS—and diminishes wound healing as well as lowering our immunity (Glaser, 2005). Moreover, when the body is exhausted there is an increased likelihood of "diseases of adaptation" (i.e., illnesses resulting from our inability to adapt to stress), such as peptic ulcers and high blood pressure (Segerstrom & Miller, 2004).

ALLOSTATIC LOAD   Some scientists believe that the fight-or-flight explanation for stress is too simplistic and that the GAS model isn't inclusive enough with regard to other processes involved in stress reactions, such as hormone production (Monroe, 2008). As such, they believe that the physiological reactions to stress are better explained by the concepts of allostasis and allostatic load (McEwen, 2005). **Allostasis** means *achieving stability through changes via a process that maintains balance among the physiological factors essential for life,* such as hormones and the immune system. **Allostatic load** refers to *cumulative changes that reflect the cost to the body of adapting repeatedly to demands (i.e., stresses) placed upon it.* This view takes into account a time frame. Over the short run, bodily functions associated with allostasis provide *protective effects against stress,* but over the long run, stressors can have *damaging effects* and adversely affect our life by resulting in poorer health (Almeida, 2005).

For example, the hypothalamic–pituitary–adrenal (HPA) axis is a network of tissues and glands in which the hypothalamus, pituitary gland, and adrenal gland are the central components. In response to stressful situations, the HPA axis releases hormones, such as cortisol, into the bloodstream (McCrory, De Brito, & Viding, 2010). But cortisol is a toxin, and as such, sustained exposure to it can damage nerve cells, muscle, and tissue. It is believed that the body's production of this potentially toxic hormone motivates us to reduce stress. In fact cortisol levels decrease after a stressor has been effectively dealt with (Golubchik, Mozes, Maayan, & Weizman, 2009). However, if stressors do not go away, then the presence of cortisol in the body becomes problematic. Put another way, allostasis helps us physiologically manage stress, but chronic allostatic overload means we eventually become too distressed. It is the difference between being "stressed" and "stressed out."

Psychological Stress Reactions

Unlike the body's stress reactions, our psychological reactions typically are shaped by learning and are heavily dependent on the way we perceive our world. Included here are a wide variety of cognitive, emotional, and behavioral responses to stress.

DEFENSE MECHANISMS Because most stressors evoke **anxiety**—*the vague, unpleasant feeling that something bad is about to happen*—common psychological reactions to stress are meant to defend us from the psychological pain associated with the perceived threat. Such reactions are called **defense mechanisms**—*automatic unconscious mechanisms that protect us from the awareness of anxiety, thereby helping us to maintain a sense of self-worth in the face of threat.* Here's an example of one such defense mechanism, **rationalization**, in which we *justify our unacceptable behavior with "good" reasons.* After failing a test in psychology because he didn't study, Nate thinks to himself, "Well, I didn't want to be a Psych major anyway. You can make more money with a business degree." Table 13–2 provides a description of additional defense mechanisms used to ward off the anxiety associated with stress. Remember, defense mechanisms are meant to fool *the self,* not other people.

Each of us relies on such mechanisms at one time or another, especially when we feel threatened; and regardless of whether the situation actually warrants it. As emergency reactions, defense mechanisms diminish our awareness of anxiety and help us maintain our sense of adequacy and self-worth in the face of threat. However, because defense mechanisms also involve self-deception and a distortion of social reality, habitual reliance on them can prove maladaptive and can stifle personal growth.

PERCEIVED LEVEL OF STRESS How people behave under stress depends partly on the level of stress experienced. Mild stress can energize us to become more alert, active, and resourceful. Medium stress tends to have a disruptive effect on our lives, especially on complex behaviors such as writing a term paper. Very high levels of stress can be extremely troublesome. Under such stress, people become less sensitive to their surroundings, easily irritated, and more apt to resort to unhealthy coping devices such as consuming too much alcohol or staying up all night watching TV. Stress also evokes a wide range of emotions, ranging from a sense of exhilaration in the face of minor, challenging stressors to the more familiar negative emotions of anxiety, anger, fear, jealousy, and discouragement. Moreover, severe stress tends to inhibit behavior and may lead to apathy and immobility, as in clinically depressed individuals who feel helpless in the face of overwhelming frustration or deprivation (Monroe & Reid, 2009). In addition, survivors of traumatic events, such as rape victims, assault, and combat, may cope well at the time of the trauma, but several months later experience a delayed emotional reaction known as posttraumatic

Table 13–2	A Few Recognized Defense Mechanisms	
Defense Mechanism	**Definition**	**Example**
Repression	Excluding unacceptable ideas or feelings from consciousness.	You can't remember details of a wedding for a marriage that ended in divorce.
Denial	Not accepting (denying) the reality of a painful or embarrassing situation.	Despite the fact that you failed a drug test and lost your job, you refuse to believe that you have a drug problem.
Regression	Reverting to a form of behavior that was more appropriate at an earlier stage of development.	Upon the birth of a sibling a 10-year old starts to crawl around on the floor and make baby sounds.
Projection	Attributing our unacceptable ideas or feelings to others.	You complain about your roommate being vain, but you're the one who is really concerned about looks and appearance.
Displacement	Redirecting threatening ideas or impulses onto less threatening objects.	Mad at your boss because you didn't get a coveted promotion at work, you go home and yell at your kids.
Sublimation	Channeling socially unacceptable urges into acceptable behaviors.	Desires to cause pain and suffering in others are expressed through writings about the zombie apocalypse.
Reaction formation	Developing conscious feelings and behaviors opposite to the unconscious, anxiety-arousing ones.	A parent who likes one of their two children better than the other, gives more positive attention to the child they're least fond of.

stress disorder. **Posttraumatic stress disorder (PTSD)** is *a severe anxiety disorder character-*
ized by symptoms of anxiety and avoidance behavior, resulting from an unusually distressing
event. Box 13–2 discusses PTSD in more detail.

BOX 13–2   Focus on Wellness: Posttraumatic Stress Disorder

PTSD is an anxiety disorder that can develop after exposure to a terrifying event or ordeal in which
grave physical harm occurred or was threatened. The types of events that trigger PTSD usually lie
outside the realm of ordinary human loss and grief. Examples are plane crashes, earthquakes, floods,
assaults, rapes, hostage taking, torture, murders, and military combat.

Incidence

The most frequent cause of PTSD for Americans is automobile accidents (Blanchard & Hickling, 2003).
However, the incidence of PTSD is much higher in veterans than in the general populations. Case in
point, nearly 14 percent of Iraq veterans suffer from PTSD (Tanielian & Jaycox, 2008). And although
nearly half of the U.S. adult population is exposed to at least one traumatic event during their lifetime,
only 7 percent will develop this disorder (National Institute of Mental Health, 2012; Ozer & Weiss,
2004). In fact, we now know that many adults do successfully navigate disastrous events (Bonanno,
Galea, Bucciarelli, & Vlahov, 2007). These individuals have spawned the growth of studies on resilience, which is discussed later in this chapter.

(Continued)

BOX 13–2 (Continued)

Symptoms

The symptoms of PTSD can begin immediately after the traumatic event or 3 to 6 months later. However, it is not unusual for the symptoms to emerge only after a much longer period, which is characteristic of the chronic or delayed forms of the disorder (Horowitz, 2011). Victims involuntarily re-experience the past traumatic event in dreams, which include "flashbacks" of the event accompanied by the original emotions of fear, shock, and horror. Flashbacks are especially likely to occur when they encounter reminders of the trauma. They also experience an emotional numbness toward their everyday world. Frequently, they have trouble concentrating at work during the day and difficulty sleeping at night. Feeling alienated from others, they may also lose interest in people. Angry outbursts and irritability are also signs of PTSD. The possibility of PTSD is greatest for those who have suffered additional traumas prior to the current one (Ai, Evans-Campbell, Santangelo, & Cascio, 2006). Interestingly, scientists using brain imaging and other sophisticated techniques have found neural changes in victims of PTSD; these physiological changes may account for some of the more chronic symptoms mentioned above, such as flashbacks and blunted emotions (Rougemont-Bücking et al., 2011).

Exploration 13.2: Trauma and Stress

www.apa.org The American Psychological Association's online public information site. It includes material on trauma, stress, and hardiness.

How Do You React to Stress?

Imagine that you just failed a test, or that your significant other just broke up with you. What do you do? Do you seek out friends for comfort and support or do you just get mad? Your answer may very well depend on your gender (Taylor, Manganello, Lee, & Rice, 2000). Here's why: Women are more likely than men to cope with stress through social support; "tend and befriend" as it is often called (i.e., sharing emotions and stressful experiences with their friends). In contrast, stressful situations cause many men to become angry, hostile, or avoidant (Darling et al., 2007). Of note, women also react to a wider range of stressors and say they feel stress more often than men (Eaton & Graham, 2008).

REACTIONS BASED ON PERSONALITY TYPE Beauty isn't the only thing that "is in the eye of the beholder" as stress is too. In fact, how you perceive a given stressor may make it more or less stressful (Monroe, 2008). Some people take criticism of their work as a personal attack, become highly distressed and waste a lot of energy defending themselves. Other people may take similar criticism as a challenge to improve their work, thereby experiencing less stress. Additional factors, such as the tendency to worry and emotional instability, can also affect the experience of stress—with higher levels of these two traits associated with greater stress responding (Zautra, Affleck, Tennen, Reich, & Davis, 2005). Of course, one of the most well-known differences in the perception of stress is between those with Type A and Type B behavior patterns.

People with a **Type B behavior pattern** are *patient, relaxed, and easy going*. In contrast, those with a **Type A behavior pattern** tend to be *competitive, argumentative, time-urgent, ambitious, impatient, and hostile*. They also tend to judge themselves and others by rigorous standards (Jamal, 2005). When others fail to maintain the high standards set by the Type A individual, they can be nasty. As a result, Type A people often keep themselves (and others) under more frequent and constant stress than do **Type B** individuals (Mohan, 2006). Not surprisingly, Type A behavior pattern has been linked with heart disease and other stress-related illnesses. However, it is worth noting that it is the hostility aspect of the Type A behavior pattern, and not the achievement-related components, that best predict health problems (Kent & Shapiro, 2009). What type of behavior pattern best describes you? Complete Activity 13–1 to find out.

ACTIVITY 13–1

What's Your Behavior Pattern Type: A or B?

INSTRUCTIONS: *For each of the following statements, indicate your level of agreement by circling the appropriate number below the statement.*

1. When another student is doing better than me in class, I make sure that I catch up and get a higher grade.

   Strongly disagree   1   2   3   4   5   6   7   Strongly agree

2. When I have somewhere to go, I still take time to "stop and smell the roses."

   Strongly disagree   1   2   3   4   5   6   7   Strongly agree

3. When I am being driven somewhere and I know a good shortcut, I get very irritated if the driver doesn't listen to my suggestion.

   Strongly disagree   1   2   3   4   5   6   7   Strongly agree

4. I find it difficult to relax because there is always something for work or school I could be doing.

   Strongly disagree   1   2   3   4   5   6   7   Strongly agree

5. I only take on projects that I know I can excel at.

   Strongly disagree   1   2   3   4   5   6   7   Strongly agree

6. I never do work on a vacation; after all, it wouldn't really be a vacation if I did.

   Strongly disagree   1   2   3   4   5   6   7   Strongly agree

7. I don't sweat the small stuff; and it's all small stuff.

   Strongly disagree   1   2   3   4   5   6   7   Strongly agree

8. I like to make friends with people who can help me do better in school or advance at work.

   Strongly disagree   1   2   3   4   5   6   7   Strongly agree

9. I tune people out when what they say no longer interests me.

   Strongly disagree   1   2   3   4   5   6   7   Strongly agree

10. I feel at ease most of the time.

   Strongly disagree   1   2   3   4   5   6   7   Strongly agree

SCORING: First, reverse score Questions 2, 6, 7, and 10 (1 = 7; 2 = 6; 3 = 5 . . .). Now tally up your score for all items. The higher the score, the more likely you engage in a Type A behavior pattern. This self-assessor was designed specifically for this book, so please use caution when interpreting the results.

More recently, psychologists have begun looking into the relationship between stress and another personality characteristic, **persistence**, which refers to *continued attempts to reach a goal in the face of adversity.* An example of persistence would be not going to bed until you figure out how to solve the math problem that you've been working on for the past few hours. Persistence, while essential in modicum to happiness and success, may become detrimental when we cannot disengage from unattainable goals. We need to know when to give up a losing battle; otherwise the stress of continued failures can mount. Ultimately, excessive persistence can lead to the development of stress-related illnesses (Miller & Wrosch, 2007).

ARE YOU STRESS PROOF?   Some individuals seem better able to take stress in stride; that is they demonstrate **psychological hardiness**—*the attitude that allows them to make the most of the situation.* The three trademarks of hardy individuals are feelings of *challenge* (instead of threat), *commitment* (rather than alienation), and *control* (as opposed to powerlessness). Those who do well with stress feel stimulated by change and stress (challenge); they are also intensely involved in what they are doing (commitment); and they are not usually overcome by feelings of powerlessness even in very difficult situations (control). The last issue, control, is especially noteworthy. In probing the relationship among stress, physical illness, and psychological disorders, the importance of personal control recurs again and again. Being able to acknowledge heightened stress, as well as its effects on you, while maintaining reasonable control of yourself and, if possible, the situation at hand is vital to managing stress successfully (Maddi, 2005).

A concept similar to hardiness is **resilience**, defined as *positive growth or positive adaptation following extreme adversity.* Resilience was once thought to be rare. Today, however, it is the most common trajectory observed following distress and trauma (Almedom, 2005; Bonanno et al., 2007). Of note, *resilience* is quite different from *recovery* after trauma. Resilience is characterized by a relatively *mild and short-lived disruption*, followed by a period of growth and healthy functioning. In contrast, recovery after trauma is typified by a significant disruption in normal functioning that declines only gradually (Bonanno, Papa, Lalande, Zhang, & Noll, 2005). In other words, resilient individuals bounce back from stressful experiences more quickly and effectively than others (Tugade & Fredrickson, 2004). Such people use humor, positive emotions, replacing negative thoughts with positive ones, social support, and optimism to cope with adversity (Southwick, Vythilingam, & Charney, 2005). The important message here is that individuals can and do experience personal growth during adverse times.

By taking the self-assessment in Activity 13–2, you can begin to identify your own stress-coping style.

PHEW!—MANAGING STRESS

LEARNING OBJECTIVES

 13.9 Discuss strategies for reducing stress by modifying your environment.
13.10 Describe different ways to reduce stress by altering your lifestyle.
13.11 Explain how stress can promote personal growth.

Stress occurs daily; and it will continue to do so for the rest of our lives. At times, the stress will be intense while at others it will be relatively minor. But one thing is for certain, stress is unavoidable. Distress, however, *is* avoidable. Managing stress means taking charge, directing and controlling our responses to stressors, thereby modifying the overall experience of stress. While there are many other ways to cope with stress, most of them fall under two major headings: modifying your environment and altering yourself or your response.

Modifying Your Environment

Soon after his boss berated Nate, a camera he had on special order finally arrived. He quickly discovered it was not exactly what he wanted. What should he do? What would you do? You

ACTIVITY 13–2

WHAT'S YOUR STRESS STYLE?

INSTRUCTIONS: *For each of the following statements, indicate your level of agreement by circling the appropriate number below the statement.*

1. When I am under stress, I become angry more quickly than usual.

   Strongly disagree   1   2   3   4   5   6   7   Strongly agree

2. During stressful times, my health habits (such as maintaining a good diet) decline.

   Strongly disagree   1   2   3   4   5   6   7   Strongly agree

3. When I am under stress, I have difficulty concentrating.

   Strongly disagree   1   2   3   4   5   6   7   Strongly agree

4. Despite being in sticky situations, I find I can resort to humor or positive thinking to help myself get through it.

   Strongly disagree   1   2   3   4   5   6   7   Strongly agree

5. When I am under stress, I react with more anxiety than do other people.

   Strongly disagree   1   2   3   4   5   6   7   Strongly agree

6. At times of stress, my nervous habits (such as nail biting or hair twisting) become more prevalent.

   Strongly disagree   1   2   3   4   5   6   7   Strongly agree

7. Stress makes my memory worse.

   Strongly disagree   1   2   3   4   5   6   7   Strongly agree

8. When I am under stress, I become easily frustrated and tense.

   Strongly disagree   1   2   3   4   5   6   7   Strongly agree

9. Stress makes me cry more easily than at other times.

   Strongly disagree   1   2   3   4   5   6   7   Strongly agree

10. I have a harder time learning as well as studying for exams when under stress.

    Strongly disagree   1   2   3   4   5   6   7   Strongly agree

11. I find stress challenging at times and sometimes even exhilarating.

    Strongly disagree   1   2   3   4   5   6   7   Strongly agree

12. After a distressing event, I take a few quiet moments to learn about myself and my reaction.

    Strongly disagree   1   2   3   4   5   6   7   Strongly agree

SCORING: *Emotional reactions to stress are measured in Questions 1, 5, and 8. Behavioral reactions to stress are measured in Questions 2, 6, and 9. Cognitive reactions to stress are measured in Questions 3, 7, and 10. Resilient reactions to stress are measured in Questions*

4, 11, 12. Add up your points for each reaction cluster, and write your total for that cluster in the space provided below:

Emotional reactions 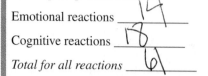 14   Behavioral reactions 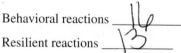 16

Cognitive reactions 18   Resilient reactions 13

Total for all reactions 61

Now decide if the scale did an accurate job measuring your typical reaction. For example, would your family or best friend concur with your scores? If you scored highest for emotional reactions, would they agree that you are emotional in stressful situations? Also, consider your total score. In some ways it indicates whether your reactions to stress are too strong or perhaps whether you are under high levels of stress. Now think about ways that you can better react or cope with stress and how you can reduce the total amount of stress that you have. Remember, this measure was designed specifically for this book. Your findings, therefore, should be used only as a tool to stimulate critical thinking about how you cope with stress.

Exploration 13.3: Stress Management

www.stressrelease.com   This website contains lots of information on stress, such as the reasons for it and tips on stress management. Make sure you check out the online resources section.

could return to the store and tell the clerk a mistake had been made and then proceed to order the correct model of camera. Or you could simply accept the camera on hand and leave, making sure never to buy anything in that store again. There's yet another option: You could refuse to accept the order and, instead, choose another camera more to your liking from among those already in stock. These responses illustrate some of the basic ways to modify your environment: assertiveness, withdrawal, or compromise. They are considered *environmental* rather than personal responses to stress because they either change your environment or change the responses of others who are creating stress for you. Let's look at each of these strategies.

ASSERTIVENESS   **Assertiveness** is the preferred way to manage stress whenever there is a reasonable possibility of success. Assertiveness is *the expression of one's rights and feelings in a direct way without violating the rights of others.* Such an approach consists of direct attempts at modifying the stressful situation itself. Common examples are returning a defective product to a store or speaking up in response to an unreasonable request. Assertiveness is a rational and constructive way of handling stress, which in turn tends to alleviate the stress involved.

WITHDRAWAL   **Withdrawal** means *removing oneself physically or emotionally from an activity, organization, or person.* Withdrawal may be an appropriate response to stress, especially when a stressful situation cannot be successfully modified through assertiveness or compromise (discussed next). An example of withdrawal would be the consumer who actively shops at a different store after getting no satisfaction from the first store's customer service center. Withdrawal is neither good nor bad in itself. Much depends on how it is used. On the one hand, if someone habitually withdraws from stressful situations, that person may drift into a constricted lifestyle that prevents adequate adjustment or personal growth. On the other hand, the use of withdrawal as a temporary strategy may be a valuable means of coping with stress that has become overwhelming or detrimental to one's health. Some examples of temporary withdrawal are as follows: A destitute student drops out of school until they can earn more money and marital partners agree to a separation while they seek counseling. When no suitable solution is forthcoming, despite the best efforts of the people involved, a permanent withdrawal may be more appropriate.

COMPROMISE Compromise is still another adaptive response to stress and occurs when an adjustment is made by modifying opposing ideas or behaviors. In contrast to withdrawal, compromise allows us to remain in the stressful situation but in a less active way than does the assertive approach. Compromise is most likely to be used when someone holds a higher rank or authority than another or when both participants are at a standstill. The three most common types of compromise are conformity, negotiation, and substitution.

1. Conformity as a response to stressful situations involves a change in our behavior due to another's direct influence. Let's say Nate worked as a buyer for a large corporation that has just established a more elaborate procedure for purchasing, including much more paperwork and more signatures for approval. At the outset, he detests the change. He may comply outwardly by adopting the new procedure even though he dislikes it. Or, he could conform to the new demands because he likes his superiors and coworkers enough to accommodate the added stress. Inasmuch as jobs are not easy to get or hold, Nate may take the new procedures in stride and decide that changing his attitude is the most realistic approach, because endless strife and resentment may be more stressful than accommodation or outright assertion. The key question in any type of conformity response, however, is whether the price of the compromise is worth it.

2. Negotiation is a more active and promising way to achieve compromise in many stressful situations. Negotiation means that *we make mutual concessions with another person.* Often used in the public area of labor management and political disputes, negotiation has now become more widely used at the interpersonal level among coworkers, marriage partners, and friends. Negotiation is preferable to conformity wherever possible because it involves mutual accommodation among the participants.

3. Substitution means that *we seek alternative goals with another person.* Substitution is a way to achieve compromise with another person when negotiation or conformity is not appropriate. For instance, if a woman desires to resume her college education but has small children and cannot enroll full-time, she may decide that the best alternative is to attend part-time. In this case, a substitute means was found to achieve the same goal. At other times, it may become necessary to choose a completely different substitute goal.

Compromise itself is neither good nor bad. Much depends on the relation between the satisfaction achieved and the price paid for the reduction of stress. Habitual compromise may bring more frustration and conflict than a more assertive approach. Too many people suffer in stale jobs or conflict-ridden relationships longer than necessary because compromise has become the easy way out. A life of passive accommodation to undue stress may be more stressful than an assertive or avoidant (withdrawal) approach.

Altering Your Lifestyle

We ultimately have more control over ourselves than over our environment. As a result, we may choose to modify something about ourselves or about our behaviors as a way of better managing stress. There are many possibilities, including developing greater tolerance for stress, altering our everyday habits, learning to control distressing thoughts, acquiring problem-solving skills, and seeking social support. See Table 13–3 for a listing of the ways to reduce stress by altering your life style.

INCREASE YOUR STRESS TOLERANCE To combat stress, it is often necessary to build up a greater tolerance for it. **Stress tolerance** can be defined as *the degree of stress you can handle or how long you can put up with a demanding task without acting in an irrational or disorganized way.* Many of the competent, successful people we admire are probably under a great deal more stress than we realize; they've simply acquired a high tolerance for it. Greater tolerance for pressure—deadlines, competition, criticism from others—usually comes with greater experience and skill. People in high-pressure jobs such as entrepreneurs, police, surgeons, and

Table 13–3	Ways to Alter Your Lifestyle to Reduce Stress

- Increase your stress tolerance
- Slow down your pace of life
- Learn to control distressing thoughts
- Experience more humor
- Improve your problem-solving skills
- Learn to effectively cope with stress
- Relax, but get plenty of exercise
- Seek out social support

Remember, you can use as many as of these techniques as necessary to reduce the stress in your life!

fire fighters have learned how to stay calm in the face of stress through months and years of experience on the job (Brandstätter, 2011). Our tolerance for frustration can also be improved by selecting reasonable goals and adjusting our expectations to match the realities of the immediate situation. Likewise, expecting too much of ourselves is a frequent source of frustration. Each of us is disappointed with ourselves from time to time. Rather than wallow in self-pity, it's more helpful to ask what we can do to remedy the situation and then learn from our experience for future reference.

SLOW DOWN YOUR PACE OF LIFE   You might be bringing a lot of stress on yourself by rushing around and trying to accomplish too much in too little time. A fast pace of life makes you walk, talk, conduct business, and do almost everything quickly; often resulting in stress when things don't go as planned. And as a consequence, health can suffer. For instance, people who feel pressured for time have blood pressure that is much higher than others (Gupta, 2002). Some believe that technology has contributed to an increase in the pace of life all over the world (Wajcman, 2008). After all, e-mail, text messaging, Internet access (be it on a computer, tablet, or phone) and the like allow for a frenetic pace of life where we come to expect instant gratification for many of our needs. Moreover, we tend to get frustrated when technology fails us, and patience is required. Learning how to slow down, then, can serve us well. Frequently, we could also lighten the stress by means of better time management.

LEARN TO CONTROL DISTRESSFUL THOUGHTS   Perhaps you've had the experience of glancing at the first question on a test and muttering to yourself, "If the rest of this test is this hard, I'm going to flunk it." Ironically, such negative self-monitoring interferes with your performance, making you do worse on the test. You can control distressful thoughts by using the following strategy. First, become aware of your negative, catastrophic manner of thinking. You'll probably notice how such thoughts lead you to assume the worst, such as "I'll never make it," "How did I get into this mess?" or "What the heck am I going to do now?" Second, formulate positive thoughts that are incompatible with your distressful thoughts. Some examples are "I can do it; just take it one step at a time," and "I'll keep doing my best and see how things turn out." It also helps to relax and give yourself a mental pat on the back when you've successfully managed distressing thoughts. Take a few minutes to acknowledge to yourself, "I did it; it worked. I'm pleased with the progress I'm making."

EXPERIENCE MORE HUMOR   Humor is effective at reducing stress. As such, another way to manage distressing thoughts is to replace them with humorous ones (Cann & Etzel, 2008). Do not minimize your stress by making fun of distressing events; rather, take some time to enjoy humor. Read some cartoons, go to lunch with a friend and tell jokes, recall funny events from your life. Humor is a valuable form of coping that can have physiological as well as psychological benefits for distressed individuals. When people laugh, there is a reduction in chemicals associated with stress, and the activity of the immune system frequently is enhanced. Humor can also reduce reactions to trauma and anxiety (Martin, 2001; Szabo, Ainsworth, & Danks, 2005).

IMPROVE YOUR PROBLEM-SOLVING SKILLS Most colleges and many community agencies offer a variety of workshops on topics such as assertiveness training, job-hunting skills, and stress management. Some people are wise enough to take such training as a way of bolstering their repertoire of social skills. Others seek it only after encountering problems. Once you have developed effective problem-solving skills, you can readily use **problem-focused coping**—*the individual tries to change the environment or find a solution to the problem*—to handle stressful situations. Imagine that you have a term paper due at the end of the semester, but you've never written one and you're not quite sure where to start. Going to the campus writing center (well in advance of the due date) would be an example of problem-focused coping because you are finding a solution to the problem of not knowing how to write a term paper.

LEARN TO EFFECTIVELY COPE WITH STRESS As mentioned above, one way to tackle the stressful events in your life is to use problem-focused coping. At times, however, there may be no solution to the problem you are facing. That is to say, the solution is outside of your control, such as experiencing the loss of a loved one or being in a terrible accident. For these situations, you may want to try **emotion-focused coping,** where *the individual tries to alter the emotional reaction to stress.* Each of the following is an example of this type of coping style: ignoring the problem or

Sports and hobbies are good methods for managing stress.

denying that it even exists, venting emotions to others, and trying to turn "lemons into lemonade" through positive thinking (which can help reduce negative emotions). In the past, psychologists have considered emotion-focused coping less adaptive than problem-focused coping. However, newer studies are demonstrating that emotion-focused coping is just as adaptive (Austenfeld & Stanton, 2004). In fact, positive emotions such as gratitude and love can buffer stress during crises such airplane crashes and terror attacks (Fredrickson, Tugade, Waugh, & Larkin, 2003).

RELAX, BUT GET PLENTY OF EXERCISE   Yet another way to help control stress is to make sure you have opportunities to relax, while at the same time, getting plenty of exercise (of course, it's best to not try to do both simultaneously). Virtually all forms of exercise combat stress, including jogging, weight lifting, using the elliptical, and swimming. In addition to burning away the stress of the day, exercise releases endorphins, which are naturally occurring body chemicals that make us feel good. Moreover, the physical benefits of exercise will give you the strength you need to ward off the negative mental health effects associated with stress (Barbour, Edenfield, & Blumenthal, 2007). If it's been a while since you've exercised take it slow at first to avoid injury. Of course, relaxation can also reduce stress, whether it comes in the form of listening to soothing music, getting a massage, practicing meditation, engaging in deep breathing, or reading a book. Such techniques work for teens and adults alike (Burns, Lee, & Brown, 2011). So remember, to reduce stress you can either get moving or you can stay still. The choice is yours.

SEEK OUT SOCIAL SUPPORT   Another means for finding help is simply to turn to friends. Numerous studies have shown that we manage stress and trauma more successfully when we have the support of a spouse, close friend, or support group (Scarpa, Haden, & Hurley, 2006). Having access to friends and support groups may help to alleviate stress in several ways. First, close relationships provide the opportunity to share painful feelings, which if kept to ourselves become more burdensome. Second, friends provide emotional support through their expressions of concern and affection. Third, the understanding and reassurance of our friends may bolster our self-esteem throughout the low periods of our lives. Fourth, concerned friends and support groups may provide information and advice that may help us to reach more effective solutions to our problems. This is especially true of support groups that are oriented to a particular problem, such as the death of a spouse. Fifth, friends can enhance positive experiences in our lives (Moritsugu, Wong, & Duffy, 2010). Remember, though, we don't have to turn to friends only in times of trouble; friends can enhance the experience of joy, too.

Exploration 13.4: Stress and Well-being

www.stress.org   The site for the American Institute of Stress, which is committed to developing a better understanding of how to tap into the vast innate potential that resides in each of us for preventing disease and promoting health.

Using Stress for Personal Growth

How we choose to alter our lifestyle or modify our environment is up to us. Stress management, like stress itself, is a personal matter. Each of us faces a different combination of stressful events at work and at home. The important thing to remember is that we can do something to manage stress more effectively. We don't have to be passive victims to whom things happen. Instead, we can look at ourselves as active agents who take charge of our lives. No matter how stressful the situation, there's always something we can do to reduce the stress. Keep in mind that stress can be a valuable means of self-understanding. We don't fully know what we can do until we have to do it. Each time we successfully get through a stressful situation, like a difficult course at school or a trying problem in our love life, we gain in self-confidence. Even experiences of disappointment and failure are sometimes blessings in disguise. Perhaps we weren't ready for the task at hand, or we were pursuing the wrong goals. Sometimes, a minor failure today can save us from a bigger let down later on. Finally, we can make stress work for us. Remember that stress is not synonymous with distress or stressed out. Too little stress and we become bored and lazy. Too much and we become tense, make mistakes, and get sick more easily. To get the most out of life, each of us needs to find our optimal level of stress and the types of stress we handle best. Properly managed, stress gives zest to life. A stressful situation can challenge us to try harder, evoking our best and bringing personal growth.

Chapter Summary

OH NO!—UNDERSTANDING STRESS

13.1 Explain the concept of stress.

Stress is defined as the pattern of specific and non-specific responses an organism makes to stimulus events that disturb its equilibrium and tax its ability to cope. However, stress may have beneficial as well as harmful effects, depending on the person and the situation

13.2 Identify Selye's four variations of stress.

Whereas distress refers to events that produce a harmful effect, eustress refers to events that are stimulating, motivational, or result in personal growth. Hyperstress, or excessive stress, stretches the limits of our adaptability. In contrast, hypostress, or insufficient stress, results from a lack of stimulation.

13.3 Describe the major causes of stress.

The major causes of stress are life changes, daily hassles, catastrophic events, and economic and social conditions.

13.4 Discuss the unique aspects of college that can be stressful

New social norms and customs, different peer groups, work overload, a change in lifestyle, as well as more demands placed on their time and self-control characterize college-related stress.

YIKES!—REACTIONS TO STRESS

13.5 Explain the general adaptation syndrome

According to the general adaptation syndrome, the presence of a stressor causes an alarm reaction in which the body's defenses are mobilized. If the stress continues, the body attempts to adapt to the stress (i.e., the resistance stage), but it will eventually succumb to the negative effects of stress if it lasts too long (i.e., the exhaustion stage).

13.6 Explain the connection between stress and defense mechanisms

In an effort to ward off anxiety associated with stressful events, we use defense mechanisms to deceive ourselves and distort reality.

13.7 Discuss how reactions to stress can differ

Each of us experiences the same stressful situations somewhat differently, depending on our particular personality and coping strategies. In response to stress, women, more so than men, are likely to engage in a "tend and befriend" style of coping. Those with a Type A behavior pattern experience more stress than those with a Type B behavior pattern. Remember, persistence can become detrimental when we cannot disengage from unattainable goals.

13.8 Compare psychological hardiness and resilience

Those who are psychologically hardy possess an attitude that allows them to make the most out of any situation, even those that are bad. In contrast, resilience refers to positive growth or positive adaptation following extreme adversity.

PHEW!—MANAGING STRESS

13.9 Discuss strategies for reducing stress by modifying your environment.

The three main ways of modifying the situational sources of stress are assertiveness, the preferred response; withdrawal, when appropriate; and compromise, especially negotiation, because it involves mutual accommodation among participants.

13.10 Describe different ways to reduce stress by altering your lifestyle.

Alleviating stress by altering our lifestyle includes building greater stress tolerance, changing our pace of life, controlling distressful thoughts, experiencing humor, relaxing and exercising, acquiring problem-solving and coping skills, and seeking out emotional support.

13.11 Explain how stress can promote personal growth.

Remember that stress is not synonymous with distress. Instead, to get the most out of life, each of us needs to find our optimal level of stress and use it to our advantage. A stressful situation can challenge us to try harder, evoking our best and bringing about personal growth.

Self-Test

1. Lucy worked in a chocolate factory on an assembly line. Her job was to identify misshapen truffles and remove them from the conveyor belt. At first she liked the job, but after a while the job became extremely boring. Lucy's job is most likely to cause her which of the following types of stress?
   a. hypostress
   b. eustress
   c. hyperstress
   d. distress

2. While driving home on a country road at night, a deer jumped out in front of Thomas' car. Thomas driver swerved to miss the deer. Luckily, his quick reactions in combination with a good set of brakes resulted in him missing the deer by inches. At first Thomas was freaked out by the experience, but after a few hours he was back to normal. What type of stress did Thomas experience?
   a. chronic stress
   b. hypostress
   c. distress
   d. acute stress

3. About a year ago Del lost his $100,000 job when the company he worked for went bankrupt. He quickly went through his life savings in order to pay his oldest daughter's college tuition and the cost of caring for his parents in a nursing home. Del can't sell his home because he owes more money to the bank than the house is worth. It would be another six months before Del landed a job. Based on the above information, and prior to gaining employment, Del appears to be in a state of _____.
   a. chronic stress
   b. acute stress
   c. eustress
   d. hypostress

4. As a boss, Jeff left much to be desired. He was constantly yelling his employees, had no patience when they needed help, and felt that they were always behind in their work (even when they were not). Jeff constantly reminded his employees that they needed to "beat out" their competitors in terms of company growth and profit. What type of personality does Jeff most likely possess?
   a. Type F
   b. Type B
   c. Type A
   d. Type Z

5. For the past 5 years, on April 16 Aisha relives the last moments she spent with her dying mother: She cries and becomes overwhelmed with grief. Aisha is experiencing:
   a. an anniversary reaction
   b. reactive attachment
   c. the General Adaptation Syndrome
   d. alarm reaction

6. Which of the following is not part of the General Adaptation Syndrome?
   a. alarm reaction
   b. resistance
   c. persistence
   d. exhaustion

7. Srikar had a huge organic chemistry exam coming up. Even though he was stressed, Srikar was able to study hard for the exam. According to Selye, Srikar's behavior is an example of a:
   a. a "fight" response
   b. a "flight" response
   c. persistence
   d. allostatic load

8. Arlene was stressed. Her roommate left her clothes all over their dorm room, stayed up till all hours of the night, and kept eating her stash of Oreo cookies. To help her deal with her roommate issues, Arlene talked about the emotional consequence what was going on with her best friend. Arlene engaged in:
   a. problem-focused coping
   b. sublimation
   c. reaction formation
   d. emotion-focused coping

9. A desirable way of handling stress that involves mutual accommodation among all the participants is:
   a. denial
   b. negotiation
   c. conformity
   d. withdrawal

10. Having a high degree of _____ is essential for people who face stressful situations on a daily basis.
    a. stress tolerance
    b. defense mechanisms
    c. allostatic load
    d. alarm reaction

Exercises

1. *Take an inventory of your stress.* List the most common ways you manage stress. When you think back over the past six months, did you handle stress well? If not, why not? Do you think that if you changed how you react to stress, you would manage stress better?

2. *Daily hassles.* Jot down some of the little things in everyday life that annoy or distress you, for example, a friend who is perpetually late or being stuck in traffic. Which hassles bother you the most? Select two or three of them and suggest specific ways you could make them less troublesome.

3. *Defense mechanisms.* Think of a particular situation in which you reacted defensively. Which defense mechanism(s) did you rely on? How well did you cope with this situation? If you face a similar situation in the future, would you handle it differently? How so?

4. *Describe your most stressful experience.* In a page or so, tell what made the incident or experience so stressful and how you coped with it. How well did your coping mechanisms work in this situation?

5. *Managing stress assertively.* Recall a stressful situation that you wished you had handled in a more assertive manner. How did you react in this situation? What happened as a result? If you're faced with a similar situation in the future, how could you handle it more assertively?

Questions for Self-Reflection

1. Can you recall several instances when stress had a beneficial effect?
2. Which situations do you find most distressing?
3. What are some of the "little things" that get you down?
4. Would you agree that having some control over your work activities makes them less stressful?
5. How can you tell when you're under a lot of stress?
6. When you become defensive, how do you behave?
7. Are you inclined to abuse alcohol or drugs when under stress?
8. What are some ways you've modified your environment to decrease stress?
9. Have you tried altering your lifestyle as a way of alleviating stress?
10. Do you believe that you have the traits of hardiness and resilience?

Chapter Fourteen

Understanding Mental Disorders

*L*isa, age 23, was a happy young adult with a zest for life. She had a good job in the loan department of a bank, and was on the fast-track for a promotion. But then Lisa's father died and she had to move back home live with her mother, who was also having health problems. Although Lisa was not very pleased about this arrangement she nonetheless felt it was her duty as a good daughter—and an only child—to care for her ailing mother. Just when Lisa thought her mother was improving, she too suddenly died. The surprise of this event deepened Lisa's angst. Lisa became more depressed as she tried to manage the aftermath of her mother's death, including paying the bills, negotiating with the funeral home, and settling other matters related to her parent's estate. As if this weren't enough to worry her, there were rumors at the bank that her department would shortly be downsized. With all this bad news, Lisa soon found that she had difficulty getting out of bed each morning and, shortly thereafter, began calling in sick to work. One day Lisa did not materialize for work and neither did she call in sick. After this happened, one of her closest coworkers, Archina, went over to Lisa's house and let herself in. The place was an utter mess. There was garbage overflowing the cans, newspapers piled in front of the door, and clothing strewn everywhere. Archina found Lisa in bed, tearful, glum, and uninterested in conversation; a mere shadow of the energetic person that she once knew.

PSYCHOLOGICAL DISORDERS

LEARNING OBJECTIVES

14.1 Describe the distinguishing features of a psychological disorder.
14.2 Explain what the DSM is and how disorders are diagnosed.
14.3 Know the prevalence and incidence of mental illness in the United States.

For many people, the terms *psychological disorder* and *abnormal behavior* mean the same thing; a logical assumption to make given that numerous forms of psychopathology involve thoughts, feelings, or actions that are not considered "normal." However, in the field of psychology, these terms are not synonymous. For example, some forms of depression are too common to be labeled

---

BOX 14–1   Did you know that …

- Mental illness is more common than cancer, heart disease, or diabetes.
- Around 50 percent of all individuals will develop some form of mental illness during their life.
- Worldwide, nearly 154 million people suffer from depression and 106 million meet the criteria for substance abuse.
- The most common cause of disability among individuals in the United States, Canada, and Western Europe is mental illness.
- In the United States, the economic cost of mental illness (e.g., disability payments, poor productivity, social servicers, etc.) is about $300 billion per year.

Source: Based on "Startling Statistics About Mental Illness," from ASHA International website, 2012.

---

abnormal or statistically "out of the normal" but are nevertheless classified as psychological disorders. Other behaviors may be considered socially deviant or unusual, such as running nude across the field at a soccer game, without being considered a form of psychopathology. Consequently, we'll begin by looking at some of the common standards used in defining psychological disorders. But first, Box 14–2 presents information about the word insanity, which as it turns out, is a legal term, and not a psychological one.

BOX 14–2   Focus on Psychology: Insanity

Believing he was chosen to determine who lived and who died, Anders Behring Breivik killed 77 people in a bomb and gun rampage in Norway in the summer of 2011. He was declared insane, and under Norwegian law could not be sentenced to prison (Fouche & Klesty, 2011). More than two decades earlier, and thousands of miles away, Jeffrey Dahmer murdered 17 boys and men over the course of 13 years. His horrific crimes included sedating, strangling, and eating parts of his victims, as well as having sex with their corpses. Dahmer even attempted to turn many of his victims into living "zombies" by pouring acid or boiling water into holes he drilled into their heads. Dahmer was convicted of 15 murders and sentenced to 15 life sentences in prison; a jury rejected the claim that Dahmer was insane (Davis, 1995). Does the fact that Breivik was declared insane while Dahmer was not surprise you?

Contrary to popular belief, the word **insane** is not a psychological term; it is in fact a legal one. Although the definitions of insanity vary somewhat by state, and by country, here's the gist, being insane means that *a defendant cannot tell right from wrong when committing a crime nor can they resist impulses to act in antisocial ways*. It is important to realize that a person can be diagnosed with a psychological disorder while at the same time being considered legally sane. Attempts to have a defendant declared legally insane (i.e., the insanity defense) are rarely used in criminal court, only occurring in about 1 percent of all cases. The reason for its infrequent use is simple: in order to be declared insane the defendant must admit guilt. Moreover, when used in criminal proceedings, the insanity defense is not very successful, resulting in an acquittal only 25 percent of the time (Caplan, 2011).

Despite the rarity of its use, and general lack of success in court, the insanity defense is disliked by the general public. After all, when found *not guilty by reason of insanity,* the defendant is remanded into the custody of mental health professionals, and not the justice system. Adding to the dislike is the fact that mental health professions, and not a parole board, determine when the defendant (now a patient) is no longer considered a danger to the public and can therefore be released into the general population. Due to concerns that defendants are "getting away" with their crimes when found *non-guilty by reason of insanity*, many states have added the plea/verdict *guilty but mentally ill.* When found guilty but mentally ill, the defendant still goes to a mental health facility, but the length of stay is determined by a judge's sentence, and not the opinion of mental health professionals (Melville & Narmark, 2002).

What Are Psychological Disorders?

You may be surprised to know that there is no precise and universally agreed-on standard that identifies a psychological disorder or, for that matter, distinguishes between abnormal and normal behavior. Despite such ambiguities, patterns of behavior, thought, and emotion, can, and do, cluster together, allowing the identification of medically agreed upon psychological disorders. Probably the most widely accepted guide in these matters is the *Diagnostic and Statistical Manual of Mental Disorders* (DSM) published by the American Psychiatric Association. Because of new research findings, better diagnostic techniques, and social change, the content of the DSM goes under periodic review. To that end, the DSM has undergone numerous revisions since 1952, the most recent scheduled to occur within the next year or so with the publication of the DSM-5 (American Psychiatric Association, 2012). For now, let us define a **psychological disorder** as a *clinically significant behavioral or psychological pattern that is associated with* (1) *personal distress;* (2) *disability or impairment in one or more important areas of functioning, e.g., maladaptive behaviors;* (3) *significantly increased risk of suffering disability, pain, or death; and* (4) *the violation of social norms.*

PERSONAL DISTRESS   As noted in the definition, a major factor in diagnosing a psychological disorder is the individual's level of **personal distress**, which refers to *intense or chronic negative self-awareness that interferes with one's sense of well-being or functioning.* For instance, someone with a chronic fear of heights or a marked change in mood might meet the criteria for mental illness. On the other hand, people who behave in an unusual or eccentric way (such as converting empty cat food cans into works of art) but are otherwise happy and functional would probably not be so diagnosed. As useful as this standard of personal distress is, it isn't sufficiently comprehensive to help us define or diagnose psychopathology.

MALADAPTIVE BEHAVIOR   Another important feature in defining a psychological disorder is **maladaptive behavior**—*significant impairment in one or more areas of psychological functioning, especially the ability to work and to get along with others.* Here, the focus is on behavior that is relevant to daily living. People with mental illness usually suffer from a significant impairment in their ability to work, to care for themselves, or to get along with family and friends. For example, it was Lisa's eventual inability to care for herself and her apartment as well as her inability to get out of bed and go to work that led others to believe she was experiencing emotional problems.

DISABILITY OR IMPAIRMENT   A third issue of relevance is the individual's *increased risk for suffering disability, pain, or death.* Individuals who exhibit maladaptive behaviors and impairments in daily living put themselves at risk for harm. Case in point, people who are addicted to methamphetamines often fail to take care of their physical health (Fass, Calhoun, Glaser, & Yanosky, 2009). Lisa, too, had stopped taking care of herself; she did not take showers, comb her hair, brush her teeth, nor maintain a healthy diet. Lisa did not keep her apartment clean and so allowed the trash to pile up as she sank deeper and deeper into depression.

SOCIAL NORMS   Another dimension of mental disorder is *the violation of social norms.* **Social norms** are *generalized expectations regarding appropriate behavior in a given situation or society.* People in every society live by rules of what is acceptable and unacceptable. For example, whereas it is considered appropriate to hold the hand of your significant other while walking through the mall, society frowns upon that same couple having sex in the middle of the food court. When an individual repeatedly violates commonly accepted social norms, that person may be considered to have a psychological disorder, if other conditions also prevail. At times, such rule violations can result in the loss of freedom and control for the individual because others fear the individual will hurt themselves or others. In fact, this fear factor can lead to stigmatization

---

BOX 14–3 Focus on Wellness: Stigma

Stigma is not just a matter of using the wrong word. Stigma is about disrespect. **Stigma** is *the use of negative labels to identify a person living with a mental disorder or with another distinguishing feature and who you believe differs from you.* Stigma is a barrier, because it causes exclusion, rejection, and devaluation of the stigmatized individual (Weiss & Ramakrishna, 2006). Fear of stigma, and the resulting discrimination, discourages individuals and their families from getting the help they need (Gary, 2005). For example, an estimated 26 percent of the U.S. population experiences a mental disorder in any given year, but almost half of these individuals do not seek treatment. The following illustrates the power of stigmas related to mental illness: (1) People would rather tell employers they committed a petty crime and served time in jail than admit to having been in a psychiatric hospital; (2) Stigma can lead to fear, mistrust, and violence against people (and their families) living with a mental disorder; and (3) Stigma can cause families and friends to turn their backs on people with mental illness (Abdullah & Brown, 2011).

The information below encourages the use of positive images to refer to people with mental disorders and underscores the reality that mental disorders can be successfully treated:

Do's

- Do use respectful language.
- Do emphasize abilities, not limitations.
- Do tell someone if they express a stigmatizing attitude.

Don'ts

- Don't portray successful persons with disabilities as superhuman.
- Don't use generic labels such as *retarded* or *mentally ill.*
- Don't use terms such as *crazy, lunatic, manic-depressive,* or *slow-functioning.*

---

of those with psychological disorders. Despite increased availability of information on mental disorders, stigma against those who suffer it is still commonplace (Hinshaw & Stier, 2008). You can read more about stigma in Box 14–3.

Exploration 14.1: Stigma

stopstigma.samhsa.gov   An online resource center to designed to promote acceptance, dignity, and social inclusion associated with mental health.

VARIATIONS IN MENTAL ILLNESS ACROSS TIME AND CULTURE As the history of psychology has demonstrated, the definition of mental illness can vary across time and culture. For example, up until 1974 homosexuality was considered a diagnosable psychological disorder; it no longer is (Bayer, 1987). Although "hearing voices" is considered symptomatic of mental illness in modern Western culture, among traditional North American Indians, hearing the voices of deceased relatives is not (Kleinman & Good, 1985). Similarly, in certain Middle Eastern cultures, hearing voices and having visions are both considered normal (Al-Issa, 1995). The presence of **culture-bound syndromes**—*sets of symptoms much more common in some societies than in others*—also demonstrates the difficulties of defining psychopathology. Case in point, *grisi siknis,* which is characterized by headache, anxiety, anger, and frenzied, aimless running, is a psychological disorder primarily found in Central America (Dennis, 1985).

How Are Disorders Classified?

The DSM classifies, defines, and describes over 200 psychological disorders, using practical criteria as the basis of classification. To arrive at a **diagnosis**—*in which the problem is* *classified within a set of recognized categories of abnormal behavior*—the clinician compares the behavior of the "patient" with the description in the manual and then selects the label of the description that best fits the problem. The purpose is to provide an accurate description of the person's overall problem and functioning, along with a prediction for the course of the disorder, which helps during treatment. The diagnosis also helps professionals communicate with and understand one another.

Throughout the DSM, the emphasis is on classifying behavior patterns, *not* people, as is often thought. Thus, the manual refers to "people who exhibit the symptoms of schizophrenia" rather than to "schizophrenics." Also, the terminology refers to "mental health professionals" and "clinicians" instead of "psychiatrists," thereby acknowledging the broader range of professionals who deal with people with psychological disorders. Finally, the emphasis is on describing rather than interpreting psychological disorders, especially when the causal factors are unknown. Thus, the DSM gives clinicians a practical, behavioral approach to dealing with people exhibiting symptoms of mental illness (Townsend, 2012).

How Common Are Psychological Disorders?

INCIDENCE AND PREVALENCE   Information about the **incidence** (i.e., *new cases this year*) and **prevalence** (i.e., *the total number of active cases*) of psychological disorders primarily comes from in-depth surveys of the general population, along with admission figures to various mental health facilities such as psychiatric hospitals and community mental health clinics. The data from these sources tells us that approximately 26 percent U.S. adults currently have a diagnosable psychological disorder and close to 50 percent will develop one before they die. However, only 5 percent of Americans will develop a **serious mental disorder**, which *substantially interferes with or limits one or more of major life activities*. Table 14–1 provides information on the incidence and prevalence of some common psychological disorders in the United States. Worldwide, over 450 million people suffer from a psychological disorder, and close to 1 million people commit suicide every year. Moreover, mental illness ranks second after cardiovascular maladies in the **global burden of diseases,** which is *a measure of years of life lost to disability throughout the world* (World Health Organization [WHO], 2012).

Exploration 14.2: Prevalence of Mental Disorders

www.nimh.nih.gov/statistics/index.shtml   Here you can find out the scope of psychological disorders and treatment in the United States.

Table 14–1	Estimated Incidence and Lifetime Prevalence of Some Psychological Disorders in the Adult Population (18 and older) of the United States	
Disorder	**Last 12 Mo**	**Lifetime Prevalence**
Anxiety	42.5 million	67.6 million
Mood	22.3 million	48.8 million
Personality	21.3 million	Not Available
Schizophrenia	2.6 million	Not Available

Source: Data from "Statistics," from National Institute of Mental Health website, 2012.

ISSUES OF AGE, GENDER, AND CULTURE   People who have a psychological disorder usually experience their first symptoms by early adulthood, with three-fourths reporting their first symptoms by age 24. However, symptoms of certain disorders (discussed below), such as obsessive-compulsive behavior, bipolar disorder, and schizophrenia appear somewhat earlier, at a median age near 20 (Keller, 2008). It is worth noting, however, that gender and cultural differences influence the prevalence of mental illness. Although men and women are equally likely to suffer from psychological disorders, the patterns of disorders differ somewhat between the sexes. Women suffer more from phobias and depression; and men are more apt to abuse alcohol and drugs and exhibit long-term antisocial behavior (WHO, 2012). At the same time, women are twice as likely as men to seek help, which may have given the mistaken impression in the past that women were more troubled by mental illness than men. Additionally, the frequency of mental disorders varies from culture to culture (NIMH, 2007b). For instance, the prevalence of depression is low in China and many parts of Africa—just the opposite of its occurrence in the United States. One explanation is that in Western (or individualistic) societies, individuals are more likely to be held personally responsible for their failures and misfortunes and thus may be more susceptible to depression as they turn their focus inward to their own perceived deficits.

Putting Mental Health in Perspective

Each year the total cost of the treatment and other services associated with mental illness, including disability support and lost earnings, tally over $300 billion in the United States alone (Kessler, Berglund, Demler, Jin, & Walters, 2005; NIMH, 2012). As you can see, mental health is fundamental to our mental and physical well-being, as well as our overall level of productivity. It is the basis for successful contributions to family, community, and society. Throughout the life span, mental health is the wellspring of thinking and communication skills, learning, resilience, and self-esteem. It is all too easy to dismiss the value of mental health until problems appear.

In the rest of this chapter, we'll describe two different sets of disorders: (1) the more common disorders, such as the anxiety disorders, mood disorders, and personality disorders; and (2) the more serious but less common disorders such as schizophrenia. It is important to note that while this chapter can raise your awareness of psychological problems, it should not be used to *diagnosis* psychopathology within yourself or others. When concerns arise, please seek out an appropriate mental health professional.

ANXIETY DISORDERS

LEARNING OBJECTIVES

14.4 Know the definition of an anxiety disorder.
14.5 Distinguish between five common classes of anxiety disorders.

Whether because of work, relationships, economics, and so forth, most of us experience anxiety (or fear) repeatedly throughout our lifetime. Such reactions are a natural emotional response to stress and a normal part of life (Monroe & Reid, 2009). Although some anxiety can be energizing, extremely high levels of it can be immobilizing. High anxiety can prevent people from leaving their homes. It can also cause them to block out daily news events, avoid interacting with others, refuse to answer the phone, and in general, not enjoy everyday life. In individuals with **anxiety disorders,** *which are characterized by symptoms of excessive or inappropriate anxiety or attempts to escape from such anxiety,* the anxiety is out of all proportion to the stressful situation. In fact, anxiety may occur in the absence of any specific danger. There are five major types of anxiety disorders: generalized anxiety disorder, panic disorder, phobias, obsessive-compulsive disorder, and posttraumatic stress disorder. Let's review each of these in detail.

Exploration 14.3: Psychological Disorders I

www.mentalhelp.net   A good general resource for information on a variety of disorders. Here you'll find chat rooms, book lists, possibilities for participating in research projects, and so forth.

Generalized Anxiety Disorder

The main characteristic of **generalized anxiety disorder** is a persistent sense of "free-floating" anxiety, meaning that it follows the individual wherever they go. People who are chronically anxious can't say what they are afraid of; all they know is that they feel on edge most of the time. They generally worry a lot, anticipate that something bad is going to happen, and find it hard to concentrate or make decisions. People with this disorder may also develop headaches, muscular tension, indigestion, a strained face, and fidgeting. Frequently, they become apprehensive about their anxiety and fear their condition will cause ulcers or a heart attack or make them "go crazy" (Llera & Newman, 2010).

Panic Disorder

Anxious people can also suffer from **panic disorder,** *characterized by the repeated occurrence of severe panic* (commonly referred to as a panic attack). These terrifying attacks occur in the absence of a feared situation and usually last 15 to 30 minutes, but can last as long as an hour (Taylor, 2010). In some instances, panic attacks occur in response to a specific situation, such as driving in city traffic or speaking publicly. At other times, the panic does not seem to be produced by a specific instigator, it just happens. During a panic attack, anxiety increases to an almost intolerable level. The individual breaks out in a cold sweat, feels dizzy, exhibits an elevated heart, and may even have difficulty breathing. Victims almost always have a feeling of inescapable doom, as if they won't make it to safety or will die. Because panic attacks are unpredictable, they often create additional anxiety, and the victims avoid certain situations in which they fear losing control, being helpless, or experiencing panic. To determine your own general level of anxiety, try the scale in Activity 14–1.

Phobias

Most of us experience an irrational avoidance of selected objects, such as spiders or snakes, but it usually has no major impact on our lives. In contrast, when the avoidance becomes a *significant* source of distress to the individual and interferes with everyday behavior, the diagnosis of a phobic disorder may be warranted. **Phobic disorders** are *characterized by a persistent and irrational fear of a specific object or activity, accompanied by a compelling desire to avoid it.* There are several major types of phobic disorders: specific phobia, social phobia, and agoraphobia.

SPECIFIC PHOBIAS   **Specific phobias**—*excessive fear of specific objects or situations*—are the most common type of phobia in the general population. Frequently feared objects include animals, particularly dogs, snakes, and insects. Other specific phobias are **acrophobia,** *the fear of heights,* and **claustrophobia,** *the fear of closed places.* Most specific phobias originate in childhood and disappear without treatment. However, the more intense fears that persist into adulthood generally don't disappear without professional help (Reuther, Davis, Grills-Taquechel, & Zlomke, 2011).

SOCIAL PHOBIA   **Social phobia** is an extreme form of shyness that can interfere with an individual's daily life and *involves a chronic, irrational fear of and a compelling desire to avoid situations where they may be scrutinized.* If confronted with the necessity of entering a social situation, the person experiences marked anxiety and attempts to stay clear of it. Examples include an intense fear of speaking, performing, eating, or going to the bathroom in public, as well as writing in the presence of others. Although this type of disorder itself is rarely incapacitating,

---

ACTIVITY 14–1

How Anxious Are You?

The following scale was developed for this book, and as such is not scientific. It is designed for you to think about your characteristic level of anxiety. Place a check mark next to each statement that is typical or characteristic of you:

_____ I often have a sense of dread or impending doom but cannot always identify what it is I fear.

_____ I find that I am afraid of things others do not seem to be afraid of.

_____ My friends think I worry more than they do about examinations, meeting deadlines, and so forth.

_____ I seem to have more stomachaches, headaches, and other signs of anxiety than others do.

_____ I frequently feel restless and tense and do not sleep as well as I should.

_____ Many times, I try to avoid situations that cause me anxiety, such as public speaking or meeting strangers.

_____ I probably perspire and have rapid heartbeats when it is inappropriate (e.g., when I have not been exercising).

_____ Decisions, especially important decisions, are usually difficult for me to make.

_____ Compared to others, I feel that I have difficulty concentrating on even the simplest of tasks.

_____ My friends are not as afraid as I am of everyday situations, such as becoming lost in a new part of a city.

SCORING: Add up the number of check marks. The highest score you can receive is 10. If you scored 7 or higher, you might want to consider whether you have high anxiety levels and whether these high levels interfere with your life. If you decide "yes," you should explore ways to reduce your anxiety. Professional help or some of the techniques in the following chapter on psychotherapy may prove useful.

---

it does result in considerable inconvenience, such as avoiding a trip that involves the use of a public lavatory. Also, in an effort to relieve their anxiety, individuals with this disorder may "self-medicate," using alcohol or drugs to calm themselves down (Robinson, Sareen, Cox, & Bolton, 2011).

AGORAPHOBIA **Agoraphobia** is *a cluster of different fears, all of which evoke intense anxiety about crowds or open spaces,* such as stores, elevators, tunnels, and public transportation. Agoraphobia typically produces a severe phobic reaction and the one for which people most often seek treatment. This type of phobia tends to occur in the late teens or early 20s, although it can occur later in life. During outbreaks of this phobia, sufferers refuse to go outside and become housebound. When they finally do go out, they take great care to avoid fear-inducing situations (Wittchen, Gloster, Beesdo-Baum, Fava, & Craske, 2010). Box 14–4 presents the names and descriptions of other types of phobias.

BOX 14-4 *Focus on Wellness: Phobias*

Acrophobia—fear of heights

Coulrophobia—fear of clowns

Ergophobia—fear of work

Hypegiaphobia—fear of responsibility

Mysophobia—fear of dirt

Ophidiophobia—fear of snakes

Triskaidekaphobia—fear of the number 13

Autophobia—fear of oneself

Decidophobia—fear of making decisions

Gamophobia—fear of marriage

Monophobia—fear of being alone

Nyctophobia—fear of darkness

Topophobia—fear of performing (stage fright)

Zoophobia—fear of animals

Obsessive-Compulsive Disorder

Have you ever had a song stuck in your heard for a short period of time? Annoying wasn't it? When this happens, if there was a simple action that you could do that would stop the song from "playing" (such as snapping your fingers), odds are you would do it. Now think what it would be like to have the same song stuck in your head hundreds of times a day and snapping your fingers each time to make it stop. You've just entered the world of an individual suffering from an obsessive-compulsive disorder. The essential features of **obsessive-compulsive disorder** (OCD) involve **obsessions** (*involuntary dwelling on an unwelcome thought*) *and* **compulsions** (*the involuntary repetition of an unnecessary act*).

Obsessions often involve the fear of being contaminated and contracting a disease (e.g., being infected by germs), the fear of causing harm (e.g., not turning off a stove or locking the doors), superstitions (e.g., must do everything a certain number of times), and the need for order or perfection (e.g., the fringes on a rug, every single one of them, must be aligned). The anxiety caused by such intrusive and unwanted thoughts, causes the individual to engage in repetitive or ritualistic behaviors to make them go away. Performing these compulsive acts can also prevent

Police, fire crews, and other first responders are more likely than those not exposed to traumatic events to suffer from post-traumatic stress disorder.

the obsessive thoughts from reoccurring. Such compulsions tend to fall into several categories: *hoarders,* who collect almost anything and cannot get rid of it; *repeaters,* who feel they must repeat a behavior a set number of times; and *orderers,* who want their possessions in certain places and arranged in certain ways. The cycle of OCD can take up hours each day, thus significantly interfering with the ability to engage in normal activities (Daitch, 2011).

Posttraumatic Stress Disorder

In the previous chapter, **posttraumatic stress disorder** (PTSD) was briefly reviewed. In short, (PTSD) is a severe anxiety disorder characterized by symptoms of anxiety and avoidance behavior; this disorder results from an unusually stressful event such as being physically or sexually assaulted. PTSD can also be caused by witnessing the devastation of war, natural disasters, plane crashes, terrorism, horrific car accidents, and murders. As this list indicates, PTSD is caused by both the experience of being in a trauma, as well as by witnessing the after effects of one. Thus, people in certain professions are more likely to develop PTSD than others, with soldiers, fire and police personnel, and rescue and medical workers being particularly vulnerable (Robinaugh et al., 2011). Moreover, the extensive viewing of traumatic events on TV, such as the after effects of school shootings, can cause PTSD (Marshall et al., 2007).

PTSD is commonly typified by intense fear, flashbacks (reliving the event over and over again), and nightmares. Other signs that a person is suffering from PTSD include mood swings, irritability, depression, crying often, limited attention span, difficulty concentrating, confusion, poor work or school performance, self-medication with drugs or alcohol, headaches, sleep disturbance, and stomach problems among others (Corales, 2005).

MOOD DISORDERS

LEARNING OBJECTIVES

14.6 Explain the difference between depressive disorders and bipolar disorder.
14.7 Distinguish between three types of depressive disorders.
14.8 List the warning signs of suicide.

Most of us go through periods of time when nothing seems to go right. We may say we're "depressed," but we're usually not suffering from a diagnosable psychological disorder. Our mood is one of mild dejection or sadness that generally passes within a matter of days. In contrast, when the *emotional disturbance is more severe and persistent* it becomes a **mood disorder**, for which there are two main types: depressive disorders and bipolar disorder. Whereas depressive disorders are characterized by a pervasive negative emotional state, bipolar disorders involve exaggerated mood swings, alternating between severe depression and extreme elation. Let's take a look at each.

Depressive Disorders

MAJOR DEPRESSION **Major depression** is *characterized by intense and unrealistic sadness as well feelings of worthlessness.* In addition to these symptoms, those with major depression may also experience decreased energy, loss of interest in everyday activities, poor appetite, feelings of inadequacy, periods of crying, and a pessimistic attitude. In many instances, people experience the symptoms of depression only to a moderate degree, so they may continue their everyday activities. For others, major depression severely impedes their ability to function at work and at home, ultimately resulting in a period of hospitalization (Hanson et al., 2005). In such instances, even the simple getting out of bed can become incredibly difficult. Noteworthy is the fact that more than half of those who experience one episode of major depression will eventually have another within two years (Schrof & Schultz, 1999).

Major depression has been attributed to a variety of causes, ranging from biological factors such as genes and biochemical processes to social and cultural influences. For instance, major depression tends to run in families, suggesting that biological vulnerability can be inherited. However, major depression can also occur in people who have no family history of depression. Whether inherited or not, major depressive disorder is often associated with changes in brain structures or brain function. Cognitive theorists point out that people can make themselves depressed by negative thinking or pessimistic cognitive styles (Ingram, Atchley, & Segal, 2011).

Interestingly, women are 70 percent more likely than men to develop depression in their lifetime (NIMH, 2012). Once again, biological influences (such as hormone levels) appear to play role in this. For instance, brain imaging research has also shown that the brain region affected by depression is eight times larger in women than in men (Foote & Seibert, 1999). Just as important to major depression, however, are differences between men and women in social roles and responsibilities, as well as in stress management. Case in point, working and married women juggle multiple tasks and suffer from more work overload than men (Mayo Clinic, 2002). In fact, one study demonstrated that there is a relationship between amount of household strain, housework performed, and depressive symptoms. Women also do more childcare than men. Thus, as a result of gender differences in social roles and responsibilities, women end up carrying a greater stress burden than men. Moreover, women and men also learn to manage stress and emotions in different ways. For instance, in contrast to men, women may be less inclined to act on their problems and more inclined to dwell (ruminate) on them (Nolen-Hoeksema, 2008). These and other factors, then, are likely to contribute to the significantly higher rates of major depression in women than in men.

SEASONAL AFFECTIVE DISORDER Some people are more vulnerable to *depression at certain times of the year, especially the winter months.* They suffer from a peculiar mood disorder commonly labeled **SAD—seasonal affective disorder.** The causes remain unclear. Because more than two-thirds of those with this syndrome have a close relative with a mood disorder, genetic factors are suspected. Another theory is that gloomy winter weather disturbs the body's natural clock, affecting the production of serotonin and melatonin. During darkness, the pineal gland in the brain secretes larger amounts of the hormone melatonin, associated with drowsiness and lethargy. Light suppresses the secretion of this chemical. Although the extra melatonin secreted in winter doesn't disturb the body's chemical balance in most people, those with SAD may suffer from an overdose of this hormone. Interestingly, not everyone living in winter darkness suffers from SAD. Icelanders, for example, have lower levels of this form of depression (Raymond, 2000). Today, people with SAD are finding relief with light therapy. During the winter months, they spend time each day in front of a sun-box, a device fitted with powerful fluorescent lights that emit the full spectrum of natural daylight (Mallikarjun, 2005).

DYSTHYMIC DISORDER Dysthymia consists of long-term mild depression that does not disable. Rather, it can keep one from feeling really good or from functioning at one's best; think Eeyore, from *Winnie the Pooh.* As you might expect, the symptoms of dysthymia are similar to major depression (e.g., sadness, low energy, pessimistic outlook, low self-esteem) only less severe. In order to receive a diagnosis of dysthymia, the aforementioned symptoms need to be present for at least two years (Gureje, 2011).

Bipolar Disorder

Some people experience *an alternation of elated and depressive moods, popularly known as manic depression* but now termed **bipolar disorder.** Usually, this disorder first appears as **mania,** in which *the individual exhibits symptoms such as euphoria and excitement, increased social activity, talkativeness, sleeplessness, and reckless behavior.* While in a manic phase, individuals engage in behaviors that can be detrimental to relationships (becoming aggressive or hyper-sexual), their financial status (spending money they do not have), and self-esteem (feeling embarrassed and remorseful about their behavior once the mania has passed). Manic episodes are then followed by a period of severe depression; characterized by hopelessness and despair.

People who take their own lives or attempt to do so are very often depressed and see suicide as the only answer to life's problems.

In addition to the manic episodes, there are other characteristics that distinguish bipolar disorder from major depression. First, bipolar disorder is not as common as major depression, occurring three times less often. Second, bipolar disorder is equally prevalent among men and women. Third, although married people are less susceptible to major depression, they enjoy no such advantage in regard to bipolar disorder. Fourth, although major depression can occur at any time in life, bipolar disorder usually appears before the age of 30. And bipolar episodes tend to be briefer and more frequent than periods of major depression. Finally, bipolar disorder is more likely to run in families than major depression, suggesting that genes are more prominent in the former than in the latter (Perry, 2005).

Suicide

INCIDENCE   Suicide is more common than homicide in the United States. In fact, there are nearly twice as many suicides as homicides. Additionally, suicide outranks AIDS/HIV deaths by about three to one (NIMH, 2012). Among 15- to 24-year olds, suicide is the third leading cause of mortality, accounting for just over 12 percent of deaths each year. Especially alarming is the fact that the suicide rate for young people in this age group has tripled in the last 30 years. However, some of the highest suicide rates are for seniors over 65 (14.3 deaths per 100,000 people) and for White men aged 85 or older (47 deaths per 100,000 people). Although women attempt suicide twice as often as men, men are four times more likely than women to die as a result of the attempt, accounting for nearly 80 percent of all suicides. Men "complete" more suicides than women, partly because their attempts tend to use swifter and more violent means, such as a gun. In contrast, women are more likely to take pills/poison or turn on gas, which often allows time for intervention. With regards to race, suicide rates are highest for Native Americans (14.3 deaths per 100,000 people) and Whites (13.5 deaths per 100,000 people), doubling those of most other races (National Center for Health Statistics, 2012).

Exploration 14.4: Suicide

www.suicide.org   A valuable site on suicide, its warning signs, misconceptions about suicide, and how survivors can better cope with their loss. The website also offers crisis center contact information.

Accurate figures on suicide are even more difficult to obtain than statistics on depression. One reason is that many people who commit suicide prefer to make their deaths look accidental. If the truth were known, as many as one out of six single-car accidents might actually be a suicide. Despite incomplete statistics, official figures indicate that about 34,000 people commit suicide each year in the United States. About every five minutes someone takes his or her life. If suicide *attempts* are included, someone somewhere is contemplating self-destruction every minute. Overall, there is one suicide for every 25 attempts (National Center for Health Statistics, 2012).

BOX 14–5   Focus on Wellness: Music and Suicide

Suicidal Themes in Music

Songs about suicide are found in nearly all genres of music, including rap, country, and opera (Stack, 2002; Stack & Gundlach, 1992). However, it is heavy metal that has been consistently singled out as a potential cause of suicide during adolescence. For many, newspaper reports of teens committing suicide after listening to heavy metal (e.g., Ozzy Osbourne's "Suicide Solution") crystallized the danger associated with consuming suicide-themed music (Baker & Bor, 2008). After all, the themes of alienation, death, and despair, which frequent many heavy metal songs, would seem to put adolescents' mental health at risk (Recours, Aussaguel, & Trujillo, 2009). For instance, lyrics in the Alice in Chains' song "Dirt" extol suicidal thoughts: "I want to taste dirty, a stinging pistol, in my mouth, on my tongue; I want you to scrape me from the walls and go crazy like you've made me." Such lyrics are shocking and disturbing, but do they influence suicidal behavior?

Is there a Connection between Music and Suicide?

During the 1990s, the American Academy of Child and Adolescent Psychiatry recommended that youth demonstrating a preoccupation with heavy metal music with destructive themes, such as death and suicide, undergo psychiatric evaluation (Alessi, Huang, James, Ying, & Chowhan, 1992). At that time, the basis for a medical decision to hospitalize a suicidal adolescent often included an evaluation of the adolescent's musical preferences (Rosenbaum & Prinsky, 1991). Two decades later, a preference for heavy metal music is no longer listed as a significant risk factor for suicide (Scheel & Westefeld, 1999).

Nevertheless, a preference for musical themes of death and suicide, such as those mentioned above, are considered relevant to suicidal behavior because the liking of themes of death and self-destruction may indicate the presence of **suicidal ideation** which *refers to both nonspecific thoughts of death and specific thoughts involving the intent to die accompanied by a plan of action*. Thus, an adolescent's focus on the death or suicide-related lyrical content in heavy metal music could be thought of as suicidal ideation involving nonspecific death thoughts. However, it is important to remember that, although suicidal ideation is predictive of suicidal behavior, its presence does not mean that a suicide attempt is imminent (Rustad, Small, Jobes, Safer, & Peterson, 2003).

WHY PEOPLE COMMIT SUICIDE It probably comes as no surprise to learn that people who take their own lives, or attempt to do so, are very often depressed (Williams, Crane, Barnhofer, van der Does, & Segal, 2006); thus, our discussion of suicide is subsumed under the topic of mood disorders. However, more than 90 percent of those who attempt suicide have major depression *or* one of the following diagnoses: bipolar disorder, alcohol and/or drug abuse, PTSD, eating disorders, personality disorders and schizophrenia (AFSP.org, 2012). Of note, suicide is more prevalent in affluent societies, so much so that it has been described as a disease of civilization. At the level of individual behavior, many possible motives have been suggested: escaping from pain or stress, trying to eliminate unacceptable feelings, turning aggression inward, punishing others by making them feel guilty, and acting impulsively on momentary feelings of desperation. Suicidal people often suffer from "tunnel vision"—the misperception that suicide is the *only* alternative to seemingly unsolvable problems in living. The tragedy is that such problems are often transitory, whereas the solution of suicide is permanent (Simon, 2011). Curiously, severely depressed people are more likely to take their lives *as their situations improve.* When they are most depressed, they may not have sufficient energy to take their own lives. In addition, autopsies of suicide victims have found abnormally low levels of **serotonin**—*a neurotransmitter that has been linked to depression*—suggesting that biochemical deficiencies may play a role in suicide. Box 14–6 alerts you to some of the other warning signs of an impending suicide.

SUICIDE PREVENTION For decades, the high-profile suicides of celebrities such as Ernest Hemingway (1961), Freddie Prinz (1977), Kurt Cobain (1994), and Richard Jeni (2007), as well as more recent suicides by teenage victims of bullying, have reminded the public about the importance of suicide prevention. Environmental approaches include tightening control of prescription sedatives, restricting gun purchases through legislation, and increasing protective measures (e.g., putting fencing around the observation platform of the Empire State Building in New York City). Another approach is to increase community awareness and resources for dealing with suicide. Many communities now have suicide and crisis intervention hotlines available 24 hours a day. Volunteers at these crisis services usually have specific goals, such as determining the seriousness of the suicide threat, establishing and conveying empathy, understanding of the caller's problems, describing available resources, and getting some sort of agreement that the caller will seek help. One such crisis center, the National Suicide Prevention Lifeline, can be reached at 1-800-273-8255.

BOX 14–6 **Focus on Health Care: Warning Signs of Suicide**

- Expression of suicidal thoughts or a preoccupation with death
- Prior suicide attempts
- Death of a close friend or family member
- Giving away prized possessions
- Depression
- Despair over a chronic illness
- Social isolation
- Change in sleeping and eating habits
- Marked personality changes
- Abuse of alcohol or drugs
- Sense of hopelessness
- Neglect of personal welfare
- Self-inflicted injury or other reckless behavior
- Divorce or stress in the family
- Job loss or loss of esteem or sense of security

Exploration 14.5: Suicide Prevention

www.suicidepreventionlifeline.org   Here you can find general information about suicide as well as contact information for those currently in crisis and contemplating suicide. Online chat with a crisis counselor is also available.

WHAT TO DO WHEN SOMEONE YOU KNOW IS SUICIDAL   Contrary to the myth that people who threaten to kill themselves seldom do so, most people who commit suicide express some suicidal intent, directly or indirectly, several months prior to their deaths. It helps to recognize the warning signs, as noted in Box 14–6. If you notice the warning signals of suicide in a family member or friend, do your best to see that he or she gets professional help. Here are some tips from the American Foundation for Suicide Prevention (AFSP) on what you can do when you first find out that someone you know is suicidal.

- Talk to the person you are concerned about (even if they are reluctant) and let him or her know you care and understand about what they are going through.
- Listen to what the person has to say and then tell him or her that their suicidal feelings are temporary, that their depression can be treated, and that their problems can be solved. Note that their feelings won't "just pass," and that they'll need help getting through this. Avoid saying things like, "You have so much to live for," or "Your suicide will hurt your family."
- Ask the person if they have a specific plan for committing suicide and about any preparations he or she has already made. As long as it is safe to do so, try to remove any firearms, drugs, or sharp objects that could be used for suicide.
- Immediately get profession help. Go with the person to a crisis center or an emergency room. At the very least contact a suicide prevention hotline via phone or online chat. Most importantly, do not leave the person alone. If they refuse to talk with someone or go the hospital, you may need to call the police
- Follow-up with the person to make sure they are going to counseling and taking medications that may have been prescribed (AFSP.org, 2012).

OTHER DISORDERS

LEARNING OBJECTIVES

14.9 Compare anorexia nervosa, bulimia nervosa, and binge eating.
14.10 Explain what a personality disorder is.
14.11 Distinguish between narcissistic, antisocial, and borderline personality disorders.
14.12 Define schizophrenia.
14.13 Explain the diathesis-stress hypothesis.

The DSM describes hundreds of psychological disorders, covering almost every conceivable complaint, from compulsive gambling to feelings of unreality; and as such, we cannot possibly review all of them. So, in the remainder of this chapter, we'll describe three types of disorders that are of special interest because they are commonly misunderstood or are found with some frequency among college students: eating disorders, personality disorders, and schizophrenia.

Exploration 14.6: Psychological Disorders II

www.helpguide.org   Contains information about all types of mental disorders. The information includes symptoms, treatments, and relevant research on each.

Eating Disorders

When Pam was 17 years old, she was somewhat overweight for her age. Her fear of getting fatter coupled with a desire to become socially attractive led her to experiment with strict diets. Pam was also "thin-spired" by ultra-skinny models and television stars. As a result, Pam's weight recently plunged from 153 pounds to 102 pounds in less than a year. Unlike Pam, Cheryl, who is 5 feet 8 inches tall, is at a healthy weight. For the past several years, however, she has begun to indulge in binge eating followed by purges of the consumed food. For instance, Cheryl will eat a quart of ice cream and a plate of brownies, gobbling the food down quite rapidly, with little chewing. Once she has started to eat, she feels a loss of control. She feels as though she cannot stop eating. Later, in secret, she induces vomiting by sticking her finger down her throat. The vomiting decreases the physical pain of overeating, thereby allowing continued eating. The entire cycle is followed by self-criticism ("Why do I eat so much?") and depression ("I'll never be able to stop myself; I am a failure"). Although very different, the eating patterns of Pam and Cheryl are both characteristic of an **eating disorder**—*a serious disturbance in everyday diet, such as eating too little or too much food, coupled with severe distress or concern about body weight or shape.* Below, the three major types of eating disorders are discussed: anorexia nervosa, bulimia nervosa, and binge eating.

ANOREXIA NERVOSA   Pam's condition, **anorexia nervosa,** is *characterized by a severe loss of appetite and weight. The essential features of this eating disorder are a fear of becoming fat along with a disturbance in body image and a refusal to maintain normal weight.* In other words, the individual relentlessly pursues thinness. Eating disorders are not due to a failure of will or behavior. Rather, they are real, treatable illnesses in which certain maladaptive patterns of eating take on a life of their own. Being 85 percent of normal body weight, along with other physical signs such as the suspension of menstrual periods, is usually sufficient for this diagnosis. Weight loss is often accomplished by a reduction in total food intake, especially foods high in carbohydrates and fats, use of laxatives or diuretics, and sometimes excessive strenuous exercise. The 1 percent of the population that suffer from this disorder (most of them girls) fear getting and feeling fat, and they do not realize they are getting dangerously thin, even when they examine themselves in the mirror (Allen & Dalton, 2011). "Dangerously thin" is not a misstatement, as up to 20 percent of people who have an eating disorder die from it. In fact, among all forms of mental illness, eating disorders have the highest mortality rate (Anred.com, 2012).

BULIMIA NERVOSA   Cheryl's condition, **bulimia nervosa,** is *characterized by excessive overeating or uncontrolled binge eating followed by self-induced vomiting.* This disorder is closely related to but different from anorexia, which is more common. Whereas the aim of the anorexic is to lose weight, the bulimic attempts to eat without gaining weight. The essential features of this disorder are episodic eating sprees, or binges, accompanied by an awareness that this eating pattern is abnormal—a fear of not being able to stop eating voluntarily and a depressed mood and self-disparaging thoughts. "You have no self-control—shame on you!" criticizes the little voice in the bulimic's head. The bulimic is also unhappy with her body image, as is the anorexic (Joiner, Wonderlich, Metalsky, & Schmidt, 1995). But unlike underweight anorexics, bulimics are typically at a healthy weight or slightly overweight. Individuals who suffer from bulimia sometimes diet excessively between binges.

Like anorexia, bulimia is more common among girls, especially those in the middle and upper socioeconomic groups. Although the estimated frequency of bulimia is around 3 percent in women (and less than 1 percent for men), about one in four college-age women are involved in bulimic behavior, which may or may not reach the level of a disorder (Anred.com, 2012). However, these findings are qualified by race. In comparison to Whites, African-American women (who tend to be less critical of their bodies) are less likely to develop an eating disorder (Powell & Kahn, 1995).

BINGE EATING   A third type of eating disorder, **binge eating** is *characterized by eating an excessive amount of food within a discrete period of time and by a sense of lack of control over eating* *during the episode.* Whereas most overweight people generally consume more calories than they expend over the course of each day, compulsive overeaters or binge eaters consume large amounts of food in a very short time without the subsequent use of purges or exercise. Often, the binge eater eats alone due to embarrassment about the loss of control. It is estimated that about one-third or more of all individuals in weight-control programs report frequent episodes of compulsive overeating. Compulsive overeaters exhibit a higher-than-average incidence of psychological problems, especially depression. Eating more often in response to positive or negative emotional states, compulsive overeaters also tend to experience greater mood fluctuations during the course of the day. Binge eating is commonly triggered by tension, hunger, consumption of any food, boredom, craving for specific foods, and solitude or loneliness (Mitchell, Devlin, de Zwaan, Crow, & Peterson, 2008).

Personality Disorders

Personality traits are *enduring patterns of thinking, feeling, acting, and relating to others that we exhibit in a wide range of situations.* However, when a person exhibits *personality traits that are so inflexible and maladaptive that they cause marked impairment in their social and occupational life,* they may have a **personality disorder.** These disorders are generally longstanding and result in a pattern of deviation from accepted social norms. Moreover, they are highly resistant to change. Unlike most form of psychopathology, personality disorders are unique in that they tend to cause less distress to the self than to those who live and work with them. As a result, these individuals resist getting professional help. Scientists now believe that many of the personality disorders described below are caused by childhood abuse and neglect (Battle et al., 2004).

NARCISSISTIC PERSONALITY DISORDER The **narcissistic personality** is *a disorder characterized by an undue sense of self-importance, often accompanied by a sense of inferiority.* Whereas a certain degree of self-interest may shield us from the effects of criticism or failure, excessive self-interest can be maladaptive, especially when the cravings for affection and reassurance become insatiable. People with this disorder generally exhibit a grandiose sense of self-importance in behavior or fantasy, often accompanied by a sense of inferiority. They exaggerate their talents and accomplishments and expect to be treated as special without the appropriate achievements. Moreover, narcissists are likely to lie and cheat without guilt or remorse in their personal lives, at work, and at school (Brunell, Staats, Barden, & Hupp, 2011). They are, however, hypersensitive to others' evaluation and react to criticism with arrogance and contempt. They believe they are unique and can be understood only by special people.

ANTISOCIAL PERSONALITY DISORDER One of the most unsettling personality disorders is the **antisocial personality,** *characterized by long-standing habits of maladaptive thought and behavior that violate the rules of society*—formerly called the psychopathic or sociopathic personality. These people have a history of chronic antisocial behavior, in which they show little concern for the welfare of others, readily taking advantage of or treating them cold-heartedly. Those with an antisocial personality also tend to be impulsive, for example, stealing a pack of cigarettes or a can of soda—whichever seems easier at the moment. Nevertheless, most people with antisocial personalities do not break the law. However, they are manipulative and irresponsible; and they act this way with little strain on their conscience, feeling no guilt or remorse for their misdeeds (Chen, Fu, Peng, Cai, & Zhou, 2011). You might ask, "How can people get away with such outrageous behavior?" One explanation may be their superficial charm, poise, and intelligence, all of which disarm their victims. Moreover, Western society may encourage antisocial tendencies by glamorizing fame and success, so that superficial charm and lack of concern for others may help antisocial people get ahead. In many cases, they have grown up in a family in which they have been under-socialized, with one or more of their parents exhibiting antisocial behavior themselves, such as harsh punishment, abuse, or frequent emotional rejection (Kantor, 2006).

BORDERLINE PERSONALITY DISORDER Those with a **borderline personality disorder** *show impulsive behaviors and unstable social relationships as well as unstable self-image.* Their impulsive behaviors, such as substance use, unsafe sexual activity, and reckless driving, are often self-damaging. Individuals with this disorder may also make suicidal threats or may self-mutilate in a desperate move to capture the attention of those who might abandon them. Moreover, the mood of those with borderline personalities is unstable, with intense or inappropriate episodes of irritability, anxiety, combativeness, and even euphoria. These symptoms occur in a variety of settings such as work or home. Because of wide ranging shifts in attitudes towards others (e.g., from high praise to extreme dislike) and out-of-control emotions, this disorder is very disturbing to those close to the borderline individual. It frequently strains interpersonal relationships to the breaking point (Manning, 2011). Psychotherapists often find it difficult to work with such individuals because those with borderline personalities tend to be very manipulative and want help at all times of the day or night (Perry, 1997). Box 14–7 delineates other prevalent personality disorders.

Schizophrenia

Schizophrenia is *a group of related psychotic disorders characterized by severe disorganization of thoughts, perceptions, and emotions; bizarre behavior; and social withdrawal.* Schizophrenics may hear voices; see things that aren't really there; believe in the patently unbelievable; remain motionless for hours; or expressive emotions that are inconsistent with the situation around them. Most of us can understand what it's like to be panic-stricken or depressed, but the unsettling behavior of a schizophrenic often remains a mystery to us. In fact, when people think about "being insane" or "going crazy" it is often the schizophrenic that comes to mind.

SYMPTOMS OF SCHIZOPHRENIA   Because *schizophrenia* is a label given to a group of related disorders, it's difficult to describe the "typical" person with schizophrenia. The essential features of these disorders include **psychotic symptoms,** *symptoms that are signs of psychosis and that include hallucinations such as hearing voices, marked impairment in self-care and social relationships, and other signs of severe disturbance.* Below are the general classes of symptoms that schizophrenics can experience.

   1. *Disorders of speech.* One of the most striking features of individuals suffering from schizophrenia is their peculiar use of language—in both the form and the content of thought and speech. There is a loosening of associations of thought and rambling, disjointed speech. Words that have no association beyond the fact that they sound alike—such as *clang* and *fang*—may be juxtaposed with each other.

   2. *Distorted beliefs.* This major disturbance in the content of thought involves **delusions**— *beliefs that have no basis in reality.* For example, individuals may feel they are being spied on or plotted against by their families.

BOX 14–7   **Other Personality Disorders**

Paranoid personality disorder: This disorder is characterized by a basic distrust of others. However, usually such distrust and suspiciousness is without basis.

Schizoid personality disorder: Evidenced by social isolation and shallow emotions. Those with this disorder tend to lack close friends or confidants.

Histrionic personality disorder: Characterized by attention seeking and excessive emotionality. Individuals with this type of personality disorder use dramatic behaviors and physical appearance to draw attention to themselves.

Avoidant personality disorder: Demonstrated by social constriction, low self-esteem, and extreme avoidance of negative self-appraisals.

Obsessive-compulsive personality disorder: Not to be confused with OCD, this disorder is marked by the need to maintain control and order. Their preoccupation with perfection, details, rules, and so forth interferes with task completion.

3. *Distorted perceptions.* Individuals suffering from schizophrenia seem to perceive the world differently from other people. They have difficulty focusing on certain aspects of their environment while screening out other information. Instead, their inner world is flooded with an undifferentiated mass of sensory data, resulting in odd associations, inner confusion, and bizarre speech. In addition, many schizophrenics experience **hallucinations**—*sensory perceptions that occur in the absence of any appropriate external stimulus.* The most common hallucination is hearing voices that characteristically order these people to commit some forbidden act or that accuse them of having done some terrible misdeed.

4. *Blunted or inappropriate emotions.* Schizophrenia is characterized by blunted effect (emotions), or in more severe cases, a lack of emotions. Schizophrenic individuals may stare with a blank expression or speak in a flat, monotonous voice. Or they may display inappropriate emotions, such as giggling when talking about some painful experience.

5. *Social withdrawal.* People who eventually have a schizophrenic episode tend to be loners, preferring animals, nature, or inanimate objects to human company. Perhaps they are preoccupied with their inner world, or having learned that they are often misunderstood, they prefer to keep to themselves. When in the presence of others, they avoid eye contact and tend to stand or sit at a greater distance from people than others do. They are also emotionally distant, making it difficult to establish satisfying close relationships with them.

The initial onset of schizophrenia usually occurs in adolescence or early adulthood. Schizophrenia may appear abruptly, with marked changes in behavior in a matter of days or weeks, or there may be a gradual deterioration in functioning over many years. During this initial phase, individuals with schizophrenia are socially withdrawn. They display blunted or shallow emotions and have trouble communicating with others. They may neglect personal hygiene, schoolwork, or jobs. By this time, such individuals may have begun to exhibit the bizarre behavior and psychotic symptoms signaling the onset of the active phase. The *active phase* of the disorder is often precipitated by intense psychological stress, such as the loss of a job, rejection in love, or the death of a parent. During this period, the psychotic symptoms become prominent. Schizophrenic individuals begin to hallucinate, hold delusions, and exhibit incoherent and illogical thought and bizarre behavior. However, no one person manifests all these symptoms; each individual exhibits a somewhat different pattern.

In the *residual phase,* individuals with schizophrenia may recover from the acute episode in a matter of weeks or months. Some of the psychotic symptoms, such as hallucinations or delusions, may persist, although they are no longer accompanied by intense emotion. These individuals may continue to exhibit eccentric behavior and odd thoughts, for example, believing they are able to control events through magical thinking. As a result, many of them are not ready to fully resume everyday responsibilities, such as holding a job or running a household.

FACTS ABOUT SCHIZOPHRENIA Based on the above symptoms, it is easy to see why schizophrenia is such disabling disorder. Here are some addition facts about schizophrenia (Mueser & Jeste, 2008):

- Rates of schizophrenia are very similar from country to country—about 1 percent of the population.
- Schizophrenia ranks among the top 10 causes of disability in developed countries worldwide.
- The risk of suicide is serious in people with schizophrenia.
- In the past, people with schizophrenia where thought to be possessed by demons or spirits.
- Around one-third of schizophrenics require long-term stays in mental health facilities.

CAUSES AND CONSEQUENCES OF SCHIZOPHRENIA Despite extensive research, the causes of schizophrenia are not fully understood. For a long while, a dysfunctional family environment was regarded as a major cause of this disorder, but in recent years there has been increasing evidence that genetic, neurological, and biochemical factors may play an even greater role. Nevertheless,

---

BOX 14–8 Outlook for Recovery

How well an individual recovers from the active phase of schizophrenia depends on a variety of factors, especially the following:

1. *Premorbid adjustment.* The more adequately the person functioned before the disorder, the better the outcome.
2. *Triggering event.* If the disorder is triggered by a specific event, such as the death of a loved one, the possibility of recovery is more favorable.
3. *Sudden onset.* The more quickly the disorder develops, the more favorable the outcome.
4. *Age of onset.* The later in life the initial episode of schizophrenia appears, the better. Men are more at risk before the age of 25; women are more at risk after 25.
5. *Affective behavior.* Symptoms of anxiety and other emotions, including depression, are favorable signs. A state of hopelessness not accompanied by depression is a poor sign.
6. *Content of delusions and hallucinations.* The more delusions involve feelings of guilt and responsibility, the better the outlook. Conversely, the more the delusions and hallucinations blame others and exonerate the individual, the more severe the disorder.
7. *Type of schizophrenia.* Paranoid schizophrenia, the most common type, has a better outlook, mostly because the individual's cognitive functioning remains relatively intact compared with other types of schizophrenia.
8. *Response to the disorder and the treatment.* The more insight individuals have concerning what makes them ill, the more responsive they are to the medication; the more cooperative they are with their therapists, the better their chances of recovery.
9. *Family support.* The more understanding and supportive these individuals' families are, the better their chances of a good recovery.

---

about half of identical twins (i.e., both twins share the same genes) with a schizophrenic sibling do not develop this disorder (Mueser & Jeste, 2008). Thus, a predisposition by itself does not appear sufficient for the development of schizophrenia. The **diathesis-stress hypothesis** views *schizophrenia as the interaction of a genetic vulnerability (the diathesis or predisposition) with environmental stressors.* That is, schizophrenic individuals tend to inherit a lower threshold to certain types of stress, which, if exceeded, may precipitate an acute episode of the disorder. If an individual manages to keep the level of environmental stress well below a particular threshold, despite a genetic predisposition, that person may never become symptomatic.

There is a considerable difference of opinion about the outlook for individuals who have suffered an acute schizophrenic episode. Traditionally, clinicians adhered to the principle of thirds; that is, about one-third of the people who have experienced a schizophrenic episode make a good recovery, another one-third make a partial recovery with occasional relapses, and still another one-third remain chronically impaired. However, with improved methods of treatment, powerful antipsychotic drugs, more favorable attitudes toward those afflicted with this disorder, and more sophisticated research strategies, a larger proportion of schizophrenic individuals are making at least a partial recovery. How well an individual recovers from an acute schizophrenic episode depends on many factors. Refer to Box 14–8, which details some of the other factors that predict who possibly will recover from schizophrenia.

APPLYING THIS TO YOURSELF

LEARNING OBJECTIVE

14.14 Apply the concepts learned in this chapter to your own lives.

What does all this mean for you? First, it is important to remember that we should never dismiss the experiences of those with mental illness nor stigmatize them. Second, if you think you are having emotional problems, seek help. It is estimated that three-quarters of all college students suffer some symptoms of major depression during college, one-quarter of them at any given time. In almost half of these students, the depression is serious enough to require professional care. Major depression may be triggered by the stress of student life, academic pressures, and the felt need to make a career decision. Major depression is often brought on by cognitive distortions, such as exaggerating the importance of getting good grades or the loss of a love relationship. In addition to depression, the stress associated with college can also cause both acute and chronic anxiety (Haas et al., 2008). Most find that it is better to get professional help than to ignore the problem or attempt to self-medicate through alcohol and drug use.

As you will read in the next chapter, there is lots of care available to those in need of it. If you are attending an educational program in a community unfamiliar to you, your campus counseling center, the dean of students, a dormitory adviser, or a psychology professor can help you find appropriate assistance. If you are a community member, you probably have a community mental health center nearby. Finally, psychologists know that every now and then all of us experience some sort of mental health issue. Psychologists are currently working to enhance our own overall well-being, and not just by reducing the incidence and prevalence of disorders (Huppert, 2009) or by alleviating the distress of those who suffer from them. There is little reason all of us cannot feel more mentally healthy.

Chapter Summary

PSYCHOLOGICAL DISORDERS

14.1 Describe the distinguishing features of a psychological disorder.

We began the chapter by noting that there is no simple way to determine whether someone has a psychological disorder. In practice, professionals rely on a combination of standards, such as the presence of personal distress, significant impairment in behavior, the social acceptability of the behavior, and an important loss of personal control.

14.2 Explain what the DSM is and how disorders are diagnosed.

The DSM is the authoritative guide for all medically recognized psychological disorders. In the DSM, the emphasis is on describing the characteristic behavior patterns of the various disorders rather than interpreting the possible causes, which are often unknown.

14.3 Know the prevalence and incidence of mental illness in the United States.

Millions of Americans suffer from psychological disorders, with approximately 26 percent U.S. adults currently have a diagnosable psychological disorder and close to 50 percent developing one before they die.

ANXIETY DISORDERS

14.4 Know the definition of an anxiety disorder.

In an anxiety disorder, the level of anxiety experienced is out of proportion to the stressful situation or may occur in the absence of any actual danger. Anxiety may be experienced in different ways in the various disorders.

14.5 Distinguish between five common classes of anxiety disorders.

In generalized anxiety disorder, a chronic sense of diffuse or free-floating anxiety becomes the predominant disturbance, and the person is anxious most of the time. Panic disorder involves the sudden onset of sheer terror. In contrast, the phobic disorders are characterized by a chronic, irrational fear of a specific object or activity, together with a compelling desire to avoid it. The essential features of obsessive-compulsive disorder are recurrent obsessions or compulsions or both, as seen in people preoccupied with various checking and cleaning rituals. PTSD, which is characterized by symptoms of anxiety and avoidance behavior, occurs as a result of unusually stressful events.

MOOD DISORDERS

14.6 Explain the difference between depressive disorders and bipolar disorder.

Whereas depressive disorders involve pervasive negative emotional states, bipolar disorder (popularly known as manic depression) involves depression alternating with extreme elation.

14.7 Distinguish between three types of depressive disorders.

Major depression is characterized by intense and unrealistic sadness as well feelings of worthlessness. Seasonal affective disorder is a form of depression that seems to be caused by the short and dark winter days in some parts of the world. Dysthymia consists of long-term mild depression that does not disable.

14.8 List the warning signs of suicide.

The warning signs of suicide include the expression of suicidal thoughts or a preoccupation with death, a prior suicide attempt, the death of a close friend or family member, the giving away of prized possession, depression or hopelessness, despair over a chronic illness, social isolation, a change in sleeping and eating habits, marked personality changes, abuse of alcohol or drugs, neglect of personal welfare, self-inflicted injury or other reckless behavior, divorce or stress in the family, and job loss or loss of esteem or sense of security.

OTHER DISORDERS

14.9 Compare anorexia nervosa, bulimia nervosa, and binge eating.

Anorexia nervosa is characterized by a disturbance in body image and eating habits and results in a loss of normal body weight. Bulimia nervosa involves episodic eating binges accompanied by a fear of not being able to stop eating voluntarily, eventually followed by a depressive mood. Binge eaters consume large amounts of food in a very short time without the subsequent use of purgatives or exercise.

14.10 Explain what a personality disorder is.

People with personality disorders are characterized by maladaptive behavior patterns that impair their social and occupational lives. The disorder may be more noticeable to those around the individual rather than to the individual.

14.11 Distinguish between narcissistic, antisocial, and borderline personality disorders.

Those with a narcissistic personality disorder have an exaggerated sense of self-importance and need constant reassurance to maintain their inflated esteem. In contrast, those with an antisocial personality disorder get into trouble because of their predatory attitude toward people and their disregard for others' rights. The borderline personality is impulsive, has disturbed interpersonal relationships, is manipulative, and can be self-damaging.

14.12 Define schizophrenia.

Schizophrenia is a group of related psychotic disorders characterized by severe disorganization of thoughts, perceptions, and emotions; bizarre behavior; and social withdrawal.

14.13 Explain the diathesis-stress hypothesis.

According to the diathesis-stress hypothesis, schizophrenia develops as the interaction of a genetic vulnerability (the diathesis or predisposition) and environmental stressors.

14.14 Apply the concepts learned in this chapter to your own lives.

First, it is important to remember that we should never dismiss the experiences of those with mental illness nor stigmatize them. Second, you should seek help if you think you or anyone else needs it. Try not to self-medicate or ignore your problems. Psychologists are now working on enhancing our well-being, not just focusing on those individuals who have a mental disorder.

Self-Test

1. Which of the following is not considered to be an aspect of psychological disorder?
   a. maladaptive behaviors
   b. social norms are followed
   c. personal distress
   d. an important loss of personal control
2. Grisi Siknis, which is characterized by headache, anxiety, anger, and aimless running, is a psychological disorder rarely found outside of Nicaragua. This is an example of a:
   a. culture-bound syndrome
   b. Central-American psychosis
   c. culture-centric fugue
   d. culture-free disorder
3. While Michelle groomed her dog in the garage, a spider dropped down in front of her, dangling by a silk thread. Michelle screamed as loud as she could, ran into her bedroom, and started to cry. Both her rate of breathing and her pulse sky rocketed. For months afterwards, Michelle refused to go into the garage. And even talking about spiders made her feel anxious. Michelle is probably suffering from:
   a. obsessive-compulsive disorder
   b. phobic disorder
   c. posttraumatic stress disorder
   d. general anxiety disorder
4. Pittacus had to do everything in fours. He drained his soda in four gulps, he used four sheets of toilet paper and wiped himself four times when in the bathroom, and he repeatedly counted by fours in his head. Pittacus did these things because he felt that something terrible would happen if he didn't. Pittacus appears to have:
   a. general anxiety disorder
   b. posttraumatic stress disorder
   c. obsessive-compulsive disorder
   d. phobic disorder
5. Every winter Janet is overcome with sadness. Each spring, her feelings of hopelessness and despair go away. Janet appears to have:
   a. bipolar disorder
   b. major depression
   c. dysthymia
   d. seasonal affective disorder
6. Which of the following statements regarding suicide is not true?
   a. people who threaten to kill themselves rarely do
   b. suicide is most common among teens and the aged

c. each year there are more suicides than homicides

d. typically men and women attempt suicide in different ways

7. Karen is 5'8" and weighs 90 pounds. But when Karen looks in the mirror she feels fat. She refuses to gain weight and eats very little for fear of getting fat. Karen appears to have:

a. schizophrenia

b. anorexia nervosa

c. bulimia nervosa

d. generalized anxiety disorder

8. Harvey is charming man who frequently manipulates people for his own benefit. At work, he blames others if things go bad and takes sole credit when things go well. Even though his actions hurt other people he never feels guilty or remorse. Harvey probably has:

a. narcissistic personality disorder

b. disorganized schizophrenia

c. antisocial personality disorder

d. major depression

9. Eve believes that the FBI has tapped her phone and that her roommate, Fergie is in on an elaborate plot to "get her." She also frequently hears voices that tell her to "watch her back." Assuming none of this is true, Eve is suffering from:

a. anorexic disturbance

b. schizophrenia

c. dissociative identity disorder

d. histrionic personality

10. Both Susan and Anna recently experienced a devastating loss of a loved one. Although Susan's family has a genetic history of schizophrenia, Anna's family does not. In turn, only Susan develops schizophrenia. Although both women experienced environmental stressors, only one of them was biologically predisposed to a psychological disorder, resulting in the two women experiencing the stressor differently. This explanation for the causes of psychological disorders is called the _____.

a. Diathesis-Stress hypothesis

b. Cannon-Bard hypothesis

c. Atkinson-Shiffrin model

d. Culture-Bound model

Exercises

1. *Have you ever experienced a panic attack?* Even if you've only experienced intense anxiety, write a page or so describing what it was like. Be sure to include what occasioned the anxiety and how it affected you. Also, write about how well you cope with similar situations today.

2. *Are you bothered by an intense fear or phobia?* If you were to list your worst fears, which ones would you include? Do you share some of the more common fears, such as the fear of snakes or spiders? Or are you bothered by other fears? What are you doing to overcome your fears?

3. *Managing the "blues."* Most of us have times when we feel down. The important thing is knowing how to handle ourselves so that we can snap out of such low moments. Write a page or so describing how you cope with discouragement and depression. How effective is your approach?

4. *Suspecting that a friend is suicidal.* At this point, do you think you're better able to recognize individuals with a high risk for suicide? If you suspected someone was suicidal, what would you do?

5. *Feeling better.* When you feel down, do you try to think of happier moments? What makes you happy? What makes you sad? Do the two "triggers" have anything in common, or does each moment have its own trigger?

Questions for Self-Reflection

1. Do you believe society tolerates greater deviance than in the past? What are the advantages and disadvantages of greater tolerance?

2. When you become anxious about something, how does this affect you? Does anxiety energize you? When you are relaxed, how do you feel? How is your behavior different in these two situations?

3. How do you cope with occasional feelings of despondency or depression? Do you live in a climate that might induce seasonal affective disorder? Do you suffer from it? What can you do about this disorder?

4. Do you think women are more apt to seek professional help for their mental disorders than men? Why?

5. Would you agree that depression among men is often masked by drinking or drug problems?

6. Do you know someone who has attempted suicide or who succeeded? How did the suicide affect you?

7. How would you account for the high suicide rate among older White men? Do you think the reasons adolescents and the elderly commit suicide are different?

8. What are some of the chronic self-destructive behaviors people engage in? Why do you think people engage in these behaviors? Can people change voluntarily, or do most people need professional help?

9. Are you aware that some individuals who have experienced acute schizophrenic episodes resume normal lives? What do you think brings on remission from schizophrenia? Can you imagine what it is like to live as an individual with schizophrenia?

10. What are some ways that you could help reduce the stigma associated with mental illness.

Chapter Fifteen

If You Go for Help

*S*ince moving back home three months ago, Sergei has been at odds with his parents, who emigrated with him from Russia when Sergei was 5. Sergei admits he's going through a difficult time in his life. He recently lost his job—again—and is having trouble making the payments for his car. To make matters worse, he has just asked his father for another small loan to help him through his present financial crisis. Sergei's parents see things differently. They feel that Sergei is floundering and has no sense of direction in his life. His friends think he is depressed, as seen in his constant but vague complaints, fatigue, and boredom. Since the recent breakup with his girlfriend, Sergei has been staying out late and drinking heavily several evenings each week and then refusing to get up in the morning. Sergei's friends are concerned and insist he get therapy. Sergei agrees very reluctantly after they apply much pressure to him. "Alright, I'll go, but just once," he says, "mostly to prove that I'm not crazy." Sergei's friends insist that he should give the therapist a chance. "Okay, okay, I'll give it a try. But I'm not making any promises."

PSYCHOTHERAPY: WHAT IS IT? WHO USES IT?

LEARNING OBJECTIVES

15.1 Define psychotherapy.
15.2 Explain the role that culture plays in treatment.

Why are people like Sergei so reluctant to seek professional help? The answers vary from one person to another, with the fear of being committed or having to take medicine leading the list. Some individuals resist getting help because of the stigma associated with mental disorders. In the popular mind, psychotherapy is for people who are "nuts." **Psychotherapy** is *the helping process in which a trained therapist performs certain activities that will facilitate a change in the client's attitudes and behaviors.* Others do not seek treatment because they simply don't know where to turn for help or because of the cost. See Figure 15–1 for a more complete list of reasons.

In practice, psychotherapy is more likely to be used by people with the milder disturbances, who seek it as a means of personal growth, as well as for the relief of troublesome symptoms.

BOX 15–1 Did you know that ...

- Only half of children with mental health issues receive treatment.
- Compared to children, teens are 90 percent more likely to use mental health services.
- Around 8 percent of adults with a psychological disorder are admitted to hospitals for short-term or long-term 24-hour care.
- The most common treatment for a mental health issue is medication.
- About one-third of inmates diagnosed with a psychological disorder receive treatment while in jail.

Source: "Statistics," from National Institute of Mental Health website, 2012.

Currently, just over 30.2 million adults (13.3 percent of those over age 18) in the United States receive treatment for mental health issues. In any event, only about one in five adults with a serious psychological problem will seek help from a mental health professional such as a psychiatrist or psychologist. Family physicians, clergy, and other types of counselors, such as social workers, will see many other individuals.

GENDER DIFFERENCES IN ADULTHOOD Would it surprise you to learn that adult females are nearly twice as likely as adult males to get the help they need (NIMH, 2012). In the United States,

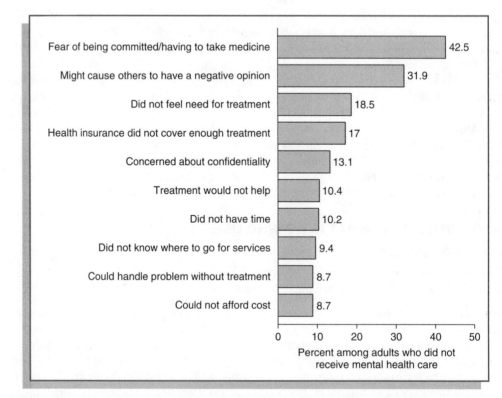

FIGURE 15–1   Reasons for not receiving mental health services in the past year (2009).
Source: Adapted from Figure 2.12 of Results from the 2009 National Survey on Drug Use and Health: Mental Health Findings (HHS Publication No. SMA 10-4609). Substance Abuse and Mental Health Services Administration, U.S. Department of Health and Human Services, 2010.

and other individualistic societies (which place a high value on self-sufficiency), psychological treatment may be seen as an admission of weakness. And because of societal differences in expectations for males and females, it is more acceptable for women than men to express their emotions, admit their faults, and seek out care. In contrast, society often dictates that men be strong and independent, handling difficulties on their own; an attitude that not only results in the avoidance of mental health services, but also a failure to acknowledge that psychological problems even exist (Mackenzie, Gekoski, & Knox, 2006).

Exploration 15.1: Mental Illness Advocacy

http://www.nami.org   The website for the National Alliance for the Mentally Ill, an advocacy group for the mentally ill and their families.

TREATMENT OF CHILDREN   During childhood, gender differences in the likelihood of receiving psychotherapy also exist; though the pattern that emerges is the exact opposite of what is seen during adulthood. Specifically, boys are 50 percent more likely than girls to receive treatment. Why the difference across development? Quite simply, during childhood the mental health issues of boys are more likely to be disruptive to those around them (such as family members and classmates) relative to the problems experienced by girls. As a result, parents have more troubles handling their boys at home and teachers have more difficulties with them in school. And because the "squeaky wheel gets the grease," boys are more likely than girls to be referred for treatment. It's not that girls don't have mental health issues, rather, it's just that their problems are less likely to be noticed by teachers and parents; and youth with problems that go unnoticed do not receive the care that they need (Coles, Slavec, Bernstein, & Baroni, 2012).

CULTURAL ISSUES   Culture also plays a pivotal role in mental health services. With a seemingly endless range of cultural subgroups and individual variations, culture is important because it bears upon what *all* people bring to the clinical setting. It can account for variations in how clients communicate their symptoms during therapy, which ones they report, and even how they are interpreted by their therapists. For example, passive behavior and difficulty talking about thoughts and feelings could be viewed as uncooperative behavior for someone from a Western culture, but appropriate for someone from a traditional Asian culture (Kim, Liang, & Li, 2003).

More often, culture bears upon whether people even seek help in the first place; what types of help they seek; what coping styles and social supports they have; and how much stigma they attach to mental disorder. Cultural issues are not just limited to individuals with mental disorders and their families. They can also affect the professionals who provide treatment. Health care providers may view symptoms, diagnoses, and treatments in ways that sometimes differ from their clients' views, especially when their cultural backgrounds are dissimilar. This divergence of viewpoints can create barriers to effective care. As such, mental health care providers need to understand, be sensitive to, and respectful of the various cultures of their clients (Mollersen, Sexton, & Holte, 2009).

Such concerns have led to the pairing up of clients and therapists based on race and ethnicity—a cultural congruence, if you will. And hands down, clients prefer to have therapists matching their own racial and ethnic identity. But not only that, clients also rate therapists of similar race and ethnicity more positively than those of different races and ethnicities. But here's the rub, for most clients, the overall success (or failure) of therapy is generally unrelated to having a racially and ethnically matched therapist. However, for clients with strong racial and ethnic preferences, and for those with a profound mistrust of

The old asylums were usually dark, grim institutions that offered little by way of beneficial treatment.

other races and ethnicities, psychotherapy outcomes improve when matched with a therapist of their own race and ethnicity. Thus, as long as there is racial and ethnic bias, discrimination, and prejudice, there will be a need for the racial and ethnic pairing of clients and therapists (Cabral & Smith, 2011). Box 15–2 discusses the issue of diversity and mental disorder in more detail.

BOX 15–2   Focus on Health Care: Disparities in Treatment

In the United States, the prevalence of mental disorders for racial and ethnic minorities is similar to that of whites. Nevertheless, there are several important disparities in the mental health care received by racial and ethnic minorities in comparison to whites:

- Minorities have less access to and availability of mental health services.
- Minorities are less likely to receive needed mental health services.
- Minorities in treatment often receive a poorer quality of mental health care.
- Minorities are underrepresented in mental health research.

Moreover, a constellation of barriers deters minorities from reaching treatment. Many of these barriers operate for all Americans: cost, fragmentation of services, lack of availability of services, and societal stigma of mental disorders. Additional barriers that deter racial and ethnic minorities from seeking care include: mistrust and fear of treatment, racism and discrimination, and differences in language and communication (Nelson, 2006). Ethnic and racial minorities collectively experience a greater disability burden (e.g., lost workdays, limitation in daily activities) from mental disorders than do Whites. This higher level of burden stems from minorities' receiving less care and poorer quality of care, rather than from their disorders being inherently more severe or prevalent in the community (Moritsugu, Wong, & Duffy, 2010).

APPLYING IT TO YOURSELF   Would you recognize when to seek help? If you have been in counseling, have you reassessed yourself lately to see if you could use a mental health tune-up? Do you have friends who would encourage you to seek assistance if they thought you were depressed or were drinking too much? Or would you do what millions of Americans do, avoid therapy because of the stigma, cost, or inconvenience? To assess your attitude about seeing a therapist for emotional problems complete the assessment found in Activity 15–1.

ACTIVITY 15–1

ATTITUDES TOWARD THERAPY

INSTRUCTIONS: *The following items measure your attitude toward seeking professional help for mental health issues. Please mark the extent of your agreement by circling the appropriate answer.*

1. If I thought I was having serious mental health issues, my first thought would be to seek out a therapist.

   Agree   Partly Agree   Partly Disagree   Disagree

2. Talking with a therapist about problems is not a very good way to solve emotional issues.

   Agree   Partly Agree   Partly Disagree   Disagree

3. If I were having significant emotional difficulties, I believe that therapy could help me.

   Agree   Partly Agree   Partly Disagree   Disagree

4. Having an attitude that emotional conflicts can be resolved without seeing a therapist is admirable.

   Agree   Partly Agree   Partly Disagree   Disagree

5. If things really bothered me for a long period of time, I would want to go to a therapist.

   Agree   Partly Agree   Partly Disagree   Disagree

6. In the future, I might want to see a therapist.

   Agree   Partly Agree   Partly Disagree   Disagree

7. People with emotional problems are more likely to solve them by seeing a therapist than by trying to figure them out on their own.

   Agree   Partly Agree   Partly Disagree   Disagree

8. For me, the time, effort, and cost of going into therapy isn't worth it.

   Agree   Partly Agree   Partly Disagree   Disagree

9. Therapy should be a last resort. First, people should try to solve their emotional problems by themselves.

   Agree   Partly Agree   Partly Disagree   Disagree

10. Like many things, emotional difficulties tend to resolve themselves on their own, without needing the help of a professional.

    Agree   Partly Agree   Partly Disagree   Disagree

SCORING: For items 1, 3, 5, 6, 7 score as follows: agree = 1, partly agree = 2, partly disagree = 3, disagree = 4. For items, 2, 7, 8, 9, 10 using the following scores: agree = 4, partly agree = 3, partly disagree = 3, disagree = 4.

A. Total for Items 1, 3, 5, 6, 7: _____
B. Total for Items 2, 4, 8, 9, 10: _____
Total Score: Add A & B together: _____

Lower scores may indicate a greater willingness to seek out professional help for emotional problems, if they were to occur.

Source: Adapted from Fischer, E. H., & Farina, A. (1995). Attitudes towards seeking professional psychological help: A shortened form and considerations for research. *Journal of College Student Development, 36,* 368–373.

INSIGHT THERAPIES—THE TALKING CURE

LEARNING OBJECTIVES

15.3 Summarize the main features of insight therapy.
15.4 Compare psychoanalysis with modern psychodynamic therapy.
15.5 Describe person-centered therapy.

A major problem in choosing a **therapist**—*a person trained to help people with psychological problems*—is sorting through the various approaches to therapy. Currently, there are hundreds of different forms of therapy available to clients. Whereas some therapies put more emphasis

Before the advent of psychotherapy and psychotropic medications, individuals with mental disorders were treated by other means, such as this antique apparatus designed to provide light therapy.

on adjustment, others may concentrate on growth or address emotional responses. Despite their differences, most therapies share a common goal: the relief of symptoms, such as intolerable anxiety or depression. In addition, many therapies offer clients a better understanding of their thoughts, feelings, motives, and relationships. And by doing so, help clients modify their problem behaviors, such as excessive fear (e.g., phobias) or compulsive gambling, and improve their interpersonal relationships at home and work. We'll commence our review with **insight therapies**—*therapies that bring change by increasing self-understanding.*

Psychoanalysis

According to Sigmund Freud, the founder of psychoanalysis, psychological disturbances are the result of *hidden* conflicts residing in our unconscious, such as inappropriate sexual and aggressive desires. If not expressed directly, these unconscious impulses and conflicts seek *in*direct release in all kinds of symptoms, such as anxiety and depression. Thus, **psychoanalysis** involves *psychotherapy aimed at helping the person gain insight and mastery over unconscious conflicts by bringing them into consciousness, where they can be dealt with directly* (Stern, 2006).

THE IMPORTANCE OF TRANSFERENCE The core of the psychoanalytic approach is the analysis of **transference**—*the unconscious tendency of clients to project onto the therapist their feelings and fantasies, both positive and negative, about significant others in their childhood.* Therapists deliberately foster the development of a transference relationship with their clients through their own neutrality and relative passivity. Over time, the client's unconscious desires shift from a conflicted relationship in their past to the current one with the therapist. For example, a male client may view his female analyst as a mother-figure, transferring on to her any emotions, desires, and beliefs associated with his own mother. Then, as the therapy proceeds, the therapist addresses transference issues to help the client achieve insight into the influence of the past on their present behavior (Meissner, 2008).

TECHNIQUES USED IN PSYCHOANALYSIS "Working through" the transference relationship, which involves an exploration of unconscious material and defenses, is accomplished via the use of a variety of techniques. One of the historically earliest of these is **free association**. In classic psychoanalysis, the individual is asked to lie down on a couch, relax, clear the mind of everyday thoughts, and then *say whatever comes to mind regardless of how trivial it sounds*. Sometimes, clients are encouraged to talk about their dreams. Although these recollections might appear irrelevant, the well-trained analyst may use dream interpretation to shed light on the clients' problems. *When an individual hesitates or is reluctant to talk about some painful experience,* this is seen as a sign of **resistance** (Carrere, 2008). For example, during therapy Sergei was reluctant to discuss his relationship with his mother. By analyzing resistances, the therapist helps clients see how they handle anxiety-provoking material. Today, the concept of resistance has been accepted by other practitioners and therapists, although the assumed causes and methods for dealing with them may differ (Grabhorn, Kaufhold, Michal, & Overbeck, 2005).

Exploration 15.2: Dream Interpretation

www.dreamforth.com This site provides a searchable database for interpreting dreams. Please use for entertainment purposes only.

PSYCHODYNAMIC THERAPY Traditionally, psychoanalysis involved hour-long sessions three to five times a week, with the course of treatment often lasting several years. In addition to being incredible time consuming, at the level of current fees, this schedule would make psychoanalysis prohibitively expensive for all but a privileged few. As a result, there have been many changes in this approach, resulting in a new form of treatment called **psychodynamic therapy**, which aims to *discover and resolve unconscious conflicts through insight*. During both psycho-analysis and psychodynamic therapy, the therapist is responsible for producing well-being in the client by explaining to them where their problems originated and what they need to do to effect change.

Modern psychodynamic therapy may involve only one or two sessions a week and often lasts only 20 or 30 sessions. The therapist sits facing the client and takes a more active role in therapy compared to the impenetrable "mirror" role advocated by Freud. Moreover, rather than focusing on unconscious sexual and aggressive conflicts as the cause of mental health prob-lems, psychodynamic therapies emphasize other issues, such as relationships with caregivers during childhood or current relationships with spouses, friends, and family. Psychodynamic therapists are also likely to be more eclectic than in the past, using techniques from other thera-peutic approaches when appropriate. At the same time, the emphasis remains on gaining insight and self-mastery of the unconscious forces affecting one's behavior. Psychodynamic therapies are most effective with clients who are ruminative, self-reflective, and introspective (Blatt & Shahar, 2004).

The Person-Centered Approach

Rather than directing the course of therapy, as psychoanalysts do, Carl Rogers believed that therapists should follow the lead of their clients, reflecting back to the client what they say during therapy and clarifying issues that come up along the way. Hence, in the end, it is the journey of self-discovery that ultimately produces the client's well-being. Toward the end of his career, Rogers (1980) changed the name of his approach from *client-centered therapy* to **person-centered therapy**, as a way of indicating that the same principles apply to a variety of fields of human interaction as well as to psychotherapy. According to this view, *the helper's genuineness, acceptance, and empathic understanding of the client are necessary and sufficient conditions for producing therapeutic change.*

Rogers developed his view of therapy out of his own experience as a therapist. Early in his career he was counseling a mother about her son, who was having problems. No matter what strategy he tried, he got nowhere. Finally, he admitted his failure. As the mother walked toward the door, she turned and asked Rogers if he ever saw adult clients. Then the woman returned to her seat and began pouring out her own problems. She spoke of her own sense of confusion and failure and her despair about her marriage, all of which were more pertinent to her son's problems than the sterile case-history approach they had followed before. After many more interviews, the woman felt better about her marriage and her son's problem behaviors soon stopped. Rogers felt the improvement had come because he had followed her lead, because he had listened and understood rather than imposed his diagnostic understanding on her. This was the first of many experiences that gradually led Rogers to the view that therapeutic progress comes mostly from respecting and responding to the client's own frame of reference and inherent potential for growth.

ROGERIAN THERAPY   Therapists using the Rogerian approach believe that all of us have within ourselves vast resources for self-understanding and for altering our behavior; and that these re-sources can be tapped if the proper climate for change can be provided. According to Rogers (1980), *three* conditions must be present for a growth-producing therapeutic climate. All of them pertain to the client–therapist relationship (Overholser, 2007).

- *First, the therapist must be genuine, or "congruent."* That is, there should be close match-ing between what the therapist experiences at the gut level and what is expressed to the clients.
- *The second essential is an attitude of acceptance and caring.* It is believed that when the therapist is accepting of and caring toward the clients, therapeutic change is most likely to occur. Therapists accept clients unconditionally, so that they are free to feel what is going

on at the moment—whether confusion, resentment, fear, or love. This *positive, unconditional acceptance* (and caring for) clients is called **unconditional positive regard.**

- *The final feature of any therapeutic relationship is empathic understanding.* In order to accomplish this task, the therapist must be able to sense the emotions and personal meanings that the clients are experiencing. Moreover, the therapist needs to be able to effectively compute this understanding to them.

Research has confirmed that Rogerian therapy promotes client and therapist co-thinking and co-experiencing. Other studies demonstrate support for the importance of the therapeutic relationship to client well-being, and that empathy and unconditional positive regard are critical elements of effective therapy. Finally, similar to psychodynamic therapy, the person-centered approach is most effective with clients who are introspective and self-reflective (Bohart & Byock, 2005; Kirschenbaum & Jourdan, 2005).

There are new approaches to therapy, not just insight therapy, developing every decade. Box 15–3 highlights some non-traditional approaches to the treatment of mental illness.

COGNITIVE AND BEHAVIORAL THERAPIES

LEARNING OBJECTIVES

15.6 Compare cognitive, behavioral, and cognitive-behavioral therapies.
15.7 Explain how to effectively use a token economy.

Today, a large and diverse group of therapists characterize their orientation as *either behavioral or cognitive, which, respectively, attempt to modify maladaptive behavior or faulty thinking.* These psychologists practice behavioral therapy, cognitive therapy, or cognitive-behavioral therapy. Each of these will be discussed in turn.

Behavioral Therapies

Rather than searching for the underlying causes of the client's difficulties, as is done in insight therapies, behavioral therapists focus directly on the problem behaviors involved. For example, instead of focusing on Sergei's Russian childhood and his reticence about disclosing personal information to strangers, behavioral therapists would focus on his present problems of drinking too much, being unemployed, and being adversarial toward his well-intentioned parents. Their aim would be to help Sergei replace his maladaptive behaviors with more appropriate and satisfying ones. Typically, **behavioral therapy** involves *discovering the factors that trigger and reinforce the problem behavior, specifying a target behavior to replace it, and then, by manipulating these factors, bringing out the desired behavior.* In the process, behavioral therapists help clients to develop the necessary skills or behaviors to cope more effectively with their life situations. Behavioral therapists draw on a repertoire of behavioral methods of proven effectiveness, for example, the token economy and desensitization.

THE TOKEN ECONOMY   In a **token economy** *good behaviors are rewarded with small tokens that can be exchanged for a larger reward later.* One type of token economy frequently used by parents and teachers alike is the sticker chart. Here are some keys to its effective use.

1. Pick a "currency" (not money) important to your child; examples include candy, toy cars, dolls, and going to a special place.
2. Keep the rules simple (see step 3); they need to be easy enough for a child to understand.
3. Decide how many stickers are needed to win a "special prize" (i.e., the currency from step 1). For example, if you are trying to promote sharing behavior during playtime, you might start by telling children that every time they share with another child, they will get a sticker; and after 2 (or 3 or 4 or more) stickers, they can trade them in for the coveted prize. Note: For particularly difficult problems (such as hitting when angry), you might have to

BOX 15–3	Focus on: Health Care: What Are Alternative Forms of Therapy?

An alternative approach to mental health care is one that emphasizes the interrelationship between mind, body, and spirit. Although some alternative approaches have a long history, many remain controversial. The National Center for Complementary and Alternative Medicine at the National Institutes of Health was created in 1992 to help evaluate alternative methods of treatment and to integrate those that are effective into mainstream health care. It is crucial, however, to consult with your health care provider about the approaches you are using, or would like to use, in order to achieve mental wellness. Also, before receiving alternative services, check to be sure the provider is properly certified by an appropriate accrediting agency. Table 15–1 provides a list of some popular forms of alternative therapies.

Table 15–1	Alternative Therapies

General Therapies

Name of Therapy	General Description	Example
Diet and Nutrition Therapy	Altering the amount and type of food consumed.	Eliminating the consumption of foods with artificial flavoring and coloring in order to increase attention and reduce hyperactivity.
Animal-Assisted Therapy	Involves one or both of the following: (1) animal caretaking and (2) animal companionship.	Caring for horses to improve self-esteem, communication, and problem-solving abilities.

Relaxation and Stress-Reduction Techniques

Name of Therapy	General Description	Example
Biofeedback	Physiological monitoring systems provide feedback on bodily functions (e.g., brain waves, heart rate, blood pressure). The patient can then observe how changes in bodily functions correspond to their changes in their thoughts and feelings.	Monitoring heart rate and blood pressure in order to see how altering thought processes (e.g., through guided imagery) can reduce PTSD-related symptoms.
Massage Therapy	Massage is the manipulation of soft-tissue structures throughout the body.	Receiving weekly massages in order to reduce stress and elevate mood.
Yoga/Meditation	Attaining insight through body positioning (i.e., poses), breathing techniques, and meditation.	Participating in a yoga practice with the hope of improving body image, reducing stress, and lifting symptoms of depression.

Expressive Therapies

Name of Therapy	General Description	Example
Art Therapy	Expressing thoughts and feelings through visual art media (e.g., paint, clay, crayon, etc.) in a therapeutic setting.	Previously hidden feelings of loneliness and sadness can be addressed once they have been represented in a painting.
Dance/Movement Therapy	Movement and Dance are used to express feelings	Participating in dance class in an attempt to reduce stress and general feelings of anxiety.
Music/Sound Therapy	Using musical expression, song writing, and music listening in a therapeutic setting to enhance well-being.	Using improvisational drumming to enhance self-esteem and elevate mood.

start with instant gratification (such that every time the child shows self-restraint when angry they get the special prize) before transitioning into a sticker chart.

4. Be consistent. Give stickers when they are deserved, and don't change the rules in the middle of a chart. Also, once earned, stickers should not be taken away; failure to earn a sticker is penalty enough to a child.

5. At home put the sticker chart where the child can see it. In school, sticker charts should be private. When charts are available to all to see in a classroom, competition, teasing, and bullying can result.

6. After a behavior has been demonstrated for a week or so, slowly transition away from the chart. To do this, simply require that more stickers be earned in order to get a prize. After weeks of transitioning, the child will probably continue to demonstrate the desired behavior, even forgetting that they earn stickers for performing it.

7. Remember, it takes longer to transition a child off a sticker chart than it does to earn a prize. When stopped too hastily, undesirable behaviors quickly return.

Token economies are extremely useful in both starting good behaviors (such as brushing teeth, making a bed, practicing an instrument) and stopping bad ones (such as whining, talking back, teasing). Moreover, this form of behavioral therapy can be used at any age. Though, children younger than 4 years of age may have difficulty understanding the rules. And although adolescents may balk a token economy at first, a valued currency can be useful in motivating a teen to try one out (Antony & Roemer, 2011).

DESENSITIZATION   In contrast to the reward-based system of the token economy, **desensitization** (sometimes known as exposure-based therapy), is a *method of controlling anxiety by learning to associate an incompatible response, like relaxation, with the fear-provoking stimulus.* By linking (e.g., exposing) the feared object or situation to something pleasant, such as relaxation, the client becomes "desensitized" to the fearful situation (Wolpe, 1973). Desensitization is especially effective with fears and phobias. To accomplish this, the therapist develops a hierarchy of feared situations, starting with the least fearful and ending with the one that causes the greatest anxiety. The client then learns relaxation techniques, which are applied during each step of the hierarchy. Eventually, the client will remain calm during what used to be the most feared situation imagined. Here's an example: Liz entered desensitization therapy because of her profound anxiety related to taking examinations, which had resulted in repeated failures. The hierarchy of imagined situations started with seeing the exam date on a calendar and culminated with the day of the examination. Liz then learned how to relax her body muscles and gradually associate the relaxed state with each of the feared situations. After 10 sessions, Liz felt free from anxiety at the highest level of the hierarchy.

VIRTUAL REALITY THERAPY   Technological advances have brought desensitization techniques into the twenty-first century. Now, rather than just simply *imagining* feared objects and situations, **virtual reality therapy** allows clients to encounter them. During virtual reality therapy, *individuals don goggles to view a three-dimensional environment in which they can move about and interact with the objects within that setting.* For instance, when standing on a ledge, many people get a little nervous, but a person suffering from a fear of heights (acrophobia) may experience symptoms similar to those of a heart attack, such as chest pains and difficulty breathing. To help overcome their fear, acrophobics use virtual reality to enter a three-dimensional environment in which they move around and experience the world from different heights. Similar to standard desensitization therapy, the client learns to relax as they get further and further away from the ground (Da Costa, Sardinha, & Nardi, 2008). In addition to treating phobias, virtual reality has successfully been used to help those suffering from combat-related PTSD. For example, in the therapeutic simulation "Virtual Iraq" clients return to the sights, sounds, and even the smells of war-torn Iraq, and in doing so, learn how to overcome the stress, anxiety, and fear that can follow combat (Rizzo et al., 2011).

Cognitive Therapies

Cognitive therapy *focuses on faulty cognitive processes as the crucial element in maladaptive behavior.* A major tenet of this form of therapy is the belief that cognitive processes—such as attention, perception, thoughts, and beliefs—may affect behavior independently of the stimuli traditionally emphasized by behavioral therapies. Indeed, cognitive therapists claim that people's actions are often shaped more by their own interpretation and reactions to external events than to the events themselves (Beck, 1979). Stated another way, cognitive therapy proposes that individuals' beliefs affect their interpretation and response to various life circumstances, thereby contributing to emotional adjustment or maladjustment. Cognitive therapists thus differ from insight therapists in that they do not probe for deep-seated causes of their client's problems.

The goal of cognitive therapy, then, is to help people change the way they think; replacing maladaptive thoughts with ones that can promote growth. Take Mel, for example, who discovered that he had earned a low grade on his first psychology test. He felt discouraged and soon engaged in some self-defeating thinking: "How stupid can I be! I'll never make a good grade in this course. I might as well drop it." A cognitive therapist might point out that Mel is overreacting to his poor performance. The therapist would point out a more realistic evaluation of his situation, for example: "This was just the first test, not the final exam; besides, your grades in other classes are quite good." The therapist might instruct Mel how to monitor his self-defeating thoughts and correct his thinking. At some point during our lives, most of us will catastrophize, that is, make matters out to be far worse than they actually are. Do any of the statements in Activity 15–2 frequently pop into your head?

ACTIVITY 15–2

ARE YOU A CATASTROPHIZER?

INSTRUCTIONS: *Place a check mark next to each statement that describes your worrisome thought processes.*

_____ 1. When I am driving in a strange place, I am sure I will get lost.

_____ 2. On the very day I don't do the reading assignment, the professor will call on me.

_____ 3. I just know when I meet someone new that person will not like me.

_____ 4. My alarm clock is least likely to work when I have an early morning commitment.

_____ 5. When I get sick, I know I'll feel worse before I feel better.

_____ 6. I am certain that if I buy something, I'll soon find it elsewhere at a better price.

_____ 7. When I most have to perform well, I perform the worst.

_____ 8. At work, when a piece of technological equipment starts to act up, it spells doom for me.

_____ 9. Unlike others, I find I have a cloud hanging over my head much of the time.

_____ 10. When my car makes a strange noise, I just know it will be something expensive.

How many check marks did you end up with? Even one check mark might indicate that you have a tendency to catastrophize, which can lead to self-defeating behaviors. For example, if you become extremely anxious about having a car accident, you just might! For each statement where a check mark appears, recast the statement in such a way that it represents a more rational, reasonable, or positive view of life, which can lead to more competent, gratifying behavior and less anxiety on your part.

Cognitive-Behavioral Therapy

Cognitive-behavioral therapy *combines elements from behavioral and cognitive therapies.* As such, this approach focuses on both replacing maladjusted thoughts as well as modifying behavior. Let's return to Mel, who failed his first psychology test. Similar to what occurs in cognitive therapy, a cognitive-behavioral therapist would also help Mel alter his cognitions, replacing the faulty ones with growth-promoting ones. But beyond that, the cognitive-behavioral therapist would also support Mel in taking positive behavioral steps to improve his performance, such as talking to the professor to discover the particular reasons he did poorly on the test, getting suggestions for improving his performance on the next test, and finding out what his chances are for eventually earning a good grade in the course. Cognitive-behavioral therapy has been shown in improve client functioning in both the short-term and the long-term, for a variety of disorders, especially those related to depression and anxiety (Northey, 2009).

OTHER APPROACHES TO TREATMENT

LEARNING OBJECTIVES

 15.8 **Know about the various forms of multiperson therapy, such as family therapy.**
 15.9 **Discuss the importance of community-based services for comprehensive mental health care.**
15.10 **Describe the major categories of biomedical therapy.**

In addition to the individual therapies discussed so far, there are a wide variety of other types of interventions. For instance, **group therapy**—*therapeutic format where treatment takes place in groups*—has mushroomed in the past several decades. Groups not only offer opportunities for people to interact with others with similar problems but also are more cost-efficient, saving time and money—an important consideration today. We'll specially examine family therapy because the disruption of marriages and families has become a major source of stress in our society. Also, the gains in medicine and technology have produced more powerful drugs and sophisticated biomedical therapies, which have become an integral part of many treatment programs, so we'll examine them, too. Finally, one of the most dramatic changes in regard to treating individuals with mental disorders is the shift away from prolonged stays in large institutions to the use of community-based services, as you will see shortly. Box 15–4 provides information about mutual-help or self-help groups in which laypersons assist one another. Sometimes, the help of a professional is not necessary; a good friend can be just as healing.

Exploration 15.3: Self-Help Groups

selfhelpgroups.org   This website, sponsored by The American Self-Help Clearinghouse, provides a directory for a variety of self-help groups.

Family, Couples, and Relationship Therapy

RELATIONSHIP THERAPY   Married and unmarried couples alike usually come to relationship therapy because of some crisis—such as infidelity on the part of one partner—or a breakdown in communication. Although each person tends to blame their partner for the current predicament, therapists tend to focus more on the partners' interaction and relationship. For instance, if one person has engaged in an extramarital affair, instead of joining in the blame, the therapist may ask each partner what he or she thinks caused this situation. Perhaps the offending partner has a personality problem or wants to "get back at" the other partner. Either way, the therapist helps both of them become more aware of how they treat each other; how they may unwittingly hurt each other; and most important, how they may nurture each other. The therapist often has to help

| BOX 15–4 | Focus on Health Care: Mutual-Help Groups |

Today, more than 12 million people participate in an estimated 500,000 **self-help** or **mutual-help groups**—*groups whose members share a common problem and meet regularly to discuss their concerns without the guidance of professionals.* Although these groups frequently have multiple functions, such as fostering self-help and lobbying for reform, most have the same underlying purpose—to provide social support as well as practical help in dealing with a problem common to all members. A major assumption is that no one understands you or can help you better than someone who has the same problem, whether it's obesity, depression, or alcoholism. New members may approach their first meeting with apprehension, wondering what the group can do for them or what it will ask in return. Experienced members, well aware of these mixed emotions, encourage new members to feel relaxed and welcome. In an atmosphere that is friendly and compassionate, new members soon realize that their participation is voluntary, with no strings attached. Moreover, to help members speak freely there is usually an unwritten code of confidentiality within the group. Even when there is a series of steps to recovery, as in the various "Anonymous" groups, members can proceed at their own pace. Some groups, especially those that deal with addictive behavior or emotional disorders, may use a "buddy" or "sponsor" system so that a new member can count on a familiar person for encouragement and support. All in all, mutual-help groups provide an atmosphere of acceptance and support that encourages their members to communicate more openly, view their problems more objectively, and find more effective coping strategies. Research demonstrates that most mutual-help groups are effective in producing positive member change (Moritsugu et al., 2010).

the couple clarify the extent to which they really want to work at the marriage and, if so, how to proceed. Therapies, such as this one, that go beyond individual intervention are more complex because of the various relationships and alliances involved. Despite the complexity, research reveals strong evidence for its effectiveness (Becvar, 2008).

FAMILY THERAPY **Family therapy,** as the name implies, *involves the larger family unit, including children and adolescents, on the assumption that the disturbance of one family member reflects problems in the overall family patterns.* There are now dozens of different types of family therapy, which vary in their theoretical approaches, range of techniques, and procedures. Some therapists prefer to see the entire family from beginning to end. Others may see the parents for a couple of sessions, then the children for a couple of sessions, and finally bring them all together. Still others, such as contextual therapists, who adhere to an intergenerational approach, may even involve members of the extended family, such as grandparents. Implicit in all such therapies is the assumption that families function as systems, so the individual's problems are best understood and treated as an integral part of the family milieu (Sexton, 2011).

Here's an example: Suppose a teenager is having trouble in school or is doing something that indicates a problem. The usual course of events is to make the teenager the client, leaving untouched the larger background of problems at home. However, professionals oriented to family therapy may discover upon further investigation that the teenager is simply a sensitive and vulnerable person who has become the scapegoat in a troubled family. When this is the case, it may be necessary to see other members of the family to get a better understanding of the family's dynamics.

Community-Based Services

Is your stereotype of a person with a mental disorder that of a homeless person, sleeping on the streets, carting around possessions in a stolen grocery cart? Does your stereotype include the person begging, urinating on the street, and curling up on apartment house stoops during cold snaps? This is the image we often hold of the mentally ill. This description need not be the case but sometimes is (Moritsugu et al., 2010).

Exploration 15.4: Community Mental Health

www.thenationalcouncil.org/cs/_overview   In addition to providing a searchable database of community mental health programs by state, this site also offers information on a wide range of topics related to community mental health care.

Source: Courtesy of National Council for Community Behavioral Healthcare.

REASONS FOR COMMUNITY-BASED SERVICES   The introduction of antipsychotic drugs, along with convincing evidence that custodial care in large mental hospitals is detrimental, led to the release of large numbers of ex-patients into the community over the past 40 years. Even recent studies of institutionalized individuals with mental disorders indicate that much of the time spent in the hospitals is spent in loneliness, without treatment, and without interaction with others (Yawar, 2008). Because most of these individuals require some type of treatment, as do others in the community who wish to avoid hospitalization, mental health professionals have responded by providing more **community-based services** (Rosenberg & Rosenberg, 2006). This is a general term meaning that *mental health services are located in the individual's own community or nearby.* The passage of the Community Mental Health Centers Act in 1963 aimed to create a **community mental health center** for every 50,000 people in the United States. These include *a variety of mental health services located in the patient's own community.* Everyone in the catchment area (an area of geographical coverage) for the center would have access to the needed psychological services at the center at affordable fees, without having to leave the community. Not surprisingly, these centers have been a major factor in the nationwide shift away from hospitalization to community-based care (Auxier, Farley, & Seifert, 2011).

Community-based services often fall short of what is really needed due to inadequate funding and lack of coordinated programming.

TYPES OF COMMUNITY-BASED SERVICES As you might expect, outpatient services are the most heavily used services of local mental health centers. The goal of **outpatient services** is to *provide help for individuals without disrupting their normal routine.* Most mental health centers offer short-term therapy for individuals in the community with a variety of problems, ranging from domestic disputes to severe emotional disturbances. The more comprehensive centers also provide alternatives to hospital care, such as day hospitals, halfway houses, and emergency or crisis services.

Day hospitals, which *offer part-time care in a hospital setting for those with mental disorders,* provide the needed therapeutic care to patients from morning until late afternoon and then allow them to return to their families in the evening. Another type of agency that has proliferated in recent years is the **halfway house**—*a residence in which newly released patients and ex-addicts can live under supervision for a short period of time while they make the crucial transition in their lives from a setting with close supervision and other restrictions* to one of greater independence and freedom. Halfway houses are also called *group homes* and *board-and-care homes.* The best halfway houses are small residences that are staffed by paraprofessionals who help the residents learn to live together and acquire the appropriate skills for returning to community life (Browne & Courtney, 2007). **Crisis intervention** has also emerged in response to a widespread need for *immediate treatment for those who are in a state of acute crisis but do not need treatment for many sessions.* Most people who come for short-term crisis counseling do not continue in treatment for more than a few sessions. In addition, a variety of telephone hotlines are now available in many communities. And police, who are frequently the first to come in contact with a person in distress, often receive some crisis intervention training (Rath, 2008).

EFFECTIVENESS OF COMMUNITY-BASED SERVICES Despite the best of intentions, community-based services often fall short of what is needed. Typically, deficiencies arise because of insufficient funding and the resultant inadequacies in facilities, staffing, and carefully thought-out and coordinated programs that address the needs of the community (Moritsugu et al., 2010). Because of these insufficiencies, the return of former patients to the community has slowed significantly. Even when individuals return to the community, they often lack the necessary supervision and support to stay there (NAMI, 2006). In large cities, many of them become "street people" before returning to the hospital—hence, our stereotype. As a result, *the number of admissions to mental hospitals has increased rather than decreased, leading to a "revolving-door" syndrome* or **transinstitutionalization**. The revolving-door syndrome and the presence of so many former mental patients in jails, on the streets, and in nursing homes reminds us that although comprehensive community-based care is an excellent idea, it is far from achieving its original goals (Swartz, 2010).

Biomedical Therapies

In contrast to the various forms of talking therapy, **biomedical therapies** are *strategies that rely on direct physiological intervention to treat the symptoms of psychological disorders.* In recent years, there has been a rapid accumulation of evidence that many disorders are related to biochemical abnormalities, especially unusually high or low levels of **neurotransmitters**—*chemical substances* (or messengers) *involved in the transmission of neural impulses between neurons.* As a result, psychoactive drugs have especially become an indispensable part of treatment. Many of those with severe disorders such as schizophrenia may be treated primarily with drugs. Those with less severe disorders may be treated with medication, but often in conjunction with the other therapies discussed so far. In fact, psychotherapy *combined with* biomedical treatment has been shown to produce better outcomes than either psychotherapy or biomedical treatments alone. Combined therapy is now the most common mode of treatment in psychiatry and is currently considered *the* standard of care for a wide range of mental disorders (Cuijpers, van Straten, Warmerdam, & Andersson, 2009). The three major classes of biomedical therapies are psychotropic medications, electroconvulsive therapy, and psychosurgery. Let's look at each.

Exploration 15.5: Drug Side Effects and Dangers

www.drugs.com   When it comes to finding out information about the side effects and dangers of prescription and non-prescription drugs, this site has it all. It's searchable too.

PSYCHOTROPIC MEDICATIONS   The prescription of **psychotropic medications**—*medication used to treat psychological disorders*—continues to be the most widely used form of biomedical therapy. Currently, 20 percent of adults in the United States take at least one psychiatric medication (Cassels, 2011). There are three major psychotropic medication categories: antianxiety, antidepressants, and antipsychotics (NIMH, 2012). Each will be discussed below. But first, Box 15–5 presents information on a growing problem on college campuses, the use of so-called **"study" drugs**—*stimulant medications taken by people without a prescription in an attempt to improve their focus while studying.*

Antianxiety drugs, which *alleviate anxiety*, are the most commonly prescribed psychoactive drugs in the United States. Xanax (alprazolam), Klonopin (clonazepam), and Ativan (lorazepam) are common psychotropic medications used to treat a wide range of anxiety disorders. As useful as these medications are, they do not cure anxiety, and they are not without side effects, including drowsiness, upset stomach, impaired thinking, and depression. Also, when used in combination with alcohol or other central nervous system depressants, these drugs can be dangerous or even fatal (Phillips et al., 2012). Finally, the most common criticism of antianxiety medications is that they may provide such prompt alleviation of symptoms that people avoid solving their problems in behavioral or social ways.

Antidepressants *are used to treat depression and elevate mood,* usually by increasing the level of certain neurotransmitters, especially norepinephrine and serotonin. There are numerous antidepressants available on the market, including Cymbalta (duloxetine), Paxil (paroxetine), and Wellbutrin (bupropion). These drugs help to relieve many of the typical symptoms of depression, such as sleeplessness or excessive sleepiness, chronic fatigue, loss of appetite, sadness, and feelings of worthlessness, but again do not provide a cure. As with all medications, there are side effects to be concerned about, such as weight gain, anxiety, insomnia, and decreased sex drive. A significant disadvantage of these drugs is that they do not begin to take effect for about two to four weeks—which can be a long time for seriously depressed people waiting for relief.

BOX 15–5   Focus on Wellness: "Study" Drugs

Andrea has a big test tomorrow, but she's finding it hard to stay on task while studying. She's thinking about her "ex," the party she wants to go to later, her favorite music group, and just about a million other little things. Andrea has a friend with **attention deficit hyperactivity disorder (ADHD)**—*characterized by a longstanding pattern of inattention, impulsivity, and hyperactivity*—who takes Adderall to reduce the symptoms of the disorder. She thinks to herself: "If Adderall can make a guy with ADHD focus, imagine what it can do for me!" Like Andrea, around 6.4 percent of college students admit to taking Adderall without a prescription (SAMHSA, 2009). The problem is that Adderall and many other drugs for treating the symptoms of ADHD (e.g., Ritalin, Concerta, Vyvanse) are amphetamine based. As such, they are habit forming, can cause agitation/anxiety, hostility, and aggression, as well as negative and psychotic thoughts; even after taking just one pill. In Andrea's case, taking Adderall caused her to have a panic attack which prevented her from studying; and as a result, she failed her exam the next day. Other side effects of Adderall use include irregular heartbeat, seizures, and rapid breathing. Remember, you should never take Adderall, or any other psychotropic medication, without a prescription. Incidentally, Adderall and the like are considered to be controlled substances. Selling such drugs (even with a prescription) is considered to be a felony under state and federal law (Concha, 2011).

> **BOX 15–6** Focus on Wellness: Alleviating Depression through Exercise
>
> Dozens of studies link regular physical exercise with lower levels of depression. It is not exactly clear how or why exercise affects depression. Some explanations focus on the changes in body and brain chemistry, resulting in rising levels of endorphins in the blood during exercise. Other explanations suggest that the sense of mastery over one's body gained through exercise may contribute to a greater sense of personal control over other aspects of one's life as well, thereby alleviating the passivity and helplessness often found in depressed people. Because the more severe types of depression typically result from a complex interaction of genetic, physiological, and psychological factors, exercise is best seen as only one facet in the overall treatment of depression—but one that should not be overlooked (Sutherland, Sutherland, & Hoehns, 2003).

Newer, quicker-acting antidepressants have been introduced, but it remains to be seen whether they will be as effective. Antidepressants are the medication class whose use has most dramatically increased in recent years (Olfson, Marcus, Druss, & Pincus, 2002). You may be wondering whether you can improve depression without taking a pill and without going into therapy. For some, the answer is yes, as you will see in Box 15–6.

Antipsychotic drugs, as the name suggests, are used to treat the symptoms of severe disorders such as schizophrenia. *These medications primarily relieve the symptoms of psychoses, such as extreme agitation, hyperactivity, hallucinations, and delusions.* As mentioned earlier, the use of antipsychotic drugs is often the primary treatment for patients with schizophrenia, especially those chronically impaired. These drugs are thought to work by blocking the activity of dopamine and other neurotransmitters, thereby reducing hallucinations, delusions, and bizarre behavior. However, they do not cure the apathy, social withdrawal, or interpersonal difficulties found in people with schizophrenia, for which psychotherapy is usually helpful.

Antipsychotic drugs also have several side effects. In producing calm, they may produce apathy as well, reducing the patient to a zombielike state. Also, a small proportion of patients develop **tardive dyskinesia,** *characterized by jerking movements around the neck and face and involuntary protrusions of the tongue.* Today, newer medications with fewer side effects are available. These are called *atypical antipsychotics* and appear to be more effective than older medications. Despite the disadvantages and the criticisms surrounding the use of such drugs, antipsychotic drugs have been the single biggest factor in reducing the institutionalized patient population in the United States from over half a million in the 1950s to about one-third that number today. Over two-thirds of individuals with schizophrenia who regularly take their medication can remain out of the hospital. Consequently, most professionals who work with them believe the value of the drugs outweighs their potential for adverse side effects (Hamden, Newton, McCauley-Elsom, & Cross, 2011).

ELECTROCONVULSIVE THERAPY **Electroconvulsive therapy (ECT)** *involves the administration of an electric current to the patient's brain to produce a convulsion.* ECT, for reasons that are not completely understood, helps to relieve severe depression in some patients. Although people often react negatively when it is mentioned, ECT has been refined and is done in a more humane manner than in the past (Rosedale, 2011). For severely depressed individuals for whom medication is ineffective, ECT usually involves 6 to 10 treatments, spaced over a period of several weeks. An electric current of approximately 70 to 130 volts is administered to the temple area for a fraction of a second. Within half an hour, the patient awakens and remembers nothing of the treatment. The most common side effect is memory loss, especially the recall of events before the treatment. Despite the controversy over ECT, its effectiveness in treating severe illness is recognized as useful by the American Psychiatric Association and similar organizations in other countries (NIMH, 2009a).

PSYCHOSURGERY **Psychosurgery** is a drastic surgical procedure *designed to destroy or disconnect brain tissue in an attempt to regulate abnormal behavior.* Psychosurgery is aimed at reducing abnormal behavior. In the earlier prefrontal lobotomies, the surgeon severed the nerves connecting the frontal lobes of the brain with the emotion-controlling centers. Although many severely disturbed patients became calm, others emerged from surgery in a vegetative state. As a result, professionals welcomed the introduction of antipsychotic drugs, which produce similar results in a safer, reversible manner. Since then, newer surgical procedures have been identified. For instance, in **deep brain stimulation** *surgeons implant electrodes deep into the brain that when activated send electrical impulses into the surrounding tissues.* So far, this new technique has been used to successfully treat those with severe OCD and depressed, suicidal patients who have not responded to other treatments. Although newer techniques are showing promising results, psychosurgery is still the treatment of *last resort* and is used only rarely (Sachdev & Chen, 2009; Schlaepfer, Bewernick, Kayser, & Lenz, 2011).

HOW WELL DOES THERAPY WORK?

LEARNING OBJECTIVES

15.11 Explain the effectiveness of psychotherapy.

Have you ever wondered if therapy would work for you? Better yet, have you ever questioned whether psychotherapy works at all? For many years, hardly anyone bothered to ask such a question. Therapists and clients alike held a kind of blind faith that therapy does work. Then after reviewing various studies on the subject, Hans Eysenck (1966) shocked the world of therapy by concluding that over time, clients *not in therapy* improved as much clients *in therapy.* Eysenck's claims were hotly contested and challenged by others. Since that time, scientists have typically asked three main questions about the effectiveness of therapy:

1. Is therapy better than no therapy?
2. Is one particular type of therapy generally more effective than others?
3. Are certain disorders more amenable to certain therapies?

Let's address these questions in order of presentation.

IS PSYCHOTHERAPY EFFECTIVE? Extensive early studies confirmed that therapy tends to have positive effects. For example, the American Psychiatric Association, which developed a commission on psychotherapy, says that based on research, at the end of therapy, the average treated patient is better off than 80 percent of untreated patients (Gabbard & Lazar, 2004). Another study found that 50 percent of patients noticeably improved after eight sessions, while 75 percent of the individuals in psychotherapy improved by the end of six months (American Psychological Association, 1998).

Research has also attempted to provide some idea about what elements make therapy effective, no matter what the theoretical underpinning (Kolden et al., 2006). One important aspect found over and over again is *the match or quality of fit between the client and the therapist,* known as the **therapeutic alliance** (Meissner, 2008). One way to provide a good match is for *the client to become an active consumer of information,* that is, to ask questions about the therapist's qualifications, for explanations about the diagnosis, and so forth. Therapy is not exclusively dependent on the therapist's skills, the disorder, and the type of therapy. The client's traits and motives are also important. The type of person likely to benefit most from psychotherapy is someone who is articulate, motivated, anxious to change, capable of becoming personally involved in therapy, and believes in psychological processes as explanations for behavior (Nietzel, Bernstein, & Milich, 1991; Vogel, Wester, Wei, & Boysen, 2005). Another important ingredient is *length of treatment,* with longer treatments yielding better results (Seligman, 1995). In research on the number of sessions required for treatment, 20 or fewer sessions seem to be the norm today for effective treatment, with some researchers arguing that even a single session can promote growth (Miller, 2008). Assigning "homework," focusing on skills building and problem solving, and repeating assessments also appear to contribute to effective interventions (O'Donohue, Buchanan, & Fisher, 2000).

IS ONE TYPE OF PSYCHOTHERAPY GENERALLY MORE EFFECTIVE THAN ANOTHER? Somewhat surprisingly, in terms of overall effectiveness, that there is little difference among specific types of interpersonal psychotherapies (Wampold, Minami, Tierney, Baskin, & Bhati, 2005). However, an increasing number of therapists characterize themselves as using an **eclectic approach**—*treatment based a combination of techniques and principles from various forms of therapy,* which appears to be more effective than any single form of therapy used by itself (Kensit, 2000).

IS ONE TYPE OF THERAPY BETTER OR WORSE FOR ANY PARTICULAR DISORDER? Although more research is merited on all of these issues, the answer to this third question at this point seems to be "yes." The following is a list of **evidence-based therapies,** that is, *therapies proven effective through rigorous research methodologies.* Cognitive therapies can successfully treat depression and anxiety. Behavior therapies work for phobias, OCD, depression, bed-wetting, and modifying the behavior of people with developmental disabilities. Cognitive-behavior therapies appear to be highly effective for anxiety disorders, depression, bulimia nervosa, and substance abuse disorders (Galanter & Kleber, 2008; Rachman, 2008). Psychotropic drugs are most effective for treating schizophrenic disorders (Hollon, Thase, & Markowitz, 2002), while a combination of medication and psychotherapy appears most effective for the treatment of depression (Cuijpers et al., 2009). As more answers become available through research, psychotherapists may increasingly offer specific treatments for particular problems or integrate different approaches that may be more effective than a single approach (Antony & Barlow, 2010).

FINDING HELP

LEARNING OBJECTIVES

15.12 List the important questions that need to be asked when thinking about getting professional help.

Being knowledgeable about psychotherapy is one thing. Knowing how to get professional help for yourself and others is another matter. Should you or someone you know have the occasion to seek professional help, you might consider the following questions addressed below:

- When should you seek professional help?
- Where do you find help?
- What should you look for in a therapist?
- What can you expect from therapy?
- How long must you go?

When Should You Seek Professional Help?

As you might expect, there is no simple answer to this question, as so much depends on the particular person and the situation. However, a simple rule is this: Whenever your problems begin to interfere with your work and personal life, it's time to seek professional help. Also, when your present methods of coping with your problems no longer work, that's another sign that you may need help, especially when your family or friends are tired of being used as therapists and become openly concerned about you. Most important, whenever you feel overwhelmed and desperate and don't know what to do, it's best to seek help.

Where Do You Find Help?

Help is available in a wide variety of settings, with a large proportion of therapists working in comprehensive mental health centers. Staffed by a combination of psychiatrists, psychologists, social workers, and counselors, these centers offer a variety of services, including emergency help, all at a nominal fee that depends on income and ability to pay.

See Box 15–7 for a description of the various types of mental health professionals available.

Many therapists work in private practice, either in a group or individual setting. They are usually listed in the yellow pages by their respective professions, for example, psychiatrists, psychologists, social workers, or family therapists. Although some are expensive, you may be reimbursed for part of the fee, depending on the type of insurance you have. Of note, the Mental Health Parity Act of 2008 requires that most employer-provided group health plans offer the same level of coverage for mental illness and drug abuse treatment as for other medical conditions. If you don't have insurance, some clinics provide low-cost or free services.

Many private social service or human service agencies provide short-term counseling and support for such matters as family problems, addiction problems, and career counseling. Also, many private and public hospitals offer emergency help for psychological problems. Then, too, most high schools and colleges have counseling centers, which provide psychological help as well as academic guidance and career counseling. If all else fails, the American Psychological Association Practice Directorate at 800-374-2723 can aim you toward an appropriate state organization that can make a local referral.

BOX 15–7   Focus on Health Care: Who Are the Therapists?

Unlike law or medicine, in which there is a single path to professional practice, there are many routes to becoming a psychotherapist. Because few states regulate the practice of psychotherapy as such, the question of who may legitimately conduct psychotherapy is governed by state law or professional boards within the respective professions.

- **Psychiatrists** *are medical doctors who specialize in the treatment of mental illness.* They usually spend three to four years training in a clinical setting following their medical degree and can treat the psychological disorders requiring drugs and hospitalization.
- **Psychoanalysts** *are psychiatrists or other mental health professionals who have received several years of additional training in personality theory and the therapeutic methods of one of the founding analysts,* such as Freud, Jung, Adler, or Sullivan.
- **Psychologists** *receive clinical training in the methods of psychological assessment and treatment as part of a program in clinical, counseling, or school psychology.* They may have a Ph.D., Ed.D., or Psy.D. degree.
- **Psychiatric (or clinical) social workers** *receive supervised clinical training as part of their master's degree program in the field of social work, and some earn a doctorate as well.* They tend to be community oriented and usually work as part of a clinical team, though many now enter private practice.
- **Counselors** *receive training in personality theory and counseling skills, usually at the master's degree level. Their counseling emphasis tends to reflect their respective professional affiliations, depending on whether they are doing marriage counseling, career counseling, pastoral counseling (clergy), or some other type.*
- **Paraprofessionals** (*para meaning "akin to"*) *have two- or four-year degrees (or sometimes no degree at all) and work in the mental health field.* Sometimes as many as half the staff members of a community mental health center work at the paraprofessional level, assisting in the helping process in a variety of ways.

<table>
<tr><td>BOX 15–8</td><td>Focus on Health Care: Computers and Therapy</td></tr>
</table>

An increasing number of psychotherapists are offering online help; in fact, technology may become an important part of psychotherapy delivery in the next decade. There are now so many online therapists that no one quite knows what to name this new form of therapy: e-therapy, e-counseling, cybertherapy, telecounseling, remote therapy, or Internet-based therapy. Many therapists are setting up websites accessible to millions of Americans with credit cards and computers.

Cybertherapists claim that Internet clients can avoid stigma, obtain treatment at almost any time or place, and proceed at their own pace. Others, however, provide the caveat that cybertherapy does not allow for as detailed probing as does face-to-face intervention and that ethical issues are beginning to emerge; for example, confidentiality may be betrayed if the wrong person receives an electronic message either to or from the therapist or client. Critics also argue that (1) the client may know little about the online therapist's qualifications because of the geographic distance between client and therapist and (2) clients who are not computer savvy may feel uncomfortable with cybertherapy (Fitzgerald, Hunter, Hadjistavropoulos, & Koocher, 2010). Contrary to many criticisms, however, technology need not necessarily compromise the all-important therapeutic alliance between client and therapist (Newman, 2004).

What Should You Look for in a Therapist?

Among the major considerations for choosing a therapist should be (a) whether the therapist is professionally trained and certified and (b) how comfortable you feel with this person. Ordinarily, people must be properly qualified to list themselves as psychiatrists, psychologists, or social workers in the telephone directory. Also, professionals are encouraged to display their state license and other certificates in a prominent place in their office. But you will also want to feel comfortable talking to the therapist. Does this person really listen to you? Is the person warm and empathic without being condescending? Does this person understand and appreciate your particular point of view? Box 15–8 discusses a rapidly growing trend that will make therapy seemingly available to everyone, no matter how remote a region they live in. This trend involves therapy via computers and the Internet.

What Can You Expect From Therapy?

Most therapies provide certain common benefits, such as an empathic, caring, and trusting relationship; hope for the demoralized; and a new way of understanding yourself and the world. Beyond this, a lot depends on the goals and progress made in your particular therapy. People seeking relatively short-term therapy usually acquire a better understanding of their problems as well as the necessary skills to cope with a personal or family crisis. Those undergoing relatively long-term therapy, such as psychoanalytic therapy, aspire to more fundamental changes in their personality and may remain in therapy longer.

How Long Must You Go?

In the past, the lack of objective guidelines made it difficult for therapists and clients alike to know how long therapy should last. However, the recent trend toward short-term therapies and the increased concern for containing health care costs have made the length of therapy a major issue. At the same time, the rate of improvement varies considerably among different types of clients. Consequently, the appropriate length of treatment often becomes an empirical issue to be decided by clients and their therapists with some interference from insurance carriers.

As a practical guide for deciding when to terminate therapy, consider two key questions: First, is the crisis or problem that brought you to therapy under control? You need not have resolved all of your difficulties, but you should have more understanding and control over your life so that your difficulties do not interfere with your work and personal activities. Second, can you maintain the gains acquired in therapy on your own? It's best to discuss these two issues with your therapist before deciding to terminate therapy. At the same time, bear in mind that in therapy (as in all close relationships) there will be both unsettling as well as gratifying occasions.

Chapter Summary

PSYCHOTHERAPY: WHAT IS IT? WHO USES IT?

15.1 Define psychotherapy.
Psychotherapy is the helping process in which a trained therapist performs certain activities that will facilitate a change in the client's attitudes and behaviors.

15.2 Explain the role that culture plays in treatment.
Therapists may view symptoms, diagnoses, and treatments in ways that sometimes diverge from their clients' views, especially when their cultural backgrounds are different. Therapists need to understand, be sensitive to, and respectful of the various cultures of their clients.

INSIGHT THERAPIES—THE TALKING CURE

15.3 Summarize the main features of insight therapy.
Insight-oriented therapies bring about change by increasing self-understanding.

15.4 Compare psychoanalysis with modern psychodynamic therapy.
Psychoanalysis arrived at insight by bringing clients' unconscious sexual and aggressive desires/conflicts into consciousness. Psychodynamic therapists focus more on personal relationships to help clients achieve insight into and self-mastery of the unconscious forces in their lives.

15.5 Describe person-centered therapy.
Rogers's person-centered approach assumes that individuals have within themselves vast resources for self-understanding and growth, which may be actualized within a caring and empathic relationship conducive to change.

COGNITIVE AND BEHAVIORAL THERAPIES

15.6 Compare cognitive, behavioral, and cognitive-behavioral therapies.
Cognitive therapies tend to focus on the irrational thoughts and beliefs that contribute to problem behaviors. Behavioral therapists focus directly on the client's problem behaviors, with the aim of replacing maladaptive behaviors with more appropriate and satisfying ones. Cognitive-behavioral techniques have the goal of modifying faulty assumptions and thought patterns and then relying on established behavioral procedures such as relaxation training to help modify the problem behavior.

15.7 Explain how to effectively use a token economy.
In a token economy, good behaviors are rewarded with small tokens that can be exchanged for a larger reward later. Keys to its effective use include (1) picking a currency of value; (2) keeping rules simple; (3) deciding on the number of tokens needed to earn the larger prize; (4) being consistent in its use; (5) at home, putting the sticker chart where the child can see it; in school, keeping it private; (6) after a behavior has been learned, slowly transitioning the child away from the token economy; and (7) remembering that undesirable behaviors return with token economies are incorrectly stopped.

OTHER APPROACHES TO TREATMENT

15.8 Know about the various forms of multiperson therapy, such as family therapy.
The various group therapies, including family and couples therapy, deal with the individual as a function of group dynamics or family structure and utilize the group process to help members achieve mutually satisfying solutions.

15.9 Discuss the importance of community-based services for comprehensive mental health care.
One of the most dramatic changes in mental health care has been the marked shift from prolonged stays in large institutions to the use of community-based services. Although the latter have expanded to include a variety of services, such as day hospitals and halfway houses, outpatient services continue to be the most widely used. Community-based programs increase the availability of mental health services for all.

15.10 Describe the major categories of biomedical therapy.
Biomedical therapies treat the symptoms of psychological problems with direct physical intervention through medication, electroconvulsive therapy, and psychosurgery.

HOW WELL DOES THERAPY WORK?

15.11 Explain the effectiveness of psychotherapy.
Studies tend to show that psychotherapy generally works better than no therapy, and clients who have had therapy are better off than untreated clients. Also, some approaches appear to be especially well suited to certain problems, such as the cognitive-behavioral approach for people anxiety disorders, depression, bulimia nervosa, and substance abuse disorders.

FINDING HELP

15.12 List the important questions that need to be asked when thinking about getting professional help.
Individuals who are considering professional help might benefit from asking the following questions: (1) When should I seek professional help? (2) Where can I find it? (3) What should I look for in a therapist? (4) What can I expect from therapy? and (5) How long must I stay in therapy?

Self-Test

1. As a therapist, Jenny felt that the only way to truly cure someone of psychopathology is to increase the client's self-understanding. Jenny's belief is consistent with:
   a. psychoanalysis
   b. systematic desensitization
   c. insight therapy
   d. psychosurgery
2. During the course of treatment, Bob started to feel that his therapist didn't like him, that he thought he was stupid, and that he believed that he wouldn't be amount to much in life. In reality, these feelings reflected how Bob felt about his father. Bob was experiencing:
   a. transference
   b. insight
   c. counter-transference
   d. free association
3. According to Carl Rogers, which of the following is not needed to establish a growth-producing therapeutic climate?
   a. The therapist must be "genuine"
   b. The therapist must provide an environment filled with acceptance and caring
   c. The therapist must engage in empathetic understanding
   d. The therapist must challenge the patients self-defeating thoughts and emotions
4. Treating a phobia with desensitization therapy involves:
   a. depriving a client of any access to an addictive drug
   b. associating a pleasant relaxed state with anxiety-arousing stimuli
   c. replacing a positive response to a harmful stimulus with a negative response
   d. associating unwanted behaviors with unpleasant experiences
5. A therapist treating depression with cognitive therapy is most likely to:
   a. attempt to change a client's self-defeating ways of thinking
   b. encourage clients to value their own unique moment-to-moment feelings
   c. focus attention on each client's unique positive and negative feelings toward the therapist
   d. emphasize that relaxation is a healthy antidote for depression
6. Alfred has recently become a behavior problem at school. The school counselor believes that Alfred's issues primarily caused problems with this parents and difficulties with his sister. The therapist believes that in order for Alfred to improve in school, his experiences with his parents and sister need to change as well. Based on the information, what type of therapy will the school counselor suggest for Alfred?
   a. cognitive therapy
   b. biomedical therapy
   c. family therapy
   d. person-centered therapy
7. Sara has been on antipsychotic medication for so many years that she has developed tardive dyskinesia. We will most likely see Sara:
   a. protruding her tongue and jerking movements around the neck
   b. developing tolerance to her medication
   c. loosing control of her limbs
   d. having trouble staying and falling asleep
8. Melissa suffers from auditory hallucinations and falsely believes that her former high school teachers are trying to kill her. Melissa's symptoms are most likely to be relieved by _____ drugs
   a. antipsychotic
   b. antianxiety
   c. antimanic
   d. antischizophrenic
9. Tyrell suffered from severe depression. Months of therapy and antidepressants have done little to help lift his mood. He has even started to have suicidal thoughts. So, Tyrell is going to undergo a procedure in which an electric current passes through his brain. The procedure Tyrell is having is called:
   a. psychosurgery
   b. prefrontal lobotomy
   c. electroconvulsive therapy
   d. SAT
10. When searching the Internet in the hopes of finding a type of therapy that might work, it is important to avoid gimmicks and unproven therapies. Rather, you should look for therapies that have been demonstrated through research to work. Such therapies are known as:
    a. evidence-based therapies
    b. therapeutic alliance therapies
    c. transinstitutionalization
    d. anecdotal therapies

Exercises

1. *How do you feel about getting help?* Write a paragraph describing your attitude toward getting help for a psychological problem. To what extent do you feel that psychological help is a sign of personal weakness? How severe would the problem have to be before you sought help? Be honest.

2. *To whom would you turn for help?* Suppose you needed psychological help immediately. To whom would you turn? Write down the name, address, and telephone number of the person or agency. If you're unable to do so, you might ask for appropriate referrals from your state psychological association or a local employee assistance program at work. You might also think about why you selected this person or agency.

3. *Distinguishing between psychiatrists and psychologists.* People often confuse these two professionals. Write a paragraph or so describing the differences between these two types of professionals. What services are usually reserved for psychiatrists? What types of problems or psychological disorders are most appropriate for psychologists?

4. *First-person account of therapy.* If you've participated in counseling or therapy, write a page or two describing your experience. In what ways was it beneficial? Do you have any misgivings about it? On the basis of your experience, what suggestions would you make to those considering therapy? If you have never been in therapy, imagine that you have been for counseling and write about why you think it might be beneficial or not.

5. *Mutual-help groups.* Perhaps you've participated in a group like Parents Without Partners or Alcoholics Anonymous. If yes, write a page or so describing your experience. If not, which type of mutual-help group would you be most interested in joining and why? You might visit the website for the American Self-Help Clearing House to obtain a list of such groups (http://selfhelpgroups.org).

Questions for Self-Reflection

1. Do you believe that friends can be good medicine?
2. If you were looking for a therapist, either for yourself or someone else, where would you seek advice?
3. What are some personal qualities you would look for in a therapist? Professional qualities?
4. Have you ever considered using desensitization to reduce your own anxieties or fears?
5. Do you think some of your limitations or problems might be related to family patterns, present or past?
6. Have you ever belonged to a mutual-help or self-help group?
7. Would you agree that people have to want to change in order to benefit fully from therapy?
8. Do you think that asking for help when you need it is itself a mark of maturity? Weakness?
9. Are you aware that many people experience personal growth (as well as the relief of symptoms) in psychotherapy? How can therapy help people grow?
10. If you went for help, what kind of therapy (e.g., person-centered) would you seek? Why?

Chapter Sixteen

Death, Dying, and Grief

*T*hroughout most of his 62 years of marriage to Joanna, Nathaniel was a fun-loving, hard-working, out-of-doors kind of person. But then Nathaniel was diagnosed with skin cancer, which left him disabled and eventually put him in a coma. Nathaniel's health disintegrated so quickly that he was unable to tell Joanna what his last wishes were. In the final days of his life, Nathaniel was on intravenous painkillers and sustained by a feeding tube. At that point, Joanna, together with her grown children, decided to have the feeding tube removed. They all knew that Nathaniel would not want to continue existing in this way. Shortly thereafter Nathaniel died; his family at his side. As Joanna grieved over her husband, she talked openly with her friends about how much she missed him. She regularly tended to the plants at the family plot. Knowing that her husband never liked being alone, she sometimes paused by his grave to talk to him. "Don't worry," she would say, "I'll be with you one day." At times, she would glance at the unused gravesite adjacent to her husband's, the one with a headstone on which her name was already engraved, and smile.

DEATH AND DYING

LEARNING OBJECTIVES

16.1 List some of the leading causes of death.
16.2 Explain the connection between mortality salience and death anxiety.
16.3 Describe how people come to terms with their own mortality.
16.4 Identify the physical and mental changes that occur near the end of life.

Some approach death and dying, like Joanna, with an open mind and matter-of-fact attitude. Others rely on denial to avoid thinking about the inevitable. Actually, some denial of death is probably necessary *and* normal to function effectively. Death, especially the possibility of our own demise, is such a harsh reality that many find this issue difficult to face directly. Denial, therefore, helps to keep anxiety and despondency at low, manageable levels. It can also help us avoid the pain associated with being separated from loved ones, in no longer being able to share with them in joys and sorrows, and in the recognition of a future without their presence. For those who believe in heaven or an afterlife, death is just the next step in a journey that will continue. But for those who aren't so sure, death can be a most unpleasant thought—and one worth avoiding, at least for a short while.

> ### BOX 16–1 Did you know that . . .
>
> - The annual death rate in the United States is about 8 percent
> - The average cost of a funeral is about $7000
> - The cremation rate in the United States is 37 percent, in Canada its nearly 68 percent
> - Funeral homes generate around $12 billion annually
> - Nearly 60 percent of mortuary science students are female
>
> *Source:* Data from "Trends and Statistics," from the National Funeral Director Association website, 2012.

Nevertheless, an excessive or inappropriate denial of death tends to be counterproductive. Case in point, people who constantly reassure themselves that "It can't happen to me" or who insist "I don't want to think about it" may continue to smoke, abuse drugs and alcohol, eat unhealthy foods, and take unnecessary risks, all of which increase the likelihood of dying early. For some, the denial of death is so strong that it causes them to avoid the aged, the seriously ill, and anyone or situation (such as funerals) that serves as a reminder of their own mortality (Routledge & Juhl, 2010; Sherman, Norman, & McSherry, 2010). Remember, though, *behaving* as if you can live forever can lead to the postponement of doing the things that really matter, which in the end can impede personal growth and result in a more superficial life.

We'll begin this chapter by considering some of the realities of death, such as the everyday risks of dying, death anxiety, and the experience of dying. In the middle section, we'll examine some of the ethical and practical issues associated with dying, such as advanced directives and hospice care. Then in the final section, we'll describe the process of grief and the importance of working through emotions associated with personal loss.

Risks of Dying

As you might suspect, the risk of dying varies greatly from one person to another depending on a variety of factors. Health habits and lifestyles, as mentioned elsewhere in this book, are especially important. For example, people who smoke a pack or more of cigarettes a day can expect to die six to nine years sooner than those who don't smoke (Prescott et al., 1998). Personality and stress management are also important, as individuals who are intense, hostile, and easily angered tend to die sooner than those who are relaxed and easy going (Cohen & Pressman, 2006; White, 2008). Heredity also affects our life expectancy. It is well known that people with long-lived parents and grandparents tend to live longer than those whose close relatives die young (Matteini et al., 2010). However, if your relatives are not noted for their longevity, you need not become fatalistic. Instead, you might make even greater efforts to adopt healthier eating and exercise habits. Table 16–1 lists some of the leading causes of death in the United States. Notice that the first few reasons are related to unhealthy lifestyles such as smoking.

Awareness of Death

Suppose you were asked, "How often do you think about your own death?" If your reply is "once in a while," you've got a lot of company. About 75 percent of people report thinking about this issue every now and then; and 25 percent do so frequently. Thus, despite attempts at denial, each of us has some *awareness of our own mortality*—that is, **mortality salience** (Vicary, 2011). As you might expect, because of events happening around us, our personal awareness of death fluctuates daily. National and international tragedies, accidents and homicides, as well as the death of family members and friends can increase our own mortality salience (Boulahanis & Heltsley, 2004). Being aware of our own mortality is one thing; understanding what it means to be dead is quite another. At what age do children truly understand the concept of death. Box 16–2 addresses this very issue.

Table 16–1	Leading Causes of Death in the United States
Cause	**Number of Deaths**
Heart disease	616,067
Cancer	562,875
Stroke	135,952
Chronic lower respiratory disease	127,924
Accidents	123,706
Alzheimer's disease	74,632
Diabetes	71,382
Pneumonia/influenza	52,717
Kidney disease	46,448

Source: Data from "Mortality Data," from Centers for Disease Control website, 2012.

BOX 16–2 Focus on Psychology: Children's Understanding of Death

The death of a loved one, especially if it is a parent, is one of the most painful experiences children can have, disrupting and irrevocably changing their lives, as well as causing profound suffering and confusion. However, it is important to realize that the impact of any loss on a child is partly affected by their understanding of death as a concept. To an adult, a common definition of **death** is *the cessation of life as measured by the absence of breathing, heartbeat, and electrical activity of the brain.* For children, death means different things depending upon their age. Here's what to expect at various ages across development.

- ***Under three years of age*** Children under the age of three do not possess the cognitive maturity to comprehend the concept of death. However, very young children can still notice the absence of loved ones and miss them terribly.
- ***Three to five years of age*** During the preschool years, children do not understand the biological underpinnings of death. As such, they believe death to be temporary, reversible, and occurring as an altered state of living, where the dead can dream, hear, see, etc., as well as still needing food, water, and oxygen. Young children think of heaven as a location that can be returned from, and get confused when the loved one fails to do so. Also, when talking to children about the concept of death, be careful about the language used to signify it. Terms such as "eternal rest" and "resting in peace" can cause a fear of sleep. Moreover, telling a child that a loved one has "gone away" can make a child feel abandoned and/or hopeful that the loved one will return.
- ***Six to ten years of age*** Between the ages of five and ten, knowledge of death increases in complexity. Below are five components of death that children come to understand as they age. It is believed that during the elementary school years these concepts are acquired in the order listed below.
  1. Death is inescapable—all living creatures die at some point in time.
  2. Death happens to everyone—there are no exceptions, every living thing will die eventually.
  3. Death is irreversible—the dead remain dead; they cannot return to life.
  4. Death stops bodily processes—after death, bodily processes no longer function.
  5. Death is biological—death is caused by a breakdown in the physiological functioning of the body.

Adolescents

With an understanding of death completely in hand, teenagers use death to spark an interest in the meaning of life.

Source: Based on "Death Understanding and Fear of Death in Young Children" by Virginia Slaughter and Maya Griffiths, from *Clinical Child Psychology and Psychiatry,* October 2007, Volume 12(4).

DEATH ANXIETY   In addition to simply thinking about death, at times people *fear death*, a phenomenon called **death anxiety**. Although death anxiety can occur at any age, people in their 20s are typically the most fearful (Harrawood, White, & Benshoff, 2009). Perhaps this occurs because young adults have their whole lives ahead of them and that the leading causes of death for this age group—accidents, homicide, and suicide—emphasize the cruel and tragic nature of death. Similar to mortality salience, large-scale disasters, terrorist attacks, and the deaths of those around us can increase death anxiety for everyone (Bartalos, 2009; Halpern-Felshner & Millstein, 2002). As individuals reach late adulthood, they generally think about death more often and talk about it more openly. Nevertheless, those in late adulthood are usually less fearful of death than other age groups. In fact, many elderly are more afraid of the *process* of dying, and the lack of dignity it can bring, than of death itself (Chochinov et al., 2002).

Of note, people who believe that their lives were full of meaning and/or examine life's events with a thankful attitude exhibit less death anxiety (Lau & Cheng, 2011; Routledge & Juhl, 2010). And those with a deep religious faith, including a belief in some kind of afterlife, are also generally less fearful of death (Krause, 2005). To become more aware of your level of death anxiety, you can complete the Death Anxiety Scale in Activity 16–1. After you know your score, contemplate how your level of death anxiety affects your life, if at all.

ACTIVITY 16–1

WHAT'S YOUR LEVEL OF DEATH ANXIETY?

INSTRUCTIONS: *For each of the following statements, indicate your degree of agreement by circling the appropriate number below the statement.*

1. As I read this chapter on death and grief, I feel uncomfortable.

    Strongly disagree   1   2   3   4   5   6   7   Strongly agree

2. I am not distressed by the thought of planning my own funeral.

    Strongly disagree   1   2   3   4   5   6   7   Strongly agree

3. When I know someone is terminally ill, I find it difficult to visit.

    Strongly disagree   1   2   3   4   5   6   7   Strongly agree

4. If I knew it would save me money, I would buy a burial plot in advance.

    Strongly disagree   1   2   3   4   5   6   7   Strongly agree

5. I prefer not to attend funerals or other death-related events.

    Strongly disagree   1   2   3   4   5   6   7   Strongly agree

6. Thoughts of my own death do not significantly trouble me.

    Strongly disagree   1   2   3   4   5   6   7   Strongly agree

7. I am careful not to take physical risks; other, more adventurous people might take.

    Strongly disagree   1   2   3   4   5   6   7   Strongly agree

8. The sight of cemeteries and funeral homes does not bother me.

    Strongly disagree   1   2   3   4   5   6   7   Strongly agree

9. I worry greatly that after death, there is nothingness.

Strongly disagree   1   2   3   4   5   6   7   Strongly agree

10. I try to attend the calling hours for friends and family who have recently died.

Strongly disagree   1   2   3   4   5   6   7   Strongly agree

SCORING: The even-numbered items need to be reverse scored so that disagreement signals higher death anxiety; that means for even-numbered items, a 1 becomes a 7, a 2 becomes a 6, and so on.

Total for odd-numbered items: _____
Total for even-numbered items (after reverse scoring) _____
Grand total _____

INTERPRETATION: A high score does not necessarily mean there is something wrong with you or that you suffer tremendous death anxiety. A low score does not necessarily mean that you manage the idea of death well. Instead, this scale is designed to stimulate you to think about death-related anxiety. Remember, this scale was developed for this book and has no scientific validity.

70–55 = You may have high levels of death anxiety.
54–40 = You may have moderately high levels of death anxiety.
39–25 = You probably are neither comfortable nor uncomfortable with the topic of death.
24–10 = You may be only somewhat distressed by the topic of death.
9 and below = You may be at peace with the idea of death, or, on the other hand, uncaring.

The Experience of Dying

Death is the final journey in life, and one that each person approaches in their own unique way. Thus, during the **experience of dying**—*the physical and psychological changes experienced by individuals nearing death*—nothing is set in stone. Nevertheless, there are some common experiences shared by many, namely: (1) coming to terms with mortality and (2) the physical and cognitive changes that occur at the very end of life. Each is addressed below. Note, the experience of dying is very different from a near-death experience (NDE), which is discussed in Box 16–3.

Exploration 16.1: Near-Death Experiences

www.near-death.com   A site with much information on near-death experiences and the afterlife.

COMING TO TERMS WITH MORTALITY   Although death is inevitable, learning that we are going to die in the near future can send shockwaves through our system, requiring significant adjustment. In coming to terms with their own mortality, Elisabeth Kübler-Ross (1993) noted that individuals tend to go through several stages.

1. The first stage consists of a **denial of death,** *with people characteristically feeling, "No, not me; this cannot happen to me."* Such denial protects them from the deep emotions associated with death and provides time to cope with the disturbing facts (Zimmerman, 2004). Later, individuals tend to show small signs that they are now willing to talk about death.

2. In the second stage, denial eventually gives way to the emotions of anger and **resentment,** *especially toward individuals who are healthy.* "Why me?" people ask. The sight of others

| BOX 16–3 | Focus on Psychology: Near-Death Experiences |

The book, *Heaven if for Real* (Burpo & Vincent, 2010) tells the story of 4-year-old Colton Burpo, who claims that while under anesthesia (during emergency surgery) he visited heaven, met Jesus, and encountered some deceased relatives, such as his grandfather who died 30 years before he was born. The book struck a chord with the American public, selling millions of copies and topping the *New York Times* bestseller list. Colton, like nearly 10 to 18 percent of cardiac arrest survivors (van Lommel, van Wees, Meyers, & Elfferich, 2001), lived through a **near-death experience (NDE)**—*the memory of events associated with being brought back to life from the verge of death.*

Across gender, age, and culture, accounts of NDE show striking similarities. Initially, individuals experience a detachment from their bodies and are pulled through a dark tunnel. Then they find themselves in another kind of "spiritual body," in which physical objects present no barrier and movement from one place to another is almost instantaneous. While in this state, they may have a reunion with long-lost friends and loved ones. One of the most incredible elements is the appearance of a brilliant light, perceived as a warm, loving "being of light," which fosters a kind of life review in a nonjudgmental way. Finally, people report being drawn back through the dark tunnel and undergoing a rapid re-entry into their bodies. It is worth noting, however, that not everyone has an enjoyable NDE, as some people have NDEs similar to nightmares, complete with demonic creatures. Other negative NDEs include being completely alone in an empty space and feeling out of control during the out-of-body experience (Greyson & Bush, 1996).

Although many who have had NDE prefer to view them as spiritual encounters, researchers are taking the mysticism out of such occurrences by claiming that the physiological events, hallucinations, and other changes in perception are created by the nervous system or anesthesia. Critics claim that research on NDE is replete with research problems (e.g., when dying individuals know about NDEs, they are more likely to report them; Agrillo, 2011). Others, such as Elisabeth Kübler-Ross (1993), believe that near-death phenomena are an integral part of the more inclusive experience of dying, including the physical level (loss of consciousness), psychic level (out-of-body awareness), and spiritual level (glimpse of nonjudgmental light or the realm of God). Regardless of cause, for most people, an NDE brings a profound change in attitudes. They not only become less fearful of death but are also more concerned with loving and valuing the life they have. There is also an increase in spirituality as well as more concern for others and less concern for material possessions. Regardless of age, race, sex, and education level, an NDE appears to be personally transforming (Agrillo, 2011).

---

enjoying their health can evoke feelings of envy, jealousy, and anger. The dying often take their feelings out on those closest to them, mostly because of what these people represent—life and health. Consequently, it is important for those nearby not to take these remarks personally, but to help dying individuals express their feelings.

3. The third stage characteristically consists of attempts to **bargain for time** in *which the dying individual attempts to negotiate with others (e.g., God) who might help him or her live longer.* Individuals at this stage often say, "I know I'm dying but. . . ." Then they indulge in a bit of magical thinking or negotiation: "If I cooperate with the doctor or my family, maybe God will let me live until my daughter graduates or my son gets married."

4. When individuals tend to drop the "but" and admit, "Yes, I'm dying," they enter the fourth stage, **depression,** *characterized by intense and sometimes unrealistic sadness.* In a sense, this is a natural response to the threat of losing one's life, and it is very important to allow the dying to grieve and express their sadness. One of the worst things a friend or family member can do is deny these feelings and say, "Cheer up." Thus, it is important for everyone to come to terms with their own feelings about death so that they can help dying people accept their own mortality without dwelling on it unduly.

5. The final stage is the **acceptance** of death, though not all dying persons reach this stage. By this time, most *people who are dying have pretty much accepted death and have disengaged themselves from others.* They may ask for fewer visitors and, at times, are difficult

to interact with. Nevertheless, at the end of life most people do not want to die alone. Although most people prefer to die at home (Administration on Aging, 2012), they are more likely to die in a hospital. In fact, much of the pain of dying comes from mental anguish, especially the fear of being separated from loved ones.

Elisabeth Kübler-Ross (1975) was the first to point out that the experience of dying is not a fixed, inevitable process and that many people do not follow the aforementioned stages (Wright, 2002). For some, anger remains the dominant mood throughout, whereas others are depressed until the end. And at any point during the process, the dying person may revisit old memories, evaluate how they lived their life, and sort through any regrets. Consequently, each person experiences the dying process in a unique way because of a variety of factors, such as life experience, age, personality differences, as well as cultural backgrounds and the course of the illness that will ultimately take their life (Quigley & Schatz, 1999).

PHYSICAL AND MENTAL CHANGES AT THE END OF LIFE   What follows is a description of the physical and mental changes that typically occur during the last three months of a terminally ill person's life.

Between one to three months prior to death, the body begins to slow down, requiring less energy from food. As a result, appetite and thirst decrease, and there is a corresponding loss in weight. For some, changes in their body chemistry produce a sense of euphoria. People who are dying also tend to sleep more, and when they are awake, they rarely engage in activities that they once enjoyed.

About one to two weeks prior to death, the dying person begins to spend most of their time sleeping. And when they are awake disorientation, delusions (e.g., paranoia), hallucinations (e.g., seeing or speaking to people who aren't there), and agitation are quite common. Speaking decreases and eventually stops altogether. Also, body movements and actions, such as hand waving, occur without purpose. There are numerous physiological changes as well: (1) body temperature lowers by a degree or more; (2) blood pressure decreases; (3) the pulse becomes irregular; (4) the person sweats more; (5) circulation becomes poor, resulting in changes in skin tone; (6) congestion builds up, causing a rattling cough; and (7) breathing becomes more rapid and labored.

During the final few days and hours of life, the physical changes mentioned above intensify. Breathing becomes more irregular, and at times the dying person will engage in "Cheyne-Stokes" breathing, characterized by rapid breathes followed by periods of no breathing at all (up to 45 seconds). Congestion continues to build. Hands and feet are cool to the touch and appear blotchy and purplish. The lips and skin under the fingernails change color as well. There is also a loss of bowel and bladder control. Usually, the person becomes unresponsive to the environment (even if their eyes are partially open). However, hearing is usually the last sense to go, so caregivers are encouraged to keep talking to their loved ones. Eventually, breathing will cease altogether, the heart will stop, and the brain will no longer function; death has occurred (HospiceFoundation.org, 2012).

LIFE AND DEATH IN PERSPECTIVE

LEARNING OBJECTIVES

16.5 Explain the right to die.
16.6 Discuss the value of advanced directives.
16.7 Compare the reasons for and against physician-assisted suicide.
16.8 Summarize hospice care.

In 1955, the average life expectancy in the United States was 48 years of age, by 1995 it was 65, and now it is 78 (Kleespies, 2004; The World Bank, 2012). As the average life expectancy increases, more people are apt to suffer from chronic illnesses, such as cancer, heart disease, and stroke. In fact, seven out of ten American deaths are the result of a chronic condition (Kung, Hoyert, Xu, & Murphy, 2008). For sufferers of chronic disease, death comes slowly, often occurring in hospitals, which are geared more to the treatment of acute illnesses and prolonging of life. Although improvements in medical care and technological advances can postpone death, they do not necessarily guarantee a life of quality. As such, ethical issues surrounding the appropriate use of lifesaving machines and the right to die in a dignified manner have arisen (Haddad, 2003). Examining such matters may help us put life and death in better perspective.

The Right to Die

At times, a terminally ill patient's quality of life, or lack thereof, can create an ethical dilemma with regard to treatment choices, both for the families making the decisions and for the doctors administering care. As an example, family members of patients in irreversible comas are often torn between their desire to be loyal to their loved ones, religious beliefs, and the emotional and financial realities of supporting someone in a permanent vegetative state (Doka, 2005). Doctors also face conflicts between their duty to sustain life, their obligation to relieve suffering, and the legal consequences of doing otherwise (Jauhar, 2003). The American Medical Association's Council on Ethical and Judicial Affairs (2010) has provided guidelines for doctors in such situations. Specifically, it is considered appropriate, and ethical, for doctors to withhold or withdraw life-sustaining measures for patients who have decided to forgo such treatments. When patients are incapacitated (as is the case with coma) and therefore cannot express their end-of-life wishes, physicians are told to honor the choices made by surrogate decision makers, typically a designated family member. In other words, doctors are told to respect a patient's right to die. The **right-to-die** is *the legal and ethical view that competent individuals who are able to understand treatment choices and their consequences have the right to decide their own fate, such as withholding of treatment that would delay death.*

ADVANCED DIRECTIVES Widespread societal support for the right-to-die has resulted in the growing use of **advanced directives**, *which allow patients to communicate health care preferences, in advance, in the event that they are no longer able to make these decisions.* The most comprehensive type of advanced directive is the **living will,** which *instructs doctors on the types of life-sustaining procedures that should be stopped or prevented in the event of a terminal condition.* Living wills (also known as health care proxies) cover a wide range of health care procedures, including those affecting brain, liver, kidney, heart, and lung functioning, as well as the provision of food and water. Another type of advance directive, but one that is far more limited in scope, is a **do not resuscitate (DNR)** order, which *prohibits doctors from using advanced cardiac life support and cardio pulmonary resuscitation (CPR) should the patient have a cardiac arrest or stop breathing.* A DNR order, however, does not prohibit the use of other medical treatments that can prolong life.

Health care professionals support the use of advanced directives because they encourage peace of mind in the dying, allow caregivers to honor patient wishes, and stimulate better communication among all concerned (Thompson, Barbour, & Schwartz, 2003). Currently, around 15 percent of American adults have an advanced directive (Sabatino, 2007). To encourage more people to do so, all federally funded hospitals, nursing homes, and hospices are required to tell incoming patients of their right to create a living will. Overall, this requirement has resulted in the making of advanced directives by a large percentage of the infirmed elderly. According to a recent survey, 65 percent or nursing home residents and 88 percent of those in hospice care have advanced directives. And as people get older, the likelihood of creating an advanced directive increases (Jones, Moss, & Harris-Kojetin, 2011). Clearly, one of the most powerful influences in the decision to make an advanced directive is the likelihood of dying in the near future. But ask yourself this, should it be?

Exploration 16.2: Living Wills

www.mayoclinic.com/health/living-wills/HA00014   A site with links to lots of information on living wills and related issues.

PHYSICIAN-ASSISTED SUICIDE   The end-of-life measures mentioned above are applicable for patients in vegetative states and for those who are terminally ill where death is about to happen (e.g., occurring in a few weeks or days). This type of end-of-life care is designed to reduce suffering and increase the comfort of the patient. Far more controversial, however, is when proactive measures are taken to end the lives of people who are in chronic, excruciating pain or are suffering from a terminal illness where death is not imminent. When such an event happens, it is called a **physician-assisted suicide**, defined as *a physician helping a patient end their life by providing the physical means, and/or information, necessary to do so.* For example, with the knowledge that a patient wants to commit suicide, a physician provides him or her with a prescription for pain killers and information on lethal doses.

Arguments abound on both sides of this emotional and contentious issue. Those in favor of physician-assisted suicide contend that it allows the patient to die with dignity, improves the end-of-life experience by eliminating unbearable pain and suffering, prompts family members to say their goodbyes, and allows the patient to determine their own fate (Smith, Goy, Harvath, & Ganzini, 2011). Those opposed physician-assisted suicide also provide a variety of reasons to justify their position, including: it is immoral; it goes against religious doctrine (e.g., it's a sin); sometimes terminally ill patients recover; advances in medical care can lessen pain and suffering, therefore negating the need for suicide; and finally, those who are suicidal have diminished mental capacity, and therefore should not be making life-and-death decisions (Chadwick, Have, & Meslin, 2011). Moreover, the American Medical Association views physician-assisted suicide as unethical, as it is incompatible with the physician's role as a healer (American Medical Association, 2010).

Although legislators in 25 different states have tried to legalize physician-assisted suicide over 120 times since 1994, currently, it is lawful in only three states: Oregon, Washington, and Montana (PatientRightsCouncil.org, 2012). As you can see, the public debate over physician-assisted suicide is far from over. In the end, everyone (regardless of their position) wants to improve the end-of-life experience for the dying as well as the quality of care that they receive. The hospice movement for the terminally ill represents a giant step toward the kind of humane and supportive community needed for a dignified death.

Exploration 16.3: Hospice Care

www.hospice-america.org   A site that includes a consumer guide to hospice care.

Hospice Care

The term "hospice" refers to a place or method for taking care of those approaching the end of their lives. Specifically, **hospice** is *a system of care that integrates a physical facility for the terminally ill with the patient's family and home to enable the patient to die with dignity.* As mentioned earlier, much of the suffering of the terminally ill consists of the treatments, the impersonal atmosphere, and the sense of isolation experienced in hospitals. In contrast, the hospice is a community that helps people to live, not merely exist, while they are dying. In addition to helping with such practical matters as pain control and preparing meals, hospice personnel also give emotional support and guidance to family members. The aim throughout is to provide a humane and supportive community in which the patient may die with dignity (Hospice Foundation of America, 2012).

Although beneficial for both patients and their families, hospice stays are often too short. The recommended amount of time necessary to provide adequate physical and psychological

Table 16–2	Hospice Care in the United States
• Number of hospice programs	5,000
• Number of hospice patients	1.6 Million
• Percent of in-home hospice patients	68
• Leading need for hospice care	Terminal cancer
• Average stay in hospice care	69 days

Source: Data from *NHPO Facts and Figure: Hospice Care in America*, 2011 Edition. National Hospice and Palliative Care Organization, 2012.

support is three months (Shockett, Teno, Miller, & Stuart, 2005). However, as you read in Table 16–2, the typical stay is much shorter. One reason is that exact time of death is never clearly predictable in terminal illnesses. Also, physicians may be reluctant to make early referrals to hospice because the patient and the family have not fully accepted that the illness is terminal. Table 16–2 provides you with some interesting statistics about hospice care in the United States.

Begun in England, the hospice movement has since spread to other countries, including the United States and Canada. The increasing population of elderly people and rising costs of hospitalization are such that the hospice movement is likely to expand in the years ahead. Besides health care professionals, the families, friends, and other volunteers in the community provide much care to the dying. Box 16–4 discusses who these caregivers are, the immense stress they experience, and the need for caregivers to care for themselves.

CAREGIVING IN NUMBERS   More than 65 million U.S. households report that their homes include someone who cannot care for themselves; if not for volunteers the annual cost of health care related services for the infirmed would be $375 billion. Caregivers are frequently family members—typically women or grown daughters. Caregivers might also be neighbors, friends, or other members of the community. Overall, there are more nonpaid caregivers in the United States than paid or professional caregivers. In addition to providing 20 hours of care per week (on average), around 60 percent of caregivers are also employed. Frequently, however, paying jobs do not provide enough income to cover the financial expense of caring for a loved one. In fact, nearly 47 percent of caregivers use up all or most of their lifesavings tending to a family member. Because the financial, emotional, and psychological stress of long-term caregiving can be enormous, individuals who have been caregivers for extended periods of time report high levels of stress, depression, poor eating habits, and hostility. One study even found that heart disease is more prevalent in caregivers than noncaregivers (*Health & Medicine Week*, 2003; National Family Caregivers Association, 2012).

CARING FOR THE CAREGIVERS   As the statistics above painfully reveal, caregivers often need to help themselves, at the very least requiring a break from their many responsibilities. In addition,

BOX 16–4	Focus on Health Care: Caregivers

Older Americans, those dying from terminal illnesses, the disabled, and others often need assistance from professional and lay caregivers. Some recipients require permanent care; others need assistance during convalescence. Friends and families often become the primary caregivers. They are not professional caregivers like home health aides, yet they are often expected to perform some of the very same duties. Dependent individuals typically cannot do their own shopping, bathing, or cooking, and as such, they rely on caregivers. Caregivers also act as chauffeurs, fill out insurance forms, give medications, take care of financial arrangements, and act as physical or emotional therapists, among other duties.

most caregivers could benefit from emotional and social support, as well as from training in a variety of medical procedures. To assist caregivers, local support groups are springing up all around the country. These groups offer advice, support, and respite care, in which another member takes over their duties for a few hours a week (Savard, Leduc, Lebel, Beland, & Bergman, 2006). If you are a caregiver or expect to be, you can join the National Family Caregivers Association (www.thefamilycaregiver.org). There are also specialized national groups for people taking care of those with AIDS, Alzheimer's, physical disabilities, the elderly, and others requiring specialized assistance in living. Most of these organizations maintain easily accessible websites. In any event, if you become or are a caregiver, don't forget to take care of yourself.

Exploration 16.4: Assisting Caregivers

www.familycaregiving101.org/index.cfm   A site dedicated to assisting family caregivers.

BEREAVEMENT AND GRIEF

LEARNING OBJECTIVES

16.9 Explain grief work.
16.10 Describe the experience of unresolved grief.
16.11 Summarize good grief.
16.12 Discuss how the grief may give new meaning to one's life.

To lose a loved one or friend through death is to lose part of oneself. It's an emotionally painful experience comprised of three related concepts: bereavement, grief, and mourning. **Bereavement** ("to be deprived of") is *the process of adjusting to the experience of loss, especially to the death of friends or loved ones.* It involves the overall experience of loss. **Grief** refers to *the intense emotional suffering that accompanies our experience of loss,* and **mourning** refers to *the outward expressions of bereavement and grief.*

Mourning Customs

Because death is one of the universal rites of passage, most societies have mourning customs to facilitate the expression of grief. In the past, American widows dressed in black and widowers wore black armbands. Such clothing explained the show of grief on the part of the bereaved and afforded them an opportunity to talk about their loss and to receive the needed sympathy. Today, many of these customs have been modified (e.g., wearing a black ribbon) or replaced with new ones (e.g., displaying a montage of pictures of the deceased). In most societies, parting with the dead is recognized by some kind of **funeral**—*the ceremonies and rituals associated with the burial or cremation of the dead*—with the particulars varying by ethnicity, cultural norms, and religious canons. For example, cremation is the preferred method of body disposition in China and India; during a Mexican-American funeral, relatives throw a handful of dirt on the coffin before the grave is filled; and during a modern wake, family and friends celebrate the deceased during a joyful gathering. Regardless of culture, religion, or ethnicity, such rites enable survivors to maintain order and experience a form of closure (Funeralwise.com, 2012). Table 16–3 presents a summary of funeral customs by religion.

Grief Work

Grief work consists of *the healthy process of working through the emotions associated with loss, freeing ourselves emotionally from the deceased, readjusting to life without that person, resuming ordinary activities, and forming new relationships.* The grief process can parallel the experience of dying and involves many of the same stages (Maciejewski, Zhang, Block, & Prigerson, 2007). Grief work takes time and, for some, is never fully completed (Boerner, Wortman, & Bonanno, 2005). Although there are large individual differences in how people grieve, we will describe the typical experience here.

Table 16–3	Funeral Customs					
Religion	**Embalming Allowed**	**Cremation Allowed**	**Traditional Source of Prayers**	**Open Casket**	**Return to Work**	**Period of Mourning**
Baptist	Yes	Yes	King James Bible	Usually	7 days	60 days
Buddhist	Yes	Yes	Sutras	Always	No specific time	90 days
Catholic	Yes	Yes	New American Standard Bible	Depends	7 days	7 days
Episcopal	Yes	Yes	The Book of Common Prayer	Rarely	7 days	Depends
Hindu	Yes	Yes	Sanskrit Blessings	Yes	10–30 days	10–30 days
Islam	No	No	Quran	No	3 days	40 days
Jewish	No	No	Siddur	No	7 days	365 days
Methodist	Yes	Yes	New Revised Standard Version of Bible	Usually	Depends	Depends

Source: Based on "Funeral Customs," from Funeralwise website, 2012.

Exploration 16.5: Grief

journeyofhearts.org/index.html   A site offering information on grief and coping.

Initially, people may react to a person's death with a sense of shock and disbelief, especially when death occurs unexpectedly (Houck, 2007). When death has been anticipated, as is the case with terminal illness, the initial response may be subdued and accompanied by a sense of relief, which may then turn to guilt as a result of feeling "relieved" at the loved one's passing. At other times, people undergo survivor guilt, defined as feeling guilty because one is still alive while others are not. As mentioned in the chapter on stress (Chapter 13), survivor guilt is typically experienced after traumatic incidents causing multiple deaths (e.g., war, automobile accidents). However, it can also occur after recovering from an illness that others have died from (such as brain cancer). In these situations, the survivor feels undeserving of life, questions why they survived when others didn't, and may even come to idealize those who died. It is important to remember, though, that survivor guilt is part of the grieving process and that acknowledging this fact can promote healing (Matsakis, 1999).

The emotional intensity of grief in these early stages often appears in the disguise of physical symptoms, such as crying, depressed feelings, lack of appetite, and difficulties concentrating at work or at home. Another common symptom of grief is lack of interaction with others (Monk, Houck, & Shear, 2006). In order to avoid the negative emotions and physical symptoms associated with grief, some people rely on sleeping pills, tranquilizers, and alcohol during their bereavement, all of which can pose health risks if relied on too much or too often. Although grief is not a disease, it is associated with increased health problems and increased likelihood of the griever's own death (Stroebe, Schut, & Stroebe, 2007). However, gender differences are present, with men dying sooner than women. Moreover, widowed men between the ages of 55 and 65 die at a 60 percent higher rate than married men of the same age. The most likely explanation is that the quality of life changes more drastically for men than for women, possibly because of their greater reliance on wives for their emotional and daily needs. Women also tend to have a better support system (family and friends) for coping with their grief.

After a deadly shooting at their school and despite their own grief, the Amish astonished the world by forgiving the shooter and attending his funeral.

In the final stage of grief, we usually come to terms with our loss (acceptance) and resume our everyday activities. This stage may occur anytime from a few months to a year or more after the initial loss, depending on how close we were to the person and the circumstances surrounding their death. About one year is the normal length of time required for grief work, with the most intense and negative emotions peaking by six months (Lindstrom, 1995). For many, normal grief can be present for an extended period of time, intensifying on important dates, such as birthdays, wedding anniversaries, and the death date of the loved one (Davis, 2001). Depression and other emotional reactions generally decline over the first year (Grad & Zavasnik, 1999). From that time on, we're likely to recall the deceased person with pleasant memories. Though, in some ways, we never fully get over the death of a loved one, such as a parent, child, or spouse. The more fully we work through our grief, however, the more likely we'll be able to move on with our normal lives.

Unresolved Grief

Unresolved grief is *a psychological state in which a person's emotional reaction to loss remains repressed, often being manifested in unexplained physical or psychological symptoms.* Also called **complicated grief,** this prolonged and impairing type of grief may assume a variety of forms, from unexplained physical complaints to psychological symptoms, such as anxiety and depression (Boelen & van den Bout, 2007). In some instances, the psychological reactions are obviously related to the loss. For example, some people avoid their grief; they can't bring themselves to return to the house, hospital, or room where a person has died because of unresolved grief. In other cases, unresolved grief may be more disguised as in unexplained outbursts of anger (Bonanno, Papa, Lalande, Zhang, & Noll, 2005).

On the other hand, some individuals do just the opposite. Instead of thinking too little about their loved one or their death, they think too much about their grief and the loss they have experienced. Rumination or preoccupation with the death of a loved one can be detrimental to well-being (Michael & Snyder, 2005). Though such cases rarely occur, individuals who ruminate or constantly rehash details of the death (especially when they have few social supports and many other stressors) experience more depression and pessimism than those who don't ruminate (Nolen-Hoeksema, Parker, & Larson, 1994). Bereavement experts suggest that this type of prolonged or complex grieving is problematic for well-being and thus requires special attention by professionals (Boelen, de Keijser, van den Hout, & van den Bout, 2007; Bonanno & Kaltman, 2001).

Good Grief

GRIEF AND PERSONAL GROWTH   So far, we've seen that it is sometimes better to go through the full experience of bereavement, however painful it may be, than to get over it too quickly or to ruminate too intently. There are, however, some positive aspects of grief. Grief can increase our appreciation of loved ones and friends more fully, despite their shortcomings. Grief also helps us value our relationships with those still living. In short, **good grief** means *that we have learned and grown in our bereavement.* Bereavement, then, has the potential to contribute to personal growth (Cadell, Regehr, & Hemsworth, 2003). Know that growth-oriented theories of bereavement contend that grief represents only a part of the self, the emotional self (Rothaupt & Becker, 2007). Therefore, grief doesn't just involve mourning; it also includes reflecting on the person who died as well as the anticipated changes for the bereaved. In this model, the survivor assimilates the reality that the deceased is gone, expresses the emotional pain of the loss, cultivates new strategies for coping in a world without the loved one, and develops new beliefs and attitudes about life, death, love, and compassion.

POSITIVE EXPRESSIONS OF GRIEF   There are several ways to make the experience of bereavement more effective: talking it out, acting it out, and feeling it out. Even though it may be very difficult to talk about the death of a loved one for the first several weeks, this may be exactly when talking it out can be most helpful. A friend should attempt to listen and help the bereaved person to talk out feelings rather than cut the mourner off. Although you may be uncomfortable discussing death, the bereaved person may well need someone to talk to. Those who grieve with

Visiting the cemetery of the deceased and tending to the grave are methods for coping with grief.

adequate social support are less likely to be depressed and may recover from their grief faster, too (Nolen-Hoeksema et al., 1994; Stroebe, Zech, Stroebe, & Abakoumkin, 2005).

Another way of resolving grief is to express it in other relevant ways. Sometimes just sheer physical activity, such as a brisk walk, helps to alleviate the tension and sadness of bereavement, at least temporarily. Funeral rituals also can afford an outlet for grief. Despite being burdensome, taking care of the affairs of the deceased may be therapeutic as well as helpful. After all, closing out the affairs of a loved one is one of the few tangible things that can be done on behalf of the departed. Finally, **grief therapy,** which *assists the bereaved to cope with the death of a loved one*, can help survivors cope with the intense emotions associated with grief (Boelen et al., 2007).

GRIEF AND YOU Through the process of grief, we often think about our own mortality. Far from being morbid, thinking about your own death may give you a new perspective on life and an opportunity for growth. For instance, if you were told you had only a limited time to live, how would you spend the time? What unfinished business would you be most concerned about? Which people would you most want to be with? Pondering the answers to such questions may help you to clarify what is really important to you. You should plan to do these things before it's too late. Elisabeth Kübler-Ross (1975) stated that the greatest lesson we may learn from dying is simply "LIVE, so you do not have to look back and say, 'God, how I wasted my life'" (p. xix).

Chapter Summary

DEATH AND DYING

16.1 List some of the leading causes of death.

Illnesses, such as heart disease, cancer, stroke, and lower respiratory disease, as well as accidents, account for more deaths than other biological or environmental causes.

16.2 Explain the connection between mortality salience and death anxiety.

In heightened times of mortality salience (during which we are acutely aware that we can die), the fear of death (i.e., death anxiety) also increases.

16.3 Describe how people come to terms with their own mortality.

Terminally ill people tend to go through several stages of dying—denial, anger, bargaining, depression, and acceptance—with considerable overlapping between the stages and with the stages sometimes out of this order. Each person experiences the dying process somewhat differently, however, depending on such factors as personality and type of illness.

16.4 Identify the physical and mental changes that occur near the end of life.

Near the end of a terminal illness, the dying go through significant physical and cognitive changes. These changes start between one and three months prior to death, and intensify as death approaches. Physical changes include decreases in hunger, thirst, body temperature, and speaking. Breathing becomes more rapid and irregular, and congestion, agitation, and the need for sleep all increase. Cognitive changes include disorientation, hallucinations, and delusions. Eventually, the person becomes unresponsive to the environment.

LIFE AND DEATH IN PERSPECTIVE

16.5 Explain the right to die.

The increased use of lifesaving technology poses critical questions about prolonging life or letting someone die rather than suffer unduly. The right to die helps ensure that those approaching death can die with dignity. The right to die also provides legal and ethical guidance to both family members and physicians.

16.6 Discuss the value of advanced directives.

Now that people live longer, they are more apt to suffer from chronic and life-threatening illnesses. As a result, patients are being encouraged to express their own wishes through advanced directives, such as the living will and the DNR order. Creating an advanced directive can help the dying make sure that their end-of-life wishes are known and they can decrease the distress felt by family members in having to make life and death decisions for a loved one. Making an advanced directive can improve communication between family members regarding issues that most want to avoid talking about.

16.7 Compare the reasons for and against physician-assisted suicide.

Physician-assisted suicide is emotional and divisive issue. Those in favor of physician-assisted suicide contend that it allows the patient to die with dignity, improves the end-of-life experience, prompts family members to say their goodbyes, and allows the patient to determine their own fate. Those opposed contend that it is immoral, that it goes against religious doctrine, that sometimes the terminally ill recover, that medical advances can reduce pain, that those who are suicidal have diminished mental capacity, and that the American Medical Association does not condone its use.

16.8 Summarize hospice care.

The importance of providing terminally ill people with a humane and supportive community has led to the hospice movement. Hospice care provides the patient with support in daily living matters, and with emotional, psychological, and medical issues. Hospice personnel also give emotional support and guidance to family members. The primary aim of hospice care is to help the patient die with dignity.

BEREAVEMENT AND GRIEF

16.9 Explain grief work.

Grief work is the healthy process of working through the emotions associated with loss, freeing ourselves emotionally from the deceased, readjusting to life without that person, resuming ordinary activities, and forming new relationships. Some experts believe it is important for the bereaved to engage actively in grief work, a process that parallels the experience of dying and involves many of the same emotions.

16.10 Describe the experience of unresolved grief.

Unresolved grief is a psychological state in which a person's emotional reaction to loss remains repressed. People who have not been able to resolve their grief may exhibit various symptoms, ranging from physical complaints to more persistent psychological symptoms. Those who live alone are especially likely to have difficulty working through their grief.

16.11 Summarize good grief.

Healthy grief consists of talking about our grief, sharing our feelings, and taking part in the rituals and activities that may eventually alleviate grief.

16.12 Discuss how the grief may give new meaning to one's life.

It appears that grief, which leads to a more realistic awareness of death as an inevitable companion of life, far from being morbid, may help each of us put our lives in better perspective and to live more fully.

Self-Test

1. Compared to young adults, older adults tend to
   a. become more fearful of death.
   b. think of death more often.
   c. become less religious.
   d. think of others' death, not their own.

2. Ellen almost drowned while swimming last year. If not for resuscitation effects of the life guards she would have died. During this event, Ellen felt as though she was floating outside her body, approaching a white light, while dead relatives lined the pathway to the light. Ellen had experienced a:
   a. near-death experience
   b. near-life experience
   c. transcendental dying experience
   d. transcendental living experience

3. Which of the following is not a stage associated with the experience of dying according to Elisabeth Kübler-Ross?
   a. denial of death
   b. bargaining
   c. life review
   d. resentment

4. Months after learning that he had inoperable brain cancer Elton was experiencing intense feelings of sadness. According to Elisabeth Kübler-Ross, what stage associated with the experience of dying is Elton in?
   a. denial of death
   b. depression
   c. resentment
   d. bargaining

5. Sandra's husband died six months ago. Currently, Sandra is working through the emotions associated with his loss, freeing herself emotionally from him, and readjusting to life without him. Sandra appears to be experiencing:
   a. a life review
   b. the stage of denial
   c. the benefits of bereavement therapy
   d. grief work

6. David lost his wife to heart disease about two years ago. He's been having a rough time since. He won't get rid of her cloths (refusing to even clean out the dresser drawers) or put away the makeup that she left on the bathroom counter. Her robe still hangs on the back of the closet door as well. To move forward with his life, David may want to consider participating in:
   a. transcendental therapy
   b. desensitization therapy
   c. grief therapy
   d. behavioral therapy

7. Paulina was diagnosed with terminal bone cancer. After battling the disease for five years, she was told she had less than six months to live. To make matters worse, the cancer caused Paulina to experience unbearable pain. Even with medication, the only time Paulina wasn't in pain was when she was unconscious. Paulina, along with her family, decided to discuss with her doctors the possibility of ending her life with a morphine overdose. The issue surrounding this difficult decision is called:
   a. para-suicide
   b. right to life

c. right to die

d. dying will

8. Before Paulina could discuss the issues with her doctors, she fell into an irreversible coma. But because she had created a _____, the doctors, and her family, knew exactly the type of end-of-life treatment that Paulina wanted.

a. dying will

b. living will

c. right to life document

d. end-of-life trust

9. For many, the idea of spending their last few months of life in a hospital is unthinkable. They would rather die at home or in a comfortable facility that feels more like home. Such people would benefit from _____ care.

a. hospice

b. assisted living

c. end-of-life clinic

d. facilitated

10. The loss of a loved one is never easy. But through the process of bereavement many will experience personal growth. Such individuals are said to have experienced:

a. para-grief

b. para-bereavement

c. good grief

d. beneficial bereavement

Exercises

1. *Subjective life expectancy.* Simply knowing a person's age does not tell you how that person feels about his or her future. To discover this information, try the following exercise in subjective life expectancy. You may want your friends or other individuals to try it as well.

1. I expect to live to age (circle your answer)

   30 35 40 45 50 55 60 65 70 75 80 85
   90 95 100

2. I want to live to age (circle your answer)

   25 30 35 40 45 50 55 60 65 70 75 80
   85 90 95 100

Are there discrepancies between your expressed desire and expectation? If so, what are the possible reasons? Usually, findings have shown that those past middle age expect and wish to live to a later age than younger people do. Did you find this to be true? When people expect to live less than the average life expectancy for their age, do they have a good reason? Did you find that some people were afraid to specify an age for fear it would somehow make death occur at that time?

2. *Your attitudes toward death.* Analyze your attitudes toward death. First, write down your actual experiences with death, such as the loss of a friend or loved one, the age and circumstances at which it occurred, and so forth. Then describe some of your feelings and attitudes toward death. Include your own responses to the subjective life expectancy exercise as well.

3. *Reflections on the experience of bereavement.* Recall a personal experience of bereavement, whether the loss of a loved one or that of a friend. Then describe your experience in a page or so. To what extent did your experience include the grief work process described in the chapter? In what ways was your experience unique? Finally, how has your experience of grief affected your life? Has it made you more cautious and, perhaps, bitter toward life? Or has it eventually become "good grief," leading you to make the most of life and to reach out to others in a more meaningful way?

4. *Organ donation.* Have you thought about donating organs from your body before you die? After you die? If so, which organs? Are you interested in leaving your body for medical science? Why or why not?

5. *Write your own obituary.* This isn't as strange as it may seem. Major newspapers have a file of obituaries written while celebrities and national figures are still alive, and then they update these accounts at the time of death. Try writing your own obituary in two or three paragraphs. In addition to giving the standard information, such as your name, age, and position at work, point out some of your major accomplishments. Which community activities would you mention? Who are your survivors? In addition, list your funeral and burial plans. What day and time do you prefer to be buried? Where is your service being held? Do you have any preferences regarding financial contributions to charities in lieu of flowers? Where do you want to be buried or have your ashes deposited?

Questions for Self-Reflection

1. Do you occasionally think about the possibility of your own death?

2. Have you ever had a close brush with death?

3. Are you afraid of dying? Why? How do you cope with the thought?

4. How often do you think of someone who is dead?

5. Is there something you would especially like to do before you die? Why have you not done this thing?

6. Can you recall your first experience of grief? Whose death was it?

7. Have you experienced good grief?

8. Have you made a will? Do you have a health care proxy? Have you signed an organ donor card? Why or why not?

9. What kind of after-death service would you like, if any?

10. What do you believe happens to us after we die?

ANSWERS TO THE SELF-TESTS

Chapter	Questions									
	1	2	3	4	5	6	7	8	9	10
1	b	d	c	a	a	a	b	a	a	c
2	a	b	a	b	b	c	c	a	c	b
3	d	d	a	b	d	a	a	c	d	c
4	b	c	a	a	d	b	b	c	b	d
5	d	a	b	d	a	d	a	c	c	d
6	a	b	d	c	c	c	a	d	c	b
7	d	a	a	d	a	c	b	d	a	d
8	c	a	b	d	a	a	b	a	b	a
9	a	a	b	d	c	c	a	c	a	b
10	c	a	b	d	a	a	a	c	d	b
11	c	d	b	b	a	c	a	c	d	b
12	c	b	a	a	b	a	b	c	d	a
13	a	d	a	c	a	c	a	d	c	a
14	b	a	b	c	d	a	b	c	b	a
15	c	a	d	b	a	c	a	a	c	a
16	b	a	c	b	d	c	c	b	a	c

GLOSSARY

acceptance. The final stage of death and dying, in which dying people have somewhat accepted death and have disengaged themselves from others.

achievement motivation. The desire to accomplish or master something difficult or challenging as independently and successfully as possible.

acculturative stress. The stress related to the process of adapting to the beliefs, languages, practices, and values of a dominant culture.

acrophobia. An irrational fear of heights.

activity theory of aging. The belief that the more active a person remains, the more satisfied and better adjusted that person is likely to be, regardless of age.

acute stress. Stress that is a momentary response to imminent danger and is relieved when the danger is over.

acupuncture. The clinical insertion and manipulation of thin needles in specific body sites.

adherence to treatment regimens. The degree to which a person's behavior (e.g., taking medications, attending treatment sessions, etc.) coincides with medical or health advice.

adoption. The legal establishment of a new, permanent parent–child relationship.

advanced directives. Legal documents which detail a patient's health care preferences, in advance, in the event that they are no longer able to make these decisions.

affective affirmation. The communication of loving, accepting attitudes or the unconditional approval of one's mate.

affiliate. To be with others who are often similar to us or whom we like.

ageism. Negative attitudes toward and treatment of older adults.

age-related changes. Changes that tend to occur at a given age, such as puberty.

agoraphobia. Classically known as "*fear of open spaces*," is typically the most severe phobic reaction and the one for which people most often seek treatment.

AIDS. Acquired immune deficiency syndrome, which is caused by a virus known as HIV and transmitted primarily through body fluids.

alarm reaction. Part of Selye's notion of the general adaptation syndrome of stress; the initial emergency response to stress-provoking agents when the body attempts to restore its normal functioning.

allostasis. Achieving stability through changes via a process that maintains balance among the physiological factors essential for life.

allostatic load. Cumulative changes that reflect the cost to the body of adapting repeatedly to demands placed upon it.

altruism. A desire to help others at a cost to the helper.

Alzheimer's disease. A debilitating cognitive disorder that may, in fact, begin to develop in midlife but is often associated with old age.

anecdotal evidence. Information presented in favor of an argument that is based on casual observations rather than data collected using more objective and scientific methods.

anger. The feeling of extreme displeasure or resentment over (perceived) mistreatment.

anniversary reaction. An individual's response to unresolved grief resulting from significant losses.

anorexia nervosa. An eating disorder characterized by a severe loss of appetite and weight. The essential features of this eating disorder are a fear of becoming fat along with a disturbance in body image and a refusal to maintain normal weight.

antianxiety drugs. Drugs that are used primarily for alleviating anxiety; including minor tranquilizers.

antidepressants. Drugs that are used to treat depression and elevate mood, usually by increasing the level of certain neurotransmitters.

antipsychotic drugs. Drugs that are used primarily to relieve symptoms of psychoses, such as extreme agitation, hyperactivity, hallucinations, and delusions.

antisocial personality. A personality disorder characterized by long-standing habits of maladaptive thought and behavior that violates the rights of others.

anxiety. A vague, unpleasant feeling that serves as an emotional alarm signal, warning us of an impending threat or danger.

anxiety disorders. A group of disorders characterized by symptoms of excessive or inappropriate anxiety or attempts to escape from such anxiety.

anxious (attachment style). An attachment style in which the individual experiences emotional extremes such as jealousy but in which the individual also desires extreme closeness.

arbitrators. Neutral third parties who, using the same techniques as mediation, assist the parties with the conflict, hope that the parties can resolve their differences, but if they cannot, render a binding decision upon the parties.

assertiveness. The expression of one's rights and feelings in a direct way without violating the rights of others.

attachment. A close, emotional tie with another person.

attachment style. Our typical style of becoming involved with others.

attention deficit hyperactivity disorder (ADHD). Psychological disorder characterized by a longstanding pattern of inattention, impulsivity, and hyperactivity.

attribution. Searching for the causes of our own or someone else's behavior.

aversion to sex. Anxiety, disgust, repulsion, and other negative emotions toward sex.

avoidance (as related to illness). A pattern an individual utilizes to minimize or deny that there are symptoms of illness to notice.

avoidant (attachment style). An attachment style that results in the individual's feeling uneasy when other people get too close.

bargain for time. The third stage of death and dying in which individuals attempt to negotiate with others who might help them live longer.

battering. A pattern of behavior used to establish power and control over another person through fear and intimidation, often including the threat or use of violence.

behavioral therapy. Therapy that involves discovering the factors that trigger and reinforce the problem behavior; specifying a target behavior to replace it; and then, by manipulating these factors, bringing out the desired behavior.

bereavement. The process of adjusting to the experience of loss, especially the death of friends or loved ones.

best possible self. Thinking about the self in an imaginary future in which everything has turned out in the most optimal way.

binge drinking. Consuming five or more drinks in a short period of time for men, four or more for women.

binge eating. Eating an excessive amount of food within a discrete period of time and with a sense of lack of control over eating during the episode.

biological perspective. Many of our personal attributes and much of our personal development may be attributable to genetic and other biological influences.

biomedical therapies. Therapeutic strategies that rely on direct physiological intervention to treat the symptoms of psychological disorders.

bipolar disorder. An emotional disorder characterized by alternation of elated and depressive moods, popularly known as manic depression.

bisexual, bisexuality. Preference for sexual activity with partners of either sex.

blended families. Families that involve the children from a previous marriage of one spouse or both.

body image. Refers to the mental image we form of our own bodies.

body leakage. The leaking of the true emotion through body postures rather than the face.

borderline personality disorder. A personality disorder in which the individual shows impulsive behavior and unstable social relationships as well as an unstable self-image.

bulimia nervosa. An eating disorder characterized by excessive overeating or uncontrolled binge eating followed by self-induced vomiting.

bullying. Repeated, unprovoked, harmful actions by one child or children against another.

burnout. A psychological syndrome of emotional exhaustion, depersonalization, and reduced personal accomplishment that occurs among individuals, especially those who do "people work."

calories. A measurement of energy produced by food when oxidized, or "burned," in the body.

career. The purposeful life pattern of work, as seen in the sequence of jobs and occupations held throughout life.

catastrophic events. The same life change happens to many people at the same time, disrupting lives and causing death and destruction.

catharsis. Venting (releasing) anger.

centralized communication networks. Communication in groups in which one or two individuals control the flow of information.

charismatic leader. This type of leader inspires social change, is visionary, and appeals to followers' self-concepts and values.

child pornography. A visual depiction of a minor engaging in sexually explicit conduct, especially one lacking serious literary, artistic, political, or scientific value.

chlamydia. A bacterium that is spread by sexual contact and that affects both males and females.

chronic stress. The self-perception of "global" (or generalized and pervasive) stress in our lives.

claustrophobia. An irrational fear of closed places.

climacteric. The loss of reproductive capacity.

co-branding. An advertising technique in which two companies work together to cross-promote products or services.

cognitive-behavioral therapies. A large and diverse group of therapies that characterize their orientation as either behavioral or cognitive or both and that attempt to modify faulty thinking or maladaptive behavior.

cognitive therapy. Therapy in which the central assumption is that the emotional and behavioral problems result from the individual's distorted thoughts and reactions to external events rather than from the events themselves.

cohabitation. The practice of unmarried persons living together, sharing bed and board.

cohabitation effect. An effect whereby couples that cohabit first have greater marital instability than couples that do not cohabit.

collectives. A large group that is unlikely to have a true leader or clear rules.

collectivist societies (cultures). Societies in which collective or societal gain is cherished over individual advancement.

coming out. When an individual accepts his or her sexual orientation as homosexual (or bisexual) and then tells others.

commitment. The pledge or promise to make something work, as in committing ourselves to a career or relationship. In love relationships, commitment is the cognitive aspect of love, which includes both a short-term affirmation of love and a long-term commitment to maintain love.

community-based service. The general term meaning that mental health services are located in the individual's own community or nearby.

community mental health center. A center designed to provide a variety of mental health services located in the patient's own community.

companionate love. Love based primarily on emotional closeness and commitment, rather than sexual intimacy.

compliance. A change in behavior in response to a direct request from another person to do so.

complicated grief. A psychological state in which a person's emotional reaction to loss remains repressed, often being manifested in unexplained physical or psychological symptoms.

compulsion. An act that the individual feels compelled to repeat again and again, usually in ritualistic fashion or according to certain rules.

confederates. Agents of the experimenter who were told in advance how to behave.

conformity. A change in behavior due to the real or imagined influence (pressure) of other people.

confrontation (as related to illness). A pattern an individual utilizes to directly note that there are symptoms of illness present.

consummate love. A complete and balanced love characterized by emotional closeness, sexual intimacy, and commitment between the partners.

contempt (in sexual relationships). A tactic in which insults are used to denigrate a partner's sexuality.

contingency theory of leadership. The theory identifies two attributes or styles of leaders known as people-oriented or task-oriented, which are effective at leading in different situations.

core of the self-concept. Those aspects of ourselves we regard as very important to us.

counselors. Professionals who receive training in personality theory and counseling skills, usually at the master's degree level. Their counseling emphasis tends to reflect their respective professional affiliations, depending on whether they are doing marriage counseling, career counseling, pastoral counseling (clergy), or some other type.

couple adjustment. The changes and adjustments in a couple's relationship during the course of their committed or married life.

crisis intervention. A treatment for those who are in a state of acute crisis but do not need treatment for many sessions.

criticism (in sexual relationships). A response pattern related to human sexuality in which one partner attacks or criticizes the other partner's character.

cultural diversity. The cultural pattern by which people from different cultural and ethnic backgrounds maintain in varying degrees both their national and their ethnic identities.

culture. The ideas, customs, arts, and skills that characterize a group of people during a given period of history.

culture-bound syndromes. Sets of symptoms much more common in some societies than in others.

cultural display rules. Rules that influence the expression of emotions that are influenced by one's culture.

cyber-bullying. Repeated, unprovoked, harmful actions by one person (or persons) against another via the Internet.

cyberslacking. The overuse of the Internet in the workplace for purposes other than work.

daily hassles. Everyday difficulties that cause stress.

day hospitals. Hospitals that provide part-time care for those with mental disorders during regular working hours and then allow them to return to their families in the evening.

death. The cessation of life as measured by the absence of breathing, heartbeat, and electrical activity of the brain.

death anxiety. The fear of death and dying.

decentralized communication networks. Communication in groups in which individuals can communicate relatively freely with one another.

decision making. The process of gathering information and relevant alternatives and making an appropriate choice.

deep brain stimulation. Surgeons implant electrodes deep into the brain that when activated send electrical impulses into the surrounding tissues.

defense mechanisms. Automatic unconscious mechanisms that protect us from the awareness of anxiety, thereby helping us to maintain a sense of self-worth in the face of threat.

defensiveness (in sexual relationships). A tactic in which we make excuses or refuse to take responsibility for our sexuality or use some other self-protective defense.

defensive pessimism. Setting unrealistically low expectations and thinking through the worst-case outcomes of an upcoming event.

delusions. Beliefs that have no basis in reality.

denial of death. The first stage of death and dying, in which people characteristically feel that death cannot happen to them.

depression. An emotional state characterized by intense and unrealistic sadness that may assume a variety of forms, some more severe and chronic than others.

desensitization. The method of controlling anxiety by learning to associate an incompatible response, like relaxation, with the fear-provoking stimulus.

desire for success. The urge to succeed. A social motive in which the individual hopes for achievement and success; in some individuals this motive competes with another social motive, the fear of failure.

development. The relatively enduring changes in people's capacities and behavior as they grow older because of biological growth processes and people's interaction with their environment, including their social environment.

devil (horns) effect. Inferring uniformly negative traits from an appearance of a few negative traits.

diagnosis. The classification of a disorder within a set of recognized categories of abnormal behavior.

diathesis-stress hypothesis. A proposal that views schizophrenia as the interaction of a genetic vulnerability (the diathesis or predisposition) with environmental stressors.

discounting. The significance of an ability traditionally valued by society is lessened.

discrimination. Applying unfair or negative treatment to groups on the basis of such features as age, sex, or race.

disengagement theory of aging. The theory that individuals tend to disengage from society with advancing age, with psychological disengagement usually preceding social withdrawal by about 10 years.

distress. Stress that has a harmful effect.

divorce. The legal dissolution of a marriage.

do not resuscitate (DNR). A legal order which prohibits doctors from using advanced cardiac life support and CPR.

door-in-the-face effect. The requester first issues a large, unreasonable request. When the respondent answers "no," the requester makes the truly desired but smaller and more reasonable demand.

downward comparison (as related to health issues). A pattern of behavior individuals utilize to compare their own situation to others who are worse off.

early adulthood. The initial stage of adult development, from the late teens or early 20s through the 30s, characterized by the establishment of personal and economic independence.

earnings gap. Inequity between men and women in terms of their pay.

eating disorder. A serious disturbance in everyday diet, such as eating too little or too much food, coupled with severe distress or concern about body weight or shape.

ecological perspective. A perspective which emphasizes the influence of the contexts (i.e., settings) on development on the individual.

eclectic approach. Treatment based on a combination of techniques and principles from various forms of therapy.

electroconvulsive therapy (ECT). The administration of an electric current to the patient's brain to produce a convulsion; sometimes used in the treatment of severe depression.

emotion. A complex pattern of changes that include physiological changes, subjective feelings, cognitive processes, and behavioral reactions.

emotional intelligence (EI). The ability to regulate one's own emotions and to be empathic for others' emotions.

emotional self-regulation. The process by which one inhibits or moderates one's emotional responses in order to remain engaged in thoughtful interaction.

emotion-focused coping. The attempt by the distressed individual to alter the emotional reaction to stress.

emotion-focused therapy (EFT). A cognitive therapy that provides a technique for changing basic thought and emotional patterns.

entrapment. The process of throwing more time, energy, or money into a bad situation.

envy. Feelings of inferiority, longing, resentment, and disapproval.

e-recruiting. A process in which job candidates are screened by phone, video, or computer.

erectile inhibition. In sexuality, this is known as impotence or the inability of the man to experience erection.

eustress. Stress that has a beneficial effect.

evaluation apprehension. The fear of others' appraisals of us.

evidence-based therapy. Therapy proven effective through rigorous research methodologies.

excitement (stage in the sexual response cycle). A stage of sexual arousal that causes increased muscle tension, engorgement of the genitals with blood, and increased heart rate.

exosystem. The social settings that the child is not part of, yet can still influence the child's development.

experience of dying. The sequence of physiological and psychological changes experienced by individuals who are dying, such as those with a terminal illness.

external locus of control. The belief by an individual that something outside of him- or herself, such as other individuals, fate, or various external situations, controls life events.

extrinsic motivation. The desire to engage in an activity because it is a means to an end and not because an individual is following his or her inner interests.

extroverts. Individuals who tend to be warm, outgoing, and involved in life.

face-saving. Saving one's own or someone else's image.

false consensus effect. An assumption that others feel or believe as we do.

family therapy. An approach that includes the larger family unit, including children and adolescents, on the assumption that the disturbance of one family member reflects problems in the overall family patterns.

feared self. The negatively viewed self that would result if you don't succeed.

fear of failure. Fear that we will be humiliated by shortcoming.

felt security. Feeling comforted by an attachment figure without actual contact.

female orgasmic disorder. Delay or absence of orgasm in a woman.

fight-or-flight response. Confronting the stressor or fleeing from the stressor.

first impression. The initial perception we form of others, in which we tend to judge them on the basis of very little information.

fixation. The emotional fixation of the personality at a particular anxiety-ridden stage that influences the individual to continue to act out symbolically any wishes that were overly inhibited or indulged.

flash mobs. Social media is used to organize the appearance, and accompanying performance, of a group of strangers.

forbidden fruit effect. Warning labels and restrictive age classifications create a desire for the prohibited content in consumers.

forming (stage). The initial stage of group development, in which the members come together to form the group.

free association. Saying whatever comes to mind regardless of how trivial it sounds.

frenemy. A person who acts like a friend, but in reality, has little concern for your personal welfare.

friends with benefits. Friendships that involve recurrent sexual activity.

friendship. The affectionate attachment between two or more people.

fundamental attribution error. The tendency to overattribute people's behavior to their personality (traits) rather than to their circumstances or situations.

funerals. The ceremonies and rituals associated with the burial or cremation of the dead.

gender identity. Self-identification as male or female.

gender roles. Social and cultural expectations about what is appropriate for males and females.

gender stereotypes. Widely held generalizations about the characteristics and behavior of men and women that exaggerate the differences between the sexes.

general adaptation syndrome. According to Selye, nonspecific physiological mechanisms as a reaction to stress, which include three progressive stages—alarm reaction, stage of resistance, and stage of exhaustion.

generalized anxiety disorder. A chronic state of diffuse or free-floating anxiety.

genital herpes. A type of herpes viral infection that is primarily transmitted through sexual contact.

genital human papillomavirus (HPV). A virus that infects the genital areas of men and women, and over time can result in the eruption of painless warts.

glass cliff. A situation where women may be set up for failure as a leader more often than are men.

global burden of disease. A measure of years of life lost to disability throughout the world.

gonorrhea. A common sexually transmitted bacterial infection that sometimes produces a cloudy, smelly discharge and a burning sensation upon urination.

good grief. Grief that leads to learning and growth in our bereavement.

great man theory (of leadership). A theory suggesting that great leaders are born with a certain common set of traits.

grief. The intense emotional suffering that accompanies our experience of loss.

grief therapy. A form of therapy that assists the bereaved to cope with the death of a loved one.

grief work. The healthy process of working through emotions associated with loss and death; freeing ourselves emotionally from the deceased, readjusting to life without that person, resuming ordinary activities, and forming new relationships.

GRIT (graduated and reciprocated initiatives in tension reduction). A conflict resolution technique in which each side gradually concedes something to the other side.

group polarization effect. Groups are likely to shift to either a more conservative or a riskier decision than individuals alone make.

group therapy. Therapeutic format where treatment takes place in groups.

groupthink. The tendency for groups to reach a consensus prematurely because the desire for harmony overrides the process of critical thinking and the search for the best decision.

guided imagery. A procedure that helps a person shut off the outside world and bypass the censor we call the brain, enabling the person to see, experience, and learn from an intuitive, feeling, unconscious nature. (See also **visualization**.)

halfway house. A residence in which newly released patients and ex-addicts can live under supervision for a short period of time while they make a crucial transition in their lives from a setting with close supervision and other restrictions. Also called group homes and board-and-care homes.

hallucinations. Sensory perceptions that occur in the absence of any appropriate external stimulus.

halo effect. Inferring uniformly positive traits from the appearance of a few positive traits.

happiness. A state with a preponderance of positive thoughts and feelings about one's life.

happy-face advantage. A phenomenon in which positive emotions are more quickly identified than negative ones.

hate crimes. Crimes motivated by biases based on race, religion, sexual orientation, ethnicity/national origin, and disability.

heredity. The transmission of traits from parents to offspring.

heterosexual, heterosexuality. Emotional and sexual preference for partners of the opposite sex.

heuristics. Mental shortcuts or guidelines for making complex decisions.

hierarchy of needs. According to Maslow, the hierarchical manner in which needs and motives function in relation to each other, so that the lowest level of unmet needs remains the most urgent.

hindsight bias. A biased representation of events or information once they have happened or after the fact.

homophobic. Term describing individuals who are afraid of homosexuals or hold negative attitudes toward homosexuals.

homosexual, homosexuality. Emotional and sexual preference for partners of the same sex.

hospice. A system of care that integrates a physical facility for the terminally ill with the patient's family and home to enable the patient to die with dignity.

humanistic perspective. A group of related theories and therapies that emphasize the values of human freedom and the uniqueness of the individual.

hyperstress. An excessive amount of stress.

hypoactive (inhibited) sexual desire. Lack of interest in sex.

hypochondriacs. People who habitually complain of unfounded ailments or exhibit an undue fear of illness.

hypostress. Insufficient stress.

hypothalamus. A small but important structure at the core of the brain that governs many aspects of behavior, such as eating and hormonal activity.

ideal self. The self we'd like to be including our aspirations, moral ideals, and values.

ill-being. Psychological distress, such as anxiety and depression.

illusion of control. The mistaken belief that we can exercise control over chance-determined events.

illusion of invulnerability. A symptom of groupthink; the group members believe they are invincible and can do no wrong.

"I" messages. Honest but nonjudgmental expressions of emotions about someone whose behavior has become a problem.

immune system. A complex surveillance system, including the brain and various blood cells, that defends our bodies by identifying and destroying various foreign invaders.

incidence (of disorders). The number of new cases of disorders reported during a given period.

individualistic societies (cultures). Societies in which individual gain (needs, wants, and autonomy) is appreciated more than general societal gain.

infantilized. Treated like infants, as, for example, when other adults speak to older adults in baby talk.

ingratiation. Managing the impressions we leave on others so that they will like us and comply with our requests. An example is flattery.

in-group. The group with which we identify.

inhibited sexual arousal. Insufficient sexual arousal, such as the male's difficulty in sustaining an erection of his penis or the female's difficulty in generating sufficient vaginal lubrication.

inhibited vaginal lubrication. When insufficient vasocongestion and insufficient lubrication occur in women.

insane. A defendant cannot tell right from wrong when committing a crime nor can they resist impulses to act in antisocial ways.

insight therapies. Any therapy that aims to bring change by increasing self-understanding.

integrative solutions (for conflicts). Solutions that take into account the needs of both sides in a conflict such that both sides can win something.

interdependence. Mutual dependence among individuals in a given group or society.

internal locus of control. An individual's belief that something within him- or herself controls life events.

intersexed persons. People who are born with chromosomal or hormonal birth defects that cause them not to readily fit into "male" or "female" categories.

intimacy. The emotional aspect of love that includes closeness, sharing, communication, and support.

intrinsic motivation. Active engagement with tasks that people find interesting and that, in turn, promote growth and are freely engaged in out of interest.

jealousy. A complex emotion that occurs when we fear losing a close relationship with another person or have lost it already.

job satisfaction. People's feelings about different aspects of their jobs; how well one likes a given job, depending on such factors as pay and coworkers.

joint (shared) custody. Joint decision making by divorced parents about the child's care.

late adulthood. The final stage of adult development, from the mid-60s to death, characterized by adjustment to changing health, income, and social roles.

learned helplessness. Maladaptive passivity that frequently follows an individual's experience with uncontrollable events.

learned optimism. A learned way of explaining both good and bad life events that in turn enhances our perceived control and adaptive responses to them.

leisure. Time free from work or duty that may be spent in recreational activities of one's choice.

libido. The psychic energy of the sex drive.

life change. A significant change in a person's life.

life review. A naturally occurring process of self-review prompted by the realization that life is approaching an end.

living will. An instrument that instructs doctors and family members to stop using life-sustaining procedures in the event of a terminal condition.

love. Deep and tender feelings of affection for or attachment to one or more persons.

macrosystem. The socio-cultural context in which development takes place, including cultural, sub-cultural, and social-class distinctions.

major depression. A type of depressive disorder characterized by intense and unrealistic sadness as well as feelings of worthlessness.

maintenance activities. Nonleisure and nonwork time spent in activities necessary for the maintenance of life, such as preparing meals and sleeping.

maladaptive behavior. Significant impairment in one or more areas of psychological functioning, especially the ability to work and to get along with others.

male impotence. The inability to experience an erection.

mania. A disorder in which the individual exhibits such symptoms as an expansive mood, increased social activity, talkativeness, sleeplessness, and reckless behavior.

marital satisfaction. The sense of gratification and contentment in a marriage, especially in the personal relationship between the partners.

marriage. The state of being married; usually the legal union between two people.

mediators. Neutral third parties who intervene in conflict and who help the two disputing parties come to common agreements via communication, creative problem solving, and other techniques.

menopause. The period in a woman's life that includes the cessation of monthly menstrual cycles.

mesosystem. Refers to the linking of different microsystems (note, the child is in each setting, but at a different time).

microexpressions. Fleeting facial expressions that last only a fraction of a second.

microsystem. The setting that the child is currently in, such as the home or daycare center.

middle adulthood. The middle stage of adult development, from the late 30s to the mid-60s, characterized by the fulfillment of career and family goals.

midlife transition. The period of personal evaluation that comes sometimes with the realization that one's life is about half over.

mindguards. A situation in groupthink in which individuals in the group take it upon themselves to censor dissenters in the group.

minority stress. The psychological and social stress associated minority status.

mistaken impression. The false or erroneous perception of others, often based on insufficient evidence.

mnemonic neglect. Poor recall (or forgetting) of negative feedback that is inconsistent with core aspects of the self-concept.

mood disorder. An emotional disturbance that is severe and persistent.

mortality salience. Awareness of our own mortality.

motherhood penalty. Refers to the fact that working mothers are viewed as less competent and less committed to work than non-mothers.

motivation. A general term referring to the forces that energize and direct our efforts toward a meaningful goal.

motive. Goal-directed activity that energizes and directs behavior.

motive targets. The people toward whom our attention or motives are directed.

mourning. The outward expressions of bereavement and grief, such as the wearing of black.

multiple orgasms. Experiencing two or more climaxes within a short period of time.

mutual-help groups. Groups whose members share a common problem and meet regularly to discuss their concerns without the guidance of professionals.

narcissistic personality. A personality disorder characterized by an undue sense of self-importance, often accompanied by a sense of inferiority.

near-death experience. The distinctive state of recall associated with being brought back to life from the verge of death.

needs. Tension states that arouse us to seek gratification.

negotiation. Making mutual concessions with another person.

networking. Using personal contacts to establish career opportunities.

neurotransmitter. Chemical substances that transmit neural impulses.

non-age-related changes. Events and influences that are unique to each of us and may occur at any age or not at all, such as divorce or the decision to change careers.

norm of reciprocity. An unwritten rule that guides reciprocal behavior related to the granting of favors.

norming (stage). The third stage of group formation in which the group comes to consensus about the rules under which it will operate.

norms. Unwritten standards or rules by which groups function and by which groups exert pressure on nonconforming members.

nutrition. Eating a proper, balanced diet to promote health.

obedience. Following a direct order or command.

obesity. An excessive amount of body fat, usually defined as exceeding the desirable weight for one's height, build, and age.

obesity stigma. Refers to the negative attitudes, stereotypes, and discriminatory behavior directed at overweight individuals.

observational learning. The process in which people learn by observing other people and events without necessarily receiving any direct reward or reinforcement.

obsession. A thought or image that keeps recurring in the mind, despite the individual's attempts to ignore or resist it.

obsessive-compulsive disorder. The condition characterized by the involuntary dwelling on an unwelcome thought or the involuntary repetition of an unnecessary act.

occupation. The activities and responsibilities necessary to perform given work tasks in a particular line of work, such as nursing or marketing.

orgasm (stage in the sexual response cycle). The climax of sexual excitement that is pleasurable and releases tension.

outpatient services. Therapeutic settings that provide help for individuals without disrupting their normal routine.

out-group. Any group we perceive as being different from (outside of) our own group.

panic disorder, panic attacks. The type of anxiety disorder characterized by the occurrence of severe panic.

paralinguistics. Unspoken but important features of spoken communications, such as gestures.

paraprofessionals. Individuals who have two- or four-year degrees (or sometimes no degree at all) and work in the mental health field.

parental monitoring. The degree to which parents know about their children's whereabouts, day-to-day activities, and activity partners.

passion. The emotional or motivational aspect of love that involves physiological arousal and an intense desire to be united with the loved one.

pathological (obsessional) jealousy. Repeated, and unfounded, suspicion of a partner's fidelity.

people- or relationship-oriented leaders. Leaders who concern themselves with their group members' feelings and relationships.

perceived control. The belief that we can influence the occurrence of events in our environment that affect our lives.

performing (stage). The final stage of group development, when the group functions better and performs its business.

personal control. The achieved amount of control we have over our lives; this term is often synonymous with perceived control.

persistence. Continued attempts to reach a goal in the face of adversity.

personal distress. Intense or chronic negative self-awareness that interferes with one's sense of well-being or functioning.

personal growth. Personal change or development in a desirable direction, including the fulfillment of one's inborn potential.

personality disorders. When personality traits are so inflexible and maladaptive that they cause marked impairment in individual's social and occupational life.

personality traits. Enduring patterns of thinking, feeling, acting, and relating to others that we exhibit in a wide range of situations.

person-centered therapy. According to Carl Rogers, the view that the helper's genuineness, acceptance, and empathic understanding of the client are necessary and sufficient conditions for producing therapeutic change.

phenomenal self. An individual's overall self-concept available to awareness.

phobic disorders. The conditions characterized by a persistent and irrational fear of a specific object or activity, accompanied by a compelling desire to avoid it.

physical fitness. A human's ability to function efficiently and effectively, including both health-related and skill-related fitness components.

physician-assisted suicide. A physician helping a patient end their life by providing the physical means, and/or information, necessary to do so.

plateau (stage in the sexual response cycle). The stage just before orgasm; in this phase, sexual arousal becomes more pronounced.

positive psychology. An umbrella term for the study of positive emotions, positive character traits, and enabling institutions.

positive regard. Acceptance by others.

post-decision regret. The regret that can be experienced shortly after we have finally made a particularly difficult choice or decision.

posttraumatic stress disorder. A severe anxiety disorder characterized by symptoms of anxiety and avoidance behavior, resulting from an unusually distressing event such as being assaulted.

power distance. The idea that people in groups accept the concept that people in an organization rightly have different levels of power and authority. The more status and privileges they ascribe to those in authority, the greater the power distance.

prejudice. An unfair, often negative attitude toward another person or group based solely on group membership.

premature ejaculation. Early orgasm in a man.

prevalence (of a disorder). The total number of active cases that can be identified in a given population at a particular time.

primary control. Actions directed at attempting to change the world to fit one's needs and desires.

primary (basic) emotions. The initial and direct emotional response to an experience.

primary group. This group is important because it is small, intimate, and interacts face-to-face.

problem-focused coping. The attempts by the distressed individual to change the environment or find a solution.

propinquity. Physical closeness.

psychiatric (clinical) social workers. Social workers who receive supervised clinical training as part of their master's degree program in the field of social work, and some earn a doctorate as well.

psychiatrists. Medical doctors who specialize in the treatment of mental illness.

psychoanalysis. Psychotherapy aimed at helping the person gain insight and mastery over unconscious conflicts. Also referred to as Freudian theory.

psychoanalysts. Psychiatrists or other mental health professionals who have received several years of additional training in personality theory and the therapeutic methods of one of the founding analysts.

psychodynamic perspective. The belief that personality and behavior result from unconscious forces, especially those originating in childhood.

psychodynamic therapy. A form of therapy which aims to discover and resolve unconscious conflicts through insight.

psychological disorder. A clinically significant behavioral or psychological pattern that is associated with (1) present personal distress; (2) disability or impairment in one or more important areas of functioning, such as, maladaptive behavior; (3) significantly increased risk of suffering disability, pain, or death; and (4) an important loss of freedom or personal control.

psychological hardiness. The attitude that allows individuals to make the most of what are often bad situations. A characteristic of individuals who cope successfully with stress.

psychologists. Professionals who receive clinical training in the methods of psychological assessment and treatment as part of a program in clinical, counseling, or school psychology.

psychosexual stages. According to Freud, the sequence of critical stages in the developmental process; the way in which individuals handle the conflicts among their pleasure-seeking impulses, inhibitions, and environmental restrictions that becomes decisive for adult personality.

psychosurgery. Surgery designed to destroy or disconnect brain tissue in an attempt to regulate abnormal behavior.

psychotherapy. A helping process in which a trained, socially sanctioned therapist performs certain activities that will facilitate a change in the client's attitudes and behaviors.

psychotic symptoms. Symptoms that are signs of psychosis (e.g., schizophrenia) and that include hallucinations such as hearing voices, marked impairment in self-care and social relationships, and other signs of severe disturbance.

psychotropic medications. Medication used to treat psychological disorders.

rationalization. Occurs when we justify our unacceptable behavior with "good" reasons.

reactance. An oppositional response that occurs when our personal freedom is restricted.

refractory period. The period of time following an orgasm when added stimulation will not result in orgasm.

reinforcement. The addition of something that increases the likelihood of a behavior.

relapse. A return to a previous state; in psychology, the return to a former problematic behavior.

relational aggression. Aggressive acts which attempt to hurt another person's social relationships or level of group inclusion.

reminiscence. Thinking about oneself and reconsidering past events and their meaning.

resentment. The second stage of death and dying, in which dying individuals resent those who are healthy.

resilience. Positive growth or adaptation following brief periods of stress after some stressful disruption or extreme adversity.

resistance. In therapy, when an individual hesitates or is reluctant to talk about some painful experiences.

resolution phase (stage in the sexual response cycle). The stage immediately following orgasm, in which the body returns to its normal, nonexcited phase.

responsibility diffusion. A phenomenon in which individuals in groups feel less responsible for the risk so are willing to make riskier decisions in groups.

retarded ejaculation. A delay or absence of orgasm in a man.

Right-to-die. The legal and ethical view that competent individuals who are able to understand treatment choices and their consequences have the right to decide their own fate, such as withholding of treatment that would delay death.

risky shift. A phenomenon in which groups coming to consensus make riskier decisions than individuals.

role. A set of rules that defines how an individual in a particular post in a group will behave.

romantic love. Love characterized by closeness and passion.

schizophrenia. A group of related psychotic disorders characterized by severe disorganization of thoughts, perceptions, and emotions; bizarre behavior; and social withdrawal.

seasonal affective disorder (SAD). A depression that is more likely to occur at certain times of the year, usually the winter months.

secondary control. Involves the individual utilizing processes directed at making him- or herself fit into the world better.

secondary (complex) emotion. Emotional experiences that are reflective, involve evaluation of the self, and typically follow primary emotions.

secondary erectile inhibition. When a man has previously experienced erections but is consistently unable to have an erection of sufficient firmness to penetrate the woman's vagina.

secondary group. This group is usually larger than a primary group, has a formal or contractual reason for coming together, often disbands when the reason for its existence disappears; members are less likely to engage in regular face-to-face interaction.

securely attached. An attachment style by which people develop happy and trusting love relationships.

self-actualization/self-actualized. The process of fulfilling our inborn potential, involving a biological growth tendency as well as self-conscious efforts at growth.

self-alienation. The failure to acknowledge or accept certain aspects of ourselves; the feeling these qualities are foreign to us and we project them onto others, whom we then dislike.

self-clarity. The extent to which one's individual self-beliefs is clearly and confidently defined, internally consistent, and stable.

self-complexity. The extent to which one's self-concept is comprised of many differentiated self-aspects.

self-concept. The overall image or awareness we have of ourselves. It includes all those perceptions of "I" and "me," together with the feelings, beliefs, and values associated with them.

self-consistency. The tendency to perceive our experiences in a manner that is consistent with our self-concept; experiences that are not consistent with the self are distorted or denied to awareness.

self-direction. The need to learn more about ourselves and our world as a means of directing our lives more effectively.

self-disclosure. The sharing of intimate or personal information with others.

self-efficacy. The belief in one's capabilities to organize and execute courses of action required to produce give attainments.

self-enhancement. Seeking out positive feedback to affirm ideas about one's positive qualities.

self-esteem. The sense of personal worth associated with one's self-concept.

self-fulfilling prophecy. A prophecy that is fulfilled when people's expectations become a reality by virtue of their own behavior.

self-handicappers. Those who make up excuses for a poor performance before the event has even taken place.

self-help groups. Groups whose members share a common problem and meet regularly to discuss their concerns without the guidance of professionals.

self-image. The personal evaluation of ourselves and the resulting feelings of worth associated with our self-concept.

self-immunization. The trivialization of threatening information, such as failure, by making the behavior seem less important.

self-recognition. A child's ability to differentiate him- or herself from others in the social environment.

self-serving attributional bias. Attributions that glorify the self or conceive of the self as causing the good outcomes that come our way.

self-verification. Attempts to preserve the positive and negative images of the self through feedback from others.

sensation-seeking motive. The tendency to seek out stimulating and novel experiences, partly because of biological factors.

serious mental disorder. A mental disorder with substantially interferes with or limits one or more of major life activities.

serotonin. A neurotransmitter that has been linked to depression.

sexting. Sending sexually explicit messages or photos via electronic communication.

sexual assault. Unwanted sexual activity, including the touching of body parts as well as oral, anal, and vaginal sex under conditions of actual or threatened force.

sexual dysfunction. A persistent problem that prevents the individual from engaging in or enjoying sexual intercourse.

sexual harassment. Any unwanted attention of a sexual nature occurring in the workplace that interferes with a person's ability to work.

sexual intercourse. The penetration of the vagina by the penis.

sexually transmitted infections (STIs). Infections transmitted primarily by sexual intercourse.

sexual orientation. A component of sexuality and is characterized by enduring emotional, romantic, or sexual attraction to a particular gender.

sexual prejudice. Negative attitudes based on sexual orientation, whether the target is homosexual, bisexual, or heterosexual.

sexual response cycle. The basic sexual response patterns of men and women, as in sexual intercourse.

sexual victimization. Being coerced to engage in sexual acts under duress or force, such as rape.

shyness. The tendency to avoid contact or familiarity with others.

sibling rivalry. A sibling relationship characterized by jealousy and resentment.

simple phobia. A most common type of phobia in which individuals are irrationally afraid of common objects such as dogs, snakes, insects, stairs, etc.

skill. The ability to perform a task well. It is usually developed over time through training or experience.

social anxiety (social phobia). Extreme shyness that may severely interfere with a person's life.

social changes. Changes in the social patterns and institutions in society.

social comparison. The process of using others to compare ourselves in order to understand who we are relative to them.

social influence. Efforts on the part of one person to alter the behavior or attitudes of one or more others.

social learning. Social learning is a process in which we learn by observing events and other people, or "models," without receiving any direct reward or reinforcement.

social loafing. Contributing less to a group effort than would be contributed to an individual effort.

social norms. The generalized expectations regarding appropriate behavior in a given situation or society.

social phobia. An extreme form of shyness that can interfere with an individual's daily life and involves a chronic, irrational fear of and a compelling desire to avoid situations where others may scrutinize the individual.

social self (selves). The way we feel others see us.

social support. A process whereby one individual or group offers comfort and advice to others who can use it as a means of coping.

specific phobia. Excessive fear of specific objects or situations

spotlight effect. Refers to the situation in which we overestimate how prominent our own behaviors, appearance, and emotions are to others.

stage of exhaustion. Stage of Selye's notion of the general adaptation syndrome response to stress in which the body is unable to continue secreting hormones at an increased rate, so the organism can no longer adapt to chronic stress. Body defenses break down, adaptation energy runs out, and the physical symptoms of the alarm reaction reappear.

stage of resistance. Stage of Selye's notion of the general adaptation syndrome response in which the human organism develops an increased resistance to the stressor.

stereotypes. Widespread generalizations about people (based solely on their group membership) that have little if any basis in fact.

stigma. The use of negative labels to identify a person living with a mental disorder or with another distinguishing feature and whom you believe differs from you.

storming. The second stage in group formation in which group members disagree or often openly conflict when they learn about each other's opinions.

stress. The pattern of responses individuals make to stimulus events that disturb their equilibrium or exceed their coping abilities.

stressors. The collective label for the variety of external and internal stimuli that evoke stress.

stress-related illness. Any illness that is affected in an important way by one's emotions, lifestyle, or environment.

stress tolerance. The degree of stress you can handle or how long you can put up with a demanding task without acting in an irrational or disorganized way.

"study" drugs. Stimulant medications taken by people without a prescription in an attempt to improve their focus while studying.

subjective well-being. A state with a preponderance of positive thoughts and feelings about one's life.

substance abuse. Misuse or dependence on a psychoactive substance like alcohol.

substitution. A conflict resolution strategy whereby we seek alternative goals with another person.

suicidal ideation. Refers to both nonspecific thoughts of death and specific thoughts involving the intent to die accompanied by a plan of action.

survivor guilt. Feeling guilty simply because one is still alive while others are not.

syphilis. A sexually transmitted and serious disease caused by a spiral-shaped bacterium, or spirochete.

tardive dyskinesia. A side effect of antipsychotic drugs, characterized by jerking movements around the neck and face and involuntary protrusions of the tongue.

task-oriented leaders. Leaders who are primarily concerned with getting the job done well and in a timely fashion.

technophobia. A fear of technology.

telework. Periodic or regular work for one's employer performed at home or another remote location.

temperament. An individual's characteristic pattern of emotional response and behavioral reactivity to situations and stressors.

therapeutic alliance. The match or quality of fit between the client and the therapist.

therapist. A person trained to help people with psychological problems.

tobacco abuse. The abuse of tobacco to such an extent that heart, respiratory, and other health-related problems develop.

token economy. A form of behavior therapy where good behaviors are rewarded with small tokens that can be exchanged for a larger reward later.

transference. The unconscious tendency of clients to project onto the therapist their feelings and fantasies, both positive and negative, about significant others in their childhood.

transformational leader. A leader who stimulates interest among colleagues and followers to view their work from a new perspective. The leader does this by generating awareness of the mission or vision of the organization and helps members to look beyond their own interests.

transinstitutionalization. The revolving-door syndrome in which mental patients find themselves housed in one institution after another, often including jails and prisons.

transition (stage in the sexual response cycle). The gradual shift from a nonsexual state to a sexual state of being and includes the awakening of sexual desire and a readiness for sexual arousal.

transitional objects. Objects that help the child transition from dependence on a caregiver for comfort and support to more independent forms of coping.

Transgendered persons. People who believe that they were born into the body of the wrong sex. They sometimes want to change this situation through hormone therapy and gender reassignment surgery.

triangular theory of love. A theory of love that suggests there are three components to love—intimacy, passion, and commitment.

trust. People's abstract but positive expectations that they can count on friends and partners to care for them and be responsive to their needs, now and in the future.

Type A behavior pattern. People who tend to be competitive, argumentative, time-urgent, ambitious, impatient, and sometimes hostile. They are heart-attack prone.

Type B behavior pattern. Individuals who are relaxed and easygoing, rather than competitive and impatient.

unconditional leisure. Any activity freely chosen, excluding work and maintenance activities.

unconditional positive regard. Unconditional positive acceptance; generally utilized in person-centered therapy.

underemployed. Working in a job beneath one's abilities or education.

unresolved grief. A psychological state in which a person's emotional reaction to loss remains repressed, often being manifested in unexplained physical or psychological symptoms.

virtual reality therapy. Patients don goggles to view a three-dimensional environment in which they can move about and interact with the objects within that setting.

viral advertising. A marketing technique in which advertisers rely on pre-existing social networks (e.g., blogs, e-mail, etc.) to promote products by encouraging users to voluntarily pass along web links, video clips, Flash games, etc.

visualization. A procedure that helps a person shut off the outside world and bypass the censor we call the brain, enabling the person to see, experience, and learn from an intuitive, feeling, unconscious nature. (See also **guided imagery**.)

voluntary marriage. The assumption that two people will remain married only as long as they are in love.

wellness. The positive ideal of health in which one strives to maintain and improve one's health.

withdrawal. To remove oneself physically or emotionally from an activity, organization, or person. In sexual relationships, a response pattern in which one partner ignores the other.

workplace. Place of paid employment outside the home.

work values. Those values that bring you the most enjoyment and satisfaction in a career or job.

REFERENCES

Abdullah, T., & Brown, T.L. (2011). Mental illness stigma and ethnocultural beliefs, values, and norms: An integrative review. *Clinical Psychology Review, 31*(6), 934–948.

Abramovitz, M. (2002, February). Mirror in your head: Your mental picture of your body can have a direct effect on your self-esteem and your behavior. *Current Health, 2,* 26–30.

Acharya, N., & Joshi, S. (2011). Achievement motivation and parental support to adolescents. *Journal of the Indian Academy of Applied Psychology, 37*(1), 132–139.

Administration on Aging. (2012). *Aging statistics.* Retrieved February 9, 2012, from http://www.aoa.gov/AoARoot/Aging_Statistics/index.aspx.

Adoption.com. (2012). *Fosterparenting.* Retrieved February 14, 2012, from http://adoption.com.

Advani, A. (2011). Introduction: Men's health. *Journal of Pharmacy Practice, 24*(3), 297.

AFSP.org. (2012). When you fear someone may take their life. *American Foundation of Suicide Prevention.* Retrieved February 12, 2012, from http://www.afsp.org/index.cfm?page_id=F2F25092-7E90-9BD4-C4658F1D2B5D19A0.

Agrillo, C. (2011). Near-death experience: Out-of-body and out-of-brain? *Review of General Psychology, 15*(1), 1–10.

Ahlfinger, N.R., & Esser, J.K. (2001). Testing the groupthink model: Effects of promotional leadership and conformity predisposition. *Social Behavior and Personality, 29,* 31–41.

Ahmed, S.R., Kia-Keating, M., & Tsai, K.H. (2011). A structural model of racial discrimination, acculturative stress, and cultural resources among Arab American adolescents. *American Journal of Community Psychology, 48*(3/4), 181–192.

Ai, A.L., Evans-Campbell, T., Santangelo, L.K., & Cascio, T. (2006). The traumatic impact of the September 11, 2001, terrorist attacks and the potential protection of optimism. *Journal of Interpersonal Violence, 21,* 689–700.

Ainsworth, M.S., Blehar, M.C., Waters, E., & Wall, S. (1978). *Patterns of attachment: A psychological study of the strange situation.* Oxford, England: Lawrence Erlbaum.

Akkirman, A.D., & Harris, D.L. (2005). Organizational communication satisfaction in the virtual workplace. *Journal of Management Development, 24,* 397–409.

Albano, A.M., & Hayward, C. (2004). *Social anxiety disorder.* New York: Oxford University Press.

Alessi, N., Huang, M., James, P., Ying, J., & Chowhan, N. (1992). The influence of music and rock videos. Facts for families (No. 40). *Psychiatry Star, American Academy of Child and Adolescent Psychiatry, Facts for Families Index.*

Alfano, C.A., & Beidel, D.C. (2011). *Social anxiety in adolescents and young adults: Translating developmental science into practice.* Washington, DC, US: American Psychological Association.

Alfano, M. (2011). Explaining away intuitions about traits: Why virtue ethics seems plausible (even if it isn't). *Review of Philosophy and Psychology, 2*(1), 121–136.

Al-Issa, I. (1995). The illusion of reality or reality of illusion: Hallucinations and culture. *British Journal of Psychiatry, 166*(3), 368–373.

Allen, L. (2009). Disorders of sexual development. *Obstetrics and Gynecological Clinics of North America, 36,* 25–45.

Allen, S., & Dalton, W.T. (2011). Treatment of eating disorders in primary care: A systematic review. *Journal of Health Psychology, 16*(8), 1165–1176.

Almedom, A.M. (2005). Resilience, hardiness, sense of coherence, and posttraumatic growth: All paths leading to "light at the end of the tunnel"? *Journal of Loss & Trauma, 10,* 253–265.

Almeida, D.M. (2005). Resilience and vulnerability to daily stressors assessed via diary methods. *Current Directions in Psychological Science, 14,* 64–68.

Alterman, J. (Speaker). (1999). The social/cultural dimension of the information revolution. Retrieved January 10, 2006, from http://www.rand.org/content/dam/rand/pubs/conf_proceedings/CF154/CF154.chap6.pdf.

Alzheimer's Association. (2009). *2009 Alzheimer's disease facts and figures.* Retrieved July 10, 2009, from http://www.alz.org.

Alzheimer's Association. (2012). *Alzheimer's facts and figures.[0]* Retrieved July 21, 2012, from http://www.alz.org/alzheimers_disease_facts_and_figures.asp.

Amato, P.R., Johnson, D.R., Booth, A., & Rogers, S.J. (2003). Continuity and change in marital quality between 1980 and 2000. *Journal of Marriage & the Family, 65,* 1–22.

American Gastroenterological Association. (2008). AGA technical review on obesity. *Gastroenterology, 123*(3), 882–932.

American Medical Association's Council on Ethical and Judicial Affairs. (2010). *Code of medical ethics of the American Medical Association.* Chicago, IL: American Medical Association.

American Psychiatric Association. (2012). *DSM.* Retrieved October 4, 2012, from http://www.psych.org/practice/dsm.

American Psychological Association. (2010). *Stress in America infographics and images.* Retrieved December 19, 2011, from http://www.apa.org/news/press/releases/stress/infographics-images.aspx.

American Psychological Association. (1998, October). *How therapy helps.* http://helping.apa.org/therapy/psychotherapy.htm.

Amichai-Hamburger, Y. (2009). *Technology and psychological well-being.* New York, NY: Cambridge University Press.

Anastasio, P.A., Rose, K.C., & Chapman, J. (1999). Can the media create public opinion? A social-identity approach. *Current Directions in Psychological Science, 8,* 152–155.

Anderson, C.A., & Bushman, B.J. (2001). Effects of violent video games on aggressive behavior, aggressive cognition, aggressive affect, physiological arousal, and prosocial behavior: A meta-analytic review of the scientific literature. *Psychological Science, 12,* 353–359.

Anderson, C.J. (2003). The psychology of doing nothing: Forms of decision avoidance result from reason and emotion. *Psychological Bulletin, 129,* 139–168.

Anderson, S.M., & Berk, M.S. (1998). The social-cognitive model of transference: Experiencing past relationships in the present. *Current Directions in Psychological Science, 7,* 109–115.

Anred.com. (2012). *Anorexia and related eating disorders.* http://anred.com.

Antony, M.M., & Barlow, D.H. (2010). *Handbook of assessment and treatment planning for psychological disorders* (2nd ed.). New York, NY, US: Guilford Press.

Antony, M.M., & Roemer, L. (2011). *Behavior therapy.* Washington, DC, US: American Psychological Association.

App, B., McIntosh, D.N., Reed, C.L., & Hertenstein, M.J. (2011). Nonverbal channel use in communication of emotion: How may depend on why. *Emotion, 11*(3), 603–617.

Arnold, J.A. (2007). Influence of third party expertise on disputants' reactions to mediation. *Psychological Reports, 10,* 407–418.

Aron, E.N. (2010). *Psychotherapy and the highly sensitive person: Improving outcomes for that minority of people who are the majority of clients.* New York, NY, US: Routledge/Taylor & Francis Group.

Asch, S.E. (1951). Effects of group pressure upon the modification and distortion of judgments. In H. Guetzkow (Ed.), *Groups, leadership, and men.* Pittsburgh, PA: Carnegie Press.

Asher, S.R., & Paquette, J.A. (2003). Loneliness and peer relations in childhood. *Current Directions in Psychological Science, 12,* 75–78.

Ashman, O., Shiomura, K., & Levy, B.R. (2006). Influence of culture and age on control beliefs: The missing link of interdependence. *International Journal of Aging & Human Development, 62,* 143–157.

Aspinwall, L.G., & Taylor, S.E. (1992). Modeling cognitive adaptation: A longitudinal investigation of the impact of individual differences and coping on college adjustment and performance. *Journal of Personality and Social Psychology, 63,* 989–1003.

Associated Press. (2011). *Collegiate major tied to earning potential.* Retrieved October 11, 2011, from http://www.washingtontimes.com/news/2011/may/24/collegiate-major-tied-earning-potential/?page=all.

Atlas, G.D. (1994). Sensitivity to criticism: A new measure of responses to everyday criticisms. *Journal of Psychoeducational Assessment, 12*(3), 241–253.

Attwood, F. (2005). What do people do with porn? Qualitative research into the consumption, use, and experience of pornography and other sexually explicit media. *Sexuality & Culture, 9,* 65–86.

Atwater, E. (1992). *I hear you: A listening skills handbook.* New York: Walker & Company.

Austenfeld, J.L., & Stanton, A.L. (2004). Coping through emotional approach: A new look at emotion, coping, and health-related outcomes. *Journal of Personality. Special Issue: Emotions, Personality, and Health, 72,* 1335–1363.

Auxier, A., Farley, T., & Seifert, K. (2011). Establishing an integrated care practice in a community health center. *Professional Psychology: Research and Practice, 42*(5), 391–397.

Avellar, S., & Smock, P.J. (2005). The economic consequences of the dissolution of cohabiting unions. *Journal of Marriage and Family, 67,* 315–327.

Ayalon, L. (2008). Volunteering as a predictor of all-cause mortality: What aspects of volunteering really matter? *International Psychogeriatrics, 20,* 1000–1013.

Ayman, R., Korabik, K., & Morris, S. (2009). Is transformational leadership always perceived as effective? Male subordinates' devaluation of female transformational leaders. *Journal of Applied Social Psychology, 39,* 852–879.

Azar, B. (2000, January). What's in a face? *Monitor on Psychology,* 44–45.

Baghurst, T., Carlston, D., Wood, J., & Wyatt, F.B. (2007). Preadolescent male perceptions of action figure physiques. *Society for Adolescent Medicine, 41,* 613–615.

Bagwell, C.L., Bender, S.E., Andreassi, C.L., Kinoshita, T.L., Montarello, S.A., & Muller, J.G. (2005). Friendship quality and perceived relationship changes predict psychosocial adjustment in early adulthood. *Journal of Social and Personal Relationships, 22,* 235–254.

Bailey, D.C., Larson, L.M., Borgen, F.H., & Gasser, C.E. (2008). Changing of the guard: Interpretive continuity of the 2005 Strong Interest Inventory. *Journal of Career Assessment, 16,* 135–155.

Baker, F., & Bor, W. (2008). Can music preference indicate mental health status in young people? *Australasian Psychiatry, 16*(4).

Baker, K., & Raney, A.A. (2007). Equally super? Gender-role stereotyping of superheroes in children's animated programs. *Mass Communication & Society, 10,* 25–41.

Baker, L.R., & Oswald, D.L. (2010). Shyness and online social networking services. *Journal of Social and Personal Relationships, 27*(7), 873–889.

Baker, S.R. (2004). Intrinsic, extrinsic, and amotivational orientations: Their role in university adjustment, stress, well-being, and subsequent academic performance. *Current Psychology: Developmental, Learning, Personality, Social, 23,* 189–202.

Baldas, T. (2007). Age bias suits on the rise with older employees working longer. *The National Law Journal.* Retrieved June 15, 2009, from http://www.law.com/jsp/article.jsp?id=1173949426492.

Ballentine, L.W., & Ogle, J.P. (2005). The making and unmaking of body problems in Seventeen magazine, 1992–2003. *Family and Consumer Sciences Research Journal, 33,* 281–307.

Balsam, K.F., Beauchaine, T.P., Mickey, R.M., & Rothblum, E.D. (2005). Mental health of lesbian, gay, bisexual, and heterosexual siblings: Effects of gender, sexual orientation, and family. *Journal of Abnormal Psychology, 114,* 471–476.

Bandura, A. (1965). Influence of models' reinforcement contingencies on the acquisition of imitative responses. *Journal of Personality and Social Psychology, 1,* 589–595.

Bandura, A. (1973). *Aggression.* Englewood Cliffs, NJ: Prentice Hall.

Bandura, A. (1986). *Social foundations of thought and action.* Englewood Cliffs, NJ: Prentice Hall.

Bandura, A. (1997). *Self-efficacy: The exercise of control.* New York: W.H. Freeman.

Banks, S., Van Dongen, H., & Dinges, D.F. (2010). Effect of sleep dose on recovery sleep stage and slow wave energy dynamics following chronic sleep restriction. *Sleep, 33*(8), 1013–1026.

Bar, M., & Neta, M. (2006). Humans prefer curved visual objects. *Psychological Science, 17,* 645–648.

Barber, B.L. (2006). To have loved and lost . . . adolescent romantic relationships and rejection. In A.C. Crouter, & A. Booth (Eds.), *Romance and sex in adolescence and emerging adulthood: Risks and opportunities* (pp. 29–40). Mahwah, NJ: Lawrence Erlbaum.

Barbour, K.A., Edenfield, T.M., & Blumenthal, J.A. (2007). Exercise as a treatment for depression and other psychiatric disorders: A review. *Journal of Cardiopulmonary Rehabilitation and Prevention, 27*(6), 359–367.

Bargal, N., Ben-Shakhar, G., & Shalev, A.Y. (2007). Posttraumatic stress disorder and depression in battered women: The mediating role of learned helplessness. *Journal of Family Violence, 22,* 267–275.

Barnes, B.L., & Srinivas, R. (1993). Self-actualization in different sex subgroups. *Journal of Personality and Clinical Studies, 9,* 19–24.

Baron, R.A., & Byrne, D. (1997). *Social psychology.* Boston: Allyn & Bacon.

Barsky, A.J., Peekna, H.M., & Borus, J.F. (2001). Somatic symptom reporting in women and men. *Journal of General Internal Medicine, 16,* 266–275.

Bartalos, M.K. (2009). *Speaking on death: America's new sense of mortality.* Westport, CT: Praeger/Greenwood.

Bartels, L. (2004). Harris home up for sale. *RockyMountainNews.com.* Retrieved December 27, 2011, from http://www.rockymountainnews.com.

Basow, S.A., & Rubenfield, K. (2003). "Troubles talk": Effects of gender and gender-typing. *Sex Roles, 48,* 183–187.

Batada, A., & Wootan, M.G. (2007). Nickelodeon markets nutrition-poor foods to children. *American Journal of Preventive Medicine, 33,* 48–50.

Battle, C.L., Shea, M.T., Johnson, D.M., Yen, S., Zlotnick, C., & Zanarini, M.C., et al. (2004). Childhood maltreatment associated with adult personality disorders: Findings from the collaborative longitudinal personality disorders study. *Journal of Personality Disorders, 18,* 193–211.

Bauer, J.J., McAdams, D.P., & Sakaeda, A.R. (2005). Interpreting the good life: Growth memories in the lives of mature, happy people. *Journal of Personality and Social Psychology, 88,* 203–217.

Baum, N. (2007). "Separation guilt" in women who initiate divorce. *Clinical Social Work Journal, 35,* 47–55.

Baum, S., Ma, J., & Payea, K. (2010). *Education pays 2010.* College Board Advocacy and Policy Center. Retrieved January 20, 2012, from http://trends.collegeboard.org/downloads/Education_Pays_2010.pdf.

Bauman, S. (2011). *Cyberbullying: What counselors need to know.* Alexandria, VA: American Counseling Association.

Baumeister, R.F., Campbell, J.D., Krueger, J.I., & Vohs, K.D. (2003). Does high self-esteem cause better performance, interpersonal success, happiness, or healthier lifestyles? *Psychological Science in the Public Interest, 4,* 1–44.

Baumeister, R.F., Campbell, J.D., Krueger, J.I., & Vohs, K.D. (2005, December 20). Exploding the self-esteem myth. *Scientific American, 292.*

Baumgardner, S.R., & Crothers, M.K. (2009). *Positive Psychology.* Upper Saddle River, NJ: Prentice Hall.

Baumrind, D. (1991). Parenting styles and adolescent development. In J. Brooks-Gunn, R. Lerner, & A. Petersen (Eds.), *The encyclopedia of adolescence* (pp. 746–758). New York: Garland.

Bayer, R. (1987). *Homosexuality and American psychiatry: The politics of diagnosis* (2nd ed.). Princeton, NJ: Princeton University Press.

Bazzett, T.J. (2008). *An introduction to behavior genetics.* Sunderland, MA: Sinauer Associates.

Beaupré, M.G., & Hess, U. (2005). Cross-cultural emotion recognition among Canadian ethnic groups. *Journal of Cross-Cultural Psychology, 36*, 355–370.

Bebetsos, E., Chroni, S., & Theodorakis, Y. (2002). Physically active students' intentions and self-efficacy towards health eating. *Psychological Reports, 91*, 485–495.

Beck, A.T. (1979). *Cognitive therapy and emotional disorders.* New York: American Library.

Becker, A.E., Burwell, R.A., Gilman, S.E., Herzog, D.B., & Hamburg, P. (2002). Eating behaviours and attitudes following prolonged exposure to television among ethnic Fijian adolescent girls. *British Journal of Psychiatry, 180*, 509–514.

Becker, A.E., Burwell, R.A., Herzog, D.B., Hamburg, P., & Gilman, S.E. (2002). Eating behaviours and attitudes following prolonged exposure to television among ethnic Fijian adolescent girls. *British Journal of Psychiatry, 180*, 509–514.

Becvar, D.S. (2008). From the editor: The complexity of working with families. *Contemporary Family Therapy: An International Journal, 30*, 181–182.

Bedell-Avers, K.E., Hunter, S.T., & Mumford, M.D. (2008). Conditions of problem-solving and the performance of charismatic, ideological, and pragmatic leaders. *Leadership Quarterly, 19*, 89–106.

Beilock, S.L., Kulp, C.A., Holt, L.E., & Carr, T.H. (2004). More on the fragility of performance: Choking under pressure in mathematical problem solving. *Journal of Experimental Psychology: General, 133*, 584–600.

Beitel, M., Ferrer, E., & Cecero, J.J. (2005). Psychological mindedness and awareness of self and others. *Journal of Clinical Psychology, 61*, 739–750.

Bell, B.T., Lawton, R., & Dittmar, H. (2007). The impact of thin models in music videos on adolescent girls' body dissatisfaction. *Body Image, 4*, 137–145.

Benenson, J.F., & Alavi, K. (2004). Sex differences in children's investment in same-sex peers. *Evolution and Human Behavior, 25*, 258–266.

Bergstrom, R.L., Neighbors, C., & Lewis, M.A. (2004). Do men find "bony" women attractive? Consequences of misperceiving opposite sex perceptions of attractive body image. *Body Image, 1*, 183–191.

Berndt, T.J. (2002). Friendships' quality and social development. *Current Direction in Psychological Science, 11*, 7–10.

Bernstein, E. (2011). Secrets of a successful second marriage: Beat the 8-year itch. *Wall Street Journal.* Retrieved February 28, 2012, from http://online.wsj.com/article/SB100014240531 11904106704576580652976268350.html.

Beste, S.A., Bergner, R.M., & Nauta, M.M. (2003). What keeps love alive? An empirical investigation. *Family Therapy, 30*(3), 125–141.

Bevan, J.L. (2003). Expectancy violation theory and sexual resistance in close, cross-sex relationships. *Communication Monographs, 70*, 68–82.

Biesanz, J.C., Human, L.J., Paquin, A., Chan, M., Parisotto, K.L., Sarracino, J., & Gillis, R.L. (2011). Do we know when our impressions of others are valid? Evidence for realistic accuracy awareness in first impressions of personality. *Social Psychological and Personality Science, 2*(5), 452–459.

Bigler, M., Neimeyer, G., & Brown, E. (2001). The divided self revisited: Effects of self-concept differentiation on psychological adjustment. *Journal of Social and Clinical Psychology, 20*, 396–415.

Bing, N.M., Nelson, W.M., III, & Wesolowski, K.L. (2009). Comparing the effects of amount of conflict on children's adjustment following parental divorce. *Journal of Divorce & Remarriage, 50*, 159–171.

Bjornsen, S. (2005). *The single girl's guide to marrying a man, his kids, and his ex-wife: Becoming a stepmother with humor and grace.* London: Penguin Books.

Bjornstad, R. (2006). Learned helplessness, discouraged workers, and multiple unemployment equilibria. *The Journal of Socio-Economic, 35*, 458–475.

Blackshaw, T. (2010). *Leisure.* New York, NY, US: Routledge/ Taylor & Francis Group.

Blanchard, E., & Hickling, E.J. (2003). *After the crash: Psychological assessment and treatment of survivors of motor vehicle accidents.* Washington, DC: American Psychological Association.

Blank, H., Musch, J., & Pohl, R.F. (2007). Hindsight bias: On being wise after the event. *Social Cognition, 25*, 1–9.

Blatt, S.J., & Shahar, G. (2004). Psychoanalysis—With whom, for what, and how? Comparisons with psychotherapy. *Journal of the American Psychoanalytic Association, 52*, 393–447.

Blum, D. (1998, May/June). Finding strength: How to overcome anything. *Psychology Today*, 32–38, 66–73.

Bobrow, D., & Bailey, M.J. (2001). Is male homosexuality maintained via kin selection? *Evolution and Human Behavior, 22*, 361–368.

Boelen, P.A., & van den Bout, J. (2007). Examination of proposed criteria for complicated grief in people confronted with violent or non-violent loss. *Death Studies, 31*, 155–164.

Boelen, P.A., de Keijser, J., van den Hout, M.A., & van den Bout, J. (2007). Treatment of complicated grief: A comparison between cognitive-behavioral therapy and supportive counseling. *Journal of Consulting and Clinical Psychology, 75*, 277–284.

Boerner, K., Wortman, C.B., & Bonanno, G.A. (2005). Resilient or at risk? A 4-year study of older adults who initially showed high or low distress following conjugal losses. *Journals of Gerontology: Series B: Psychological Sciences and Social Sciences, 60B*, 67–73.

Bohart, A.C., & Byock, G. (2005). Experiencing Carl Rogers from the client's point of view: A vicarious ethnographic investigation. I. extraction and perception of meaning. *Humanistic Psychologist, 33*, 187–212.

Bolles, R.N. (2011). *What color is your parachute? A practical manual for job hunters and career seekers.* Berkeley, CA: Ten Speed Press.

Bonanno, G.A., & Kaltman, S. (2001). The varieties of grief experience. *Clinical Psychology Review, 21*, 705–734.

Bonanno, G.A., Galea, S., Bucciarelli, A., & Vlahov, D. (2007). What predicts psychological resilience after disaster? The role of demographics, resources, and life stress. *Journal of Consulting and Clinical Psychology, 75*, 671–682.

Bonanno, G.A., Papa, A., Lalande, K., Westphal, M., & Coifman, K. (2004). The importance of being flexible: The ability to both enhance and suppress emotional expression predicts long-term adjustment. *Psychological Science, 15*, 482–487.

Bonanno, G.A., Papa, A., Lalande, K., Zhang, N., & Noll, J.G. (2005). Grief processing and deliberate grief avoidance: A prospective comparison of bereaved spouses and parents in the United States and the People's Republic of China, *Journal of Consulting and Clinical Psychology, 73*, 86–98.

Bond, C.F., Jr., & DePaulo, B.M. (2008). Individual differences in judging deception: Accuracy and bias. *Psychological Bulletin, 134*(4), 477–492.

Bond, R. (2005). Group size and conformity. *Group Processes & Intergroup Relations, 8*, 331–354.

Bookwala, J., & Jacobs, J. (2004). Age, marital processes, and depressed affect. *The Gerontologist, 44*, 328–338.

Bouchard, T.J., Jr. (2004). Genetic influence on human psychological traits: A survey. *Current Directions in Psychological Science, 13*(4), 148–151.

Boulahanis, J.G., & Heltsley, M.J. (2004). Perceived Fears: The Reporting Patterns of Juvenile Homicide in Chicago Newspapers. *Criminal Justice Policy Review, 15*(2), 132–160.

Bouton, M.E. (2007). *Learning and behavior: A contemporary synthesis.* Sunderland, MA, US: Sinauer Associates.

Bowlby, J. (1977). The making and breaking of affectional bonds: I. aetiology and psychopathology in the light of attachment theory. *British Journal of Psychiatry, 130*, 201–210.

Boyatzis, C.J., Matillo, G.M., & Nesbitt, K.M. (1995). Effects of "The Mighty Morphin Power Rangers" on children's aggression with peers. *Child Study Journal, 25*, 45–55.

Brandstätter, H. (2011). Personality aspects of entrepreneurship: A look at five meta-analyses. *Personality and Individual Differences, 51*(3), 222–230.

Brewis, A., & Meyer, M. (2005). Marital coitus across the life course. *Journal of Biosocial Science, 37*, 499–518.

Broad, K.L. (2011). Coming out for parents, families and friends of lesbians and gays: From support group grieving to love advocacy. *Sexualities, 14*(4), 399–415.

Broadcasting Standards Authority. (2008). *Seen and heard: Children's media use, exposure, and response.* Retrieved July 28, 2011, from www.bsa.govt.nz.

Brody, J.E. (2002, November 19). Adding some heft to the ideal feminine form. *The New York Times*, p. D7.

Bronfenbrenner, U. (1993). The ecology of cognitive development: Research models and fugitive findings. In R. Wonziak & K. Fischer (Eds.), *Development in context: Acting and thinking in specific environments* (pp. 3–44). Hillsdale, NJ: Erlbaum.

Brown, G.D.A., Gardner, J., Oswald, A.J., & Qian, J. (2008). Does wage rank affect employees' well-being? *Industrial Relations: A Journal of Economy & Society, 47*, 355–389.

Brown, K.T. (2004). The power of perception: Skin tone bias and psychological well-being for Black Americans. In G. Philogène (Ed.), *Racial identity in context: The legacy of Kenneth B. Clark* (pp. 111–123). Washington, DC: American Psychological Association.

Brown, T.M., & Miller, C.E. (2000). Communication networks in task-performing groups: Effects of task complexity, time pressure, and interpersonal dominance. *Small Group Research, 31*(2), 131–157.

Browne, G., & Courtney, M. (2007). Schizophrenia housing and supportive relationships. *International Journal of Mental Health Nursing, 16*(2), 73–80.

Bruch, M.A., & Belkin, D.K. (2001). Attributional style in shyness and depression: Shared and specific maladaptive patterns. *Cognitive Theory and Research, 25*, 247–259.

Brunell, A.B., Staats, S., Barden, J., & Hupp, J. (2011). Narcissism and academic dishonesty: The exhibitionism dimension and the lack of guilt, *Personality and Individual Differences, 50*(3), 323–328.

Buchanan, N.T., & Fitzgerald, L.F. (2008). Effects of racial and sexual harassment on work and the psychological well-being of African American women. *Journal of Occupational Health Psychology, 13*, 137–151.

Buettner, L., Shattell, M., & Reber, M. (2011). Working hard to relax: Improving engagement in leisure time activities for a healthier work-life balance. *Issues in Mental Health Nursing, 32*(4), 269–270.

Bullock, J.R. (2002). Bullying among children. *Childhood Education, 3*, 130–133.

Burger, J.M., Girgis, Z.M., & Manning, C.C. (2011). In their own words: Explaining obedience to authority through an examination of participants' comments. *Social Psychological and Personality Science, 2*(5), 460–466.

Burns, J.L., Lee, R.M., & Brown, L.J. (2011). The effect of meditation on self-reported measures of stress, anxiety, depression, and perfectionism in a college population. *Journal of College Student Psychotherapy, 25*(2), 132–144.

Burns, J.W., Quartana, P.J., Gilliam, W., Matsuura, J., Nappi, C., & Wolfe, B. (2012). Suppression of anger and subsequent pain intensity and behavior among chronic low back pain patients: The role of symptom-specific physiological reactivity. *Journal of Behavioral Medicine, 35*(1), 103–114.

Burpo, T., & Vincent, L. (2010). *Heaven is for real: A little boy's astounding story of his trip to heaven and back.* Nashville, TN: Thomas Nelson.

Burton, C.M., & King, L.A. (2008). Effects of (very) brief writing on health: The two-minute miracle. *British Journal of Health Psychology, 13*, 9–14.

Bushman, B.J., & Baumeister, R.F. (1998). Threatened egotism, narcissism, self-esteem, and direct and displaced aggression: Does self-love or self-hate lead to violence? *Journal of Personality and Social Psychology, 75*, 219–229.

Bushman, B.J., & Stack, A.D. (1996). Forbidden fruit versus tainted fruit: Effects of warning labels on attraction to television violence. *Journal of Experimental Psychology Applied, 2*, 207–226.

Buunk, A.P., Solano, A.C., Zurriaga, R., & González, P. (2011). Gender differences in the jealousy-evoking effect of rival characteristics: A study in Spain and Argentina. *Journal of Cross-Cultural Psychology, 42*(3), 323–339.

Buys, L.R. (2001). Life in a retirement village: Implications for contact with community and village friends. *Gerontology, 47*, 55–59.

Cabral, R.R., & Smith, T.B. (2011). Racial/ethnic matching of clients and therapists in mental health services: A meta-analytic review of preferences, perceptions, and outcomes. *Journal of Counseling Psychology, 58*(4), 537–554.

Cacioppo J.T., & Patrick, W. (2008). *Loneliness: Human nature and the need for social connection.* New York: W. W. Norton.

Cadell, S., Regehr, C., & Hemsworth, D. (2003). Factors contributing to posttraumatic growth: A proposed structural equation model. *American Journal of Orthopsychiatry, 73*, 279–287.

Cafferty, J. (2010). *$10 billion spent on cosmetic procedures despite recession.* Retrieved May 1, 2012, from http://cafferty-file.blogs.cnn.com.

Cameron, A.F., & Webster, J. (2004). Unintended consequences of emerging communication technologies: Instant messaging in the workplace. *Computers in Human Behavior, 21*, 85–103.

Campbell, B.C., Dreber, A., Apicella, C.L., Eisenberg, D.T.A., Gray, P.B., Little, A.C., et al. (2010). Testosterone exposure, dopaminergic reward, and sensation-seeking in young men. *Physiology & Behavior, 99*(4), 451–456.

Canli, T., & Gabrieli, J.D.E. (2004). Imaging gender differences in sexual arousal. *Nature Neuroscience, 7*, 325–326.

Cann, A. & Etzel, K.C. (2008). Remembering and anticipating stressors: Positive personality mediates the relationship with sense of humor. *Humor: International Journal of Humor Research, 21*, 157–178.

Caplan, L. (2011). The insanity defense post-Hinckley. *New York Times.* Retrieved November 28, 2011, from http://www.nytimes.com/2011/01/18/opinion/18tue4.html.

Cappelleri, J.C., Bell, S.S., Althof, S.E., Siegel, R.L., & Stecher, V.J. (2006). Comparison between sildenafil treated subjects with erectile dysfunction and control subjects on the Self-Esteem and Relationship questionnaire. *The Journal of Sexual Medicine, 3*, 274–282.

Cardona-Coll, D. (2003). Bargaining and strategic demand commitment. *Theory and Decision, 54*, 357–374.

Carducci, B.J., & Zimbardo, P.G. (1995, November/December). Are you shy? *Psychology Today, 34*–40.

Carey, A.R., & Ward, S. (2000, January 1). Thinking of retirement. *USA Today,* 1B.

Carnaghi, A., & Maass, A. (2007). In-group and out-group perspective in the use of derogatory group labels: Gay versus fag. *Journal of Language and Social Psychology, 26*, 142–156.

Carr, A. (2011). *Positive psychology: The science of happiness and human strengths* (2nd ed.). New York, NY, US: Routledge/Taylor & Francis Group.

Carr, J.L. (2005, February). *American College Health Association campus violence white paper.* Baltimore, MD: American College Health Association.

Carrere, R.A. (2008). Reflections on psychoanalysis conducted as a talking cure. *Contemporary Psychoanalysis, 44*, 400–418.

Carstensen, L.L., & Charles, S.T. (1998). Emotion in the second half of life. *Current Directions in Psychological Science, 7*, 144–149.

Caspi, A., & Herbener, E.S. (1990). Continuity and change: Assortative marriage and the consistency of personality in adulthood. *Journal of Personality and Social Psychology, 58*, 250–258.

Caspi, A., & Silva, P.A. (1995). Temperamental qualities at age three predict personality traits in young adulthood: Longitudinal evidence from a birth cohort. *Child Development, 66*(2), 486–498.

Cassels, C. (2011). America's use of psychotropic medications on the rise. *Medscape Medical News.* Retrieved December 8, 2011, from http://www.medscape.com/viewarticle/753789.

Cassidy, C., O'Connor, R.C., Howe, C., & Warden, D. (2004). Perceived discrimination and psychological distress: The role of personal and ethnic self-esteem. *Journal of Counseling Psychology, 5,* 329–339.

Cassidy, J., & Shaver, P.R. (2008). *Handbook of attachment: Theory, research, and clinical applications* (2nd ed.). New York: Guilford Press.

CBC News. (2011). *Riots erupt in Vancouver after Canucks loss.* Retrieved February 5, 2012, from http://www.cbc.ca/news/canada/british-columbia/story/2011/06/15/bc-stanley-cup-fans-post-game-7.html.

Centers for Disease Control and Prevention. (CDC). (2005). *Physical activity for everyone: The importance of physical activity.* Retrieved August 7, 2006, from http://www.cdc.gov/nccdphp/dnpa/physical/importance/index.htm.

Centers for Disease Control and Prevention. (2011). *Sexually transmitted diseases.* Retrieved July 2, 2011, from http://www.cdc.gov/std/.

Centers for Disease Control and Prevention. (2012). *Healthy weight- It's not a diet it's a lifestyle!* Retrieved September 15, 2012, from http://www.cdc.gov/healthyweight/assessing/bmi/index.html.

Chadwick, R.F., Have, H., & Meslin, E.M. (2011). *The SAGE handbook of health care ethics: Core and emerging issues.* Los Angeles: SAGE.

Chapman, M.A. (1999, September/October). Bad choices: Why we make them. How to stop. *Psychology Today, 36–39,* 71.

Chapman, K.L., Kertz, S.J., & Woodruff-Borden, J. (2009). A structural equation model analysis of perceived control and psychological distress on worry among African-American and European-American young Adults. *Journal of Anxiety Disorders, 23,* 69–76.

Chen, I. (2009, June). The social brain. *Smithsonian,* 38–43.

Chen, S., & Fu, Y. (2008). Leisure participation and enjoyment among the elderly: Individual characteristics and sociability. *Educational Gerontology, 34,* 871–889.

Chen, Z., Fu, L., Peng, Y., Cai, R., & Zhou, S. (2011). The relationship among childhood abuse, parenting styles, and antisocial personality disorder tendency. *Chinese Journal of Clinical Psychology, 19*(2), 212–214.

ChildStat.gov. (2012). *America's children in brief: Key national indicators of well-being, 2012.* Retrieved April 16, 2012, from http://www.childstats.gov/americaschildren/index.asp.

Chivers, M.L., Rieger, G., Latty, E., & Bailey, J.M. (2004). A sex difference in the specificity of sexual arousal. *Psychological Science, 15,* 736–744.

Childwise. (2010). *Childwise news* (Issue 3). Retrieved July 18, 2011, from http://childwise.co.uk.

Cho, H., & Wilke, D.J. (2005). How has the violence against women act affected the response of the criminal justice system to domestic violence? *Journal of Sociology & Social Welfare, 32,* 125–139.

Chochinov, H.M., Hack, T., Hassard, T., Kristjanson, L.J., McClement, S., & Harlos, M. (2002). Dignity in the terminally ill: A cross-sectional, cohort study. *The Lancet, 360,* 2026–2030.

Christakis, N.A., & Fowler, J.H. (2007). The spread of obesity in a large social network over 32 years. *New England Journal of Medicine, 357*(4), 370–379.

Christensen, T.C., Wood, J.V., & Barrett, L.F. (2003). Remembering everyday experience through the prism of self-esteem. *Personality and Social Psychology Bulletin, 29,* 51–62.

Christie-Mizell, C.A., Pryor, E.M., & Grossman, E.R.B. (2008). Child depressive symptoms, spanking, and emotional support: Differences between African American and European American youth. *Family Relations, 57,* 335–350.

Chrobot-Mason, D., Ruderman, M.N., Weber, T.J., Ohlott, P.J., & Dalton, M.A. (2007). Illuminating a cross-cultural leadership challenge: When identity groups collide. *International Journal of Resource Management, 18,* 2011–2036.

Chung, D. (2005). Violence, control, romance and gender equality: Young women and heterosexual relationships. *Women's Studies International Forum, 28,* 445–455.

Cialdini, R.B., & Goldstein, N.J. (2004). Social influence: Compliance and conformity. *Annual Review of Psychology, 55,* 591–621.

Cohan, C.L., & Kleinbaum, S. (2002). Toward a greater understanding of the cohabitation effect: Premarital cohabitation and marital communication. *Journal of Marriage and the Family, 64,* 180–192.

Cohen, A.B. (2009). Many forms of culture. *American Psychologist, 64,* 194–204.

Cohen, D. (2011). Barely half of U. S. adults are married: A record low. *Pew Social & Demographic Trends.* Retrieved February 20, 2012, from http://www.pewsocialtrends.org/2011/12/14/barely-half-of-u-s-adults-are-married-a-record-low/

Cohen, S., & Pressman, S.D. (2006). Positive affect and health. *Current Directions in Psychological Science, 15,* 122–125.

Cohen-Bendahan, C.C.C., van de Beek, C., & Berenbaum, S.A. (2005). Prenatal sex hormone effects on child and adult sex-typed behavior: Methods and findings. *Neuroscience & Biobehavioral Reviews, 29,* 353–384.

Cohn, M.A., Fredrickson, B.L., Brown, S.L., Mikels, J.A., & Conway, A.M. (2009). Happiness unpacked: Positive emotions increase life satisfaction by building resilience. *Emotion, 9,* 361–368.

Colarusso, C.A. (2010). *The long shadow of sexual abuse: Developmental effects across the life cycle*. Lanham, MD, US: Jason Aronson.

Coles, E.K., Slavec, J., Bernstein, M., & Baroni, E. (2012). Exploring the gender gap in referrals for children with ADHD and other disruptive behavior disorders. *Journal of Attention Disorders, 16*(2), 101–108.

Collins, R.L., Martino, S.C., Elliott, M.N., & Miu, A. (2011). Relationships between adolescent sexual outcomes and exposure to sex in media: Robustness to propensity-based analysis. *Developmental Psychology, 47*(2), 585–591.

Collins, R.L., Elliott, M.N., Berry, S.H., Kanouse, D.E., Kunkel, D., Hunter, S.B., et al. (2004). Watching sex on television predicts adolescent initiation of sexual behavior. *Pediatrics, 114*, 280–289.

Concha, M. (2011). "Study" drug's downside. *Miami Herald*. Retrieved December 20, 2011, from http://www.miamiherald.com/2011/12/06/2532768/study-drugs-downside.html.

Contrada, R.J., & Baum, A. (2011). *The handbook of stress science: Biology, psychology, and health*. New York, NY: Springer Publishing Co.

Conway, L.G., III, & Schaller, M. (2005). When authorities' commands backfire: Attributions about consensus and effects on deviant decision making. *Journal of Personality and Social Psychology, 89*, 311–326.

Conway, T.L., Vickers, R.R., & French, J.R. (1992). An application of person-environment fit theory: Perceived versus desire control. *Journal of Social Issues, 48*, 95–107.

Cook, C.R., Gresham, F.M., Kern, L., Barreras, R.B., Thornton, S., & Crews, S.D. (2008). Social skills training for secondary students with emotional and/or behavioral disorders: A review and analysis of the meta-analytic literature. *Journal of Emotional and Behavioral Disorders, 16*, 131–144.

Coontz, S. (2005). *Marriage, a history*. New York, NY: Viking.

Cooper, H., Okamura, L., & McNeil, P. (1995). Situation and personality correlates of psychological well-being, social activity, and personal control. *Journal of Research in Personality, 29*, 395–417.

Corales, T.A. (2005). *Focus on posttraumatic stress disorder research*. Hauppauge, NY, US: Nova Science Publishers.

Corpus, J.H., McClintic-Gilbert, M.S., & Hayenga, A.O. (2009). Within-year changes in children's intrinsic and extrinsic motivational orientations: Contextual predictors and academic outcomes. *Contemporary Educational Psychology, 34*, 154–166.

Correll, S.J., Benard, S., & Paik, I. (2007). Getting a job: Is there a motherhood penalty? *American Journal of Sociology, 112*, 1297–1338.

Coulson, M. (2004). Attributing emotion to static body postures: Recognition accuracy, confusions, and viewpoint dependence. *Journal of Nonverbal Behavior, 28*, 117–139.

Coultas, J.C. (2004). When in Rome … an evolutionary perspective on conformity. *Group Processes & Intergroup Relations, 7*, 317–331.

Court, A. (2003, September 5–7). Out of Africa. *USA Weekend*, 5.

Crandall, C.S. (1994). Prejudice against fat people: Ideology and self-interest. *Journal of Personality and Social Psychology, 66*, 882–894.

Crane, R.D., Soderquist, J.N., & Gardner, M.D. (1995). Gender differences in cognitive and behavioral steps toward divorce. *American Journal of Family Therapy, 23*, 99–105.

Crittenden, P.M., & Landini, A. (2011). *Assessing adult attachment: A dynamic maturational approach to discourse analysis*. New York, NY: W. W. Norton & Co.

Crocker, J., & Knight, K.M. (2005). Contingencies of self-worth. *Current Directions in Psychological Science, 14*, 200–203.

Crocker, J., & Park, L.E. (2004). Reaping the benefits of pursuing self-esteem without the costs? Reply to DuBois and Flay (2004), Sheldon (2004), and Pyszczynski and Cox (2004). *Psychological Bulletin, 130*, 430–434.

Crone, D., Smith, A., & Gough, B. (2005). 'I feel totally at one, totally alive and totally happy': A psycho-social explanation of the physical activity and mental health relationship. *Health Education Research, 20*, 600–611.

Crooks, R.L., & Bauer, K. (2008). *Our sexuality*. Belmont, CA: Wadsworth.

Crozier, W.R. (2005). Measuring shyness: Analysis of the revised cheek and buss shyness scale. *Personality and Individual Differences, 38*, 1947–1956.

Csank, P., & Conway, M. (2004). Engaging in self-reflection changes self-concept clarity: On differences between women and men, and low-and high-clarity individuals. *Sex Roles, 50*, 469–480.

CubbiesBaseball.com. (2012). *Chicago Cub curses*. Retrieved February 5, 2012, from http://www.cubbiesbaseball.com/chicago-cubs-curses.

Cuijpers, P., van Straten, A., Warmerdam, L., & Andersson, G. (2009). Psychotherapy versus the combination of psychotherapy and pharmacotherapy in the treatment of depression: A meta-analysis. *Depression and Anxiety, 26*, 279–288.

Cushner, K. (2005). Conflict, negotiation, and mediation across cultures: Highlights from the fourth biennial conference of the international academy for intercultural research. *International Journal of Intercultural Relations. Special Issue: Conflict, Negotiation, and Mediation across Cultures: Highlights from the Fourth Biennial Conference of the International Academy for Intercultural Research, 29*, 635–638.

D'Augelli, A.R., Hershberger, S.L., & Pilkingston, N.W. (1998). Lesbian, gay and bisexual youth and their families: Disclosure of sexual orientation and its consequences. *American Journal of Orthopsychiatry, 68*, 361–371.

Da Costa, R.T., Sardinha, A., & Nardi, A.E. (2008). Virtual reality exposure in the treatment of fear of flying. *Aviation, Space, and Environmental Medicine, 79*(9), 899–903.

Dahlen, E.R., & Martin, R.C. (2005). The experience, expression, and control of anger in perceived social support. *Personality and Individual Differences, 39*, 391–401.

Daitch, C. (2011). *Anxiety disorders: The go-to guide for clients and therapists.* New York, NY: W. W. Norton & Co.

Damon, W., & Hart, D. (1988). *Self-understanding in childhood and adolescence.* New York, NY, US: Cambridge University Press.

Darling, C.A., McWey, L.M., Howard, S.N., & Olmstead, S.B. (2007). College student stress: The influence of interpersonal relationships on sense of coherence. *Stress and Health: Journal of the International Society for the Investigation of Stress, 23*, 215–229.

Davalos, D.B., Davalos, R.A., & Layton, H.S. (2007). Content analysis of magazine headlines: Changes over three decades? *Feminism & Psychology, 17*, 250–258.

Davis, D. (1995). *The Jeffrey Dahmer story: An American nightmare.* New York: St. Martin's Paperbacks.

Davis, G.F. (2001). Loss and the duration of grief (Letter to the editor). *The Journal of the American Medical Association, 285*, 1152.

Davis, M., Markus, K.A., Walters, S.B., Vorus, N., & Connors, B. (2005). Behavioral cues to deception vs. topic incriminating potential in criminal confessions. *Law and Human Behavior, 29*, 683–704.

Davis, S. (1996, July/August). The enduring power of friendship. *American Health*, 60–63.

Davis, S. (2003). Sex stereotypes in commercials targeted toward children: A content analysis. *Sociological Spectrum, 23*, 407–424.

De Bruyn, E.H., Cillessen, A.H.N., & Wissink, I.B. (2010). Associations of peer acceptance and perceived popularity with bullying and victimization in early adolescence. *The Journal of Early Adolescence, 30*(4), 543–566.

De Dreu, C.K.W. (2005). A PACT against conflict escalation in negotiation and dispute resolution. *Current Directions in Psychological Science, 14*, 149–152.

Dearborn, K. (2002). Studies in emotional intelligence redefine our approach to leadership development. *Public Personnel Management, 31*, 523–530.

Decaluwé, K., Pauwels, B., Verpoest, S., & Van de Voorde, J. (2011). New therapeutic targets for the treatment of erectile dysfunction. *Journal of Sexual Medicine, 8*(12), 3271–3290.

Deci, E.L., & Moller, A.C. (2005). *The concept of competence: A starting place for understanding intrinsic motivation and self-determined extrinsic motivation.* New York: Guilford Publications.

Deci, E.L., & Ryan, R.M. (2008). Self-determination theory: A macrotheory of human motivation, development, and health. *Canadian Psychology/Psychologie Canadienne. Special Issue: Social Psychology and Self-Determination Theory: A Canadian Contribution, 49*, 182–185.

DeHart, G.B., Sroufe, L.A., & Cooper, R.G. (2004). *Child development: Its nature and course* (5th ed.). New York: McGraw-Hill.

Delle Fave, A., Massimini, F., & Bassi, M. (2011). *Psychological selection and optimal experience across cultures: Social empowerment through personal growth.* New York, NY: Springer Science.

Dennerstein, L., & Hayes, R.D. (2005). Confronting the challenges: Epidemiological study of female sexual dysfunction and the menopause. *Journal of Sexual Medicine, 2*, 118–132.

Dennis, P. (1985). Grisi siknis in Miskito culture. In R.C. Simons & C.C. Hughes (Eds.), *The culture-bound syndromes* (pp. 289–306). Dordrecht, Holland: D. Reidel Publishing.

Denrell, J. (2005). Why most people disapprove of me: Experience sampling in impression formation. *Psychological Review, 112*, 951–978.

Dentinger, E., & Clarkberg, M. (2002). Informal caregiving and retirement timing among men and women. *Journal of Family Issues, 25*, 857–879.

Derenne, J.L., & Beresin, E.V. (2006). Body image, media, and eating disorders. *Academic Psychiatry, 30*, 257–261.

De-Souza, G., & Klein, H.J. (1995). Emergent leadership in the group goal-setting process. *Small Groups Research, 26*, 475–496.

Di Mattei, V.E., Prunas, A., Novella, L., Marcone, A., Cappa, S.F., & Sarno, L. (2008). The burden of distress in caregivers of elderly demented patients and its relationship with coping strategies. *Neurological Sciences, 29*, 383–389.

Diener, E., & Seligman, M.R.P. (2002). Very happy people. *Psychological Science, 13*, 81–84.

DiGuiseppe, R., & Tafrate, R.C. (2003). Anger treatment for adults: A meta-analytic review. *Clinical Psychology: Science and Practice, 10*, 70–84.

Dijkstra, P., Gibbons, F.X., & Buunk, A.P. (2010). Social comparison theory. In J.E. Maddux & J.P. Tangney (Eds.), *Social psychological foundations of clinical psychology*. New York, NY, US: Guilford Press.

Dimberg, U., Thunberg, M., & Elmehed, K. (2000). Unconscious facial reactions to emotional facial expressions. *Psychological Science, 11*, 86–89.

Ditommaso, E., Brannen, C., & Burgess, M. (2005). The universality of relationship characteristics: A cross-cultural comparison of different types of attachment and loneliness in Canadian and visiting Chinese students. *Social Behavior and Personality, 33*, 57–68.

Doerr, H.O. (2007). *Selected theories of development*. Ashland, OH: Hogrefe & Huber Publishers.

Doka, L.K. (2005). Ethics, end-of-life decisions and grief. *Mortality. Special Issue: Ethical concerns involving end-of-life issues in the United States—Introduction: Ethics and end-of-life issues, 10*, 83–90.

Donnell, A.J., Thomas, A., & Buboltz, W.C. (2001). Psychological reactance: Factor structure and internal consistency of the Questionnaire for the Measurement of Psychological Reactance. *The Journal of Social Psychology, 141*, 679–687.

Donnelly, J.E., Blair, S.N., Jakicic, J.M., Manore, M.M., Rankin, J.W., & Smith, B.K. (2009). Appropriate physical activity intervention strategies for weight loss and prevention of weight regain for adults. *Medicine and Science in Sports and Exercise, 41*(2), 459–469.

Donovan, R.J., & Jalleh, G. (2000). Positive versus negative framing of a hypothetical infant immunization: The influence of involvement. *Health Education and Behavior, 27*, 82–95.

Doss, B.D., Rhoades, G.K., Stanley, S.M., & Markman, H.J. (2009). The effect of the transition to parenthood on relationship quality: An 8-year prospective study. *Journal of Personality and Social Psychology, 96*, 601–619.

Dovidio, J.F., Glick, P., & Rudman, L.A. (Eds.). (2005). *On the nature of prejudice: Fifty years after Allport*. Malden, MA: Blackwell Publishing.

Downey, L., & Van Willigen, M. (2005). Environmental stressors: The mental health impacts of living near industrial activity. *Journal of Health and Social Behavior, 46*, 289–305.

Drentea, P. (2002). Retirement and mental health. *Journal of Aging and Health, 14*, 167–194.

Drentea, P., & Moren-Cross, J.L. (2005). Social capital and social support on the web: The case of an internet mother site. *Sociology of Health & Illness, 27*, 920–943.

Drew, L.M., & Silverstein, M. (2007). Grandparents' psychological well-being after loss of contact with their grandchildren. *Journal of Family Psychology, 21*, 372–379.

Dubrovsky, V.J., Kiesler, S., & Sethna, B.N. (1991). The equalization phenomenon: Status effects in computer mediated and face-to-face decision-making groups. *Human Computer Interaction, 6*, 119–146.

Duffy, A.L., & Nesdale, D. (2009). Peer groups, social identity, and children's bullying behavior. *Social Development, 18*(1), 121–139.

Dunkel, C.S., Harbke, C.R., & Papini, D.R. (2009). Direct and indirect effects of birth order on personality and identity: Support for the null hypothesis. *The Journal of Genetic Psychology: Research and Theory on Human Development, 170*(2), 159–175.

Dunn, J., O'Connor, T.G., & Cheng, H. (2005). Children's responses to conflict between their different parents: Mothers, stepfathers, nonresident fathers, and nonresident stepmothers. *Journal of Clinical Child and Adolescent Psychology, 34*, 223–234.

Dunn, M.S. (2005). The relationship between religiosity, employment, and political beliefs on substance use among high school seniors. *Journal of Alcohol and Drug Education, 49*, 73–88.

Dunne, G.A. (2000). Lesbians as authentic workers? Institutional heterosexuality and the reproduction of gender inequalities. *Sexualities. Special Issue: Speaking from a Lesbian Position: Opening up Sexuality Studies, 3*, 133–148.

Dunning, D., Heath, C., & Suls, J.M. (2004). Flawed self-assessment: Implications for health, education, and the workplace. *Psychological Science in the Public Interest, 5*, 69–106.

Durrant, J.E., & Smith, A.B. (2011). *Global pathways to abolishing physical punishment: Realizing children's rights*. New York: Routledge.

Durrant, J.E. (2008). Physical punishment, culture, and rights: Current issues for professionals. *Journal of Developmental & Behavioral Pediatrics, 29*, 55–66.

Dweck, C.S. (1999). Caution—Praise can be dangerous. *American Educator, 23*, 4–9.

Dweck, C.S. (2008). Can personality be changed? The role of beliefs in personality and change. *Current Directions in Psychological Science, 17*, 391–394.

Dwyer, K.M., Fredstrom, B.K., Rubin, K.H., Booth-LaForce, C., Rose-Krasnor, L., & Burgess, K.B. (2010). Attachment, social information processing, and friendship quality of early adolescent girls and boys. *Journal of Social and Personal Relationships, 27*(1), 91–116.

Dykas, M.J., & Cassidy, J. (2011). Attachment and the processing of social information across the life span: Theory and evidence. *Psychological Bulletin, 137*(1), 19–46.

Eagly, A.H. (2007). Female leadership advantage and disadvantage: Resolving the contradictions. *Psychology of Women Quarterly, 31*, 1–12.

Eaton, R.J., & Graham, B. (2008). The role of gender and negative affectivity in stressor appraisal and coping selection. *International Journal of Stress Management, 15*, 94–115.

Economos, C.D., Hildebrandt, L.M., & Hyatt, R.R. (2008). College freshman stress and weight change: Differences by gender. *American Journal of Health Behavior, 32*, 16–25.

Edwards, R. (1998). The effects of gender, gender role, and values on the interpretation of messages. *Journal of Language and Social Psychology. Special Issue: The Language of Equivocation, 17*, 52–71.

EEOC. (2012). *Sexual harassment charges*. Retrieved January 29, 2012, from http://www.eeoc.gov/eeoc/statistics/enforcement/sexual_harassment.cfm.

Efrati-Virtzer, M., & Margalit, M. (2009). Students' behaviour difficulties, sense of coherence and adjustment at school: Risk and protective factors. *European Journal of Special Needs Education, 24*, 59–73.

Eggermont, S. (2005). Young adolescents' perceptions of peer sexual behaviours: The role of television viewing. *Child: Care, Health and Development, 31*, 459–468.

Ehrensaft, M.K. (2009). Family and relationship predictors of psychological and physical aggression. In K.D. O'Leary & E.M. Woodin (Eds.), *Psychological and physical aggression in couples: Causes and interventions* (pp. 99–118). Washington, DC: American Psychological Association.

Eisenberger, N.I., Lieberman, M.D., & Williams, K.D. (2003). Does rejection hurt? An fMRI study of social exclusion. *Science, 302*, 290–292.

Ekman, P. (1985). *Telling lies.* New York: W. W. Norton.

Elias, M. (1999, November 23). Culture affects choice on post-menopause estrogen. *USA Today,* D1.

Ellis, J.A., & Sinclair, R.D. (2008). Male pattern baldness: Current treatments, future prospects. *Drug Discovery Today, 13*, 791–797.

Epstein, M., & Ward, L.M. (2008). "Always Use Protection": Communication boys receive about sex from parents, peers, and the media. *Journal of Youth & Adolescence, 37*, 113–126.

Erikson, E.H. (1964). *Childhood and society* (2nd ed.). New York: W. W. Norton.

Eriksson, U., Starrin, B., & Janson, S. (2008). Long-term sickness absence due to burnout: Absentees' experiences. *Qualitative Health Research, 18*, 620–632.

Erol, R.Y., & Orth, U. (2011). Self-esteem development from age 14 to 30 years: A longitudinal study. *Journal of Personality and Social Psychology, 101*(3), 607–619.

Eyal, K., Kunkel, D., Biely, E.N., & Finnerty, K.L. (2007). Sexual socialization messages on television programs most popular among teens. *Journal of Broadcasting & Electronic Media, 51*(2), 316–336.

Eysenck, H.J. (1966). *The effects of psychotherapy.* New York: International Science Press.

Farquhar, J.C., & Wasylkiw, L. (2007). Media images of men: Trends and consequences of body conceptualization. *Psychology of Men & Masculinity, 8*, 145–160.

Fass, D., Calhoun, G.B., Glaser, B.A., & Yanosky, D.J. (2009). Differentiating characteristics of juvenile methamphetamine users. *Journal of Child & Adolescent Substance Abuse, 18*(2), 144–156.

Fay, N., Garrod, S., & Carletta, J. (2000). Group discussion as interactive dialogue or as serial monologue: The influence of group size. *Psychological Science, 11*, 481–486.

FBI. (2012). *Hate crime statistics, 2010.* Retrieved February 5, 2012, from http://www.fbi.gov/about-us/cjis/ucr/hate-crime/2010.

Fehr, B. (2004). Intimacy expectations in same-sex friendships: A prototype interaction-pattern model. *Journal of Personality and Social Psychology, 86*, 265–284.

Feldman, J., Miyamoto, J., & Loftus, E.F. (1999). Are actions regretted more than inactions? *Organizational Behavior and Human Decision Processes, 78*, 232–255.

Fernandez, A.M., Vera-Villarroel, P., Sierra, J.C., & Zubeidat, I. (2007). Distress in response to emotional and sexual infidelity: Evidence of evolved gender differences in Spanish students. *Journal of Psychology: Interdisciplinary and Applied, 141*, 17–24.

Ferrari, J.R., & Dovidio, J.F. (2000). Examining behavioral processes in indecision: Decisional procrastination and decision-making style. *Journal of Research in Personality, 34*, 127–137.

Fincham, F.D. (2003). Marital conflict: Correlates, structure, and context. *Current Directions in Psychological Science, 12*, 23–27.

Fink, B., Hamdaoui, A., Wenig, F., & Neave, N. (2010). Hand-grip strength and sensation seeking. *Personality and Individual Differences, 49*, 789–793.

Finkel, E.J., Eastwick, P.W., Karney, B.R., Reis, H.T., & Sprecher, S. (in press). Online dating: A critical analysis from the perspective of psychological science. *Psychological Science in the Public Interest.*

Fischer, C.S. (2008). What wealth-happiness paradox? A short note on the American case. *Journal of Happiness Studies, 9*, 219–226.

Fischer, C.S. (2011). *Still connected: Family and friends in America since 1970.* New York, NY: Russell Sage Foundation.

Fischer, C.T. (2003). Infusing humanistic perspective into psychology. *Journal of Humanistic Psychology, 43*, 93–105.

Fischer, P.M., Schwart, M.P., Richards, J.W., Goldstein, A.O., & Rojas, J.T. (1991). Brand logo recognition by children aged 3 to 6 years: Mickey Mouse and Old Joe the Camel. *Journal of the American Medical Association, 266*, 3145–3153.

Fisk, A.D., & Rogers, W.A. (2002). Psychology and aging: Enhancing the lives of an aging population. *Current Directions in Psychological Science, 11*, 107–110.

Fitness.gov. (2012). *Resources.* Retrieved April 9, 2012, from http://fitness.gov/resource-center/

Fitzgerald, T.D., Hunter, P.V., Hadjistavropoulos, T., & Koocher, G.P. (2010). Ethical and legal considerations for internet-based psychotherapy. *Cognitive Behaviour Therapy, 39*(3), 173–187.

Fleck, C. (2011). *Older workers may never recover from great recession.* AARP.org. Retrieved November 5, 2011, from http://www.aarp.org/work/retirement-planning/info-05-2011/recession-ppi-study.html.

Fleming, L.C., & Jacobsen, K.H. (2010). Bullying among middle-school students in low and middle income countries. *Health Promotion International, 25*(1), 73–84.

Flett, G.L., Hewitt, P.L., Blankstein, K.R., & Mosher, S.W. (1991). Perfectionism, self-actualization, and personal adjustment. *Journal of Social Behavior and Personality. Special Issue: Handbook of Self-Actualization 6,* http://fitness.gov/resource-center/147–160.

Fleury-Steiner, R.E., Bybee, D., Sullivan, C.M., Belknap, J., & Melton, H.C. (2006). Contextual factors impacting battered women's intentions to reuse the criminal legal system. *Journal of Community Psychology, 34*(3), 327–342.

Flynt, S.W., & Morton, R.C. (2004). Bullying and children with disabilities. *Journal of Instructional Psychology, 31,* 330–333.

Foote, D., & Seibert, S. (1999, Spring/Summer). The age of anxiety. *Special Issue: Newsweek,* 68–72.

Fouche, G., & Klesty, V. (2011). Norwegian mass killer ruled insane, likely to avoid prison. *Reuters.* Retrieved November 30, 2011, from http://www.reuters.com/article/2011/11/29/us-norway-killer-idUSTRE7AS0PY20111129.

Fowler, J.H., Settle, J.E., & Christakis, N.A. (2011). Correlated genotypes in friendship networks. *Proceedings of the National Academy of Sciences of the United States of America, 108*(5), 1993–1997.

Fox, S. (2008, August 26). *The engaged E-patient population: People turn to the internet for health information when the stakes are high and the connection fast.* http://www.pewinternet.org/Reports/2008/The-Engaged-Epatient-Population.aspx.

Frankl, V. (1978). *The unheard cry for meaning.* New York: Simon & Schuster.

Fredrickson, B.L., Tugade, M.M., Waugh, C.E., & Larkin, G.R. (2003). What good are positive emotions in crisis? A prospective study of resilience and emotions following the terrorist attacks on the United States on September 11th, 2001. *Journal of Personality and Social Psychology, 84,* 365–376.

Friedman, M.J. (2005). Introduction: Every crisis is an opportunity. *CNS Spectrums, 10,* 96–98.

Fries, J.F. (2002). Reducing disability in older age. *Journal of the American Medical Association, 288,* 3164–3166.

Fromm, E. (1963). *Escape from freedom.* New York: Holt.

Fry, R. (2011). Living together: The economics of cohabitation. *Pew Social & Demographic Trends.* Retrieved February 20, 2012, from http://www.pewsocialtrends.org/2011/06/27/living-together-the-economics-of-cohabitation/.

Fudge, A.K., Knapp, M.L., & Theune, K.W. (2002). Interaction appearance theory: Changing perceptions of physical attractiveness through social interaction. *Communication Theory, 12,* 8–40.

Funeralwise.com. (2012). *Funeral customs by religion, ethnicity, and culture.* Retrieved April 19, 2012, from http://www.funeralwise.com/customs/.

Gabbard, G.O., & Lazar, S.G. (2004). *Efficacy and cost effectiveness of psychotherapy.* Report prepared for the APA Commission on Psychotherapy by Psychiatrists. http://www.psych.org/psych_pract/ispe_efficacy.cfm.

Galanter, M., & Kleber, H.D. (2008). *The American Psychiatric Publishing textbook of substance abuse treatment: Cognitive behavioral therapies.* Arlington, VA: American Psychiatric Publishing.

Gann, C. (2012). Sex life of older adults and rising STDs. *ABC News.* Retrieved February 7, 2012, from http://abcnews.go.com/blogs/health/2012/02/03/older-people-getting-busy-and-getting-stds/.

Gary, F.A. (2005). Stigma: Barrier to mental health care among ethnic minorities. *Issues in Mental Health Nursing, 26,* 979–999.

George, H.R., Swami, V., Cornelissen, P.L., & Tovee, M.J. (2008). Preferences for body mass index and waist-to-hip ratio do not vary with observer age. *Journal of Evolutionary Psychology, 6,* 207–218.

Gibbs, J.L., Ellison, N.B., & Heino, R.D. (2006). Self-presentation in online personals: The role of anticipated future interaction, self-disclosure, and perceived success in internet dating. *Communication Research, 33*(2), 152–177.

Gilbert, D.T., Brown, R.P., Pinel, E.C., & Wilson, T.D. (2000). Three kinds of control. *Journal of Personality and Social Psychology, 79,* 690–700.

Giles, L.C., Glonek, G.F.V., Luszcz, M.A., & Andrews, G.R. (2005). Effect of social networks on 10 year survival in very old Australians: The Australian longitudinal study of aging. *Journal of Epidemiology & Community Health, 59,* 574–579.

Gilovich, T., & Medvec, V.H. (1995). The experience of regret: What, when, and why. *Psychological Review, 102,* 379–395.

Gilovich, T., & Savitsky, K. (1999). The spotlight effect and the illusion of transparency: Egocentric assessments of how we are seen by others. *Current Directions in Psychological Science, 8,* 165–168.

Gino, F., Sharek, Z., & Moore, D.A. (2011). Keeping the illusion of control under control: Ceilings, floors, and imperfect calibration. *Organizational Behavior and Human Decision Processes, 114*(2), 104–114.

Glantz, S.A. (2003). Smoking in movies: A major problem and a real solution. *Lancet, 362,* 258–259.

Glaser, R. (2005). Stress-associated immune dysregulation and its importance for human health: A personal history of psychoneuroimmunology. *Brain, Behavior and Immunity, 19,* 3–11.

Gobeski, K.T., & Beehr, T.A. (2009). How retirees work: Predictors of different types of bridge employment. *Journal of Organizational Behavior, 30,* 401–425.

Goldin-Meadow, S. (2006). Talking and thinking with our hands. *Current Directions in Psychological Science, 15*, 34–39.

Goldman, L. (2008). *Coming out, coming in: Nurturing the well-being and inclusion of gay youth in mainstream society.* New York, NY: Routledge/Taylor & Francis Group.

Gologor, E. (1977). Group polarization in a non-sick-taking culture. *Journal of Cross-Cultural Psychology, 8*, 331–346.

Golub, A., & Johnson, B.D. (2002). The misuse of the "gateway theory" in US policy on drug abuse control: A secondary analysis of the muddled deduction. *International Journal of Drug Policy, 13*(1), 5–19.

Golubchik, P., Mozes, T., Maayan, R., & Weizman, A. (2009). Neurosteroid blood levels in delinquent adolescent boys with conduct disorder. *European Neuropsychopharmacology, 19*(1), 49–52.

Gomez, J., Miranda, R., & Polanco, L. (2011). Acculturative stress, perceived discrimination, and vulnerability to suicide attempts among emerging adults. *Journal of Youth and Adolescence, 40*(11), 1465–1476.

Goodwin, R., & Engstron, G. (2002). Personality and the perception of health in the general population. *Psychological Medicine, 32*, 325–332.

Gordon, K.C., Friedman, M.A., Miller, I.W., & Gaertner, L. (2005). Marital attributions as moderators of the marital discord-depression link. *Journal of Social & Clinical Psychology, 24*, 876–893.

Gordon, T., & Sands, J.S. (1984). *P.E.T. in action.* New York: Bantam.

Gottman. (2012). *Research FAQs.* The Gottman Relationship Institute. Retrieved February 11, 2012, from http://www.gottman.com/49853/Research-FAQs.html.

Gottman, J., & Carrere, S. (2000, September 23). Welcome to the love lab. *Psychology Today*, 42–47, 87.

Grabhorn, R., Kaufhold, J., Michal, M., & Overbeck, G. (2005). The therapeutic relationship as reflected in linguistic interaction: Work on resistance. *Psychotherapy Research, 15*, 470–482.

Grad, O.T., & Zavasnik, A. (1999). Phenomenology of bereavement process after suicide, traffic accident and terminal illness (in spouses). *Archives of Suicide Research, 5*, 157–172.

Granvold, D.K. (2001). Promoting long term sexual passion. *Constructivism in the Human Sciences, 6*, 73–83

Graves, S.B. (1999). Television and prejudice reduction: When does television as a vicarious experience make a difference? *Journal of Social Issues, 55*, 707–727.

Gray, N. (2008). Health information on the internet: A double-edged sword. *Journal of Adolescent Health, 42*, 432–433.

Green, B.C. (2005). Homosexual signification: A moral construct in social contexts. *Journal of Homosexuality, 49*, 119–134.

Green, K.E., Groves, M.M., & Tegano, D.W. (2004). Parenting practices that limit transitional object use: An illustration. *Early Child Development and Care, 174*, 427–436.

Green, S., & Pritchard, M.E. (2003). Predictors of body image dissatisfaction in adult men and women. *Social Behavior and Personality, 31*(3), 215–222.

Greenberg, M.T., Cicchetti, D., & Cummings, E.M. (1990). *Attachment in the preschool years: Theory, research, and intervention.* The John D. and Catherine T. MacArthur Foundation series on mental health and development. Chicago: University of Chicago Press.

Greene, K., & Faulkner, S.L. (2005). Gender, belief in the sexual double standard, and sexual talk in heterosexual dating relationships. *Sex Roles, 53*, 239–251.

Greene, S.M., Anderson, E.R., Doyle, E.A., & Riedelbach, H. (2006). Divorce. In G.G. Bear & K.M. Minke (Eds.), *Children's needs III: Development, prevention, and intervention* (pp. 745–757). Washington, DC: National Association of School Psychologists.

Greve, W., & Wentura, D. (2003). Immunizing the self: Self-concept stabilization through reality-adaptive self-definitions. *Personality and Social Psychology Bulletin, 29*, 39–50.

Greyson, B., & Bush, N.E. (1996). Distressing near-death experiences. In L.W. Bailey & J. Yates (Eds.), *The near-death experience: A reader.* New York: Routledge.

Grobani, N., Krauss, S.W., Watson, P.J., & Le Briton, D. (2008). Relationship of perceived stress with depression. Complete mediation by perceived control and anxiety in Iran and the United States. *International Journal of Psychology, 43*, 958–968.

Gruenewald, T.L., Karlamangla, A.S., Greendale, G.A., Singer, B.H., & Seeman, T.E. (2009). Increased mortality risk in older adults with persistently low or declining feelings of usefulness to others. *Journal of Aging and Health, 21*, 398–425.

Gu, X., Solmon, M.A., Zhang, T., & Xiang, P. (2011). Group cohesion, achievement motivation, and motivational outcomes among female college students. *Journal of Applied Sport Psychology, 23*(2), 175–188.

Guendelman, M.D., Cheryan, S., & Monin, B. (2011). Fitting in but getting fat: Identity threat and dietary choices among U.S. immigrant groups. *Psychological Science, 22*(7), 959–967.

Guerrero, L.K. (1997). Nonverbal involvement across interactions with same-sex friends, opposite-sex friends and romantic partners: Consistency or change. *Journal of Social and Personal Relationships, 14*, 31–58.

Guerrero, L.K., & Andersen, P.A. (1998). The dark side of jealousy and envy: Desire, delusion, desperation, and destructive communication. In B.H. Spirtzberg & W.R. Cupach (Eds.), *The dark side of close relationships* (pp. 33–70). Mahwah, NJ: Lawrence Erlbaum.

Guindon, M.H. (Ed.). (2010). *Self-esteem across the lifespan: Issues and interventions.* New York, NY: Routledge/Taylor & Francis Group.

Guo, Y., Wang, S., Johnson, V., & Diaz, M. (2011). College students' stress under current economic downturn. *College Student Journal, 45*(3), 536–543.

Gupta, S. (2002, December 2). A hurry-up lifestyle can hurt the young: Even if you're only 18, impatience can mean hypertension later on. And that can be bad news for your heart. *Time,* 103.

Gureje, O. (2011). Dysthymia in a cross-cultural perspective. *Current Opinion in Psychiatry, 24*(1), 67–71.

Guttmacher Institute. (2004). *Contraception in the United States: Current use and continuing challenges.* Retrieved May 04, 2006, from http://www.guttmacher.org/presentations/contraception-us.html.

Guzzo, K.B. (2009). Marital intentions and the stability of first cohabitations. *Journal of Family Issues, 30,* 179–205.

Haas, A., Koestner, B., Rosenberg, J., Moore, D., Garlow, S.J., Sedway, J., et al. (2008). An interactive web-based method of outreach to college students at risk for suicide. *Journal of American College Health, 57,* 15–22.

Haberfellner, E.M. (2007). A review of the assessment of antidepressant-induced sexual dysfunction used in randomized, controlled clinical trials. *Pharmacopsychiatry, 40,* 173–182.

Haddad, A. (2003). Ethics in action (acute care decisions). *RN, 66,* 27–29.

Halberstadt, J. (2003). The paradox of emotion attribution: Explanation biases perceptual memory for emotional expressions. *Current Directions in Psychological Science, 12*(6), 197–201.

Halevy, N., Bornstein, G., & Sagiv, L. (2008). "In-group love" and "out-group hate" as motives for individual participation in intergroup conflict: A new game paradigm. *Psychological Science, 19,* 405–411.

Halford, J.C.G., Boyland, E.J., Hughes, G., Oliveira, L.P., & Dovey, T.M. (2007). Beyond-brand effect of television (TV) food advertisements/commercials on caloric intake and food choice of 5–7-year-old children. *Appetite, 49,* 263–267.

Halford, W.K., O'Donnell, C., Lizzio, K., & Wilson, A.L. (2006). Do couples at high risk of relationship problems attend premarriage education? *Journal of Family Psychology, 20,* 160–163.

Hall, W.D., & Lynskey, M. (2005). Is cannabis a gateway drug? Testing hypotheses about the relationship between cannabis use and the use of other illicit drugs. *Drug and Alcohol Review, 24*(1), 39–48.

Halpern-Felshner, B.L., & Millstein, S.G. (2002). The effects of terrorism on teens; perceptions of dying: The new world is riskier than ever. *Journal of Adolescent Health, 30,* 308–311.

Hamden, A., Newton, R., McCauley-Elsom, K., & Cross, W. (2011). Is deinstitutionalization working in our community? *International Journal of Mental Health Nursing, 20*(4), 274–283.

Hamilton, M.C., Anderson, D., Broaddus, M., & Young, K. (2006) Gender stereotyping and under-representation of female characters in 200 popular children's picture books: A twenty-first century update. *Sex Roles, 55,* 757–765.

Hanley, S.J., & Abell, S.C. (2002). Maslow and relatedness: Creating an interpersonal model of self-actualization. *Journal of Humanistic Psychology, 42,* 37–56.

Hansen, J.C., & Dik, B.J. (2005). Evidence of 12-year predictive and concurrent validity for SII occupational scale scores. *Journal of Vocational Behavior, 67,* 365–378.

Hanson, M.S., Fink, P., Søndergaard, L., & Frydenberg, M. (2005). Mental illness and health care: A study among new neurological patients. *General Hospital Psychiatry, 27,* 119–124.

Harder, B. (2005). Potent medicine: Can Viagra and other lifestyle drugs save lives? *Science News, 168,* 124–126.

Harper, K., Sperry, S., & Thompson, J.K. (2008). Viewership of pro-eating disorder websites: Association with body image and eating disturbances. *International Journal of Eating Disorders, 41,* 92–95.

Harrawood, L.K., White, L.J., & Benshoff, J.J. (2009). Death anxiety in a national sample of United States funeral directors and its relationship with death exposure, age, and sex. *Omega: Journal of Death and Dying, 58,* 129–146.

Harrison, K., & Hefner, V. (2006). Media exposure, current and future body ideals, and disordered eating among preadolescent girls: A longitudinal panel study. *Journal of Youth and Adolescence, 35,* 153–163.

Harter, S. (1987). Developmental and dynamic changes in the nature of self-concept: Implications for child psychotherapy. In S.R. Shirk (Ed.), *Cognitive development and child psychotherapy* (pp. 119–160). New York: Plenum.

Harter, S. (2006). The self. In N. Eisenberg, W. Damon, & R.M. Lerner (Eds.), *Handbook of child psychology: Vol. 3, Social, emotional, and personality development* (6th ed., pp. 505–570). Hoboken, NJ: John Wiley & Sons.

Hartman, M., & Warren, L.H. (2005). Explaining age differences in temporal working memory. *Psychology and Aging. Special Issue: Emotion-Cognition Interactions and the Aging Mind, 20,* 645–656.

Harvard Health Letter, (2006, January). Patient, protect thyself? 1–2.

Haselton, M.G. (2003). The sexual overperception bias: Evidence of a systematic bias in men from a survey of naturally occurring events. *Journal of Research in Personality, 37,* 34–47.

Hatfield, J., & Fernandes, R. (2009). The role of risk-propensity in the risky driving of younger drivers. *Accident Analysis & Prevention, 41*(1), 25–35.

Hatton, E., & Trautner, M.N. (2011). Equal opportunity objectification? The sexualization of men and women on the cover of Rolling Stone. *Sexuality & Culture: An Interdisciplinary Quarterly, 15*(3), 256–278.

Hauslohner, A. (2011). Out of a village in Egypt: Portrait of a Facebook rebel. *Time.com*. Retrieved February 12, 2012, from http://www.time.com/time/world/article/0,8599,2049646,00.html.

Hawkley, L.C., Thisted, R.A., & Cacioppo, J.T. (2009). Loneliness predicts reduced physical activity: Cross-sectional & longitudinal analyses. *Health Psychology, 28*, 354–363.

Hazan, C., & Shaver, P. (1994). Attachment as an organizing framework for research on close relationships. *Psychological Inquiry, 5*, 1–22.

Health & Medicine Week. (2003, June 10). Role of chronic stress clarified, 3.

Healthline.com. (2012). *Infertility*. Retrieved March 5, 2012, from http://www.healthline.com/adamcontent/infertility.

Hébert, R. (2005). Vacation: Not what you remember. *APS Observer, 18*, 12–19.

Heiman, J.R. (2008). Treating low sexual desire—New findings for testosterone in women. *New England Journal of Medicine, 359*, 2047–2049.

Heiser, N.A., Turner, S.M., Beidel, D.C., & Roberson-Nay, R. (2009). Differentiating social phobia from shyness. *Journal of Anxiety Disorders, 23*, 469–476.

Helgeson, V.S. (1990). *The female advantage: Women's ways of leadership*. New York: Doubleday Currency.

Helgeson, V.S. (1994). Long-distance romantic relationships: Sex differences in adjustment and break-up. *Personality and Social Psychology Bulletin, 20*, 254–265.

Helson, R., & Soto, C.J. (2005). Up and down in middle age: Monotonic and nonmonotonic changes in roles, status, and personality. *Journal of Personality and Social Psychology, 89*, 194–204.

Hendrick, S.S. (2006). *Love, intimacy, and partners*. New York: Oxford University Press.

Henningsen, D.D., Henningsen, M.L.M., Eden, J., & Cruz, M.G. (2006). Examining the symptoms of groupthink and retrospective sensemaking. *Small Group Research, 37*, 36–64.

Hess, U., Senecal, S., Kirouac, G., Herrera, P., Philippot, P., & Kleck, R.E. (2000). Emotional expressivity in men and women: Stereotypes and self-perception. *Cognition and Emotion, 14*, 609–642.

Heth, J.T., & Somer, E. (2002). Characterizing stress tolerance: "Controllability awareness" and its relationship to perceived stress and reported health. *Personality and Individual Differences, 33*, 883–895.

Hethcock, B. (2011). Match.com faces class-action suit. *Dallas Business Journal*. Retrieved February 14, 2012, from http://www.bizjournals.com/dallas/news/2011/08/08/matchcom-faces-class-action-suit.html.

Hilbrecht, M., Shaw, S.M., Johnson, L.C., & Andrey, J. (2008). "I'm home for the kids": Contradictory implications for work-life balance of teleworking mothers. *Gender, Work & Organization, 15*, 454–476.

Hill, A., & McKie, R. (2008). Ten years on: It's time to count the cost of the Viagra revolution. *The Observer*, p. 30.

Hill, S.D., & Tomlin, C. (1981). Self-recognition in retarded children. *Child Development, 52*(1), 145–150.

Hinshaw, S.P., & Stier, A. (2008). Stigma as related to mental disorders. *Annual Review of Clinical Psychology, 4*, 367–393.

Hinsz, V.B., & Jundt, D.K. (2005). Exploring individual differences in a goal-setting situation using the motivational trait questionnaire. *Journal of Applied Social Psychology, 35*, 551–571.

Hobara, M. (2003). Prevalence of transitional objects in young children in Tokyo and New York. *Infant Mental Health Journal, 24*, 174–191.

Hoffman, K.R. (2002, May 3). Are girls meaner than boys? *Time for Kids*, 4–5.

Hoffmann, H., Kessler, H., Eppel, T., Rukavina, S., & Traue, H.C. (2010). Expression intensity, gender and facial emotion recognition: Women recognize only subtle facial emotions better than men. *Acta Psychologica, 135*(3), 278–283.

Hogarth, R.M. (2005). Deciding analytically or trusting your intuition? The advantages and disadvantages of analytic and intuitive thought. In T. Betsch, & S. Haberstroh (Eds.), *The routines of decision making* (pp. 67–82). Mahwah, NJ: Lawrence Erlbaum.

Hogue, M., & Lord, R.G. (2007). A multilevel, complexity theory approach to understanding gender bias in leadership. *Leadership Quarterly, 18*, 370–390.

Holland, J.M., & Neimeyer, R.A. (2010). An examination of stage theory of grief among individuals bereaved by natural and violent causes: A meaning orientated contribution. *Omega: Journal of Death and Dying, 61*, 103–120.

Hollon, S.D., Thase, M.E., & Markowitz, J.C. (2002). Treatment and prevention of depression. *Psychological Science in the Public Interest, 3*, 39–77.

Holmberg, D., & Blair, K.L. (2009). Sexual desire, communication, satisfaction, and preferences of men and women in same-sex versus mixed-sex relationships. *Journal of Sex Research, 46*, 57–66.

Holmes, T.H., & Rahe, R.H. (1967). The social readjustment rating scale. *Journal of Psychosomatic Research, 11*, 213–217.

Hong, Y., Wyer, R.S., & Fong, C.P.S. (2008). Chinese working in groups: Effort dispensability versus normative influence. *Asian Journal of Social Psychology, 11*, 187–195.

Hopko, D.R., Crittendon, J.A., Grant, E., & Wilson, S.A. (2005). The impact of anxiety on performance IQ. *Anxiety, Stress & Coping: An International Journal, 18*, 17–35.

Hornsey, M.J., & Jetten, J. (2005). Loyalty without conformity: Tailoring self-perception as a means of balancing belonging and differentiation. *Self and Identity, 4*, 81–95.

Horowitz, M.J. (2011). *Stress response syndromes: PTSD, grief, adjustment, and dissociative disorders* (5th ed.). Lanham, MD: Jason Aronson.

Horrigan, J.B. (2008). *Seeding the cloud: What mobile access means for usage patterns and online content.* www.pewinternet. org/~/media//Files/Reports/2008/PIP_Users.and.Cloud.pdf.

HospiceFoundation.org. (2012). *A caregivers guide to the dying process.* Hospice Foundation of America: Washington, DC.

Houck, J.A. (2007). A comparison on grief reactions in cancer, HIV/AIDS, and suicide bereavement. *Journal of HIV/AIDS & Social Services, 6*, 97–112.

Huang, G. (2011). College freshman face increasing stress levels. *The Dartmouth.* Retrieved December 21, 2011, from http://the-dartmouth.com/2011/02/07/news/stress.

Huddy, L., Khatib, N., & Capelos, T. (2002). The polls—Trends: Reactions to the terrorist attacks of September 11, 2001. *Public Opinion Quarterly, 66*, 418–451.

Huesmann, L.R. (2007). The impact of electronic media violence: Scientific theory and research. *Journal of Adolescent Health, 41*, S6–S13.

Hugenberg, K. (2005). Social categorization and the perception of facial affect: Target race moderates the response latency advantage for happy faces. *Emotion, 5*, 267–276.

Hugenberg, K., & Bodenhausen, G.V. (2003). Facing prejudice: Implicit prejudice and the perception of facial threat. *Psychological Science, 14*, 640–643.

Hugill, N., Fink, B., & Neave, N. (2010). The role of human body movements in mate selection. *Evolutionary Psychology, 8*, 66–89.

Hugill, N., Fink, B., Neave, N., Besson, A., & Bunse, L. (2011). Women's perception of men's sensation seeking propensity from their dance movements. *Personality and Individual Differences, 51*(4), 483–487.

Huntington, S.P. (1999, June/July). When cultures collide. *Civilization,* 76–77.

Huppert, F.A. (2009). A new approach to reducing disorder and improving well-being. *Perspectives on Psychological Science, 4*, 108–111.

Hyde, J.S., & DeLamater, J. (1997). *Understanding human sexuality.* New York: McGraw-Hill.

Iidaka, T., Nogawa, J., Kansaku, K., & Sadato, N. (2008). Neural correlates involved in processing happy affect on same race faces. *Journal of Psychophysiology, 22*, 91–99.

Ingram, R.E., Atchley, R.A., & Segal, Z.V. (2011). *Vulnerability to depression: From cognitive neuroscience to prevention and treatment.* New York, NY, US: Guilford Press.

InternetWorldStatistics.com. (2012). *The big Internet picture.* Retrieved January 13, 2012, from http://www.internetworld-stats.com/stats.htm.

Israel, G.E., & Tarver, D.E. (2001). *Transgender care: Recommended guidelines, practical information and personal accounts.* Philadelphia, PA: Temple University Press.

Iyengar, S.S., Wells, R.E., & Schwartz, B. (2006). Doing better but feeling worse: Looking for the "best" job undermines satisfaction. *Psychological Science, 17*, 143–150.

Jaccoby, S. (1999, September/October). Great sex: What's age got to do with it? *Modern Maturity,* 41–45.

Jackson, L.M., Pratt, M.W., Hunsberger, B., & Pancer, S.M. (2005). Optimism as a mediator of the relation between perceived parental authoritativeness and adjustment among adolescents: Finding the sunny side of the street. *Social Development, 14*, 273–304.

Jackson, T., Flaherty, S.R., & Kosuth, R. (2000). Culture and self-presentation as predictors of shyness among Japanese and American female college students. *Perceptual and Motor Skills, 90*, 475–482.

Jackson, T., Weiss, K.E., Lundquist, J.J., & Soderlind, A. (2002). Perceptions of goal-directed activities of optimists and pessimists: A personal projects analysis. *Journal of Psychology, 136*, 521–532.

Jamal, M. (2005). Short communication: Personal and organizational outcomes related to job stress and type-A behavior: A study of Canadian and Chinese employees. *Stress and Health: Journal of the International Society for the Investigation of Stress, 21*, 129–137.

James, V.H., & Owens, L.D. (2005). "They turned around like I wasn't there": An analysis of teenage girls' letters about their peer conflicts. *School Psychology International, 26*, 71–88.

Janis, I.L. (1982). *Groupthink* (2nd ed.). Boston: Houghton Mifflin.

Jansz, J., & Martis, R.G. (2007). The Lara phenomenon: Powerful female characters in video games. *Sex Roles, 56*, 141–148.

Jauhar, S. (2003, March 16). When doctors slam the door. *The New York Times Magazine,* 32–35.

Jayson, S. (2009). More women wait to start families. *USA Today.* Retrieved September 13, 2011, from http://www.usatoday.com/news/health/2009-08-12-latebirths12_N.htm.

Jewell, R.D., & Kidwell, B. (2005). The moderating effect of perceived control on motivation to engage in deliberative processing. *Psychology & Marketing, 22*, 751–769.

Johnson, S.P., Slater, A., & Hocking, I. (2011). Theoretical Issues in Child Development. In A.M. Slater and J.G. Bremner

(Eds.) *An Introduction to Developmental Psychology* (pp. 1–38). Oxford: Blackwell Publishing.

Johnson, S., & Patz, A. (2003, March/April). Save your relationship. *Psychology Today*, 50–58.

Johnson, S.D., Phelps, D.L., & Cottler, L.B. (2004). The association of sexual dysfunction and substance use among a community epidemiological sample. *Archives of Sexual Behavior, 33*, 55–63.

Johnson, S.K., Murphy, S.E., Zewdie, S., & Reichard, R. (2008). The strong, sensitive type: Effects of gender stereotypes and leadership prototypes on the evaluation of male and female leaders. *Organizational Behavior and Human Decision Processes, 106*, 39–60.

Joiner, T.E., Wonderlich, S.A., Metalsky, G., Schmidt, N.B. (1995). Body dissatisfaction: A feature of bulimia, depression, or both? *Journal of Social and Clinical Psychology, 14*, 339–355.

Jones, A.L., Moss, A.J., & Harris-Kojetin, L.D. (2011). *Use of advance directives in long-term care populations*. NCHS Data Brief, 54.

Jones, D. (1995). Sexual selection, physical attractiveness, and facial neoteny: Cross-cultural evidence and implication. *Current Anthropology, 36*, 723–748.

Jones, G. (2002). *Killing monsters: Why children need fantasy, super heroes, and make-believe violence*. New York: Basic Books.

Jones, S.M., & Burleson, B.R. (2003). Effects of helper and recipient sex on the experience and outcomes of comforting messages: An experimental investigation. *Sex Roles, 48*, 1–19.

Johnson, T., Kulesa, P., Cho, Y.I., & Shavitt, S. (2005). The relation between culture and response styles: Evidence from 19 countries. *Journal of Cross-Cultural Psychology, 36*, 264–277.

Jorm, A.F. (2005). Social networks and health: It's time for an intervention trial. *Journal of Epidemiology & Community Health, 59*, 537–538.

Judge, T.A., Hurst, C., & Simon, L.S. (2009). Does it pay to be smart, attractive, or confident (or all three)? Relationships among general mental ability, physical attractiveness, core self-evaluations, and income. *Journal of Applied Psychology, 94*, 742–755.

Jung, K., & Steil, R. (2012). The feeling of being contaminated in adult survivors of childhood sexual abuse and its treatment via a two-session program of cognitive restructuring and imagery modification: A case study. *Behavior Modification, 36*(1), 67–86.

Kahr, B. (2008). *Who's been sleeping in your head? The secret world of sexual fantasies*. New York: Basic Books.

Kaiser Family Foundation. (2011). *Sexual health of adolescents and young adults in the United States*. Retrieved January 2, 2012, from http://www.kff.org/womenshealth/upload/3040-05-2.pdf.

Kalmijn, M. (2005). Attitude alignment in marriage and cohabitation: The case of sex-role attitudes. *Personal Relationships, 12*, 521–535.

Kanemasa, Y., & Daibo, I. (2003). Effects of early adult attachment styles on intimate opposite-sex relationships. *Japanese Journal of Social Psychology, 19*, 59–76.

Kantor, M. (2006). *The psychopathy of everyday life: How antisocial personality disorders affects all of us*. Westport, CT, US: Praeger Publishers/Greenwood Publishing Group.

Kaplan, R.E., & Kaiser, R.B. (2003). Rethinking a classic distinction in leadership: Implications for the assessment and development of executives. *Consulting Psychology Journal: Practice and Research. Special Issue: Leadership Development: New Perspectives, 55*, 15–25.

Kasser, T., & Ryan, R.M. (1996). Further examining the American dream: Differential correlates of intrinsic and extrinsic goals. *Personality and Social Psychology Bulletin, 22*, 280–287.

Katz, J., & Myhr, L. (2008). Perceived conflict patterns and relationship quality associated with verbal sexual coercion by male dating partners. *Journal of Interpersonal Violence, 23*(6), 798–814.

Kayes, A.B., Kayes, D.C., & Kolb, D.A. (2005). Experiential learning in teams. *Simulation & Gaming, 36*, 330–354.

Kayes, D.C. (2005). The destructive pursuit of idealized goals. *Organizational Dynamics, 34*, 391–401.

Kazdin, A.E., & Benjet, C. (2003). Spanking children: Evidence and issues. *Current Directions in Psychological Science, 12*, 100–103.

Keery, H., Boutelle, K., van den Berg, P., & Thompson, J.K. (2005). The impact of appearance-related teasing by family members. *Journal of Adolescent Health, 37*, 120–127.

Keller, A., Ford, L.H., & Meacham, J.A. (1978). Dimensions of self-concept in preschool children. *Developmental Psychology, 14*(5), 483–489.

Keller, M.C. (2008). The evolutionary persistence of genes that increase mental disorders risk. *Current Directions in Psychological Science, 17*, 395–399.

Kelly, N.R., Bulik, C.M., & Mazzeo, S.E. (2011). An exploration of body dissatisfaction and perceptions of black and white girls enrolled in an intervention for overweight children. *Body Image, 8*(4), 379–384.

Kennedy, K.A., & Pronin, E. (2008). When disagreement gets ugly: Perceptions of bias and the escalation of conflict. *Personality and Social Psychology Bulletin, 34*, 833–648.

Kensit, D.A. (2000). Rogerian theory: A critique of the effectiveness of pure client-centered therapy. *Counseling Psychology Quarterly, 13*, 345–351.

Kent, L.K., & Shapiro, P.A. (2009). Depression and related psychological factors in heart disease. *Harvard Review of Psychiatry, 17*(6), 377–388.

Kessler, R.C., Berglund, P., Demler, O., Jin, R., & Walters, E.E. (2005). Lifetime prevalence and age of-onset distributions of DSM-IV disorders in the National Comorbidity Survey Replication. *Archives of General Psychiatry, 62*, 593–602.

Kessler, R.C., Molnar, B.E., Feurer, I.D., & Applebaum, M. (2001). Patterns and mental health predictors of domestic violence in the United States: Results from the National Comorbidity Survey. *International Journal of Law and Psychiatry, 24*, 487–509.

Keyes, K.M., Hatzenbuehler, M.L., & Hasin, D.S. (2011). Stressful life experiences, alcohol consumption, and alcohol use disorders: The epidemiologic evidence for four main types of stressors. *Psychopharmacology, 218*(1), 1–17.

Kieffer, K.M., Cronin, C., & Gawet, D.L. (2006). Test and study worry and emotionality in the prediction of college students' reasons for drinking: An exploratory investigation. *Journal of Alcohol and Drug Education, 50*, 57–81.

Kim, B.S.K., Liang, C.T.H., & Li, L.C. (2003). Counselor ethnicity, counselor nonverbal behavior, and session outcome with Asian American clients: Initial findings. *Journal of Counseling & Development, 81*, 202–207.

Kim, J., Park, S., & Emery, C.R. (2009). The incidence and impact of family violence on mental health among South Korean women: Results of a national survey. *Journal of Family Violence, 24*, 193–202.

Kim, J.L., Collins, R.L., Kanouse, D.E., Elliott, M.N., Berry, S.H., Hunter, S.B., et al. (2006). Sexual readiness, household policies, and other predictors of adolescents' exposure to sexual content in mainstream entertainment television. *Media Psychology, 8*, 449–471.

Kim, S.K., & Hyunsu, B. (2010). Acupuncture and immune modulation. *Autonomic Neuroscience: Basic and Clinical, 157*, 38–41.

Kirk, J., & Belovics, R. (2006). Making e-working work. *Journal of Employment Counseling, 43*, 39–46.

Kirschenbaum, H., & Jourdan, A. (2005). The current status of Carl Rogers and the person-centered approach. *Psychotherapy: Theory, Research, Practice, Training, 42*, 37–51.

Kirsh, S.J. (2010). *Media and youth: A developmental perspective*. Oxford, UK: Wiley-Blackwell.

Kirsh, S.J. (2012). *Children, adolescents, and media violence: A critical look at the research* (2nd ed.). Thousand Oaks, CA: Sage.

Kitayama, S., & Uchida, Y. (2005). Interdependent agency: An alternative system for action. In R.M. Sorrentino, D. Cohen, J.M. Olson, & M.P. Zanna (Eds.), *Ontario symposium on personality and social psychology*, June 2002, University of Western Ontario, London, Canada; an earlier version of this paper was presented at the aforementioned symposium (pp. 137–164). Mahwah, NJ: Lawrence Erlbaum.

Kito, M. (2005). Self-disclosure in romantic relationships and friendships among American and Japanese college students. *Journal of Social Psychology, 145*, 127–140.

Kleespies, P.M. (2004). Life and death decisions: Psychological and ethical considerations in end-of-life care. In P.M. Kleespies (Ed.), *Life and death decisions: Psychological and ethical considerations in end-of-life care*. Washington, DC: American Psychological Association.

Kleinman, A., & Good, B. (1985). *Culture and depression: Studies in the anthropology and cross-cultural psychiatry of affect and disorder*. Berkeley: University of California Press.

Kneip, T., & Bauer, G. (2009). Did unilateral divorce laws raise divorce rates in Western Europe? *Journal of Marriage and Family, 71*(3), 592–607.

Knox, D., & Zusman, M.E. (2001). Marrying a man with "baggage": Implications for second wives. *Journal of Divorce and Remarriage, 35*, 67–79.

Koch, S.C. (2005). Evaluative affect display toward male and female leaders of task-oriented groups. *Small Group Research, 36*, 678–703.

Koenig, M.A., & Jaswal, V.K. (2011). Characterizing children's expectations about expertise and incompetence: Halo or pitchfork effects? *Child Development, 82*(5), 1634–1647.

Kohut, A., & Wike, R. (2008, Spring). Assessing globalization: Benefits and drawbacks of trade and integration. *Harvard International Review*. www.harvardir.org/index.php?page=article&id-1727.

Kolata, G. (2002, November 19). Is frailty inevitable? Some experts say no. *The New York Times*, p. D5.

Kolden, G.G., Chisholm-Stockard, S.M., Strauman, T.J., Tierney, S.C., Mullen, E.A., & Schneider, K.L. (2006). Universal session-level change processes in an early session of psychotherapy: Path models. *Journal of Counseling and Clinical Psychology, 74*, 327–336.

Koltko-Rivera, M.E. (2006). Rediscovering the later version of Maslow's hierarchy of needs: Self-transcendence and opportunities for theory, research, and unification. *Review of General Psychology, 10*(4), 302–317.

Koman, E.S., & Wolff, S.B. (2008). Emotional intelligence competencies in the team and team leader: A multi-level examination of the impact of emotional intelligence in team performance. *Journal of Management Development, 27*, 55–75.

Kormanik, M.B., & Rocco, T.S. (2009). Internal versus external control of reinforcement: A review of the locus of control construct. *Human Resource Development Review, 8*(4), 463–483.

Kornblush, K. (2003, January–February). The parent trap: Working American parents have twenty-two fewer hours a week to spend with their kids than they did thirty years ago. Here's how to help the new "juggler family." *The Atlantic Monthly,* 111–112.

Kovan, N.M., Chung, A.L., & Sroufe, L.A. (2009). The intergenerational continuity of observed early parenting: A prospective, longitudinal study. *Developmental Psychology, 45*(5), 1205–1213.

Kraaij, V., Pruymboom, E., & Garnefski, N. (2002). Cognitive coping and depressive symptoms in the elderly: A longitudinal study. *Aging & Mental Health, 6,* 275–281.

Krause, N. (2005). God-mediated control and psychological well-being in late life. *Research on Aging, 27,* 136–164.

Krause, N. (2006). Exploring the stress-buffeting effects of church-based and secular social support on self-rated health in late life. *The Journals of Gerontology, 61,* 35–43.

Krebs, C.P., Lindquist, C.H., Warner, T.D., Fisher, B.S., & Martin, S.L. (2007). *The campus sexual assault survey.* Report commissioned by the National Institutes for Justice.

Kruger, J., Epley, N., Parker, J., & Ng, Z. (2005). Egocentrism over e-mail: Can we communicate as well as we think? *Journal of Personality and Social Psychology, 89,* 925–936.

Kübler-Ross, E. (1975). *Death.* Englewood Cliffs, NJ: Prentice Hall.

Kübler-Ross, E. (1993). *On death and dying.* New York: Collier Books.

Kühnel, J., & Sonnentag, S. (2011). How long do you benefit from vacation? A closer look at the fade-out of vacation effects. *Journal of Organizational Behavior, 32*(1), 125–143.

Kung, H.C., Hoyert, D.L., Xu, J.Q., & Murphy, S.L. (2008). Deaths: Final data for 2005. *National Vital Statistics Reports, 56*(10).

Kurdek, L.A. (2005). What do we know about gay and lesbian couples? *Current Directions in Psychological Science, 14,* 251–254.

Labre, M.P. (2005). Burn fat, build muscle: A content analysis of men's health and men's fitness. *International Journal of Men's Health, 4*(2), 187–200.

Labre, M.P., & Walsh-Childers, K. (2003). Friendly advice? Beauty messages in web sites of teen magazines. *Mass Communication & Society, 6,* 379–396.

Lachman, M.E., Neupert, S.D., & Agrigoroaei, S. (2011). The relevance of control beliefs for health and aging. In K.W. Schaie & S.L. Willis (Eds.), *Handbook of the psychology of aging* (7th ed., pp. 175–190). San Diego, CA: Academic Press.

Ladd, G.W. (2005). *Children's peer relations and social competence: A century of progress.* New Haven, CT: Yale University Press.

LaFrance, M., Hecht, M.A., & Paluck, E.L. (2003). The contingent smile: A meta-analysis of sex differences in smiling. *Psychological Bulletin, 129,* 305–334.

Lagus, K.A., Bernat, D.H., Bearinger, L.H., Resnick, M.D., & Eisenberg, M.E. (2011). Parental perspectives on sources of sex information for young people. *Journal of Adolescent Health, 49*(1), 87–89.

Lamb, D. (2009, June). Children of the dust. *Smithsonian,* 28–37.

Lambert, A.J., Payne, B.K., Jacoby, L.L., Shaffer, L.M., Chasteen, A.L., & Khan, S. (2003). Stereotypes as dominant responses: On the "social facilitation" of prejudice in anticipated public contexts. *Journal of Personality and Social Psychology, 84,* 277–295.

Landy, S. (2009). *Pathways to competence: Encouraging healthy social and emotional development in young children* (2nd ed.). Baltimore, MD: Paul H. Brookes Publishing.

Langlois, J.H., Kalakanis, L., Rubenstein, A.J., Larson, A., Hallam, M., & Smoot, M. (2000). Maxims or myths of beauty: A meta-analytic and theoretical view. *Psychological Bulletin, 126,* 390–423.

Lantz, A. (2001). Meetings in a distributed group of experts: Comparing face-to-face, chat and collaborative virtual environments. *Behaviour and Information Technology, 20,* 111–117.

Larzelere, R.E. (2008). Disciplinary spanking: The scientific evidence. *Journal of Developmental & Behavioral Pediatrics, 29,* 334–335.

LaSala, M. (2002). Walls and bridges: How coupled gay men and lesbians manage their intergeneration relationships. *Journal of Marital and Family Therapy, 28,* 327–339.

Lasser, J., Tharinger, D., & Cloth, A. (2006). Gay, lesbian, and bisexual youth. In G.G. Bear, & K.M. Minke (Eds.), *Children's needs III: Development, prevention, and intervention* (pp. 419–430). Washington, DC: National Association of School Psychologists.

Lau, R.W.L., & Cheng, S. (2011). Gratitude lessens death anxiety. *European Journal of Ageing, 8*(3), 169–175.

Lauglo, J. (2011). Political socialization in the family and young people's educational achievement and ambition. *British Journal of Sociology of Education, 32*(1), 53–74.

Lauzen, M.M., & Dozier, D.M. (2005). Recognition and respect revisited: Portrayals of age and gender in prime-time television. *Mass Communication and Society, 8,* 241–256.

Lavie, C.J., Milani, R.V., & Ventura, H.O. (2009). Obesity and cardiovascular disease. *Journal of the American College of Cardiology, 53,* 1925–1932.

Lazarus, R.S. (1993). From psychological stress to the emotions: A history of changing outlooks. *Annual Review of Psychology, 44*, 1–21.

Ledgerwood, A., & Chaiken, S. (2007). Priming us and them: Automatic assimilation and contrast in group attitudes. *Journal of Personality and Social Psychology, 93*, 940–956.

Lehmiller, J.J., VanderDrift, L.E., & Kelly J.R. (2011). Sex differences in approaching friends with benefits relationships. *The Journal of Sex Research, 48*, 275–284.

Leiter, M.P., & Maslach, C. (2005). *Banishing burnout: Six strategies for improving your relationship with work*. San Francisco, CA: Jossey-Bass.

Lenderking, W.R. (2005). The psychology of quality of life. *Quality of Life Research: An International Journal of Quality of Life Aspects of Treatment, Care & Rehabilitation, 14*, 1439–1441.

Lepore, L., & Brown, R. (2002). The role of awareness: Divergent automatic stereotype activation and implicit judgment correction. *Social Cognition, 20*, 321–351.

Leppänen, J., Tenhunen, M., & Hietanen, J. (2003). Faster choice-reaction times to positive than to negative facial expressions. *Journal of Psychophysiology, 17*, 113–123.

Levine, R., Sato, S., Hashimoto, T., & Verma, J. (1995). Love and marriage in eleven cultures. *Journal of Cross-Cultural Psychology, 26*, 554–571.

Leviton, C.D., & Leviton, P. (2004). What is guided imagery? The cutting-edge process in mind/body medical procedures. *Annuals of the American Psychotherapy Association, 7*, 22–29.

Levy, B.R., Ding, L., Lakra, D., Kosteas, J., & Niccolai, L. (2007). Older persons' exclusion from sexually transmitted disease risk-reduction clinical trials. *Sexually Transmitted Disease, 34*, 541–544.

Lewis, M. (1997). The self in self-conscious emotions. In J.G. Snodgrass, & R.L. Thompson (Eds.), *The self across psychology: Self-recognition, self-awareness, and the self concept* (pp. 119–142). New York, NY, US: New York Academy of Sciences.

Lewis, M., & Brooks-Gunn, J. (1979). *Social cognition and the acquisition of self*. New York: Plenum Press.

Libby, L.K., Eibach, R.P., & Gilovich, T. (2005). Here's looking at me: The effect of memory perspective on assessments of personal change. *Journal of Personality and Social Psychology, 88*, 50–62.

Lindgren, A. (2002). Career development strategies for workers in their 60s. *Knight Ridder/Tribune News Service*, K4958.

Lindgren, K.P., Parkhill, M.R., George, W.H., & Hendershot, C.S. (2008). Gender differences in perceptions of sexual intent: A qualitative review and integration. *Psychology of Women Quarterly, 32*, 423–439.

Lindstrom, T.C. (1995). Anxiety and adaptation in bereavement. *Anxiety, Stress, and Coping: An International Journal, 8*, 251–261.

Lippke, S., & Ziegelmann, J.P. (2006). Understanding and modeling health behavior: The multi-stage model of health behavior change. *Journal of Health Psychology, 11*, 37–50.

Liu, Y., & Yussen, S.R. (2005). A comparison of perceived control beliefs between Chinese and American students. *International Journal of Behavioral Development, 29*, 14–23.

Livingston, G., & Parker, K. (2010). Since the start of the great recession, more children raised by grandparents. *Pew Research Center*. Retrieved March 1, 2012, from http://www.pewsocialtrends.org/2010/09/09/since-the-start-of-the-great-recession-more-children-raised-by-grandparents/.

Llera, S.J., & Newman, M.G. (2010). Effects of worry on physiological and subjective reactivity to emotional stimuli in generalized anxiety disorder and nonanxious control participants. *Emotion, 10*(5), 640–650.

Lleras, C. (2008). Employment, work conditions, and the home environment in single-mother families. *Journal of Family Issues, 29*, 1268–1297.

Lo, V., & Wei, R. (2005). Exposure to Internet pornography and Taiwanese adolescents' sexual attitudes and behavior. *Journal of Broadcasting & Electronic Media, 49*(2), 221–237.

Lofshult, D. (2006). Caloric restriction is for the birds. *IDEA Fitness Journal, 3*, 79–80.

Lopes, P.N., Brackett, M.A., Nezlek, J.B., Schütz, A., Sellin, I., & Salovey, P. (2004). Emotional intelligence and social interaction. *Personality and Social Psychology Bulletin, 30*, 1018–1034.

Lorenzo, G.L., Biesanz, J.C., & Human, L.J. (2010). What is beautiful is good and more accurately understood: Physical attractiveness and accuracy in first impressions of personality. *Psychological Science, 21*(12), 1777–1782.

Lucas, R.E. (2005). Time does not heal all wounds: A longitudinal study of reaction and adaptation to divorce. *Psychological Science, 16*, 945–950.

Lucas, T.W., Wendorf, C.A., Imamoglu, E.O., Shen, J., Parkhill, M.R., & Weisfeld, C.C., et al. (2004). Marital satisfaction in four cultures as a function of homogamy, male dominance and female attractiveness. *Sexualities, Evolution & Gender, 6*, 97–130.

Luce, M.F. (2005). Decision making as coping. *Health Psychology. Special Issue: Basic and Applied Decision Making in Cancer Control, 24*, S23–S28.

Luszczynska, A., Benight, C.C., & Cieslak, R. (2009). Self-efficacy and health-related outcomes of collective trauma: A systematic review. *European Psychologist, 14*, 51–62.

Luszczynska, A., Scholz, U., & Schwarzer, R. (2005). The general self-efficacy scale: Multicultural validation studies. *Journal of Psychology: Interdisciplinary and Applied, 139*, 439–457.

Lyons, J.B., & Schneider, T.R. (2005). The influence of emotional intelligence on performance. *Personality and Individual Differences, 39*, 693–703.

Lyubomirsky, S., & Lepper, S.H. (1999). A measure of subjective happiness: Preliminary reliability and construct validation. *Social Indicators Research, 46*, 137–155.

Lyubomirsky, S., Sheldon, K.M., & Schkade, D. (2005). Pursuing happiness: The architecture of sustainable change. *Review of General Psychology. Special Issue: Positive Psychology, 9*, 111–131.

Ma, Y., & Qin, H. (2009). Regular and frequent sexual intercourse for elderly men could preserve erectile function. *Medical Hyphotheses, 72*, 370.

Maccoby, E.E., & Martin, J.A. (1983). Socialization in the context of the family: Parent–child interaction. In E.M. Hetherington (Ed.) & P.H. Mussen (Gen Ed.), *Handbook of child psychology. Socialization, personality, and social development* (4th ed., Vol. 4, pp. 1–102). New York: Wiley.

Maciejewski, P.K., Zhang, B., Block, S.D., & Prigerson, H.G. (2007). An empirical examination of the stage theory of grief. *Journal of the American Medical Association, 297*, 716–723.

MacKay, K.A., & Kuh, G.D. (1994). A comparison of student effort and educational gains of Caucasian and African-American students at predominantly white colleges and universities. *Journal of College Student Development, 35*, 217–223.

Mackenzie, C.S., Gekoski, W.L., & Knox, V.J. (2006). Age, gender, and the underutilization of mental health services: The influence of help seeking attitudes. *Aging and Mental Health, 10*, 574–582.

Macklem, G.L. (2008). *Practitioner's guide to emotion regulation in school-aged children.* New York, NY: Springer Science + Business Media.

MacNab, B., MacLean, J., Brislin, R., Aguilera, G.M., Worthley, R., Ravlin, E., Galperin, B.L., Tiessen, J.H., Jenner, S., Bess, D. Lituchy, T.R., & Turcotte, M.F. (2007). Culture and ethics management: Whistle-blowing and internal reporting within a NAFTA country context. *International Journal of Cross Cultural Management, 7*, 5–28.

Maddi, S.R. (2005). On hardiness and other pathways to resilience. *American Psychologist, 60*, 261–262.

Maher, B. (2003, January). Patching up the American family. *The World and I, 56*–58.

Main, M., & Solomon, J. (1990). Procedures for identifying infants as disorganized/disoriented during the Ainsworth strange situation. In M.T. Greenberg, D. Cicchetti, & E.M. Cummings (Eds.), *Attachment in the preschool years: Theory, research,* *and intervention* (pp. 121–160). Chicago: University of Chicago Press.

Major, B., & Eccleston, C.P. (2005). Stigma and social exclusion. In D. Abrams, M.A. Hogg, & J.M. Marques (Eds.), *The social psychology of inclusion and exclusion* (pp. 63–87). New York: Psychology Press.

Major, B., Kaiser, C.R., & McCoy, S.K. (2003). It's not my fault: When and why attributions to prejudice protect self-esteem. *Personality and Social Psychology Bulletin, 29*, 772–781.

Mallikarjun, P. (2005, February). Understanding seasonal affective disorder. *The Practitioner, 249*, 116–124.

Malmberg, J., Miilunpalo, S., Pasanen, M., Vuori, I., & Oja, P. (2005). Characteristics of leisure time physical activity associated with risk of decline in perceived health—A 10-year follow-up of middle-aged and elderly men and women. *Preventive Medicine: An International Journal Devoted to Practice and Theory, 41*, 141–150.

Mandal, B., & Roe, B. (2008). Job loss, retirement and the mental health of older Americans. *Journal of Mental Health Policy and Economics, 11*, 167–176.

Manning, S.Y. (2011). *Loving someone with borderline personality disorder: How to keepout-of-control emotions from destroying our relationship.* New York, NY: Guilford Press.

Manning, W.D. (2010). *Trends in cohabitation: Twenty years of change, 1987-2008 (FP-10-07).* National Center for Family & Marriage Research. Retrieved February 15, 2012, from http://ncfmr.bgsu.edu/pdf/family_profiles/file87411.pdf.

Mansfield, A.K., Addis, M.E., & Courtenay, W. (2005). Measurement of men's help seeking: Development and evaluation of the barriers to help seeking scale. *Psychology of Men & Masculinity, 6*, 95–108.

Marano, H.E. (2005). What's a shy guy to do? *Psychology Today, 38*, 14.

Marazziti, D., Di Nasso, E., Masala, I., Baroni, S., Abelli, M., & Mengali, F., et al. (2003). Normal and obsessional jealousy: A study of a population of young adults. *European Psychiatry, 18*, 106–111.

Marcus, B. (1999). The efficacy of exercise as an aid for smoking cessation in women: A randomized, controlled study. *Archives of Internal Medicine, 159*, 1229–1234.

Markus, H., & Kitayama, S. (1991). Culture and the self: Implications for cognition, emotion, and motivation. *Psychological Review, 98*, 224–253.

Markus, H.R., & Kitayama, S. (2003). Culture, self, and the reality of the social. *Psychological Inquiry, 14*, 277–283.

Marshall, R.D., Bryant, R.A., Amsel, L., Suh, E.J., Cook, J.M., & Nerial, Y. (2007). The psychology of ongoing threat: Relative risk appraisal, the September 11th attacks, and terrorism-related fear. *American Psychologist, 62*, 304–316.

Martin, A.J., Marsh, H.W., & Debus, R.L. (2001). Self-handicapping and defensive pessimism: Exploring a model of predictors and outcomes from a self-protection perspective. *Journal of Educational Psychology, 93,* 87–102.

Martin, R.A. (2001). Humor, laughter, and physical health: Methodological issues and research. *Psychological Bulletin, 127,* 504–519.

Martinez, F., Le Floch, V., Gaffié, B., & Villejoubert, G. (2011). Reports of wins and risk taking: An investigation of the mediating effect of the illusion of control. *Journal of Gambling Studies, 27*(2), 271–285.

Martini, K., & Reed, C. (2010). *Thank you for firing me!: How to catch the next wave of success after you lose your job.* New York: Sterling.

Martsch, M.D. (2005). A comparison of two group interventions for adolescent aggression: High process versus low process. *Research on Social Work Practice, 15,* 8–18.

Marzillier, S.L., & Davey, G.C.L. (2004). The emotional profiling of disgust-eliciting stimuli: Evidence for primary and complex disgusts. *Cognition & Emotion, 18,* 313–336.

Masche, J.G. (2008). Reciprocal influences between developmental transitions and parent-child relationships in young adulthood. *International Journal of Behavioral Development, 32,* 401–411.

Mask, L., & Blanchard, C.M. (2011). The effects of "thin ideal" media on women's body image concerns and eating-related intentions: The beneficial role of an autonomous regulation of eating behaviors. *Body Image, 8*(4), 357–365.

Maslow, A.H. (1954). *Motivation and personality.* Harper and Row: New York.

Maslow, A.H. (1968). *Toward a psychology of being* (2nd ed.). New York: Van Nostrand Reinhold.

Maslow, A.H. (1971). *The farther reaches of human nature.* New York: Viking.

Mason, W.A., Conrey, F.R., & Smith, E.R. (2007). Situating influence processes: Dynamic, multidirectional flows of influence within networks. *Personality and Social Psychology Review, 11,* 279–300.

Masood, N., Okazaki, S., & Takeuchi, D.T. (2009). Gender, family, and community correlates of mental health in south Asian Americans. *Cultural Diversity and Ethnic Minority Psychology, 15*(3), 265–274.

Masters, W., & Johnson, V. (1966). *Human sexual response.* Boston: Little, Brown.

Masters, W., & Johnson, V. (1979). *Homosexuality in perspective.* Boston: Little, Brown.

Masters, W.H., Johnson, V.E., & Kolodny, R.C. (1988). *Human sexuality* (3rd ed.). Boston: Little, Brown.

Masters, W.H., Johnson, V.E., & Kolodny, R.C. (1995). *Human sexuality.* New York: HarperCollins.

Mather, M., & Adams, D. (2007). *The crossover in female-male college enrollment rates.* Retrieved June 5, 2009, from http://www.prb.org/Articles/2007/CrossoverinFemaleMale CollegeEnrollmentRates.aspx.

Mather, M., & Carstensen, L.L. (2005). Aging and motivated cognition: The positivity effect in attention and memory. *Trends in Cognitive Sciences, 9,* 496–502.

Matsakis, A. (1999). *Survivor guilt: A self-help guide.* Oakland, CA, US: New Harbinger Publications.

Matsumoto, D. (2000). *Culture and psychology.* Pacific Grove, CA: Brooks/Cole.

Matsumoto, D. (2002). Methodological requirements to test a possible ingroup advantage in judging emotions across cultures: Comments on Elfenbein and Ambady and evidence. *Psychological Bulletin, 128,* 236–342.

Matsumoto, D. (2003). The discrepancy between consensual-level culture and individual-level culture. *Culture & Psychology, 9,* 89–95.

Matsumoto, D. (2007). Culture, context, and behavior. *Journal of Personality, 75,* 1285–1320.

Matteini, A.M., Fallin, M.D., Kammerer, C.M., Schupf, N., Yashin, A.I., Christensen, K., et al. (2010). Heritability estimates of endophenotypes of long and health life: The long life family study. *The Journals of Gerontology: Series A: Biological Sciences and Medical Sciences, 65A*(12), 1375–1379.

Mauss, I.B., Tamir, M., Anderson, C.L., & Savino, N.S. (2011). Can seeking happiness make people unhappy? Paradoxical effects of valuing happiness. *Emotion, 11*(4), 807–815.

Mayerowitz, S. (2010). Americans afraid to take full vacations. *ABCNews.* Retrieved December 7, 2011, from http://abcnews.go.com/Travel/americans-refuse-vacation-days-lag-rest-world/story?id=11361600#.TyQHLFyiF2A.

Mayo Clinic. (2002, September 4). *Women and depression: Understanding the gender gap.* http://www.mayoclinic.com.

Mayo Clinic. (2005). *Obesity.* Retrieved August 7, 2006, from http://www.mayoclinic.com/health/obesity/d500314.

Mayseless, O., & Popper, M. (2007). Reliance on leaders and social institutions: An attachment perspective. *Attachment & Human Development, 9,* 73–93.

McCabe, M.P. (2005). Boys want sex, girls want commitment: Does this trade-off still exist? *Sexual and Relationship Therapy, 20,* 139–141.

McCarthy, B., & McCarthy, E. (2009). *Discovering your couple sexual style: Sharing desire, pleasure, and satisfaction.* New York: Routledge/Taylor & Francis Group.

McConatha, J.T., Lightner, E., & Deaner, S.L. (1994). Culture, age, and gender as variables in expression of emotions. *Journal of Social Behavior and Personality, 9*, 481–488.

McConnell, A.R., Renaud, J.M., Dean, K.K., Green, S.P., Lamoreaux, M.J., & Hall, C.E., et al. (2005). Whose self is it anyway? Self-aspect control moderates the relation between self-complexity and well-being. *Journal of Experimental Social Psychology, 41*, 1–18.

McCrory, E., De Brito, S.A., & Viding, E. (2010). Research review: The neurobiology and genetics of maltreatment and adversity. *Journal of Child Psychology and Psychiatry, 51*(10), 1079–1095.

McDonald-Miszczak, L., Maki, S.A., & Gould, O.N. (2000). Self-reported medication adherence and health status in late adulthood: The role of beliefs. *Experimental Aging Research, 26*, 189–207.

McGillis, D. (1997). *Community mediation programs: Developments and challenges.* Washington, DC: U.S. Department of Justice.

McGuckin, C., Cummins, P.K., & Lewis, C.A. (2009). Bully/victim problems in Northern Ireland's schools: Data from the 2003 young persons' behavior and attitude survey. *Adolescence, 44*(174), 347–358.

McGuire, K.M.B., Greenberg, M.A., & Gevirtz, R. (2005). Autonomic effects of expressive writing in individuals with elevated blood pressure. *Journal of Health Psychology. Special Issue: Psychological Interventions in Chronic Illness, 10*, 197–209.

McIntosh, E., Gillanders, D., & Rodgers, S. (2010). Rumination, goal linking, daily hassles and life events in major depression. *Clinical Psychology & Psychotherapy, 17*(1), 33–43.

McKay, D.R. (2012). *Ten myths about choosing a career.* Retrieved January 20, 2012, from http://careerplanning.about.com/od/careerchoicechan/a/myths_choice.htm.

McEwen, B.S. (2005). Stressed or stressed out: What is the difference? *Journal of Psychiatry & Neuroscience, 30*, 315–318.

Meana, M., & Nunnink, S.E. (2006). Gender differences in the content of cognitive distraction during sex. *Journal of Sex Research. Special Issue: Scientific Abstracts, World Congress of Sexology 2005, 43*, 59–67.

Meevissen, Y.M.C., Peters, M.L., & Alberts, H.J.E.M. (2011). Become more optimistic by imagining a best possible self: Effects of a two week intervention. *Journal of Behavior Therapy and Experimental Psychiatry, 42*(3), 371–378.

Mehra, B., Merkel, C., & Bishop, A.P. (2004). The internet for empowerment of minority and marginalized users. *New Media & Society, 6*, 781–802.

Meissner, W.W. (2008). Reply to commentary by M.H. Spero. *Psychoanalytic Psychology, 25*, 197–199.

Mellor, D., Hayashi, Y., Firth, L., Stokes, M., Chambers, S., & Cummins, R. (2008). Volunteering and well-being: do self-esteem, optimism, and perceived control mediate the relationship? *Journal of Social Service Research, 34*, 61–70.

Melville, J.D., & Narmark, D. (2002). Punishing the insane: The verdict of guilty but mentally ill. *Journal of the American Academy of Psychiatric Law, 30*, 553–555.

Menec, V.H. (2003). The relation between everyday activities and successful aging: A 6-year longitudinal study. *The Journals of Gerontology, Series B, Psychological Sciences and Social Sciences, 58*, 74–83.

Michael, S., & Snyder, C.R. (2005). Getting unstuck: The roles of hope, finding meaning, and rumination in adjustment to bereavement among college students. *Death Studies, 29*, 435–458.

Michalos, A.C. (1991). *Global report on student well-being (Vol. 1): Life satisfaction and happiness.* New York: Springer-Verlag.

Milgram, S. (1974). Obedience to authority. *Human Relations, 18*, 57–76.

Miller, C.H., & Quick, B.L. (2010). Sensation seeking and psychological reactance as health risk predictors for an emerging adult population. *Health Communication, 25*(3), 266–275.

Miller, G.E., & Wrosch, C. (2007). You gotta know when to fold'em: Goal disengagement and systemic inflammation in adolescence. *Psychological Science, 18*, 773–777.

Miller, J.G. (1999). Cultural psychology: Implications for basic psychological theory. *Psychological Science, 10*, 85–91.

Miller, J.K. (2008). Walk-in single session team therapy: A study of client satisfaction. *Journal of Systemic Therapies, 27*, 78–94.

Miller, S., Gorman-Smith, D., Sullivan, T., Orpinas, P., & Simon, T.R. (2009). Parent and peer predictors of physical dating violence perpetration in early adolescence: Tests of moderation and gender differences. *Journal of Clinical Child and Adolescent Psychology, 38*(4), 538–550.

Miller, T.W. (2010). *Handbook of stressful transitions across the lifespan.* New York: Springer.

Misra, R., McKean, M., West, S., & Russo, T. (2000). Academic stress of college students: Comparison of student and faculty perceptions. *College Student Journal, 34*, 236–245.

Mitchell, J.E., Devlin, M.J., de Zwaan, M., Crow, S.J., & Peterson, C.B. (2008). *Binge-eating disorder: Clinical foundations and treatment.* New York, NY, US: Guilford Press.

Mitchell, T. (2003, September 5–7). After 9/11. *USA Weekend,* 4.

Moen, P., & Roehling, P. (2005) *The career mystique: Cracks in the American Dream.* Lanham, MD: Rowman & Littlefield.

Mohan, J. (2006). Cardiac psychology. *Journal of the Indian Academy of Applied Psychology. Special Issue:*

Commemoration of the 10th International and 41st National Conference of IAAP, 32, 214–220.

Mohr, R.D., & Zoghi, C. (2006). Is job enrichment really enriching? Retrieved August 09, 2006, from bls.gov/ore/pdf/ec060010.pdf.

Mokdad, A.H., Marks, J.S., Stroup, D.F., & Gerberding, J.L. (2004). Actual causes of death in the United States. *Journal of the American Medical Association, 291,* 1238–1245.

Mollersen, S., Sexton, H., & Holte, A. (2009). Effects of client and therapist ethnicity and ethnic matching: A prospective naturalistic study of outpatient mental health treatment in Northern Norway. *Nordic Journal of Psychiatry, 63,* 246–255.

Monk, T.H., Houck, P.R., & Shear, M.K. (2006). The daily life of complicated grief patients—What gets missed, what gets added? *Death Studies, 30,* 77–85.

Monroe, S.M. (2008). Modern approaches to conceptualizing and measuring human life stress. *Annual Review of Clinical Psychology, 4,* 33–52.

Monroe, S.M., & Reid, M.W. (2009). Life stress and major depression. *Current Directions in Psychological Science, 18,* 68–72.

Moore, N.B., & Davidson, J.K., Sr. (2000). Communicating with new sex partners: College women and questions that make a difference. *Journal of Sex & Marital Therapy, 26*(3), 215–230.

Moreau, D. (2002, November). Payday: Sooner or later? *AARP Bulletin,* 26.

Moritsugu, J., Wong, F.Y., & Duffy, K.G. (2010), *Community psychology,* Boston, MA: Allyn & Bacon.

Morris, J.A., Brotheridge, C.M., & Urbanski, J.C. (2005). Bringing humility to leadership: Antecedents and consequences of leader humility. *Human Relations, 58,* 1323–1350.

Morris, M., Nadler, J., Kurtzberg, T., & Thompson, L. (2002). Schmooze or lose: Social friction and lubrication in e-mail negotiations. *Groups Dynamics. Special Issue: Group and Internet, 6,* 89–100.

Morry, M.M. (2005). Allocentrism and friendship satisfaction: The mediating roles of disclosure and closeness. *Canadian Journal of Behavioural Science, 37,* 211–222.

Mroczek, D.K., & Spiro, A., III. (2005). Change in life satisfaction during adulthood: Findings from the Veterans Affairs normative aging study. *Journal of Personality and Social Psychology, 88,* 189–202.

Mueller, K.A., & Yoder, J.D. (1997). Gendered norms for family size, employment, and occupation: Are there personal costs for violating them? *Sex Roles, 36,* 207–220.

Mueser, K.T., & Jeste, D.V. (2008). *Clinical handbook of schizophrenia.* New York, NY, US: Guilford Press.

Mulvaney, M.K., & Mebert, C.J. (2007). Parental corporal punishment predicts behavior problems in early childhood. *Journal of Family Psychology, 21*(3), 389–397.

Mundell, E.J. (2002). Sitcoms, videos make even fifth-graders feel fat. *Reuters Health.* Retrieved January 30, 2012, from http://story.news.yahoo.com.

Murray, S.L., & Holmes, J.G. (2011). *Interdependent minds: The dynamics of close relationships.* New York, NY: Guilford Press.

Murray, S.L. (2005). Regulating the risks of closeness: A relationship-specific sense of felt security. *Current Directions in Psychological Science, 14,* 74–78.

Murray, S.L., Holmes, J.G., & Griffin, D.W. (2000). Self-esteem and the quest for felt security: How perceived regard regulates attachment processes. *Journal of Personality and Social Psychology, 78,* 478–498.

Myers, D.G. (1998). *Social psychology.* New York: McGraw-Hill.

Myers, D.G., & Diener, E. (1995). Who is happy? *Psychological Science, 6,* 10–19.

Nail, P.R., Misak, J.E., & Davis, R.M. (2004). Self-affirmation versus self-consistency: A comparison of two competing self-theories of dissonance phenomena. *Personality and Individual Differences, 36,* 1893–1905.

National Center for Chronic Disease Prevention and Health Promotion. (2011). *Tobacco use: Targeting the nation's leading killer.* Retrieved November 1, 2011, from http://www.cdc.gov/chronicdisease/resources/publications/aag/pdf/2011/Tobacco_AAG_2011_508.pdf.

National Center for Health Statistics. (2011). *Unmarried childbearing.* Retrieved March 3, 2011, from http://www.cdc.gov/nchs/fastats/unmarry.htm.

National Center for Missing and Exploited Children. (2006). *Child pornography—What is it?* Retrieved May 11, 2006, from http://www.cybertipline.com/missingkids/servlet/pageservlet.

National Family Caregivers Association. (2012). *Caregiving statistics.* Retrieved February 12, 2012, from http://www.Thefamilycaregiver.org.

National Institute of Mental Health. (2006). *When someone has schizophrenia.* Retrieved July 5, 2006, from http://www.nimh.nih.gov/publicat/schizosoms.cfm.

National Institute of Mental Health. (2007a, January 17). *New insights on how mental health is influenced by culture and immigration status.* Retrieved June 8, 2009, from http://www.nimh.nih.gov/science-news/2007/new-insights-on-how-mental-health-is-influenced-by-culture-and-immigration-status.shtml.

National Institute of Mental Health. (2007b, October 16). *Science Update: National survey tracks prevalence of personality disorders in U.S. Population.* http://www.nimh.nih.gov/science-news/2007/national-survey-tracks-prevalence-of-personality-disorders-in-us-population.shtml.

National Institute of Mental Health. (2009). *How is depression detected and treated: Electroconvulsive therapy.* Retrieved June

10, 2009, from http://www.nimh.nih.gov/health/publications/depression/how-is-depression-diagnosed-and-treated.shtml

National Institute of Mental Health. (2012). *Prevalence of serious mental illness among U.S. adults by age, sex, and race.* Retrieved June 3, 2012, from http://www.nimh.nih.gov/statistics/SMI_AASR.shtml.

National Institute on Drug Abuse. (2007). *Monitoring the future: National results on adolescent drug use, overview of key findings.* NIH Pub. No. 01-4923.

National Institute on Drug Abuse. (2009). *Principles of drug addiction treatment* (2nd ed.). NIH Publication No. 09–4180.

NationMaster.com. (2012). *Age of women at first childbirth (most recent) by country.* Retrieved February 17, 2012, from http://www.nationmaster.com/graph/hea_age_of_wom_at_fir_chi-health-age-women-first-childbirth

Navarro, J., & Karlins, M. (2008). *What every BODY is saying: An ex-FBI agent's guide to speed-reading people.* New York, NY: Collins Living.

Neff, L.A., & Karney, B.R. (2005). To know you is to love you: The implications of global adoration and specific accuracy for marital relationships. *Journal of Personality and Social Psychology, 88*(3), 480–497.

Neili, R.K. (2008). Diversity's discontents: the "contact hypothesis" exploded. *Academic Questions, 21,* 409–430.

Nelson, C.A. (2006). Of eggshells and thin-skulls: A consideration of racism-related mental illness impacting Black women. *International Journal of Law and Psychiatry, 29,* 112–136.

Neugarten, G.L. (1986). The aging society. In A. Pifer & L. Bronte (Eds.), *Our aging society.* New York: W. W. Norton.

Newman, M.G. (2004). Technology in psychotherapy: An introduction. *Journal of Clinical Psychology, 60,* 141–145.

Nielsen, M., Suddendorf, T., & Slaughter, V. (2006). Mirror self-recognition beyond the face. *Child Development, 77*(1), 176–185.

Niemiec, C.P., Ryan, R.M., & Deci, E.L. (2009). The path taken: Consequences of attaining intrinsic and extrinsic aspirations in post-college life. *Journal of Research in Personality, 43*(3), 291–306.

Nielsen, K., Randall, R., Yarker, J., & Brenner, S.O. (2008). The effects of transformational leadership on followers' perceived work characteristics and psychological well-being: A longitudinal study. *Work & Stress, 22*(1), 16–32.

Nietzel, M.T., Bernstein, D.A., & Milich, R. (1991). *Introduction to clinical psychology.* Englewood Cliffs, NJ: Prentice Hall.

Nieuwenhuizen, A.G., & Rutters, F. (2008). The hypothalamic-pituitary-adrenal-axis in the regulation of energy balance. *Physiology & Behavior, 94,* 169–177.

Nije Bijvank, M., Konijn, E.A., Bushman, B.J., & Roelofsma, P.H.M.P. (2009). Age and content labels make video games forbidden fruit for youth. *Pediatrics, 123,* 870–876.

Nishina, A., Juvonen, J., & Witkow, M.R. (2005). Sticks and stones may break my bones, but names will make me feel sick: The psychosocial, somatic, and scholastic consequences of peer harassment. *Journal of Clinical Child and Adolescent Psychology, 34,* 37–48.

Nolen-Hoeksema, N., Parker, L.E., & Larson, J. (1994). Ruminative coping with depressed mood following loss. *Journal of Personality and Social Psychology, 67,* 92–104.

Nolen-Hoeksema, S. (2008). It is not what you have; it is what you do with it: Support for *Addis's gendered responding framework. Clinical Psychology: Science and Practice, 15,* 178–181.

Norem, J. (2002). Defensive pessimism, optimism, and pessimism. In E.C. Change (Ed.), *Optimism & pessimism: Implications for theory, research and practice* (pp. 77–100). Washington, DC: American Psychological Association.

Norem, J.K., & Cantor, N. (1986). Defensive pessimism: Harnessing anxiety as motivation. *Journal of Personality and Social Psychology, 51,* 1208–1217.

Northey, W.F. (2009). Effectiveness research: A view from the USA. *Journal of Family Therapy, 31,* 75–84.

O'Donohue, W., Buchanan, J.A., & Fisher, J.E. (2000). Characteristics of empirically supported treatments. *Journal of Psychotherapy Practice and Research, 9,* 69–74.

Oetzel, J.G., & Ting-Toomey, S. (2003). Face concerns in interpersonal conflict: A cross-cultural empirical test of the face negotiation theory. *Communication Research, 30,* 599–624.

Office of National Drug Control Policy. (2004). *The economic costs of drug abuse in the United States, 1992–2002.* Washington, DC: Executive Office of the President (Publication No. 207303). Available at https://www.ncjrs.gov/ondcppubs/publications/pdf/economic_costs.pdf.

Ogden, C.L., Carroll, M.D., Curtin, L.R., McDowell, M.A., Tabak, C.J., & Flegal, K.M. (2006). Prevalence of overweight and obesity in the United States, 1999–2004. *Journal of the American Medical Association, 295,* 1549–1555.

Oishi, S., Hahn, J., Schimmack, U., Radhakrishan, P., Dzokoto, V., & Ahadi, S. (2005). The measurement of values across cultures: A pairwise comparison approach. *Journal of Research in Personality, 39,* 299–305.

Oka, Y., Suzuki, S., & Inoue, Y. (2008). Bedtime activities, sleep environment, and sleep/wake patterns of Japanese elementary school children. *Behavioral Sleep Medicine. Special Issue: Pediatric Sleep Medicine: Next Steps in Research, Patient Care, Policy, and Education, 6*(4), 220–233.

Olfson, M., Marcus, S.C., Druss, B., & Pincus, H.A. (2002). National trends in the use of outpatient psychotherapy. *The American Journal of Psychiatry, 159,* 1914–1920.

Olivola, C.Y., & Todorov, A. (2010). Fooled by first impressions? Reexamining the diagnostic value of appearance-based inferences. *Journal of Experimental Social Psychology, 46*(2), 315–324.

Onguardonline.gov. (2012). *Be smart online.* Retrieved March 15, 2012, from http://onguardonline.gov/.

OpenDNS. (2011). *OpenDNS 2010 report web content filtering and phishing.* Retrieved January 17, 2012, from opendns.com.

Orange, L.M., & Brodwin, M.G. (2005). Childhood sexual abuse: What rehabilitation counselors need to know. *The Journal of Rehabilitation, 71*, 5–11.

Orr, E.S., Sisic, M., Ross, C., Simmering, M.G., Arseneault, J.M., & Orr, R.R. (2009). The influence of shyness on the use of Facebook in an undergraduate sample. *CyberPsychology and Behavior, 12*, 337–340.

Orth, U., Robins, R.W., & Soto, C.J. (2010). Tracking the trajectory of shame, guilt, and pride across the life span. *Journal of Personality and Social Psychology, 99*(6), 1061–1071.

Ortiz, S.Y., & Roscigno, V.J. (2009). Discrimination, women, and work: Processes and variations by race and class. *Sociological Quarterly, 50*, 336–359.

Osgood, C.E. (1962). *An alternative to war or surrender.* Urbana, IL: University of Illinois Press.

Ostbyte, T., & Taylor, D.H., Jr. (2004). The effect of smoking on years of healthy life lost among middle-aged and older Americans. *Health Services Research, 39*, 531–551.

Osterberg, L., & Blaschke, T. (2005). Drug therapy: Adherence to medication. *New England Journal of Medicine, 353*, 487–497.

Oswald, D.L., & Clark, E.M. (2003). Best friends forever? High school best friendships and the transition to college. *Personal Relationships, 10*, 187–196.

Overholser, J. (2007). The central role of the therapeutic alliance: A simulated interview with Carl Rogers. *Journal of Contemporary Psychology, 37*, 71–78.

Owen, J., & Fincham, F.D. (2011). Effects of gender and psychosocial factors on "friends with benefits" relationships among young adults. *Archives of Sexual Behavior, 40*(2), 311–320.

Owen, S.S. (2004). Corporal punishment experiences and attitudes in a sample of college students. *Psychological Reports, 94*, 348–350.

Oxley, N.L., Dzindolet, M.R., & Miller, J.L. (2002). Sex differences in communication with close friends: Testing Tannen's claims. *Psychological Reports, 91*, 537–544.

Ozer, E.J., & Weiss, D.S. (2004). Who develops posttraumatic stress disorder? *Current Directions in Psychological Science, 13*, 169–172.

Özkan, S., Alatas, E.S., & Zencir, M. (2005). Women's quality of life in the premenopausal and postmenopausal periods. *Quality of Life Research: An International Journal of Quality of Life Aspects of Treatment, Care & Rehabilitation, 14*, 1795–1801.

Pacey, S. (2005). Step change: The interplay of sexual and parenting problems when couples form stepfamilies. *Sexual and Relationship Therapy, 20*, 359–369.

Palmer, E.L., & Carpenter, C.F. (2006). Food and beverage marketing to children and youth: Trends and issues. *Media Psychology, 8*, 165–190.

Palmer, J.K., & Loveland, J.M. (2008). The influence of group discussion on performance judgments: Rating accuracy, contrast effects, and halo. *Journal of Psychology: Interdisciplinary and Applied, 142*, 117–130.

Pardo, J.S., Gibbons, R., Suppes, A.S., & Krauss, R.M. (2012). Phonetic convergence in college roommates. Revision under review at *Journal of Phonetics, 40*, 190–197.

Park, H., & Antonioni, D. (2007). Personality, reciprocity, and strength of conflict resolution strategy. *Journal of Research in Personality, 41*, 110–125.

Park, H.S., Lee, H.E., & Song, J.A. (2005). "I am sorry to send you SPAM": Cross-cultural differences in use of apologies in email advertising in Korea and the U.S. *Human Communication Research, 31*, 365–398.

Park, L.E., Crocker, J., & Mickelson, K.D. (2004). Attachment styles and contingencies of self-worth. *Personality and Social Psychology Bulletin, 30*, 1243–1254.

Parker, J., Rubin, K.H., Erath, S., Wojslawowicz, J.C., & Buskirk, A.A. (2006). Peer relationships and developmental psychopathology. In D. Cicchetti & D. Cohen (Eds.), *Developmental psychopathology: Risk, disorder, and adaptation* (2nd ed., Vol. 2, pp. 419–493). New York: Wiley.

Parker-Hope, T. (2009). When sex leaves the marriage. *New York Times.* Retrieved January 15, 2012, from http://well.blogs.nytimes.com/2009/06/03/when-sex-leaves-the-marriage/.

Parrott, W.G., & Smith, R.H. (1993). Distinguishing the experiences of envy and jealousy. *Journal of Personality and Social Psychology, 64*, 906–920.

PatientsRightsCouncil.org. (2012). *Assisted suicide laws in the United States.* Retrieved July 15, 2012, from http://www.patientsrightscouncil.org/site/assisted-suicide-state-laws/.

Patterson, C.L., & Singer, J.A. (2007). Exploring the role of expectancies in the mental and physical health outcomes of written self-disclosure. *Imagination, Cognition and Personality, 27*, 99–115.

Pawaskar, M.D., & Sansgiry, S.S. (2006). Over-the-counter medication labels: Problems and needs of the elderly population. *Journal of the American Geriatrics Society, 54*, 1955–1956.

Pearsall, M.J., Christian, M.S., & Ellis, A.P.J. (2010). Motivating interdependent teams: Individual rewards, shared rewards, or something in between? *Journal of Applied Psychology, 95*(1), 183–191.

Pecchioni, L.L., & Croghan, J.M. (2002). Young adults' stereotypes of older adults with their grandparents as the targets. *Journal of Communication, 52,* 715–731.

Pedro-Carroll, J.L. (2005). Fostering resilience in the aftermath of divorce: The role of evidence-based programs for children. *Family Court Review. Special Issue on Prevention: Research, Policy, and Evidence-Based Practice, 43,* 52–64.

Peisah, C., Latif, E., Wilhelm, K., & Williams, B. (2009). Secrets to psychological success: Why older doctors might have lower psychological distress and burnout than younger doctors. *Aging & Mental Health, 13,* 300–307.

Pell, M.D. (2005). Nonverbal emotion priming: Evidence from the "facial affect decision task." *Journal of Nonverbal Behavior, 29,* 45–73.

Perilloux, C., & Buss, D.M. (2008). Breaking up romantic relationships: Costs experienced and coping strategies deployed. *Evolutionary Psychology, 6,* 164–181.

Perkins, A.M., & Corr, P.J. (2005). Can worriers be winners? The association between worrying and job performance. *Personality and Individual Differences, 38,* 25–31.

Perry, P. (1997, July/August). Personality disorders: Coping with the borderline. *The Saturday Evening Post,* 44–52.

Perry, P. (2005). New strategy for diagnosing bipolar disorder: Can diagnostic brain scans help identify patients with bipolar disorder? Interview with Dr. John D. Port. *Saturday Evening Post, 277,* 64–68.

Peterson, C., & Vaidya, R.S. (2001). Explanatory style, expectations, and depressive symptoms. *Personality and Individual Differences, 31,* 1217–1223.

Peterson, K. (2002, July 8). Cohabiting can make marriage an iffy proposition. *USA Today,* D1–D2.

Peterson, K.S. (1999, September 29). A hostile start makes the argument for divorce. *USA Today,* p. D1.

Petkoska, J., & Earl, J.K. (2009). Understanding the influence of demographic and psychological variables on retirement planning. *Psychology and Aging, 24,* 245–251.

Petrecca, L. (2009). Many people satisfied with their jobs despite tough times. *USAToday.com.* Retrieved February 5, 2012, from http://www.usatoday.com/money/economy/2009-03-12-money-worries-side_N.htm.

Pettigrew, T.F., & Tropp, L.R. (2008). How does intergroup contact reduce prejudice? Meta-analytic tests of three mediators. *European Journal of Social Psychology, 38,* 922–934.

Pettit, M.L., & DeBarr, K.A. (2011). Perceived stress, energy drink consumption, and academic performance among college students. *Journal of American College Health, 59*(5), 335–341.

Pfaffenberger, A.H. (2005). Optimal adult development: An inquiry into the dynamics of growth. *Journal of Humanistic Psychology, 45,* 279–301.

Phillips, J.A., & Sweeney, M.M. (2005). Premarital cohabitation and marital disruption among White, Black, and Mexican American women. *Journal of Marriage and Family, 67,* 296–314.

Phillips, L. (2005). Both specific functions and general ability can be useful: But it depends on what type of research question you ask. *Cortex, 41,* 236–237.

Phillips, L., Dillon, C., Baskys, A., Dickey, R., Dumontet, J., Elbe, D., et al. (2012). *Clinical handbook of psychotropic drugs* (19th rev. ed.). Cambridge, MA, US: Hogrefe Publishing.

Pienta, A.M., & Hayward, M.D. (2002). Who expects to continue working after age 62? The retirement plans of couples. *Journal of Gerontology: Series B: Psychological Sciences and Social Sciences, 57,* 199–208.

Pierson, M.R., & Glaeser, B.C. (2002). Self-concept: Differences among adolescents by gender. *Academic Exchange Quarterly, 6,* 152–157.

Pinquart, M., & Schindler, I. (2007). Changes of life satisfaction in the transition to retirement: A latent-class approach. *Psychology and Aging, 22,* 442–455.

Platow, M.J., Byrne, L., & Ryan, M.K. (2005). Experimentally manipulated high in-group status can buffer personal self-esteem against discrimination. *European Journal of Social Psychology. Special Issue: In Honour of Ken Dion, 35,* 599–608.

Plomin, R., DeFries, J.C., McClearn, G.E., & McGuffin, P. (2008). *Behavioral Genetics* (5th ed.). New York, NY: Worth Publishers,

Plutchik, R. (2001). The nature of emotions. *American Scientist, 89,* 344–350.

Polansky, J.R., & Glantz, S.A. (2004) *First-run smoking presentations in U.S. movies 1999–2003.* University of California San Francisco Center for Tobacco Control Research and Education. Retrieved May 15, 2008, from http://www.medscape.com.

Polivy, J., & Herman, C.P. (2000). The false-hope syndrome: Unfulfilled expectations of self-change. *Current Directions in Psychological Science, 9,* 128–131.

Porter, S. & ten Brinke, L. (2010). The truth about lies: What works in detecting high-stakes deception? Invited Review in a Special Issue of *Legal and Criminological Psychology, 15,* 57–75.

Porter, S., & ten Brinke, L. (2008). Reading between the lies: Identifying concealed and falsified emotions in universal facial expressions. *Psychological Science, 19,* 508–514.

Potter-Efron, R.T. (2005). *Handbook of anger management: Individual, couple, family, and group approaches.* Binghamton, NY: Haworth Clinical Practice Press.

Pound, P., Britten, N., Morgan, M., Yardley, L., Pope, C., & Daker-White, G., et al. (2005). Resisting medicines: A synthesis of qualitative studies of medicine taking. *Social Science & Medicine, 61*, 133–155.

Powell, A.D., & Kahn, A.S. (1995). Racial differences in women's desires to be thin. *International Journal of Eating Disorders, 17*, 191–195.

Powell, G.N., Butterfield, D.A., & Parent, J.D. (2002). Gender and managerial stereotypes: Have times changed? *Journal of Management, 28*, 177–193.

Prentky, R.A., Knight, R.A., & Lee, A.F.S. (2006). Child sexual molestation: Research issues. In C.R. Bartol, & A.M. Bartol (Eds.), *Current perspectives in forensic psychology and criminal justice* (pp. 119–129). Thousand Oaks, CA: Sage Publications.

Prescott, E., Osler, M., Hein, H.O., Borch-Johnsen, K., Schnohr, P., & Vestbo, J. (1998). Life expectancy in Danish women and men related to smoking habits: Smoking may affect women more. *Journal of Epidemiology and Community Health, 52*(2), 131–132.

Previti, D., & Amato, P.R. (2004). Is infidelity a cause or a consequence of poor marital quality? *Journal of Social and Personal Relationships, 21*, 217–230.

Prinstein, M.J., & Dodge, K.A. (2008). *Understanding peer influence in children and adolescents*. New York: Guilford Press.

Pritchard, M.E., & Wilson, G.S. (2006). Do coping styles change during the first semester of college? *Journal of Social Psychology, 146*, 125–127.

PRWEB. (2011). *U.S. weight loss market worth $60.9 billion.* Retrieved May 29, 2011, from http://www.prweb.com/releases/2011/5/prweb8393658.htm.

P.R. Newswire. (June, 2009). *New Match.com mobile dating application available for the new Palm Pre.* Retrieved July 15, 2009, from http://www.prnewswire.com.

Puhl, R.M., & Latner, J.D. (2007). Stigma, obesity, and the health of the nation's children. *Psychological Bulletin, 133*, 557–580.

Puterbaugh, D. (2005, May). Why newborns cause acrimony and alimony. *USA Today Magazine, 133*, 26–29.

Pyszczynski, T., & Cox, C. (2004). Can we really do without self-esteem? Comment on Crocker and Park (2004). *Psychological Bulletin, 130*, 425–429.

Quast, L. (2011). Taking a new look at "The Motherhood Penalty." *Forbes.* Retrieved October 16, 2011, from http://www.forbes.com/sites/lisaquast/2011/06/27/taking-a-new-look-at-the-motherhood-penalty/.

Quigley, D.G., & Schatz, M.S. (1999). Men and women and their responses in spousal bereavement. *Hospice Journal, 14*, 65–78.

Quinn, K.A., & Macrae, C.N. (2011). The face and person perception: Insights from social cognition. *British Journal of Psychology, 102*(4), 849–867.

Rachman, S. (2008). Psychological treatment for anxiety: The evolution of behavior therapy and cognitive behavior therapy. *Annual Review of Clinical Psychology, 5*, 97–119.

Rape, Abuse, & Incest National Network. (RAINN). (2012). *Statistics.* Retrieved March 17, 2012, from http://www.rainn.org/statistics.

Rath, J. (2008). Training to be a volunteer rape crisis counselor: A qualitative study of women's experiences. *British Journal of Guidance & Counseling, 36*(1), 19–32.

Ratliff, K.A., & Nosek, B.A. (2011). Negativity and outgroup biases in attitude formation and transfer. *Personality and Social Psychology Bulletin, 37*(12), 1692–1703.

Raymond, N. (2000, July/August). Mood: Blues around the world. *Psychology Today, 12.*

Raynor, D.A., Phelan, S., Hill, J.O., & Wing, R.R. (2006). Television viewing and weight maintenance: Results from the National Weight Control Registry. *Obesity, 14*(10), 1816–1824.

Raynor, D.A., Wing, R.R., & Phelan, S. (2007). Depression and adherence to medical advice. In A. Steptoe (Ed.), *Depression and physical illness.* Cambridge, UK: Cambridge University Press.

Recours, R., Aussaguel, F., & Trujillo, N. (2009). Metal music and mental health in France. *Culture, Medicine and Psychiatry, 33*(3), 473–488.

Regan, P.C., & Atkins, L. (2006). Sex differences and similarities in frequency and intensity of sexual desire. *Social Behavior and Personality, 34*, 95–102.

Regan, P.C., Durvasula, R., Howell, L., Ureño, O., & Rea, M. (2004). Gender, ethnicity, and the developmental timing of first sexual and romantic experiences. *Social Behavior and Personality, 32*, 667–676.

Reid, A. (2004). Gender and sources of subjective well-being. *Sex Roles, 51*, 617–629.

Reifschneider, M.J., Hamrick, K.S., & Lacey, J.N. (2011). Exercise, eating patterns, and obesity: Evidence from the ATUS and its eating & health module. *Social Indicators Research, 101*(2), 215–219.

Reiss, S., & Havercamp, S.M. (2005). Motivation in developmental context: A new method for studying self-actualization. *Journal of Humanistic Psychology, 45*, 41–53.

Rennison, C.M. (2003). *Intimate partner violence: Crime data brief.* Washington, DC: Bureau of Justice Statistics.

Reuters. (2010). *Boomerang kids, boomerang budgets.* Retrieved October 15, 2011, from http://www.reuters.com/article/2010/11/08/us-dp-boomerang-idUSTRE6A73T720101108/.

Reuther, E.T., Davis, T.E., Grills-Taquechel, A.E., & Zlomke, K.R. (2011). Fear of anxiety in fearful adults: An analysis of heterogeneity among phobia types. *Current Psychology: A Journal for Diverse Perspectives on Diverse Psychological Issues, 30*(3), 268–274.

Reynolds, B.M., & Repetti, R.L. (2006). *Adolescent girls' health in the context of peer and community relationships.* New York: Oxford University Press.

Reynolds, J.R., & Turner, R.J. (2008). Major life events: Their personal meaning, resolution, and mental health significance. *Journal of Health and Social Behavior, 49*, 223–237.

Richards, J.M. (2004). The cognitive consequences of concealing feelings. *Current Directions in Psychological Science, 13*, 131–134.

Rideout, V.J., Foehr, U.G., & Roberts, D.F. (2010). *Generation M2: Media in the lives of 8- to 18-Year-Olds.* The Henry J. Kaiser Family Foundation. Retrieved May 2, 2010, from http://www.kff.org/entmedia/mh012010pkg.cfm.

Ritter, B.A., & Yoder, J.D. (2004). Gender differences in leader emergence persist even for dominant women: An updated confirmation of role congruity theory. *Psychology of Women Quarterly, 28*, 187–193.

Rizzo, A., Parsons, T.D., Lange, B., Kenny, P., Buckwalter, J.G., Rothbaum, B., et al. (2011). Virtual reality goes to war: A brief review of the future of military behavioral healthcare. *Journal of Clinical Psychology in Medical Settings, 18*(2), 176–187.

Roberts, D.F., Henriksen, L., & Christenson, P.G. (1999). *Substance use in popular movies and music.* Washington, DC: Office of National Drug Control Policy.

Roberts, S. (2010). Facing a financial pinch, and moving in with mom and dad. *New York Times.* Retrieved October 14, 2011, from http://www.nytimes.com/2010/03/22/nyregion/22singles.html.

Robinaugh, D.J., Marques, L., Traeger, L.N., Marks, E.H., Sung, S.C., Gayle Beck, J., et al. (2011). Understanding the relationship of perceived social support to post-trauma cognitions and posttraumatic stress disorder. *Journal of Anxiety Disorders, 25*(8), 1072–1078.

Robins, R.W., & Trzesniewski, K.H. (2005). Self-esteem development across the lifespan. *Current Directions in Psychological Science, 14*, 158–162.

Robinson, E., Tobias, T., Shaw, L., Freeman, E., & Higgs, S. (2011). Social matching of food intake and the need for social acceptance. *Appetite, 56*(3), 747–752.

Robinson, H.M., & Hood, S.D. (2007). Social anxiety disorder— A review of pharmacological treatments. *Current Psychiatry Reviews, 3*, 95–122.

Robinson, J., Sareen, J., Cox, B.J., & Bolton, J.M. (2011). Role of self-medication in the development of comorbid anxiety and substance use disorders: A longitudinal investigation. *Archives of General Psychiatry, 68*(8), 800–807.

Roelofs, J., Meesters, C., Ter Huurne, M., Bamelis, L., & Muris, P. (2006). On the links between attachment style, parental rearing behaviors, and internalizing and externalizing problems in non-clinical children. *Journal of Child and Family Studies, 15*, 331–344.

Roese, N.J., & Summerville, A. (2005). What we regret most … and why. *Personality and Social Psychology Bulletin, 31*, 1273–1285.

Rogers, C.R. (1961). *On becoming a person.* Boston: Houghton Mifflin.

Rogers, C.R. (1980). *A way of being.* Boston: Houghton Mifflin.

Rogge, R.D., Bradbury, T.N., Hahlweg, K., Engl, J., & Thurmaier, F. (2006). Predicting marital distress and dissolution: Refining the two-factor hypothesis. *Journal of Family Psychology, 20*, 156–159.

Rohrbaugh, J.B. (2008). *A comprehensive guide to child custody evaluations: Mental health and legal perspectives.* New York: Springer.

Rokach, A., & Neto, F. (2005). Age, culture, and the antecedents of loneliness. *Social Behavior and Personality, 33*, 477–494.

Rosario, M., Schrimshaw, E.W., & Hunter, J. (2009). Disclosure of sexual orientation and subsequent substance use and abuse among lesbian, gay, and bisexual youths: Critical role of disclosure reactions. *Psychology of Addictive Behaviors, 23*, 175–184.

Rosario, M., Schrimshaw, E.W., Hunter, J., & Braun, L. (2006). Sexual identity development among lesbian, gay, and bisexual youths: Consistency and change over time. *Journal of Sex Research. Special Issue: Scientific Abstracts, World Congress of Sexology 2005, 43*, 46–58.

Rosedale, M. (2011). Our patients' lives are worth fighting for and electroconvulsive therapy (ECT) saves lives: A compendium of the evidence. *Journal of the American Psychiatric Nurses Association, 17*(3), 209–211.

Roseman, I.J. (2008). Motivations and emotivations: Approach, avoidance, and other tendencies in motivated and emotional behavior. In A.J. Elliot (Ed.), *Handbook of approach and avoidance motivation* (pp. 343–366). New York: Psychology Press.

Rosenbaum, J.L., & Prinsky, L. (1991). The presumption of influence: Recent responses to popular music subcultures. *Crime and Delinquency, 37*, 528–535.

Rosenberg, J., & Rosenberg, S. (Eds.). (2006). *Community mental health: Challenges for the 21st century.* New York, NY, US: Routledge.

Rosenfeld, M.J., & Thomas, R.J. (2010, September). *Meeting online: The rise of the Internet as a social intermediary.* Unpublished manuscript, Department of Sociology, Stanford University, Stanford, CA.

Ross, M., & Wilson, A.E. (2003). Autobiographical memory and conceptions of self: Getting better all the time. *Current Directions in Psychological Science, 12,* 66–69.

Rothaupt, J.W., & Becker, K. (2007). A literature review of Western bereavement theory: From decathecting to continuing bonds. *The Family Journal, 15,* 6–15.

Rothbart, M.K. (2011). *Becoming who we are: Temperament and personality in development.* New York, NY, US: Guilford Press.

Rougemont-Bücking, A., Linnman, C., Zeffiro, T.A., Zeidan, M.A., Lebron-Milad, K., Rodriguez-Romaguera, J., et al. (2011). Altered processing of contextual information during fear extinction in PTSD: An fMRI study. *CNS Neuroscience & Therapeutics, 17*(4), 227–236.

Routledge, C., & Juhl, J. (2010). When death thoughts lead to death fears: Mortality salience increases death anxiety for individuals who lack meaning in life. *Cognition and Emotion, 24*(5), 848–854.

Rubin, K.H., & Coplan, R.J. (2010). *The development of shyness and social withdrawal.* New York, NY, US: Guilford Press.

Rudman, L.A., & Goodwin, S.A. (2004). Gender differences in automatic in-group bias: Why do women like women more than men like men? *Journal of Personality and Social Psychology, 87,* 494–509.

Ruscher, J.B., Cralley, E.L., & O'Farrell, K.J. (2005). How newly acquainted dyads develop shared stereotypic impressions through conversation. *Group Processes & Intergroup Relations, 8,* 259–270.

Russell, D.P. (2007). Recruiting and staffing in the electronic age: A research-based perspective. *Consulting Psychology Journal: Practice and Research, 59,* 91–101.

Russo, N.F. (2008). Call to action: Reducing interpersonal violence across the lifespan. *American Journal of Orthopsychiatry, 78,* 383–385.

Rustad, R.A., Small, J.E., Jobes, D.A., Safer, M.A., & Peterson, R.J. (2003). The impact of rock videos and music with suicidal content on thoughts and attitudes about suicide. *Suicide and Life-Threatening Behavior, 33,* 120–131.

Ryan, C., Russell, S.T., Huebner, D., Diaz, R., & Sanchez, J. (2010). Family acceptance in adolescence and the health of LGBT young adults. *Journal of Child and Adolescent Psychiatric Nursing, 23*(4), 205–213.

Ryan, M.K., Haslam, S.A., & Postmes, T. (2007). Reactions to the glass cliff: Gender differences in the explanations for the precariousness of women's leadership positions. *Journal of Organizational Change Management, 20,* 182–197.

Ryan, S., Franzetta, K., Manlove, J., & Holcombe, E. (2007). Adolescents' discussions about contraception or STDs with partners before first sex. *Perspectives on Sexual and Reproductive Health, 39,* 149–157.

Ryan, T., & Xenos, S. (2011). Who uses Facebook? An investigation into the relationship between the big five, shyness, narcissism, loneliness, and Facebook usage. *Computers in Human Behavior, 27*(5), 1658–1664.

Saad, L. (2010). *Americans' acceptance of gay relations crosses 50% threshold.* Gallup. Retrieved January 29, 2012, from http://www.gallup.com/poll/135764/americans-acceptance-gay-relations-crosses-threshold.aspx.

Sabatino C. (2007). *Advance directives and advance care planning: Legal and policy issues.* Report prepared for the U.S. Department of Health and Human Services; Assistant Secretary for Planning and Evaluation; Office of Disability, Aging and Long-Term Care Policy, Washington, DC.

Sachdev, P.S., & Chen, X. (2009). Neurosurgical treatment of mood disorders: Traditional psychosurgery and the advent of deep brain stimulation. *Current Opinion in Psychiatry, 22*(1), 25–31.

Safdar, S., Friedlmeier, W., Matsumoto, D., Yoo, S.H., Kwantes, C.T., Kakai, H., et al. (2009). Variations of emotional display rules within and across cultures: A comparison between Canada, USA, and Japan. *Canadian Journal of Behavioural Science/ Revue Canadienne Des Sciences Du Comportement, 41,* 1–10.

Sakuragi, T. (2004). Association of culture with shyness among Japanese and American university students. *Perceptual and Motor Skills, 98,* 803–813.

Salerno, S. (2005). *SHAM: How the self-help movement made America helpless.* New York, NY: Crown Trade Paperbacks/ Crown Publishers.

Substance Abuse and Mental Health Services Administration. (2009). Adderal and college students. *SAMHSA News, 17*(3). http://www.samhsa.gov/samhsaNewsletter/Volume_17_Number_3/Adderall.aspx.

Samons, S.L. (2009). *When the opposite sex isn't: Sexual orientation in male to female transgender people.* New York, NY, US: Routledge/Taylor & Francis Group.

Sanchez, D.T., & Crocker, J. (2005). How investment in gender ideals affects well-being: The role of external contingencies of self-worth. *Psychology of Women Quarterly, 29,* 63–77.

Santesso, D.L., Schmidt, L.A., & Fox, N.A. (2004). Are shyness and sociability still a dangerous combination for substance use? Evidence from a U.S. and Canadian sample. *Personality and Individual Differences, 37,* 5–17.

Sargent, J.D., Wills, T.A., Stoolmiller, M., Gibson, J., & Gibbons, F.X. (2006). Alcohol use in motion pictures and its relation with early-onset teen drinking. *Journal of Studies on Alcohol, 67,* 54–65.

SART.org. (2012). *Society for assisted reproductive technologies.* Retrieved January 16, 2012, from http://sart.org/affiliates/sart/default.aspx?id=2377.

Sassaroli, S., Gallucci, M., & Ruggiero, G.M. (2008). Low perception of control as a cognitive factor of eating disorders: Its independent effects on measures of eating disorders and its interactive effects with perfectionism and self-esteem. *Journal of Behavior Therapy and Experimental Psychology, 39*, 467–488.

Saunders, P.L., & Chester, A. (2008). Shyness and the internet: Social problem or panacea? *Computers in Human Behavior, 24*, 2649–2658.

Savard, J., Leduc, N., Lebel, P., Beland, F., & Bergman, H. (2006). Caregiver satisfaction with support services: Influence of different types of services. *Journal of Aging and Health, 18*, 3–27.

Saxton, T.K., DeBruine, L.M., Jones, B.C., Little, A.C., & Roberts, S.C. (2011). A longitudinal study of adolescents' judgments of the attractiveness of facial symmetry, averageness and sexual dimorphism. *Journal of Evolutionary Psychology, 9*(1), 43–55.

Sayer, L.C. (2005). Gender, time and inequality: Trends in women's and men's paid work, unpaid work and free time. *Social Forces, 84*, 285–303.

Saylor, C.F., Cowart, B.L., Lipovsky, J.A., Jackson, C., & Finch, A.J. (2003). Media exposure to September 11. *The American Behavioral Scientist, 46*, 1622–1642.

Scarpa, A., Haden, S.C., & Hurley, J. (2006). Community violence victimization and symptoms of posttraumatic stress disorder: The moderating effects of coping and social support. *Journal of Interpersonal Violence, 21*, 446–469.

Scealy, M., Phillips, J.G., & Stevenson, R. (2002). Shyness and anxiety as predictors of patterns of internet usage. *CyberPsychology and Behavior, 5*, 507–515.

Schachter, S., & Singer, J. (1962). Cognitive, social, and physiological determinants of emotional state. *Psychological Review, 69*, 379–399.

Scheel, K.R., & Westefeld, J.S. (1999). Heavy metal music and adolescent suicidality: An empirical investigation. *Adolescence, 34*, 253–259.

Scheier, M.F., & Carver, C.S. (1993). On the power of positive thinking: The benefits of being optimistic. *Psychological Science, 4*, 26–30.

Schein, E.H. (2006). *Career anchors: Self-assessment.* Hoboken, NJ: Pfeiffer. Besides providing a self-survey to discover your own strengths and talents, this book includes basic career descriptions so that readers can find the jobs with which they are most compatible.

Schlaepfer, T.E., Bewernick, B., Kayser, S., & Lenz, D. (2011). Modulating affect, cognition, and behavior–prospects of deep brain stimulation for treatment-resistant psychiatric disorders. *Frontiers in Integrative Neuroscience, 5.*

Schlenker, B.R., Pontari, B.A., & Christopher, A.N. (2001). Excuses and character: Personal and social implications of excuses. *Personality and Social Psychology Review, 5*, 15–32.

Schmitt, D.P., & Allik, J. (2005). Simultaneous administration of the Rosenberg self-esteem scale in 53 nations: Exploring the universal and culture-specific features of global self-esteem. *Journal of Personality and Social Psychology, 89*(4), 623–642.

Schooler, D. (2008). Real women have curves: A longitudinal investigation of TV and the body image development of Latina adolescents. *Journal of Adolescent Research, 23*, 132–153.

Schooler, D., Ward, L.M., Merriwether, A., & Caruthers, A. (2004). Who's that girl: Television's role in the body image development of young White and Black women. *Psychology of Women Quarterly, 28*, 38–47.

Schrof, J.M., & Schultz, S. (1999, March 8). Melancholy nation. *U.S. News & World Report*, 56–63.

Schug, J., Yuki, M., & Maddux, W. (2010). Relational mobility explains between- and within-culture differences in self-disclosure to close friends. *Psychological Science, 21*(10), 1471–1478.

Schuler, A.J. (2003). *Tips for successful cross cultural communication.* Retrieved February 1, 2012, from http://www.SchulerSolutions.com.

Schulz, R., & Heckhausen, J. (1996). A life span model of successful aging. *American Psychologist, 51*, 702–714.

Schunk, D.H., & Pajares, F. (2009). Self-efficacy theory. In K.R. Wentzel & A. Wigfield (Eds.), *Handbook of motivation at school* (pp. 35–53). New York: Routledge.

Schutte, N.S., Malouff, J.M., Bobik, C., Coston, R.D., Greeson, C., Jedlicka, C., & Rhodes, E., et al. (2001). Emotional intelligence and interpersonal relations. *The Journal of Social Psychology, 141*, 523–536.

Schützwohl, A. (2006). Sex differences in jealousy: Information search and cognitive preoccupation. *Personality and Individual Differences, 40*, 285–292.

Schwartz, P. (2002, May/June). Love is all you need. *Psychology Today*, 56–62.

Schwartz, S.H., & Rubel, T. (2005). Sex differences in value priorities: Cross-cultural and multimethod studies. *Journal of Personality and Social Psychology, 89*, 1010–1028.

Scioli, A., Ricci, M., Nyugen, T., & Scioli, E.R. (2011). Hope: Its nature and measurement. *Psychology of Religion and Spirituality, 3*(2), 78–97.

Scott, S.B., Jackson, B.R., & Bergeman, C.S. (2011). What contributes to perceived stress in later life? A recursive partitioning approach. *Psychology and Aging, 26*(4), 830–843.

Sczesny, S., Bosak, J., Neff, D., & Schyns, B. (2004). Gender stereotypes and the attribution of leadership traits: A cross-cultural comparison. *Sex Roles, 51*, 631–645.

Sedikides, C., & Koole, S.L. (2004). In defense of the self. *Social Cognition, 22*, 1–3.

Sedikides, C., Gaertner, L., & Vevea, J.L. (2005). Pancultural self-enhancement reloaded: A meta-analytic reply to Heine (2005). *Journal of Personality and Social Psychology, 89,* 539–551.

Segerstrom, S.C., & Miller, G.E. (2004). Psychological stress and the human immune system: A meta-analytic study of 30 years of inquiry. *Psychological Bulletin, 130,* 601–630.

Seligman, M.E.P. (2011). *Flourish: A visionary new understanding of happiness and well- being.* New York, NY: Free Press.

Seligman, M.E.P. (1981). A learned helplessness point of view. In L.P. Rehm (Ed.), *Behavior therapy for depression.* New York: Academic Press.

Seligman, M.E.P. (1992). *Learned optimism.* New York: Knopf.

Seligman, M.E.P. (1995). The effectiveness of psychotherapy: The Consumer Reports study. *American Psychologist, 50,* 965–974.

Selye, H. (1991). History and present states of the stress concept. In A. Monat & R.S. Lazarus (Eds.), *Stress and coping: An anthology* (3rd ed., pp. 21–35). New York: Columbia University Press.

Senko, C., & Harackiewicz, J.M. (2005). Regulation of achievement goals: The role of competence feedback. *Journal of Educational Psychology, 97,* 320–336.

Sexton, T.L. (2011). *Functional family therapy in clinical practice: An evidence-based treatment model for working with troubled adolescents.* New York, NY, US: Routledge/Taylor & Francis Group.

Shackelford, T.K., Goetz, A.T., Buss, D.M., Euler, H.A., & Hoier, S. (2005). When we hurt the ones we love: Predicting violence against women from men's mate retention. *Personal Relationships, 12,* 447–463.

Shah, A. (2007). *Global computer usage, cell phone ownership jump.* The Pew Global Attitudes Project. http://pcworld.about.come/gi/dynamic/offside.htm?=http://pewglobal.org/reports/pdf/258.pdf.

Sharma, S.K., & Sharma, A. (2010). Examining the relationship between organisational culture and leadership styles. *Journal of the Indian Academy of Applied Psychology, 36*(1), 97–105.

Sharpe, J.P., Martin, N.R., & Roth, K.A. (2011). Optimism and the big five factors of personality: Beyond neuroticism and extraversion. *Personality and Individual Differences, 51*(8), 946–951.

Sheets, V.L., & Lugar, R. (2005). Sources of conflict between friends in Russia and the United States. *Cross-Cultural Research: The Journal of Comparative Social Science, 39,* 380–398.

Sheffield, M., Carey, J., Patenaude, W., & Lambert, M.J. (1995). An exploration of the relationship between interpersonal problems and psychological health. *Psychological Reports, 76,* 947–956.

Sheldon, K.M., Elliot, A.J., Ryan, R.M., Chirkov, V., Kim, Y., & Wu, C., et al. (2004). Self-concordance and subjective well-being in four cultures. *Journal of Cross-Cultural Psychology, 35,* 209–223.

Sheldon, K.M., Kasser, T., Houser-Marko, L., Jones, T., & Turban, D. (2005). Doing one's duty: Chronological age, felt autonomy, and subjective well-being. *European Journal of Personality, 19,* 97–115.

Sherman, D.W., Norman, R., & McSherry, C.B. (2010). A comparison of death anxiety and quality of life of patients with advanced cancer or AIDS and their family caregivers. *JANAC: Journal of the Association of Nurses in AIDS Care, 21*(2), 99–112.

Sherman, J.W., Stroessner, S.J., Conrey, F.R., & Azam, O.A. (2005). Prejudice and stereotype maintenance processes: Attention, attribution, and individuation. *Journal of Personality and Social Psychology, 89,* 607–622.

Shmotkin, D. (2005). Happiness in the face of adversity: Reformulating the dynamic and modular bases of subjective well-being. *Review of General Psychology, 9,* 291–325.

Shochat, T., Flint-Bretler, O., & Tzischinsky, O. (2010). Sleep patterns, electronic media exposure and daytime sleep-related behaviours among Israeli adolescents. *Acta Paediatrica, 99*(9), 1396–1400.

Shockett, E.R., Teno J.M., Miller S.C., Stuart B. (2005). Late referral to hospice and bereaved family member perception of quality of end-of-life care. *Journal of Pain and Symptom Management, 30,* 400–407.

Simon, R.I. (2011). *Preventing patient suicide: Clinical assessment and management.* Arlington, VA, US: American Psychiatric Publishing.

Simonton, D.K. (1987). *Why presidents succeed: A political psychology of leadership.* New Haven, CT: Yale University Press.

Singh, A., & Upadhyay, A. (2008). Age and sex differences in academic stress among college students. *Social Science International, 24,* 78–88.

Singh, R., & Joshi, H.L. (2008). Suicidal ideation in relation to depression, life stress and personality among college students. *Journal of the Indian Academy of Applied Psychology, 34*(2), 259–265.

Sinno, S.M., & Killen, M. (2011). Social reasoning about 'second-shift' parenting. *British Journal of Developmental Psychology, 29*(2), 313–329.

Skyving, M., Berg, H., & Laflamme, L. (2009). A pattern analysis of traffic crashes fatal to older drivers. *Accident Analysis & Prevention, 41,* 253–258.

Slaughter, V., & Griffiths, M. (2007). Death understanding and fear of death in young children. *Clinical Child Psychology and Psychiatry, 12*(4), 525–535.

Sleebos, E., Ellemers, N., & de Gilder, D. (2006). The carrot and the stick: Affective commitment and acceptance anxiety as motives for discretionary group efforts by respected and disrespected group members. *Personality and Social Psychology Bulletin, 32,* 244–255.

Slowik, G. (2011). What is hormone replacement therapy (HRT). *Ehealthmed.com.* Retrieved December 5, 2011, from http://ehealthmd.com/content/what-hormone-replacement-therapy-hrt.

Smith, A., Thurston, M., & Green, K. (2011). Propinquity, sociability and excitement: Exploring the normalisation of sensible drug use among 15-16-year-olds in north-west England and north-east Wales. *Journal of Youth Studies, 14*(3), 359–379.

Smith, D.E., & Cogswell, C. (1994). A cross-cultural perspective on adolescent girls' body perception. *Perceptual and Motor Skills, 78,* 744–746.

Smith, K., Goy, E., Harvath, T., & Ganzini, L. (2011). Quality of death and dying in patients who request physician-assisted death. *Journal of Palliative Medicine, 14*(4), 445–450.

Smith, P.B., & Bond, M.H. (1993). *Across cultures.* Boston: Allyn & Bacon.

Smith, R.A., & Weber, A.L. (2005). Applying social psychology in everyday life. In F.W. Schneider, J.A. Gruman & L.M. Coutts (Eds.), *Applied social psychology: Understanding and addressing social and practical problems* (pp. 75–99). Thousand Oaks, CA, US: Sage Publications.

Smith, T.J., & Campbell, C. (2009). The relationship between occupational interests and values. *Journal of Career Assessment, 17,* 39–55.

Smith, T.W. (2003). *American sexual behavior: Trends, sociodemographic differences, and risk behavior.* Chicago, IL: University of Chicago, National Opinion Research Center.

Smock, P.J., Manning, W.D., & Porter, M. (2005). "Everything's there except money": How money shapes decisions to marry among cohabitors. *Journal of Marriage and Family, 67,* 680–696.

Solomon, R.S. (2005). Name that feeling: Sabini and Silver on emotional names. *Psychological Inquiry, 16,* 41–44.

Somers, C.L., & Surmann, A.T. (2004). Adolescents' preferences for source of sex education. *Child Study Journal, 34,* 47–59.

Sonenklar, C. (2011). *Anorexia and bulimia.* Minneapolis: Twenty-First Century Books.

Sonnentag, S., & Zijlstra, F.R.H. (2006). Job characteristics and off-job activities as predictors of need for recovery, well-being, and fatigue. *Journal of Applied Psychology, 91,* 330–350.

Sood, A., & Tellis, G.J. (2005). Technological evolution and radical innovation. *Journal of Marketing, 69,* 152–168.

Southwick, S.M., Vythilingam, M., & Charney, D.S. (2005). The psychobiology of depression and resilience to stress: Implications for prevention and treatment. *Annual Review of Clinical Psychology, 1,* 255–291.

Spector, P.E. (2002). Employee control and occupational stress. *Current Directions, 11,* 133–136.

Spencer, S.M., & Patrick, J.H. (2009). Social support and personal mastery as protective resources during emerging adulthood. *Journal of Adult Development, 16*(4), 191–198.

Spiegel, A. (2010). Traces of Katrina: New Orleans suicide rate still up. *NPR.org.* Retrieved December 27 from http://www.npr.org/templates/story/story.php?storyId=129482180.

Spiers, A., & Walker, G.J. (2009). The effects of ethnicity and leisure satisfaction on happiness, peacefulness, and quality of life. *Leisure Sciences, 31,* 84–99.

Spindler, S.R. (2001). Reversing the negative genomic effects of aging with short-term caloric restriction. *The Scientific World, 1,* 544–546.

Spotts, E.L., Pederson, N.L., Neiderhiser, J.M., Reiss, D., Lichtenstein, P., & Hansson, K., et al. (2005). Genetic effects on women's positive mental health: Do marital relationships and social support matter? *Journal of Family Psychology, 19,* 339–349.

St. Clair, M. (2011). *So much, so fast, so little time: Coming to terms with rapid change and its consequences.* Santa Barbara, CA: Praeger.

Stack, S. (2002). Opera subculture and suicide for honor. *Death Studies, 26*(5), 431–437.

Stack, S., & Gundlach, J. (1992). The effect of country music on suicide. *Social Forces, 71,* 211–218.

Stambor, Z. (2006). Stressed out nation. *Monitor on Psychology, 37,* 28.

Stankiewicz, J.M., & Rosselli, F. (2008). Women as sex objects and victims in print advertisements. *Sex Roles, 58,* 579–589.

Stanley, S.M., Amato, P.R., Johnson, C.A., & Markman, H.J. (2006). Premarital education, marital quality, and marital stability: Findings from a large, random household survey. *Journal of Family Psychology, 20,* 117–126.

Stapel, D.A., & Johnson, C.S. (2007). When nothing compares to me: How defensive motivations and similarity shape social comparison effects. *European Journal of Social Psychology, 37,* 824–838.

Starcevic, V. (2005). *Anxiety disorders in adults: A clinical guide.* New York: Oxford University Press.

Starker, S. (1989). *Evil influences: Crusades against the mass media.* New Brunswick, NJ: Transaction Publishers.

Stassen Berger, K. (2007). Update on bullying at school: Science forgotten? *Developmental Review, 27,* 90–126.

Stearns, P.N. (2006). *Childhood in world history.* New York: Routledge.

Steinberg, L., Lambom, S.D., Darling, N., Mounts, N.S., & Dombusch, S.M. (1994). Over-Time changes in adjustment and competence among adolescents from authoritative, authoritarian, indulgent, and neglectful families. *Child Development, 65*, 754–770.

Steiner, A. (2002). Got time for friends? *Utne Reader, 67*–71.

Stern, S.R. (2005). Messages from teens on the big screen: Smoking, drinking, and drug use in teen-centered films. *Journal of Health Communication, 10*, 331–346.

Stern, J. (2006). A short introduction to psychoanalysis. *Psychoanalytic Psychotherapy, 20*, 65–68.

Sternberg, R.J. (2004). *A triangular theory of love*. Philadelphia: Taylor & Francis.

Sternglanz, R.W., & DePaulo, B.M. (2004). Reading nonverbal cues to emotions: The advantages and liabilities of relationship closeness. *Journal of Nonverbal Behavior. Special Issue: Interpersonal Sensitivity, Part II, 28*, 245–266. 55.

Stolz, H.E., Barber, B.K., & Olsen, J.A. (2005). Toward disentangling fathering and mothering: An assessment of relative importance. *Journal of Marriage and Family, 67*, 1076–1092.

Streich, M., Casper, W.J., & Salvaggio, A.N. (2008). Examining couple agreement about work-family conflict. *Journal of Managerial Psychology, 23*, 252–272.

Stroebe, M., Schut, H., & Stroebe, W. (2007). Health outcomes of bereavement. *Lancet, 370*, 1960–1973.

Stroebe, W., Zech, E., Stroebe, M.S., & Abakoumkin, G. (2005). Does social support help in bereavement. *Journal of Social and Clinical Psychology, 24*, 1030–1050.

Strom, P., & Strom, R. (2005). Parent-child relationships in early adulthood: College students living at home. *Community Journal of Research and Practice, 29*, 517–529.

Subrahmanyam, K., Smahel, D., & Greenfield, P. (2006). Connecting developmental constructions to the internet: Identity presentation and sexual exploration in online teen chat rooms. *Developmental Psychology, 42*(3), 395–406.

Substance Abuse and Mental Health Services Administration. (2006). *Youth drug use continues downward slide older adult rates of use increase*. Retrieved June 6, 2008, from http://www.samhsa.gov/news/newsreleases/060907_nsduh.aspx.

Suh, E.J., Moskowitz, D.S., Fournier, M.A., & Zuroff, D.C. (2004). Gender and relationships: Influences on agentic and communal behaviors. *Personal Relationships, 11*, 41–59.

Sulkowski, M.L., Dempsey, J., & Dempsey, A.G. (2011). Effects of stress and coping on binge eating in female college students. *Eating Behaviors, 12*(3), 188–191.

Sullivan, A. (2003, August 11). Beware the straight backlash. *Time*, 35.

Sullivan, K.T., Pasch, L.A., Johnson, M.D., & Bradbury, T.N. (2010). Social support, problem solving, and the longitudinal course of newlywed marriage. *Journal of Personality and Social Psychology, 98*(4), 631–644.

Sum, S., Mathews, R.M., Hughes, I., & Campbell, A. (2008). Internet use and loneliness in older adults. *CyberPsychology & Behavior, 11*, 208–211.

Sunnafrank, M., Ramirez, A.J., & Metts, S. (2004). At first sight: Persistent relational effects of get-acquainted conversations. *Journal of Social and Personal Relationships, 21*, 361–379.

Sutherland, J.E., Sutherland, S.J., & Hoehns, J.D. (2003). Achieving the best outcome in treatment of depression. *The Journal of Family Practice, 52*(3), 201–209.

Swanbrow, D. (2009). *Living together: The best way to divorce-proof a marriage?* University of Michigan News Services. Retrieved March 1, 2012, from http://ns.umich.edu/new/releases/7276.

Swartz, M.S. (2010). Advancing research at the intersection of two systems. *Psychiatric Services, 61*(5), 431.

Szabo, A., Ainsworth, S.E., & Danks, P.K. (2005). Experimental comparison of the psychological benefits of aerobic exercise, humor, and music. *Humor: International Journal of Humor Research, 18*, 235–246.

Takano, Y., & Sogon, S. (2008). Are Japanese men more collectivistic than Americans? Examining conformity in in-groups and the reference-group effect. *Journal of Cross-Cultural Psychology, 39*, 237–250.

Tangney, J.P. (1999). The self-conscious emotions: Shame, guilt, embarrassment and pride. In T. Dalgleish & M.J. Power (Eds.), *Handbook of cognition and emotion* (pp. 541–568). Chichester, England: Wiley.

Tanielian, T., & Jaycox, L.H. (2008). *Invisible wounds of war: Psychological and cognitive injuries, their consequences, and services to assist recovery*. Santa Monica, CA: RAND Corporation.

Taylor, C.B. (2010). Panic disorder. In C.B. Taylor (Ed.), *How to practice evidence-based psychiatry: Basic principles and case studies* (pp. 147–155). Arlington, VA, US: American Psychiatric Publishing.

Taylor, C.A., Manganello, J.A., Lee, S.J., & Rice, J.C. (2010). Mothers' spanking of 3-year-old children and subsequent risk of children's aggressive behavior. *Pediatrics, 125*(5), e1057–e1065.

Taylor, S.E., Klein, L.C., Lewis, B.P., Gruenewald, T.L., Gurung, R.A., & Updegraff, J.A. (2000). Biobehavioral responses to stress in females: Tend-and-befriend, not fight-or-flight. *Psychological Review, 107*, 411–429.

Taylor, S.E., & Brown, J.D. (1994). Positive illusions and well-being revisited: Separating fact from fiction. *Psychological Bulletin, 116*, 21–27.

Techniques. (2000, March). Stressed out on campus. *Techniques*, 9.

Teichert, N.W. (2002). *Nation faces inadequate care for seniors as baby boomers age.* Knight Ridder/Tribune Business News, Item 02333003.

Tennen, H., & Affleck, G. (1987). The costs and benefits of optimistic explanations and dispositional optimism. *Journal of Personality, 55*, 377–393.

Thanakwang, K. (2009). Social relationships influencing positive perceived health among Thai older persons: A secondary data analysis using the national elderly survey. *Nursing & Health Sciences, 11*(2), 144–149.

The National Highway Traffic Safety Administration. (2012). *Research on drowsy driving.* Retrieved March 1, 2012, from http://www.nhtsa.gov/Driving+Safety/Distracted+Driving/Research+on+Drowsy+Driving.

The World Bank. (2012). *Life expectancy at birth, total (years).* Retrieved March 7, 2012, from http://data.worldbank.org/indicator/SP.DYN.LE00.IN.

Thomas, A., & Chess, S. (1984). Genesis and evolution of behavioral disorders: From infancy to early adult life. *The American Journal of Psychiatry, 141*(1), 1–9.

Thomas, J.L., Patten, C.A., Decker, P.A., Croghan, I.T., Cowles, M.L., & Bronars, C.A., et al. (2005). Development and preliminary evaluation of a measure of support provided to a smoker among young adults. *Addictive Behaviors, 30*, 1351.

Thompson, K.M., & Yokota, F. (2004). Violence, sex, and profanity in films: Correlation of movie ratings with content. *General Medicine, 6.* Retrieved January 15, 2005, from http://www.medscape.com.

Thompson, V.S.S. (2002). Racism: Perceptions of distress among African Americans. *Community Mental Health Journal, 38*, 111–118.

Thompson, T.D.B., Barbour, R.S., & Schwartz, L. (2003). Health professionals' views on advance directives: A qualitative interdisciplinary study. *Palliative Medicine, 17*, 403–409.

Tice, D.M., & Baumeister, R.F. (1997). Longitudinal study of procrastination, performance, stress and health: The costs and benefits of dawdling. *Psychological Science, 8*, 454–458.

Tiggemann, M. (2004). Body image across the adult life span: Stability and change. *Body Image, 1*, 29–41.

Tirodkar, M.A., & Jain, A. (2003). Food messages on African American television shows. *American Journal of Public Health, 93*, 439–441.

Toates, F. (2009). An integrative theoretical framework for understanding sexual motivation, arousal, and behavior. *Journal of Sex Research, 46*, 168–193.

Toker, S., Shirom, A., Shapira, I., Berliner, S., & Melamed, S. (2005). The association between burnout, depression, anxiety, and inflammation biomarkers: C-reactive protein and fibrinogen in men and women. *Journal of Occupational Health Psychology, 10*, 344–362.

Tolan, P.H., Gorman-Smith, D., & Henry, D.B. (2003). The developmental ecology of urban males' youth violence. *Developmental Psychology. Special Issue: Violent Children, 39*, 274–291.

Tomberg, T., Toomela, A., Pulver, A., & Tikk, A. (2005). Coping strategies, social support, life orientation and health-related quality of life following traumatic brain injury. *Brain Injury, 19*, 1181–1190.

Townsend, M.C. (2012). *Psychiatric mental health nursing: Concepts of care in evidence-based practice.* Philadelphia: F.A. Davis Co.

Trakhtenberg, E.C. (2008). The effects of guided imagery on the immune system: A critical review. *International Journal of Neuroscience, 118*, 839–855.

Tsai, J.L., Knutson, B., & Fung, H.H. (2006). Cultural variation in affect valuation. *Journal of Personality and Social Psychology, 90*, 288–307.

Tuckman, B.W. (1965). Development sequences in small groups. *Psychological Bulletin, 63*, 384–399.

Tugade, M.M., & Fredrickson, B.L. (2004). Resilient individuals use positive emotions to bounce back from negative emotional experiences. *Journal of Personality and Social Psychology, 86*, 320–333.

Tummala-Narra, P., Inman, A.G., & Ettigi, S.P. (2011). Asian Indians' responses to discrimination: A mixed-method examination of identity, coping, and self-esteem. *Asian American Journal of Psychology, 2*(3), 205–218.

Tylka, T.L. (2011). Refinement of the tripartite influence model for men: Dual body image pathways to body change behaviors. *Body Image, 8*(3), 199–207.

U.S. Bureau of the Census. (2012). *The 2012 statistical abstract: USA statistics in brief.* Retrieved April 16, 2012, from http://www.census.gov/.

U.S. Bureau of the Census. (2012). *Income, Poverty, and Health Insurance Coverage in the United States: 2011.* Retrieved October 1, 2012, from http://www.census.gov/prod/2012pubs/p60-243.pdf.

U.S. Department of Agriculture. (2012). Retrieved January 11, 2012, from http://www.choosemyplate.gov.

U.S. Department of Commerce. (2002). *A nation online: Executive summary.* http://www.ntia.doc.gov/legacy/ntiahome/dn/html/EXECSUM.htm.

U.S. Department of Health and Human Services. (2007). *The Surgeon General's call to action to prevent and reduce underage drinking.* Department of Health and Human Services, Office of the Surgeon General. Retrieved February 12, 2012, from http://www.surgeongeneral.gov; http://www.hhs.gov/od.

U.S. Department of Health and Human Services, Administration for Children and Families, Administration on Children,

Youth and Families, Children's Bureau. (2011). *Child Maltreatment 2010.* Available from http://www.acf.hhs.gov/programs/cb/resource/child-maltreatment-2010.

U.S. Department of Labor, Bureau of Labor Statistics. (2011). *College enrollment and work activity of 2010 high school graduates.* Retrieved December 19, 2011, from http://www.bls.gov/news.release/hsgec.nr0.htm.

U.S. Department of Labor, Bureau of Labor Statistics. (2012). *Occupational outlook handbook.* http://www.bls.gov.

U.S. Department of Labor. (2012). *Women in the labor force: A databook.* http://www.bls.gov/cps/wlf-databook-2011.pdf.

Ulijn, J., Rutkowski, A.F., Kumar, R., & Zhu, Y. (2005). Patterns of feelings in face-to-face negotiation: A Sino-Dutch pilot study. *Cross Cultural Management, 12,* 103–118.

Ulrich-Lai, Y.M., Christiansen, A.M., Ostrander, M.M., Jones, A.A., Jones, K.R., Choi, D.C., et al. (2010). Pleasurable behaviors reduce stress via brain reward pathways. *Proceedings of the National Academy of Sciences of the United States of America, 107*(47), 20529–20534.

Underwood, N. (2002, January 21). The happy divorce. *McLean's,* 25–29.

Valkenburg, P.M., Peter, J., & Schouten, A.P. (2006). Friend networking sites and their relationship to adolescents' well-being and social self-esteem. *CyberPsychology & Behavior, 9,* 584–590.

van Assema, P., Martens, M., Ruiter, A.C., & Brug, J. (2001). Framing of nutrition education messages in persuading consumers of the advantages of a healthy diet. *Journal of Human Nutrition and Dietetics, 14,* 435–442.

van den Bulck, J., Beullens, K., & Mulder, J. (2006). Television and music video exposure and adolescent 'alcopop' use. *International Journal of Adolescent Medicine and Health, 18,* 107–114.

Van Emmerik, H., Euwema, M.C., & Wendt, H. (2008). Leadership behaviors around the world: The relative importance of gender versus cultural background. *International Journal of Cross-Cultural Management, 8*(3), 297–315.

Vangelisti, A.L., & Gerstenberger, M. (2004). Communication and marital infidelity. In J. Duncombe, K. Harrison, G. Allan, & D. Marsden (Eds.), *The state of affairs: Explorations in infidelity and commitment* (pp. 59–78). Mahwah, NJ: Lawrence Erlbaum.

van Harreveld, F., van der Pligt, J., & Nordgren, L. (2008). The relativity of bad decisions: Social comparison as a means to alleviate regret. *British Journal of Social Psychology, 47,* 105–117.

van Lommel, P., van Wees, R., Meyers, V., & Elfferich, I. (2001). Near-death experience in survivors of cardiac arrest: A prospective study in the Netherlands. *The Lancet, 358,* 2039–2045.

Vandebosch, H., & Van Cleemput, K. (2009). Cyberbullying among youngsters: Profiles of bullies and victims. *New Media & Society, 11*(8), 1349–1371.

Veríssimo, M., Santos, A.J., Vaughn, B.E., Torres, N., Monteiro, L., & Santos, O. (2011). Quality of attachment to father and mother and number of reciprocal friends. *Early Child Development and Care, 181*(1), 27–38.

Verkuytenm, M., &Thijs, J. (2004). Global and ethnic self-esteem in school context: Minority and majority groups in the Netherlands, *Social Indicators Research, 67,* 253–281.

Vermeire, E., Hearnshaw, H., Van Royen, P., & Denekens, J. (2001). Patient adherence to treatment: Three decades of research. *Journal of Clinical Pharmacy and Therapeutics, 26,* 331–342.

Vicary, A.M. (2011). Mortality salience and namesaking: Does thinking about death make people want to name their children after themselves? *Journal of Research in Personality, 45*(1), 138–141.

Vincent, G.K., & Velkoff, V.A. (2010). *The next four decades: The older population in the united states: 2010 to 2050.* Retrieved, April 16, 2012, from http://www.census.gov/prod/2010pubs/p25-1138.pdf.

Vitello, P. (2006). A ring tone meant to fall on deaf ears. *New York Times.* Retrieved October 19, 2011, from http://www.nytimes.com/2006/06/12/technology/12ring.html?ex=1307764800&en=2a80d150770df0df&ei=5090&partner=rssuserland&emc=rss.

Vittengl, J.R., & Holt, C.S. (2000). Getting acquainted: The relationship of self-disclosure and social attraction to positive affect. *Journal of Social and Personal Relationships, 17,* 53–66.

Vogel, D.L., Wester, S.R., Wei, M., & Boysen, G.A. (2005). The role of outcome expectations and attitudes on decisions to seek professional help. *Journal of Counseling Psychology, 52,* 459–470.

VolunteeringinAmerica.gov. (2012). *What's new.* Retrieved January 28, 2012, from http://www.volunteeringinamerica.gov/.

Vrij, A., Granhag, P.A., & Porter, S. (2010). Pitfalls and opportunities in nonverbal and verbal lie detection. *Psychological Science in the Public Interest, 11*(3), 89–121.

Vroom, V.H., & Jago, A.G. (2007). The role of the situation in leadership. *American Psychologist: Special Issue: Leadership, 62,* 17–24.

Wadsworth, M.E., Raviv, T., Santiago, C.D., & Etter, E.M. (2011). Testing the adaptation to poverty-related stress model: Predicting psychopathology symptoms in families facing economic hardship. *Journal of Clinical Child and Adolescent Psychology, 40*(4), 646–657.

Wagner, N., Hassanein, K., & Head, M. (2010). Computer use by older adults: A multi-disciplinary review. *Computers in Human Behavior, 26*(5), 870–882.

Wajcman, J. (2008). Life in the fast lane? Towards a sociology of technology and time. *British Journal of Sociology, 59*, 59–77.

Wallace, B., & Fisher, L.E. (2003). *Consciousness and Behavior* (4rd ed.). Needham Heights, MA: Allyn & Bacon.

Wallerstein, J.S., & Lewis, J.M. (2005). The reality of divorce. Reply to Gordon (2005). *Psychoanalytic Psychology, 22*, 452–454.

Walsh, J. (2002). Shyness and social phobia: A social work perspective on a problem in living. *Health and Social Work, 27*, 137–144.

Walther, J.B., Van Der Heide, B., Kim, S., Westerman, D., & Tong, S.T. (2008). The role of friends' appearance and behavior on evaluations of individuals on Facebook: Are we known by the company we keep? *Human Communication Research, 34*, 28–49.

Wampold, B.E., Minami, T., Tierney, S.C., Baskin, T.W., & Bhati, K.S. (2005). The placebo is powerful: Estimating placebo effects in medicine and psychotherapy from randomized clinical trials. *Journal of Clinical Psychology, 61*, 835–854.

Wang, S., & Wu, P. (2008). The role of feedback and self-efficacy on web-based learning: The social cognitive perspective. *Computers & Education, 51*, 1589–1598.

Wang, W. (2012). *The rise of intermarriage.* Pew Social & Demographic Trends. Retrieved February 20, 2012, from http://www.pewsocialtrends.org/2012/02/16/the-rise-of-intermarriage/.

Wansink, B., Painter, J.E., & North, J. (2005). Bottomless bowls: Why visual cues of portion size may influence intake. *Obesity Research, 13*(1), 93–100.

Want, S.C. (2009). Meta-analytic moderators of experimental exposure to media portrayals of women on female appearance satisfaction: Social comparisons as automatic processes. *Body Image, 6*, 257–269.

Ward, L.M. (2003). Understanding the role of entertainment media in the sexual socialization of American youth: A review of empirical research. *Developmental Review, 23*, 347–388.

Warr, P., & Clapperton, G. (2010). *The joy of work? jobs, happiness, and you.* New York, NY, US: Routledge/Taylor & Francis Group.

Weaver, A.D., MacKeigan, K.L., & MacDonald, H.A. (2011). Experiences and perceptions of young adults in friends with benefits relationships: A qualitative study. *Canadian Journal of Human Sexuality, 20*, 41–53.

Wechsler, H., & Nelson, T.F. (2008). What we have learned from the Harvard School of Public Health college alcohol study: Focusing attention on college student alcohol consumption and the environmental conditions that promote it. *Journal of Studies on Alcohol and Drugs, 69*(4), 481–490.

Weiner, B., Panton, S., & Weber, M. (1999, April 28). *New study first to quantify illicit drug and substance use in movies and music popular among youth.* http://www.mapinc.org/drugnews/v99.n458.a04.html/ghdex.

Weiss, M.G., & Ramakrishna, J. (2006). Stigma interventions and research for international health. *Lancet, 367*, 536–538.

Werner, N.E., Bumpus, M.F., & Rock, D. (2010). Involvement in internet aggression during early adolescence. *Journal of Youth and Adolescence, 39*(6), 607–619.

Westerhof, G.J., & Barrett, A.E. (2005). Age identity and subjective well-being: A comparison of the United States and Germany. *Journals of Gerontology: Series B: Psychological Sciences and Social Sciences, 60B*, 129–136.

Wethington, E. (2000). Expecting stress: Americans and the "midlife crisis." *Motivation and Emotion, 24*, 85–103.

Wheelan, S.A. (2009). Group size, group development, and group productivity. *Small Group Research, 40*, 247–262.

Whitbourne, S.K., Whitbourne, S.B., & Whitbourne, S.K. (2011). *Adult development and aging: Biopsychosocial perspectives.* Hoboken, NJ: Wiley.

White, K.S. (2008). Cardiovascular disease and anxiety. In M.J. Zvolensky & J.A.J. Smits (Eds.), *Anxiety in health behaviors and physical illness.* New York: Springer Science.

Whitty, M.T., & Carr, A.N. (2006). New rules in the workplace: Applying object-relations theory to explain problem internet and email behaviour in the workplace. *Computers in Human Behavior, 22*, 235–250.

Wierda-Boer, H.H., Gerris, J.R.M., & Vermulst, A.A. (2009). Managing multiple roles: Personality, stress, and work-family interference in dual-earner couples. *Journal of Individual Differences, 30*, 6–19.

Wigman, S.A., Graham-Kevan, N., & Archer, J. (2008). Investigating sub-groups of harassers: The roles of attachment, dependency, jealousy and aggression. *Journal of Family Violence, 23*, 557–568.

Wilde, A., & Diekman, A.B. (2005). Cross-cultural similarities and differences in dynamic stereotypes: A comparison between Germany and the United States. *Psychology of Women Quarterly, 29*, 188–196.

Williams, J.M.G., Crane, C., Barnhofer, T., van der Does, A.J.W., & Segal, Z.V. (2006). Recurrence of suicidal ideation across depressive episodes. *Journal of Affective Disorders, 91*, 189–194.

Willoughby, B.L.B., Malik, N.M., & Lindahl, K.M. (2006). Parental reactions to their sons' sexual orientation disclosures: The roles of family cohesion, adaptability, and parenting style. *Psychology of Men & Masculinity, 7*, 14–26.

Wills, T.A., Sargent, J.D., Stoolmiller, M., Gibbons, F.X., Worth, K.A., & Dal Cin, S. (2007). Movie exposure to smoking cues and adolescent smoking onset: A test for mediation through peer affiliations. *Health Psychology, 26*, 769–776.

Wilson, G.A., Zeng, Q., & Blackburn, D.G. (2011). An examination of parental attachments, parental detachments and self-esteem across hetero-, bi-, and homosexual individuals. *Journal of Bisexuality, 11*(1), 86–97.

Wilson, J., Peebles, R., & Hardy, K.K. (2006). Surfing for thinness: A pilot study of pro-eating disorder web site usage in adolescents with eating disorders. *Pediatrics, 118*, 1635–1643.

Wilson, J.M., Straus, S.G., & McEvily, B. (2006). All in due time: The development of trust in computer-mediated and face-to-face teams. *Organizational Behavior and Human Decision Processes, 99*, 16–33.

Wilson, T.D., & Gilbert, D.T. (2005). Affective forecasting: Knowing what to want. *Current Directions in Psychological Science, 14*, 131–134.

Wincze, J.P. (2009). *Enhancing sexuality: A problem-solving approach to treating dysfunction: Therapist guide* (2nd ed.). New York, NY, US: Oxford University Press.

Wing, R.R., & Raynor, D.A. (2006). Lifestyle modifications in the obese patient with cardiovascular disease. In M.K. Robinson & A. Thomas (Eds.), *Obesity and cardiovascular disease*. New York: Taylor & Francis.

Wingfield, A., Tun, P.A., & McCoy, S.L. (2005). Hearing loss in older adults: What is it and how it interacts with cognitive performance. *Current Directions in Psychological Science, 14*, 144–148.

Winnicott, D.W. (1953). Transitional objects and transitional phenomena; a study of the first not-me possession. *International Journal of Psycho-Analysis, 34*, 89–97.

Wiseman, H., Mayseless, O., & Sharabany, R. (2006). Why are they lonely? Perceived quality of early relationships with parents, attachment, personality predispositions and loneliness in first-year university students. *Personality and Individual Differences, 40*, 237–248.

Wittchen, H., Gloster, A.T., Beesdo-Baum, K., Fava, G.A., & Craske, M.G. (2010). Agoraphobia: A review of the diagnostic classificatory position and criteria. *Depression and Anxiety, 27*(2), 113–133.

Wojcieszak, M., & Price, V. (2009). What underlies the false consensus effect? How personal opinion and disagreement affect perception of public opinion. *International Journal of Public Opinion Research, 21*, 25–46.

Wolak, J., Mitchell, K., & Finkelhor, D. (2007). Unwanted and wanted exposure to pornography in a national sample of youth Internet users. *Pediatrics, 119*, 247–257.

Wolpe, J. (1973). *The practice of behavior therapy*. New York: Pergamon.

Women's Way. (2006). Power skills: How volunteering shapes professional success. Retrieved August 9, 2006, from http://www.volunteermatch.org/volunteers/resources/surveyfnl.pdf.

Wood, N.D., Crane, D.R., Schaalje, G.B., & Law, D.D. (2005). What works for whom: A meta-analytic review of marital and couples therapy in reference to marital distress. *American Journal of Family Therapy, 33*, 273–287.

Woods, S., & White, E. (2005). The association between bullying behaviour, arousal levels and behaviour problems. *Journal of Adolescence, 28*, 381–395.

Workman, M. (2007). The effects from technology-mediated interaction and openness in virtual team performing measures. *Behaviour & Information Technology, 26*, 355–365.

World at Work. (2011). *Telework 2010*. Retrieved January 15, 2012, from www.worldatwork.org.

World Health Organization. (2011). *WHO report on the global tobacco epidemic, 2011: Warning about the dangers of tobacco*. Available from http://www.who.int/tobacco/global_report/2011/en/index.html.

World Health Organization. (2012). *Women and mental health*. Retrieved April 2, 2012, from http://www.who.int/mediacentre/factsheets/fs248/en/.

WorldHeartFederation.org. (2007). *Children, adolescents and obesity*. Retrieved May 19, 2008, from http://www.world-heart-federation.org/press/facts-figures/children-adolescents-and-obesity.

Worldhunger.org. (2012). *2011 world hunger and poverty facts and statistics*. Retrieved January 19, 2012, from http://www.worldhunger.org/articles/Learn/world%20hunger%20facts%202002.htm.

Worldwatch.org. (2012). *World watch institute*. Retrieved February 22, 2012, from http://www.worldwatch.org.

Wright, C.E., Kunz-Ebrecht, S.R., Iliffe, S., Foese, O., & Steptoe, A. (2005). Physiological correlates of cognitive functioning in an elderly population. *Psychoneuroendocrinology, 30*, 826–838.

Wright, K. (2002, June). Six degrees of speculation. *Discover*, 19–21.

Xie, G., & Lee, M.J. (2008). Anticipated violence, arousal, and enjoyment of movies: Viewers' reactions to violent previews based on arousal-seeking tendency. *Journal of Social Psychology, 148*, 277–292.

Yamaguchi, S., Gelfand, M., Ohashi, M.M., & Zemba, Y. (2005). The cultural psychology of control: Illusions of personal versus collective control in the United States and Japan. *Journal of Cross-Cultural Psychology, 36*, 750–761.

Yamawaki, N., Tschanz, B.T., & Feick, D.L. (2004). Defensive pessimism, self-esteem instability, and goal strivings. *Cognition and Emotion, 18*(2), 233–249.

Yancy, K.B. (2011). Most U.S. Workers don't use all vacation days. *USAToday.com*. Retrieved December 5, 2011, from http://

travel.usatoday.com/destinations/dispatches/post/2011/11/most-us-workers-dont-use-all-vacation-days/567951/1.

Yawar, A. (2008). Time and humanity on psychiatric wards. *Lancet, 37,* 285–286.

Ybarra, O. (2001). When first impressions don't last: The role of isolation and adaptation processes in the revision of evaluative impressions. *Social Cognition, 19,* 491–520.

Yoquinto, L. (2012). Sex life becomes more satisfying for women after 40. *MyHealthNewsDaily.com.* Retrieved February 3, 2012, from http://www.myhealthnewsdaily.com/2083-women-sex-life-age.html.

Yuen, C.N., & Lavin, M.J. (2004). Internet dependence in the collegiate population: The role of shyness. *CyberPsychology & Behavior, 7,* 379–383.

Zaccaro, S.J. (2007). Trait-based perspectives of leadership. *American Psychologist. Special Issue: Leadership, 62,* 6–16.

Zautra, A.J., Affleck, G.G., Tennen, H., Reich, J.W., & Davis, M.C. (2005). Dynamic approaches to emotions and stress in everyday life: Bolger and Zuckerman reloaded with positive as well as negative affects. *Journal of Personality. Special Issue: Advances in Personality and Daily Experience, 73,* 1–28.

Zayas, V., Mischel, W., Shoda, Y., & Aber, J.L. (2011). Roots of adult attachment: Maternal caregiving at 18 months predicts adult peer and partner attachment. *Social Psychological and Personality Science, 2*(3), 289–297.

Zeidner, M., & Matthews, G. (2005). Evaluation anxiety: Current theory and research. In A. Elliot & C. Dweck (Eds.), *Handbook of competence and motivation* (pp. 141–163). New York: Guilford Press.

Zimmerman, C. (2004). Denial of impending death: A discourse analysis of the palliative care literature. *Social Science & Medicine, 59,* 1769–1780.

Zuckerman, M., Knee, C.R., Kieffer, S.C., & Gagne, M. (2004). What individuals believe they can and cannot do: Explorations of realistic and unrealistic control beliefs. *Journal of Personality Assessment, 82,* 215–232.

Zurbriggen, E.L., & Yost, M.R. (2004). Power, desire, and pleasure in sexual fantasies. *Journal of Sex Research, 41,* 288–300.

Zurbriggen, E.L., Collins, R.L., Lamb, S., Roberts, T.A., Tolman, D.L., Ward, L.M., et al. (2007). *Report of the APA task force on the sexualization of girls.* Washington, DC: American Psychological Association. Retrieved May 28, 2009, from http://www.apa.org/pi/wpo/sexualizationrep.pdf.

PHOTO CREDITS

Chapter 1

Pages 2: Olga Hmelevskaya

Page 8: Karen Grover Duffy

Page 18: Susan Shuman

Chapter 2

Pages 22, 30, 31: Karen Grover Duffy

Chapter 3

Pages 44, 51, 57 : Karen Grover Duffy

Chapter 4

Page 62: Olga Hmelevskaya

Page 66: Susan Shuman

Page 75: Supri Suharjoto/Shutterstock

Chapter 5

Page 80: Shaun Robinson/Shutterstock

Page 84: Marina Konstantinova

Pages 86, 101: Karen Grover Duffy

Chapter 6

Pages 106, 118: Karen Grover Duffy

Page 109: Steven Platte

Chapter 7

Page 126: Bette Adelman

Page 130: Karen Grover Duffy

Page 142: Andrew Hmelevskii

Chapter 8

Page 150: Elena Elisseeva/Shutterstock

Pages 158, 159: Karen Grover Duffy

Page 166: John Paul Marchand

Chapter 9

Page 170: Zhiltsov Alexandr/Shutterstock

Page 178: Susan Shuman

Pages 182, 190: Shutterstock

Chapter 10

Pages 194, 203: Karen Grover Duffy

Page 210: Andrew Lever/Shutterstock

Chapter 11

Page 216: Ekaterina Pokrovsky/Shutterstock

Page 219: Andrew Hmelevskii

Page 226: Susan Shuman

Chapter 12

Page 240: Andrew Hmelevskii

Page 250: Karen Grover Duffy

Chapter 13

Page 264: Olga Hmelevskaya

Page 267: Karen Grover Duffy

Page 281: Susan Shuman

Chapter 14

Page 286: Susan Shuman

Page 295: Karen Grover Duffy

Page 298: Alexandre Boavida/Shutterstock

Chapter 15

Page 310: Karen Grover Duffy

Page 314: Shutterstock

Page 316: Karen Grover Duffy

Page 325: Steve Lovegrove/Shutterstock

Chapter 16

Page 336: Hofhauser/Shutterstock

Pages 349, 350: Karen Grover Duffy

NAME INDEX

SUBJECT INDEX